Thomas Robinson

Homiletical commentary on the book of Job

Thomas Robinson

Homiletical commentary on the book of Job

ISBN/EAN: 9783337735944

Printed in Europe, USA, Canada, Australia, Japan

Cover: Foto ©ninafisch / pixelio.de

More available books at **www.hansebooks.com**

HOMILETICAL

COMMENTARY

ON

THE BOOK OF JOB.

BY

THOMAS ROBINSON, D.D.,

Author of "Suggestive and Homiletic Commentary on the Epistle to the Romans,"
"The Evangelists and the Mishna," &c.

LONDON:
RICHARD D. DICKINSON,
FARRINGDON STREET.

1876.

PREFACE.

THE following work was originally intended to form part of Dr. Van Doren's "Suggestive and Homiletic Commentary on the Old and New Testaments;" and consequently to be accompanied with critical notes similar to those in the Author's Commentary on the Epistle to the Romans, already published in connection with that series. That undertaking, however, having been given up by Dr. Van Doren, it was proposed to the writer by the Editors of the "Homiletical Commentary on the Books of the Old and New Testaments" to reconstruct and adapt his work, so that it might be admitted as part of their series. The object of the Editors of the "Homiletical Commentary," however, was rather to aid in the use of existing commentaries than to produce a new one, intending their series to contain as little as possible of what might be found in other expositions. The writer is deeply conscious of the many imperfections adhering to his work; he has, however, made it his endeavour, as far as he was able, to carry out the object of the Editors; and, at the same time, to prepare an expository and homiletical work on what is acknowledged to be one of the most difficult books of the Bible, which may, by the Divine blessing, be useful both to ordinary readers of the Word and to those who have to minister to others.

In the preparation of his work the Author has availed himself of all the critical and practical aids within his reach, in order that it might exhibit the results of the studies of the most eminent Biblical scholars and expositors of the Word up to the present time. He is sorry that, owing to the change of plan, he is not able to present to the student the views and opinions of others on the various *loci difficiles* of the book, as he had done in his Commentary on the Romans. If he has thus appeared in any place to adopt sentiments which have been expressed by living writers before him, without mentioning their names, he takes this opportunity of expressing his obligations and of soliciting their kindly condonance. In connection with the first two chapters, he was especially pleased with remarks found in some papers of the "Homilist" on the Book of Job, probably from the pen of the accomplished editor, Dr. Thomas.

Those who are best acquainted with the nature of the Book of Job, as one of the most ancient books in the world, if not itself the most ancient, and with the difficulties connected with the original language of the composition, will be most disposed to make allowance for the imperfections discoverable in the present work. If he shall have succeeded in any degree in aiding the readers of the Word in the spiritual understanding of this frequently obscure, but most precious, portion of it, or in assisting any in expounding it to others, the writer will have had his desire accomplished, and will ascribe all the praise to Him "of whom, and through whom, and to whom are all things: to whom be glory for ever and ever. Amen."

MORPETH,

June 19*th*, 187

HOMILETIC COMMENTARY

JOB.

Introduction.

I. The General Character of the Book. One of the grandest portions of inspired Scripture. A heaven-replenished storehouse of comfort and instruction. The Patriarchal Bible, and a precious monument of primitive theology. Is to the Old Testament what the Epistle to the Romans is to the New. Job's history well known to early Christians as an example of patience (Jam. v. 11). Understood by them typically and allegorically of Christ. From the second century the book read in the churches in Passion Week. Stands unique and independent among the books of the Bible. In its prose parts so simple and easy that a child may understand it; in its poetic portion, the deepest and obscurest book in the Old Testament. Contains milk for babes and strong meat for those of full age. Studded with passages of grandeur and beauty, tenderness and pathos, sublimity and terror. Acknowledged to surpass in sublimity and majesty every other book in the world. In recent times studied as a master-piece of poetry. A fountain from which some of the greatest poets have drawn their inspirations. To suffering believers the sound of Faithful's voice to Christian in the Valley of the Shadow of Death.

2. Author. Uncertain. Long believed by most to be Moses. Moses well acquainted with Egypt; "learned in all the wisdom of the Egyptians, and mighty in words and deeds" (Acts vii. 22); capable of writing sublime poetry (as Ex. xv.; Deut. xxxii. and xxxiii.); himself trained in the school of affliction (Heb. xi. 25); had opportunities in Midian for obtaining the knowledge of the history and composing the poem. Parts of the book probably in previous existence as traditional poetry, maxims, or sayings of earlier sages (*e.g.* xii. 13—25; xv. 20—35). The human authorship uncertain, no doubt about the Divine. The author of the greatest and sublimest poem in the world unknown.— *Little matter that our names are forgotten, if our works live.*

II. Period of Composition. Opinions divided. Two periods principally assigned. 1. That of Moses (see above); 2. That of David and Solomon. Views of scholars and critics now more generally in favour of the latter; (1) From the style and character of the composition; (2) The advanced state of art and civilization indicated; (3) The occurrence of certain expressions; (4) The prevalence of the idea of "Wisdom;" (5) The similarity of sentiment and language to those in Psalms and Proverbs, particularly as regards the state of the dead; *e.g.* in Psalm lxxxviii. and lxxxix. (the works of Heman and Ethan (1 Kings v. 11).

III. Character of the Book. A true history poetically treated. Proofs; (1) Job mentioned as a historical person with Noah and Daniel (Ezek. xiv. 14; James v. 11;)— (2) The localities real, and names of persons not significant, except that of Job himself; —(3) Extended fiction not according to the spirit of high antiquity, and especially to that of the Bible. Probably the facts given substantially, though not exactly, as they occurred. The speeches not necessarily given *verbatim*.

IV. Species of Composition. A drama, but only in a loose sense. A didactic narrative, for the most part in a poetic and dramatic form. The discussion of a grave and solemn question the body of the book. The controversy carried on in poetry, the introduction and conclusion in prose. Poetry the earliest form of composition, as best retained in memory. Sentiments and maxims preserved in the East in a terse, proverbial, and poetic form. The book exhibits the chief characteristic of Hebrew poetry, viz. *parallelism*, or the slightly varied repetition of the same sentiment in parallel clauses. Earliest examples of it in Gen. iv. 23 ; Jude 14. Parallelism a key to the interpretation. The poetry of Job also *strophaic*,—arranged, though irregularly, in strophes or stanzas, each containing more or less verses or connected parallel clauses.

V. Genuineness and Integrity of the Book. The whole now generally admitted to be from one and the same author. The three parts,—introduction, controversy, and conclusion—intimately connected with and necessary to each other. The speeches of Elihu necessary as a complement to the others, and as preparatory to the address of Jehovah. Possibly, as in some other books of Scripture, a second inspired hand may have completed the book as we now have it. A dislocation of some passages also possible; the instances noted in the commentary.

VI. Canonicity and Inspiration. Universally admitted. Its inspiration not prejudiced by our ignorance of the human author. The book apparently known by Ezekiel six hundred years before Christ (Ezek. xiv. 14). Translated into Greek, as part of the Hebrew Scriptures, two hundred and seventy years before Christ. Included in the Scriptures used and referred to by Jesus and the apostles as the inspired word of God. Quoted twice by the apostle (Heb. xii. 5 ; 1 Cor. iii. 19) ; in the latter case with the usual form of Scripture quotation, "It is written." Its morality and theology in harmony with the other books of Scripture. Completes the canon by presenting a view of the Patriarchal Dispensation. In the development of the history of Redemption, stands midway between the Fall and the Crucifixion.

VII. Subject of the Book. The trial of Job; its occasion, nature, endurance, and issue. The trial of man as recovered by Divine grace from Adam's fall. Proof given against Satan that there is such a thing as disinterested piety in the world. To afford this proof, Job visited with varied, intense, and accumulated suffering. Keen discussion arising out of this between Job and his three friends, as to why he is thus treated. The cause, according to the friends, some secret sins on the part of Job; according to Job himself, God's mere arbitrary will. Another reason hinted at by one of the three and maintained by a fifth speaker,—the benevolent design of suffering though induced by sin (ch. v. 17; xxxiii. 19—30). The book, the story of an elect one in early patriarchal days, taught by suffering to learn practically the life of faith. The nest in which he thought to die, rifled of everything. Job righteous, but not yet prepared for such a change. To be made, by trial, a member of the pilgrim family. Job, like Abraham, to be one of God's strangers in the world (Heb. xi. 13). Chastened to be made a partaker of God's holiness (Heb. xii. 10). Made to have resurrection in his experience as well as in his creed.

VIII. Design of the Book. Probably manifold. (1) To show the reality of true religion, the nature and the power of faith. (2) To exhibit the blessedness of the godly however assailed by affliction. (3) To show that true piety is wisdom, the only way to man's real and highest welfare. (4) To display the Providence of God in its inscrutableness, justice, and mercy. (5) To show that in the case of the righteous, "behind a frowning Providence" God "hides a smiling face." (6) To exhibit the consistency between the truths of Revelation and the dealings of Providence. (7) To afford an example of patience and trust in God under sorest trials, and so to minister

2

comfort and hope to tried believers. (8) To exhibit a child of God set to learn through trials the power of his heavenly calling. (9) To illustrate the fact of human depravity even in the best. (10) To teach the final conquest over Satan and the triumphs of righteousness and peace in the earth. (11) To exhibit a picture of man's fall and his redemption through faith in the Redeemer. (12) To present in Job a type of Christ, the righteous sufferer for man's sake. The same type exhibited in many of the Psalms, as the twenty-second and sixty-ninth. The sufferings of Christ and the glory that should follow, the central truth of Old Testament Scriptures (1 Pet. i. 11). The testimony of Jesus the spirit of prophecy (Rev. xix. 10; Luke xxiv. 27). This book, like the rest of the Old Testament, written that through patience and comfort of the Scriptures we might have hope (Rom. xv. 4). Profitable, like all inspired Scripture, for doctrine, for reproof, for correction, and for instruction in righteousness (2 Tim. iii. 16).

IX. **Divisions.** Three general divisions with many subordinate ones; viz., the introduction or prologue (ch. i. ii.); the controversy, including Job's lamentation as the occasion of it (iii-xlii., 6); the conclusion or epilogue (xlii. 7, &c.). Two parts in the controversy:—the Controversy proper between Job and his three friends; and the Solution of it, in the speeches of Elihu and the address of Jehovah.

X. **Analysis of Contents.**—I. FIRST DIVISION: historical introduction (in prose) (ch. i. ii.) (1) Job's character, prosperity, and walk (i. 1—5). (2) Jehovah's purpose to prove Job by suffering (i.) through loss of property (i. 16—17; (ii.) loss of children (18, 19); (iii.) loss of health (ii. 1—8). (3) Job's perseverance in his piety (i. 20—22; ii. 9, 10.) (4) The visit of his friends as the preparation for the conflict (ii. 11—13).

II. SECOND DIVISION: The Controversy and its Solution (in poetry). (1) Job's desponding lament, the immediate occasion of the controversy (ch. iii). (2) The controversy proper, in three cycles or courses of dialogues.

First Course: Commencement of the controversy (iv.—xiv.).

First Dialogue—Eliphaz and Job (iv.—vii.). (1) Eliphaz accuses Job and exhorts him to repentance (iv., v). (2) Job justifies his lament and complains of his friends (vi., vii).

Second Dialogue—Bildad and Job (viii.—x.). (1) Bildad reproves Job and reminds him of the end of wickedness (viii.). (2) Job maintains his innocence and complains of God's mysterious severity (ix., x.).

Third Dialogue—Zophar and Job (xi.—xiv.). (1) Zophar severely charges Job and urges him to repentance (xi). (2) Job attacks his friends as wanting in wisdom and justice, and addresses himself to God, still maintaining his innocence, and complaining of the general lot of humanity (xii.—xiv.).

Second Course: Growth of the controversy (xv.—xxi.).

First Dialogue—Eliphaz and Job (xv.—xvii.). (1) Eliphaz reproves Job's obstinacy in maintaining his innocence, and asserts God's righteous retribution on evil doers (xv.) (2) Job bemoans his forlorn condition, but expresses the confident hope of a future acknowledgment of his innocence (xvi., xvii.).

Second Dialogue—Bildad and Job (xviii., xix.). (1) Bildad rebukes Job as an empty boisterous talker, and reminds him of the fate of the ungodly (xviii.) (2) Job retorts on his friends, bewails his sufferings, but expresses confidence in God as his Redeemer and Avenger, and warns his friends of the consequence of their uncharitableness (xix.).

Third Dialogue—Zophar and Job (xx., xxi.). (1) Zophar maintains the short-lived prosperity and bitter end of the ungodly (xxi.). (2) Job in reply asserts their frequent prosperity and the afflictions of the godly (xxi.).

Third Course: Height of the controversy (xxii.—xxvii.).

First Dialogue—Eliphaz and Job (xxii.—xxiv.). (1) Eliphaz openly accuses Job of great sins and warns him to repent (xxii.). (2) Job expresses his wish that God would appear and decide the case Himself, but bemoans His withdrawal from him, recounting at the same time similiar cases of apparent inequality of divine procedure (xxiii., xxiv.).

Second Dialogue—Bildad and Job (xxv., xxvi.). (1) Bildad briefly declares God's greatness and purity, and man's vileness (xxv.). (2) Job ridicules Bildad's common-places, and enlarges much more fully on God's sovereignty and power (xxvi.).

Job alone in the field (xxvii., xxviii.). (1) Solemnly re-asserts his innocence, and declares his joy in God, with the certain miserable end of the ungodly (xxvii.). (2) Intimates that the wisdom which can solve the problem is only found with and through means of true piety (xxviii.).

The Solution of the controversy.

First Step in the Solution : *Guilt cannot be the cause of those peculiar sufferings.* Job's soliloquy (xxix.—xxxi.). (1) Longing retrospect of former prosperity (xxix.). (2) Mournful description of his present condition (xxx.). (3) Solemn protestation of his freedom from open and secret sins (xxxi.).

Second Step: *Afflictions of the righteous chastening and purifying.* Elihu's speech (xxxii. —xxxvii.). (1) His introduction by the poet, in prose (xxxii. 1—6). (2) His motive and reasons for joining in the controversy (6—22).

His first speech (xxxiii.). (1) Invites Job's attention to himself as a mild judge of his case (1—7). (2) Blames his confidence in his innocence (8—11). (3) Declares God's gracious dealings with men to bring them to repentance (12—30).

His second speech (xxxiv.). (1) Blames Job for doubting God's righteousness (1—9). (2) Maintains that righteousness, as necessary to the government of the world (10—30). (3) Reproves Job's sin and folly in charging God with injustice, and in calling on Him to decide the controversy (31—37).

His third speech (xxxv.). Blames Job for thinking piety useless to its possessor (1—5). Gives reason for the continuance of sufferings (9—16).

His fourth speech (xxxvi.—xxxvii.). (1) Defends the righteousness of God on the ground of His benevolent object in afflicting (1—21), and of His wise and mighty operations in nature (22—37; xxxvii. 1—13). (2) Shows the lessons from these operations (14—24).

Third Step in the Solution: *None may dispute against God.* Jehovah's speeches, with Job's confession (xxxviii., xlii. 1—6).

Jehovah's appearance and challenge to Job (xxxviii. 1—3).

His first speech (xxxviii.—xxxix.). (1) Challenges Job to answer various questions relative to creation (4—15); to the visible universe and powers of nature (16—27); to the wind and starry heavens (28—38); to the preservation and propagation of wild animals (xxxix. 1—30). (2) Conclusion of speech, with Job's humble reply (xl. 1—5).

Jehovah's second speech (xl. 6, &c., xli.). (1) Reproves Job for doubting God's righteousness (xl. 7—14). (2) Points to humbling proofs of his weakness in relation to certain animals, as the Behemoth and Leviathan (xl. 15, &c., xli.).

Job's humble confession of the divine power and his own guilt and folly (xlii. 1—6).

III. Third Division. Historical conclusion, in prose (xlii. 7—15). (1) Jehovah's justification of Job before his friends (7—10). (2) Job's restoration to former honour and dignity (11, 12). (3) The doubling of his estate and children (12—17).

CHAPTER I. 1—3.

FIRST PART OF PROSE INTRODUCTION TO THE BOOK OR POEM.

1. Job's personality (verse 1). "There was a man," &c.

1. *His actual existence.* Job a historic, not a fictitious character. Mentioned with Noah and Daniel (Ez. xiv. 14). Lived in the time of the patriarchs. Died about 200 years old; Abraham, 175; his father Terah, 205. No apparent allusion in the Book to the Exodus or the Giving of the Law. Worship, manners, and customs, those of patriarchal times. *His existence a proof God never left Himself without a witness.*

2. *His residence.* "In the land of Uz." Uz, east or south-east of Palestine. Adjacent to the Edomites, who appear at one time to have occupied it (Lam. iv. 21). Probably in Arabia Deserta, between Palestine and the Euphrates. Uz the name of a son of Aram the son of Shem (Gen. x. 23); of the firstborn of Nahor, Abraham's brother (Gen. xxii. 21); and of the grandson of Seir the Horite (Gen. xxxvi. 28). The country named from one of these. Job's country, like Abraham's, at that time tending to idolatry (ch. xxxi. 26—28). *Grace found flourishing in the most unfavourable situations.* Job, like Abraham and Daniel, found "faithful among the faithless." *To be godly among the ungodly a high excellence and honour.* So Obadiah in Ahab's court and the saints in Cesar's palace (1 Kings xviii. 12; Phil. iv. 22).

3. *His name.* "Whose name was Job." Denotes "the persecuted," or "the penitent." Names in the east often significant, —descriptive of character or history. Sometimes given from events connected with the birth, as Jabez, Ichabod, &c. Sometimes changed for another in after-life, as Jacob for Israel, Jedidiah for Solomon. Benoni, "son of my affliction," changed by Jacob to Benjamin,—"son of my right hand" (Gen. xxxv. 18). Job thought by some to be the same with Jobab (Gen. x. 29). "Job" also the name of one of the sons of Issachar (Gen. xlvi. 13). Job's name a memento of the possible or actual reverse to his prosperity (ch. iii. 25, 26). His afflictions to be remembered as waters that have passed away (ch. xi. 16). *Profitable, as well as pleasant, to remember past troubles* (Ps. xlii. 6, 8).

II. His character. "That man was perfect," &c. *The question not so much what a man* DOES *as what he* IS. Grace mentioned before greatness. *A gracious character and spiritual blessings a man's choicest possessions.*

"Perfect." Implies: 1. *Completeness.* Job complete in all the parts of his moral character (Jam. i. 4). Like a human body with no member or organ wanting or imperfect. A man's morality and religion to be characterized by *symmetry and thoroughness. Attention not to be given to one class of duties to the neglect of another.*—Job conscientious in the discharge of all the duties of life (Ps. cxix. 6). Kept, like Paul, a conscience void of offence both towards God and man (Acts xxiv. 16). Believers to be sanctified wholly, throughout body, soul, and spirit (1 Thess. v. 23.) *Are actually sanctified in every part, though every part not wholly sanctified.* A perfect man, in the New Testament sense, an advanced, mature, and fully instructed Christian (Phil. iii. 15; 1 Cor. ii 6; Eph. iv. 13; James iii. 2).

2. *Sincerity.* Job's perfection rather that of purpose than performance. Aimed constantly at perfection. Not sinless but sincere. Without guile (John i. 57). Without hypocrisy towards God or double-dealing towards man. *Sincerity the foundation of a gracious character.* Gives religion all its worth and beauty. Godly sincerity is Gospel perfection. Sincere and sound-hearted believers in God's sight "perfect."

3 *Blamelessness.* The character of Zechariah and Elizabeth (Luke i. 6). No fault found in Daniel, even by his enemies (Dan. vi. 4). Moral integrity is Bible perfection. Paul lived in all good conscience (Acts xxiv. 2). Job blameless though not sinless. Reproved by Jehovah (ch. xlii. 5, 6). Noah said to be perfect (Gen. vi. 9).—God's testimony to Job's blamelessness (ch. ii. 3). His own (ch. xxxi *throughout*).

Christian Perfection.

A certain perfection belonging to saints both in Old and New Testaments. The holiness of believers on earth, *partial and progressive.* Christ the only absolutely righteous and perfect One. Believers perfect and complete in Him, now *representatively,* hereafter *personally* (Col. ii, 10). Have here a *begun* perfection in conformity to Christ's image (Rom.

5

viii. 9. 20). That conformity to be in time absolute and complete (2 Cor. iii. 18). Christ made to those who are in Him both "wisdom" and "sanctification" (1 Cor. i. 30). Believers only made perfect in love (1 John iv. 18). Job's case (ch. xxix 11, 16; xxxi. 16, 20). Love the fulfilling of the law (Rom. xiii. 10). Perfection required by God in all his children (Matt. v. 48; Gen. xvii. 1; Jam. i. 4). To be constantly pressed after by them (Phil. iii. 12, 14). Desire and endeavour after it a test of sincerity. Not usually to be attained without afflictions (Heb. v. 8; xii. 10, 11). The Captain of our salvation himself made perfect through suffering (Heb. ii. 10). Job perfect and upright *before* his trials, humble and contrite *after* them (ch. xl. 4; xlii. 6.

"Upright." Refers to heart and life. Or, "perfect" internally, "upright" externally.— Job outwardly what he was inwardly, and *vice versâ*. *Uprightness of life and conduct the best proof of inward sincerity.* When the heart is sincere towards God, the actions will be just towards men. "Upright" = straight. Job held the straight path of rectitude. Sin's ways crooked. Joshua not to turn to the right hand or to the left (Joshua i. 7). Like Daniel, Job did what was right, regardless of consequences (Dan. vi. 10). "Perfect" and "upright" connected also in the Psalms (Psalm xxxvii. 37). The two complete the moral character of a man of God.

"One that feared God." Another element in his character, and accounting for the preceding. *Religion, or the fear of God, the true basis of morality.* The first table of the law the foundation of and preparation for the second. *A morality without religion is a body without a soul.*—Job profoundly religious. The horizon of his soul filled with God (ch. xxix. 3, 4; xxxi. 23). Looked at all things in their relation to God and His will (ch. xxxi. 2, 14, 15, 28). Reverenced His majesty, regarded His authority, dreaded His wrath. Feared *God*, not the idols of his countrymen (ch. xxxi. 26, 27). So Cornelius (Acts x. 2.) Feared Him, not with a slavish but a filial fear—a fear coupled with confidence and love. *The fear of the saints, rather the fear of offending than the dread of suffering.* Believers fear God for His *goodness* as well as His *greatness* (Hos. iii. 5). Saints fear God because He *pardons*, sinners because He *punishes* (Ps. cxxx. 4). *Filial fear the product of God's free grace revealed in the Gospel* (Jer. xxxii. 39, 40; Rom. viii. 15). The root of all true religion. Holiness perfected in it (2 Cor. vii. 1. Forgiveness through the blood of Jesus imparted with a view to it (Ps. cxxx. 4). That fear required by God (Jer. v. 22). Due to Him (Ps. lxxxix. 7). Casts out the fear of

man (Heb. xi. 27; Dan. iii. 16—18).—*The fear of God the secret of true courage and endurance.* — Fabius Maximus, a Roman general, sought to impress his soldiers with reverence for the gods as the best means of confirming their valour [*Plutarch*].

"Eschewed evil." Heb., "Departed from evil," from its practice and presence. Hurried away from it as from the presence of a monster. Avoided it as offensive to God, and in itself loathsome and abominable. *Sometimes more difficult to avoid evil than to practice good.* Evil often fashionable. Followed by the multitude (Exod. xxiii. 2; Matt. vii. 13). To depart from evil the effect and evidence of the fear of God (Ps. iv. 4; Prov. viii. 13; xvi. 6). Exhibits the spirituality and strength of holiness. The spirit active against evil in order to depart from it. Believers while on earth beset with temptations to evil. Job eschewed *all* evil. Every appearance of it to be abstained from (1 Thess. v. 22). Evil to be departed from in its *pleasing* as well as its *repulsive* forms. Not only evil itself to be eschewed, but its occasions, temptations, and incentives (Prov. iv. 14, 15; Matt. v. 29, 30). Job withdrew his *eyes* from evil as well as his hands and feet (ch. xxxi. 1). To depart from evil necessary in order to persevere in good. Grace received to be carefully guarded and preserved. Job's perfection not sinlessness, but a constant striving against sin.

III. His prosperity.

In three particulars (verse 2).

1. *His children.* "There were born to him." Children esteemed a great part of a man's prosperity and happiness, especially in O. T. times. Viewed as a mark of the Divine favour and blessing (Ps. cxxvii. 3—5; cxxviii. 3, 4). Mentioned first as the chief part of Job's outward prosperity. His happiness, however, not merely in having children, but having them *godly* (verse 5). "Born *to* him." His children comforts and blessings to him. *Job eminent for holiness, yet not a hermit or recluse.*

"Seven sons and three daughters." In number and sex the ideal of a perfect family. Both numbers, as well as their sum, mystic and symbolical. "Seven," indicative of *perfection*; "ten," of *multitude*. The more children, if gracious, the greater blessing. More sons than daughters, an enhancement of his property. *A large family no hindrance to piety, uprightness, and charity* (ch. xxix. 11—17; xxxi. 13—20, 39). So Enoch walked with God 300 years, and begat sons and daughters (Gen. v. 22).

2. *His property.* "His substance was seven thousand sheep," &c. Job described as an Arab prince, emir or sheikh. His

possession in *cattle*, though not a wandering Bedowin (ch. xxix. 7). No land or houses mentioned, though living in or near a city. Appears, like Isaac, to have cultivated land belonging to others (ch. xxxi. 39). Wealth, in earliest times, reckoned not by extent of land but number of cattle (Gen. xii. 61; xxiv. 35; xxx. 43). *Heavenly wisdom the only real "substance"* (Prov. viii. 21; xxiii. 5). *Piety and charity ordinarily the best way of thriving even in this world.* Prayer whets the tools, oils the wheels, and brings a blessing. Riches an evil only in their *abuse*. In the *hand* a *blessing*, in the *heart* a *curse*. Riches *not bad*, therefore given to the *good; not the best*, therefore given also to the *bad*. Taken from the good for *trial*, from the bad for *conviction or punishment*. Not money, but the *love* of it, the root of all evil (1 Tim. vi. 10). Job's grace seen in his having riches without setting his heart on them (ch. xxxi. 24, 25; Ps. lxii. 10). One of the few examples in which the camel gets through the needle's eye (Matt. xix. 24). In the N.T., the poor of this world often chosen as heirs of the kingdom (Jam. ii. 5). The Master himself without a place on which to lay his head (Matt. viii. 20). Enough for the servant that he be as his Lord (Matt. x. 25). Job pious, and his piety acting as a friend to his prosperity; prosperous, and his prosperity giving a lustre to his piety [*Henry*.]

"Household." Body of servants or slaves required for cattle and agriculture. Job's slaves or servants treated by him with justice and humanity (ch. xxxi. 13). Re-

garded by him as in God's sight on the same footing with himself (ch. xxxi. 14). Could all bear honourable testimony to his conduct and character (ch. xxxi. 31). Like Abraham, doubtless, had them trained for *God's* service as well as *his own* (Gen. xiv. 14).

3. *His dignity*. "So that" (or, "and") "he was the greatest," &c. A new feature in his prosperity. Probably indicates his eminence and rank as a prince or magistrate. Job not only the *richest* but the most *respected* in the land (Gen. xxiv. 35; xxvi. 13; Ecc. ii. 9). A man of great authority, not only from his *possessions* but his *character*. His greatness not only that of *wealth*, but of intellectual and moral *worth* (ch. xxix. 11 16; xxxi. 16—20). Mentioned to show the greatness of his fall and his grace in bearing it. Job, like David and Daniel, an example of grace coupled with earthly nobility. *Grace graces the highest position. Goodness, the fairest jewel in an earthly coronet.* Grace found in every station. Not many noble are called, yet always some (1 Cor. i. 26). Poor Lazarus reposes in rich Abraham's bosom. Goodness appears the more excellent when associated with worldly greatness. Has then most to overcome and can most diffuse its influence.

"Men of the East." "The East" applied to countries east of Palestine, as the north of Arabia. *Heb.*, "Sons of the East." Noted for their riches, yet Job the richest of them all. Easy with God to make his children the *greatest*, yet in love often places them among the *least* in this world (1 Cor. i. 27, 28).

CHAPTER I. 4, 5.

SECOND PART OF PROSE INTRODUCTION.

I. Job's happiness in his children (verse 4).

"And his sons went," &c. Their feasting the medium of social intercourse and of maintaining friendly relations with each other. Shows (1) the social habits of his children; (2) the love and harmony prevailing among them. An exemplification of Ps. cxxxiii. 1. Contrasted with the family of Adam (Gen. iv. 8); of Abraham (Gen. xxi. 9; of Isaac (Gen. xxvii. 41); of Jacob (Gen. xxxvii. 4); of David (2 Sam. xiii. 28).

Festivity.

"Feasting" lawful,—when (1) moderate; (2) seasonable; (3) in the fear of God; (4) with thankful acknowledgment of his good ness; (5) without offence to others; (6) with charitable remembrance of the poor and needy

(Luke xiv. 12—14. Ecc. iii. 4). The general rule of Christian feasting (1 Cor. x. 31). Its limitation (Rom. xiv. 20, 21; 1 Cor. viii. 13; x. 32, 33). Unseasonable times for feasting (Amos vi. 4—6; Joel ii. 16; Is. xxii. 12, 13). Christ's presence and miracle at Cana a sanction to special seasons of temperate festivity (John ii. 1—11). The creature given not only for necessity but delight (Ps. civ. 14, 15).

Job's sons feasted (1) in their own houses; indicating their wealth, order, and harmony; —also, the maturity of their age. Enhances the calamity of their death. (2) "Each on his own day," *i. e.* his birthday, or the day on which it was his turn to entertain the rest. Birthdays in the East days of great rejoicing (Gen. xl. 20; Matt. xiv. 6). (3.) They sent and called for their "three sisters," supposed, like women in the East, to be living with their mother, in their own tent or apartment (Gen. xxiv. 67 ; xxxi. 33, 34 ; Esther ii. 9—14). Beautiful picture of fraternal harmony and affection. *Proof of how Job had trained up his family.*

II. Job's spiritual care over his children (verse 5).

"And it was so, when," &c. At the conclusion of each feast Job offers special sacrifices for his children. Uncertain whether his sons were present, though probable. "He sent and sanctified them ;" (1) Doing what is immediately after related ; or, (2) Exhorting them to prepare themselves for the approaching solemnity. In O. T language, people often said to *do* that which they *enjoin to be done.* The members of the family usually present at the family sacrifice (1 Sam. xx. 6, 29).—Hence learn :—

1. *Christians to see that their families observe God's worship as well as themselves.* Family worship an institution of God. An acknowledgment of God as the God of the family and the author of family blessings: A prayerless family an unblessed one. A family without worship, a garden without a fence. The presence of the children at daily family worship calculated to produce (1) Reverential fear and filial confidence towards God ; (2) Dutiful regard, submission, and obedience towards their parents ; (3) Harmony, affection, and sympathy towards each other.

2. *Preparation necessary for solemn services and approaches to God* (Ex. xix. 10, 14 ; Ps. xxvi. 2). As men measure to God in *preparation*, God measures to men in *blessing* [*Trapp*]. God not to be worshipped carelessly and slovenly, but in the best manner possible (Ecc. v. 1). Jews had their preparation and fore-preparation for the Passover. Before Christ, such preparation both moral and ceremonial (Gen. xxxv. 2). After Christ, only moral (Ps. xxvi. 2).

Job took measures to keep his children in a pure and pardoned state. *Parents cannot make their children spiritual worshippers, but can bring them to spiritual ordinances.* Cannot give converting grace, but can employ the means through which God may impart it.

Job recognized and sought to discharge his responsibilities as a father. Realized his children's relation to God and eternity. Hence more concerned that they should have *grace in their heart* than *gold in their house ;* should stand in the favour of *God* than enjoy the smiles of the *world ;* should be *sanctified* for the *next* world than be *accomplished* for *this.* Job's solicitude contrasted with Eli's indifference (1 Sam. ii. 29). *A parent's*

responsibility for his children does not cease with their childhood. Though no longer sheltered by the parent's *roof*, they can and ought to be sheltered by the parent's *prayers.* "Rose up early." His zeal and earnestness. Impatient till God was reconciled to his children. An early hour required by the *largeness* of the work as well as the *solemnity* of it. Sacrifices usually offered early in the morning (Ex. xxxii. 6). *Not safe to let sin be unrepented of and unforgiven.* The Psalmist's resolution (Ps. lxiii. 1). Abraham's practice (Gen. xxii. 3). That of Moses (Ex. xxiv. 4; of Jesus Christ (Mark i. 35). Has special promise attached to it (Prov. viii. 17). What our hands find to do, to be done with our might (Ecc. ix. 10). *Well to begin the day with prayer and application of the Atonement.* God, the author of *every day*, ought to have the *first hour* of it. The mind then freshest and freest from earthly cares and distractions. Early worship taught by the light of nature. Practised by the heathen (1 Sam. v. 3, 4).

III. Job's faith in the Atonement.

"Offered burnt offerings," as the head of the family. Patriarchal custom. So Abraham (Gen. xii. 7, 8); Isaac (Gen. xxvi. 25); Jacob (Gen. xxxiii. 20; xxxv. 6). The Law with a priestly family not yet instituted.

Sacrifices.

The "burnt-offering" a victim slain and burnt entire on the altar (Lev. i. 9.) Under the law, might be either a bullock, a lamb, a goat, or turtle doves (Lev. i. 2, 10, 14). Burnt-offerings the only sacrifices mentioned in Patriarchal times. Sacrifices offered from the earliest period. Found in Adam's family (Gen. iv. 4). Probably prescribed by God himself on the day man fell. The first sacrifices probably the beasts with whose skins God provided coats for our first parents (Gen. iii. 21). The first express direction from God regarding sacrifice given to Abraham (Gen. xv. 9.) Intended to keep in view the promised Seed, to be bruised in man's stead (Gen. iii. 15). Offered with every special approach to God. No worship without sacrifice. Without shedding of blood no remission, and without remission no acceptable approach to God. Sacrifices told (1) Of guilt; (2) Of punishment; (3) Of substitution. Sometimes *Eucharistic*, or connected with *thanksgiving.* So Noah's (Gen. viii. 20). Sometimes *Federative*, or connected with a *covenant* (Ex. xxiv. 4 8). In Job's case, simply *Expiatory*, or with a view to *forgiveness of sin.* Hence his faith (Heb. ii. 4). Sacrifice, as a substitute for the offender, a *natural instinct.* Hence, as well as from *tradition*, universal in the heathen world. *There,* sometimes human ones offered, as of more supposed value than dumb animals. Impossible for the blood of bulls and goats to take away sin (Heb. x. 4). The insufficiency of all such sacrifices deeply felt in the conscience (Mic. vi. 6, 7). *Every bloody sacrifice a finger pointing to the only sufficient one on Calvary* (John i. 29). Hence the cry on the cross, "It is finished," and the rent veil (John xix. 30; Matt. xxvii. 51.)

"Die man, or justice must, unless for him
  Some other *able* and as *willing,* pay
  The rigid satisfaction, death for death."
                              Milton.

"According to the number of them all." A victim for each of the seven sons. Job no niggard in God's service. *Children to be prayed for individually and specifically.* Each has his particular temper and circumstances, trials and temptations, sins and wants. *Christ's one offering sufficient for all and for all time* (Heb. x. 12—14). *Particular application of the atonement to be made by and for each.* Each sinner needs a *substitute for himself* or a *personal interest* in the great universal one. "He gave Himself a ransom for *all,*" to be followed by—"He gave Himself for *me*" (1 Tim. ii. 6; Gal. ii. 20).

"For Job said," within himself or to others. Special reason why Job now sacrificed. Religious duties to be *grounded on intelligent reasons.* God requires a reasonable service (Rom. xii. 1). Not *ignorance,* but *intelligence,* the mother of true devotion. "Call him wise whose actions, words, and steps are all a clear *because* to a clear *why*" [*Lavater*].

"It may be my sons have sinned,"—during their festivities. A bloody sacrifice rendered necessary by *sin,* which can only be washed out by blood (Heb. ix. 22). Sin such an outrage on God's universe that only blood can atone for it [*Talmage*]. "It *may* be." *Suspicion* of sin, much more the *consciousness* of it, ought to send us at once to Christ's blood. A blessing to have a tender conscience. To be without *allowed sin,* the holiness of *earth;* to be without *sin at all,* the holiness of *heaven. Sin easily committed in the tumult and rush of pleasure.* The time of

security the time for greatest *apprehension.* Job's sons usually devout. Their sinning now only a *contingency;* but a very possible one. Their danger that of—(1) Vain thoughts; (2) Excited feelings; (3) Unguarded words. Cause for Job's concern —(1) In the depravity of the heart; (2) In the frailty and folly of youth; (3) in the temptations incident to a feast. Wine a mocker; sin easily committed under its influence (Prov. xx. 1; xxxiii. 29—35). A double guard needed in the social use of it.—"Cursed God in their hearts;"—reproached or renounced Him for the moment. Same word usually rendered "bless." Sometimes also the opposite, as 1 Kings xxi. 10. Blessing in the East customary on parting as well as meeting (Gen. xlvii. 7—10; 1 Kings viii. 66). Hence, or from a peculiar Hebrew usage, the probable double meaning of the word here as well as in chap. ii. 9. *Allowed sin a temporary renouncement of God. Sin itself an element of separation between God and the soul. Great danger of such renouncement in festivity and worldly pleasure.* "In their hearts;"—(1) thinking lightly of God's favour in comparison with present enjoyment: the contrast of Psalm iv. 6, 7; (2) forgetting and not acknowledging God as the author of all their mercies. *Heart or secret sins not to be lightly thought of* (Ps. xix. 12; 1 Cor. iv. 4). Such sins are (1) Dangerous; (2) Deserving condemnation; (3) Need atoning blood. The morality of Job's children. Job apprehensive only of *heart sins.*

IV. The habit and continuance of Job's piety.

"Thus did Job continually." Marg.: "All the days;" either, while the feast lasted; or rather, at the conclusion of every such feast. Job's piety habitual and constant. Mark of his sincerity. He who serves God uprightly will serve Him continually [*M. Henry*]. The same occasions always liable to bring the same sins. Same corrupt nature always present. *Fresh sins require fresh pardon.* Renewed pardon requires renewed application to the atoning blood. The blood of Jesus a fountain ever full and ever free. *Prayer and care to follow the godly through life.* Constant washing of the feet needed (John xiii. 10).

CHAPTER I. 6—12

THIRD PART OF PROSE INTRODUCTION.

I. The celestial council (verse 6). "There was a day." *What God decrees in eternity has its day of accomplishment in time.* "Everything has its hour" [*Hebrew Proverb*].

"The sons of God came." Representation of God's court and administration. So 1 Kings xxii. 19. The veil separating the visible from the invisible drawn aside.

9

Reveals an assembly of God's angelic ministers and Himself among them. *All Job's trials the result of transactions in heaven.* The same true of the sufferings and death of Job's great Antitype (Acts ii. 23; vi. 27, 28); and of the trials of the least of His suffering members (Rom. viii. 28—30).

Angels.

"Sons of God," *i.e.*, angels, celestial spirits. So xxxviii. 7. All ministering spirits employed in Jehovah's service (Ps. ciii. 21; Heb. i. 14) Perhaps including the spirits of departed believers (Rev. vii. 13; xxii. 8, 9; Acts xii. 14, 15). "Sons of God," from their *nature;* "angels," or messengers, from their *office.* "Sons of God," by *creation;* "angels," by Divine *appointment.* "Sons of God," as resembling God,—(1) in spirituality of substance; (2) in intellectual, moral, and physical qualities (Ps. ciii. 20). Of various ranks and orders, and invested with various powers and charges (Rom. viii. 38; Eph. i. 21; Col. i. 16; 2 Peter iii. 22; Rev. xiv. 18; xvi. 5; xix. 17).—"Present themselves before the Lord," as His ministers or attendants (Prov. xxii. 29; Zech. vi. 5; Luke i. 19). Ready to receive and execute His orders and to render their account. "Thousands at His bidding speed, and post o'er land and ocean." *As supreme Governor, God takes cognizance of all that is done in this and other worlds. Mighty spirits the ministers and executioners of His behests.* Such employed in the destruction of the cities of the plain (Gen. xix. 1, 12, 13); in the promulgation of the law on Mount Sinai (Gal. iii. 19; Acts vii. 53; Ps. lxviii. 17); in the destruction of the Assyrian army and deliverance of Jerusalem (Is. xxxvii. 36); in the restoration of the Jewish church and state after the captivity (Dan. 20, 21; Zech. i. 10, 11, 20, 21; vi. 1—8); in the establishment and spread of the Gospel (Luke ii. 9—12; John i. 51); in the destruction of the kingdom of Antichrist (Rev. xix. 14); in the transactions of the last day (Matt. xiii. 41, 49, 50); in the service of individual believers (Heb. i. 14; Acts xii. 7); preeminently in that of their incarnate Head (Ps. xci. 11, 12; Matt. iv. 11).

"The Lord." *Heb.,* "Jehovah." Always with this meaning when printed in capitals. Indicates (1) The self-existing, eternal, unchangeable Being (Ex. iii. 14); (2) The faithful fulfiller of covenant relations and engagements. Not practically known to the patriarchs before Moses by this name (Ex. vi. 3). Appeared only at the Burning Bush as the promise-fulfilling God. The name applied to and appropriated by Jesus (Rom. xiii. 10

—12; Rev. i. 8). Given specifically to the One True God who adopted the descendants of Abraham, Isaac, and Jacob for His people, when the world was apostatizing into idolatry. The name never applied to a false God or to any mere creature. Given however to an angel who is called "the angel of the Lord" or the "angel Jehovah," being the second person in the Godhead; the Messenger of the Covenant and Mediator between God and men, who afterwards became incarnate.

II. Satan's Presence.

"And Satan came also among them."

Satan.

Here first introduced under this name. Observe—

1. *His name.* Denotes "the adversary." The devil so called (1 Pet. v. 8). The name without the article applied to an adversary in a court of justice (Ps. cix. 6). Other names—the Devil or Slanderer; the Old Serpent; the Great Dragon; the Tempter; the Wicked One; Beelzebub; Apollyon; the Prince and god of this world.

2. *His personality.* His personal existence is (1.) *In accordance with reason.* (i) Existences may be *above* as well as *below* man. (ii.) These existences *may fall* and become unholy as truly as man. (iii.) Fallen intelligent beings usually the *tempters of others.* (2) *Testified by the whole of Scripture.* The truth regarding him gradually developed in the Old Testament. Marked out as a serpent in the temptation of our first parents. Probably the lying spirit in the mouth of the false prophets (1 Kings xxii. 21). The name itself given, 1 Chron. xxi. 1; Zech. iii. 1. His personality pre-eminently taught by the Lord Jesus Himself in the Gospels. (3) *Confirmed by universal belief.* The belief in the existence of such a spirit common to all nations.

3. *His nature and character.* A created spirit; probably one of the highest. A son of God by creation, like the other angels, and originally holy; but fell, apparently through pride (1 Tim. iii. 6; Jude vi.). Has become the tempter and accuser of men, especially of the good (Rev. xii. 10). The most finished specimen of unsanctified intelligence. His nature,—*great intellect employed for selfish and wicked purposes.* Designated by Christ a *liar* and a *murderer* (John viii. 44). Christ's whole life a conflict with him, according to the promise (Gen. iii. 15). The life of every believer a similar conflict (Eph. vi. 11—17; 1 Pet. v. 8). Believers made the theatre of Christ's continued victory over him. Already overcome by Christ on their behalf (Col. ii. 15). To be bruised under their feet shortly

(Rom. xvi. 20). Meantime to be steadfastly resisted (1 Pet. v. 9). Times of signal victory over him indicated in Luke x. 18.; Rev. xii. 10. Seeks every advantage over us (2 Cor. ii. 11). Transforms himself into an angel of light (2 Cor. xi. 14). Is overcome by the word of God and faith in the blood of Christ (Rev. xii. 11). Law and justice, through sin, on Satan's side against man; (Heb. ii. 14); but through Christ's death, once more on man's side against Satan (Is. xlii. 21; li. 8; Rom. viii. 32—34). Believers to reckon on his repeated and sometimes sudden assaults. The more faithful and walking in the light, the more exposed to them.

4. *His works.* The agent in Adam's fall (2 Cor. ii. 3)—a wide-spread tradition. Sought to overthrow Christ and to draw Him into sin (Matt. iv). He blinds men's minds against the light of the Gospel (2 Cor. iv. 4). Seeks to catch away the seed of the word from the hearts of the hearers (Matt. xiii. 19). Aims at beguiling men's minds from the simplicity of Christ's doctrine (2 Cor. ii. 3). Affects men's bodies with diseases and infirmities (Luke xiii. 16). Endeavours to thwart the preachers of the Gospel (1 Thess. ii. 18). Employs his messengers to buffet Christ's servants (2 Cor. xii. 7). *Probably much of the unsteadfastness and discomfort of believers due to his agency [Homilist].* In regard to Satan, the book of Job in close analogy with the whole Bible. Job's happiness the object of his envy, like that of Adam in Eden. Lying spirits, as well as ministering angels, sent forth from God's presence (also in 1 Kings xxii. 19). The thorn in the flesh from Satan, alike in the case of Job and Paul.—"Came also." Satan not less than other spirits subject to God's authority. Like them also employed in executing the divine purposes. An intruder into all sacred places (1 Kings xxii. 19, &c.; Luke, iv. 31). His punishment only gradually inflicted. Still allowed to move at large. —"Among them." As Judas among the Apostles. Still found in the assemblies of God's children. No place on earth too holy for his intrusion. Public ordinances special occasions for the exertion of his power. Present to distract the thoughts, defile the imagination, and harden the heart.

III. **Jehovah's challenge regarding Job** (verse 7).

" The Lord said unto Satan, whence comest thou?" The highest fallen spirit amenable to Jehovah. *No creature able to outgrow his responsibility.* That responsibility not diminished by a course of sin. God's questions not for information to the questioner but conviction to the questioned. Similar questions to Adam (Gen. iii. 2); and to Cain (Gen. iv. 9). The question intended to open the way to Job's desired trial. At the same time lays bare Satan's character and doings. *The most secret malice open to the eye of Omniscience.* "From going to and fro." Marks (1) Satan's *present circumstances.* Allowed still to roam at large, though ever in chains. Only *reserved* to the judgment of eternal fire (Jude vi.; Matt. xxv. 52). (2) His *terrible activity.* Satan no laggard. Ever on the wing. In constant quest of opportunities of mischief (1 Peter v. 8). A true Apollyon; assiduous in his endeavours to *destroy.* (3) His *homelessness and unrest.* Like Cain, a vagabond in the earth. Seeks rest and finds none (Matt. xii. 45). *No rest for a depraved spirit* (Is. lvii. 20, 21). (4) His *constant increase of knowledge.* Same word implies "*Search*" (Num. xi. 8; 2 Sam. xxiv. 2). Satan ever prying into the ways and circumstances of men. Constantly increasing his knowledge with a view to destroy.—"In the earth." This earth now the permitted sphere of his activity. No place therefore secure from his attacks. *Good to remember we are in a world where Satan is, and is ever active.* —"Going up and down in it." Intensifies his activity and restlessness. Satan's name among the Arabs, *El Harith,* "The Active," or "The Zealous." Seems to glory in his work. Knows he has but a short time (Rev. xii. 12). Goes up and down in the earth but finds no home in it. *Satan and all his children homeless wanderers in the universe.* His answer in keeping with his character. Tells only part of the truth. Says nothing of the evil he does and seeks to do. Unable to report any good deed, and unwilling to own to any evil one. His work had been to draw men away from their allegiance to God and to destroy their souls.—"Hast thou considered?" &c. Satan questioned as no unconcerned spectator. Allusion to his character as a spy, enemy, and accuser of good men. —"My servant Job." *God never ashamed to own his faithful servants. An interested spectator of a good man's ways and actions.* A faithful servant of God the most considerable object in the world to God and angels. "*A servant of God*" the most honourable and distinguishing title. May be mean and contemptible *without,* but all glorious *within* (Ps. xlv. 13). Job God's servant *consciously* and by *choice;* Nabuchadnezzar God's servant *unconsciously* and by *constraint* (Jer. xxv. 9). God's people proved by living as *His servants,* not as *their own masters.* "My servant Job," a stinging word to Satan. A *true saint is Satan's eye-sore.* A good man the special object of his attention and malice. Job mentioned by *name.* Implies intimate

11

knowledge and special regard (Ex. xxxiii. 12; Is. xlix. 1; Jer. xiii. 11; John x. 3).—"That there is," &c. God dwells on Job's character. Delights in contemplating his saints (Zeph. iii. 17.—"None like him," in the degree of his piety and fidelity. Degrees of excellence. Job not only the greatest but the holiest. *Eminence in goodness to be aimed at.* Paul gloried in being "not a whit behind the very chiefest Apostles" (2 Cor. xi. 5). His motto, "Forward" (Phil. iii. 11—14). "On to perfection" (Heb. vi. 1). God notices not only a man's piety but the *degree* of it. Gives to each his just meed of praise.—"A perfect and an upright man." Job's good character endorsed by God. Good to have *man's* testimony in our favour,—better still to have *God's.* God more observant of the good than the evil in his people (Num. xxiii. 21).

IV. Satan's accusation and proposal (verse 9).

"Doth Job serve God for nought?" Satan true to his name, the *Devil,* or Slanderer. Accuser of the brethren (Rev. xii. 10). *A good man's praise the reproach and torment of the bad.* Satan *exalts* a man's piety to make him *proud,* denies it to make him *sad.* Cannot deny Job's *religion,* but challenges the *ground and reality* of it. *A mark of Satan's children to be a detractor of true godliness.* Satan's method to begin by *questioning. Insinuates,* then directly *charges.* Always a liar. In Eden, called evil good, now calls good evil. Satan's insinuation the immediate occasion of Job's trial.—"For nought." Either (1) Without sufficient cause (John xv. 25); or, (2) Without regard to his own interest (Gen. xx 15). Job's religion charged with mercenary motives—his piety mere selfishness. *Bad men judge of others by themselves.* With carnal men *piety* is *policy.* A truth at the bottom of Satan's insinuation, though false in regard to Job. *Everything lies in the motive. A selfish piety no deity.* Common with Satan's children to call God's saints hypocrites. *An evil conscience makes men suspicious of others' sincerity.* Satan's charge against Job implicitly one against God himself and the plan of Redemption. If Job's religion is hollow, *all* religion is, and *Redemption is a failure.*—Satan's words true as a *fact,* though false as *motive. No man serves God for nought.* Godliness profitable unto all things (1 Tim. iv. 8; vi. 6). In keeping God's commandments is great reward (Ps. xix. 11). God himself the exceeding great reward of His servants (Gen. xv. 1). True godliness consistent with "respect to the recompense of the reward" (Heb. xi. 26). Past and present mercies also not excluded from the motives to godliness (Rom. xii. 1). Yet true religion *more* than *gratitude for past*

or *regard to future* good (Ps. cxix. 120, 140). Satan well acquainted with *mankind,* but ignorant of the *nature of true grace.* Not only a *deceiver* but, like all unregenerate men, *deceived* (Tit. iii. 3)—"Hast thou not made a hedge about him" (ver. 10). *Satan speaks truth when it serves his purpose.* The saint's happiness and enjoyment of the divine favour the object of his hatred and envy. God's protection of his servants a blessed truth. (Ps. xci.; cxxi.). His angels and still more *Himself* the hedge of His people (Ps. xxxiv. 7; cxxi. 3; Zach. ii. 5). Either is Himself the hedge or makes one. Satan would leap the hedge, but dare not, and cannot without permission.—"And about His house." Not only the godly but *their belongings* the object of divine care. Horses and chariots of fire around Elisha's residence (2 Kings vi. 17).—"On every side." Satan a wolf prowling round the fold and vexed to find no means of entrance.—"Hast blessed the work of His hands." Satan well aware of the source of Job's prosperity (Prov. x. 22). Satan no atheist. Practical atheism makes men deny what Satan admits. "The work of his hands," —his undertakings and engagements, as a man, a master, and a magistrate. Job diligent in business as well as fervent in spirit (Rom, xii. 11. *God's blessing not with the idle but with the industrious.* All toil *bootless* which is *unblest by God* (Ps. cxxvi. 12). Peter toils all night but catches nothing till Christ enters the boat (Luke v. 5, 6).—"But put forth thine hand now" (ver. 11). Satan's impudence equal to his malice. Gives God the lie and challenges Him to a trial. Asserts Job's hypocrisy and offers to prove it. Adopts the language of a suppliant. Satan prays, but in malice. Eager to see Job a sufferer and proved to be a hypocrite. Unable to put forth his own hand without permission.— "Touch all that he hath,"—children and possessions. The touch intended to be a destructive one (Ps. cv. 15). Satan's mercies cruel. *Earthly possessions subject to God's disposal.* Prosperity vanishes at his *touch,* (Ps. civ. 32). —"He will curse thee,"—reproach or renounce thee, as in ver. 5. The natural result, on the principle of *selfishness.* Common with unrenewed nature. Heathens in misfortune vilify their gods. Pompey, after a defeat, said there had been a mist on the eyes of Providence. *Margin,* "If he curse thee not." Probably an oath or imprecation, but partly suppressed. Profanity the devil's language; yet in God's presence keeps back from fear what men fear not to utter.—"To thy face," —boldly and openly. Job's fear for his sons that they might have done it in their *hearts. Boldness and openness an aggravation of sin.* Charity thinketh no evil; malice thinks *all* evil.

V. The Permission (ver. 12). "Behold." Marks (1) the strangeness of the thing; (2) the impudence of the demand; (3) the purpose of God to make the whole conspicuous. God's thoughts and ways above man's. His judgments a great deep. Makes the wrath of man and devil to praise Him. Glory to God and blessing to man by the permission now given to Satan.—"All that he hath is in thy power." Satan's prayer granted, and himself to be thine instrument. A double gratification, but to issue in his own confusion. *Not always a mercy for a man to have his prayer answered* (Ps. cvi. 15; Hos. xiii. 10, 11). Job now, like the disciples, to be for a time in Satan's sieve (Luke xxii. 31). To be cast into the furnace, not to be consumed, but proved and purified. Not understood at the time, though sometimes for a moment apprehended (xxiii. 10). His ignorance of the fact the cause of his disquietude and perplexity. *Believers often ignorant of the cause and object of their trials* (John xiii. 7). God's *heart* always *towards* his people even when his *hand* seems *against* them. His dearest saints sometimes apparently for a time abandoned by Him (Ps. xxii. 1; 2 Chron. xxxii, 31). The most crushing trials neither inconsistent with His grace *in* us nor His love *to* us. The cup drunk by the Head often tasted by the members, though for a different object (Matt. xx. 23; xxvi. 39). Satan God's scullion for scouring the vessels of His household [*Trapp*].—"On himself put not forth thine hand." Satan a chained lion, and the chain in our Father's hand. *Believers tried no farther than is necessary.*—"So Satan went forth." Gladly and eagerly as a wolf with permission to enter the fold. Thought every hour two till he had sped his commission [*Trapp*]. *His diligence in doing evil to be emulated by us in doing good.*—"From the presence of the Lord,"—having been, like Doeg, detained against his will (1 Sam. xxi. 7). *God's presence no place for an unholy nature.* To "see God," the happiness only of the "pure in heart" (Matt. v. 8; 1 John iii. 1, 3; Rev. xxii. 4).

CHAPTER I. 13—19.

FOURTH PART OF INTRODUCTION.—INFLICTION OF THE TRIAL.

I. Occasion of the trial (verse 16). "There was a day." Satan watches for the time best suited for his designs. The occasion chosen that the trial might fall the more grievous (Is. xxvii. 4). Diabolical wisdom in doing mischief. Satan's terrible malignity.—"His sons and his daughters were eating, and drinking wine." The children's hilarity to be an aggravation of the father's calamity. The more unexpected and unprepared for, the heavier the stroke. Satan likes to make his stroke tell. Turns mirth into mourning. Job's children to die when most likely to be sinning (ver. 5). Satan's object to destroy both body and soul at one stroke. Satan as well as Job knew the dangers incident to wine. *God's judgments often come when men are most secure* (Luke xii. 19, 20; 1 Thes. v. 2). Good to rejoice as though we rejoiced not (1 Cor. vii. 30). The Saviour's caution (Luke xxi. 3, 4). Changes in circumstances to be prepared for (Prov. xxvii. 1). *A day may have a fair beginning and a foul ending.* 'In the greatest calm provide for a storm' [*Queen Elizabeth*]—"In their elder brother's house." Hence no ordinary feast. The celebration of the eldest son's birthday chosen with characteristic malignity.

II. The trial itself in its four particulars. 1. *Attack of the Sabeans on the oxen and asses* (ver. 14, 15). "There came a messenger,"—spared in Satan's malice to carry the news. A "cruel messenger" to be sent to Job, as if a "rebellious man" (Prov. xvii. 11).—"The oxen." Satan begins with the cattle. The trial must rise in a climax. —"Were ploughing,"* preparing for the next year's crop, thus also to be lost.—"Asses feeding beside them," so arranged that both might share the same fate. The picture of security and repose heightens by contrast the calamity of the attack.—"Sabeans." A warlike marauding people in the north parts of Arabia Deserta. Those in *South* Arabia, or Arabia Felix, *merchants*, not *marauders* (vi. 19; 1 Kings x. 1). Bedoween incursions able to reduce a rich man to poverty in a few days. *Satan at no loss for instruments to do his work.* Possesses a mysterious power to influence men's minds to evil. The ungodly already prepared for that influence.

---

* Oriental ploughing, as in the south of Europe, done by oxen. Plough of wood, consisting of a share, two handles, and a pole or beam. Drawn by two oxen yoked together, and guided by a ploughman using a goad.

Satan's temptations suited to men's natural inclinations. Bad men often used by God for the trial and chastening of his children.—"Fell on them,"—rushed on them with a view to spoil. An unprovoked attack. Exceptions to the general rule in Prov. xvi. 7.—"Slain the servants." *Preparation for death to be taken into daily duties.* Blessed to be ready when the Master calls. *Sudden death then sudden glory.*—"I only am escaped," by God's special Providence and Satan's malice. Some escape from danger as "brands plucked out of the burning". (Amos iv. 11).

2. *Destruction of the sheep by lightning* (ver. 16). "While he was yet speaking." Fiendish rapidity of Satan's work. Aims at stunning and overwhelming the sufferer. Trials often like rapidly succeeding billows. Deep calleth unto deep (Ps. lxii. 7). Troubles seldom single. "Welcome misfortune, if you come alone" [*Basque Proverb*].—"Fire of God."—*Marg.*, "a great fire," (like Ps. civ. 16). "Hot thunderbolts" (Ps. lxxviii. 48). Rapid lightnings, apparently sent by God though really by Satan. A cut in the words put into the mouth of the shepherds. Act of an angry God. The object to represent God as cruel and unjust, and so bring Job to curse Him. A limited mysterious power given to Satan over the elements of nature (Eph. ii. 2).—"From heaven." From the upper regions of the air, but apparently from *God.* The air or lower heavens the place of Satan's special presence and operations (Luke x. 8; Eph. ii. 2; vi. 12).—"Sheep." The greatest part of Job's wealth (ver. 3.) Most frequently used in sacrifice. Smitten, though sanctified by frequent offerings. God's ways often dark and mysterious.

3. *Capture of the camels* (verse 17). "Chaldæans," *Heb.* "Chasdim." The name related to that of Chesed, Abraham's nephew (Gen. xxii. 22). Two such peoples mentioned in Genesis:—(1) The old Semitic Chaldæans of the mountains, in the north of Assyria and Mesopotamia (Gen. x. 22; xi. 28, 31); Abraham himself of these (Gen. xi. 28). (2) The later Chaldæans of Mesopotamia, descended from Nahor, Abraham's brother (Gen. xxii. 22). Called by Jeremiah an "ancient nation" (Jer. v. 15). A fierce and warlike people (Heb. i. 16, 11). First subdued by the Assyrians. In time overcame their masters, and formed the Chaldæan or Babylonian Empire under Nabopolassar, a viceroy in Babylon, about 600 B.C. Their empire overthrown by Cyrus, who took Babylon, 583 B.C. In Job's time a body of hardy mountaineers. Always strong enough to make such a raid. More fierce and powerful than the Sabeans.

Strokes increase in severity. *Satan inflames his instruments with his own murderous passions.*—"Three bands." To attack in various directions and let nothing escape. (So Gen. xiv. 15). Three bands under so many captains, Satan really commander-in-chief.—"Fell upon the camels." *Marg.* "rushed." Made a raid upon them, as 1 Sam. xxiii. 27; xxx. 14. Arabs sometimes make a raid twenty or thirty days' march from their tents.—"Carried them away." Three thousand camels no slight loss. *Satan goes the full length of his cord.* More grievous to be stripped of riches than to be always poor.

4. *Loss of all his children* (verses 18, 19). "While he was yet speaking." Satan never at rest till he has done all the mischief he is permitted. *Good to be always ready for another and a worse encounter.* Seneca says, 'Cæsar sometimes put up his sword, but never put it off.'—"Thy sons." The trial reaches its climax. His sons the object of his greatest solicitude. The subjects of so many prayers might have been expected to be spared, or at least *some* of them. The mystery increases.—"Were eating and drinking." When Job feared most they might be sinning (verse 5). *Possible to be taken from the festive board to the Judgment-seat. Festivity unsafe without God and His blessing in it.* Well to be prepared to pass from earthly joys to heavenly ones.—"Behold." Marks the greatness of the calamity. Seven sons and three daughters,—the whole of Job's children,—all arrived at maturity,—all prosperous and happy,—cut off at one stroke,—suddenly and unexpectedly,—amid the hilarity of a feast! —"A great wind." A tornado, cyclone, or whirlwind. Common in the East. Mysterious power of Satan to excite the atmosphere into a storm. 'Prince of the power of the air.' Wind in God's hand, but now for His own purpose, partially and for a time, transferred to Satan's" (Prov. xxx. 4). —"From the wilderness." Whence the fiercest winds came (Jer. iv. 11; xiii. 24). From the south part of the great North Arabian Desert (Is. xxi. 1; Hos. xiii. 15).— "Smote the four corners of the house." At once or successively; coming with force and steady aim as under Satan's direction. All the appearance of the work of an angry God.—"And it fell." The object for which Satan raised the storm. Such catastrophes not uncommon in the East. Houses of comparatively frail construction (Matt. vii. 27). Well-known violence of tornadoes. One in England, in 1811, tore up plantations and levelled houses with the ground, carried large trees, torn up by the roots, to the distance of twenty or thirty yards; lifted

cows from one field to another; and carried haystacks to a considerable distance. Camels sometimes lifted off their legs by Eastern whirlwinds. *God able to make our plagues wonderful* (Deut. xxviii. 59).—"Upon the young men." Mentioned as more likely to overwhelm the father; sisters included. —"And they are dead." Crushing tidings for a father's ears. *All* dead,—dead *all at once*,—dead *prematurely*,—dead by a *sudden*, *unusual*, and *miserable death*,—dead *as if by the hand of God Himself*, as Bildad regarded them,—dead *at the time that Job had most need of their comfort under his other calamities.* Job reduced, in one short day, from being one of the happiest of fathers to a state of childlessness and misery. *Our heaviest trials often through our sweetest comforts.* The sharpest thorns on the same tree with the loveliest flowers. The *beauty of all earthly blessings quickly blasted* (Is. lx. 6, 8). *Too much* not to be expected from *God*, nor *too little* from the *creature.*

CHAPTER I. 20—22.

FIFTH PART OF INTRODUCTION—THE RESULT OF SATAN'S ATTEMPTS.

I. Job's grief (ver. 20). "Then Job arose." Probably found by the tidings in the usual posture of Orientals. Aroused from wonted calmness. His nature now stirred to its depths. *Deeply moved*, but *not prostrated* by his calamities.—"Rent his mantle," or robe; long outer garment worn by men of rank (1 Sam. xv. 27; xviii. 4), and by priests (1 Sam. xxviii. 14; Ex. xxviii. 13); still worn by wealthy Arabs. Rent it in token of sorrow and humiliation (Gen. xxxvii. 34). Job neither too insensible to feel grief, nor too proud to acknowledge it. *Piety not stoicism;* sharpens rather than blunts sensibility. As little virtue in *not feeling* sorrow as in *being overcome* by it. Not to feel is to be either more or less than a man. Jesus wept. Insensibility under chastening reproved as a sin (Jer. v. 3; Hosea vii. 9). When God afflicts us we should afflict ourselves (Jer. xxxi. 18). Grace teaches us, not to be *without* sorrow, but to *moderate* it, and to connect with it *penitence and submission, faith and hope* (2 Cor. vii. 11; 1 Thess. iv. 13).—"Shaved his head." Another token of mourning (Ezra ix. 3; Is. xv. 2; xxii. 12; Jer. vii. 29; xli. 5). Forbidden by the law only in certain cases and in certain forms (Lev. xix. 27; xxxi. 5; Deut. xiv. 1). Nature demands some external sign of grief, and religion does not forbid it.— "Fell down upon the ground." (1) In grief; so Joshua (Josh. vii. 6); (2) In humiliation; (3) In adoration. *Trouble a blessing when it leads to self-abasement before God.* Satan expected to see Job standing on his feet and cursing the author of his troubles.

II. His piety (ver. 20, 21). "And worshipped." Praised God and acknowleged his sovereignty. Bowed submissively to His will and dispensations. Instead of cursing God Job adores His justice, goodness, and holiness. *Afflictions draw a godly man nearer to God instead of driving him from Him.* A sign of a gracious state to be *worshipping* when God is *chastising.* The best way to bear and be benefited by trials is to take them to God. *That trouble cannot but be blest which brings us to our knees.* Faith calms the crushed spirit by conducting it to a God in Christ.—"And said." Job opens his mouth, but not as Satan expected. *Serious and suitable considerations to be employed under trouble.* Truths suggested by religion to quiet the spirit and preserve it in patience. —"Naked came I forth," &c. Job's first consideration. Nothing originally ours. Man by nature destitute even of clothes for his body. The truth in the text the apostle's argument for contentment (1 Tim. vi. 7). —"Naked shall I return thither." Second consideration. Earth not our home. We return to our parent dust. Reference to Gen. iii. 19. These words probably copied or referred to in Ecc. v. 14, and xii. 7. *Our condition in this world of less consequence as we are so soon to leave it.*—Third consideration. We must leave the world naked as we entered it (1 Tim. vi. 7). Death strips Dives of his fine linen and Lazarus of his filthy rags. *Grace the only riches we can carry out of the world with us.* To be stripped of earthly possessions only a *question of time.* "Thither,"—unto my mother's womb, used figuratively for the earth. So the "lower parts of the earth" used for the womb (Ps. cxxxix. 15). The same term sometimes used both literally and figuratively in the same sentence. So Matt. viii. 22.— "The Lord gave." The language of truth and piety. Contrasted with that of pride and atheism,—"My own hand hath gotten me this wealth" (Deut. viii. 17). Heathens by the light of nature called God the "Giver of good things." Power to get wealth the gift of God (Deut. viii. 18; Prov. x. 22). "Gave," and therefore has the right to withdraw at his pleasure. *What we possess we hold only as stewards of another's goods* (Luke xvi. 1—12; 1 Peter iv. 10.)—"The Lord hath taken away." God's hand in our losses as well as our gains. Divine philosophy. So Joseph Gen. xlv. 5—8; David, Ps. xxxix. 9; Eli, 1 Sam. iii. 18. "The Lord,"—not the Sabeaus and Chaldæans, the lightning or the whirlwinds. *The philosophy that rests on second causes or natural laws a philosophy falsely so called.* Satan only the author of Job's calamities as he received permission from God. *The arrows God's, whoever shoots them.* Evil as well as good from God either directly or permissively (Is. xlv. 7; Amos iii. 6). Man's and Satan's sin overruled by God for good; not therefore the less sinful (Acts ii. 23). God's hand in trouble *seen by the eye of faith,* an alleviation; otherwise au aggravation.

III. The Victory.

1. *Positive* side. *Job blesses God instead of cursing Him* (ver. 21). "Blessed be the Name of the Lord." The word chosen with reference to Satan's charge. The same word used, but in its opposite and proper sense. Satan thus entirely defeated. Every word of Job gives the lie to his slander. Power of grace that teaches us to bless God in troubles and adversities (2 Sam. xv. 26). *No* ground, even in the worst times, to *murmur* against God, *much to bless* Him. Such grounds are: (1) Often greater love and richer blessing when He takes away than when He gives. *Our greatest trials and losses often our richest mercies.* "For all I bless Thee, most for the severe" [*Young*].—2. In the greatest sufferings and losses the believer's main interests are secure. The pieces of silver may be lost, the casket of jewels remains safe. (3.) The sufferings of believers are seeds to bear precious fruit both here and hereafter (Rom. viii. 24; Heb. xii. 10, 11). Believers therefore strengthened "unto all patience and long suffering *with joyfulness*" (Col. i. 11). *True Christian piety the purest heroism.* Widely different from stoical insensibility and pride. Believers *weep,* but *bless God through their tears.* Job's blessing God must have sent an echo through the heaven of heavens. Unprecedented trials, heightened by the contrast of unprecedented prosperity, meet not merely with submission, but with blessing on the Author of both. To bless God in prosperity is only natural; to bless Him in adversity and trouble is music that fills heaven and earth with gladness. Job's calamities appeared only to argue God against him. Mighty faith that blesses God while smiting our comforts to the ground. The grace enjoined on N. T. believers, exemplified in this O. T. saint (1 Thess. v. 18). To bless God in our comforts the way to have

them increased; to bless Him in our afflictions the way to have them removed [*Augustine*]. A thankful and pious spirit the true philosopher's stone—turns all things into gold. *Faith gilds our crosses and sees a silver lining in the darkest cloud.*—Matter for praise under the most trying dispensations:—(1) The past enjoyment of undeserved mercies so long continued; (2) The present enjoyment of *some* mercies however few; (3) The possession of God Himself as in Christ our God and portion; (4) The assurance that the heaviest trials work together for our good; (5) The hope of a better and enduring inheritance reserved for us in heaven.—"The name of the Lord,"—the Lord Himself as revealed to us in the Word. Here "Jehovah," the ever-living faithful covenant God of His people. The name here thrice repeated. Perhaps not without a mystery, like Num. vii. 24—27, compared with Matt. xxviii. 19; 2 Cor. xiii. 14; 1 John v. 7. The name fondly dwelt upon by the afflicted patriarch. *The name of the Lord the tried believer's sweetest consolation and strongest support.* A strong tower into which the righteous runs and is safe (Prov. xviii. 10.)

2. *Negative* side of victory. *In all these trials Job kept from sinning* (ver. 22.) "Sinned not," as Satan desired and declared he would. Glorious triumph of grace to keep from sinning in such circumstances. Sinned not, either by impatience or passion. Reference to the case in hand. Grace given to keep us from sin, not absolutely, but relatively and comparatively. Sin more or less in all a believer's actions, though all his actions not sinful. Scripture written that the believer sin not (1 John ii. 1). Looking to *Christ,* Peter walked on the water; looking to the *wind,* he began to sink in it (Matt. xiv. 28—31). The flesh or old nature in a believer *must* sin; the spirit or new nature in him *cannot.* (1 John iii. 9). A constant struggle between the spirit and the flesh (Gal. v. 17). A believer's duty and privilege to walk in the spirit, and so be kept from fulfilling the desire of the flesh (Gal. v. 16). *I feel and grieve,* but by the grace of God I *fret* at nothing [*John Wesley*].—"Nor charged God foolishly." (1) Imputed no folly, injustice, or impropriety to God; (2) Vented no foolish and impious murmurs against Him. Ascribed nothing to God unworthy of His justice, goodness, and wisdom. Entertained no *dishonourable thought,* uttered no *murmuring word* against Him. *Impiety the greatest folly.* To murmur against God's dealings is as foolish as it is wicked. *To misconstrue God's character and conduct, the great sin to be guarded against under heavy trials.*

CHAPTER II. 1—6.

SIXTH PART OF INTRODUCTION.—PREPARATION FOR JOB'S FURTHER TRIAL.

I. Second Celestial Council (verse 1). "Again there was a day," some time after the events already related. Not said how long. Heavenly things represented under the figure of earthly ones, in condescension to our capacity. In heaven no succession of day and night (Rev. xxi. 25).—"The sons of God came," &c. Same scene represented as before. *God's providence continually exercised, and extending to all times and events.* His angelic ministers continually serving Him in their respective spheres (Rev. xxii. 3). "His state is kingly; thousands at his bidding speed," &c. Good to remember—"They also serve who only stand and wait." *Angels intensely interested in the salvation of men, and employed in helping to promote it* (Acts viii. 26; x. 3).—"Satan also came." Summoned, or expecting a fresh permission. Like Saul of Tarsus, "breathing out threatening and slaughter," and eager to get out a fresh commission of destruction (Acts ix. 1).—"To present himself before the Lord," having previously received a commission. This, therefore, omitted in the former account. *Men, angels, and devils, amenable to God.*

II. God's testimony to Job's steadfastness (verse 2). "From whence comest thou?" Happy for us that God's eye is continually on Satan's movements (Luke xxii. 31, 32).—"From going to and fro." Active and restless as ever. Says nothing of the harm he has done. *An evil doer seldom has the courage to speak the whole truth* (2 Kings v. 25).—"Walking up and down in it." God says the same thing of him, but tells us *how* (1 Peter v. 8). As Job still retained his *integrity*, so Satan his *assiduity*. Believers neither to be ignorant of his *devices*, nor forgetful of his *zeal.*— (Verse 3). "Hast thou considered my servant Job?" Job still God's servant. *God's estimate of His people not diminished by their sufferings.* Precious testimony to the poor persecuted church at Smyrna (Rev. ii. 9)—."Still holdeth fast his integrity." Perfect and upright as before. "Still," notwithstanding these severe and accumulated trials. "Holdeth fast," implying exertion. Hard to hold out in such a storm. *Satan's efforts to rob Job of his integrity, Job's to retain it. Whatever a godly man loses he will keep his integrity.* "If you love my soul away with it," said a

martyr at the stake, when tempted with a pardon to recant. Two things never to be let go—*Christ's righteousness, and a good conscience.* The Epistle to the Hebrews written to strengthen tried believers to hold fast their profession (Heb. iii. 14; iv. 14; x. 23, 35, 39). *God a concerned and compassionate observer of his people's conduct under trials* (Jer. xxxi. 18; Hos. xiv. 8). Commends their conduct *in* them, without at once delivering them *from* them. What is well done is sure, sooner or later, to receive His approving testimony. God neither conceals our graces nor our *improvement* of them. *To continue good while suffering evil, the crown of goodness.* A good man persevering in evil times an object of Divine admiration [*Seneca*].—God's further commendation of Job now enlarged. *Grace grows in conflict.* "Although thou movedst me against him." Implies successful urgency (So 1 Kings xxi. 25). Spoken after the manner of men. Satan an excellent orator if he but have an audience [*Trapp*].—"Thou movedst me." God "afflicteth not willingly" (Lam. iii. 33). Satan an earnest pleader *against* the saints: Christ as earnest *for* them (John xvii. 11, 15, 17). Satan's malice and calumny the occasion of Job's sufferings, and so of his subsequent glory. God's *secret purpose* to exhibit the reality and preciousness of His servant's faith. All questioning of the efficacy of Christ's redemption and the power of Divine grace, to be for ever silenced. *Not only events themselves purposed by God, but the way and occasion of their occurrence.*—"To destroy him," Marg., "to swallow him up." Satan's cruel intention. Satan's object in trial is to *destroy*; God's, to *prove and purify. God's sympathy with His suffering people.* What Satan called a *touch*, God calls *destruction. Awful judgment to be left in the hands of the roaring lion* (1 Peter v. 8).—"Without cause." (1.) *Without any special sin of his to merit it.* This testimony to be remembered throughout the book. Believed and maintained by Job; denied by his three friends. The cause of his perplexity and distraction aggravated by their opposition. *Tried believers often ignorant of God's thoughts concerning them, and of the cause and object of their trial.*—(2.) *Without ground or necessity for it.* Satan's charge proved by the result to be unfounded.

2　　　　　　　　　　　　　　　　　　17

III. Satan's farther accusation (verse 4). "Satan answered the Lord." Satanic impudence. Though defeated, he has still an answer for God. *Boldness acquired by a course of iniquity.* A whore's forehead (Jer. iii. 3).—"Skin for skin." A proverbial expression. A mere question of barter. Job has yet a whole skin. He will part with anything to save his life. Will give up what he *has*, to save *himself*. "We must give up our beards to save our heads" [*Turkish Proverb*].—"All that a man hath he will give for his life." Not only his property and children, but probably his religion too. The test not yet sufficiently severe. The screw needs only to be driven a little farther. Satan argues still on the principles of man's selfishness. His words too often verified in fallen humanity. Peruvians sacrificed their firstborn to redeem their own life when the priest pronounced them mortally sick. Cranmer, in a moment of weakness, at first recanted in order to escape martyrdom. Abraham, when left to himself to save his life, gave up Sarah, and instigated her to tell a lie (Gen. xii. 12, 13). Yet the statement a libel upon the race. Satan true to his character. *Self-preservation a powerful instinct, but not supreme.* With a good man, subordinate to the principles of morality and religion. Yields to faith, hope, and charity. Paul counted not his life dear to him that he might finish his course and ministry with joy (Acts xx. 24). Daniel, Stephen, and all "the noble army of martyrs" give Satan the lie. Men and *women* have died, "refusing to accept deliverance, to obtain a better resurrection" (Heb. xi. 35). "Welcome, death!" said *Hugh M'Kail*, on the martyr's scaffold. "Welcome, if need be, the axe or the gibbet; but evil befall the tongue that dares to make me so infamous a proposal," said *Kossuth*, in reply to the Sultan's proposal to save his life by renouncing Christianity.—"Touch his bone and his flesh" (verse 5). Strike home at his person. Person nearer than property or children.

Intensest pain and suffering intended. The iron to enter the soul. Satan's cruelty. A merciless tormentor (Matt. xviii. 34). Unwearied in his efforts to destroy *Always needful to prepare for new assaults.* Satan acquainted with the tendency of great bodily suffering. *Pain, a powerful means of disquieting and weakening the mind.* Without disordering its faculties, able to exhaust its energies and sink it into despondency. A piercing shaft in Satan's quiver. A thorn in the flesh Paul's great temptation (2 Cor. xii. 7, 9). Men "blasphemed God because of the *pain*" (Rev. xvi. 9). This Satan's expectation in regard to Job.—"He will curse thee," &c. Same assertion as before. Satan unwilling to yield. *Men, lost to all right principle themselves, have no faith in the virtue of others.*

IV. The renewed permission (verse 6). "He is in thine hand." *Before,* only his property and children; *now,* himself. *Saints, for trial, mysteriously given for a time into Satan's hand.* The persecuted church at Smyrna (Rev. ii. 10). Unknown to us how far bodily affliction may be from Satan's hand (Luke xiii. 16). Though God *lengthens* Satan's chain, he never *loosens* it. *The saints never in Satan's hand without Christ being with them* (Dan. iii. 25; Ps. xxiii. 4; xci. 15; Is. xliii. 2).—"But save his life." Satan's permission in regard to the saints always limited. He might scratch with his paw, but not fasten his fang [*Trapp*]. Job's life to be endangered, but not destroyed. Life and death in *God's* hand, not *Satan's.* A mercy to have life spared (Jer. xxxix. 18). Precious blessings still for Job to experience, and important work still for him to do. A man immortal till his work is done. The limit set in *Job's* case, not prescribed in *Christ's.* Christ, as the Shepherd, smitten to *death* in the room of the sheep (Zech. xiii. 7; John x. 11).

CHAPTER II. 7—10.

SEVENTH PART OF INTRODUCTION; JOB'S FURTHER TRIAL.

I. Satan's use of God's permission (verse 7).

"So went Satan forth." Glad in obtaining his wish, like Saul on his way to Damascus. Resolved to use his liberty to the utmost. Gets his will, but with limitation (Luke xxii. 31, 32).—"From the presence of the Lord." Like Cain (Gen. 4—16). His object not to serve God, but torture man.—"Smote Job."

Implies suddenness and vehemence. The hand heavy, though unseen. So Herod smitten by the angel (Acts xii. 23). Such smiting often ascribed to God, whoever the instrument (Deut. xxviii. 35). Satanic ingenuity in smiting the body yet preserving life and mental faculties. *Piety and patience under one trial, no security against another and a heavier.* Heavy burdens laid on strong shoulders. God knows the metal He gives Satan to ring [*Trapp*]. Our comfort is, that He lays no trial on His children beyond what He enables them to bear (1 Cor. x. 13).

II. Job's Disease.

"Sore boils." *Heb.*, a bad, malignant ulcer, or inflammatory ulceration. Worst kind of leprosy. Inflicted on the Egyptians and threatened to the Israelites (Deut. xxviii. 27). Prevalent both in Arabia and Egypt. Made the sufferer loathsome to himself and his nearest relations (ch. xix. 13, 19). Appeared to make him out as an object of the Divine displeasure; as Miriam, Gehazi, and King Azariah. In an advanced stage, fingers, toes, and hands, gradually fall off (ch. xxx. 17, 30). Attended with great attenuation and debility of body (xvi. 8; xix. 20; xxx. 18). Restless nights and terrifying dreams (xxx. 17; vii. 13, 14). Anxiety of mind and loathing of life (vii. 15). Foul breath and difficult respiration (vii. 4; xiii. 15; xxx. 17). The skin itchy, of great tenseness, full of cracks and rents, and covered with hard or festering ulcers, and with black scales (ii. 8; xix. 20; xxx. 18; vii. 5; xxx. 30). The feet and legs swollen to an enormous size; hence the disease also called *Elephantiasis*. The mouth swollen and the countenance distorted, giving the patient a lion-like appearance; hence another name to the disease, *Leontiasis*. Contagious through the mere breath. Often hereditary. As a rule, incurable. In any case, one of the most *protracted* as well as dreadful diseases.—"From the crown," &c. So in Deut. xxviii. 35. The body one continued sore. Job escaped with the skin of his teeth—sores everywhere else (xix. 20). The *tongue* left free for an obvious reason. Satan's mercies cruel. Rare spectacle for angels; the holiest man on earth the most afflicted. Astounding sight for men; the richest and greatest man in the land made at once the most loathsome and miserable. *Impossible to say to what extent God may allow his dearest children to be afflicted.* After Job, no saint need be staggered at his suffering. Yet all Job's sufferings under Divine inspection and admeasurement (Is. xxvii. 8).— A circumstance marking the extremity of Job's affliction (verse 8). "And he took him a potsherd." As near at hand. Arab jars thin and frail, and easily broken—sometimes by merely putting them down on the floor. Hence fragments of broken jars found everywhere (Is. xxx. 14). A potsherd used by Job instead of a napkin. Possibly, however, an instrument still used in the East for similar purposes. Required to remove the purulent matter from his sores, and perhaps to allay their irritation. His hands and fingers themselves affected, or the foulness of his sores

forbidding the touch. Without friend, physician, or relative to attend to his disease. In the case of Lazarus, dogs supplied the place of the potsherd (Luke xvi. 20—21). *God's dearest saints often reduced to the greatest extremities.*—"Sat down among the ashes." In token of mourning (xlii. 6; Jon. iii. 6; Matt. xi. 21); and of abasement (Jer. vi. 26; Is. xlvii. 3; lviii. 5; Ezek. xxvii. 30). The ash-heap probably outside the city. Dung-hills still similarly used in the East. One part of the leper's affliction, that he was to be removed from society (Lev. xiii. 46; Num. xii. 14—15; 2 Kings xv. 5).

1. *Increased affliction calls for increased humiliation.*

2. *Self-abasement the certain way to Divine exaltation* (Jam. iv. 9—10).

III. Job's trial from his wife (verse 9).

"Then said his wife." Amazed at her husband's sufferings and piety. Herself already tempted and overcome. Spared by Satan to aid him in his attempts upon her husband. Another of his cruel mercies. She who should have been a comforter now becomes a tormentor. Her former piety now staggered at her husband's trials. Weak professors readily offended. The case of Adam and Eve expected to be repeated. Satan wise in selecting his instruments.

1. *Those who fall themselves usually employed in tempting others.*

2. *Strongest temptations and keenest trials often from nearest friends.*

"Dost thou still retain thine integrity?" Already affirmed by God (verse 3). *What is highly esteemed by God often reproached by man, and vice versa* (Luke xvi. 15). Job, in his wife's eyes, "perversely righteous and absurdly good" [*Sir R. Blackmore*]. *Perseverance in piety under heavy crosses a mystery to the world.*—"Curse God and die." Three horrid temptations—infidelity, blasphemy, and despair. Same word used as in i. 11; but properly denoting "to bless." Perhaps a bitter taunt, referring to i. 21—"Go on with your fine religion!" Probably—"Renounce God, who treats you so vilely." Includes the idea of uttered reproach and blasphemy (1 Kings xxi. 10). Job urged by his wife to fulfil Satan's grand desire.

1. *Satan's great work to set men against their Maker and His service.*

2. *His fiercest temptations often reserved for the time of greatest affliction.*

3. *Satan tempts men to put the worst construction on God's dealings, and prompts to the worst means of relief.* Points Job to the gulf of Atheism as the only refuge [*Davidson*].

4. *The holiest saints liable to the most horrid and blasphemous temptations.*

5. *The flesh in ourselves and others always*

an antagonist to faith and holiness (Matt. xvi. 22—23). "And die." As the end of all your trouble. So Satan tempted Saul, Ahithopel, and Judas Iscariot. *No suggestion so horrid but Satan may inject it into a believing mind.* Job afterwards still pressed with the same temptation to suicide (vii. 15). *One of Satan's lies, that death ends all.* His object to make men die in an act of sin, without time or opportunity for repentance. *His friendliest proposals tend to damnation and destruction.* Would make men imitators of his blasphemy and partakers of his despair.

IV. Job's continued patience and piety (verse 10). "But he said unto her." Did not curse God, and then use Adam's excuse (Gen. iii. 12).—"Thou speakest," &c. Reproves with mingled gentleness and firmness. So Christ reproved Peter (Mat. xvi. 23). *Dishonour done to God to be at once discountenanced and reproved* (Lev. xix. 17; Prov. xxvii. 5; xxix. 15).—"As one." A gentle form of reproof. Husbands to love their wives, and not be *bitter* against them (Col. iii. 19). No fierce or furious language here. Her present speech not like her usual self. Speaks out of her ordinary character.

1. *Believers liable to be drawn into sin.*
2. *Love to be mingled with, and to moderate, reproof* (Eph. iv. 15).
3. *Reproof to be respectful, especially when addressed to relatives and seniors* (1 Tim. v. 1).

"As one of the foolish women speaketh." "Foolish," in the Old Testament, used for "sinful or ungodly." The language of Job's wife, that of foolish, profane, wicked women.

1. *The part of a fool to deny God and reproach His Providence* (Ps. xiv. 1).
2. *Folly to judge of a man's condition from God's outward dealings with him.*
3. *Unworthy thoughts of God the mark of a carnal, foolish spirit.*
4. *Sin not only vile but foolish,*—as truly opposed to *man's interests* as to *God's honour.*
5. *Impatience and passion under trouble the greatest foolishness.* Hard, and therefore senseless, to kick against the pricks (Acts ix. 5). Idolaters wont to reproach their gods in misfortune.

"What! shall we receive," &c.? What is sinful is to be put down, not with *rage* but with *reason.* Satan's horrid and blasphemous temptations not to be listened to for a moment. *Sharp reproof consistent with love and sometimes required by it* (Tit. i. 13). He who knows not how to be angry knows not how to love [*Augustine.*]—"Shall we receive good at the hand of God?" *Present miseries not to obliterate past mercies.* The greatest sufferer already the recipient of unnumbered benefits. God's mercies "new every morning." To sinners all is mercy on this side of hell. Mercy written on every sunbeam that gilds and gladdens the earth.—"And shall we not receive evil also?" "Evil" put for affliction and adversity. All comforts and no crosses, unreasonable to expect and undesirable to receive. Evil as well as good to be not only *expected,* but thankfully *accepted.* The question points to the *manner of receiving,* as well as the *matter received.* Both equally *dispensed* by God, therefore both to be reverentially *accepted* by *us.* Both worthy of God to *dispense,* and beneficial for us to *receive.* The part of faith and love, to accept troubles as from a Father's hand. The true spirit of adoption, to kiss the rod and the hand that holds it. *Thankfully to accept of good is merely human, thankfully to accept of evil is Divine.* In everything to give thanks, *God's will in Christ concerning us* (1 Thess. v. 13). Job here greater than his miseries. More than a conqueror. One of heaven's as well as earth's heroes.—"In all this," his increased calamities as well as his wife's taunts and temptations. Job now lying under a quaternion of troubles—adversity, bereavement, disease, and reproach. More, however, yet remained for Satan to inflict and for Job to suffer. *Continuance of suffering often much more trying than suffering itself. Inward* affliction to be added to the *outward.* Much more trying. The spirit of a man will sustain his infirmity, but a *wounded spirit* who can bear? (Prov. xviii. 14). A hint, perhaps, here given of further trial, with a less gratifying result. — "Sinned not with his lips." Vented no reflection on God's character and procedure. The greatest temptation in such circumstances to sin with the lips. The thing Satan desired, endeavoured after, and waited for. The temptation to murmur *present,* but *resisted and repressed.* Job still by grace a conqueror over corrupt nature. Not always thus walking on the swelling waters of innate corruption. Man's weakness to be exhibited, even in a state of grace. Hitherto Job shown to be the "perfect man" God declared him to be (Jam. iii. 2). The Old Testament ideal of a perfect man and a suffering saint. An illustrious type of Christ in His suffering and patience (Is. liii. 7; 1 Pet. ii. 23). The type afterwards fails, that in all things Christ may have the pre-eminence (Col. i. 18).

CHAPTER II. 11—13.

CONCLUDING PART OF PROSE INTRODUCTION.—VISIT OF JOB'S FRIENDS.

I. The Friends. (Verse 11.) "Now when Job's three friends heard." Rather, "three friends of Job." Probably friends most intimate with him, and from whom he had most to expect (ch vi. 14, 15). Perhaps connected with him by kindred as well as acquaintance and religion. Worshippers of the true God. Eminent in their day and country for wisdom and piety. Their religious views those of the age. Regarded retribution as very much a thing of this life. Hence their unfavourable view of Job's *character* from his *condition*. Much older than Job. Intending comfort, they become under Satan's influence, and from their narrow mistaken views, his severest trial. Instead of soothing they add to his grief,— by uncharitable suspicions, false reasonings, unseasonable admonitions, and their re-proofs. *Good easily perverted to evil by Satan's malice.* Satan used Job's wife to *jeer* him out of his religion, and his friends to *dispute* him out of it [*Caryl.*]—"Came,"—probably, when his disease was now considerably advanced (vii. 4). Affliction should draw us *to* our friends, not drive us *from* them. *Adversity one of the best tests of friendship* (Prov. xvii. 17). Good manners to be an unbidden guest in the house of mourning. [*Caryl*]. *True friendship shewn in self-denying effort.* "Eliphaz." An old Edomite name. A district also so called (Gen. xxxvi. 11, 15). Denotes "my God is strength." Indicates his parent's piety.—"Temanite." From the stock he sprung from, or the place (Teman) where he lived. Temanites celebrated for their wisdom (Jer. xlix. 7; Obad. viii. 9). —"Shuhite." Of Shuah, in the east part of North Arabia. Shuah one of the settlements of the sons of Keturah (Gen xxv. 2). —"Naamathite." From Naamah, probably a district in Syria. The town in Judah so named (Jud. xv. 41), too far distant.

II. Object of the Friends' visit. "Had made an appointment together." Probably living not far apart from each other. *Good to unite together in works of charity and mercy* (Mark ii. 3).—"To mourn with him." *Sympathy in sorrow an instinct of humanity and a Christian duty* (Rom. xii. 15). Example of Jesus (John ii. 33, 34). Job's own character (ch. xxx. 25). *Tears shed with our own, often the most soothing balm in sorrow.* A world of meaning in the child's

words,—"I only cried with her."—"And to comfort him." The motive good, though the execution faulty. *A friend in trouble one of our choicest blessings.* A brother born for adversity. Comfort of mourners one of the objects of the Lord's ministry (Is. lxi. 2). See His mode of dispensing it, Is. xlii. 3; Matt. xi. 28—30. *To comfort in trouble one of the leading parts of Christian duty* (1 Thess. v. 18; vi. 11; Jam. i. 27; Matt. xxv. 36). Job's own character and practice (ch. xxix. 25). —Verse 12, "Lifted up their eyes afar off." Where yet they might easily have recognised him. So the father of the prodigal (Luke xv. 20). Job apparently now in the open air, and, as a leper, outside the city.—"Knew him not." So altered by his disease, his sorrow, and his place among the ashes. Marks the depth of his calamity. Unrecognizable by his friends. *When men know us least, is the time that God knows us best.* (Ps. xxxi. 7.)

III. Their Sympathy. Verse 12. "They lifted up their voice and wept." Marks their deep sympathy and their friend's deep sorrow. In the east, full vent usually given to grief (Gen. xxvii. 38; xxix. 11; Jud. ii. 4; Ruth i. 9; 1 Sam. xxiv. 16).—"Sprinkled dust upon their heads towards heaven." Casting it into the air, so as to fall down on their heads (Acts xxii. 23). Token of grief, astonishment, and humiliation towards God under a great sorrow (Josh. vii. 6; Neh. ix. 1; Sam. iv. 10). Their feeling, consternation and sorrow at the sight of so sad a change.—"Sat down with him upon the ground" (verse 13). Another token of sympathetic grief (2 Sam. xii. 16; Is. iii. 26; Lam. ii. 10; Ezra ix. 3). True sympathy to sit down on the ground with one so loathsome in himself, and apparently an object of the Divine displeasure.—"Seven days." Usual time of mourning for the dead (Gen. l. 10; 1 Sam. xxxi. 13). Job's children dead, and himself virtually so. So in time of great affliction (Ezek. iii. 15). Depth of Job's calamity marked by that of his friends' sympathy.—"None spake a word unto him." True sympathy expressed by silence as well as tears. Silence usual and becoming in presence of deep distress (Lam. ii. 10). "A reverence due to such prodigious woe" [*Sir R. Blackmore*]. Unseasonable words an aggravation of the sufferer's grief. The

21

friends confounded at Job's calamity and unable to speak to it. Ignorant as to the cause, and apprehensive of Divine displeasure. *Prudence and skill required in administering consolation.*—"For they saw." His affliction apparently much greater than they had anticipated. The heart affected by the eye. *Good to place ourselves in the presence of sorrow* (Ecc. vii. 2).—"That his grief was very great." The stroke as heavy as it was possible for Satan to inflict, and the grief proportionate. *No sin for our feelings to keep pace with God's dealings.*

Lessons from Job's grief and the occasion of it :—

1. God's dearest children and most faithful servants may be the subjects of deepest suffering.

2. No part of piety to render the sou insensible to calamity.

3. The sudden removal of all earthly comforts possible, and to be prepared for.

4. Much of the sufferings of God's servants the probable result of Satan's malice.

5. Patience and submission to God's will consistent with the deepest grief.

Job in his deep distress a type of the "Man of Sorrows." His soul "exceeding sorrowful, even unto death." In an agony, prayed the more earnestly that the cup might, if possible, pass from Him, yet meekly submitted. His bloody sweat, the result of a frame like our own convulsed by inward distress (Matt. xxvi. 37, 39; Luke xxii. 44).

CHAPTER III.

COMMENCEMENT OF FIRST GREAT DIVISION OF THE POEM.

Job's bitter complaint and outburst of despondency—the more immediate occasion of the Controversy between him and his friends.

I. Job breaks the prolonged silence (verses 1, 2).

"After this,"—viz.: the visit of his friends and the seven days' silence.—"Job opened his mouth." Denoting—(1) freeness of speech (Ezek. xvi. 62; xxix. 4); (2) earnestness in speaking (Prov. xxxi. 5, 6; Is. lii. 7); (3) deliberate and grave utterance (Ps. lxxviii. 2; Prov. iii. 6). Orientals speak seldom, and then gravely and sententiously. Job long silent from his extraordinary calamity. Profound grief shuts the mouth (Ps. lxxvii. 4). Pent up anguish now finds a vent. His sufferings probably increasing, and his feelings now irrepressible. Patient till God's anger seems to sink into his soul [*Chrysostom*]. Satan, to exasperate his feelings and depress his spirits, now acts on his *mind* and *imagination*, both *directly* and through his *disease*. The moment now arrived that Satan had been waiting for. *Usually great danger in giving vent to pent up fee'ings.* A double prayerful watch then needed not to sin with one's tongue (Ps. xxxix. i; cxli. 3). Danger of speaking rather from heat of passion than light of wisdom. Better for Job had he kept his mouth close still [*Trapp*]. "Either say nothing or what is better than nothing" [*Greek Proverb*]. When God's hand is on our back, our hand should be on our mouth [*Brookes*]. The maturity of grace proved by the management of the tongue (Jam. iii. 2).—"Job spake and said." Every expression in Job's speeches not to be vindicated. The rashness of his language

acknowledged by himself (ch. vi. 3). Job in the end not only hushed but humbled for what he had said (ch. xl. 5). In judging of his language however we are to remember :—

1. *The extremity of his sufferings and the depth of his distress.* His language extravagant but natural. Stunned by his calamities. Great sufferings naturally generate great passions. Job's sufferings to be viewed in connection with—(1) His high unblemished character; (2) His previous long continued prosperity; (3) The prevalent ideas as to Divine retribution.

2. *The time of his suffering also a time of spiritual darkness.* Satan's permission extended to the mind as well as the body. Mental confusion often the result of Satan's buffetings. *Times of outward trouble often those also of inward conflict.*

3. *The period at which Job lived.* Twilight as compared with that of the Gospel. Topics of consolation limited. No suffering Forerunner and Example to contemplate. Prospects dim as regarded the future world. No Scriptures with examples written for patience and comfort.

4. *The usually depressing nature of Job's disease.*

5. *The fact that the holiest saint is nothing except as strengthened and upheld by Divine grace.*

6. *Even in Job's complaint, no reproach is uttered against either the Author or instruments of his trouble.*

II. Job curses the day of his birth (verses 1—3, &c.).
"Cursed his day." Vilified, reproached, and execrated the day of his birth. A different word from that in i. 5, 11; ii. 5, 9; but the proper Hebrew word for cursing. Wished it to be branded as an evil, doleful, unhappy day. Similar language used by Jeremiah under less trying circumstances (Jer. xx. 14—18). The words mark:—

1. *Satan's defeat.* Job curses his *day;* Satan expected him to curse his *God.* Under *law,* Satan conquers; under *grace,* suffers defeat.

2. *Job's fall.* The language a contrast with i. 21; ii. 10. A secret and indirect reflection on Divine Providence. Job hitherto "a perfect man;" is he so now? (Jam. iii. 2). An end seen to all human perfection (Ps. cxix. 96). *A believer's fall consistent with final conquest* (Mic. vii. 8). Faith and patience may both suffer eclipse without perishing (Luke xxii. 32). A sheep may *fall* into the mire, while a swine *wallows* in it [*Brookes*]. *Satan's sieve brings out the saint's chaff.* The Scripture verified (Eccles. vii. 20; 1 Kings viii. 46; Prov. xx. 9; Jam. iii. 2). The man Christ Jesus the only Righteous One (1 John ii. 2). Tempted in all points, yet without sin (Heb. iv. 15). The greatest sufferer, yet His only cry: "My God, my God, why hast Thou forsaken me" (Matt. xxvii. 46). Endured anguish and temptation without abatement of love or trace of impatience. Thought also of the day of His birth, but with thankfulness and praise (Ps. xxii. 9, 10).

3. *The presence of the flesh in believers.* In ch. i. 21 and ii. 10, the *Spirit* spoke in Job; in iii. 3, &c., the *flesh.* The flesh in Job cursed the day of his birth; the spirit in David blessed God for the same thing (Ps. cxxxix. 14—17). *The believer is like Rebekah with two nations in her womb* (Gen. xxv. 23). These in perpetual conflict with each other (Gal. v. 17; Rom. vii. 25). Hence "out of the same mouth proceedeth blessing and cursing" (Jam. iii. 10).

4. *The folly and wickedness of sin.* Foolish to curse a day at all; wicked to curse one's birthday. *Every* day is God's creature; our *birthday*, His creature to us for *good.* Under a dispensation of mercy, every man's birthday either a blessing, or *may* be such. *Present misery not to obliterate the remembrance of past mercy.* The very thing which Job had formerly reproved in his wife (ch. ii. 10).

5. *The passionate vehemence of Job's grief.* Seen in the language and figures he employs. Verse 5. "Let darkness and the shadow of death stain it." Take away its beauty and make it abominable; or rather, as the *margin*: "Claim it for its own;" take it back and keep entire possession of it. Allusion to primeval

chaotic darkness (Gen. i. 2). — "Let a cloud dwell upon it;" or, "let a mass of clouds pitch their tent over it." The utterance of a deeply moved and excited spirit. Words similar in sense heaped together to intensify the idea. The eloquence of grief.—"Let the blackness of the day terrify it." Let whatever tends to obscure the day, as eclipses, storms, clouds, hot winds, &c., make it dismal and frightful. The day on which Christ suffered, thus "terrified," not by a natural but a supernatural darkness. "Surely nature is expiring, or the God of nature is suffering,"—said on that solemn occasion by a heathen philosopher.—Verse 6. "Let it not come into the number of the months;"—let it disappear from the calendar; be made to drop out of memory and existence.—Verse 7. "Let that night be solitary," ungladdened by a single birth, and destitute of all social converse and festivity. Returns to the night of his conception. Sublime accumulation of poetic figures and tragic expressions. — "Let no joyful noise be heard therein;" no song or sound of mirth; no voice of natal or of nuptial joy. Let it be devoted to the wail of sorrow, or to deep perpetual silence.—Verse 8. "Let them curse it that curse the day,"—either hired mourners, astrologers, or unhappy desperate persons; those accustomed to execrate daylight, the day of some special calamity, the day of their own birth, or that of some friend's death. All such to be employed in execrating the day of Job's birth.—"Who are ready to raise up their mourning;" or rather, as in the *margin*,—"to raise up a Leviathan,"—the crocodile or other monster (Is. xxvii. 1). Same persons described. Probable reference to some popular superstition, or practice in lamentation and execration. Job wishes his birthday to be execrated by such persons in the strongest and most energetic language.—Verse 9. "Neither let it see the dawning of the day." The Hebrew full of poetic beauty,—"Let it not see the eyelids of the morning." No cheerful rays of morning light glancing forth from the rising sun, to succeed that baleful night. Picture of eternal darkness. *Heaven a nightless day, hell a dayless night* [*Trapp*].

III. Job wishes he had never been, or had died when he began to live (verse 11).
"Why died I not from the womb?" In the impetuosity and perplexity of his spirit, puts it in the form of a question. Questions often asked by a troubled spirit in petulance and rebellion. These questions among the things confessed by Job with humiliation and repentance (ch. xlii. 6). "God's judgments a great deep; and he who asks *why*, will be

driven out on this deep, for there is no chart to guide us" [*Beecher*]. That our times are in God's hand quieted David's spirit, but failed to quiet Job's (Ps. xxxi. 15). Observe:—

1. *Times may come when the sweetest truths fail to comfort a child of God.* Unbelief and passion shut out the light and refuse to be comforted.

2. *Job's language the common lament of fallen and suffering humanity.* Heathen philosophy concluded that, in the view of the troubles of life, the best thing is not to be born at all; the next best is, to get out of the world as soon as possible.

3. *Job's question unanswerable but for the birth in Bethlehem.* Better not to have been born at all, if not *born again.* With a Saviour provided and offered, our birth either a blessing, or *might* be. Under an economy of grace, life spared in mercy (Lam. iii. 22; 2 Pet. iii. 15).

4. *A solemn question for each, Why did I not die from the womb?* Life invested with the most solemn responsibilities. A solemn thing to *die*, perhaps more so to *live*. Important and mysterious purposes connected with each one's life. The babe in the mother's arms may prove a Moses, a David, or a Paul. "What will ever come of it?" said one to Franklin in reference to the first discovered balloon. "What will ever come of that?" replied Franklin, pointing to a baby in its cradle. Job ignorant, when he asked the question, that his name should become a synonym for suffering patience.

IV. Job describes the grave and state of the dead (verses 13—19).

The description grand, tragic, and poetical. Given according to outward appearance and in relation to earthly experience.

Death and the Grave.

1. *Death a state of quiet sleep* (verse 13). A sleep as regards the animal frame. Gives the grave an attractiveness in a world of tumult and sorrow. Death a boon in such a world. The churchyard a hallowed resting place, where—"The rude forefathers of the hamlet sleep." Only sin disturbs this beautiful idea. Sin plants thorns and deadly nightshade among roses and evergreens. *Jesus takes away the sting of death, and makes the grave a bed of rest.* The death of a believer pre-eminently a sleep (1 Cor. xv. 51; 1 Thess. iv. 14; v. 10). The sleep in Jesus followed by a blessed awaking (1 Thess. v. 16).

2. *The grave a place of general rendezvous* (verses 14, 16, 19). "The small and great,"—infants that never saw the light, with kings

and their counsellors of state, all gather in the common ante-room of the grave, waiting the resurrection summons. In the great cemetery of Cairo, the magnificent mausoleums of the caliphs are mingled with the humble graves of the poor. Common receptacle for "the wise and foolish, cowards, and the brave."

3. *A place of absolute equality* (verse 19). "The small and great are there;" or, "are there the same." On the same level, and in the same condition. The bones of the prince undistinguished in the charnel-house from those of the peasant. "Dust to dust" pronounced over the coffin of the monarch as well as that of the pauper. The burial place of Alexander the Great shown in an obscure corner in Alexandria. *The only distinction in the next world determined by our character and conduct in this.*

4. *A place where the wicked cease from their oppression* (verses 17, 18). The grave an effectual check to the wrongs of the tyrant, the slave-owner, and the persecutor. Herod smitten in the midst of his murders and eaten up of worms (Acts xii. 23).

5. *A place of rest for the suffering and weary* (verses 17—19). "The prisoners rest together;"—hearing no more "the cruel voice nor sounding rod." Prisoners in the gold mines of Egypt, like slaves in more recent times, were driven to their work by the lash, their taskmasters being barbarian soldiers, who spoke a foreign language.— "The servant is free from his master." Slavery viewed as, in most cases, worse than death. To make the repose of the grave real and complete was the mission of Jesus, (Matt. xi. 28). The true rest in death taught in Heb. iv. 9; Rev. xiv. 13. The grave a sweet resting place only to those who have found rest in Christ. To believers, a place of rest—(1) From the cares and troubles of life; (2) From the oppression of man and the buffetings of Satan; (3) From the burden of a carnal and sinful nature; (4) From the conflict with sin and the flesh; (5) From painful labours in the service of Christ and humanity. *Do your work, and God will send you to rest in good time* [*Trapp*].

6. *A place exhibiting the vanity of earthly glory and riches* (verse 14). Kings and counsellors of the earth among the tenants of the tomb (Is. xiv. 6; Ez xxxii. 21, &c.). "Earth's proudest triumphs end in 'Here he lies.'" "This" (a shroud fastened and carried at the top of a lance by his own command), "this is all that remains to Saladin the Great of all his glory." "Conquer the whole earth, and in a few days such a spot as this (six feet of earth) will be all you have" [*Constantine the Great to a miser*]. All the glory of Napoleon

24

dwindled down to a pair of military boots, which he insisted on having on when dying. Death and corruption mock "the pride of heraldry and the pomp of power." The bodies of Egyptian kings and statesmen embalmed and preserved for thousands of years. Wealth and art may preserve the body's *form*, but neither its life nor beauty. —"Which built desolate places for themselves." Only *that*. Their gain and glory for which they laboured, only a *desolation*. Palaces to become ruins,—pyramids and mausoleums to be rifled of their contents. The ruins of Cæsar's Golden Palace at Rome now partly covered with a peasant's garden; those of Cleopatra's palace at Alexandria scarcely distinguishable. The great pyramid at Ghizeh still standing, but shorn of its original beauty. The marble casing stripped from its sides to adorn a neighbouring city. Its granite sarcophagus, once containing the dust of Cheops, its royal founder, long empty. In the second pyramid, the body of its founder, Cephren, discovered a few years ago and brought to England. The Egyptian tombs themselves usually built in or near a desert. These tombs generally built on a scale of great extent and magnificence. Often hewn out of the solid rock and highly decorated. The rock-hewn tombs at Thebes about two miles in extent. Of the pyramids at Ghizeh, the largest occupies an area of 13 acres; the second 11. The whole one solid mass of masonry, with a small chamber or two in the centre. The height of the Great Pyramid, 479 feet, or 119 higher than St. Paul's Church in London. These pyramids built *by the kings themselves*, and *for* themselves. Begun at their accession, enlarged each successive year of their reign, and closed, as if for ever, at their death. More care bestowed by the Egyptians on their tombs than on their dwellings. In Persia, royal sepulchres, apart from others, cut out high up in the face of steep cliffs. Shebna's vanity (Is. xxii. 16). Some take more care about their sepulchres than their souls [*Caryl*]. A heathen poet says: "Light is the loss of a sepulchre;" but *who can calculate the loss of a soul?* (Matt. xvi. 26). —(Verse 15). "With princes that had gold." *Had* gold. Their riches a thing of the past. Their gold unable to bribe away death. —"Who filled their houses with silver," which should rather have filled the *hungry*. Gold and silver often preserved to be a witness against its possessor. Treasure heaped together for the last days (Jam. v. 3). Perhaps ordered by the possessors to be deposited with them in their tombs, also called their *houses* (Is. xxii. 16; xiv. 18, 19). Its presence there a bitter mockery, its former possessor able neither to use nor recognize it.

IV. Job complains that life is continued to the suffering and sorrowing (verse 20.)

"Wherefore is light given to them that are in misery?" &c. A tacit reflection on his Maker's goodness, justice, and wisdom. Another of those things that Job repented of "in dust and ashes," (v. 26).

Life

Wisely and graciously continued even to sufferers.

1. If *unprepared* for death, the sufferer is spared in mercy *for such preparation*. Death to the unprepared the harbinger of death eternal. An infinitely greater evil to be *cut off in sin* than to be *spared in suffering*. The life of *nature* mercifully continued, that the life of *grace* may be obtained *here*, and the life of *glory hereafter*.

2. If *prepared*, the sufferer's life is continued for *various wise and gracious purposes*.

(1.) For *proof and trial of his state*. Suffering a touchstone of sincerity. *Affliction the fire that tries the moral metal of the soul*. God uses not *scales* to *weigh* our graces, but a *touchstone* to *try* them [*Brookes*].

(2.) For *further sanctification*. Afflictions God's goldsmiths. The rising waves lifted the ark nearer heaven. Affliction the Christian man's divinity. Deepens repentance for sin, the cause of all suffering. Promotes the exercise of Christian graces, especially meekness, patience, and submission. Even Christ learned obedience by the things which He suffered. Trials develope and strengthen Christian character. Each succeeding wave hardens the oyster-shell that encloses the pearl.

(3.) For *enhancement of future glory and happiness*. As we suffer with Christ we shall be glorified with him. Labour makes rest sweeter and the crown brighter.

(4.) For *the benefit and edification of others*. Suffering meekly borne by a believer exhibits the sustaining power of grace and so encourages others. The believer's lamp often trimmed afresh at a fellow-christian's sick bed. Christian animated to persevere through the Valley of the Shadow of Death by the sound of Faithful's voice before him. Four hundred persons converted to Christ by witnessing Cæcilia's demeanour under suffering.

(5.) For *the glory of Him who is both the Author and Finisher of faith*. Affliction meekly endured exhibits the faithfulness and love of God, and so leads both ourselves and others to praise Him (Is. xxiv. 15; 1 Pet. i. 7).—Suffering a *blessing to society, and one of its regenerating forces*. Tends to humble pride and check evil-doers. Exhibits the evil of sin, the vanity of the world, and the certainty of death. Affords room for the exercise of sympathy, compassion, and benevolence. Gives scope to self-sacrifice, the noblest form of humanity.

V. Job expresses his longing for death (verse 21).

"Which long for death, &c." Said to be especially true of those who laboured in the gold mines of Egypt. A peculiar feature of Job's disease. Probably suicide the temptation presented to him by Satan through his wife. *Suicide Satan's recipe for the ills of humanity.* Job longs for death but is kept by grace from doing anything to procure it.

Death.

Our time in *God's* hand, not our own. *He is ill fitted to die who is unwilling to live.* Physical death only a blessing to him who has been delivered from *spiritual* death, and so secured against death *eternal.* Death a monster only to be safely encountered when deprived of his sting. His terrors only quenched in the blood of Christ. Death only to be desired—(1.) When our work is done; (2.) When God pleases to call us; (3.) That we may be freed from sin; (4.) That we may be with Christ (Phil. i. 23). *To bear life's burden well is better than to be delivered from it.* Grace makes a man willing to *live,* amidst life's greatest *privations and sufferings;* willing to *die,* amidst its greatest *enjoyments and comforts.*—"And it cometh not." The extreme of misery to desire death and not be able to find it (Rev. ix. 6). The misery of the damned. *Endless existence the crown of hell's torments.* Salted with fire (Mark. ix. 49). The *first* death drives the soul out of the body; the misery of the *second* death is, that it *keeps the soul in it.*

VI. Job plaintively dwells on his sad condition (verse 23).

Describes himself as "A man whose way is hid, and whom God hath hedged in,"—visited with troubles which he cannot understand, and from which he sees no way of escape. *The soul in darkness misreads all God's dealings, and only looks on the dark side.* Satan had said of Job what Job here says of himself, but with greater truth. Satan truly but enviously viewed God as hedging Job round with *protection and blessing;* Job views God as unkindly hedging him round with *darkness and trouble.* Job ascribes to God what was really done by *Satan* with God's *permission,* or by *God* only at Satan's *instigation.* The memory of past good too

26

often obliterated by the experience of present evil.—Represents his present calamities as the realisation of his worst fears (verse 25). "The thing which I greatly feared is come upon me." A tender conscience fears reverses in the height of prosperity, and in consequence of it. A fall after great felicity an instinct of human nature. Paulus Emilius, a Roman general, on the death of his two sons immediately after an unusually splendid triumph, said: "I have always had a dread of fortune; and because in the course of this war she prospered every measure of mine, the rather did I expect that some tempest would follow so favourable a gale." A wise man feareth, but a fool rageth and is confident" (Prov. xiv. 16).

Fear of the Future.

Apprehension of future evil right and profitable—

(1.) When it preserves from carnal and careless security (Ps. xxx. 6, 7); (2.) When it incites to the use of right means to prevent it (Prov. xiv. 16); (3.) When it leads us to prepare for it by seeking strength to endure it; (4.) When it arises from the conviction of the uncertainty of earthly good (Prov. xxvii. 24); (5.) When it produces earnestness in securing a better and enduring portion (Matt. vi. 20); (6.) When it leads to fidelity in the improvement of present benefits. Such apprehension wrong and hurtful;—(1.) When arising from undue anxiety about the continuance of present mercies; (2.) When attended with anxiety and distrust about the future (Phil. iv. 6); (3.) When preventing the thankful enjoyment of present blessings (Eccl. ii. 23, 24); (4.) When leading to undue means to preserve them.

Apprehension and freedom from security no prevention of the evil (verse 26). "Yet trouble came." Learn — (1) *Prayer and piety are no security against trouble.* God has not promised to preserve his people *from* trouble, but to *support* them *in* it; (2) *No human caution or foresight is able to secure men against calamity.* The race not to the swift nor the battle to the strong. (3) *To sit loose to earthly comforts is the best way to retain them, or to bear their removal.* To God's people no trouble comes *unsent,* or *without a blessing in its bosom.* Trouble in the believer's inventory (1 Cor. iii. 21, 22). Among the "all things" that work together for his good (Rom. viii. 28). Unable to separate him from Christ's love (Rom. viii. 39). The storm makes the traveller wrap himself more closely in his mantle.

Trouble and its Uses to the Believer.

To believers trouble is,—

1. *Purifying.* Affliction is God's furnace for purging away our dross; his thorn for piercing through our pride. The Jews clung to idols till they were carried captive to Babylon. The three captives lost nothing in the furnace but their *bonds.*

2. *Preservative.* Often preserves from greater evils. Augustine missed his way, and so escaped intended mischief. *The Christian's armour rusts in time of peace.* Salt brine preserves from putrefaction.

3. *Fructifying.* Affliction makes both fragrant and fruitful. God's rod, like Aaron's buds, blossoms, and bears almonds. Flowers smell sweetest after a shower. Vines said to bear the better for bleeding. Believers often most internally fruitful when most externally afflicted. Manasseh's chain more profitable to him than his crown. Many trees grow better in the shade than the sunshine.

4. *Teaching.* Trouble teaches by experience. God's rod a speaking one. At eventide light. Stars shine when the sun goes down. Some scriptures not understood by Luther till he was in affliction. God's house of correction His school of instruction.

5. *Brings consolation. Suffering* times often the believer's *singing* times. Songs in the night. As our tribulations in Christ, so our consolations. Every stone thrown at Stephen drove him nearer to Christ. Jacob's most blessed sleep when he had only stones for his pillow. Paul's sweetest epistles written when a prisoner at Rome. The most of Heaven seen by John when a lonely exile at Patmos. The darker the cloud the brighter the rainbow. God's presence changes the furnace of trial into a fire of joy. God's rod, like Jonathan's staff, brings honey on its point.

6. *Conforms us to Christ.* God had one son without sin, but none without suffering. All His members to be conformed to His suffering image, though some resemble Him more than others [*Rutherford*].

7. *Is the way to the Kingdom.* Affliction only a dark passage to our Father's house,— a dark lane to a royal palace. The short storm that ends in an everlasting calm [*Brookes*].

CHAPTER IV.

COMMENCEMENT OF THE CONTROVERSY BETWEEN JOB AND HIS THREE FRIENDS.

First Course of the Speeches. First Dialogue,—Eliphaz and Job.

First Speech of Eliphaz.

Eliphaz censures Job for his impatience, and hints at sin as the cause of his suffering. Verse 1. "Then Eliphaz the Temanite," &c. First of the three in age and experience. The mildest of Job's accusers, and superior to the rest in discernment and delicacy. His tone friendly and modest, but pours vinegar rather than oil on Job's wounds. A wise man of the class of Solomon, Heman, and Ethan (1 Kings, iv. 30, 31). Maintains that no innocent person is ever left to perish (verse 7). His statements sound in themselves, but false in their application. His speech the product of a genuine, pious, wise man of the east. Characterized by the legality and narrowness of the age in which he lived. Sadly wanting in sympathy and heart. Eliphaz immensely Job's inferior in intelligence, though his superior in age.

I. Introduction (verse 2).

"If we assay," &c. Begins with gentleness and courtesy. *Reproof to be given, not only with love in the heart, but tenderness on the tongue.* The razor cuts cleanest when whetted with oil. Tenderness especially due to sufferers.—"Wilt thou be grieved," or "take it ill?" As difficult to bear reproof in trouble as it is to give it. *Patiently to bear reproof, the sign of an honest, if not a gracious heart* (Prov. xvi. 32). Next to the *not deserving* of a reproof is the *well taking* of it [*Bishop Hall*]. No little grace required to say "Let the righteous smite me, it shall be a kindness" (Ps. cxli. 5).— "But who can withhold himself," &c. The reason of his speaking. Compelled by conscience. Good to speak and act only from conviction of duty. Care to be taken, however, that that conviction be an *enlightened* one. *Compulsion* from *our own* spirit not to be mistaken for *impulsion* from *God's. Better not to speak at all than not to speak to the purpose.*

II. The Reproof. Contains—1. *A testimony to Job's past character and conduct,* (v. 3, 4). "Thou hast instructed many," &c.

Job's conduct to others in similar circumstances to his own. "Instructed,"—"strengthened," "upheld."—Noble testimony—(1.) To his *sympathy and warmth of heart;* (2.) To his *wisdom and intelligence*—"hast instructed"; (3.) To his *zeal and self-denying activity* on behalf of others—"instructed *many*"; (4.) To his *experience in the things of God,* fitting him for a spiritual comforter. Job's character not merely one of *uprightness and integrity,* but of *kindness and benevolence.* Eliphaz endorses the testimony—a "perfect" as well as an "upright" man. Does this, however, less to praise his *past,* than to censure his *present* conduct. Confirms Job's own testimony of himself (xxix. 13, &c.; xxx. 25). Job the opposite of a selfish character. Improved his prosperity and influence for the comfort and benefit of others. A true priest and minister to the neighbourhood in which he lived. Not only prayed and sacrificed *for* others, but imparted instruction and consolation *to* them. Not only feared God *himself,* but sought to lead *others* to do the same. Sought to stimulate to duty and to strengthen under trial. Performed for those in trouble the part of Jonathan to David (1 Sam. xxiii. 16). His conduct enjoined as a New Testament duty (Is. xxxv. 3; Heb. xii. 12). Practised by Christians as a New Testament grace (Rom. xv. 14; 1 Cor. xvi. 15; Heb. vi. 10; 1 Thess. v. 11). The work and ministry of Christ himself, Job's antitype (Is. xlii. 3; lxi. 1-3). Instruction placed *first,* as the means and foundation of the rest. The *word of truth* the medium to be employed in healing sick and wounded spirits (Ps. cvii. 20).

Christian Ministry

Especially one of instruction and consolation (Is. xl. 12). Requires an enlightened mind, a tender heart, and a gracious tongue. Abundant room for such a ministry in a sinning and suffering world. Dark minds, weak hands, and tottering knees to be met with everywhere. The feeble, the falling, and the fallen, the church has with it always. The whole creation travailing together in pain; and believers, with the first fruits of the Spirit, groaning within themselves (Rom. viii. 22, 23). Cases especially requiring such a ministry:—1. *Affliction,* personal or domestic; 2. *Bereavement*; 3. Temporal *losses and misfortunes;* 4. *Persecution* and *cruel treatment* from others; 5. *Spiritual darkness and temptation;* 6. *Sorrow* and *contrition for sin;* 7. *Infirmities of age* and *approaching dissolution.* "Till tears are wiped away, and hearts cease to ache, and sin no longer desolates, every believer has a mission in this world" [*Beecher*]. Grounds of consolation and support in the character

and truth of God (1 Sam. xxiii. 16. The Old and New Testaments the storehouse of Divine consolations (Rom. xv. 4). Lamentations iii., Romans viii., and Hebrews xii. especially rich in such topics. The believer and well-instructed scribe to be always ready to draw out of this treasury (Matt. xiii. 52).—Topics of consolation in time of trouble and affliction:—(1.) The *character of God, as compassionate and faithful;* (2.) The *hand of God in all our afflictions;* (3.) *God's gracious purposes* in sending trouble; (4.) The *shortness and lightness of affliction* as compared with the "eternal weight of glory" for which it is preparatory; (5.) The *promises* of pardon, grace, guidance, provision, and protection to the end; (6.) *Christ Himself* as our Redeemer, in whom we have all things; (7.) *His example* as a *sufferer;* (8.) His *sympathy in our affliction.*

2. The *censure.* "But now," &c. To commend with a "but" is a wound rather than a consolation [*Trapp*]. Christ's reproofs, however, sometimes given with such a "but" (Rev. ii. 14).—"Now it is come upon thee," —viz., trouble. Storms proving the ship's seaworthiness.—"And thou faintest." Same word as in verse 2, rendered "grieved." An unfeeling reproach. Eliphaz a sorry imitator of what he had just commended in Job. Forgets the unprecedented character of Job's sufferings. Charges him with being either a pretender to the virtue he had not, or a neglector of what he had. Job's antitype similarly taunted,—"He saved others," &c. (Matt. xxvii. 42). Yet suggests an important truth both for Christians and ministers.

Ministerial Consistency.

Heed to be taken not to preach to others without practising ourselves. The people's ears not to be holier than the preacher's heart. Jewish Rabbies condemned for teaching others whilst not teaching themselves (Rom. ii. 21). Self application of enforced truth the preacher's duty as well as the people's. The exhortation of the *lips* to be seconded by the testimony of the *life. Present doings* not to shame *former sayings* [*Trapp*]. One said of Erasmus, "There is more of Christ's soldier in his *book* than in his *bosom.*" The easiest thing to give good counsel, the hardest to act on it. Self application of Divine truth man's duty, but God's gift. Sustaining grace needed by the strongest as well as the weakest. The saddest fall, that "when a standard bearer fainteth" (Is. xvi. 18). To "faint" in the day of adversity proves our strength is small (Prov. xxiv. 10). *The believer's duty to do each day's work with Christian diligence, and to bear each day's*

28

cross with Christian patience. The charge of Eliphaz though not the kindest, yet true. Job had both "fainted," and was "troubled," or confounded. The language of chap. iii. a sad contrast to that of chap. i. and ii. The shield of faith vilely cast away. How is the mighty fallen!—*Faith and patience in the greatest saints subject to eclipse.* Job had with Peter walked on the water; but now, with Peter, begins to sink in it.—*Inconstancy written on all creature-excellence.* Only One able to say "I change not," (Mal. iii. 6). David's mountain stands strong till God hides His face, and he is troubled (Ps. xxx. 7). Job to learn that his own strength is weakness, and that his righteousness is of God and not of himself. The strong man must glory only *in the Lord* (ch. xxix. 20; Jer. ix. 23, 24). Job, like Paul, to be shorn of his strength, that the power of Christ may rest upon him (2 Cor. xii. 9). Only he who waits on the Lord renews his strength, so as to walk without fainting (Is. xl. 31). In spite of dashing waves the limpet clings to the rock through its own emptiness. —(Verse 6). "Is not this thy fear," &c. Apparently a cruel charge of hypocrisy. Probably, however, not so decided and direct as appears in our version. Perhaps more correctly read: "Is not thy fear [of God] thy confidence, and thy hope, the uprightness of thy ways?" That is, "Should it not be so?" Doctrine: *A man's religion ought to give him confidence in time of trouble.* Like his former statement, the question of Eliphaz a testimony to Job's piety. An endorsement of ch. i. 1. Job admitted to have been distinguished for his fear of God and integrity of life. The only question now, "Is it real?" Eliphaz begins to suspect it. —The "fear of God" another word for religion. That fear, when genuine, coupled with "uprightness" of life. *True religion ever accompanied with its twin-sister, morality.* True piety ought to give "confidence" in regard to the *present*, and "hope" in regard to the *future.* The words of Eliphaz a great truth falsely applied. The 46th Psalm an exemplification of that truth. Habakkuk's Song another (Hab. iii. 17, 18). For this result, however, the fear of God to be coupled with

Faith in God.

Job's *fear of* God unshaken, but his *faith in* God beclouded. A *past* religious and moral life in itself not sufficient to stay the mind in trouble. The peace of God that keeps the heart and mind, the result of *faith in Jesus Christ* (Phil. iv. 7). Not a blameless or God-fearing life, but a mind *stayed on God* and *trusting in Him*, keeps the soul in perfect peace (Is. xxvi. 3). Such a *trust*,

however, the usual outcome and accompaniment of such a *life.* Faith *in* God, and the fear *of* God make the soul triumph in every trouble. "Let us sing the 46th Psalm, and let them do their worst" [*Luther, when threatened by enemies*]. "My father is at the helm," enough to quiet the soul in every storm. "He has nothing to fear who has Cæsar for his friend" (*Seneca*). For *Cæsar*, substitute *Christ.* *The privilege of believers, eagle-like, to hold on their career through storms and tempests.* "The righteous is as bold as a lion," *i. e.*, with faith in exercise. Job's faith, like that of the disciples, tested in a storm and found defective (Mark iv. 40). Sometimes, however, breaks through the cloud, and triumphs over all opposition (xxiii. 10; xvi. 19; xix. 25—27; xiii. 15). *There are times when the believer's faith is scarcely able to keep head above water.*

III. Exhortation, with veiled Reproof (verse 7).

"Remember, I pray thee," &c. Skilfully ambiguous. May serve either for conviction or consolation. *History a useful teacher, but requires intelligence to read its lessons.* The part of true wisdom to mark, record, and improve God's dealings in Providence (Ps. cvii. 43). His works made to be remembered (Ps. cxi. 4). Asaph's and David's conduct in times of trouble (Ps. lxxvii. 11, 12; cxliii. 5).—"Whoever perished being innocent?" Literally: "Who is that innocent person who hath perished?" Asks for any such known example. Eternity not in view. "Perished" by some signal judgment. "Cut off" by some sudden catastrophe. Reference to Job's own case. Job *not yet* "cut off;" hence *consolation* in the question. The innocent "cast down but not destroyed." Paul's experience (2 Cor. iv. 9; vi. 9). David's (Ps. lxxi. 20). Job *all but* "cut off;" hence the question for *conviction.* Can Job be an innocent person? No such person has ever perished. No example, according to Eliphaz, of a godly man cut off by any signal judgment or overwhelming catastrophe. The opposite side maintained by Job. The godly fall with the ungodly (ch ix. 22, 23). Same truth taught, Ecc. ix. 2, 3; Ez. xxi. 3. The godly often suffer while the wicked prosper (xii. 5, 6; xxi. 7; Ps. lxxiii. 3, 12). The first recorded death of a believer a violent and bloody one. Saints at times "killed all the day long," and their "blood shed like water" (Ps. xliv. 22; lxxix. 3). Paul glories in the long martyrroll of the *Old* Testament, as the church has since done in that of the *New* (Heb. xi. 35-37). Thousands of the faithful "cut off" in the persecution of Antiochus Epiphanes

(Dan. xi. 33). Still, Job's case an unusual one, and not belonging to any of these classes. His crushing calamities apparently direct from the hand of God. Everything seemed to proclaim him an object of the Divine anger. "God smites, hence there is guilt,"— an instinct of humanity (Acts, xxviii, 3, 4). Hence the suspicion of his friends, and Job's own perplexity (ch. xiii. 24; xvi. 9—14; xix. 10, 11). *Faith has often a hard battle to fight against appearances and carnal reasoning.* Job's friends instead of aiding his buffeted and sometimes staggering faith, help his unbelief. Their object, to make him out, and bring him to acknowledge himself to be, other than he had appeared. The experience of Job a foreshadowing of that of Jesus (Is. liii. 3, 4; Matt. xxvii. 43, 46).

V. Eliphaz adduces his own observation for Job's conviction (verse 8).

"Even as I have seen." *Useful for the preacher to substantiate his arguments and appeals by facts of his own observation.*

Sin and its Consequences.

1. *Sin.* "They that plough iniquity,"— practise *wrong*, especially in relation to others. A cruel thrust at Job, as if this had been his character, and that for which he was now suffering. "*Plough*" iniquity—practise it carefully, industriously, painfully, perseveringly, and with expectation of profit (Prov. xxii. 8; Hos. viii. 7; vi. 13. Sinners sore labourers (Prov. xvi. 17; Is. lix. 5; Jer. ix. 5). *Satan the worst master; keeps his servants at hard work with miserable wages.*—"And sow wickedness," or "mischief;"—continue to prosecute wicked and oppressive schemes. The character of tyrants to oppress others with the view of enriching themselves. *Sin gradual and progressive. One sin prepares the way for another.* Ploughing prepares for sowing. The sinner urged on to persevere in sin. One sin to be followed by another, *in order to gain the result,* as ploughing by sowing. "Evil men and seducers wax worse and worse" (2 Tim. iii. 13). *Sin is never at a stay; if we do not retreat from it, we advance in it* [*Barrow*].

2. *Its consequences.* "Reap the same;" (1.) The profit of their sin. (2.) The punishment of it. Retribution corresponding with the sin, constantly recognised in the Bible (Is. xxxiii. 1; Rev. xiii. 10; Matt. vii. 2; Jam. ii. 13). Exemplified in Adonibezek (Jud. i. 7); and in the persecutors of the church (Rev. xvi. 6). The Egyptians, who drowned Israel's infants in the Nile, are themselves drowned in the Red Sea. Countries distinguished for persecution, as Spain with its Inquisition, and France with its Bartholomew Massacre, dis-

tinguished also for the horrors of bloody revolutions and civil wars. Charles IX. of France, who ordered the Massacre of 1575, expired in a bloody sweat, exclaiming, "What blood! What murders! What shall I do? I am lost for ever." Under God's government, *sin followed by suffering as a body by its shadow* (Num. xxxii. 23). Men constantly sowing either to the flesh or the spirit (Gal. vi. 7, 8). The crop according to the seed.

(Ver. 9). The fate of the prosperous wicked. Cruelly held forth by Eliphaz as if to terrify Job and identify his case with theirs. The case of Job and his children terribly resembling it. *Truth misapplied assumes the nature and produces the effect of error.* "By the blast (or breath) of God they perish." *A mere breath of God sufficient for the destruction of the ungodly.* "Thou didst blow with thy wind," sung over the ruin of Pharaoh's host and of the Spanish Armada. *The whirlwind that overthrows the dwelling and wrecks the ship, but the breath of the Almighty.* The wicked driven away by God's breath as so much dust or chaff before the wind (Ps. i. 4). The breath that made the world can as easily destroy it (Ps. xxxiii. 6).—"By the breath of his nostrils are they consumed," like vegetation scorched and burnt up by the hot wind of the desert (Jer. iv. 11; Ez. xvii. 10; Hos. xiii. 15). The life of the ungodly is— (1.) *Laborious and painful in its efforts;* (2.) *Often prosperous for a time in its results;* (3.) *Miserable in its end.* "Consumed," by Divine judgments in this life, or by the experience of His wrath in the life to come. The former mainly intended by Eliphaz, without exclusion of the latter. True, as to what *frequently* happens. Examples,—the Antediluvians, and the Cities of the Plain. Its *universality* implied by Eliphaz, but denied by Job (ch. xxi. 7—14; xii. 6). Sentence against an evil work not always speedily executed (Ecc. viii. 11). *Some* wicked men punished here, to save God's *providence; only* some to save his *patience* and *promise of future judgment* [*Augustine*]. The preservation of the ungodly only a reservation. God's forbearance no acquittance. Divine justice slow but sure. Has leaden heels but iron hands. The longer in drawing the arrow, the deeper the wound. [*Brookes.*]

(Verse 10). Same truth poetically set forth under another figure. "The roaring of the lion and the voice of the fierce lion,"—supply "is silenced." The *threatening of the rich oppressor and the terror inspired by it come to an end.* "Lions" used in Scripture as the symbol of cruel and rapacious men (Ps. lvii. 4; Jer. l. 17; Zeph. iii. 3). The figure common in Arab poetry for the rich and powerful. Furnished by the deserts of Arabia in which Eliphaz lived. The reference cruelly intended by him to Job and his three sons.—" The teeth of the young lions are broken." *The means of wicked men's doing mischief and practising oppression ultimately taken from them.* The teeth of the tyrant and persecutor sooner or later broken. Examples :—Belshazzar (Dan. v. 22, 30) ; Herod (Acts xii. 23) ; Nero (2 Tim. iv. 17). Heartless allusion to the condition of Job and his family.—(Verse 11). "The old lion perisheth." Various aspects, and perhaps species, of the lion indicated. Usual with Arab poets to express the same thing by several synonymous terms ; each, however, with a variety of idea. Various forms and degrees of wickedness, and various classes of persecutors and oppressors ; as lions differ in ferocity, age, and strength. *Common with Scripture to represent moral character under the figure of various animals :* cruelty by the lion and bear ; rapacity by the wolf and the leopard ; subtlety by the fox and the serpent ; uncleanness by the swine and the dog ; innocence by the dove ; meekness by the lamb ; industry by the ant. Some animals with natures and habits for imitation, others the reverse. *The inferior creatures, in the variety of their natures and habits, the divinely-constituted symbols of the various characters and dispositions of men.* The natural world a Divine mirror of the moral and spiritual.

VI. The vision (verse 12).
"Now a thing was secretly brought to me," &c. The vision related by Eliphaz :— (1.) To gain authority to his own reasoning and doctrine ; (2.) To reprove Job's murmuring, and sinful reflection on the Divine procedure ; (3.) To humble his apparent self-righteousness, and convince him he was a sinner. The doctrine of the vision true but misapplied by the narrator. Visions frequently afforded in patriarchal times in the absence of a written revelation (ch. xxxiii. 15, 16). One of the " divers manners " (Heb. i. 1). Such communications given " secretly," in the absence of other parties, (Dan. x. 7, 8). Eliphaz probably awake and revolving past midnight visions,—" in thoughts," &c. The description allowed to excel all others of a similar kind in sublimity and horror. Sublime without being obscure, circumstantial without being mean [*Kitto*]. Wonderful grouping of impressive ideas. Midnight—solitude—deep silence—approach of the spectre—its gliding and flitting motion —its shadowy, unrecognisable form—its final stationary attitude—the voice—the awful silence broken by the solemn question of the spirit—the chill horror of the spectator—

trembling in all his limbs—the hair of his body standing up from fear. *Much more connected with the earth than is ordinarily visible.* Man surrounded with a countless invisible population of intelligent creatures. "Myriads of spiritual beings walk the earth " [*Milton*]. *Man an object of intense interest both to good and bad spirits.* Communication with the spirit world at present confined within narrow limits ; partly through our physical nature, still more through our fallen condition. Man in his present state naturally alarmed at spiritual and supernatural appearances (Dan. x. 7, 8). Special strength required to endure such appearances and receive such communications (Dan. x. 17—19). Flesh·and blood unable to inherit the kingdom of God (1 Cor. xv. 50). Man's natural body to be changed into a spiritual one to hold fellowship with the spirit world (1 Cor. xv. 44). —" Mine ear received a little thereof ;" Heb., " a whisper." The amount received, only a whisper as compared with a full out-spoken speech. All we know of God, a mere whisper in comparison with mighty thunder (ch. xxvi. 14). Little of Divine truth communicated compared with what is to be known (1 Cor. xiii. 9). The greatest part of what we know, the least part of what we know not. Things heard by Paul in Paradise unlawful or impossible to be uttered (2 Cor. xii. 4). Truth communicated only as we are able to receive it (Mark, iv. 33 ; John xvi. 12). " Even in the Scripture, I am ignorant of much more than I know " [*Augustine*]. — (Verse 16). " There was silence and I heard a voice ; " or, " Silence, and a voice I heard," *i.e.* a still small voice, as 1 Kings xix. 12. Deep silence the result of the spectre's appearance, and the preparation for its communication. Silence within the hearer's soul as well as in the world without. Enjoined in the Divine presence and in receiving Divine communications (Hab. ii. 20). Silence in heaven before the sounding of the seven trumpets (Rev. viii. 1). The " foot " to be " kept," and silent attention to be maintained in the house of God (Eccles. v. 1, 2). Preparation of heart necessary for receiving Divine truth (Ps. lxxxv. 8 ; 1 Sam. iii. 9). Silence from—(1.) The voice of pride and self conceit ; (2.) The opinions and wisdom of the flesh ; (3.) The desires and cravings of corrupt nature ; (4.) The impatient clamourings of selfwill.

The Spectre's Communication.

(Verse 17). "Shall mortal man be more just than God,"—or, " be just before God ? " The object of the communication on the part of the spirit,—(1.) *To silence man's murmurings*

31

against the Divine procedure, as if man were more just than God (ch. iii. 10—23 ; xxxv. 2; xl. 8). *To murmur under trouble is to reflect on the Divine wisdom and goodness, and to make ourselves more righteous than God.* In the view of Eliphaz, this the sin into which Job had fallen. The sin to which great and accumulated suffering especially exposes our fallen nature. That into which Asaph had nearly fallen (Ps. lxxiii. 2). *God as righteous when he afflicts a good man as when he punishes a bad one.* Jeremiah's Divine philosophy,—" Wherefore doth a living man complain?" (Lam. iii. 39). It is "of God's mercies" that a saint as well as a sinner is "not consumed" (Lam. iii. 22). One single sin, seen in its real character, enough to shut the mouth of every complainer. Just views of the character of God and of the nature of sin calculated to silence murmurs under heaviest troubles. (2.) *To humble man's pride, and to prove every man in God's sight a sinner.* The object of the first three chapters of the Epistle to the Romans. The lesson Job was intended to learn, and *did* learn (ch. xlii. 5). Taught Isaiah by the vision of the Divine glory in the Temple (Is. vi. 1, &c.); and Peter by the miraculous draught of fishes (Luke v. 8). The object of the Gospel to teach how a man may be just before God. *The law-fulfilling and justice-satisfying work of Christ, God's way of making a man righteous before Him.* God justifies only "the *ungodly* that believe in Jesus" (Rom. iv. 40; Luke xviii. 10, 54). The reason obvious (Rom. iii. 10, 23). To become righteous, a man must take the place of a *sinner,*—his real character. The sinner becomes righteous before God in *accepting the righteousness of another.* RIGHTEOUS IN CHRIST,—our peace in life, our joy in death, and our passport into the New Jerusalem (Jer. xxiii. 5, 6; Is. xlv. 24; 1 Cor. i. 30; 2 Cor. v. 21). Job a "perfect man" according to law; but in order to evangelical perfection, his comeliness, like Daniel's, to be "turned into corruption" in him (Dan. x. 8). *The saint's highest attainment to know himself a poor sinner, and Christ a rich Saviour.* "I a poor sinner am, but Jesus died for me," (*Wesley's deathbed testimony*).—*The believer's perfection, thoroughly to know his absolute imperfection.* Education, example, correction, and punishment, may do much for a man, but cannot make him a poor sinner [*Krummacher*]. "A sinner is a sacred thing; the Holy Ghost has made him so" [*Hart*].

Verse 18. "Behold." Always indicating something important, and calling for special attention. Uncertain whether, in what follows, the spirit or Eliphaz himself is the speaker. The object,—to humble man, and more especially Job, as in nature and character so much inferior to the angels. The

constant aim of Job's "friends," to bring him down from his excellency (Ps. lxii. 4).—"He put no trust in his servants." Angels God's servants by way of eminence (Ps. ciii. 20—21; civ. 4). *The highest honour of a creature is to be a servant of his Creator.* God's service not only our *freedom,* but our *glory.* God's dominion over all created intelligences. The Seraphim his servants. Man as well as angel *must* serve; but he may choose his master.

"Thou canst not choose but serve; man's lot is servitude.
But thou hast thus much choice—a bad lord or a good."

God puts no trust in the angels, as being :— 1. *Mutable* and *unstable.* Many of them fell ; others might, but for sustaining grace. God alone unchangeable (Mal. iii. 6; Jam. i. 17). Angels secure, like men, only by a Divine act of election (i. Tim. v. 21). 2. *Imperfect and liable to err.* Fallibility and imperfection stamped on all creature-excellence. God only wise (Rom. xvi 27); only holy (Rev. xv. 4); only true (John xvii. 3). Infallibility a Divine attribute, claimed by the Pope while arrogating to himself, as the pretended head of the Church, the promise of the Holy Ghost made by Christ to His Apostles. —"His angels He charged with folly ;"—(1) allowed; (2) marked; (3) visited, sin in them. "Angels," so called from their *office* as God's messengers or agents. "Sons of God," from their nature (see ch. i. 6). Probable allusion in the text to the fall of some of them (Jude i. 6) ;—"kept not their first estate, but left their own habitation" (2 Peter ii. 4). *Rebellion against God the height of folly in man or angel.* Sinning angels dealt with according to their folly (Jude vi.; 2 Pet. ii. 4). The fall of *angels* as possible and as likely as the fall of *men.* Their fall a mystery, but clearly revealed. Man's fall connected with that of angels which preceded it. *Fallen intelligences, human or angelic, naturally the tempters of others.*—The angel's fall a lesson of humility to man (verse 19). "How much less," *i.e.* can He trust *men ;* or, "how much more" must He charge *men* with folly. The fallibility and imperfection of men argued from that of angels. Job pronounced and esteemed a "perfect man." His spirit and conduct under his trials at first in accordance with this character. Conscious himself of his spotless life (ch. xxix., xxxi). Too ready to glory in it (xxxi. 35—37). Appeared to maintain it in a way unbecoming in one who was a sinner (xxxiii. 9; ix. 17; x. 7). Needed to be taught more deeply the imperfection of his perfection. His perfection not even that of an imperfect angel, but of a *man.* The object of the Book of Job, as of God's dealings in general, to hide pride from man (xxxiii. 17).

The dust the place of the highest and the holiest before his maker.

Poetical and affecting description of

Man's Condition and Circumstances.

1. *As inhabiting a frail and humble body—* (Verse 19). "Who dwell in houses of clay." Oriental houses of the poorer classes usually of clay or mud dried in the sun. These naturally the frailest and humblest character. Contrasted with the houses of the great,—usually of hewn stone. Man's fleshly body so spoken of (2 Cor. v. 1). Adam = red earth. Hence used as the name of the race (Gen. ii. 15). Flesh a sign and cause of weakness (Is. xxxi. 3; Gen. vi. 3; Ps. lxxviii. 39). Contrasted with the angels, who are spirits, and therefore strong (Is. xxxi. 3; Ps. ciii. 20). Man's present body as "natural," contrasted with his resurrection body as "spiritual" (1 Cor. xiii. 42—44; 2 Cor. v. 1).

2. *Formed out of the ground and returning to it.* "Whose foundation is in the dust." The elements of man's body those of the ground on which he treads. Man frequently reminded of his origin to keep him humble. His lowly origin an enhancement of redeeming love. God's Son took not on Him (or, "took not hold of") the nature of angels, but that of Abraham (Heb. ii. 16). Man in his *creation* made *lower* than the angels; in his *regeneration*, *higher* (Ps. viii. 4, &c.). His return to dust *natural*, but not *necessary*. The Divine sentence on Adam's transgression (Gen. iii. 19; Ps. xciii. 3; Eccles. xii. 7). Hitherto but two authentic exceptions (Gen. v. 24; 2 Kings ii. 11. "'Dust to dust' concludes earth's noblest song."

3. *Weak and easily destroyed.* "Crushed before the moth." Crushed to death *as easily* as a moth is crushed between the fingers; or, crushed "in presence of a moth," which can prove his death. Man's body so frail that the slightest accident can terminate his existence. Pope Adrian actually choked by a gnat. A dish of lampreys the death of an English king. Man's continued existence the result of Divine preservation (ch. xix. 12). "Strange that a harp of thousand strings," &c.

4. *Constantly liable to death, and on the way to it* (verse 20). "They are destroyed from morning to evening." Liable every moment to accident, disease and death. A continual tendency to dissolution. The seeds of disease and death inherent in man's frame. Death the immediate consequence of the fall (Gen. ii. 17). Man's life itself is death in constant development. "The moment we begin to live," &c. Man crushed

"between morning and evening." An insect life. Man an ephemeral; his life a day.

5. *Cut off in death from the visible world without ability to return to it.* "They perish for ever." Man's death a finality. Only *one* life. Appointed *once* to die (Heb. ix. 27). "The bourne from whence no traveller returns." Man as water spilt upon the ground, not to be taken up again (2 Sam. xiv. 14). Art can embalm and preserve the body, but not put life into it. Galvanism can move the limbs, but not restore the life. Resurrection here out of view. The text speaks of what is *apparent*, *natural, and ordinary*. Resurrection the result of a new dispensation and a second Adam. Jesus Christ the resurrection and the life. Christ the first fruits (1 Cor. xv. 20, 23). Specimens of bodily resurrection already afforded;—(1) In Christ himself; (2) In those restored to life by Himself and by others through His power; (3) In those who rose and left their graves after His resurrection (Matt. xxvii. 52, 63). The resurrection of all believers at His second coming (1 Cor. xv. 23; 1 Thess. iv. 15—17). To be followed by a general resurrection (Rev. xx. 5; John v. 28, 29). A new earth the habitation of risen saints (2 Peter iii. 13).

6. *Unnoticed in death by higher orders of beings.* "Without any regarding it;"—*i. e.*, as to any appearance of it. No attempt made by angelic beings to prevent it. No expression heard of sorrow or concern on account of it. Man dies in silence from the other world as if unnoticed and disregarded. This, however, only in appearance (see Luke xvi. 22; Ps. lxxii. 14; cxvi. 15).

7. *Stripped of all the excellence possessed on earth* (verse 21). "Doth not their excellence which was in them go away?" Not only the best and most excellent thing which was *with* them,—as riches, dignity, power, &c.,—but which was *in* them,—as beauty and strength of body, powers and endowments of mind (Ps. xlix. 14, 17; Eccles. ix. 10). True, however, only in *appearance*, and in regard to the *body*. The spirit returns to God who gave it (Ecc. xii. 7). All excellence departs from the *body*, but not from the *man*. *Excellencies of the spirit develope and bloom in a higher sphere*. A *holy character immortal, and survives the tomb.* Grace the only glory that a man can carry with him into the spirit-world.

8. *Dying without attaining to wisdom.* "They die, even without wisdom." Man attains in this life to comparatively little knowledge in *natural* things, and to still less in *spiritual* ones (1 Cor. xiii. 9—13). Sir Isaac Newton's death-bed estimate of his attainments in science,—a little child gathering pebbles on the sea-shore, with the ocean

of unexplored knowledge before him. . "The greatest part of what I know is the least part of what I know not" [*Augustine*].

Most die without true and saving wisdom (Matt. vii. 14; 2 Tim. iii. 15). Man's wisdom in life is rightly to prepare for death (Ps. xc. 12; Deut. xxxii. 29).

CHAPTER.V.

THE FIRST SPEECH OF ELIPHAZ.—CONTINUED. .

I. Application of the Vision (verse 1). "Call now, if there be any that will answer thee; and to which of the saints ('holy ones'—probably *angels*, as xv. 15; Dan. viii. 13) wilt thou turn?" Job to expect no countenance to his language either from holy men or angels.

Learn:—

1. *Vain for a sinner to appeal against God either to saints or angels.* Every angel in heaven will take God's part against the complaining sinner. Angels already taught the wickedness and woe of rebellion against God. Angels themselves charged with folly; how then dare *man* open his mouth? *The cry of a poor sinner heard in heaven, but not that of an unhumbled self-righteous complainer.* That cry heard when directed to *God*, not to angels.

2. *No ground in the text for the doctrine of angelic intercession or prayer to departed saints.* God the hearer of prayer; to *Him* all flesh are to come (Ps. lxv. 1). To pray to others in trouble or difficulty, an *insult* to God, as if either *unable* or *unwilling to answer* (2 Kings i. 3). An angel presents the prayers of saints to God, but he the "Angel of the Covenant" (Rev. viii. 3, 4; Mal. iii. 1; Zec. iii. 1—8). The only prayer in the Bible addressed to a departed saint, that of the rich man in hell, and then not heard (Luke xvi. 24, 27). *To intercede for others the part of saints on earth.* To apply for that intercession a privilege and duty (ch. xlii. 8; Jam. v. 15, 18; 1 John v. 16). Angels *ministering attendants* on believers, not *interceding priests for* them (Heb. i. 14). *One* Mediator between God and men (1 Tim. ii. 5). One Advocate with the Father (1 John ii. 1). One Priest in heaven who makes intercession for us (Rom. viii. 34; Heb. vii. 25; ix. 24). Men to come to God by *Him* (Heb. vii. 25; John xiv. 6). Angels employed by God for the benefit of his children (Ps. xxxiv. 7; xci. 11; Heb. i. 14). Prayer for that ministry to be addressed, not to the *servants*, but to the Master who sends them (Matt. xxvi. 53).

3. *Angels and departed saints to be "turned to,"* not *for help and protection, but for example* (Ps. ciii. 20; Matt. vi. 10). Angels our example:—(1) In obedience; (2) In submission; (3) In humility; (4) In reverence.

The prayer oftener uttered than realized,— "Thy will be done on earth," &c. God's will done in heaven:—(1) By *each* of its inhabitants; (2) Without *intermission* or *deviation*; (3) With *promptitude* and *cheerfulness*; (4) Without *murmuring* or *questioning*. Earth converted into heaven when this prayer is fulfilled. A consummation to be expected:—(1) From the prayer itself; (2) From express promises to that effect (2 Peter iii. 13; Is. xi. 9; Zeph. iii. 9).

II. The folly and effects of fretting against God (verse 2).

"For wrath (passion, and displeasure against God for his dealings in Providence) killeth the foolish man, and envy (*margin*, 'indignation') slayeth the silly one." Probably one of the traditional sayings of the wise in common use among the sages of Arabia. A specimen of the proverbial poetry of the ancients, and a good example of Hebrew parallelism. "Poems instead of written laws,"—one of the Bedouin's boasts. These maxims or wise sayings freely applied by Job's "comforters" against him. The present, like others, an important truth. The sentiment extended in the 37th Psalm. An unfeeling application intended by Eliphaz to the case of Job.

Learn:—

1. *It is the part only of fools to fret against God and his procedure.* To complain against God and His dealings as absurd as it is wicked. The extreme of folly for a *creature of yesterday* to find fault with or sit in judgment on the doings of the Eternal Creator. Rather may a child three years old censure the architect's plan of a palace, or an ignorant boor cavil at the complications of a steam-engine.

(2.) *Fretting against God's dealings brings its own punishment.* The complainer against God's Providence is his own executioner. The man that frets in trouble is like the bird which is said to eat its own bowels. "Envy," or impatient fretfulness, is "rottenness to the bones" (Prov. xiv. 30). Fretting and passionate complaining "kills," as—(1.) It robs of peace, which is the spirit's life; (2.) Affects the health, and hastens death; (3.) Injures the life and prosperity of the soul; (4.) Brings greater chastening and punishment from God. No greater antagonist to health than a fretful spirit; no greater help to it than a contented and submissive one. Passion and impatience in trouble more hurtful and crushing than the trouble itself. True wisdom, as well as piety, under trial is, *to commit our way to God and rest in his wisdom and goodness* (Ps. xxxvii. 5—7).

III. Testimony from personal observation as to the prosperous wicked (verse 3—5).

"I have seen the foolish (ungodly) taking root," &c. The object of Eliphaz to confirm the former statement (ch. iv. 7—9). Unfeeling allusion to the case of Job. Crushing language to come from the lips of a professed friend and comforter. The tongue that uttered it as truly guided by Satan as that of Job's wife. Even Peter, by his carnal though friendly counsel, could earn the title of "Satan" (Matt. xvi. 22, 23). The *truth* of a statement no justification of its cruel and uncharitable application. From the statement of Eliphaz, still more or less realized, we learn concerning

Providence.

1. *That the ungodly frequently prosper in this life.*—(Verse 3.) "I have seen the foolish taking root," not only prospering, but apparently firm in his prosperity. Same sentiment and figure (Ps. xxxvii. 35; Jer. xii. 2). The prosperity of the wicked often a mystery and stumbling-block to the righteous (ch. xii. 6; xxi. 7; Ps. lxxiii. 3—12; Jer. xii. 1). The lot of the righteous and the wicked in this life often a contrast to each other, but a contrast the reverse of what might at first sight be expected (Luke xvi. 25). Wise reasons with God for allowing the ungodly to prosper. (1.) It exercises the faith and patience of the godly; (2.) Teaches the great inferiority of earthly to heavenly blessings; (3.) Confirms the truth of a judgment to come. Insolvable mystery but for a future state, which clears up all (Luke xvi. 25; Jam. v. 1—7). *The godly too much beloved to receive their portion in this life.* The good things of this world only the bones cast to the dogs [*Rutherford*].

2. *That the prosperity of the ungodly is followed by a speedy and certain, if not a sudden, fall.* "Suddenly I cursed his habitation,"—soon had unexpected occasion to mark it as accursed of God and doomed to destruction. The prosperity of the ungodly as insecure and temporary as it appears fair and promising. "Thou didst set them on slippery places." The fall often in this life. Examples: Nebuchadnezzar, Haman, Napoleon. Yet not always (Ps. xvii. 14;

3—3

lxxiii. 4; Luke xii. 16—20; xvi. 19, 22, 25). Nor even generally; maintained by Job against his three friends (ch. xxi. 7—13; xii. 6). If not sooner, the fall certain in death (Luke xvi. 23, 25; xii. 20).

3. *That the children of the ungodly often participate in their fall.*—(Verse 4). "His children are far from safety, and they are crushed in the gate,"—ruined by a judicial sentence, or dying by the judgment of God (2 Kings, vii. 20). Veiled allusion to Job's children. Children often involved in the effects of their parents' sin (Lev. xxvi. 39; Is. xiv. 20, 21). A penalty embodied in the Decalogue (Exod. xx. 5). Repeated in the solemn declaration of Jehovah's name and character (Exod. xxxiv. 7). God's face set not only against the ungodly themselves, but against their family (Lev. xx. 5). Examples: Israel in the Wilderness (Num. xiv. 33); Achan (Josh. vii. 24); Ahab (1 Kings, xxi. 29); Gehazi (2 Kings, v. 27). So general as to have become a proverb in Israel (Jer. xxxi. 29; Ezek. xviii. 2). The children of the ungodly often inherit the father's punishment while imitating his sin (Is. lxv. 7). By repentance, the children escape many, if not all, the effects of their parents' conduct (Ezek. xviii. 14—17). No small part of a father's punishment, that his sin causes his children to suffer both *with* him and *after* him. A diseased constitution and a degraded position among the least of these effects. *Vicious habits and propensities often the sad inheritance bequeathed by ungodly parents to their children.* A powerful motive to such parents to repent.

4. *That the wealth of the ungodly often becomes the prey of the rapacious and covetous.* (Verse 5).—"Whose harvest (literally; or, 'what he has gathered,' *i.e.,* by a course of iniquity) the hungry catch up, and taketh even out of the thorns (though guarded ever so carefully, as by a thick thorn-hedge); and the robber (as the Sabeans and Chaldeans, or 'the thirsty') swalloweth up their substance." Another cruel thrust at Job (ch. i. 15, 17). Crops in Syria and Arabia seldom safe from plundering Bedouin. Backslidden Israel obliged to hide away their grain from the Midianites (Jud. vi. 11). Earthly treasures such as thieves can break through and steal (Matt. vi. 19). A frail tenure that by which the ungodly hold their wealth. They often taken suddenly from it or it from them (Luke xii. 20). A canker in an ungodly man's gold and silver (Jam. v. 2). Sometimes, however, unintentionally laid up for the righteous to inherit (ch. xxvii. 17). Happy they on whose treasure no robber can lay his hand (Matt. vi. 20). With Christ we have "durable riches," and an inheritance laid up for us in heaven (Prov. viii. 18; 1 Pet. i. 14).

35

IV. Poetical aphorisms as to the origin and extent of trouble (verse 67).

"Although (or 'for'), &c." Perhaps another example of the traditional sayings of the East. A commonplace, intended partly for Job's reproof and partly for his comfort. Declares the origin, universality, and unavoidableness of trouble. Foolish to complain so bitterly of what is unavoidable and as universal as the race. A consolation to know that our sufferings are only such as are common to man (1 Cor x. 13). Suffering saints reminded that the same afflictions are accomplished in their brethren that are in the world (1 Peter v. 9). Both the reproof and the consolation inapplicable to Job's case, which was both *unprecedented* and *unparalleled*. Implied on the part of Eliphaz a want of sympathy and appreciation of the depth of Job's trouble. Hence felt by Job to be only an exasperation of his grief (ch. vi. 2—7).

The passage suggests concerning

Trouble.

1. *Its origin.* Negatively.—(Verse 6). "Not from the dust" or "ground." (1.) Not from mere chance, as a weed springing up from the soil; nor (2) From anything merely external; not from the *ground* but from *ourselves.* Positively.—(Verse 7). "Born unto trouble." Trouble is—(1.) From a necessity and law imposed on our existence in this world; (2.) From sin, which is the ground of that necessity. *The origin of suffering is in man himself as a child of fallen Adam.* All suffering the consequence of sin. Man is "born to *trouble*," simply because he is "born in *sin*" (Ps. li. 5). *Sin and suffering linked by bonds of adamant.* In the government of a good and righteous God, suffering could exist only,—(1.) As a legal necessity in consequence of disobedience to His laws; or (2.) As a moral necessity for the discipline of His erring children. All suffering in the world the consequence of the first transgression (Rom. v. 12);

> ' Of one man's disobedience, and the fruit
> Of that forbidden tree, whose mortal taste
> Brought death into the world and all our
> woe."

2. *Its universality.* "Man is born unto trouble."—(Ve s : 7). Suffering co-extensive with the race. An inmate of the palace as truly as of the prison. *Tears moisten the pillow of down as well as the pallet of straw.* One of the Hebrew terms for "man" is *enosh,* or "the miserable." Trouble makes the world akin. Suffering universal, because sin is so. Follows sin as its shadow. Its

universality ought to render us—(1.) Patient under our own trouble; (2.) Sympathizing with that of others.—(i.) *Terrible evil of sin that has filled a world with suffering.* (ii.) *Heaven all the more desirable as entirely free from it.* (iii.) *Precious grace that converts it into a blessing.*

3. *Its certainty.* "As the sparks fly upward." This by a law of nature. Suffering in like manner a law of our being. Inseparable from our existence in the present life. *The hand that made us has, since the entrance of sin, made us sufferers.* Man born to *trouble* as truly as he is born to *live.* Tears track man's pathway from the cradle to the grave. No wealth can purchase, no power effect, immunity from the common lot. *Only through the incarnation and suffering of God's own Son, our suffering not necessarily eternal.* "The wages of sin is death,—the gift of God eternal life, through Jesus Christ our Lord" (Rom. vi. 23).

V. The counsel of Eliphaz (verse 8—16.

"I would seek unto God (El, the mighty One), and unto God (Elohim, plural,—denoting totality of Divine perfections, or perhaps plurality of Divine persons), would I commit my cause," &c. This to the end of the chapter the best part of Eliphaz's speech. Comes down from the place of a reprover to that of a friendly adviser. His counsel characterized by *wisdom*, if not by *warmth.* Its only fault that it implies an uncharitable and unjust reflection, as if Job was a prayerless man (*See* ch. xvi. 20; x. 2; xii. 4; xiii. 20; xiv. 6). At times, however, from darkness and confusion, Job, like other believers, hardly able to pray (xxiii. 3, 4, 15). *Our great comfort in trouble that we can address ourselves to God in it.* God to be sought unto in trouble,—(1.) For counsel and direction *in* it; (2.) For comfort and support *under* it; (3.) For grace so to bear it as to glorify God *by* it; (4.) For deliverance in His own time and way *out of* it; (5.) For the spiritual benefit and improvement intended *through* it. *True piety, and wisdom to commit our cause into God's hands* (Ps. xxxvii. 5). The very hairs of our head all numbered by Him (Matt. x. 30). Makes all things work together for good to them that love Him (Rom. viii. 28). To seek unto God in trouble an instinct of nature. Practised even by the heathen according to their knowledge (Jonah i. 5). In ordinary circumstances the Athenians sacrificed to the gods of the Pantheon, but in time of calamity prayed to the Unknown God (Acts xvii. 23). *The attributes of God such as to render Him the proper object of prayer and trust in time of trouble.* These attributes described by Eliphaz as exhibited in His works.

36

Attributes of God.

1. *His Almightiness.*—(Verse 9). "Who doeth great things and unsearchable," &c. *A God almighty to help and deliver, our great comfort in trouble* (Ps. xlvi. 1; lxii. 8; lxv. 5). Nothing impossible with God. His almightiness seen in His works of creation, providence, and grace. His works in creation "marvellous" and "unsearchable," both for greatness and minuteness, number and complexity. His works in providence "unsearchable,"—(1) In the end designed in them; (2) In the manner of its accomplishment. "Deep in unfathomable mines," &c. More now *seen* in the works of creation than could even be *imagined* in the days of Eliphaz. The discoveries of the last three centuries give an emphasis to his words undreamt of at that period. Many of the numerous *nebulæ* or dusky spots observed throughout the heavens, already resolved by the telescope into innumerable stars, each itself a sun. Reason to conclude the same of the rest, though from their distance as yet unresolved. Millions of suns, probably with systems like our own, found to compose the Milky Way of which our solar system is a part. The microscope, on the other hand, reveals *animalculæ* so minute that a thousand millions of them together do not exceed in size a grain of sand; yet each having perfect and distinct formations and all the functions essential to life. *Such a view of God's almightiness calculated not only to deepen our reverence, but to increase our trust.*

2. *His goodness and benevolence*—(Verse 10, 11). "Who giveth rain," &c. Rain a striking display of God's goodness as well as of his power and wisdom. One of his most common but precious gifts (Ps. lxv. 9, 10; Jer. xiv. 22; Amos iv. 7; Zec. x. 1; Acts xiv. 17). One of the most beautiful as well as beneficent operations in nature. The evaporation of moisture, its suspension in clouds, its condensation and descent, carried on by the operation of natural laws of which God is the author and director. The changes of temperature on which this operation depends, all in His hands, and "unsearchable" to us. *Every drop of rain comes to us as a witness-bearer of the Divine benevolence* (Ps. lxviii. 9, 10).—"To set up on high those that be low," &c. The change on the part of thousands from wretchedness and despondency to gladness and rejoicing, often, especially in the East, the result of an abundant rain. *In this, as in other respects, the natural a beautiful and instructive figure of the spiritual* (Is. xliv. 3—5; lv. 10—13; Deut. xxxii. 2).

3. *His wisdom*—(Verse 12—14). "He disappointeth the desires of the crafty," &c. His wisdom displayed in overmatching the

crafty and disappointing their schemes.—(Verse 13.) "He taketh the wise in their own craftiness." Quoted by the apostle in 1 Cor. iii. 19, to show that "the wisdom of men is foolishness with God." The deepest devices of carnal men in God's view only short-sighted contrivances of little children. Their "best laid schemes" often suddenly overturned by the slightest incident. Human "enterprises," most carefully prepared and likely to succeed, often made to collapse like houses of cards. The splendid Armada, designed by Spain for the overthrow of the Reformation in England, dissipated and destroyed by unfavourable weather. Of the three attempts of the French to effect a landing in Ireland, the first and second failed through the adverse elements, and the third by the influence of the change in Buonaparte's counsels. Haman's well laid scheme to crush Mordecai and the Jews ends in his own disgrace and ruin. At David's prayer and for David's deliverance, Ahithophel's sagacious counsel is turned into foolishness (2 Sam. xv. 31: xvi. 20—23; xvii. 1—14). The Birs Nimroud, on the plains of Babylon, a standing example of the "counsel of froward" Babel-builders "carried headlong." *Our affairs safe in the hands of One with whom the wisdom of men is only foolishness.*

4. *His compassion* (verses 14, 15). "But he saveth the poor from the sword," &c. (or, "He saveth the oppressed from their mouth, the poor from the hand," &c.) From their "mouth," open to devour, and from their "hand" lifted up to slay them. Examples: The enslaved Israelites delivered from the hand of Pharaoh and the Egyptians (Ex. xviii. 20); Peter from the hand of Herod and the expectation of the Jews (Acts xii. 11); Paul from the mouth of the lion Nero (2 Tim. iv. 17). God's *goodness* exercised towards men *in general*; His *compassion* towards the *needy and oppressed*. The helpless and afflicted especially the objects of His regard (Ps. lxxii. 12, 13; ciii. 6). An additional reason for Job's seeking unto God and committing his cause into His hands.—The results on *others* from God's compassion exercised in the deliverance of the afflicted. (Verse 16).—(1.) "The poor have hope." Job in his affliction encouraged to hope in God from his dealings with others in a similar condition. The use to be made of all God's gracious interpositions on behalf of those in trouble (Ps. xxii. 4, 5; xxxiv. 6, 8, 11; xl. 1—3). *Hope in God the object of the Scriptures and the examples of delivering mercy recorded in them* (Rom. xv. iv). Encouragement to hope, the actual result of God's dealings with Job (Jam. v. 11).—(2.) "Iniquity stoppeth her mouth" (found also in Ps. cvii. 42). Persecution and oppression often struck dumb,—

(1) by God's manifest deliverance of the poor that trusted in Him; (2) by His judgments on the wicked executed along with that deliverance (Ex. xiv. 25). God's *works* will put the ungodly to silence when His *words* do not. The time of the final deliverance of the godly that of the shame and confusion of the wicked (Dan. xii. 2).

VI. The plea of Eliphaz for Job's repentance (verses 17—18).

Holds out the benevolent object and happy effects of affliction. Job thus addressed as one needing repentance and now under the Divine correction. The statement true and applicable to Job's case, but not as Eliphaz supposed. Job's affliction not strictly a correction for sin, but to be employed as such for his spiritual benefit. His "captivity" to be "turned," and that upon his repentance. His repentance, however, not as Eliphaz thought, for *sins of life*, but for that of *cavilling at the Divine procedure*. The whole passage a fine specimen of ancient Shemitic poetry. Probably more of the wisdom of the ancients handed down in verse from the earliest times. Contains a highly coloured description of the happiness of the godly in the present· life. Generally true, according to the Old Testament platform. In harmony with other Old Testament promises, especially in the Psalms and Proverbs. *New* Testament promises rather of *inward peace* with *outward trouble;* all our need supplied, and all things working together for our good (John xiv. 27; xvi. 33; Phil. iv. 19; Rom. viii. 28). The error of Eliphaz in making earthly prosperity the uniform reward of godliness. That error seen and opposed by Job. Some of the promises held out by Eliphaz felt by Job to be a cruel mockery and an aggravation of his grief. These promises however afterwards fully realised in his experience (ch. xlii.)— "Behold," &c. Calls Job's special attention to what he is now to advance. The thing stated strange in itself and not readily believed. "Happy is the man whom God corrected." Same sentiment in nearly the same words (Ps. xciv. 12). Two modes of correction employed by God—(1) By His Word and Spirit ; (2) By His work in Providence. The latter here intended "Correcteth," or "rebukes," viz., with the "rod of affliction" (Sam. iii. 1 ; Ps. xxxix. 10 11). The text contains :—(1.) A *truth* stated ; (2.) A *lesson* drawn from it. The truth : *Blessedness found in Divine correction.* The lesson : *That correction therefore not to be despised.*

Divine Correction.

1. Its *blessedness.* Seen—(1) *In its origin.* Its origin—*Divine love* (Prov. iii. 12 ; Heb. xii. 6 ; Rev. iii. 19). Correction the

part, not of a *judge* but of a *father* (Heb. xii. 7—9). A mercy to be *corrected* when we might have been *destroyed* (Sam. iii. 22). Sad token for a man when God will not spend a rod upon him [*Brookes*]. (2) *In its object.* Our *spiritual benefit* (Heb. xii. 11) ;—Repentance (Rev. iii. 19); Removal of sin (Is. xxvii. 9); Participation in God's holiness (Heb. xii. 10). *Affliction is God's medicine to heal, and His furnace to purify His children.* (3) *In its actual result.* Affliction in itself a fruit of sin, but in God's hand a *means of good.* When God corrects His children, He—(i.) *Supports.* them *in* the affliction; (ii.) *Purifies* them *by* it ; (iii.) *Delivers* them *out of* it. "None more unhappy than he who never felt adversity" [*Seneca*].

2. Its *improvement.* Here *negatively* expressed. "Despise not thou," &c. So Prov. iii. 11; Heb. xii. 5. God's corrections are not to be—(i.) Refused as something *nauseous*; nor, (ii.) Rejected as something *hurtful*; nor, (iii.) *Slighted* as something *useless.* The exhortation implies the opposite duty. God's corrections are on the contrary to be—(1) *Highly prized*; (2) *Carefully improved.* Prized, as—(i.) From a Father's hand; (ii.) Sent in love; (iii.) Designed for our highest good. Affliction to be *improved*—(1) By *consideration* of its *object ;* (2) By *examination* into its *cause ;* (3) By *endeavour* after its *fruit* (Lam. iii. 39—42). Trials only *profitable when we are rightly exercised under them* (Heb. xii. 11). *To be benefited by God's rod, it is necessary to be taught out of God's Word* (Ps. xciv. 12). —The correction that of "the Almighty," or All-sufficient. Indicates—1. His *benevolence* in the correction ; the "Almighty" under no obligation to sinning creatures. 2. His *ability*—(1) To *sustain* us *under* it; (2) To *sanctify* us *by* it ; (3) To *deliver* us *out of* it. *God's corrections are sores which He himself will heal again.*

Verse 18. "He maketh sore and bindeth up." Same truth (1 Sam. ii. 6 ; Hos. vi. 1). All pains and griefs from God. True even in Job's case, though not as Eliphaz supposed. This thought an aggravation to Job's distress. "Maketh sore," as a surgeon amputating a limb or cutting out a gangrene. The pain no further inflicted·than is necessary (Lam. iii. 33). "And bindeth up," —as a wound or amputated limb (Ps. cxlvii. 3). God himself the Physician of souls (Ps. ciii. 3). Jehovah Rophi (Ex. xv. 26). The office assumed and executed by the incarnate Son (Luke iv. 18, 23 ; Matt. ix. 12). The bandages employed—the doctrines, promises, and consolations of the Gospel (Ps. cvii. 20).—"He woundeth," as with a surgeon's knife or lancet. God wounds to heal. His wounds faithful, as those of a friend (Prov. xxvii. 6 ; Ps. cxli. 5). Judicial wounds reserved for the head of obstinate transgressors (Ps. lxviii. 21).—" And his hands make whole".—literally, "sew up," viz., the wound. His own hands; implying —(1) *Readiness*; (2) *Tenderness*; (3) *Skill*; .(4) *Success* in the operation. Learn—(i.) *Those wounds well and lovingly sewed up that are sewed up by the hands of the Almighty.* (ii.) *We may well endure wounds that are to be sewed up by such a Physician.*

VII. Motive to repentance drawn from the promises (Verse 19, &c.).

These promises held out on the supposition of *repentance and prayer*. Most of God's promises both to saints and princes *conditional*. The blessings here enumerated both of a negative and positive nature. Most of them, according to the Old Testament dispensation, pertaining to the present life.

The Promises.

1. Negatively. *Safety and deliverance in times of trouble.* "In six troubles He shall deliver thee." "Six;" a definite number for an indefinite: many and manifold troubles " (Prov. vi. 16; 1 Pet. i. 6). "Many are the afflictions of the righteous" (Ps. xxxiv. 19). "One woe past, another woe cometh." "Lord, how are mine enemies increased" (Ps. iii. 1). Deliverance promised not in one or two troubles, but in *all*, however many (Ps. xxxiv. 19). Every new trouble needs Divine support and deliverance. "*In*" six troubles, viz.—the troubles you yourself are in; or, the dangers and calamities prevailing around you. "A thousand shall fall at thy side," &c. (Ps. xci. 7). The promise is either—(1) to be kept from *falling into the trouble*; or, (2) to be preserved from *injury by it*; or (3) to be in due time *taken out of it*. Preservation *in* trouble, support *under* it, and deliverance *out of* it, all in the believer's charter. The cross not immediately taken from the shoulder, but strength given to bear it. The time and mode of deliverance best reserved in God's own hands. Deliverance from troubles either *temporary* and *partial*, or *final* and *complete*. Only the former usually experienced in this life. Here, trouble succeeds trouble as wave succeeds wave. One past, we are to prepare for another. Final and complete deliverance only at death. *Death strikes off every link of the believer's chain, except the last one, which is itself.* That link, which binds the body to the grave, struck off at the Lord's appearing (1 Cor. xv. 52, 57).— "Yea, in seven;" however accumulated in number and excessive in severity. "Seven" the number of *fulness*. Not one, nor many, but "all thy waves and

thy billows," &c. (Is. xlii. 7). The furnace heated "seven times" more than usual for the three young captives (Dan. iii. 19). —"There shall no evil touch thee"—so as really to injure or destroy (Ps. xci. 7, 10). The lions in the den lie harmless at Daniel's feet. The fire leaves the captive's hair unsinged, while it consumes their bonds (Dan. iii. 25). Even physical evil not always a real evil. Rutherford, in his exile, dates his letters from his "palace at Aberdeen." Such evils often the prevention of greater ones, and the means of obtaining blessings. Bernard Gilpin breaks his leg by an accident, and escapes the fires of Smithfield. "Children, we should have been undone, had we not been undone," said *Themistocles, when an exile at the Persian Court.* Joseph's confinement in prison his stepping-stone to the throne of Egypt.—*Kinds of deliverance promised.* (1) From *famine* (verse 20). "In famine," (—arising from failure in the crops—) "He shall redeem thee from death." Believers may *suffer in famine*, but, as a rule, not *die from it*. The righteous not even then forsaken, nor his seed begging bread (Ps. xxxvii. 25). (2) From calumny (verse 21). "Thou shalt be hid from the scourge of the tongue"—so as not to be hurt by calumny and false accusation. The tongue often a more mischievous instrument than the sword. Slander the choice weapon of the ungodly against the faithful (Jer. xviii. 18). Times of spies and informers, when no godly man appears safe. Yet God has a pavilion to hide His people from the strife of tongues (Ps. xxxi. 20). Jeremiah, Daniel, and the three captives assailed by the tongue, but delivered. Stephen, like his Master, falls by it, but only the sooner to gain his crown. Paul smitten with it, but the sooner obtains his desire of being with Christ. *God either gives to His people what He promises, or something better.* (3) From *foreign invasion.* "Neither shalt thou be afraid (*i. e.*, have any cause to be afraid) of destruction (—desolation from an invading enemy) when it cometh,"—or is coming, either upon others or near thyself. The believer not taken *out* of the evil, but kept *above* it. Preserved from real evil in it, and from fear regarding it. *Faith grasping the promises lifts the soul above fear.* The name of the Lord a strong tower, &c. "Fear not, thou carriest Cæsar;" for Cæsar substitute *Christ.* No *cause* for fear, therefore no place to be given to it. God a wall of fire round about his people (Zec. ii. 5). Makes a dense mist or wreath of snow such a wall at his pleasure. "The providence of God is my inheritance"—inscribed on an old house in Chester, the only one in the street untouched by the plague. (Verse

22.)—"At destruction" (—the desolation as already come)—"and famine" (—scarcity of food as its attendant—) "thou shalt laugh." The promise rises in a climax, —safety — fearlessness — triumph. Faith enables believers to laugh when others weep. A holy laughter put by God Himself into the mouths of His servants (ch. viii. 21; Ps. cxxvi. 2). Believers laugh in times of calamity, not from *want of sensibility*, but from *warrant of safety*. The godly can *laugh* from satisfaction as to themselves, while they *weep* in *sympathy for others*. To laugh at destruction *without* faith, is either stoicism or cruelty; to laugh *from* faith, the highest piety. Abraham laughed *piously* from *faith*; Sarah laughed *sinfully* from *the want of it*. Faith and fidelity *give songs in the darkest night of adversity*. God's sweetest consolations often reserved for the time of sorest tribulations. (4). From *wild beasts*. "Neither shalt thou be afraid of the beasts of the earth"— ravaging a country wasted by an invading foe. The incursions of wild beasts often spoken of as a Divine judgment (Deut. xxxii. 24; 1 Kings xvii. 25; Ezek. v. 17, xiv. 21). *Then* a much greater terror in the East than now. Term probably included reptiles (Gen. iii. 1). Similar promise of Divine protection against them (Ps. xci. 13). Daniel's God able to shut the lions' mouths. Paul shakes off the viper that fastened on his hand and feels no harm (Acts xxviii. 1, &c.) Yet Polycarp and thousands more found their martyr's crown in the jaws of wild beasts. (5) From being hurt either by the *animate or inanimate creation*.—(Verse 23.) "Thou shalt be in league with the stones of the field, and the beasts of the field shall be at peace with thee." The covenant made with believers includes the beasts of the field as their friends and allies (Hos. ii. 18). *Man in rebellion against His Maker has all creation at enmity with him.* Reconciliation with God through Christ restores man to friendship with the creatures. Dominion over the lower animals lost in Adam but regained in Christ (Ps. viii. 6; Heb. ii. 8). Neither stones can hurt nor beasts devour against God's will. Stones and beasts not only *not hurtful*, but made *profitable*. The lions that refused to touch Daniel devoured his enemies. The stones of the field afforded Jacob the pillow on which he slept his sweetest sleep.

2. *Point of transition to positive blessings.* These such as are held most valuable among men. Promised to Israel while faithful to God. *Not* all of them promised to believers, with the world in its present condition and Satan as its prince. To be enjoyed in that better state, when the earth shall be full of the knowledge of the Lord (Is. lxv. 17—25; Rom. viii. 19—22; 2 Pet. iii. 13). A

for eshadowing of that state in Job's condition after his restoration (ch. xlii. 10—17.) (1) Domestic *peace and felicity* (Verse 24). "Thou shalt know," &c., i.e., by a Divine assurance and a happy experience. To *discern a mercy is itself a new mercy in its bosom* [*Brookes*]. "Thy tabernacle shall be in peace," or, "be peace,"—so thoroughly pervaded by it. In safety from others; in harmony with itself; and enjoying a general prosperity. "A peaceable habitation, a sure dwelling, and a quiet resting place," among promised blessings (Is. xxxii. 18). The voice of rejoicing and salvation in the tabernacles of the righteous (Ps. ii. 8, 15). *God's presence the only sure foundation of family peace.* That peace consistent with trial, sickness, and death in the dwelling 1 Pet. i. 6).—(2) *Safety and prosperity in our secular calling.* "Thou shalt visit thy habitation, (or perhaps,' thy fold,') and shalt not sin;" (or, 'shalt not miss any of thy property;' or, 'not be disappointed in thy hope,'—*Margin*, "Shalt not err"). "Shalt visit thy habitation," after the day's journey or toil;" or, "shalt visit thy fold or pasture," as one looking to the state of his flocks and herds (Prov. xxvii. 23). *A great mercy to have a habitation to visit; a still greater one to be made to visit it without sin.* Domestic peace a precious blessing; domestic *purity* a still more precious one, and essential to it. *Better to be kept from sinning in our habitation than from suffering in it.* God's blessing on our family and affairs connected with *diligence* in attending to them. Great mercy to find our dwelling preserved from flames within and foes without. The contrary on one occasion one of David's great trials (1 Sam. xxx. 1—5). *Promises not falsified by trials that seem to run counter to them.*—(3) *A numerous and happy offspring.* (Verse 25). "Thy seed shall be great," &c. A numerous and powerful family accounted, especially in the East, one of the greatest blessings. The Bible expresses the feelings of humanity in reference to children,—"Happy is the man that hath his quiver full of them" (Ps. cxxvii. 5). One of the most frequently promised earthly blessings in the Old Testament. The promise supposes godliness in the parents, and, as its consequence, also in the children (Ps. cxxviii. 1, 4). In the New Testament, the promise not so much of a *great* as of a *gracious* offspring (Is. xliv. 3—5). Contrary to his expectation, the text realized in Job's case, notwithstanding his bereavement (ch. xli. 13).—(4) *A ripe old age with a peaceful death and burial.* (Verse 25). "Thou shalt come to thy grave in a full age," &c. "Shalt come." indicating—(1) Willingness to die; (2) A quiet passage. "To thy grave,"—buried in the sepulchres of thy fathers. A peaceful grave and decent burial held, especially in the East, a matter of great importance. The want of it threatened as a Divine judgment (Deut. xxviii. 26; Jer. xxii. 13, 19; xxxvi. 38). Graves in the East usually hewn out in the rock or dug deep in the sand. Bodies otherwise frequently exposed to birds and beasts of prey. The promise generally fulfilled. But the godless rich man died and was buried; while nothing is said of the burial of Lazarus. The promise of a ripe old age especially an Old Testament one. Made first to Abraham (Gen. xv. 15). Made generally to the godly (Ps. xci. 16). The desire to live to a good old age an instinct of human nature. Premature death often threatened to the ungodly. Length of days in wisdom's right hand (Prov. iii. 16). The general result of a holy, peaceful, and temperate life. A course of piety in every respect favourable to it. Long life connected both in the Old and New Testament with obedience to the fifth commandment (Ex. xx. 12; Eph. v. 1—3). *A blessing to live while we can live to purpose.* Life to be measured, not so much by its *days* as by its *doings*. More important to live *well* than to live *long*. Inward development not necessarily the work of years. The promise rather of *ripeness for death* than *continuance of life. The faithful believer is satisfied with life whenever called to quit it.* Ripening for death the result of Divine grace, and found at all ages.

VIII. Application of the foregoing (verse 27).

1. *Affirmation of its truth with the grounds of it.* "Lo this—so it is." Good to speak with full conviction of the truth of what we advance. Personal conviction, however, not necessarily the proof of truth. Conviction may be more or less enlightened. Inspired utterances *always* true.—"We have searched it." Eliphaz the spokesman of the rest. Their discourses probably the result of previous conference. Their minds already made up on the subject of the Divine procedure in reference to the righteous and the wicked. The statements of Eliphaz *the result of study and examination.* The objects of his search were—(1) *The actual experience of men,* or *God's visible dealings in Providence;* (2) *The traditional maxims of wise men before him.* The examination, having little of revealed truth, both *partial* and *limited.* The period of Eliphaz the early twilight of the world. *All statements in respect to moral and religious truth to be the result of careful examination, according to the means within our reach.*

2. *Exhortation to personal self-application of the truth delivered.* "Know thou it." Truth heard, to become matter of personal experience. In order to this, it is to be— (1) Examined; (2) Pondered; (3) Received. The conduct of the Bereans (Acts xvii. 11). The tone of Eliphaz that of a monitor and teacher, as much older than Job (ch. xv. 10; xxxii. 6, 7; xlii. 16).—"For thy good." The hearer's good to be the speaker's aim (Eph. iv. 29). His duty to apply truth heard for his own advantage. The aim of Eliphaz, Job's repentance and consequent restoration to Divine favour. His motive good, but founded on a mistaken and uncharitable view of Job's character and the cause of his sufferings. Eliphaz, viewed as an example to preachers—(1) Sincere; (2) Earnest; (3) Courteous; (4) Employs variety of arguments and illustrations; (5) Adduces authorities; (6) Appeals to Divine revelation. Fails—(1) In sympathy and warmth of feeling; (2) In comprehensiveness of view; (3) In adaptation of his authorities to the case in hand; (4) In charitable judgment; (5) In appreciation of the case of his hearer.

CHAPTER VI.

JOB'S REPLY TO ELIPHAZ.

I. Justifies his complaint (verse 2). "O that my grief were thoroughly weighed," &c. Job's case neither apprehended nor appreciated by his friends. Desires fervently that his suffering and his complaining were weighed against each other; or that his calamity and the grief occasioned by it were thoroughly considered. The weight of it beyond that of the "sand" of the sea,—too numerous to be counted and too heavy to be weighed. The greatness of it beyond his ability to express, being also the cause why he had expressed himself so vehemently and inconsiderately;—"therefore my words are swallowed up," or, "were rash" or "vehement." Job's outward trials accumulated and intense beyond all precedent. These at first endured with extraordinary meekness and patience. *Now,* through the nature of his disease and Satan operating on his mind in consequence of it, all viewed on the dark side. *Our sufferings very much as we are made to view them.* The bitterest part of Job's sufferings now probably *internal* ones;

41

his external trials being viewed as sent from God, not in *love* but in unaccountable *anger*.—Describes these sufferings (verse 4) according to his views and feelings :—(1.) As "*arrows*:" Sharp and penetrating; coming swiftly, suddenly, and with great force; not one but many, coming in quick succession. (2.) "*Arrows of the Almighty.*" Shot by Him as at an enemy, or as a mere butt for His archery. The *Almighty's* arrows must be especially sharp and deadly. That they were the *Almighty's* arrows the bitterest circumstance connected with them. (3.) "*Poisoned* arrows." Hence especially deadly, and discharged by a deadly foe. Indicates the intensely painful character of his sufferings; poisoned arrows inflicting especially painful and inflammatory wounds. (4.) These arrows not only discharged against him, but abiding "*within*" him, or being "*with*" him. His distress unintermitting. (5.) The *effect* of the arrows, their poison "*drinking up his spirit*"—exhausting his vital energy; or, his spirit drinking up their deadly poison.

The Arrows of the Almighty.

No power of man or angel able to withstand these arrows. No shield but the shield of faith able to receive them. No hand but the pierced hand of Jesus able to extract them. No balm but the blood of the Cross able to heal their burning wounds. One of these arrows able to bring down the stoutest adversary. "O Galilæan, thou hast conquered,"—said by one of the most determined enemies of Christ, Julian the Apostate Emperor, while dying on the battle-field. Job's miseries scarcely half-told in the preceding history. His outward calamities rather the *occasion* than the *cause* of his intensest suffering. A believer's inward trouble in time of trial sometimes greater than the outward trouble which occasioned it. His greatest distress often from a cause entirely different from the outward trial. Heavy outward trouble often light in comparison with inward distress from spiritual and unseen causes. The rankling arrows of the Almighty much more dreadful than either the loss of property and children, or bodily affliction. A terrible aggravation of Job's outward trouble. Apprehended wrath on the part of God the greatest of all troubles to a believer. The essence of the Redeemer's suffering, as of that of the patriarch's,—"My God, my God," &c. The awful experience of the lost. No greater hell than these arrows, "sharp in the hearts of the King's enemies" (Ps. xlv. 5). Fully discharged against the Son of God while standing as the Sinner's Substitute. That Substitute accepted becomes Himself the Sinner's

Shield. The arrows felt in the conviction of sin (Acts ii. 37). Bringing the sinner to the feet of the Saviour they become arrows of *mercy*. The arrows extracted and the wounds healed by simple trust in Jesus and His blood. Discharged against the believer rather in his own *apprehension* than in *reality*. The apprehension intended as a discipline and trial of faith (Is. liv. 8; lvii. 17, 18). The experience removed when the object has been served (Jer. xxxi. 18—20). Satan, *working on our unbelief in time of trouble, able to make his own darts to be mistaken for the arrows of the Almighty.* The Almighty's arrows now in the Saviour's hand (Ps. xlv. 5; Rev. vi. 2).

Job's condition sufficient to account for his complaint. Even *beasts* do not utter their cries when they have food. (Verse 5)—"Doth the wild ass bray?" &c. The ass found in a wild state, large, fleet, and strong, in Arabia and west of the Euphrates. A hint at the want of sympathy on the part of his friends. It is easy to be quiet when suffering nothing. True sympathy makes us suffer in the distress of another (1 Cor. xii. 26). Natural to feel and utter complaint under severe suffering. Men cannot eat insipid and tasteless food without mixing salt with it. (Verse 6)—"Can that which is unsavoury?" &c. Salt so important with the Arabs as to be used as a synonym for food, their diet being chiefly vegetable. Mentions, as an example of the insipid, the "white of an egg," or perhaps the herb "*purslain*," proverbial among the Arabs for its insipidity. Perhaps Job quotes a proverb in common use. Indicates not only the naturalness of complaint, but the need of sympathy and encouragement in time of trouble. Insipid things need salt to make them palatable. Speech to be with grace seasoned with salt for the benefit of others (Col. iv. 6). "A word spoken in season, how good is it." "Heaviness in the heart of man maketh it stoop, but a good word maketh it glad" (Prov. xii. 25). The true humanity of Jesus seen in His craving for human sympathy in His distress (Matt. xxvi. 37—40). A bitter aggravation of trouble when "lover and friend are put far from us" (Ps. lxxxviii. 18). *The deepest poverty is to be without a friend to sympathize with us in our sorrow.*—Job reasserts his sad condition. (Verse 6)—"The things which my soul refused to touch," &c. Sad reverse when what we could not even touch before is now our daily but sorrowful and nauseous food. Job's loathsome ulcers now as his daily bread. Similar sentiment (Ps. cii. 9; xlii. 3; lxxx. 5). Learn: (1) *Painful reverses to be prepared for.* (2) *Moderation and humility our duty in prosperity.* Sometimes but a short step from affluence to destitution (Prov. xxiii. 5; 1 Tim. vi. 17). The beauty of health speedily exchanged for the loathsomeness of disease. A single day may put Dives in the place of Lazarus, *or a worse*. (3) *The uncertainty of earthly posses- sions and enjoyments to be improved to the securing of heavenly ones.* Grace teaches the rich man to rejoice in that he is made low (Jam. i. 10).

II. **Repeats and justifies his desire for death** (verse 8, &c.). "O that I might have my request," &c. His request a release from present suffer- ings by death. Asked also as a favour from God by Elijah under the juniper tree, and by Jonah at Nineveh (1 Kings xix. 4; Jon. iv. 3, 8). God the arbiter of life and death. Job leaves his time in God's hand (ch. xiv. 14). Satan and Job's wife would have had him taking the matter into his own. Ancient heathens believed they had a right to end their life when they pleased. Desire for death a natural feeling under deep and pro- tracted distress. Often, however, rather from the impatience of the flesh than the aspiration of the spirit. Only men's way- wardness and hardness of heart once awakened something of the feeling in Jesus (Matt. xvii. 17). Paul's desire to depart was to be with Christ (Phil. i. 23). Desire for death no proof of fitness for it. The choice be- tween life and death best referred to God Himself. *Preparation for death implies some ability to glorify God in life.* Soon enough to rest when our work is done. A favour to "cease at once to work and live." Job's request not granted. Some prayers better refused than answered. A sick child may be spared to die a felon's death.

The reason of Job's desire for death:— (1) *The comfort in the prospect of a speedy release from his extreme distress.* (Verse 10) —"Then should I yet have comfort (or, this should be my comfort); yea, I would harden myself in sorrow: let Him not spare" (or, I would leap for joy in my unsparing sorrow). (2) *The consciousness of having been God's faithful servant*: "For I have not concealed (or denied) the words of the Holy One." Implies—(i.) Fearlessness in confessing the truth; (ii.) Faithfulness in communicating it. The sin of the heathen that of "holding or keeping down the truth in unrighteous- ness." Truth inwardly believed is to be outwardly professed (Rom. x. 10). God honoured and the world benefited by a bold and consistent profession of the truth. The practice of God's faithful servants in every age (Ps. lxxi. 17; cxix. 46). Examples: Enoch, Noah, Abraham, Daniel. Truth received in order to be communicated (2 Cor. iv. 6; Phil. ii. 15, 16). The language of

Job used by David and his great Antitype (Ps. xl. 9, 10). The testimony of a good and enlightened conscience a precious com- fort in the midst of suffering and in the prospect of death (2 Cor. i. 12; 2 Tim. iv. 6—8). The testimony of Job's conscience, that he had neither by fearfulness nor faith- lessness concealed

The Words of the Holy One.

These words found in the shape of—(1) Doctrines; (2) Promises; (3) Commands. They were *God's* words, as—(1) Communicated by Him to Adam and others, and handed down to their posterity; (2) Revealed to Job him- self. "God at sundry times and in divers manners spake to the fathers" (Heb. i. 1). The Church of God in possession of such words from the beginning. Faint echoes and distorted forms of these words found everywhere among the heathen. Prominent among these was the proto-evangel of Gen. iii. 15. These words the precious treasure of the children of God in every age. A light to their feet and a comfort to their heart. Employed by Job in instructing, sustaining, and comforting others (ch. iv. 3, 4). God known in Job's time as "the Holy One." So called, Is. xl. 25; Hos. xi. 9; Heb. iii. 3. His name Holy (Is. lvii. 15). God alone holy (Rev. xv. 4). Peculiarly and essentially holy (1 Sam. ii. 2). Thrice holy (Is. vi. 3; Rev. iv. 8). Contrasted with the gods of the heathen. These acknowledged by their very worshippers to be impure and unworthy of imitation. The Greeks and Romans justified their own impurity by that of their gods. People naturally resemble the deities they worship. Solemn obligation resting on the worshippers of the true God to be holy (Lev. xi. 44; 1 Pet. i. 16). His children made partakers of his holiness (Heb. xii. 10; 2 Pet. i. 4).

Job justifies his desire for death on the ground of his grievous affliction. His strength unable to hold out under such accumulated evils (verse 11). "What is my strength,"(— or power of endurance—)"that I should hope,"(—indulge the slow protracted hope of recovery and the enjoyment of those tem- poral blessings held out by Eliphaz)? "And what is mine end"(—the end of these miseries) —"that I should prolong my life?"(—or con- tinue to exercise patience). The language of the flesh. Spoken according to *sense*. Justified by appearance and carnal reasoning. Despondency and impatience natural in the absence of faith. Faith battles with appear- ances and triumphs over them (Ps. xlii. 11; Mic. vii. 7, 8; Hab. iii. 17, 18). No time long to faith. Abraham's faith held out twenty-five years for the promised birth, till his own and his wife's body were as good as dead. Faith the mother of patience. Looks not at the weakness of the creature, but the power of the Creator. Difficulties and apparent impossibilities the true matter for faith. "Laughs at impossibilities," because leaning on Omnipotence. Faith often to seek in a storm. "Every man is a believer in a fair day" [*Rutherford*]. No express promise of recovery and restoration given to Job. The fact of God's omnipotence, and the truth that He is the hearer of prayer, that He interposes sooner or later in his servants' behalf, and that He does all things well,—enough for faith to rest upon in time of trouble. Faith at times triumphant in Job, though not with reference to any temporal deliverance (ch. xix. 25, &c.; xxiii. 10).—Verse 12. "Is my strength the strength of stones, or is my flesh of brass?"—the symbol of hardness and durability. The nature of unbelief to dwell in personal weakness. Faith looks not on human weakness but on Divine strength. Hence makes its possessor strong in his weakness. Through faith, believers "out of weakness were made strong" (Heb. xi. 34). Faith enabled Paul rather to glory in his infirmities, and to say : "When I am weak, then am I strong" (2 Cor. xii. 9, 10).

Job justifies his despondency on the ground of his thorough and apparently hopeless prostration (verse 13). "Is not my help in me? And is wisdom driven quite from me?" (Rather,—Is it not the fact that no help for me is in myself, and that recovery (or health) is quite fled from me?). Expresses his real case as viewed by the eye of sense. Abraham's faith, however, did not stagger even when the child of promise was to be offered on the altar. Our weakness and helplessness the proper theatre for the display of God's power and Christ's grace. Divine strength magnifies itself in realized weakness (2 Cor. xii. 9). A higher experience than that attained by Job reserved for God's children in the Gospel age (Heb. xi. 40 ; Matt. xi. 11). The feeble to be then like David, and the House of David as God (Zec. xii. 8 ; Is. xxx. 26).

III. Complains of his friends' want of sympathy (verses 14—21).

Kindness to the afflicted

1. *Job states a moral truth* (verse 14). "To him that is afflicted," &c.

Compassionate kindness to the suffering a dictate of humanity, and one of the first principles of religion (Jam. i. 27 ; Matt. ix. 13). The good Samaritan Christ's chosen example for His disciples, and His own commentary on the second table of the law.

Mercy accompanied with truth the essence of moral perfection, and the true spirit of Christianity (Ps. lxxxv. 10 ; lxxxix. 14). Pity to be shown to the afflicted—(1) In words of sympathy and kindness ; (2) In practical assistance, as far as in our power ; (3) In refraining from what may unnecessarily wound the feelings ; (4) In commending the sufferer's case to God (Ps. cxli. 5 ; Jam. v. 15, 16). This to be done for any in affliction, especially for a friend (Luke x 29—37 ; Prov. xvii. 17).

2. *Applies this truth to the case of his friends.* "But he forsaketh the fear," &c.,—viz., Eliphaz and the others, in their want of kindness and sympathy towards Job. *Want of love to our neighbour proves want of love to God.* Love to our neighbour enjoined by Divine authority as the second part of the law. The want of it, therefore, an evidence of the want of *fear* as well as *love* towards God. Pity is love to our neighbour in *affliction.* Our neighbour has *always* a claim on our *love*, and *in affliction* on our *pity*. That pity engendered by the fear of God, as—(1) Our neighbour is God's own offspring ; (2) Our suffering neighbour is the object of His special regard. Pity required by God towards a suffering neighbour as He has had pity on ourselves (Matt. xviii. 33—35). Mercy and compassion His own character, to be imitated by all His children (Luke vi. 36). The fear of God therefore the guarantee of right feelings towards man. The guardian of all the social and relative duties. Love to God unable to dwell in the same heart with indifference to man. Selfishness incompatible with the fear of God. After God's example, kindness and pity to be shown to the afflicted, whatever his character and religion. Illustrated by the parable of the Good Samaritan, and the legend of Abraham and the Idolater. As a motive to shew kindness to the poor and the afflicted, God has identified their cause with His own (Prov. xiv. 31; xix. 17). Pity due to an afflicted fellow-creature, still more to an afflicted friend. Duties and obligations enhanced according to relationship (Mal. i. 6 ; Prov. xvii. 17 ; xviii. 24).

The disappointing conduct of the friends touchingly set forth by a continued simile (verse 15, &c.). "My brethren have dealt deceitfully as a brook," (or wady—a narrow valley or bed of a stream between two rocky hills, filled with water in winter but usually dried up in summer)—"as the stream of brooks they (or, which) pass away," viz. in the heat of summer. Three points in the comparison :—(1) *The former profession of friendship*,—resembling the noisy, rushing wady-stream, full of water through the melted ice, and snow, and rains of winter, when less required. (Verse 16).—(2) *The failure in real kindness and sympathy when needed,*—like the drying up of the brook through the summer heat, and the entire disappearance of the waters, having vanished into vapour or been lost in the sands of the desert. (Verse 17, 18).—(3) *The bitter disappointment,*—like that of the caravans of Tema or Ishmaelites, and the trading companies of Sheba or Arabia Felix, when, contrary to their expectation, they find the stream dried up, and are unable to obtain a supply of water (verse 19, 20). Observe— (1) *The right of the afflicted to expect kindness and sympathy, especially from their friends.* (2) *Care to be taken to make a visit of condolence to correspond with its profession.* (3) *A great part of friendship, to be true in time of trouble.* Affection not to be cooled by affliction. A brother born for adversity. False friends like vermin that abandon a sinking vessel, or swallows that depart at the approach of winter. True friends like ivy that adheres to the tree in its decay. Genuine friendship, like the light of phosphorus, brightest in the dark. (4) *Our views of a friend's character not to be lightly changed, least of all by his circumstances.* Base even to suspect a friend. Love "hopeth all things" and "thinketh no evil."

The ground of his complaint (verse 21). "For now ye are nothing,"—are to me like the vanished wady-stream, as though you had never been. Friends by profession to prove themselves worthy of the name. Base to profess friendship and to be destitute of its feelings, or to withhold its offices. Love to be not in word and in tongue, but in deed and in truth (1 John iii. 18).—"Ye have seen my casting down," (my prostration and calamity) "and are afraid." Their feelings read in their faces. Only *one* had spoken with his lips, *all* with their *looks.* Their fear as if a pious dread at the signal display of Divine judgment, and horror at the discovery of secret wickedness. Afraid—(1) Of being found sympathizing with a guilty man; (2) Of being involved in the same calamity; (3) Of being called upon to relieve or defend the sufferer. Base to withhold sympathy and kindness from regard to our own comfort, credit, or convenience.

IV. Remonstrates with his friends on the baseness of their conduct (verses 22 —24).

1. *He had asked no favour at their hands* (verses 22, 23). "Did I say (or, is it because I said) Bring unto me (for my relief); or Give a reward for me of your substance (to repair my losses or obtain the favour of the judge); or, Deliver me from the enemy's hand? Or, redeem me from the hand of the mighty?"—(who have

robbed me of my property, or are now adding to my affliction). The right of the afflicted and suffering to receive not only sympathy but practical help. Afforded by Abraham to his captive nephew (Gen. xiv. 14). This a noble mind recoils from asking, though thankful in receiving. The favour Job refused to ask, afterwards liberally accorded (ch. xlii. 11). *Sometimes the only service we can render is a cordial sympathy.*

2. *They had not attempted to show him his sin* (verse 24). "Teach me and I will hold my tongue; and cause me to understand wherein I have erred." Mark of an honest and ingenuous mind to be willing to be convinced of error or wrong-doing. A prejudice or superstition simply to infer sinning from suffering. Absurd to exhort to repentance without attempting to convince of sin. Job's friends unable to point out any fault in his former life, except by inference. The language of his Antitype partially his— "Which of you convinceth me of sin?" (John viii. 46). All sin an erring or straying from the path of rectitude and the will of God. Found in all, Job not excepted; his friends only challenged to point out any breach of morality or religion as the cause of his peculiar suffering. To point out sin when we see it, is a duty we owe to our neighbour. Faithful and wise reproof required by the law of love (Lev. xix. 17). *Job's sense of the value of such reproof* (verse 25).

Right Words.

"How forcible are right words!" (Heb. "words of uprightness").

1. The *form* of such words—(1) Argument; (2) Reproof; (3) Instruction; (4) Admonition; (5) Persuasion.

2. The *character* of the words—"right." (1) *Right and true in themselves*—unmixed with error and falsehood—"sound speech that cannot be condemned" (Tit. ii. 8). In speaking to others we are to beware of doubting with untempered mortar (Ezek. xiii. 10); or of corrupting the Word of God (2 Cor. ii. 17). To speak forth only "the words of truth and soberness" (Acts xxvi. 25); "acceptable words," but also "words of truth" (Eccles. xii. 10). Arguments to be sound,—premises true, and conclusions just. Our statements to be according to the law and the testimony (Is. viii. 20). (2) *The whole truth, so far as necessary, in connection with the subject.* Nothing profitable to be kept back, either from fear or favour. No mere one-sided view of the truth to be given. Teachers not to be partial in the law (Mal. ii. 9). Truth to be exhibited in all its parts, and in their due proportions. The word of truth to be rightly divided (2 Tim. ii. 15). The mercy of God not to be enlarged upon to the ignoring of

His justice, nor the converse. The promises not to be without the precepts, nor the precepts without the promises. Faith not to be urged without works as its fruits, nor works without faith as their foundation. Not morality without religion, nor religion without morality. Not the law without the Gospel, nor the Gospel without the law. Words, to be right words, must be evangelical words—"the truth as it is in Jesus." Pardon not to be held out apart from Christ's blood which procures it. Holiness not to be urged apart from Christ's indwelling spirit as its author. (3) *Correct in their application.* Truth may be so applied as to become practical error. The fault in Job's friends. Pillows not to be sewed to all armholes; and those not to be made sad, even with truth, whom the Lord does not make sad (Ezek. xiii. 18—22). Meat to be given in season as each requires and is able to bear it. Milk to babes, strong meat to those of mature age. Some to be sharply reproved. The bruised reed to be bound up with tender hand. Not only truth to be preached, but *seasonable* truth—"the present truth," (Pet. i. 12). Sound doctrine not to be so preached as to become a *soporific.* The words of the wise to be as *goads,* therefore to be wisely *directed.* "A word spoken in season, how good is it?" (4) *Spoken in uprightness and sincerity.* Without fear or favour. Without prejudice or passion. Without self-seeking or time-serving. With simplicity and godly sincerity. As in the sight of God and in the view of eternity. The speaker to *be,* and therefore to *appear,* in earnest. Truth not to be spoken as if it were fiction, as if not believed by the speaker himself. To be spoken in *love,* in tenderness, sympathy, and concern for the hearer's welfare. The speaker's *spirit* to preach as well as his *speech,* his *manner* as well as his *matter.* The words of truth on the speaker's lips not to be falsified by the manner in which they are spoken, or by the inconsistency of his life.

3. The *efficacy* of such words. "Forcible," —powerful, efficacious. (1.) In *enlightening she understanding,* discovering truth, and *to producing faith.* "So spake that a great multitude believed." (Acts xiv. 1). A well-constructed argument having truth for its basis, irresistible [*A. Clarke*]. In *awakening the conscience,* convincing of sin, and so producing *repentance.* So Peter's words at Pentecost, and Paul's before Felix (Acts ii. 37; xxiv. 25). (3.) In *moving the affections* and will, and so restraining from sin, and persuading to *duty.* So with the awakened at Pentecost (Acts ii. 41). The Ephesians burned their ungodly books (Acts xix. 19). Herod heard John gladly and did

many things (Mark vi. 20). (4.) In *comforting the afflicted,* sustaining the weak, and succouring the tempted. "Heaviness in the heart of man maketh it stoop—a good word maketh it glad" (Prov. xii. 25). The effect of Job's own words in his former condition (chap. iv. 3, 4).

V. Complains of his friends' reproof and their conduct towards him (verses 25—27).

1. *Their argument and reproof had been pointless and profitless* (verse 25). "What doth your arguing reprove? (or, "what conviction is there in the reproof you have administered?") Eliphaz, their chief speaker, had (1) shewn no sin on the part of Job as meriting his severe treatment; (2) Exhorted to repentance without showing the grounds for its necessity. In discoursing to others we are to have a *clear aim and definite purpose.* That aim to be a *right one and important in the circumstances.* Our purpose to be prosecuted in a *wise and suitable manner.* The preacher not to speak "as uncertainly," nor to preach "as one that beateth the air."

2. *Their reproof was directed only against words uttered in deep distress and great disquietude of spirit* (verse 26). "Do ye imagine to reprove words, and the speeches of one that is desperate, which are as wind?" (or, "and to scrutinize, sift, or 'air' the speeches of one that is desperate?") The fault of Job's friends that they had attacked the words of his complaint instead of showing the evil of his life. As a rule, by our words we shall be justified or condemned (Matt. xii. 37). The reason, "out of the abundance of the heart the mouth speaketh." Ordinarily, a man is as his speech. Allowance, however, to be made for words uttered under deep distress, and in exceptionally trying circumstances. A high offence in God's sight to make a man an offender for a word (Is. xxix. 21). Observe—(1.) *Rash words, especially under provocation, an "easily besetting sin"* (Heb. xii. 1). Great temptation to such words under excited feeling. The heart to be kept with all diligence, especially in time of trouble (Prov. iv. 23). The mouth to be kept as with a bridle when God's hand is heavy on us (Ps. xxxix. 1—10). (2.) The *case of a believer may appear "desperate" to himself and others, when it appears the very opposite to God.* A child of God often writes bitter things against himself when his Father does not. A tried believer apt to judge of his case from feeling and appearance. The flesh a blind judge as to a man's real case and character. That case can never be desperate which is linked to the Almighty's throne. "Thou hast nothing to fear who hast Cæsar for thy friend." A man's case cannot be desperate who has—,

(i) a place in the Almighty's heart; (ii) his hand in His heavenly Father's; (iii) an interest in the everlasting covenant (2 Sam. ii. 3, 5).

Job strongly inveighs against his friend's conduct (verse 27). " Yea, ye overwhelm (*margin*, ' cause [a net or noose] to fall upon') the fatherless, and ye dig a pit for your friend" (seeking to catch him in ungarded words, and to make him out to be a hypocrite and transgressor). Rightly or wrongly, Job construes his friends' language and looks into *malice*. Their conduct harsh and unfeeling, but according to Job, diabolical. Strong language and exaggerated views of the conduct of others towards ourselves, a natural result of deep trouble and excited feeling. Men capable, however, of the conduct here ascribed by Job to his friends. Joseph's brethren an example. The words strictly true of the enemies of Jesus, their truest and best friend. The conduct of Job's friends all the guiltier as being—(1) Under colour of friendship; (2) Under profession of piety; (3) With considerable knowledge of Divine truth. *Cruellest feelings sometimes covered with the garb of greatest sanctity.* Example: Torquemada and the Spanish Inquisitors. Important prayer—"' Search me, O God, and know my heart " &c. (Ps. cxxxix. 23).

VI. Job's challenge to his friends (verses 28—30).

1. *Appeal of conscious integrity* (verse 28). " Now, therefore, be content, look upon me; for it is evident unto you (*margin*, ' it is before your face ') if I lie " (or, " shall I lie to your face ?") Observe :—(1) *Conscious innocence not only allows but solicits examination.* A good conscience enables a man to live in a glass-house. So Jesus—" Which of you convinceth me of sin " (John viii. 46). A mark of grace to come to the light that our deeds may be made manifest (John iii. 21). Paul prays for believers that they may be " sincere,''—able, in heart and life, to bear the scrutiny of daylight (Phil. i. 10). A child of God is careful to be truthful both in lip and life. A Christian is one who is more concerned to *be* than to *appear* such. (2) *Truth and sincerity read in the countenance.*

The face the dial-plate of the soul. *An upright heart makes an open countenance* (verse 29). " Return, I pray you, let it not be iniquity (or, ' let there no injustice '—no unjust or partial judgment); yea, return again, my righteousness is in it " (*margin*, "in this matter "—I shall be found innocent in the trial). *Truth and innocence court investigation.* The consciously upright desire only impartial and unprejudiced trial. The language of Jesus, and of those wrapped in His righteousness—"Who is he that condemneth " (Isa. l. 9; Rom. viii. 32—34). The believer a paradox—"Black but comely" —black in himself, comely in Christ; guilty and yet righteous—guilty in his own person, righteous in his righteous Head (2 Cor. v. 21). *Renounces all righteousness but Christ's in the sight of God, yet careful to maintain a spotless character in the sight of men.*

2. *The ground of Job's appeal*—his ability to distinguish and judge of moral conduct (verse 30). " Is there iniquity (literally, or, a depraved taste) in my tongue ? Cannot my taste (*margin*, ' palate ') discern perverse things ? " (am I not able to distinguish between right and wrong ?) *No small excellence to possess a correct moral judgment.* Moral sense obscured and weakened by the fall and by a course of sin. The moral judgment becomes depraved by sin as the taste by disease. The character of the ungodly to call evil good, and good evil. The mature Christian, one who has his senses exercised to discern both good and evil (Heb. v. 14). A fruit of renewing grace to know and approve "the good, the perfect, and the acceptable " (Rom. xii. 2). " Judgment " to " approve things that are excellent," or to " distinguish between things that differ," a gift of grace (Phil. i. 9, 10). A part of spiritual wisdom to understand what the will of the Lord is, and the opposite (Eph. v. 17). *Grace indicated not only by a tender, but an enlightened conscience.* The ungodly know not what at they stumble. " They know not what they do." In murdering Christ's followers, men were to think they were doing God service (John xvi. 2). Paul's former case (Acts xxvi. 9—11). Important prayer—"Cause me to know the way wherein I should walk " (Ps. cxliii. 8).

CHAPTER VII.

CONTINUATION OF JOB'S SPEECH.

Job ceases to altercate with Eliphaz and to defend himself. Resumes his complaints, and ends by addressing himself to God.

I. Complains of the general lot of humanity (verse 1).
" Is there not an appointed time (*margin*, a warfare,' or *war-service*) to man (pro-perly, to *wretched* man, Heb., ' Enosh,'—man viewed as fallen, and therefore miserable) upon earth ? Are not his days also as the days of an hireling ? " Wishes to show—

47

(1) His desire for death excusable ; (2) Suffering not peculiar to the bad. Suggests instructive views of

Human Life.

1. *As an appointed period.* War-service, and the time of a hired labourer's employment, *limited.* The term used also to express the time of a Levite's service at the tabernacle, namely, twenty years (Numb. iv. 23). Doctrine : *The bounds of man's life appointed* (ch. xiv. 5). Our days measured out by Him who created us (Psa. xxxix. 4). Our times in His hand (Psa. xxxi. 15). Not without respect to the means necessary for life's continuance. God's predestination neither interferes with *the human will* nor the *operation of second causes,* but embraces both. The means taken into view along with the appointment of the *end.* The crop not appointed without the ploughing and sowing. If the passengers' lives are to be preserved, the sailors are to do their duty (Acts xxvii. 22—31). The elect saved, but not without regeneration, repentance, and faith. If a man is to reach his "threescore years and ten," he is not to shorten them by neglect, intemperance, or crime. The wicked often do not "live out half their days,"—the days they *might* and *should* have lived. Disease as much appointed as the death it occasions. Lessons : Life an *appointed period.* Hence— (1.) *Bear meekly its trials* ; they are but for a limited time ; (2.) *Wait patiently for its termination :* it will come in God's time. Neither greatly desire nor hasten it ; (3.) *Carefully improve its continuance.* Much to be done, and but a short time to do it in (Eccles. ix. 10).

2. *As a war-service.* Such a period not one of ease, enjoyment, or indulgence ; but of hardship, privation, unrest. Job's reason for desiring its termination. Life a war-service—(1) As a time of *trouble and suffering.* Man born to trouble (ch. v. 7) ; (2) As a time of *conflict.* Sin and Satan our great enemies ; (3) As a time of *service.* Man bound to serve God as his rightful sovereign. Lessons : (1) Be *patient of hardship,* and *prepared for trial* and *suffering.* Man's, and especially a Christian's, is a *soldier's* life. "Endure hardness" (2 Tim. ii. 3). Tedious marches, camp discomforts, field duties. (2) Be *careful to be on the right side.* We must serve ; but it may be either under Christ's banner or the devil's. (3) Be *faithful, obedient, and active ;* faithful to your King, obedient to your Captain, active in discharge of your duty. (4) Be *hopeful, courageous, and enduring.* With Christ as our captain victory is certain ; and, after short and faithful service, comes long and honourable reward (2 Tim. iv. 7, 8).

48

3. *As the term of a hired servant.* We may have a hireling's *post,* without a hireling's *spirit.* Salvation by grace not inconsistent with "respect to the recompense of reward." Each believer has his work in the vineyard, and each receives "his penny." A hired labourer has—(1) *Painful and self-denying labour* to undergo ; (2) A *short and limited time* to do it in ; (3) *Due wages* to receive when it is done. Life such a service. Man must serve—either God or Satan, righteousness or sin (Rom. vi. 16—22). Each thought, word, and action, a service to one or other of these two masters. Hence—(1) "*Choose the best master.* God's service is—(i.) Honourable ; (ii.) Pleasant ; (iii.) Satisfying to the conscience. Has along with it—(*a*) Kind treatment ; (*b*) Comfortable provision ; (*c*) Liberal remuneration.—(2) *Be diligent in doing the Master's work* and *watchful in looking for the Master's coming* (Mark xiii. 34—37.)

II. Renews his complaint and describes his sad condition. Mention of the "hireling" in verse 1 suggests to him the comparison of himself to a slave or a day-labourer who longs for the evening rest (verse 2). "As the servant (or slave) earnestly desireth (*margin*—'gapeth' or pants after) the shadow [of evening], and as a hireling (hired servant, as distinguished from a slave) looketh for the reward (or finishing) of his work, so," &c.

Describes his afflicted condition in three particulars :—

1. *Comfortless days and painful nights* (verse 3). "So am I made to possess (*Heb.* 'to inherit') months of vanity (without comfort or relief to myself, and without profit either to myself, or others), and wearisome nights (*Heb.* 'nights of labour or trouble') are appointed (*Heb.* 'numbered') to me." Such days and nights the result—(1) Of his disease ; (2) Of his bereavement ; (3) Of spiritual darkness. Says not *days,* but "months" of vanity, each day appearing a month. So Jonah speaks of his three days in the fish's belly as an eternity,—"for ever" (Jon. ii. 6). "A man in great misery may so far lose his measure as to think a minute an hour" [*Locke*]. On the other hand, as grief *retards,* so joy *hastens* time. The bliss of heaven makes "eternity seem as a day." Job's troubles, however, may now have probably lasted some months. These painful days and nights spoken of as an *inheritance.* A bitter irony, yet true. Trouble handed down to us with sin as its consequence. "A sad inheritance of woe." Adheres to us as our ancestral possession. "*Made* to possess" them, as against his will. "The creature made subject to vanity, not willingly" (Rom. viii. 20). Blessed contrast to this inheritance is that found in Christ (Rom. viii. 17; Heb. ix. 15; 1 Pet. i. 4). Yet mouths of suffering not necessarily "months of vanity." These, to a child of God, among the all things working together for his good (Rom. viii. 24). Times of affliction are made times of profit, to *ourselves*, through spiritual teaching and Divine communion; to *others*, by the example afforded of patience and Divine support.

"In all my list of blessings infinite
Stands this the foremost, that my heart has bled."

2. *Restlessness of mind and body* (verse 4). "When I lie down, I say, when shall I arise, and the night be gone? (or, 'but the night is extended;' *margin*, 'and the evening be measured?') And I am full of tossings," &c. The distressing *nights* dwelt upon rather than the days. Long, weary, sleepless nights among the most painful circumstances connected with sickness or sorrow. Such nights contrasted with the refreshing rest of the worn-out slave and weary labourer. These wearisome and restless nights, however, *counted out* by God to his people. (verse 3). Not one too many, or more than He will over-rule for our good. *God an accurate dispenser of His people's sufferings and sorrow* (Is. xxvii. 8). Connected with the long sleepless nights are the "tossings to and fro upon the bed." "We change the place, but keep the pain." The nocturnal tossings in *mind* often more painful than those of the *body* (Ps. lxxvii. 2—9; Is. xxxviii. 13). Sleep God's gift to his beloved (Ps. cxxvii. 2). Its absence in sickness or trouble itself no small affliction.

"Nature's soft nurse, how have I frighted thee,
That thou no more wilt weigh my eyelids down?"

3. *Loathsomeness of body* (verse 5). "My flesh is clothed with worms and clods of dust (literally, or in appearance); my skin is broken and become loathsome;" (or, breaks [in ulcers] and dissolves [in matter]). Corruption breeding worms, ulcerous running sores, and rough ashy scales covering the body, prominent features in Job's disease. The Elephantiasis a species of leprosy (Lev. xii.. 9—17). Renders the patient loathsome to look at, and forbids contact or near approach. Similar revolting picture probably presented in Lazarus (Luke xvi. 20), and in Herod (Acts xii. 23). Something like it complained of by David (Ps. xxxviii. 3, 5, 7, 11), and by Heman (Ps. lxxxviii. 8, 18). A sad aggravation of our

affliction when it renders us loathsome to our friends.

Lessons from Job's Disease.

(1) *Terrible power of Satan.* Satan the immediate author of Job's disease. (2) *Dreadful effects of sin.* But for sin there had been no disease. Sin turns our comeliness into corruption, and covers a formerly fair and healthy body with foul putridity and worm-breeding sores. (3) *Character of our mortal body.* Soon reduced to loathsome putrefaction even while alive. "Our vile body," —the "body of our humiliation" (Phil. iii. 21). (4) The *saint as liable to the most loathsome diseases as the sinner.* Witness Job and Lazarus. (5.) The *love of Christ in assuming a body with such liabilities.* Made "in the likeness of sinful flesh" (Rom. viii. 2). "Took our infirmities and bare our sicknesses" (Matt. viii. 17, quoted from Is. liii. 4). From the same prophecy, the Messiah said by the Jews to have his place among the lepers. (6.) *Preciousness of a glorious resurrection.* Our vile body changed and fashioned like to Christ's glorious body (Phil. iii. 21.) (7.) *Affecting picture of the loathsomeness of sin.* Leprosy the most loathsome of all bodily diseases. Sin symbolized by it as the most loathsome thing in the universe. The only truly loathsome thing in the eyes of God and holy beings. Makes the soul infinitely more loathsome than Job's disease did his body. The godless rich man loathsome with his plump, well-fed, and richly-clad body; godly Lazarus beautiful and comely in his sores.

4. *The prematureness of his anticipated death* (verse 6). "My days are swifter than a weaver's shuttle (or, 'come more quickly to an end than the weaving of a web'), and are spent without hope," (viz., of extension or relief; or, 'are finished for want of thread') so Is. xxxviii. 12. Job anticipated death as the certain and not distant result of his affliction (ch. ix. 25, 26; xvii. 11). Himself, as life was *then*, still comparatively young. Probably not more than seventy,—only a third of the age then usually attained and actually attained by himself (ch. xlii. 16). A premature death, especially in Old Testament times, viewed as a grievous calamity (Is. vi. 5; xxx. 9; Is. xxxviii. 10—19. The language suggestive in regard to

Time.

1. *Its rapid flight and short duration.* Set forth in Scripture under various comparisons: —a flower, a vapour, a dream, a watch of the night, a tale that has been told, &

4—1

Here, either a *weaver's shuttle* passing quickly to and fro, or a *web*, speedily and perhaps suddenly finished from want of thread. Time represented by the ancients with *wings*, as not running but *flying*. Jacob speaks of his days as few at the age of 130. The longest life only a speck in comparison with eternity. A northern winter's day, when the sun has scarcely risen before it sets again. The sun of many sets while it is yet noon. Job, like most others, had counted on a long life (ch. xxix. 18). Now the grave seems to open its mouth for him (ch. xvii. 1). "Though death be before the old man's face, it may be behind the young man's back" [*Seneca.*] Hence the *vanity of earthly pleasures and enjoyments*. Like Jonah's gourd, these spring up in a night and perish in a night. But "for a season," and that a very short one. Earthly pleasures are, according to one who deeply plunged into them,—

"Like the snow-falls in the river,
A moment white, then melt for ever ;
Or like the rainbow's lovely form,
Evanishing amid the storm."

2. *The value of time.* Time the short seed-time for eternity. Bound up with eternal destinies. Its value seldom realised. No note taken of it but as the clock tells of its departure. Men speak of *killing* time. To destroy time is "suicide, where more than blood is spilt." Greater folly to throw away hours than empires. The value of time realised on a dying bed. "Millions of money for an inch of time" [*Queen Elizabeth on her deathbed*]. Time ceases at death, and gives place to eternity. "No clock strikes in hell, to say, Thank God, another hour is past. One gigantic clock there, without a dial-plate ; its pendulum eternally vibrating, Ever, Never ; Damnation ever, Redemption never" [*Krummacher*].
3. *The danger of delay in securing the soul's salvation.* Madness to put off till to-morrow what ought to be done to-day. "Serious things to-morrow"—cost both Cæsar and Archias their life. Procrastination the death of souls. Men "resolve and re-resolve, and die the same." Augustine was kept seven years from closing with Christ by the temptation, Time enough yet. When Hannibal *could* have taken Rome, he *would* not, and when he *would*, he *could* not. "What thy hand findeth to do, do it with thy might." The soul's salvation the one thing needful. Sad to be sowing our seed when we should be reaping our harvest [*Brooks*]. Cæsar Borgia on his deathbed said : While I lived, I provided for everything but death, and now death comes and I am unprovided for it. A promise made *to* late repentance, but no promise *of* late repentance.

"Alas, that men should lightly spend
In godless mirth or prayerless toil unblest,
Their brief inestimable day of proof,
Till the last golden sands run out."

IV. **Job turns imploringly to God** (verse 7). "O remember," &c. *Better in trouble to cry to God than to complain to man.* God sometimes appears to His suffering people to *forget* them and their case (Ps. xiii. 1 ; xliv. 24 ; Is. xlix. 14). The contrary affirmed by God for their comfort (Is. xlix. 15). Job pleads for mitigation of His sufferings on the ground—(1) Of the *frail and fleeting nature of his earthly life.* "My life is wind"—a breath or puff of air ; a "cloud" or smoke ; unsubstantial and evanescent (Ps. lxxviii. 39 ; (2) Its *speedy termination* (verse 8). "Thine eyes are upon me, and I am not." Speaks of himself as already dead, or soon to be,—a living corpse. (a) *Life terminated by a look from the Almighty.* His glance our death. So those sent to apprehend Jesus fell backward to the ground at his mere look ; (b) *Life, compared with God's eternity, only a moment*—the glance or twinkling of an eye. (3) The *impossibility of its recall* (verse 9, 10). "He that goeth down to the grave shall come up no more." The emitted breath, the cloud or smoke disappearing from the sky, never more to be recalled. Death, "the bourne from which no traveller returns." *Only one life on earth.* A few special exceptions to prove the rule. Men die but once. *Solemn responsibility connected with our one life.* No second to correct the errors, undo the mischief, or make up for the negligence, of the first. An egress from the grave in reserve for each, but no return to a mortal life. A resurrection to come, both of the just and the unjust. That resurrection, however, not in the course of nature, but by the special command and power of God (John v. 28 ; 1 Thess. iv. 16). Christ Himself the Resurrection and the Life. Resurrection committed to His hands (John xi. 25 ; vi. 54). Resurrection not unknown to the patriarchs, but seldom referred to by Job. Enoch's translation a testimony to the early ages of the existence of the body in an invisible state. His prophecy a distinct revelation of resurrection (Jude 14, 15). God's relation to the godly dead as their God, a guarantee both of the separate existence of their spirits and the future resurrection of their bodies (Matt. xxii. 31, 32). The doctrine of the resurrection, as well as of the state after death, one of gradual development. Job's age the twilight of revelation.

V. **Job's resolution to give way to complaint.** Occasioned by the consideration of his misery in the world, and his anticipated speedy, untimely, and irrevocable departure out of it (verse 11). "Therefore I will not refrain my mouth," &c. Falls again into his former temptation. His spirit like a surging sea, quiet for a little, then heaving again its angry billows. His present resolution the worst thing he could do. Tended to a continually increasing strife with God. Satan doubtless now rejoiced in his apparent advantage. So far his scheme likely to succeed. Probably thought the next thing would be that Job would "curse God to his face." Job preserved from this only by imparted and indwelling grace. *Perilous to advance so near the brink of the precipice.* Dangerous to indulge in bitter language in reference to our lot. Safest when *God's* hand is on our *back,* to keep *our* hand on our *mouth.* David's resolution in similar circumstances much wiser than Job's (Ps. xxxix. 1). *Free utterance to excited feelings only adds fuel to the fire.* Grace shutting the lips raises up a barrier to the tempest of the spirit. Passion acquires strength by indulgence and free expression. "Anguish of spirit" a very unsafe guide to speech. *Only turbid streams likely to flow from a turbid fountain.*

The result of Job's resolution, *petulant and unbecoming expostulation with God.* (Verse 12). "Am I a sea (or a desolating inundation, as of the Nile), or a whale (or sea-monster, as the crocodile), that Thou settest a watch over me (to restrain me by these terrible sufferings from doing injury)?" Very erroneous thoughts often suggested in trouble as to God's motive in sending it. We may sympathize with Job's sufferings without imitating his language. His language, however, indicates—(1) A believer readily ascribing all in his lot to God; (2) A soul moving always in the Divine presence; (3) The frequent and familiar intercourse of a child of God with his Heavenly Father.

VI. Enlarges farther on his affliction (verses 13, 14).

1. *His distressing nights* (verse 13). "When I say, My bed shall ease my complaint, then thou scarest me with dreams and terrifiest me with visions" (images presented to the imagination while half-sleeping, half-waking). These probably a natural symptom of Job's disease. A grievous aggravation of the affliction. Night, the period of rest to others, made more distressing than the day. The blessing of "tired Nature's sweet restorer, balmy sleep," seldom duly appreciated and acknowledged. Our minds accessible to Satan as well as God and good angels during sleep. Dreams either natural or supernatural; as supernatural, either diabolical or Divine. Job, in ignorance, ascribes to God what

was properly due to Satan. Satan cruelly skilful in adopting suitable means to accomplish his purpose. His object to exhaust the energies of Job's body and spirit, and by representing God as his enemy, to bring him to despair and to curse or renounce Him. For this, he employs a filthy disease and frightful dreams, and tempts him to believe them both from God. Satan a merciless tormentor. Possesses a terrible power of inflicting pain. Job's case a picture of the misery of falling into Satan's hands. Still more fearful to fall into the hands of the living God (Heb. x. 31). God able to make every organ of the body and every faculty of the mind the seat of intolerable suffering.—Earnest desire for death the effect of these sufferings on the mind of Job (verse 15). "So that my soul chooseth strangling and death rather than life" (*margin,* "than my bones,"—all that is left of me). The "soul," or mere fleshly nature, may choose death as a release from suffering; the "spirit" or renewed nature says—"Not my will but thine be done;" "All the days of my appointed time will I wait," &c. (ch. xiv. 14). *Grace the truest heroism.* Brave in the battle-field, a man may yet fly in the battle of life. *Suicide at best but moral cowardice.* To be only accounted for by the *absence* or the *eclipse* of faith. *Faith in God alone gives true courage.* The strongest mind weak when left to itself under depressing thoughts or a disturbed brain. "Do thyself no harm," a timely voice to harassed and despairing souls.

2. *The extremely reduced state of his body and the certainty of a speedy death* (verse 16). "I loathe it (*i.e.,* my life; or, 'I am wasting away'); I would not (or, 'I shall not') live always (*i.e.,* I shall soon die at any rate); let me alone (leave me to die, or cease to harass me with bodily and mental suffering), for my days are vanity" [and will soon come to an end]. Job's spirit tossed between two desires—either an immediate death as a release from his continued misery, or a relief from suffering for the few days that remained to him. The troubled and agitated spirit seldom long in one stay.

VII. Man's insignificance urged by Job as a plea for deliverance or relief (verse 17).

"What is man (*Heb.,* 'wretched man,' *enosh*) that thou," &c. Same question asked by David from an entirely different consideration (Ps. viii. 4). The same truth often viewed in different aspects and with different feelings by different persons, and by the same person at different times. The truth, dark to one or at one time, is bright to another or to the same person at another time. *Truth, like the cloud that followed Israel, presents both a dark side and a bright one.* Happy, like Israel, to be on the *bright* side. God's great attention to man produced in David *admiration and praise;* in Job *displeasure and complaint.* To the Psalmist God appears amiable as a Father delighting in blessing His children; to the Patriarch, stern as a judge, constantly examining into men's actions. Faith's office is to view the truth *as it is,* apart from personal feeling. *Feeling,* in Job, asks with *petulance*—" Why doth He visit men every morning?" *Faith,* in Jeremiah, exclaims with *thankfulness,* amid the desolations of a sacked and burned city—" His mercies are new every morning" (Sam. iii. 23). God's morning visitation a *mercy,* and should—(1) Impart *comfort;* (2) Awaken *praise.* Opens our eyes to the grateful light of day, the beauties of nature, and the faces of relatives and friends. Imparts to us health of body, soundness of mind, comfort of spirit. Continues to us day after day food, raiment, home, society of friends. Invites us every morning afresh to communion with Himself as our Father in Christ. Important and suggestive question,

What is Man?

At once the least and the greatest of God's creatures. Lower than the angels in creature-position, immensely higher in Redemption-privilege. Lives one life on earth consisting of a few months or years; a second in another sphere, which shall last for ever. Has a body that allies him to the ground on which he walks; and a spirit that connects him to the God that made him. A reed, but a reed that thinks [*Pascal*]. A worm, but a worm capable of measuring the distances of the stars and of grasping the universe. Made in the image of his Creator as to moral nature, intelligence, immortality, and dominion. Through disobedience and rebellion, reduced below the level of the brutes. Mercifully provided with deliverance from his fallen condition through the substituted obedience and death of his incarnate Creator.—Man " magnified " by God,

1. In *Creation;* his place above all the creatures around him, and second only to that of the angels that surround the Eternal's throne.

2. In *Providence;* the attention originally paid to his comfort, and the care continually exercised over him.

3. In *Redemption;* the highest possible proof of Divine regard afforded in the life, sufferings, and death of God's own Son for his deliverance and happiness.

4. In his *Glorification;* united to the Son of God and made like Him in spirit, soul,

and body; exalted as His spouse to sit with Him on His throne, and with Him to judge angels.

5. In the *Assumption of his nature by the Son of God.* Christ *the* man, the second Adam and Head of the race. In Christ man's nature taken into mysterious, intimate, and indissoluble union with the Divine. Man exalted in Christ to the throne of the universe.

VIII. Conclusion of Job's speech (verses 19—21). Contains—

1. *A peevish prayer* (verse 19) " How long wilt thou not depart (*Heb.,* 'look away') from me? nor let me alone that I may swallow down my spittle" (even for the shortest period)? Prayers in time of trial are sometimes—(1) Ignorant; (2) Injurious; (3) Requiring repentance. The flesh incapable of judging aright of God and His dealings. God viewed by Job as an adversary intent only on overthrowing him. Yet His removal, or the withdrawing of His eyes from us, our certain ruin. The same spirit moved the Gadarenes to beseech Christ to depart out of their consts. Prayer often unanswered in compassion to the offerer. Grace needed to know what to pray for (Luke xi. 1). The Holy Spirit's office (Rom. viii. 26).

2. *A partial confession* (verse 20). " I have sinned; what shall I do (or, ' What have I [thereby] done') unto thee?" A confession, but neither frank nor free. Made rather hypothetically,—" granting I have sinned," or, " If I have." Job's conscience not yet sufficiently enlightened nor his soul sufficiently subdued to make the Publican's confession. The confession rather extorted by the fact of suffering than the consciousness of sin. Job free from life sins; heart sins not yet sufficiently discovered to him. This discovery and his consequent humble confession not made till Jehovah has revealed Himself (ch. xl. 4; xlii. 5, 6). Compare Is: vi. 5; Luke v. 8.—In order to be acceptable,

Confession of Sin

must be—(1) *Free;* spontaneous, unconstrained; not extorted by suffering, or merely in order to deliverance from it, as in the case of Pharaoh (Ex. ix. 27; x. 16); (2.) *Frank;* open and sincere; without guile or desire of concealment (Ps. xxxii. 25); (3.) *Full;* thorough and without reservation (Josh. vii. 19—21); (4.) *Particular;* not merely of sin in general, or as common to the race; " I have sinned and done *this* evil in thy sight" (Ps. li. 4; (5.) *Serious and heartfelt;* with sense of the heinousness and demerit of the sin confessed

(Ps. li. 3; Luke xviii. 13). In true confession the heart is both *affected with* the sin, and *engaged against* it. Confession of sin needful in the holiest saint. Sin cleaves to the believer as ivy to the wall. The strongest believer not above the *actings* of sin, the weakest not under the *power* of it. The more we realize God's *spotlessness*, the more we discern our own *spots*. Sweet to confess sin in sight of the laver of a Saviour's blood. Confession of sin with the lips enhances the preciousness of Christ in the heart. *Concealed* sin grows—(1) In *strength*; (2) In *guilt*; (3) In *terror* (Ps. xxxii. 3, 4). Job's confession, such as it was, one rather of the *mere fact of sin*. Acknowledges no *evil* connected with it, or *demerit* attached to it. Its heinousness and malignity as *against God*, yet to be discovered. "What have I done unto thee?" The idea: What wrong have I done thee by my sin, that thou shouldst thus treat me as thine enemy? Sin to be viewed as an injury, not merely to our neighbour or ourselves, but more especially *against God.*

Sin

Is injury done to God, as—
(1.) *It robs Him of the honour due to Him* (Mal. i. 6). Man's sin may not take from God's *happiness*, but it takes from God's *honour.* Every sin strikes as truly at God's honour as at our peace. (2.) *It tramples under foot His authority.* Says with Pharaoh : "Who is the Lord that I should obey His voice?" (Ex. v. 2). (3.) *It breaks His laws.* (4.) *It disturbs the harmony and happiness of His universe.* (5.) *It introduces disorder into His government*, and, if not arrested and punished, would bring it to an end. (6.) *It interrupts and would terminate His enjoyment of His own works* (Gen. i. 31; Ps. civ. 24). (7.) *It obliterates His image in His intelligent creatures, and substitutes that of His adversary.* Treasonably effaces His image and superscription from His own coin. Job, in his confession, petulantly addresses God as the watcher and observer of His creatures—"Oh, thou preserver of men." Same word denotes "guardian" and "observer" (chap. xxvii. 18). Latter sense here favoured by the context (so chap. xiv. 16). God viewed as if carefully marking men's faults in order to punish them. Only perverted and dishonouring views of God taken by the flesh, especially under trouble. Satan's aim to foster such views in Job in order to gain his object. Job's complaint in keeping with this view. "Why hast Thou set me as a mark against Thee?" (to shoot at, or make an attack upon). The supposed result of God's close inspection of his conduct, and as in revenge for the injury done to

him. Already viewed himself as shot at by the Almighty's arrows (chapter vi 4). Speaks according to sense and appearance. *God's choicest saints often appear to be the butt of his sharpest arrows.*—The effect and meaning of these arrows; "So that I am a burden to myself" or, "and I am become a burden to thee" (both readings found, the latter probably the true one). The sinner, a burden to *God* through his *sin*, and a burden to *himself* through his *suffering*. When sin makes a man a burden to God, he is likely to become a burden to himself. A sinner left to himself the greatest burden that can be laid upon him. Suffering often a heavy burden; sin a thousand times more so. "I had rather go into hell without sin, than into heaven with it" [*Luther*]. Cain said, my *punishment* is greater than I can bear : the same word generally rendered "iniquity," as in verse 20. Judas thought to throw off the burden by hanging himself, but only made it faster and heavier. *Sin makes men a burden to the Creator as well as to themselves.* God wearied with men's iniquities (Is. xliii. 24). Pressed under them as a cart full of sheaves (Am. ii. 13). That Job was a burden *to himself* was his *own feeling*; that he was a burden to God, was *Satan's suggestion*.

3. *A passionate question and a plaintive appeal* (verse 20). "And why dost thou not pardon (*Heb.* 'take away' or remit, as a debt) my transgression, and take away (*Heb.* 'cause to pass away' as a cloud) mine iniquity?" "Transgression" and "iniquity" embrace all kinds of sin, those of commission and omission, presumption and ignorance, life and heart. The question not that of a humble penitent asking forgiveness. Job yet to be made a poor sinner. Pardon of sin a favour, not an *obligation*, or *matter of course.*

Pardon of Sin.

Often, as here, desired rather as the removal of *suffering* than of *guilt*. Only not *bestowed*, because the sinner is not prepared to *receive* it. Pride, impenitence, and unbelief shut out forgiveness as the window-shutters exclude the sun. Pardon only vouchsafed—(1) When sin is realised and sincerely confessed (1 John i. 9; Ps. xxxii. 5); (2) When its demerit and hell-deserving-ness is acknowledged (Ps. li. 4, 11); (3) When deliverance is desired from its practice and power as well as from its punishment (Ps. li. 10); (4) When pardon is humbly sought as a matter of pure mercy (Ps. li. 1; Luke xviii. 13); (5) When it is accepted as only bestowed in virtue of the suffering and death of God's Son as the sinner's

Substitute (Heb. ix. 15, 22, 28; 1 John i. 7, 9; ii. 1, 2; Rom. iii. 24—26). *The reason of Job's passionate question the prospect of a speedy death.* "For now shall I sleep in the dust." Idea: I shall soon die, and Thou must either pardon and heal me speedily or not at all. Death to the believer a *sleep*. The thought of it not unpleasant to Job. A blessed awaking the hope of the Church (Ps. xvii. 15; Is. xxvi. 19; Dan. xii. 2; 1 Thess. iv. 14—16). Job's hope (ch. xiv. 12—15; xix. 25—27). *He can calmly lay his head in the dust, whose heart is already in heaven.*—Job believes in a time of Divine relenting towards him. "Thou shalt seek me in the morning (*i.e.*, diligently), but I shall not be"—(thy desire to do me good will be too late). The picture that of a father relenting towards a suffering child. Exhibited also in Jer. xxxi. 18—20; liv. 6—10. *God's love to His people unchanging and everlasting* (Jer. xxxi. 3; John xiii. 1). His *dealings with* them may change, but not his *delight in* them. The believer, however tried, still unwilling to quit his hold of God's fatherly relationship. Faith says, "Though His *hand* be *against* me, His *heart* is still *towards* me." Job's comfort too at times (ch. xiii. 15, 16; xiv. 15; xix. 25—27; xxiii. 10).

CHAPTER VIII.

BILDAD'S FIRST SPEECH.

Bildad less courteous and considerate of Job's feelings than even Eliphaz. Commences with an unfeeling reflection on his speech. Pursues the same line of argument and address as his predecessor—(1) God is righteous—punishing the bad, and rewarding those who seek and serve Him; (2) Job exhorted to prove the latter by sincere repentance and prayer; (3) The prosperity of the wicked short-lived, and sure to end in ruin: the end of the righteous certain joy and triumph.

I. Bildad's Introduction (verse 2).

A harsh censure on Job's speech—(1) For its *length*. "How long wilt thou speak," &c. Had listened to Job with impatience. Due to every man to hear him patiently, especially a man in affliction; (2) For its *matter*. "How long wilt thou speak *these things?*" Uttered with contempt—these worthless and wicked sentiments; (3) For its *vehemence*. "And the words of thy mouth be like a *strong wind*"—recklessly bearing down all before thee, human and Divine. Intensely unfeeling thus to attack the words of a man in such deep distress. *Faultiness in another's* speech no excuse for *unfeelingness* in our *own*. Job's speech not more destitute of *sobriety* than Bildad's is of *sympathy*. Difficult even under the Gospel to have our "speech always with grace, seasoned with salt." Christians so to speak as to "minister grace to the hearer," and bring glory to God. Bildad's censure not without use to preachers. Suggests care as to—(1) The *length*; (2) The *matter*; (3) The *manner* of their discourses. Preachers to avoid—(1) Prolixity; (2) Unsound or unprofitable matter; (3) A vehement and boisterous delivery.

II. Bildad strongly asserts the Divine righteousness (verse 3).

"Doth God pervert judgment? or doth the Almighty pervert justice?" This apparently implied in Job's complaints. God essentially righteous. Incapable of injustice towards His creatures. As "the Almighty," He is beyond any temptation to act unjustly. The Judge of all the earth cannot but do right (Gen. xviii. 25). Severe complaints like Job's, a reflection on God's justice. God is righteous

1. *In punishing sin.* The reference in Bildad's mind both to Job's affliction and his children's death. Cruelly treats the latter as a probable, if not certain, instance of Divine justice (verse 4).—"If (or, 'since') thy children have sinned against Him, and He have cast them away for (*margin*, 'in the hand of') their transgression," making their sin in immoderate feasting to be its own punishment, &c. An erroneous as well as unfeeling application of the general truth. (1) Job's children had sinned, but not above all men that dwelt in the land of Uz; (2) Their sin was not the occasion of their death. No injustice on God's part, however, either to Job or his children, in allowing the calamity. Sufficient sin in each to merit more than any earthly affliction (Lam. iii. 39). Death, in the case of believers' children, their removal to a better state. To the parents, overruled for their elevation to a higher spiritual life. *Bildad's error in regarding earth as the sphere of God's retributive justice.* General tendency to view calamity as the righteous punishment of sinful conduct. The tower in Siloam. The error reproved by Jesus (Luke xiii. 1—5). The unjust reserved to the day of judgment to be punished (2 Peter ii. 9). The present

life rather the time of forbearance and mercy (2 Peter iii. 9, 15). Many apparent anomalies in the Divine procedure. Examples: Abel's murder, and Cain's long and prosperous life. A future state necessary to clear up these anomalies, and fully display the righteousness of God.

2. *In rewarding those who seek and serve Him* (verse 5).—" If thou " (emphatic, thou who art still spared) "wouldst seek unto God betimes (repair to Him earnestly and at once), and make, &c., if thou wert pure [in thy heart and motive] and upright [in thy profession and practice while so doing]; surely now [even in thy extreme misery] He would awake for thee " (and come quickly to thy help). The error and sting in all this, the supposition that Job had been a wicked man and a hypocrite. The sentiment in itself true and profitable. (1) God the only help and refuge in trouble (Ps. xlvi. 1.) (2) The duty and interest of all in trouble to betake themselves to Him. (3) This to be attended to "betimes," at once, and with all earnestness. (4) Supplication to be made to Him for pardon, deliverance, and grace (Lam. iii. 41). (5) This to be done in sincerity and uprightness, with a renouncing of all sin (Ps. lxvi .18). (6) The result a certain and speedy interposition in our behalf. A twofold promise held out: 1. A peaceful and prosperous habitation; 2. A large increase in worldly possessions (verse 7). "He would make the habitation of thy righteousness prosperous," (or, "would restore thy then righteous habitation, and endow it with perfect felicity "). Temporal blessing promised as the expression of the Divine favour. An insinuation that Job's dwelling had not formerly been a righteous one. Two great mercies indicated in this promise. (1) *A pious home* ; a home where—(i.) God is daily and duly acknowledged and worshipped; (ii.) The members of the family live in love towards each other ; (iii.) All the duties of morality and religion are carefully attended to. Such a dwelling contrasted with the "tents of wickedness" (Ps. lxxxiv. 11). (2) *A peaceful and prosperous home ;* where— (i.) The inmates are at peace with God and with one another ; (ii.) God prospers their honest endeavours to obtain a competent livelihood; (iii.) They are preserved from domestic troubles ; (iv.) All the inmates are the pardoned and accepted children of God. A pious home usually a peaceful and prosperous one. There God commands his blessing (Ps. cxxxiii. 3). The ark brought a blessing with it into Obededom's house (2 Sam. vi. 10, 11). The voice of rejoicing and salvation in the tabernacles of the righteous (Ps. cxviii. 15). A peaceful habitation a new covenant blessing (Is. xxxii. 18).

The dove of Divine peace hovers over the altar of domestic worship.

III. Bildad refers Job to the Fathers for instruction (verse 8). " Enquire, I pray thee, of the former age, and prepare thyself to the search of their fathers,"—to the examination of the records of those still further distant, as Noah, Shem, &c. The reason given : " For we (the present generation as compared with the past, or viewed as single individuals) are but of yesterday and know nothing " (—have comparatively little knowledge and experience of God's dealings with men); "because our days upon earth (as mere individuals, or as compared with those of our ancestors), are a shadow. Shall they not teach thee and tell thee [how God acts towards men in this world], and utter words out of their heart," —well-pondered sayings as the result of their careful observation and reflection? Knowledge in the earlier period of the world rather *the results of observation.* These embodied in poetical and proverbial sayings. Such sayings existed either as written records or as traditional poetry. Especially valued by the Arabs, and still esteemed by them as the strongest testimonies. Mostly, however, the productions only of human wisdom, and to be distinguished from Divine revelation. Amongst them were the utterances of inspired men, as that of Enoch (Jude 14.).

Tradition.

Such traditions to be received with deference and respect, but not as of binding authority. Their authority that of the arguments which support them. Men always fallible, except as inspired by God to deliver truth. The fathers of the race and the fathers of the Church in the same category. Their wisdom and experience neither to be disregarded nor implicitly received. Increased light obtained with the advance of ages and the increase of experience. The wisdom and experience of each generation to be valued as a contribution to that of its successors. Opinion in good men is but knowledge in the making [*Milton*]. It is only the weak who, at each epoch, believe mankind to have arrived at the culminating point of their progressive march [*Humboldt*]. The famous test of ecclesiastical tradition a safe one, if it could be found,—what has been taught *by all,* taught *always,* and taught *everywhere.* The longevity of the earlier ages favourable for wider observation. In the time of Job, human life reduced to about 200 years. Noah lived to be 950 ; Arphaxad, his grandson, only 438 ; Peleg, the great-grandson of Arphaxad, 239; Serug, Peleg's grandson, probably about the time of Job, 230; Terah, Serug's grandson and the father of Abraham, 205. The change apparent and striking to those living at the time. Hence Bildad's acknowledgment—

Human Life a Shadow.

Time measured at that time by the shadow projected by the index of a dial, a spear stuck in the ground, &c. Man's life but a solar day,—as the shadow fleeting along the dial-plate. Life mercifully reduced in consequence of sin. A long, vigorous life-time more favourable to the development of human depravity. "The heart never grows better by age: I fear, worse,—always harder" [*Lord Chesterfield*]. Great longevity only gives occasion to the godly for David's lament (Ps. cxx. 5, 6). The present extent of human life long enough for a child of God to be kept from home (2 Cor. v. 6, 8). Life, as a "*shadow*," calls for—(1) *Diligence in the improvement of it.* Momentous issues hang on the fleeting shadow. Eternal interests demand despatch. (2) *A loose hold of things of time.* Like life itself, "all here is shadow, all beyond is substance." Foolish to set the heart on a shadow. "He builds too low who builds beneath the skies." (3) *A proper estimate to be made of the troubles and joys, the possessions and pursuits, of the present life.* (4) *Earnestness in securing a solid and lasting happiness beyond the grave.*

IV. Quotation from the ancients (verses 11—19). Exhibits:
1. *The temporary prosperity of the ungodly.* Compared—(1) To the *paper-reed* of Egypt, and the *flag* of the marsh or *grass* of the meadow (verse 11). "Can the rush (or 'papyrus') grow up without mire? Can the flag ('marsh-plant,' or 'grass of the meadow,'—same word wrongly translated 'meadow' in Gen. xli. 2.) grow without water?" The papyrus of the Nile formerly used in the manufacture of garments, shoes, baskets, boats, and *paper*, whence our English word. The papyrus probably employed by the Jews of Alexandria for writing on while translating the Old Testament into Greek, having used this very word in the place of our "rush." Now only found in marshes of the White Nile in Nubia, and in one or two spots in Palestine. Such plants capable of receiving a large supply of water which they require for their nourishment. Grow tall and luxuriant while the water is supplied; but speedily die when that supply is withdrawn. Picture of worldly men who have no living principle of enduring pros-

perity within themselves, either in the love of God in them, or the blessing of God on them. Their prosperity only from favourable circumstances, which may at any time come to an end. Contrast Haman with Joseph, both attaining to the highest prosperity. (2) To a *spider's web*, constructed with the greatest care, and expected to prove a lasting support to its' possessor, but which the slightest accident may disturb and destroy (verse 14). "Whose trust (his riches, &c., in which he trusts) shall be a spider's web" —as unsubstantial and as certain speedily to perish. "The spider's most attenuated thread is cord, is cable," compared to such prosperity and trust. (3) To a *luxuriant garden-tree*, growing near a fountain and striking its numerous roots into the rocky bed on which it stands, open to the sun, and with every advantage of soil and situation (verse 16, 17). "He is green (or moist) before the sun (enjoying the warm and genial influence of its rays), and his branch shooteth forth in his garden: his roots are wrapped about the heap (or fountain), and seeth the place of stones" (enjoys the benefit of rocky strata for its support). A still more striking picture of the prosperous ungodly than the tall and luxuriant marsh-plant. Compare Ps. xxxvii. 35.

2. *The certain and speedy termination of that prosperity.* (1) The *papyrus* or *marsh-plant* suddenly withers from want of the required supply of water (verse 12). "Whilst it is yet in its greenness (promising long continuance), and not cut down (—without any hand applied to pluck or cut it down), it withereth before any other herb" (suddenly decays without giving notice of the approaching change, while other plants less dependent on a large supply of moisture continue to live). Soon ripe, soon rotten. The prosperity of the ungodly a Jonah's gourd. (2) The *spider's web*, on which he depends for his support, speedily perishes by accident or the broom (verse 15). "He (the spider, or the ungodly whom he represents) shall lean on his house (on his web, or the riches, family, &c., of the worldly figured by it), but it shall not stand; he shall hold it fast (or, lay hold of it—for its preservation, or rather for his own support), but it shall not endure." "Time destroys the well-built house as well as the spider's web" [*Arab Proverb*]. The prosperity and bliss of the worldly man perishes like that flimsy web. It is well if, like that web also, it does not bury its possessor in its ruins. (3) The *luxuriant tree*, spreading abroad its roots and branches, is suddenly struck by lightning or whirlwind, and at once becomes a leafless skeleton, or is laid prostrate on its native soil (verse 18). "If he destroy him (or, 'if he [or it]

be destroyed '—*Heb.* 'swallowed up') from his place, then it shall deny him, saying: I have not seen thee "—the place where it stood is forgotten. The application given by the Psalmist: "He (the wicked) passed away, and lo, he was not; yea, I sought him, but he could not be found" (Ps. xxxvii. 36). History full of such instances. Haman, instead of parading on the monarch's horse, is left hanging on a felon's gallows. When the Messenians saw the renowned Philopœmon stripped and dragged along with his hands ignominiously bound behind his back, "they wept, and contemned all human greatness as a faithless support, as vanity and nothing" [*Plutarch*]. The Emperor Vitellius was driven through the streets of Rome naked, and then thrown into the Tiber.

"O mighty Cæsar! dost thou lie so low!
   Are all thy conquests, glories, triumphs, spoils,
   Shrunk to this little measure?"

3. *The application* (verse 13). "So are the paths of all that forget God; and the hypocrite's hope shall perish."

Forgetfulness of God.

Those "who forget God" placed in the same class with the "hypocrite," or rather the "profane," or "wicked." Enough to characterize a man as wicked, that he "forgets God" (So Ps. ix. 17; x. 22). To forget God is—(1) Not to *think* of Him; (2) Not to *thank* Him; (3) Not to *serve and obey* Him. It is to forget—(1) His presence; (2) His Providence; (3) His precepts. Forgetfulness of another implies—(1) Want of love; (2) Want of respect. Men feel wounded on being forgotten by those whom they love, and on whose love they have a claim. Observe—
1. *Forgetfulness of God is the root and essence of all sin.* It is to ignore, and, as far as we are able, to annihilate, Him from His own universe. It is to treat Him as though there were no such Being. The fool hath said in his heart, "No God" (Ps. xiv. 1). To "remember" God equivalent to loving and serving Him (Eccles. xii. 1; Is. lxiv. 5).
2. *To forget God is to forget Him who possesses all claims to our remembrance*;—(1) From what He is *in Himself*; (2) From what He is and has been *to us*. God is—(1) The Being who is the Source and Centre of all possible excellence and loveliness; (2) Our Creator and Father; (3) Our Preserver from moment to moment; (4) Our Provider; (5) Our Protector; (6) Our Deliverer from trouble and danger; (7) Our Benefactor and best Friend; (8) In Christ our Redeemer

and Saviour from sin and all its direful consequences.
3. *In forgetting God we give our thoughts and hearts to the world, which has no attraction but what it derives from Him, and which can neither satisfy nor save us.* To forget God, therefore, is both ingratitude, robbery, and idolatry. It is to rob Him of His honour as well as ourselves of peace.
4. *To remember God is to elevate, ennoble, and purify ourselves.*

V. Conclusion of Bildad's Speech (verse 20—22).

Perhaps another of the sayings of the ancients. Same general subject—God's dealings with the righteous and the wicked. Intended, like parts of the speech of Eliphaz, either for consolation or conviction, or perhaps both. Contains—
1. *Comfort for the godly under trial* (verse 20). "Behold, God will not cast away a perfect man" (see chap. i. 1). Hence, comfort for Job, *if such*. This, however, still to be *proved*. A righteous man may be cast *down*, but not cast *away* (Ps. xciv. 14; 2 Cor. iv. 9). Hence the difficulty to Job's friends in judging of his character. For the present, to all appearance, he was cast away. Himself, his family, and his fortunes, apparently a total wreck. The question therefore natural—Has Job been what he appeared? Or has he at length in his prosperity turned his back upon God? The Divine rule—"If thou forsake Him, He will cast thee off for ever" (1 Chron. xxviii. 9). Job himself conscious this was not *his* case: but this uncertain to the others. *A truly good man proved to be such by continuing good.* Care to be taken not only to *begin*, but to *persevere* in well-doing. Not to prove a castaway, Paul kept his body under (1 Cor. ix. 27). (verse 21). "Till (or, 'while'—connecting with verse 22) he shall fill thy mouth with laughing, and thy lips with rejoicing" (*margin,* "shouting for joy.") "Till," &c., implies continuance in well-doing and well-suffering. In due time we reap, if we faint not. Sowing in tears, we reap in joy. The "shouting" of victory crowns the well-fought battle. That "shouting" one—(1) of *joy.* "The ransomed of the Lord return, and come to Zion with songs and everlasting joy on their heads" (Isa. xxxv. 10). (2) Of *praise.* "Salvation to our God that sitteth upon the throne, and unto the Lamb" (Rev. vii. 10). "Not unto us, O Lord, not unto us, but to thy name, give glory" (Ps. cxv. 1).
2. *Warning to the ungodly* (verse 20). "Neither will he help the evil-doers."—*Margin,* "take the ungodly by the hand," or, "take hold of their hand,"—*i.e.,* with the view of helping and countenancing them.

An unkind cut for poor Job, who seemed far enough from Divine help. So little can man know either love or hatred from that which s before him (Eccles. ix. 1). *Now* men see not the bright light which is in the clouds (ch. xxxvii. 21). "Judge not the Lord by feeble sense." A solemn truth in the words of Bildad. The help which the ungodly receive is not God's help. Divine help the privilege of the godly (Ps. lxiii. 7; Acts xxvi. 22). *To enjoy God's help we must employ ourselves in God's service* (verse 22).—"They that hate thee shall be clothed with shame (as Ps. xxxv. 26; cix. 29; cxxxii. 18). The ungodly, however prosperous for a time, condemned to shame. Shame the natural fruit of sin (Rom. vi. 21). Shame and contempt the characteristic and doom of the risen ungodly (Dan. xii. 2). "Shame" experienced —(1) That they madly threw away their souls for the pleasures of sin; (2) That those whom they hated and despised they now see crowned with joy and victory; (3) That they so basely fought against the God that made them.—"And the dwelling-place (*Heb.* 'tent,' as Ps. lxxxiv. 11) of the wicked shall come to nought,"—as a tent when struck leaves no trace of it behind. The "tent" of the ungodly may be a rich pavilion, but its doom is written. *Sin brings families as well as individuals to certain ruin.*

CHAPTER IX.

JOB'S REPLY TO BILDAD.

Strongly affirms the truth of Bildad's speech as to God's justice (verse 1). Declares the impossibility of fallen man establishing his righteousness with God. The same already acknowledged in reference to himself (ch. vii. 20, 21). Only maintains, as before, his freedom from such sins as to make him specially obnoxious to God's judgments. Enlarges on the majesty, power and sovereignty of God, as exhibited in His works of creation and providence. Again complains of his severe and unmerited sufferings, and his inability to plead his own cause with God.

I. **Acknowledgement of man's sinfulness and guilt in the sight of God** (verse 2). "But (or, 'and') how should a man (a fallen, mortal man, '*enosh*') be just with God? if he will contend with him, he cannot answer him one of a thousand" [of the charges to be brought against him]. The language suggests the ·

Way of a Sinner's acceptance with God.

1. *Man's state and necessity as a sinner the foundation of the Gospel.* Man is a sinner, unable to justify himself before God. The Gospel reveals a Saviour, and shows how man can obtain the justification he needs. In the Gospel is revealed "the righteousness of God"—a righteousness provided by God for man's justification; or, God's righteous way of justifying a sinner; viz., by the obedience and death of His own Son as the sinner's substitute (Rom. i. 17). To show this necessity of man and the provision made in the Gospel to meet it, Paul's object in the Epistle to the Romans.

2. *The necessity acknowledged by Job; the provision unnoticed by him as not bearing on the present controversy, and as not yet clearly known.* The way of forgiveness through vicarious suffering understood, as constantly exhibited in the sacrifices. That of a sinner standing accepted and righteous before God through the active and passive obedience of another not yet fully revealed. The "righteousness of God" better known in the time of David—"I will make mention of thy righteousness, even of thine only" (Ps. lxxi. 16). Still more clearly revealed by Isaiah— "Surely shall one say, In the Lord have I righteousness and strength; in him shall all the seed of Israel be justified and shall glory" (Is. xlv. 24, 25). The light still advancing in the time of Jeremiah, a century later: "I will raise unto David a righteous branch— and this is his name whereby he shall be called, the Lord our Righteousness" (Jer. xxiii. 5, 6). Clearer still in the time of Daniel: "We do not present our supplications before thee for our righteousnesses, but for thy great mercies"—"for the Lord's (Adonai's) sake;" "Seventy weeks are determined to make reconciliation for iniquity, and to bring in everlasting righteousness;" "Messiah shall be cut off, but not for himself" (Dan. ix. 17, 18, 24, 26).

3. *That provision "witnessed to by the law and the prophets," but only "now," in the Gospel dispensation, "manifested"* (Rom. iii. 21). Described as "the righteousness of God without the law, which is by faith in Jesus Christ, unto all, and upon all them that believe" (verse 22). The same ground and necessity of it alleged as confessed by Job: "For all have sinned and come short of the glory of God" (verse 23).

The "righteousness of God" to show that God is "just, and the justifier of him that believeth in Jesus," declared "at this time" in the "remission (or passing over) of sins that were past" (in previous generations) (verse 26).

4. "How CAN A MAN BE JUST WITH GOD?"—*the great question for humanity.* The great concern for a dying hour, therefore the great concern *now.* How we stand with men a trifle in comparison. Without the Gospel, man's views regarding it false, and his efforts vain. Men look for it—(1) From their own virtues; (2) From the efficacy of sacrifices, ceremonies, and penances; (3) From the merits and intercession of others. But men's greatest virtues still leave them sinners. No efficacy in the temporary sufferings of man or beast to atone for sin. No sinner can have merit or power with God to procure his neighbour's acceptance any more than his own. "The sufficiency of my merit is to know that my merit is insufficient" [*Augustine*].

5. *God's way of acceptance every way suited to meet the case.* Salvation and acceptance through a substitute according to reason and analogy. Common among men to allow the merit of one to avail on behalf of another. The eye of Zaleucus admitted as sufficient satisfaction to justice for that of his son. The uplifted stump of Æschylus, in testimony of his services to his country, allowed to prevail for his brother's acquittal. One permitted to take another's place in serving his country in time of war. Elements in the substitution of Christ:—(1) The Divine law receives its perfect fulfilment and righteous penalty for man's transgression in man's nature; (2) The man Christ constituted by God a second Adam and head of the race; (3) As man fell by the disobedience of one, the first Adam, he rises by the obedience of one, the second Adam; (4) The dignity of the Substitute, as the Son of God, sufficient to impart to His merits all necessary efficacy; (5) His Divine nature and supernatural birth exempted Him from sin and the liability of the race; (6) Christ, with a human mother and a Divine Father, placed both *within* the race and *outside* of it, as necessary for substitution.

6. *Righteous in the righteousness of another,* —*the only way left for a sinner's acceptance with God.* RIGHTEOUS IN CHRIST, the Gospel plan and the believer's glory. Sufficient for the acceptance and justification of the entire race. A man who is now not just and accepted before God is so only from—(1) *Ignorance* of God's plan of making a sinner righteous; (2) *Unwillingness* to accept of it; (3) *Inability* to trust in it; or (4) *Indifference* in regard to his salvation.

II. The folly of contending against God (verse 4).

"He is wise in heart and mighty in strength; who hath hardened himself against Him and prospered?" Men harden themselves against God—(1) While resisting His authority and disobeying his commands; (2) Rebelling and murmuring against His dealings in Providence; (3) Refusing the offers of His mercy in the Gospel. *Man possessed of the fearful power of hardening himself against God.* The folly of such contention seen—

1. *From the attributes of God.* God "wise in heart and mighty in strength." "Wise" to convict the offender and know how to deal with him; "Mighty" to arrest him and inflict the merited punishment. "Wise" to know and choose what is best to do; "Mighty" to accomplish it. Strength may prevail against wisdom, and wisdom against strength; but who can prevail against both combined? *Almighty strength safe in the hands of infinite wisdom.* Strength without wisdom makes a tyrant; strength with wisdom, a God. *In Christ the wisdom and strength of God are both employed on our behalf.* To His *wisdom* and *power,* as well as to His *love,* is due the plan of man's salvation (Eph. iii. 10; i. 19, 20). Christ both "the power of God and the wisdom of God" (1 Cor. i. 24).

2. *From the facts of history.* "Who hath hardened himself against Him and prospered?" The sinning angels, Pharaoh, Sennacherib's army, the infidel leaders in the first French Revolution, referred to for an answer. For a creature to oppose God is for briars and thorns to do battle against fire. Success certain in falling in with God's plan and procedure; certain ruin in opposing it. Prosperity for a time sometimes the apparent result of opposing God. That prosperity generally only the precursor of ultimate ruin. Pharaoh never appeared nearer his object than when he met with destruction.

Magnificent description of the

Power and Majesty of God,

As exhibited in the works of creation and providence (verses 5—10). The description unequalled for poetic grandeur. Its elements—

1. *The sudden overthrow of mountains* (verse 5). "Which removeth the mountains, and they know not (or, before ever they are aware), and overthroweth them in his anger" (as in righteous judgment for the sins of the people). "To remove mountains," synonymous with an impossibility. Nothing impossible with God. Hannibal

59

celebrated for making a passage over the mountains; God removes them out of the way. Through the secret operation of natural causes, as in earthquakes and otherwise, mountains sometimes split, and portions torn away from the rest, with destruction of human life. All nature under God's control, and employed by Him in mercy or in judgment.

2. *Trembling of the earth's foundations, and disappearance of portions of its surface.* (verse 6). " Which shaketh the earth out of her place, and the pillars thereof (or, its foundations,—the earth represented as a fabric or building) tremble." Nothing apparently more firm in its place than the earth; yet islands and other large portions of it frequently made to disappear, through subterraneous agencies in earthquakes, subsidences, and submersions, what was once land now becoming sea. Earthquakes and all apparently natural convulsions and changes entirely under God's control.

3. *The sun withholding its beams in obedience to His command* (verse 7). "Which commandeth the sun and it riseth not,"—sends not forth its rays; as in eclipses, dense fogs, the darkness frequently accompanying earthquakes, or when clouds and tempests darken the sky. The Divine command as powerful as at the beginning (Gen. i. 3). Joshua's command but an echo of his Master's (Josh. x. 12).

4. *The starry sky sealed up as a folded scroll.* "And sealeth up the stars." The starry heavens God's volume nightly spread open before us (Ps. xix. 1). Its characters sometimes entirely hidden by clouds, fogs, or tempests, as in Acts xxvii. 20. The nocturnal sky usually clear in the East, and the stars peculiarly brilliant. Hence the obscuration of it much more striking than with us. The clouds God's seal, not to be broken by any earthly power. The scroll to be one day folded up (Is. xxxiv. 4; 2 Pet. iii. 10; Rev. vi. 14).

5. *The firmament spread out as a canopy, and the clouds made His chariot* (verse 8). " Which alone (by His unaided power,—the one only Creator and Preserver of all) spreadeth out (or boweth) the heavens." Spread out the firmament at the beginning, still keeps it spread, and spreads it out afresh every morning as a curtain (Ps. civ. 2; Is. xl. 22). Employs the clouds as His chariot, bowing the heavens beneath Him, and putting darkness under His feet (Ps. xviii. 9; cxliv. 5). Probably a further description of a tempest. The verse a miniature of the scene so sublimely described in Ps. xviii. 7—15.

6. *The towering billows made a pathway for His feet.* "And treadeth on the waves GO

(*margin,* ' heights ') of the sea." Sublimely expresses His control over the mountain billows of the ocean, treading on them as a Conquerer and Ruler, restraining their fury, and keeping them from returning and again deluging the earth. So Christ visibly walked on the stormy lake of Galilee (Matt. xiv. 26). Comfort for the tempest-tossed mariner, to remember that the God who is love both walks on the wings of the wind and the waves of the sea. A man walking on the waves, the Egyptian hieroglyphic for impossibility. "With God all things are possible."

7. *The constellations of heaven, as His creatures, rising and setting at His will* verse 9). " Which maketh Arcturus (or the Great Bear), Orion, and the Pleiades (or Seven Stars), and the chambers of the south" (or the Constellations in the Southern Hemisphere, appearing to the Arabs only in summer). Preserves them in their original places, marshals them as His hosts, sustains and directs their apparent motions through all the successive seasons of the year.

8. *His acts wonderful, innumerable, and unsearchable* (verse 10). " Which doeth great things past finding out ; yea, and wonders without number." In creation, His works wondrous and unsearchable, both in their multitude and magnitude, their complexity and minuteness. A drop of water and a dusky spot hardly visible on the face of the sky, each reveals such wonders; the one, millions of perfectly-formed living creatures; the other millions of worlds, each world a sun. In Providence and the government of the universe, His works equally great and marvellous, innumerable and beyond our power of investigation. "His thoughts a great deep." "Deep in unfathomable mines," &c.

Lessons from this description :—

1. Ruinous to resist a Being of such power and majesty.

2. Blessed to have such a Being for our friend ; miserable to have Him for a foe.

3. Our duty and happiness to trust Him in the most trying and apparently hopeless situations.

4. His appointment and dispensations to be meekly submitted to.

5. A Being of such perfections to be reverenced, adored, and obeyed.

III. **God's Perfections and Dealings viewed by Job in relation to Himself.**

1. *Job declares God's incomprehensibleness in His dealings with him* (verse 11). "Lo, he goeth by me (is near me, in the dealings of his Providence), and I see him not ; he passeth on also (from one stroke to

another, or 'passeth through like a whirlwind,' Is. xxi. 1), but I perceive him not" (do not apprehend either His meaning or His love). A great part of Job's trial, that while God was so painfully visiting him he was entirely in the dark as to His meaning. Contrasted with his experience in former trials (chap. xxix. 3). Observe—(1) *A child of God sometimes entirely in the dark as to the meaning of God's dealings with Him.* Perplexity and bewilderment as to the cause of our trials on *God's* side, sometimes no small part of them. One of the greatest trials of a believer to be under trouble, and not to apprehend God's love in it. (2) *God's incomprehensibleness an exercise for faith.* His children to trust Him in the dark. God most glorified by such confiding faith. Abraham an example (Rom. iv. 19—21; Heb. xi. 8, 17—19). (3) *Incomprehensibleness a feature in God's character and conduct.* His ways in the sea, and His footsteps not known (Ps. lxxvii 19). His ways past finding (Rom. xi. 33). The glory of God is to conceal a thing (Ps. xxv. 2). God's dealings incomprehensible to us—(i.) as to their *reasons*; (ii.) as to their *ends.* "What I do thou knowest not now" (John xiii. 7). Part of the darkness, of sin that God is near and yet not perceived. His close and constant nearness a matter for praise and adoration (Ps. cxxxix. 5). Analogy between God's dealings in nature and in Providence. The operations and effects obvious, the agent Himself unseen. The operation of natural causes manifest; the moving power behind and under these entirely hidden (Acts xvii. 22).

2. *Job acknowledges God's sovereignty and irresistible power* (verse 12). "Behold, he taketh away, who can hinder him? (*margin* 'turn him away'). Who will say unto him, 'What doest thou?'" Observe—(1) *God takes away as He pleases.* Already acknowledged by Job in his calamities (ch. i. 21; ii. 10). Good to recognize God's hand in our losses. No evil but from God, either directly or indirectly (Is. xlv. 7; Amos iii. 6). Satan rather than God, the *immediate* author of Job's calamities. Yet Satan's action is not without God's permission. *Satan only God's instrument in accomplishing His purpose of trying His people.*—(2) *When God takes away, none can hinder Him.* God possesses not only the *right* but the *might* to do as He pleases. Our comfort to know that both are exercised in wisdom, goodness, and holiness. Good to remember that when God takes away, that—(i.) He only takes away *His own;* (ii.) He takes away *for our good.* Job a greater gainer by his losses than he had ever been by his gains. To say to God, What doest Thou? is as *ignorant* as it

is *wicked.* What God does, He does because it is best. God gives no reason to impenitent sinners either as to *what* He does or *why* He does it. A child of God *would* not hinder Him even if he *could.*—(3) *Opposition to God and His will as useless as it is wicked* (verse 13). "If God will not withdraw his anger (or simply, 'God will not withdraw,' &c.), the proud helpers do stoop under Him." God's anger not to be turned away by man's opposition, but by repentance, submission, and faith (Ps. ii. 10—12). His "anger" put for the *rod* which is the expression of it. All creature help against God and His chastisements utterly vain. Israel's sin, that when under the rod they went to Egypt for help (Is. xxx. 2; xxxi. 1). Egypt in their pride, ready to render that help (Is. xxx. 4). Both helpers and helped obliged in the end to stoop under the rod (Is. xxxi. 3). Not uncommon for the ungodly to agree to mutual help in resisting God and His purposes (Ps. ii. 1—3; lxxxiii. 5—8; Acts xxi. 28; xxiii. 12). Such confederacies frequent in the time of the Reformation. Combinations against the Protestant religion combinations against God and his truth. Pride the characteristic of such confederacies (Ex. v. 2; xv. 9). Their end seen in the overthrow of sinning angels and the destruction of Pharaoh's host (Jude 6; Ex. xv. 9). The final destruction of anti-christian combinations yet to be exhibited (Rev. xvii. 12—14; xix. 11—21). *The essence of pride to oppose oneself to God's purposes.*—(4) *Good to take warning from others not to fall into their sin* (verse 15). "How much less shall I answer him [in his charges against me], and choose out my words to reason with him" [as defendant in my cause]. *Humility learned by consideration of God's mightiness.* If the proudest opposers of God and His purposes must stoop, how then shall I dispute with Him?—(5) *Silence and submission under God's rebuke our interest as well as our duty* (verse 15). "Whom, though I were righteous, yet would I not answer [at his bar], but I would make supplication to my judge" (or to him debating with me). Man's wisdom not to *dispute with God, but to submit to Him.* God ever ready to hear the sinner when he *supplicates,* but never when he *disputes.* However blameless his conduct, or good his conscience, fallen man still a sinner before God. "FOUND WANTING," written on man's best performances. God better acquainted *with our character and conduct than we are ourselves* (1 Cor. iv. 4; 1 John iii. 20). Constant reason for humiliation and faith (Ps. xix. 12; cxxxix. 23, 24).—(6) *The tried soul ready to fall back into despondency and un-*

belief (verse 16). "If I had (or have) called [on Him to answer my complaints], and he had (or hath) answered me [by condescending to take the place of a defendant], yet would (or will) I not believe that he had (or hath) hearkened to my voice." Unbelief made the continuance of Job's sufferings an argument that God had not hearkened to his prayer. The part of the *flesh*, to reason from the *dealings* of God's *hand* to the *purposes* of God's *heart*. Prayer often *heard before the proof of it is apparent*. Faith required to believe this (Mark xi. 24). *Unbelief* must *see* the answer before it believes in it; *faith* believes in it before seeing it. *Prayer, like seed, which for a time lies buried in the earth.* God's time for answering prayer reserved in His own hand. *Prayer attended to, and prayer answered, two different things.* The former usually followed sooner or later by the latter. *Receiving* an answer to be distinguished from the *actual enjoying* of it (Mark xi. 24). Faith believes that it *receives* the blessing asked before it *sees* it: the *seeing* comes in God's time.—
(7) *Unbelief eyes outward dealings* (verse 17, 18). "For he breaketh me with a tempest (or, 'crusheth me as in a whirlwind '), he multiplieth my wounds without cause. He will not suffer me to take my breath (enjoy the least respite or relief), but filleth me with bitterness." The ground of Job's despondency and unbelief. Continued suffering forbids him to believe God regards His prayers. *Hard to believe in God's love when so terribly crushed with successive strokes of His Providence.* A tragic but true description of Job's sufferings. "Broken"—crushed, or "bruised," as in Gen. iii. 15. "With a tempest," or "in a whirlwind "—suddenly—violently—irresistibly, like one continually lifted up and then dashed down again forcibly to the ground. This as suffered "without cause" known to himself, only all the more painful. His suffering "without cause," God's own account of the matter (ch. ii. 3). The thing denied by the friends, but persistently maintained by Job, while yet acknowledging himself a sinner before God. Job ignorant of God's purpose in the affliction. What was really done by *Satan*, Job in his ignorance ascribes to *God*. Ignorant of Satan's *malice*, he can only think of God's *arbitrariness*. Satan having destroyed Job's children by one "whirlwind," thinks to destroy Job himself by another of a different nature. *Sufferings long continued and without intermission terribly exhausting and crushing to the human spirit.* The "bitterness" of Job's outward sufferings only the counterpart of the bitterness in his soul. *Heroic faith to believe in God's gracious regard in such terribly distressing circum-*

stances. Such experience and faith that of Jesus Himself (Matt. xxvi. 38; xxvii. 46). Job's faith also at times triumphant (ch. xix. 25; xxiii. 10).

IV. Job's mental agitation in respect to his case (verses 19—21).
1. *His inability to plead with God* (verse 19).—"If I speak of strength (—if the question be one of strength), lo! he is strong (or, 'a strong One is here '; or, 'the strong One saith, here am I '); and if of judgment —(if the question be of one of *right*), who shall set me a time to plead" (or, 'who shall bring him [or us] into court' [that as umpire, we may debate the case before him]. Though conscious of innocence, Job feels there is no possibility of pleading his case against God. As regards power, God is the Mighty One, with whom no creature may contend. He is sovereign and supreme, so that there can be no umpire to summon both parties to trial. No creature therefore may dispute with God. Happily, no creature *needs. Every one's case left safe in His hands.* Only agitation and unrest till this is done. Job at last, after all his tumults and tossings, is brought to this, and then has peace. The lesson for Job and all tried ones,—*not to dispute with God, but to leave the case confidingly in His hands, assured that the Judge of all the earth will do right.* The lesson that of the 37th Psalm. "Commit thy way unto the Lord; trust also in Him, and he shall bring it to pass. And he shall bring forth thy righteousness as the light, and thy judgment as the noonday " (Ps. xxxvii. 5, 6).
2. *His certainty of condemnation notwithstanding His conscious integrity* (verse 20). "If I justify myself (or, 'although I be righteous '), mine own mouth shall condemn me (—by its very utterances will shew me guilty), if I say, I am perfect (or, 'although I am upright '), it shall also prove me perverse " (or, 'He, *i.e.* God, shall declare me guilty '). A great truth *felt*, though unwillingly acknowledged by the "perfect" man. *However upright and consciously innocent, a fallen man must yet stand condemned before his Maker.* To exhibit this, one of the great objects of the book of Job. Fallen man, at his best estate, a *sinner*, and so *guilty* before God. The Apostle's declaration, as shewing the necessity for the Gospel scheme (Rom. iii. 23). No flesh living capable of being justified in God's sight (Ps. cxl. 3). "No just man on earth that doeth good and sinneth not" (Eccles. vii. 20). To be justified before God on the ground of his own merits, a man must be absolutely sinless (Gal. iii. 10; Jam. ii. 10). Such a person nowhere to be found (1 John i. 8). *The mouth that pleads "Not guilty" before God*

condemns itself. Its very language proves the man a sinner by convicting him—(1) Of pride; (2) Of rebelliousness; (3) Of falsehood. *Self-righteousness in a sinner sufficient to condemn him.* The object of the law not to justify but to silence (Rom. iii. 19). A man's salvation and peace is found—(1) In acknowledging guilt and taking the place of a lost sinner before God; (2) In casting himself entirely on His mercy as flowing through a Saviour's atoning blood (Rom. iii. 24).

3. *His resolution to maintain his integrity at all costs* (verse 21). "Though I were perfect, yet would I not know my soul (or, I am blameless and sincere, I care not for myself'); I would despise (or, I 'despise') my life." As an honest man, conscious of sincerity and uprightness, Job refuses to confess himself a hypocrite and secret transgressor, in order to obtain the restoration to temporal prosperity held out by his friends. A contest maintained by Job with his friends as well as with God. As against *God*, he was wrong; as against *men*, he was right. Before *God*, he must and does acknowledge himself a sinner; before *men*, he maintains his integrity. In asserting himself "perfect" (blameless, sincere, upright), he only does what God had done for him (chap. i. 8; ii. 3). *A man may boldly maintain his integrity before his fellow men, while he humbly abases himself as a sinner before God.* In the sight of God, Paul bows as "the chief of sinners" (1 Tim. i. 15); before a human tribunal, he declares—"I have lived in all good conscience before God until this day" (Acts xxiii. 1).

V. Perplexed thoughts as to the Divine procedure in the present world (verses 22—24).

1. *Its indiscriminateness* (verse 22). "This is one thing (or, 'it is all one'); therefore I said it, he destroyeth the perfect (the blameless or upright) and the wicked." Both classes treated, as a rule, without discrimination in the present life. Maintained by Job—(1) As against the *friends*. Calamities not confined to the wicked; (2) As against *God Himself.* No special regard had to those who serve Him. Such indiscriminate procedure maintained in the Book of Ecclesiastes (chap. ix. 2, 3). One of the *facts* in the Divine government observed by thoughtful and good men. Both classes suffer alike, as in war, famine, pestilence, earthquake, tempests, &c. Both share equally in the ills and calamities of life. A mystery and a stumblingblock. To be regarded—(1) As *an argument for a future state.* The difference between the righteous and the wicked reserved for a future day (Mal. iii. 18).—(2) As *a trial for faith in the*

Divine character. Hence the murmurings of unbelieving professors (Mal. iii. 13, 15).

2. *Its apparent indifference to the sufferings of the godly* (verse 23). "If the scourge slay suddenly (or, indiscriminately), he will laugh (or, it laugheth) at the trial of the innocent." The supposed case already asserted (verse 22). Job's own case before his view. Providence often has the appearance of cruel indifference to the sufferings of the innocent. *The feelings of God's heart not to be judged by the dealings of His hand.* Divine "love and hatred" not known by any mere outward dispensation (Eccles. ix. 1). The godly sometimes "accounted as sheep for the slaughter" (Ps. xliv. 22). The Divine sympathy for the suffering exhibited in the character of Jesus. For a time Jesus Himself also sometimes appeared indifferent to suffering (Matt. xv. 23—26; Mark iv. 38; John xi. 6). The Divine dealings in the present life are—(1) *Probative;* (2) *Disciplinary.* The trial of the righteous found at last unto praise, and honour, and glory (1 Pet. i. 7). *Precious metal proved as well as purified by the fire.* The scourge that destroys the guilty only tries the good (So Ps. xi. 5; vii. 11).

3. *Its apparently unjust partiality* (verse 24). "The earth is given into the hand of the wicked; he covereth the faces of the judges thereof." Two anomalies—(1) The wicked are exalted to power, while godly men are depressed; (2) Tyrants are allowed to reign while rightful rulers are treated with ignominy and put to death (Est. vii. 8. Same sentiment (Ps. xii. 8). The ungodly styled "the man of the earth." (Ps. x. 18). Satan himself the "prince of this world." He and his host the "rulers of the darkness of this world." Godly men in Christ earth's proper judges and rulers (1 Cor. vi. 2, 3; Rev. i. 5). Such often treated in the providence of God as malefactors. Job himself an example (ch. xxix. 7—17, 25; xxx. 10—23). God the author of civil government. The earth with its various states and governments in His hand. Given over by Him to others according to His will. Often in judgment to bad men (Dan. iv. 17). By Him kings reign. He putteth down one and setteth up another (Ps. lxxv. 7; Dan. ii. 21). Ruleth in the kingdom of men, and appointeth over it whomsoever he will (Dan. iv. 17, 25; v. 21). Does this in His invisible and mysterious providence, without infringement on man's free will or the operation of second causes. This fact one of the elements in the doctrine of "wisdom," exhibited in this and other inspired books of the same period.

4. *The mysterious certainly connected with it.* "If not (—if the case be not so), where

and who is he [who does these things]?" Or, "if the case be not thus [viz., that God does these things], who is it [that does them]?" The facts undeniable; who but One can be the author of them? Acknowledged mystery in these anomalies in the government of a righteous God. Yet none but God can be the author of them. Earth necessarily under a Supreme Ruler. That Ruler necessarily righteous. The doctrine of two co-ordinate principles not to be admitted. God the author both of good and evil—light and darkness (Is. xlv. 7). The existence and prevalence of evil in the world, including the elevation of wicked rulers, one of the mysteries in Divine Providence. God the author of evil—(1) By permission; (2) By predestination; (3) By Providence. Satan the author of evil—(1) Actually; (2) Subordinately; (3) Instrumentally. Evil under the Divine government permitted for wise and benevolent purposes. His wisdom and benevolence seen—(1) In restraining the evil; (2) In overruling it for good; (3) In employing it for the exhibition of His own perfections (Ps. lxxvi. 10). God displays His glory, while "from seeming evil still educing good." *Tyrants and evil rulers God's scourge to a guilty land.* The terrible and destructive thunderstorm the purifier of the atmosphere. The rainbow the offspring of the dark cloud behind it. The grandest scenery the product of earth's terrible convulsions. The stars shine out most brilliantly from the blackest sky. Deep shadows give effect to the picture—an occasional discord to the music. Old and fractured instruments often yield the sweetest tones. Wicked hands the agencies in man's redemption (Acts ii. 23).

VI. Reflections on his own pitiful condition (verses 25—35).

1. *The rapid termination of his prosperity and his life* (verse 25). "Now my days are (or, have been) swifter than a post (or, runner,—a state-courier carrying letters or despatches, sometimes travelling a hundred and fifty miles in less than twenty-four hours; dromedaries, able to outrun the fleetest horses, also employed (Esther viii. 14); they flee (or, have fled) away; they see (or, have seen) no good." Job had not reached the meridian of life. Lived after his troubles a hundred and forty years. His present age probably not more than the half of that. His death, which appeared at hand, therefore sadly premature. His past prosperity accordingly short-lived. In the presence of his now accumulated miseries, his days appear to have witnessed no happiness. *Present misery apt to make us overlook past mercy.* Two more comparisons to represent

the swiftness with which his life had sped to its close—(1) A reed-skiff or canoe, formed of the papyrus or the Nile, remarkable for its lightness and swiftness (verse 26). "They are (or have) passed away as the swift ships" (*margin,* "ships of desire," or, "ships of Ebeh;" more probably "ships of papyrus," like Is. xviii. 2.) (2) An eagle, swiftest of birds, eagerly pouncing down on its prey. "As the eagle hasteth," &c. A frequent comparison. (See Deut. xxviii. 49; Jer. iv. 13; Sam. iv. 19.)

Human Life a Voyage.

Each individual's life fitly compared to a swift sailing vessel speeding onwards on her voyage.—1. *Constant and rapid progress.* No stoppage till we reach the place of destination.—2. The *precise length of the voyage various* in each case.—3. The *length of the voyage and the time of its termination previously unknown.*—4. The *voyage a most important one to each.* All others comparatively insignificant. Its issue an eternity of happiness or woe.—5. The *freight an immortal spirit* with boundless capacities.—6. The *place of destination* one or other of *only two,* widely remote from each other in character and situation—a paradise of bliss and a home of glory, or a region of darkness and despair.—7. *Each vessel under the direction of an invisible power that presides at the helm.* The helmsman in each case, either the Prince of Life, or the Prince of Darkness. The object of the former is to steer the vessel to glory; that of the latter to wreck it on the shores of death. The first human vessel launched with the former at the helm. Man listening to the flattering proposals of the latter accepted him for his pilot. Since then human life has been started under the influence of the Prince of Darkness, the "god of this world." The choice made by Adam of a pilot, confirmed by his offspring who are born in his likeness. Man might have been hopelessly left to his miserable and ungrateful choice. Mercy, however, places again within his reach a change of pilots. The Prince of Life, having atoned for man's rebellion, offers again to take charge of the vessel. Conscious of their sin and misery, many thankfully accept His offer and safely reach the port of peace. Others, rejecting it, are wrecked on the rocks of eternal ruin.—Two important questions—(1) *Whither am I bound?* For heaven or for hell? (2) *Who is my pilot?* Christ or the Wicked One?

2. *The inability of his efforts to overcome his heaviness* (verses 27, 28). "If I say, I will forget my complaint (lay aside my lamentation); I will leave off my heaviness and comfort myself (or, I will put away my

sorrowful countenance and brighten up), I am afraid of all my sorrow (—I shudder at my accumulated griefs). I know that thou wilt not hold (or, treat me as) innocent" (whatever I may be or may deem myself). A painful struggle between the enlightened spirit, and the flesh aided by the depressing nature of disease and the buffetings of the invisible adversary. Similar struggle in David—"Why art thou cast down?" &c. (Ps. xlii. 5, 11; xliii. 5). *The believer often conscious that he ought to rejoice when unbelief forbids him.* Much more under the New than the Old Testament to make a child of God "lay aside his sorrowful countenance and brighten up." To "rejoice in the Lord" in the midst of trials, made much easier now than in the days of Job. The aim of Jesus to give his people ground to "rejoice in tribulation," (John xiv. 27; xv. 11; xvi. 33). Enjoined on them (Phil. iv. 1). Their actual experience (Rom. v. 3; 1 Pet. i. 6). Job kept from "brightening up" by the thought that, though *conscious of innocence,* God would still hold and treat him as *guilty.* The believer able now to rejoice in the thought that, though *conscious of guilt,* God for Christ's sake will hold and treat him as *innocent,* making him accepted in the beloved."

3. *His despair of being able to obtain acquittance with God* (verse 29). "If I be wicked (or simply, 'I am,' or 'shall be wicked;' *i.e.,* must be held and treated as such), why then labour I in vain" [to maintain a good conscience or attempt to prove my innocence]? A hard and unbelieving thought of God, suggested by his own carnal nature, and by the enemy who sought to bring him to curse his Maker as arbitrary, tyrannical, and unjust. Satan's old trade (Gen. iii. 1, 4, 5). The bitter and ungenerous thought too fondly dwelt upon by Job. Perhaps some secret consciousness of inward corruption, and of the truth as regarded himself (verse 30). "If I wash myself with snow-water (the purest to be got), and make my hands never so clean (or, 'cleanse my hands with lye'—used with oil instead of soap), yet shalt thou plunge me in the ditch (or pit), and mine own clothes shall abhor me" (*margin,* "make me to be abhorred"). The idea: All my attempts to make my heart and life pure will with Thee be utterly vain,—Thou wilt still regard me as impure and abominable. The thought probably suggested by—(1) his conscious endeavours to maintain purity of heart and life; (2) his treatment at God's hands being such as apparently to indicate the Divine condemnation. *Should* have been awakened by—(1) Conscious corruption; (2) Apprehension of the Divine purity. So Isaiah (Is. vi. 5). So Job himself afterwards (ch. xl. 4; xlii. 5, 6). The language probably now dictated by peevishness and bitterness. Yet true, though in a different sense from that intended. All man's attempts to justify and purify himself before God in vain. He still remains wicked, guilty, and abominable in the sight of a holy God. Man, as a fallen child of Adam, in his very nature corrupt and opposed to God. All self-attempts leave his nature unchanged and polluting all his actions. Such attempts themselves only the offspring of pride and self-righteousness, therefore abominable. Humility and love the only things in a creature acceptable to God. Man's self-attempts leave him destitute of both. Guilt not to be effaced but by an atonement, or satisfaction to Divine justice. The waters of the ocean unable to wash out a single blood-spot of guilt. Only Almighty power able to remove the leopard's spots or whiten the Ethiopian's skin. In Christ provision made both for the removal of guilt and impurity. His blood removes the one, His Spirit's grace the other. From His pierced side came forth both "blood and water" (John xix. 34; John v. 6, 8). The true posture of each fallen child of man in Luke xviii. 13. The prayer (Ps. li. 7). The invitation (Is. i. 18). The promise (Ez. xxxvi. 25). The acceptance (1 John i. 7. The thanksgiving (Rev. i. 5). A gracious plunging of the self-purified into the ditch, in the Divinely awakened consciousness of guilt and corruption. Saul carefully washed at Jerusalem; blessedly plunged in the ditch at Damascus (Acts ix. 9—11; xxvi. 4, 5).

4. *Job's inability to plead his cause before God* (verse 32). "For he is not a man as I am, that I should answer him [as defendant at the bar], and that we should come together in judgment" [to plead our respective causes]. Job thinks he has a case against God, as God appears to have one against him. Wishes he could have them tried, but feels that the distance between him and God precludes the thought (verse 33). "Neither is there any daysman betwixt us (*margin,* "one that should argue;" or, "an umpire;" properly, an arbitrator with authority to restrain each party, and to bind them to his decision) that might lay his hand [authoritatively] upon us both." Hence the supposed impossibility of an equal contest. What Job desiderated has, in a much better sense, been provided for sinful man. A daysman, or Mediator, has been found in the person of Jesus Christ—the fellow both of God and man (Zech. xiii. 7). Not to afford man an opportunity of vainly pleading his innocence against God, but of humbly acknowledging his guilt and obtaining mercy (1 John ii;

1 Tim. ii. 5, 6). Job imagines he could make good his case but for the Divine power and majesty that overawe him (verse 34). "Let him take his rod away from me (—his power, and perhaps the effect of it, his affliction), and let not his fear (or terrible majesty) rrify me. Then, would I speak and not ar him: but it is not so with me" (*margin* but I am not so with myself;" or, "for I am not so in mind,"—as to fear him in the controversy from any consciousness of guilt). The fear of the Divine majesty the common feeling of humanity. Even the seraphim cover their faces with their wings before God. The doors of the temple and the foundations of Sinai shook at His presence.

"A fearful thing to fall into the hands of the living God." The "rod" of God seen removed in the person and work of Him who was "meek and lowly in heart," and who "suffered for our sins, the Just one in the room of the unjust." The rays of Divine majesty softened in the God-man, Christ Jesus. The Father seen in him who was the "man of sorrows" (John xiv. 9). Jesus the way to the Father. Through Him we enter with boldness into the holiest of all (John xiv. 6; Heb. x. 19—22). Christ the true Jacob's ladder. The foot on the earth, and the top reaching to heaven (John i. 51; Gen. xxviii. 12).

CHAPTER X.

JOB'S REPLY TO BILDAD—CONTINUED.

His speech takes the form rather of an expostulation with God in regard to his afflictions. The vehemence of his spirit reaches its height in this chapter. Does not renounce God, but takes great liberty in addressing Him. The liberty, however, rather that of a child with a father whose clouded and averted face he can neither understand nor endure.

I. His impatience of life, and his resolution to give free vent to his complaints (verse 1).
"My soul is weary of (or, 'loathes,' or 'bursts in') my life; I will leave my complaint upon myself (I will give loose reins to my complaint): I will speak," &c. The language of a deeply distressed and even desperate man. Contrasted with Ps. xxxix. 1, and Lam. iii. 39; and especially with New Testament experience (Phil. iv. 5—7; Rom. v. 3; 1 Pet. i. 6—8). In Job's words we have—(1) *An unhappy state of mind allowed*—"My soul is weary of my life." So Rebekah (Gen. xxvii. 46); Elijah (1 Kings xix. 4); and Jonah (iv. 38). Believers in trouble are to possess their souls in patience. A mind stayed on God is kept "in perfect peace."—(2) *An unwise resolution formed*—"I will leave my complaint upon myself, &c." Safer and wiser to check than to indulge complaints regarding God's dealings with us. *The impatience of the flesh makes men sit under Elijah's juniper tree and Jonah's gourd.* Yet a troubled soul, familiar with God, pours out its complaints into His ear without sin (Ps. xlii. 6—11). Life in itself a mercy; yet sometimes would be little better than hell but for the hopes of heaven [*Trapp*].

II. His desire not to be treated as guilty, without knowing the grounds of it (verse 2).
"I will say unto God." Implies—(1) *Deep distress*, extorting the language. (2) *A childlike confidence and freedom towards God.* (3) *Peevishness and want of reverence.*—"Do not condemn me" (or, treat me as a guilty person). *A father's displeasure is a generous child's greatest grief.* A single sin sufficient to make us guilty before God (James ii. 10; Gal. iii. 10). Only one way for a sinner to be freed from condemnation (Rom. viii. 1, 34). Christ the Righteous suffers in the place of the condemned sinner (2 Cor. v. 21). A believer, however, still sometimes either *really* or *apparently* under God's displeasure (Isa. liv. 7—9; lvii. 17—18).—"Show me wherefore thou contendest with me." Job's trial, that God seemed to have a controversy with him while he was ignorant of the cause. *A spiritually enlightened man apprehends God has a controversy with him when there is none; an unrenewed man does not believe in it when it actually exists.*—With different classes and individuals God may have various

Grounds of Controversy.

1. With *nations and unconverted men.* The grounds—(1) Rebellion against his authority; (2) Unthankfulness for His mercies; (3) Apostacy from His religion; (4) Persecution of His cause and people; (5) Contempt of His ordinances; (6) Rejection of His Son.

2. With *churches and individual Christians.* The grounds may be—(1) Departure from

first love (Rev. ii. 4, 5); (2) Formality and hypocrisy (Rev. iii. 1); (3) Pride and self-satisfaction (Rev. iii. 1—7); (4) Lukewarmness (Rev. iii. 15, 16); (5) Unfaithfulness and unfruitfulness (John xv. 2); (6) Covetousness and wordly-mindedness (Is. lvii. 17). Troubles laid on believers may be—(1) On account of *past or present sin ;* (2) For *trial and manifestation of grace ;* (3) For *purification and spiritual growth ;* (4) For *exhibition of Divine support.*

III. **Appeal to God against His present treatment** (verses 3—12). The grounds of this appeal :
1. *Its inconsistency with God's nature and honour* (verse 3). "Is it good unto thee that thou shouldst oppress, that thou shouldst despise the work of thine hands, and shine upon the counsel of the wicked?" Three things apparently involved in Job's afflictions :—(1) Oppression on the part of God; (2) Contempt of His own works; (3) Countenance given to the sentiments and practice of ungodly men who deny His providence if not His very existence, and maintain the uselessness of religion. In Job's case there appeared no ground for such severe treatment. Though God's own creature, he seemed to be treated as unworthy of regard. As a religious man, his great afflictions might give occasion to the ungodly to harden themselves in their irreligion. All this is inconsistent with God's nature and honour. God's nature is love. A God of truth and without iniquity. Afflicts none willingly. Despises not any. Ungodliness His abomination. Observe :—(1) *God's procedure sometimes apparently at variance with His nature and character.* (2) *That inconsistency only in appearance.* God cannot act but in accordance with His nature, which is love and light, goodness, purity, and justice. (3) *God's glory and honour involved in His dealings with His creatures, and especially with His servants.* (4) *God's nature and character a rock for our feet under the most trying dispensations.*
2. *God's Omniscience* (verse 4). "Hast thou eyes of flesh? or seest thou as man seeth?" (Verse 7) "Thou knowest that I am not wicked." Conscious of innocence we can appeal to Divine omniscience for a favourable verdict. Man looks on the outward appearance ; God's eyes penetrate the heart (1 Sam. xvi. 7). Man deceived by appearances. Sees imperfectly into character and conduct. Requires lengthened observation to arrive at the truth. Often swayed by passion and partiality. God takes all into one view at once (Acts xv. 18). His eyes a flame of fire (Rev. i. 14). His servants' character and conduct often misjudged

by men. Perfectly known to God. Job's comfort (ch. xvi. 19 ; xxiii. 10). His trial that his friends read his character in his sufferings. His Antitype similarly misjudged (Is. liii. 4 ; John vii. 23). *God's* knowledge of Job's innocence already shewn in the history. Job's *own* knowledge of it as yet only from his own consciousness. This consciousness his confidence towards God. "If our hearts condemn us not," &c. (1 John iii. 21). Job a sinner, but not a "wicked" sinner. Sinned not deliberately and from choice. Not guilty of hypocrisy and secret sin. Not to love sin or allow ourselves in it, is with God not to sin at all (1 John iii. 6, 8, 9).
3. *God's eternity* (verse 5). "Are thy days as the days of man? Are thy years as man's days?" [God's eternity marked by "*years*" in contrast with man's days.] (Verse 6).—"That thou inquirest after mine iniquity, and searchest after my sin." Short-lived man requires haste to investigate and punish crime. His few years afford him but few opportunities of fully ascertaining character. The judge may die or the criminal escape. God's eternity excludes all need of haste, and secures all opportunity for knowledge. No need with God of torture to elicit confession. The severity, rapid succession, and long continuance of Job's afflictions, apparently inconsistent with this.
4. *His omnipotence* (verse 7). "Thou knowest (or, 'Although thou knowest'—*margin*,—'It is upon thy knowledge ') that I am not wicked, and there is (or, 'and that there is ') none that can deliver out of thine hand." No fear of a *rescue* on behalf of God's prisoners. Hence no need of vehement urgency in inflicting punishment. Solemn truth for the impenitent. "How shall we escape," &c? (Heb. ii. 3). "Consider this, all ye that forget God," &c. (Ps. l. 22). Precious comfort for Christ's sheep. None able to pluck them out of his hand (John x. 29, 30).
5. *His relation to man as his Creator* (verse 8). "Thine hands have made me (or, 'elaborated me,'—*margin*, 'took pains with me'), and fashioned (—exquisitely moulded and adorned) me together round about (—every part of me) ; yet thou dost destroy me." Powerful plea. Workmen respect their own work. The more pains bestowed, the more regard will be shown. The heavens the work of God's *fingers ;* man the work of his "hands." Man the most exquisite piece of Divine workmanship even in his body, still more in his soul, most of all in the union of both. The "human face Divine" an example of this exquisite moulding and adorning. The head apparently designed by nature as the cupola to the most glorious of her works [*Addison*]. Galen, the physician, converted

to the belief of a Divine Creator by the wisdom displayed in the structure of the human frame. Man God's glory as His work in creation; still more as his work in redemption (Is. xxix. 23; xlv. 11; lx. 21).

6. *Man's frailty and mortality* (verse 9). "Remember, I beseech thee, that thou hast made me as the clay; and wilt thou (or, thou wilt) bring me unto dust again?" Reference to the Creation, and to the sentence pronounced on man at the Fall. Similar terms to those in Gen. ii. 7, and iii. 19. Written documents or traditionary records of the events probably then in existence, and afterwards employed by Moses. Man's frail and shortlived existence used by Job as a plea for milder treatment. Similar plea in Ps. lxxxix. 47. An availing one with God (Ps. ciii. 14; Gen. vi. 3). God's nature compassion. Our frailty pleads with God for forbearance, with man himself for earnestness (Eccles. ix. 10).

7. *God's kindness already manifested.* (1) In our *conception* (verse 10). "Hast thou not poured me out as milk, and curdled me like cheese?" God the careful and beneficent Agent in our conception (Ps. cxxxix. 15, 16; Eccles. xi. 5). The process of nature in the womb His own, as instituted, sustained and controlled by Him. Milk coagulated into cheese an image of the formation of the embryo of the future man. (2) In the *growth of the fœtus* (verse 11). "Thou hast clothed me with skin and flesh, and fenced me with bones and sinews." The development of the embryo another of God's mysterious and beneficent operations. The order in the text that of Nature,—first the skin, then the flesh, lastly the harder parts gradually added. Among other important purposes, "bones and sinews" serve for protection to the more vital parts. (3) In the bestowment of *life* (verse 12). "Thou has granted me life." Life imparted to the embryo in the womb as a gift of God. Natural life a precious gift; how much more spiritual and eternal! That life also originally imparted to man, but lost in Adam (Rom. v. 17; 1 Cor. xv. 21). Restored in Christ who is the Life (John xiv. 6; xi. 25; 1 Cor. xv. 21; Rom. v. 17, 21; 1 John v. 11, 12. (4) In the *favour and kindness accompanying life.* "Life and favour." The kindness of God visible in every stage of our natural life. Conspicuous in infancy. "Cast upon him from the womb." Kindly watched over in a long-continued period of helplessness. Beneficent provision made in parental affection. Each individual the recipient of ten thousand mercies every day he lives. Divine goodness smiles on us in every sunbeam, and fans in every breeze. (5) In the continued *preservation of life.* "And thy visitation (provi-

dential care) hath preserved my spirit." Natural life preserved by a careful and watchful Providence. The hand that put the heart in motion sustains its pulsations. Provides the means necessary for life's support. The petition answered even before it is offered—"Give us this day our daily bread." Protects life and organs from constantly surrounding dangers. An unseen hand averts a thousand accidents each day we live. The *mind* preserved from derangement and disease as well as the body. The same Divine care that protected the brain, the seat of life and thought, by a strong, spherical, bony skull, still continued in preserving the spirit. Sleep, as needful for the mind as the body, the daily gift of a beneficent Providence.—An object of so much regard not likely to be soon despised or lightly cast away. Neither natural nor becoming for so much kindness to terminate in cruelty.

IV. Complaints against God and His procedure (verses 13—18).

1. *That his sufferings were in God's secret purpose amidst all His past kindness* (verse 13). "And these things hast thou hid in thine heart; I know that this is with thee." The comfort of believers that all events in our lot are part of God's secret counsel (Ps. cxxxix. 16; Eccles. iii. 14). A truth of natural religion that what God does in time He purposed in eternity (Acts xv. 18). Necessary and desirable in a Being infinite, eternal, and unchangeable; omnipresent, omniscient, and almighty; holy, wise, and good. Job's predetermined afflictions in *his* view an apparent contradiction to God's former kindness. Life seemed given only to make him miserable. Such ungenerous thoughts his own infirmity. God neither fickle nor cruel. All things made, according to His purpose, to work together for good to them that love Him (Rom. viii. 28). Predestined sufferings no contradiction to experienced kindness. Joseph's imprisonment under a false abominable charge was in God's secret counsel while delivering him from the pit and placing him in Potiphar's palace. Observe—(1) *The nature of the flesh is to put a wrong construction upon God's dealings.* (2) *The object of Satan is to misrepresent God, as arbitrary, cruel and tyrannical.* (3) *Hard thoughts of God a special temptation in time of trouble.*

2. *Complains of God's excessive strictness in marking and punishing offences* (verse 14). "If I sin (rather, 'have sinned'), then Thou markest (or hast marked) me, and Thou wilt not acquit me from mine iniquity." This perhaps the secret counsel complained of in preceding verse. In ignorance Job views his afflictions as the effect of God's strictness in

marking his sin. As yet no frank and humble confession. Observe—(1) *Sin often brought to mind in time of affliction.* (2) *As a fact, the sins of God's children often visited when those of others are not so.* (3) *The views of the flesh in regard to God always perverted.* According to the flesh, God is either—(1) Indifferent to men's conduct; soft and indulgent to their sins; or (2) Stern and inexorable; strict in marking and punishing every offence. (4) *In a believer, the flesh speaks at one time, and the spirit at another.* Job's present language uttered under the promptings of Satan. Yet, in itself, in a certain sense true, as (1) *Men's sins are observed and marked by God.* Men judged at last "out of those things which are written in the books." For every idle word account to be given in the day of judgment. Men receive according to the things done in the body—good or bad. The secrets of men to be one day judged by Jesus Christ (Rom. ii. 16). Every evil work and secret thing to be brought into judgment. (2) *The guilty by no means acquitted by God.* Yet *sin is forgiven and the guilty are pardoned.* The gracious provision of the scheme of Redemption. *Through the substitution and satisfaction of Christ, God can punish and yet pardon.* God a just God and yet a Saviour; just and the justifier of the ungodly that believe in Jesus. Millions of sins forgiven, yet not one unpunished. The iniquities of men laid on the one righteous man, Christ Jesus. The Just One "bruised and put to grief" as a sacrifice for the sins of the unjust. The guiltless takes the place of the guilty, and the guilty that of the guiltless (2 Cor. v. 21). The blood of Jesus able to cleanse from all sin, because the blood of God's Son (1 John i. 7). Every sin marked against the sinner answered and atoned for by the Surety. The only thing now required for the sinner's pardon is his humble and hearty acceptance of the Substitute. God is satisfied with the Surety. It only remains that the sinner be so too. Confessing his guilt and accepting the Substitute, he is at once forgiven (1 John i. 9, 12). Observe—(1) *The peculiarity of the Gospel age is that its provision is revealed with a clearness and fulness before unknown.* (2) *The Gospel a blessed contradiction to the latter part of Job's present utterance.* The *Law* declares, God cannot and will not acquit the guilty; the *Gospel* points to Calvary and says, the guiltless One became the guilty and suffered the penalty. (3) *The sinner who refuses the Surety retains his guilt, and suffers himself the punishment of it.*

3. *Complains of being treated as he is though a righteous man* (verse 15). "If I be wicked (—sin deliberately; or, 'be guilty') woe unto me: if I be righteous, yet will I

(or may I) not lift up my head." A dictate of natural religion that the guilty transgressor must be punished. "This man is a murderer whom vengeance suffereth not to live" (Acts xxviii. 4). Also the teaching of nature that the just man may lift up his head with confidence and joy. "Be just, and fear not." None, however, *in himself,* able to do this *before God.* The most upright still guilty in God's sight. Standing *righteous in Christ,* a man lifts up his head before God. Job unable at present to do this—(1) As not realizing his standing in the Surety; (2) Keeping his eyes on his affliction; (3) His sufferings, according to the popular view, seemed to proclaim him a guilty man.—" I am full (or, 'being full') of confusion (reproach or ignominy); therefore see thou (or, 'seeing as I do') mine affliction." Job's other trials greatly aggravated by reproaches from his friends. Confusion, perplexity and shame, natural results of his affliction, especially in the time in which he lived. A natural tendency to judge of a man from his circumstances. An aggravation to a good man's sufferings, that himself and religion are misjudged from them. Hence Paul's anxiety in regard to his sufferings as an apostle (Eph. iii. 13; 2 Tim. i. 8). Himself not ashamed of them (2 Tim. i. 12).

4. *Complains that his sufferings only increased in number and intensity.* Three trying circumstances in Job's afflictions. (1) Their *continual increase* from the commencement (verse 16). "For it increaseth" (rears itself up like a swelling wave; or, "should it [my head] lift itself up"). Terrible climax in Job's sufferings. Commenced with loss of oxen and asses, and increased to extreme bodily affliction, inward darkness, and apprehension of Divine wrath. Probably his disease itself increased in violence as it continued. (2) Their *intensity.* "Thou huntest me as a fierce lion; and again thou showest thyself marvellous upon me?" God's purpose seemed to be to hunt him down as a dangerous animal; or as if He Himself were a fierce lion intent on tearing him to pieces, as Is. xxxviii. 13; Hos. v. 14, xiii. 7; Ps. l. 22. His afflictions appeared like a display of what God could inflict. His plagues made wonderful (Deut. xxviii. 59). (3) Their *variety* and *constant change* (verse 17). "Thou renewest thy witnesses (or, 'weapons;' margin, 'plagues') against me; and increasest thine indignation upon me; changes and war (or, 'successions and a host,' *i.e.,* one host succeeding another) are against me." God appeared to be employing all his weapons against him, each attack a fresh "witness" produced to confront and confound him as a guilty man. One troop of troubles seemed only to succeed another, equally bent on his

destruction. Observe—(1.) *A child of God views all his troubles as from the Divine hand.* (2.) *This often an exaggeration rather than an alleviation of them.* (3.) *A fearful thing to fall into the hands of the living God.* (4.) *Blessed to have God for a friend, terrible to have him for an enemy.* (5.) *Believers not to be staggered at the heaviest troubles succeeding each other.* (6.) *No troubles to a believer but what a Father's love permits and a Father's hand metes out.*

V. A piteous lament (verses 18—22) embraces—

(1) *A regret that he had ever been born, or permitted to live* (verses 18, 19). "Wherefore then hast Thou brought me out of the womb? O that I had given up the ghost, and no eye had seen me! I should have been as though I had not been ; I should have been carried from the womb to the grave." The feeling and thoughts of his first outburst return upon him (ch. iii. 10—16). An advance in the complaint ; his birth directly ascribed to God, and charged upon him as an evil. The idea of God extracting the infant from the womb familiar in the Psalms, as Ps. xxii. 9 ; lxxi. 6. With David a matter of praise ; with Job one of regret. *Unbelief and passion cast reproach on the Author both of our being and our well-being.* Job has long ago regretted the blindness and haste which dictated these irreverent and ungrateful words.

2. *An impassioned request for a short relief from suffering, on the grounds of his speedy departure* (verse 20). "Are not my days few? Cease then, and let me alone ; that I may take comfort (brighten up, as ch. ix. 27) a little before I go." Same sentiment in the conclusion of his reply to Eliphaz (ch. vii. 19, 21). Observe—(1) *A saint, though sad and sinning, cannot be restrained from praying.* The flesh only lifts up its voice when that of the spirit is silent. The boon of a short relief testifies the depth of Job's distress. (2) *Brief respite in suffering a mercy to the sufferer.* Enables him—(i.) To rally his strength ; (ii.) To collect his thoughts ; (iii.) To recover calmness ; (iv.) To prepare himself for further suffering. (3) *Terrible doom of the lost, which admits of no such respite* (Luke xvi. 24 ; Mark ix. 44 ; Rev. xiv. 10, 11.)

3. Gloomy description of the

State of the Dead

as viewed by Old Testament saints (verses 21, 22).

1. A place of *perpetual exile* (verses 21). "I go whence I shall not return ; a land," &c. Viewed as a land or country ; its in-

habitants the shades or spirits 'of deceased men. Hence the sublime description in Is. xiv. 9, 10 ; Ez. xxxii. 21. A land from which is no return to the present world.

2. A place *without attraction.* Return from it to the present world desirable, but not practicable. Much inferior to the present life for enjoyment. Banishment to it an evil. Hence Hezekiah's sorrow and regret at the prospect of having so soon to enter it (Is. xxxviii. 3—18).

3. A place of *confusion and disorder* (verse 22). "Without any order." (1) No distinction of classes, as on earth. [Hence David's prayer, Ps. xxvi. 9.] A place of indiscriminate gathering (1 Sam. xxviii. 19). (2) No pleasing vicissitude of day and night, summer and winter. (3) No beauty or orderly arrangement. Chaotic confusion, as on the earth before the six day's creation (Gen. i. 2). (4) No exercise of religious worship. No praise or thanksgiving. This part of the prospect especially deplored by the godly (Ps. vi. 5 ; xxx. 9 ; lxxxviii. 10—12 ; cxv. 17 ; Is. xxxviii. 18).

4. A place of *darkness and gloom* (verse 21). "The land of darkness and the shadow of death," &c. A funeral pall of midnight darkness ever resting on it. Any light that penetrates it only darkness,—"The light is as darkness." The view probably borrowed from the places of Oriental sepulture, subterranean grottoes. The darkness of these sepulchral chambers transferred to the spirit-world. The experience of the disembodied spirit supposed to bear affinity to the circumstances of the body. The Sun of righteousness had not yet irradiated the world beyond the grave. The Forerunner in human nature had not yet entered within the veil. A blissful Paradise, as a home for the disembodied just, not yet known. The doctrine of a happy intermediate state reserved for the teaching of Him who is the Way, the Truth, and the Life. Perhaps the enjoyment of it reserved for the time when He Himself should return to glory, having finished the work of our Redemption (Luke xxiii. 43). It was left for Jesus to dispel the darkness that brooded over the spirit-world, and show beyond the grave the hills of celestial bliss. Life and immortality brought to light by Jesus Christ through the Gospel (2 Tim. i. 10). Jesus carried light into the darksome grave and world beyond—(1) By His teachings (Luke xvi. 22 ; xxiii. 43 ; John xiv. 2). (2) By His death, resurrection, and ascension into heaven. By His lying in the grave He has left there a perpetual light for the comfort of all His dying people [*Caryl*]. *Blessed contrast between the prospect of death to believers now, and that to those of Old Testament times.* The kingdom of heaven with all

its glory and beauty, its joy and song, its inhabitants and employments, opened to believers by the death and resurrection of Jesus. Instead of the dreary and confused abode of half-conscious spirits, the world beyond is now the believer's bright and happy home in his Father's house. Jesus has taught believers joyously to sing on the bed of death, as well as amid the enjoyments of life: "Yonder's my house and portion fair," &c. Hence a threefold duty lying on New Testament believers:—(1) Thankfulness; (2) Joyfulness; (3) Heavenly-mindedness.

CHAPTER XI.

FIRST SPEECH OF ZOPHAR.

Zophar follows in the same train with his companions. Misled by the same false principle—great sufferings prove great sins—he acts the part, not of a comforter, but of a reprover and an exhorter.

I. **His reason for speaking** (verses 2—4).
"Should not the multitude of words be answered?" &c. His reason involves Job's censure. Bitterly reproves him—(1) As a *mere talker* (verse 2). "Should a man full of talk be justified?" (2) As a *vain and lying boaster* (verse 3). "Should thy lies make men hold their peace?" (3) *As a proud despiser of others*; "When thou mockest, shall no man make thee ashamed?" (4) As a *self-righteous pretender to perfection*, both in his principle and his practice (verse 4). "For thou hast said, my doctrine (speech, teaching, principles) is pure, and I am clean in thine eyes." Observe—(1) *Even good men can speak and act towards others like the carnal and unconverted*. (2) *Religious professors very often misunderstand and misjudge God's tried people*. (3) *Believers' greatest trials sometimes from their own brethren in the faith*. Christ a *merciful* as well as *faithful* High Priest, touched with the feeling of our infirmities (Heb. ii. 17, 18; iv. 15).

II. **Zophar desiderates Divine teaching for Job's conviction** (verse 5).
"But oh that God would speak, and open his lips against thee!" God speaks with a strong hand (Is. viii. 11). "None teacheth like Him." Such teaching needed alike by saint and sinner. Necessary—(1) for conviction; (2) for consolation. Divine teaching imparts—(1) the knowledge of ourselves; (2) the knowledge of God. God opens his lips—(1) "*against*" the sinner, for his conviction; (2) *for* him, for his consolation. "Spake in time past to the fathers in divers manners." Speaks now—(1) In His Word; (2) By His Spirit. The Spirit's office to convince the world of sin, righteousness, and judgment (John xvi. 8). The Word of God sharper than any two-edged sword—a discerner of the thoughts and intents of the heart. Its office to pierce, to the dividing asunder of soul and spirit, joints and marrow (Heb. iv. 12).—Two things desired as the result of Divine teaching in Job's case; both important for shutting the mouths of complainers against God:—
1. *The discovery of God's transcendent and unsearchable wisdom* (verse 6). "That he would shew thee the secrets (hidden depths) of wisdom, that they are double to that which is" (or, "for they are manifold," or "there are doublings,"—complications or intricacies—"in his understanding").—*All complaints against the Divine procedure and our own lot proceed from ignorance of God's designs*. "What I do thou knowest not now." God's judgments a great deep. His way in the sea. "Depth of riches," both in "the wisdom and knowledge of God." His ways past finding out, yet all just and true. God not to be traced but trusted. "Judge not the Lord by feeble sense," &c.
2. *The discovery of Job's own sinfulness as much greater than his sufferings*. "Know therefore that God exacteth of thee less than thine iniquity deserveth" (or "consign to oblivion in thy favour," or "remits to thee [a part] of thy iniquity," or "punishment"). True, even in Job's case, on *the supposition that his sufferings were the punishment of his sins*. Any affliction in this life only a part of what all sin deserves. *The rich man in torments probably no worse than his neighbours* (Luke xvi. 19—23). His sin not even mentioned by the Saviour. Probably only *worldliness and self-indulgence*, with its natural consequence, *heedlessness of the wants and woes of others*. His belly and the world his God. To offend in one point of God's law makes a man guilty of all. Sin, knowingly committed, nothing less than *rebellion against God*; causeless anger and hatred against another, equivalent in God's sight to *murder*. Each subjects a man to the penalty of hell-fire (Matt. v. 22; 1 John iii. 15). Covetousness a species of idolatry (Eph. v. 5; Col. iii. 5). Earth a place of mercy and forbearance. The full punishment of sin reserved for another state.

III. Zophar chides Job's presumption, and enlarges on the unsearchableness of the Almighty (verses 7—9).

"Canst thou by searching find out God" (or, "wilt thou find out the search," or "deep wisdom" of God ?) Canst thou find out the Almighty unto perfection (or "wilt thou find out perfectly," or "penetrate to the perfection of the Almighty ?") It is as high as heaven (*margin*, "the heights of heaven"); what canst thou do [in attaining to it, viz., the deep wisdom or perfection of the Almighty], deeper than hell (Sheol, or Hades, the invisible spirit-world, supposed to be in the lower parts of the earth), what canst thou know? (or how wilt thou understand it ?) The measure thereof is longer than the earth and broader than the sea." Poetical description of the Divine wisdom and knowledge, and in general of

The Unsearchableness of God.

God unsearchable to finite creatures—
1. In His *Person*. His Nature or Essence beyond creature ken. As easy for an insect to comprehend man's nature as for man to comprehend his Creator's. The more the Grecian sage studied the question, what is God? the more he felt himself lost in it. Hence the altar of Athens with the inscription: To the Unknown God. In God is both "that which may be known," and which may *not* be known (Rom. i. 19). *That* He is, and *what* He is, may be known; *how* He is, and *how far* He is, is beyond a creature's capacity to know. God capable of being *apprehended*, but not of being *comprehended*. A little child may *apprehend* God; a seraph cannot *comprehend* Him. God is incomprehensible in His mode of being as the *One God*; still more as the *Three in One*. To know *that* God is and *what* He is, is necessary for an intelligent creature's *happiness*: to know *how* He is, were it possible, could only gratify his *curiosity*. God only known as He is pleased to reveal Himself. Reveals Himself—(1) In His works ; (2) In the human consciousness ; (3) In His word; (4) Most of all in His Son Jesus Christ. Christ the image of the invisible God; He that hath seen *Him* hath seen the Father (Col. i. 15 ; John xiv. 9). The incarnation, life, and death of Jesus Christ,—the final, full and authentic exhibition of the Divine character and perfections. Eternal life, to know the only true God and Jesus Christ whom He hath sent (John xvii. 3).
2. His *Perfections*. God's Perfections or Attributes are—(1) *Natural* or essential, as His Omniscience and Omnipotence; (2) *Moral*, as His justice and goodness. God unsearchable in both kinds. The universe a

theatre for the display of His perfections. A God everywhere present, and everywhere working,—sustaining the vibrations of an animalcule and the revolutions of a planet; watching over a sparrow, and giving orders to an archangel; and doing all in infinite wisdom, and justice, and goodness,—may well be unsearchable.
3. In His *Purposes*. The history of the world and of the universe, as well as of each individual, the evolution of these purposes (Acts xv. 18 ; ii. 23). His purposes unsearchable (Rom. xi. 33 ; Ps. xcii. 5). "Deep in unfathomable mines," &c.
4. In His *Performances*. God unsearchable in His works of creation. Examples : The contents of a drop of stagnant water, as examined with a microscope ; the starry heavens, as seen through Lord Rosse's telescope. Modern astronomy gives a meaning to the "heights of heaven" undreamt of in the days of Zophar. Geology, on the other hand, reveals displays of Divine power and wisdom in extinct worlds or creations far beneath our feet.
5. In His *Procedure*. God's dealings in providence both in regard to angels and men, the human race and the individuals composing it, unsearchable. Evil permitted in His own universe. The incarnation and death of His own Son an atonement for it. Man the object of that merciful provision ; sinning angels excluded from its benefit.

Lessons from the unsearchableness of God :—
1. *Modesty and humility* in judging of God's person or perfections, His works or His ways.
2. *Submission to His will*, and acquiescence in His providence.
3. *Implicit trust* in His wisdom and goodness.
4. *Reverential, loving, and admiring* adoration. The result of the contemplation of God's works and ways in the apostle (Rom. xi. 33—36), and in the glorified in heaven (Rev. xv. 3, 4).

IV. Adduces God's resistless power and all-seeing eye as arguments to move Job to repentance (verse 10—12).
1. His *Almighty power* (verse 10). "If He cut off" (*margin*, "make a change," as He has done in Job and his family ; or, "if He seize" as a criminal, as He has done in Job's case), and shut up (as in prison ; or, "deliver over," *i.e.*, to an officer for trial), or gather together (an assembly or court to try the criminal)—who can hinder him ? (*margin*, "turn him away.") Awful picture of a sinner arrested by Divine justice: A sinner in the hands of an angry God ! Escape or rescue equally impossible. The only hope

of safety for a sinner lies in submission. Same sentiment uttered by Job himself (ch. ix. 4, 12, 13). Argument used by God (Ps. l. 22); by Jesus (Matt. v. 25, 26); by the Apostle (Heb. ii. 3; x. 31).

2. His *Omniscience* (ver. 12). "For He knoweth vain men; He seeth wickedness also; will He not then consider it?" Another weighty argument for a sinner's repentance. To elude God's eye as impossible as to escape from His hand. "No darkness or shadow of death where the workers of iniquity may hide themselves." "All things naked and open to the eyes of Him with whom we have to do." Further considerations, however, necessary to bring a sinner to repentance. Felix "trembled," and said to the preacher: "Go thy way for this time." Only the apprehension of the mercy of God in Christ able to soften and subdue the sinner's heart. As addressed to Job, these arguments were — (1) Inapplicable; Job not the sinner Zophar supposed. (2) Useless; Job probably more keenly sensible of these truths than Zophar himself. Arguments, in order to move and benefit, need to be not only *sound and solemn*, but *suitable and seasonable.—One important part of a preacher's duty to consider the character and condition of those whom he addresses.*— Zophar's *application of the foregoing arguments* (verse 12). "For vain man would be wise (or 'but let a vain, or empty, hollow-headed man become wise') though man be born as the wild ass's colt," (or, "and let the wild ass's colt be born a man"). The latter part of the verse, as thus read, an Arab proverb. "Wild ass," used by the Arabs as a term of reproach. Probably the whole a proverbial maxim of the ancients. Apparently an exhortation rather than a statement. Contains truth in reference to man in general.

1. *Man left to himself, ever since the fall, is "vain."* Empty of real goodness and sound spiritual understanding. "There is none that understandeth; there is none that doeth good." Even the sages of antiquity "professing themselves wise became fools" (Rom. i. 22).

2. *Man is now by nature froward and self-willed "as a wild ass's colt."* Like that animal, man's disposition is to be free and uncontrolled. The child, like the man, wishes to be its own master. "Our lips are our own. Who is lord over us?" "Who is the Lord, that I should serve Him?" "Let us break their bonds asunder, and cast away their cords from us." Frowardness, self-will, and intractableness, God's frequent complaints against Israel. "All day long have I stretched out my hand towards a disobedient and gainsaying people." "The heart of man fully set in them to do evil."

"Madness in men's hearts while they live." The constant tendency of man's fallen nature to break loose from the restraints of Divine authority. Apart from grace, man, after his hardness and impenitent heart, treasures up wrath against the day of wrath (Rom. ii. 5).

3. *A change of character and disposition necessary in order to man's well-being either here or hereafter.* The vain man must become wise. The wild ass's colt—froward, self-willed, independent—must become a man, thoughtful, submissive, obedient. The second part of Christ's call in the Gospel: "Take my yoke upon you, and learn of me, for I am meek and lowly in heart; and ye shall find rest to your souls" (Matt. xi. 29).

4. *Such a change nothing less than a new birth.* The wild ass's colt must be "born" in order to become a man. A new birth necessary to froward, self-willed, independent man, in order to his entering the kingdom of God, whether on earth or in heaven. The teaching of Jesus (John iii. 7). The promise (Ez. xxxvi. 26). The prayer (Ps. li. 10). The experience of it (Tit. iii. 5). The exhortation, as addressed to Job, was—(1) *Inapplicable.* Job neither a fool nor, except perhaps in his trouble, especially when worried by his friends, a wild ass's colt. (2). *Uncharitable,* because inappropriate. "Charity thinketh no evil; hopeth all things." (3). *Rude.* No part of wisdom in a preacher or monitor to apply harsh terms and ill names, even indirectly. "Be courteous." Hearers neither to be flattered on the one hand nor libelled on the other. (4). *Unfeeling.* No consideration made of Job's intense sufferings and accumulated trials. Zophar pours vinegar instead of oil on Job's wounded spirit. Sympathy in a preacher necessary to success. Want of sympathy argues want of sense.

V. Persuasion to repentance, on the ground of personal advantage (verse 13, —20).

The whole passage a noble strain of moral Oriental poetry. Perhaps quoted from the ancients by Zophar, from its supposed applicability to Job's case. Exhibits the views prevalent at the period. The teaching that of the Old Testament or pre-Evangelical platform. Holds forth more especially the promise of earthly comfort and prosperity as the result of repentance and piety. Similar sentiments expressed by Eliphaz (ch. v. 8, 17—26); and by Bildad (ch. viii. 5—7). Frequent in the Psalms and Proverbs; as Psalms i., xxxvii. and cxxviii.; Prov. iii., iv., and viii. In order to personal profit, the passage to be read in the light of New Testament truth. *The lamp of the New*

Testament to be carried with us in exploring the dark chambers of the Old. In the New Testament, the promises of future good are mainly connected with the Lord's second appearing (Acts iii. 19—21; 1 Thess. i. 9, 10; Tit. ii. 11—13). The posture of New Testament believers that of "strangers and pilgrims on the earth;" the object of their desires and affections, the "things that are above;" their spirit, contentment with "such things as they have" (Heb. xiii. 5, 14; 1 Pet. ii. 11; Col. iii. 1, 2; 2 Tim. vi. 8). The passage contains—

1. *The terms proposed, or the duty recommended* (verse 13, 14). The condition a true turning to God. Three steps indicated—

(1). *A preparation or right disposition of the heart* (verse 13). "If thou prepare (or set right) thine heart." Always represented as the first step in seeking God (1 Sam. vii. 3; 2 Cor. xix. 3; xxx. 19; Ezra, vii. 10; Ps. lxxviii. 8, 37). Implies—(*a*) Serious consideration; (*b*) Firm purpose; (*c*) Suitable frame and disposition; (*d*) Removal of secret sin. The heart naturally *biassed*, and needs to be made *straight*; unstable, and needs to be made *steadfast*. Sincerity and earnestness essential in seeking God.

(2). *Earnest prayer.* "If thou stretch forth thine hands towards Him." A common attitude in Old Testament devotion (Ps. lxxxvi. 9; cxliii. 6; Is. i. 15). Examples: Moses (Ex. ix. 33); Ezra (ix. 5); Solomon (1 Kings viii. 22). Includes—(*a*) Confession of sin; (*b*) Supplication for mercy.

(3). *Amendment of life* (verse 14). "If iniquity be in thine hand, put it far away, and let not wickedness dwell in thy tabernacles" (or tents,—Arab chiefs required more than one for their household;—wickedness—not to be allowed in any of them. Several copies and ancient versions, however, read the word in the singular). Sin to be put away both from our persons and our premises. "Iniquity,"—injustice or wrong-doing not to remain in our *hand*; "wickedness,"—any kind of open sin—not to remain in our *house*. Zacchæus an example of the first (Luke xix. 8); David of the second (Ps. ci. 7). A man is greatly responsible for what is done in his household. Domestic, as well as personal sins, to be looked after and put away. The commendation of Abraham (Gen. xviii. 19); The neglect of Eli (1 Sam. ii.12, 17; iii. 11, 14); The resolution of David (Ps. ci. 2, 7). Observe—(1) A striking gradation in the putting away of sin;—from the *heart*, from the *hand*, from the *house*. (2) True religion begins with the *heart*, and ends with the *life*. (3) Sin not only to be put away, but "far away." Present impressions not to be trusted. All occasions and temptations to relapses to be avoided.

2. *The promises annexed* (verse 15—19). The promises suppose pardon and acceptance of the penitent, with his consciousness of it. This promised in the Old as well as in the New Testament, upon sincere confession and repentance, with faith in the Sacrifice (See Ps. xxxii. 1, 5; Prov. xxviii. 13; Is. i. 17; lv. 6, 7.) The promises here are—

1. *A cheerful confidence before God and men* (verse 15). "Thou shalt lift up thy face without spot; yea, thou shalt be steadfast, and shalt not fear." Sense of pardon gives serenity of aspect. A purged conscience makes an uplifted countenance. "Without spot,"—either of guilt or its consequences. A face unabashed by guilt or shame, unsullied by grief or tears. Spots on the conscience transfer themselves to the countenance. Spots of *guilt* removed by the sprinkled blood; spots of *grief* by the consciousness of it. Conscious guilt makes the countenance to fall; sense of pardon and acceptance lifts it up (Gen. iv. 5, 6; Luke xviii. 13; 1 John iii. 21.) The face sooner and better lifted up by *pardon* than by *prosperity*.

2. *Deliverance from present suffering* (verse 16). "Thou shalt forget thy misery and remember it as waters that pass (or, have passed) away." Inward, if not outward misery, removed by sense of pardoning mercy (Ps. xxxii. 1, 5; li. 8—14). Inward suffering sooner or later the fruit of sin. The remembrance of previous sorrow swallowed up by present joy. Trouble forgotten through long continued triumph. Remembrance of grief often only an enhancement of joy. No trace left of the winter-torrent that has passed away. "Your joy no man taketh from you." The desolating flood that has disappeared only remembered with thankful joy. So the pardoned soul has still in remembrance, "the wormwood and the gall."

3. *Abiding peace and joy* (verse 17). "Thine age shall be clearer than the noonday (or, "a period, or happy age, shall arise to thee, brighter than, &c."); and thou (or it) shalt shine forth, thou (or it) shalt be as the morning" (or, "now thou art in darkness, but then thou shalt be as the morning"). Light out of darkness, the experience of a penitent and pardoned soul (Hos. vi. 3). The light and joy of acceptance like "the noonday" for brightness; like "the morning" for increase. "The path of the just," the justified and sanctified in Christ, a light increasing in brightness "unto the perfect day" (Prov. iv. 18). The believer's joy not diminished by manifold trials (1 Peter, i. 6). Like oil poured on water, comes always to the surface. At times unspeakable and full of glory (1 Peter i. 8).

4. *Safety and security* (verse 18, 19). "Thou shalt be secure, because there is hope;

yea, thou shalt dig about thee (making preparation, according to patriarchal custom, for a new abode; or, 'now thou art ashamed but then, &c.'), and thou shalt take thy rest in safety; also, thou shalt lie down (as a shepherd with his flock), and none shall make thee afraid." Hope in God's mercy through Christ, the only foundation of real security. Divine protection one of the sweetest of new covenant blessings. Christ's sheep safe in His hands and in those of His Father (John x. 28, 30). "Kept by the power of God through faith unto salvation." Preservation of the soul an Old as well as New Testament promise (Ps. cxxi. 7). Oriental tents and travellers exposed to danger from robbers, wild beasts, and reptiles; believers' souls exposed to no less peril (2 Col. ii. 8, 18; 1 Peter v. 8; 2 Cor. xi. 3).

5. *Influence among men* (verse 19). "Many shall make suit to thee." The mark of a great, if not a good man. "Many entreat the favour of the prince" (Prov. xix. 6). The same promised to the Church or Bride of Christ (Ps. xlv. 12). So Abimelech made suit to Abraham, entreating his favour and alliance (Gen. xxvi. 26—29. Pardoned people are praying people; and praying people are Israels,—princes that have power both with God and men (Gen. xxxii. 28). God's presence with a believer the ground of true greatness. He that has power with God likely to have influence among men. "We will go with you for we have heard that God is with you (Zech. viii. 23). Believers are kings and priests to God. Their duty so to walk as to gain respect to their profession. An ill sign with a professor when nobody seeks the favour of his prayers. A believer's privilege so to carry Christ about with him that men shall feel his influence, as those who sought only to be in Peter's shadow. The true character of a pardoned and accepted person

is to have so much of Christ's loving spirit as to carry with him a constant beneflaction. Made sweet and gracious by God's favour *on* them, and His spirit *in* them, believers carry with them the unconscious influence of a sweet and gracious atmosphere. A pardoned man, walking with Christ and imbibing His spirit, as sure to be perceived as a bag that carries sweet perfume. The privilege and duty of believers to exhale so much of Christ's loving nature as, like the modest and half-hidden violets, to attract others to them by their fragrance. This, as well as the other promises, realised in Job's after experience, but not in the way imagined by Zophar (ch. xlii. 7—9).

VI. The contrasted case of the un·godly (verse 20) Includes—(1) "*Anxiety and disappointment.* "The eyes of the wicked shall fail,"—anxiously looking in vain for the possession of good and deliverance from evil. A time when it is too late to knock even at mercy's door. "They shall seek me early, but they shall not find me (Prov. i. 28. (2) *Per-plexity and hopelessness.* "They shall not escape." (*Heb.* "Refuge has perished from them"). Calamity, sooner or later, overtakes the Christless and impenitent, from which escape is impossible. "Because I called and ye refused,—I also will laugh at your calamity" (Prov. i. 24—26). "How shall we escape if we neglect so great salvation?" (Heb. ii. 3; x. 26, 27). (3) *Ruin and despair.* "Their hope shall be as the giving up of the ghost" (*margin*, "as a puff of breath"). The hope of the impenitent and Christless proves as vain and unsubstantial as a puff of breath. Their expectation terminates with their life. Having chosen death rather than life, they obtain their choice. "All they that hate me love death." (Prov. viii. 36.)

CHAPTER XII.

JOB'S REPLY TO ZOPHAR.

I. Defends himself against the charge of ignorance implied in Zophar's speech (verse 2, 3). His defence is :—.

1. *Ironical* (verse 2). "No doubt but ye are the people; and wisdom shall die with you;" the wisdom of mankind is collected in your person, and when you die wisdom must perish at the same time. Times when it may be proper to use the language of irony and sarcasm. Its proper use to put error and pretension to shame. So Elijah

to the worshippers of Baal: "Cry aloud for he is a God;" and Paul to the Corinthians: "Ye are rich; ye have reigned as kings without us" (1 Cor. iv. 8). Assumption on the part of preachers and monitors sure to render their words powerless and themselves ridiculous.

2. *Serious* (verse 3). "But I have under- standing as well as you: I am not inferior to you." Times when modesty does not forbid a man to speak in his own commenda- tion. Allowable when for our own defence,

75

or for the interests of truth. Paul compelled by his detractors to this "foolishness of boasting" (2 Cor. xii. 11). A man's duty to *know himself;* and especially to know whether he has "understanding" to "know the only true God, and Jesus Christ whom He has sent, which is life eternal" (2 Cor. xiii. 5; 1 John v. 20; John xvii. 3).

3. *Contemptuous.* "Yea, who knoweth not such things as these" (*margin,* "with whom are not such things as these?"). Conceit and pretension to be taken down. Zophar's vaunted wisdom was after all—(1) *Commonplace.* His speech mostly such moral and religious sentiments as were found in everybody's mouth. (2) *Borrowed;* second-hand maxims handed down from the fathers. Preachers to be careful—(1) Not to deal in mere commonplace sentiments, or to ring changes on a few universally admitted truths. Hearers to be taught something which they do not already know. The instructed scribe to "bring out of his treasure things new and old." Necessary to present new truths, or old ones in a new, clearer, or more impressive light. (2) Not to parade before others what is not really their own, without acknowledging it. False prophets reproved for stealing God's words, "every one from his neighbour," and passing them off as if delivered to themselves (Jer. xxiii. 30).

II. Complains of his being treated with scorn in consequence of affliction (verse 4).

"I am as one (or, 'I am one who is') mocked of his neighbour, who calleth upon God and he heareth him (or, 'that he may answer him;' or, 'and let him answer him;' possibly the taunt of his enemies, as Ps. xxii. 8; Matthew xxvii. 43); the just upright man is laughed to scorn." This treatment, according to the ordinary way of the world (ver. 5). "He that is ready to slip with his feet is a lamp despised (or a torch thrown away as useless) in the thought of him that is at ease" (or, "contempt adheres to calamity in the mind of the prosperous and secure, ready for those who slip with their feet"—who are tottering, or already fallen into adversity and trouble). Probably one of proverbial maxims referred to in verse 4, quoted by Job on *his* side of the question, and as descriptive of his own case.

1. He was *mocked.* No small aggravation of his affliction (ch. xvi. 10, 20; xvii. 2, 6; xxi. 3; xxx. 1, 9, 10). The experience of David (Ps. xxii. 7; xxxv. 16; lxix. 11, 12; and of David's Lord (Matt. xxvi. 67, 68; xxvii. 27—31; Luke, xxiii. 35). Mockery worse to bear than open violence. The bitterness of this treatment enhanced by the previous experience of honour and respect

(ch. xxix. 7—25). Believers not to be staggered at "cruel mockings," either from the world or nominal professors. Such mockery the expression of inward contempt,—"in the thought of him," &c. *The followers of a despised Christ to expect no better treatment than their Master* (Is. liii. 3; John xiii. 16).

2. Was mocked *in consequence of his affliction* (verse 5). An aggravation of the treatment. Affliction painful enough in itself, and demanding sympathy. Hard to endure, and cruel to inflict, mockery and contempt on account of it. This experience of Job also that of David, and of the great Antitype of both. *Christ was mocked by men when bruised by God.*

3. Job thus mocked *notwithstanding his uprightness and piety.* (1.) His *uprightness,*—"the just upright man." The testimony already given him by God (ch. i. 8; ii. 3). (2.) His *piety.* Manifested in his prayerfulness,—"who calleth upon God," &c. Exemplified in his conduct in reference to his children (ch. i. 5). His practice still in his affliction (ch. xvi. 20). Made at last an intercessor for his friends (ch. xii. 8, 10). *A man of piety necessarily a man of prayer.* Affliction draws a good man nearer to God, sends a bad one farther from Him. Terrible aggravation of the sin when the mocked sufferer is an upright child of God. The tremendous guilt of the Jews in relation to Jesus. Job's prayers *ordinarily* heard and answered, though *apparently not so now.* So with Jesus in his last suffering (Ps. xxii. 2; Luke xxii, 42, compared with John xi. 42). Prayer, offered believingly in the name of Christ, heard and answered, though in God's own time and way. God's answer to believers' prayers his testimony to the acceptance of their persons.

4. Job was mocked *by those who were at ease themselves* (verse 5). Another aggravation of the sin as well as of the suffering occasioned by it. To be "at ease," a common description of the ungodly. Too often applicable even to the professors of religion (Amos vi. 1). Job's complaint that of Christ's suffering church (Ps. cxxiii. 3. 4). *Suffering in ourselves the parent of sympathy for others.*

III. Re-asserts the prosperity of the ungodly (verse 6).

"The tabernacles of robbers prosper; yea, they that provoke God are secure; into whose hand God bringeth abundantly" (or, "to whom God bringeth with his hand," or, "to him who carrieth God in his hand"). Repeats more fully what he had asserted (ch. ix. 24). Perhaps quotes another maxim of the ancients. Observe—

1. The *characters spoken of.* (1) "Rob-

bers." Reference to the ungodly who put might for right. The earth, previous to the flood, filled with violence by such. The giants in those days, mighty men of renown (Gen. vi. 1). The flood the consequence of their violence and its prosperity. A similar state of things not long after that event. Nimrod, "a mighty hunter before the Lord." Hence the war of the kings (Gen. xiv). The Sabeans and Chaldeans (ch. 15—17) other specimens of these "robbers." Lust for property, power and pleasure, the natural tendency of fallen men. Hence wars and fightings (Jam. iv. 1, 2). Tyrants, despots, and great conquerors, often only robbers on a large scale. Unlawful gains, oppression of the poor, and mercantile dishonesty, other forms of "robbery" (Jer. xxii. 13; Heb. ii. 12). (2) They "*provoke God to anger.*" The effect of all ungodliness. God angry with the wicked every day. The wrath of God revealed from heaven against all ungodliness and righteousness of men (Rom. i. 18). God's anger especially provoked by cruelty and wrong. The whole life of the ungodly a continued provocation of God. Wealth treasured up against the day of wrath (Rom. ii. 5). Patience no proof of the want of provocations.

2. *What is asserted of them.* They "prosper." The prosperity of the ungodly more fully enlarged upon (ch. xxi. 7—13). The stumbling-block of Asaph (Ps. lxxiii. 2, 12); the perplexity of Jeremiah (Jer. xii. 1). (1) *Their dwellings are in outward peace and prosperity.* Their "tabernacles" prosper. A *cluster* of tents required to form an Oriental chieftain's household. The *families* of the ungodly appear to prosper (ch. xxi. 8, 9, 11). Full of children, and leaving the rest of their substance to their babes (Ps. xvii. 14). Their homes appear likely to stand for many generations. Their lands called by their own names (Ps. xlix. 11).—(2) They *enjoy abundance of earthly comforts.* Their abundance brought to them in the providence of God, though idolatrously ascribed to their own hand (Deut. viii. 17; Heb. i. 11). Observe—(i.) *Good fortune no proof of Divine favour.* Dives had his good things in this life, Lazarus his evil things. (ii.) *Earthly goods as well as trials at the Divine disposal.* These often mysteriously, always wisely, distributed. As compared with *spiritual blessings,* rather the husks that the swine eat, or the bones thrown to the dogs. Ordinarily given as incitements to repentance, gratitude, and love. When lusted after, often given in judgment rather than in mercy. The desire granted, while leanness is sent into the soul (Ps. cvi. 15).

IV. An Appeal to the irrational creation (verse 7—10).

"Ask now the beasts, and they shall teach thee, &c. Who knoweth not in all these (or, 'which among all these knoweth not') that the hand of the Lord hath wrought this?" (that God—here alone in the dialogues spoken of as "the Lord"—is both Creator and Governor of all things). Perhaps a third proverbial maxim quoted by Job.—Observe:

1. *All animate and inanimate nature man's teachers.*

The Book of Nature.

Its lessons manifold both as to faith and practice. Job, in the end, referred to its teachings by God himself. Heaven and earth an open Bible, speaking both *from* God and *of* Him. The nocturnal sky a wide unfolded scroll, with every star a character. David's delight to spell in it the glory and perfections of God (Ps. xix. 1, 2). Every rising sun proclaims anew His goodness and faithfulness (Sam. iii. 23). Solomon sent his readers to the ants for a lesson of industry. Jesus directs His disciples to the birds and the flowers to learn implicit confidence in the care of their heavenly Father. The book of nature distinctly enough written, and the voices of creation sufficiently audible and clear. But sin has dimmed our spiritual vision, dulled our hearing, and made us slow to learn either about God or ourselves.

2. *The existence of an all-pervading, all-sustaining, and all-controlling*

Providence

Insisted on by Zophar as if Job had been ignorant of it. Declared by the dust on a butterfly's wing as well as by the lustre of the Dogstar. Proclaimed by the motion of an insect as it dances in the sun-beams, as well as by the rising and setting of sun, moon, and planets. The hand that upholds the sun in the heavens guides the sparrow in its fall to the ground. "Not a fly but has had infinite wisdom concerned, not only in its structure, but in its destination." [*Young*] Nature's works designed to lead up to nature's God.—"In his hand is the soul of every living thing, and the breath (or spirit) of all mankind" (verse 10). All life in and from God. First created, and then supported and preserved by Him. "In Him we live," &c.,—not only *by* Him but *in* Him. The life of men, animals and plants, no longer continued than He pleases. The laws of existence established by Him, and still under His control. The spirit or thinking part of man as well as the soul or feeling part of animals, equally proceeding from and dependent upon Him. The highest creature no more able to prolong his existence a moment beyond His will.than to create a universe. The power of a man to *think*, as well as the sense to *feel*, and the muscles to *act*, alike from Him. A glance of His eye able to reduce creation to its original nothingness. All events under His control. Moral evil permitted, penal evil inflicted by Him. The twin truths of creation and providence everywhere taught by external nature. The truth that nature fails to teach, that which man most needs to learn. For man to learn the way of pardon and reconciliation with God, the volume of nature required to be supplemented by that of revelation.

V. The right and duty of exercising private judgment (verse 11).

"Doth not the ear try words, and the mouth taste his meat?" (or, "as the mouth tastes its food"). The office of the ear to try or judge of the statements submitted to it. The ear put for the judgment or reason which acts through it. Moral and religious truths at that time conveyed through the ear rather than the eye. Books or writings rarely, if ever, found among the people.—*Men's duty to examine and judge of what they hear.* Applicable to the quotations already, or yet to be, made from the ancients by Job and his friends, as well as to the sentiments uttered by themselves. Job bespeaks candour and attention to his speeches, and resolves to judge for himself as to what is advanced by his friends. Observe, in reference to

Private judgment,

1. *Man possesses a faculty by which to judge of moral and religious statements.* Such a faculty distinguishes man from the brutes, and allies him to angels. The faculty of reason or judgment originally given and still continued to men, though weakened and depraved by sin. Appealed to by God in His messages to men (Isaiah v. 3); by Christ (Luke xii. 57); by His apostles (1 Cor. x. 15; xi. 13—14). Lies at the foundation of all efforts to instruct, enlighten, and persuade others in reference to religious subjects. Implies the possession and the apprehension of a standard of right and wrong. Its highest office to judge of moral and religious statements by that standard. A standard of moral judgment implanted in man's nature at his creation, but now much effaced. Renewed in the moral law and in the Scriptures in general. The object of the Bible and of the Holy Spirit to exhibit that standard, and to lead men to judge, conclude, and act according to it.

2. *Man's duty to exercise that faculty in regard to all statements on moral and reli-*

gious subjects. Appeal to the law and the testimony in reference to what man teaches, enjoined by God Himself (Is. viii. 20). Men commanded to cease to hear the instruction that causeth to err from the words of knowledge (Prov. xix. 27). The apostolic injunction—"Prove all things, hold fast that which is good." "Believe not every spirit, but try the spirits, whether they be of God" (1 Thes. v. 21; 1 John iv. 1). The part of the "simple" to "believe every word." The Bereans commended for searching the Scriptures daily to see whether the things spoken by the apostles were according to them (Acts xvii. 11). Superstition and priestcraft deny to men the right of private judgment, and forbid the ear to do its office. To believe only because the Church or our forefathers have done so, is for the ear no longer to "try words." Man responsible to God for the right exercise of the judgment He has given him. When *God* speaks, the office of the judgment is to discover that He has done so, to ascertain *what* He has spoken, and then, unquestioningly, to accept it. God's announcements often *above* reason, never *contrary* to it. The judgment to be exercised on moral and religious subjects with—(1) Seriousness and attention; (2) Candour and patience; (3) Modesty and humility; (4) Impartiality and absence of prejudice; (5) Prayer for Divine enlightenment.

3. *Human authority on religious subjects to be respected, but not regarded as paramount* (verses 12, 13). "With the ancient is wisdom, and in length of days is understanding. With Him (i.e, God) is wisdom and strength, he hath counsel and understanding,"—wisdom in both its forms, speculative and practical; or, wisdom to direct and strength to accomplish. The latter verse probably the commencement of another quotation. Job's object in it—(1) To vindicate his knowledge of God as not inferior to that of his friends; (2) To show that the wisdom of God infinitely surpasses that of the wisest of men. Human wisdom acquired by study, observation and experience, —by the long-continued exercise of the judgment referred to in verse 11. By reason of use men have their senses exercised to discern good and evil, and so become men of full age in understanding, instead of children (Heb. v. 13, 14; 1 Cor. xiv. 20). That wisdom always imperfect and fallible. God the only infallible teacher. Wisdom, *in* men, as something communicated; *with* God, as something eternally and essentially abiding. In man as a stream, limited and uncertain; with God, as a perennial fountain. An appeal, therefore, to be made from man's teaching to God's. Divine teaching to be implicitly submitted

to and confided in, as that of infinite wisdom.

VI. Spirited description of God's providence in the world (verse 14—25). Probably a quotation of ancient poetry, or the production of the poet put into Job's mouth. Properly commences with verse 13. A magnificent ode or hymn on the Divine perfections and procedure in the world. The similarity in language and sentiment to parts of 107th Psalm remarkable. Celebrates especially the various .

Acts of Divine Providence.

Exhibits its operations on a grand and extensive scale. Represents God as ruling over nations as well as individuals. His Providence viewed more in its solemn and judicial aspects.

1 *In acts of destruction* (verse 14). "He breaketh down, and (or 'so that') it cannot be built again." The part of the Divine Ruler is to pull down as well as to build up—to kill as well as to make alive (Is. xlv. 7 ; Am. iii. 6 ; Deut. xxxii. 39). Breaks down houses, cities, individuals, families, nations—the earth itself. Seen in the Flood, the Cities of the Plain, perhaps the Tower of Babel. Breaks down cities, buildings, &c., by earthquakes, inundations, volcanoes, lightnings, tempests, &c ; nations and kingdoms by invasions, wars, civil discord, foolish counsels, &c ; individuals by diseases and misfortunes. Breaks down in various ways human schemes and enterprises (Gen. xi. 3—8 ; 2 Chr. xx, 36, 37). Reference to one form of destruction in verse 15. "He withholdeth the waters and they dry up ; also he sendeth them out and they overturn the earth." Exemplified in the Deluge. The windows of heaven then opened, and the fountains of the great deep broken up (Gen. vii. 11). Inundations frequent in Arabia and Egypt.

2. *In laying restraints on individuals.* "He shutteth up a man (*Heb.* 'over a man') and there is no opening." Reference to underground prisons (Jer. xxxvii. 38). God in His providence shuts up individuals as prisoners—by affliction and misfortune (Job himself an example) ; by delivering them up into the hand of enemies ; by bringing them into difficulties and straits ; by inward darkness and distress ; by insanity, as in the case of Nebuchadnezzar. When God shuts up, none but Himself can open (Is. xxii. 22).

3. *In overruling both men's misery and mischief* (verse 16). "The deceived and the deceiver are His." The deceiver can only *act*, and the deceived *suffer*, by His permission. The *deceiver* His, to restrain

his deception and employ it for His own wise purposes. The *deceived* His, to deliver him from the deception, or to correct or punish him by it. The deceiver God's instrument in trying the good and punishing the bad. Satan the deceiver of the nations (Rev. xx. 3). Lying spirits in the mouth of false prophets, God's instruments in punishing Ahab and his people (1 Kings xxii. 20). False Christs and false prophets to deceive many, but not the elect (Matt. xxiv. 11—24). Antichrist's advent to be with all deceivableness of unrighteousness in those that receive not the love of the truth (2 Thess. ii. 11).

4. *In punishing nations and their rulers* (verse 17). "He leadeth councillors away spoiled (stripped as captives taken in war, or deprived of their dignity, or as persons bereft of judgment), and maketh the judges fools ;" (—so infatuates them, that they shall give wrong judgment, and so bring the nation into trouble). So God threatened to take away from Judah the judge, and the prudent, and the councillor, and to give children to be their princes, and to cause babes to rule over them (Is. iii. 2—4). No greater woe to a land than when God in judgment gives it up to unwise rulers and statesmen (Ecc. x. 16).—Verse 18. "He looseth the bond of kings (dissolves their authority, as in the case of Rehoboam and the Ten Tribes), and girdeth their loins with a girdle" (perhaps a cord or rope, as indicative of servitude). No uncommon thing for despotic rulers to be dethroned by their oppressed and discontented subjects, and instead of the insignia of royalty to have to wear the habit of a prisoner or an exile (Jer. lii. 8—11, 31—33). Numerous examples in Europe within the last century. —(Verse 24, 25). "He taketh away the heart (or understanding) of the chief of the people of the earth (or the land), and causeth them to wander in a wilderness where there is no way, &c." Easy with God in judgment on themselves or the nation, to leave rulers and statesmen in such perplexity as not to know what to do, and to abandon them to foolish and ruinous counsels. So Rehoboam adopted the unwise counsel given him by his youthful advisers. The result of such judicial infatuation seen in foolish and hurtful wars, in the adoption of unwise public measures, in the enactment of intolerant, partial, and unjust laws, and in a short-sighted reactionary policy after one of enlightened progress.

5. *In humbling the brave, the gifted, and the great* (verse 19). "He leadeth princes (or priests—probably civil rulers, viceroys, or ministers of state) away spoiled, and overthroweth the mighty" (warriors mighty

in battle). No king saved by the multitude of a host. The battle is the Lord's, who gives the victory to whom He will. Threatened to take from Judah the mighty man and the man of war. At times turned the edge of Israel's sword, so that they could not stand in the battle (Ps. lxxxix. 43). Armies and their generals often overthrown when calculating on certain victory. God sometimes overthrows the mighty by allowing them to overthrow themselves through foolish and ambitious counsels. (Verse 20.)—"He removeth away the speech of the trusty (the eloquence of the patriotic orator), and taketh away the understanding of the aged" (the prudence and wisdom of the experienced senator). So God threatened to take away from Judah "the eloquent orator, the ancient and the honourable man" (Is. iii. 2, 3). May remove such by disease or death without supplying their places, by withholding the desire to serve their country with their gifts, or by withdrawing the gifts themselves. Persuasive eloquence and penetrating judgment not in men's own keeping. The influence of wise and confidential advisers sometimes destroyed to serve God's own purposes (2 Sam. xv. 31; xvii. 14, 23).—Verse 21. "He poureth contempt upon princes, and weakeneth the strength of the mighty." Numerous examples furnished by France and other European countries during the last hundred years.

6. *In disclosing hidden wickedness* (verse 22). "He discovereth deep things out of darkness, and bringeth out to light the shadow of death." (1) Wicked and deep-laid schemes. Examples: the diabolical contrivance of Haman for the destruction of the Jews (Book of Esther); the Gunpowder Plot for the overthrow of the Protestant religion in England. (2) Secret crimes long hidden from men. Examples: Joseph's brethren, Achan, David. The verse in this sense quoted by the Apostle, 1 Cor. iv. 5.

7. *In the increase and decay of nations* (verse 23). "He increaseth the nations and destroyeth them; He enlargeth the nations and straiteneth them again." A nation sometimes made to rise within a short time to great power and influence. Examples: Rome; Israel under David and Solomon; and in more modern times, England, America, and Prussia. Examples of decay of nations: Israel, after the death of Solomon; Rome, after the prevalence of luxury, pride and cruelty; Spain, after its persecution of the truth and exclusion of an open Bible. Changes in the condition of nations perhaps as early as the times of Job (Gen. xiv.). Egypt, a powerful monarchy at a very early period, ultimately for its idolatry, "the basest of kingdoms." The seven nations of Canaan extirpated for their wickedness and lust. Only a short period occupied by the rise and fall of each of the first three universal empires.

CHAPTER XIII.

JOB'S REPLY TO ZOPHAR—CONTINUED.

I. **Job re-asserts his knowledge of the Divine procedure as not inferior to that of his friends (verse 1, 2).** "Lo, mine eye," &c. Right in certain circumstances to maintain one's own knowledge, but without vain glory (2 Cor. xi. 6; Eph. iii. 4). Three things suggested in the words of Job as necessary to the

Acquisition of knowledge.

1. *Observation.* "Mine eye hath seen all this." Important to make a right use of one's eyes. God's works both of creation and providence to be carefully observed. To observe God's works and ways is both a part of wisdom and the means of increasing it (Ps. cvii. 43). A mark of the ungodly and a cause of their destruction, not to regard the works of the Lord nor the operation of His hand (Ps. xxviii. 5; Is. v. 12). Often the best knowlege that which is obtained by careful personal observation. "Come and

see," a common phrase in the Jewish schools, and frequently repeated in the New Testament (John i.; Rev. vi). Better to see for ourselves than to hear from others. The eyes, as well as the ears, are the purveyors for the mind.

2. *Attention to the instruction of others.* "Mine ear hath heard." Moral and religious instruction at that time mostly oral. Consisted mainly in the recitation of proverbial maxims or truths delivered in short sentences. Such frequently quoted by Job and his friends. Reference made here to such. Each individual's own personal observation necessarily limited. The testimony of others required to supplement our own observation. The privilege and duty of one to avail himself of the testimony and conclusions of another. Since the invention of printing, the extension of education, the employment of steam, and the removal of the taxes on knowledge,—the testimony and instruction of others now addressed nearly as much to the

eye as to the ear. Reading now greatly takes the place of hearing, as the means of obtaining knowledge.

3. *Reflection.* "Hath understood (or considered) it." Reflection an appropriating and assimilating process. Turns to account what is observed, read, or heard. Reading and hearing are with a view to reflection, as food is taken into the mouth only with a view to its being digested in the stomach. Food only serves the purpose of nutrition when properly masticated and digested. The eye and the ear collect the materials for the mind to work upon. Reading, as Bacon says, makes a full man; but reflection makes an intelligent, a growing, and a sure man. The want of consideration the characteristic of the way-side hearers. The reason of the Word of God, when heard, not entering the heart, and so of its being caught away by the enemy (Matt. xiii. 19).

II. His desire and resolution to address himself to God (verse 3).

"Surely, (or 'however') I would (or will) speak to the Almighty; and I desire to reason (or debate the case) with God." Observe—

1. *Great comfort to a believer in being able to take his case to God.* Many things may be poured into God's ear which may not be uttered to man's. Our comfort that in every controversy an appeal may be made from man to God. The heart in trouble eased by pouring itself out to our Father in heaven. The best way to dispose of difficulties and perplexities is to take them at once to God. Better to take our case to God than to man, as—(1) He is better acquainted with it, and can make no mistake about it ; (2) Will give a more just decision, being neither influenced by passion nor prejudice ; (3) Will shew more tenderness and sympathy in dealing with it.

2. *God's great condescension in allowing a creature to reason with Him.* His desire that we should do so (Is. i. 18 ; xli. 21 ; xliii. 26). Our privilege to plead with Him, not to *justify ourselves as righteous,* but to *be justified by Him as sinners.* In the Gospel, God permits us to plead with Him for justification and acceptance on the ground of a better righteousness than our own. His invitation (Is. i. 18) ; David's resolution (Ps. lxxi. 16) ; Paul's triumph (Rom. viii. 33, 34).

III. Vehement retort from his friends (verse 4).

"But ye are forgers of lies (or,'stitchers up of falsehood,' 'disappointing surgeons,' or 'framers of false arguments,'), ye are all physicians of no value" (or, 'of nothingness,' or 'idol physicians,' as Zech. xi.

17). They had come professedly to bind up their friend's wounds, and heal his diseased mind. In doing this they had only employed false and futile arguments. Had applied useless remedies, and misapplied good ones. Had set out on the false principle that great sufferings prove great sins, and that temporal prosperity must always accompany true piety. Had therefore concluded that Job must be both a transgressor and a hypocrite. Had consequently employed arguments to bring him to humiliation, repentance, and prayer. Among other arguments, had held out to him the promise of deliverance from trouble and restoration to prosperity. Observe—

1. *Much wisdom required in ministering to a mind diseased.* Care to be taken to employ only solid considerations and sound arguments. Only truth will satisfy and heal a troubled spirit. Preachers to beware of "daubing with untempered mortar."

2. *Scripture truth, rightly applied, the only medicine for sin-sick souls.* Scripture written that through patience and comfort from it we might have hope (Rom. xv. 4). Paul's direction to Christian mourners : "Comfort one another with these words,"—the truths he had just stated (1 Thess. iv. 18).

3. *The honour and corresponding responsibility of being made a physician of souls.* Requires—(1) Study and knowledge of cases ; (2) Knowledge of the requisite remedies ; (3) Skill in applying them ; (4) Sympathy with the sufferer. Christ the Great Physician of souls, and an example to all others. The best thing the preacher can do is to direct the Christian mourner and the sin-sick soul to Him (1 Cor. ii. 2).

VI. Keen remonstrance and reproof (verses 5–13).

1. *Begs his friends only to refrain from speaking altogether* (verse 5). "O that ye would altogether hold your peace ! and it should be your wisdom."—Verse 13. "Hold your peace, and let me alone." Application of the maxim in Prov. xvii. 28. Silence may not only give the appearance of wisdom, but is often wisdom itself. The part of a wise man either not to speak, or to speak to the purpose. Our speech to be "with grace, seasoned with salt."

2. *Bespeaks their attention to his reasoning and reproof* (verse 6). "Hear now my reasoning, and hearken to the pleadings of my lips." A duty owed to a brother both to prove and reprove—to *prove error* and *reprove sin* in him (Lev. xix. 17 ; Prov. ix. 8).

3. *Shews their sin in acting as they had done.* Their sin—(1) In *dissembling and*

6

using *false arguments, while pretending to defend God and His procedure* (verse 7). "Will ye speak wickedly for God? and talk deceitfully for him"—(speaking differently from what their consciences believed, in order to please God and uphold his cause). To make God appear just in afflicting Job, they, contrary to their convictions, wished to make him out a guilty transgressor. Observe —(i.) *God needs no false doctrine or unsound reasoning to defend Him or His doings.*—(ii.) *God's cause needs no sinful compromises or questionable measures to uphold it.* Neither the wrath nor the wrong-doing of man "worketh the righteousness of God."—(2) *In giving partial judgment for God, and presuming to make themselves His patrons, as if he needed either their favour or defence* (verse 8). "Will ye accept his person? will ye contend for God?" Good men to be God's witnesses, but not His patrons or advocates. A sin in His sight to judge, not according to the merits of the case, but the quality of the parties. Partiality in reference to *men* an injustice, in reference to *God* an insult. God's cause to be defended not with favour and partiality, but with truth and justice. Favour and acceptance of persons in judgment so obnoxious to God that He accounts it a sin, even when in reference to Himself. Only a blind, false, and superstitious regard to religion defends it with anything but truth and honesty.— 3. In *condemning what they secretly believed to be right, or maintaining with their lips what they did not believe in their hearts* (verse 9). "Is it good (or will it be for your advantage) that he search you out (examine and expose your secret motives?) Or as one man mocketh another, do ye so mock him? He will surely reprove you, if you do secretly accept persons. Shall not His excellency make you afraid (of acting thus hypocritically), and His dread fall upon you?" (or, 'is it not His majesty that makes you afraid [of speaking according to your convictions] and does not the dread of him overwhelm you?' [so as to act hypocritically in the matter]. Their condemnation of Job not from conviction of his guilt but from fear of God's displeasure, and the desire to appear on His side. Observe—(i.) *All dissimulation hateful to the God of truth.* Believers so to act as willing to bear the scrutiny of Him whose eyes are as a flame of fire. (ii.) *Fearful mockery of God to cloak our want of charity to man with a pretended zeal for God.* (iii.) *Necessary in maintaining the cause of religion, to examine our motives and the means we employ in doing so.* A good cause may be defended from evil motives, and a bad cause may be upheld under the appearance of piety. A sin to act from slavish

82

fear of the Almighty, rather than from conviction and a regard to truth. 4. *Declares the worthlessness of his friends' authorities and maxims with reference to the case in hand* (verse 12). "Your remembrances are like ashes (or, 'your memorial sayings are proverbs of ashes,'—worthless, and easily scattered by the wind); your bodies to bodies of clay" (or, "your towers, or defences,"— *i.e.*, your arguments and maxims—are "towers of mud,"—as opposed to those of stone, without strength or solidity, and easily thrown down). Probably a proverbial phrase for weak and worthless arguments. The reference to the quotations from the ancients in his friends' speeches. These called "remembrances," or "memorial sayings," as intended to be carried in the memory, and so kept ready for use. Particularly numerous among the Arabs, and taking the place of laws. Abundant in the speeches of Job and his friends, especially of the latter. Great part of Oriental wisdom and learning consisted in the knowledge and ready recitation of these traditional maxims. Their value to be decided on their respective merits. Not to be regarded as in themselves inspired productions. Probably neither their authors nor reciters inspired men. As much wisdom required in the application as in the composition of them. "A parable in the mouth of fools" proverbially worthless and injurious (Prov. xxvi. 7, 9). In the case of Job's friends the fault chiefly in the application. The maxims themselves generally good, according to the views prevalent at the period. Care to be taken by preachers and others—(1) *That quotations, especially those from Scripture, are correctly applied;* (2) *That the arguments they employ are solid ones* —not "defences of mud."

V. His Resolution to plead his cause with God at whatever risk (verse 13). "Let me alone, that I (or I myself) may speak (*viz.* to God), and let come on me what will." (Verse 14).—"Wherefore do I (or, 'come what may,'—repeated from previous verse,—'I will) take my flesh in my teeth, and put my life in mine hand." A proverbial expression for "expose myself," *viz.*, to the threatened peril of suffering for presumption in pleading his cause with God. The attempt considered by his friends as most daring and perilous. *Faith and a good conscience are courageous, even in reference to God Himself* (1 John, iii. 21). The righteous are bold as a lion (Prov. xxviii. 1). "Virtue is bold, and goodness never fearful." Job's case with God that of Esther with the king: "I will go, and if I perish I perish" (Esth. iv. 16). Abraham's case in pleading for Sodom: "I have taken upon me to speak unto the Lord, who am but dust and ashes (Gen. xviii. 27. *Necessity and love make men courageous.* —Verse 15. "Though he slay me, yet will I trust in Him (or, 'behold, he will slay me,' or 'let Him slay me, I will not expect' [anything else]—the Hebrew words for 'not' and 'in him,' the same in sound); but I will maintain (or, 'only I will prove and argue') my ways before Him." The antithesis between the third and the first and second clauses, rather than between the second and the first. Observe—

1. *The boldness of Job's faith and conscious integrity here rises to its highest pitch.* Though with only death before him as the result, he will still maintain his integrity, even at the tribunal of the Almighty. THE HEAT AND TURNING POINT OF THE CONFLICT BETWEEN GOD AND SATAN IN THESE WORDS. Satan's charge,—Job will give up all, even his religion, to save his life. Thus it will be shown that God has not a sincere disinterested servant in the world; that all religion is mere selfishness and time-serving policy. God will thus be stripped of His honour in the universe. For Job to have given up his integrity and acknowledged he was not the man he had appeared, would have given the victory into Satan's hand. Job would have been condemned out of his own mouth. Fear would have made him a liar, and to save his life he would have thrown away his religion. This the aim of Satan, and the tendency of all the arguments of his friends, cunningly suggested by himself. JOB PREFERS TO DIE, and Satan is defeated. Glorious triumph of faith and a good conscience! *Many a believer, like Job, the battle-field between God and Satan.* As he maintains faith and a good conscience, God is honoured and Satan put to shame.

2. *Job persuaded that though his daring might end in death, it would ultimately prove his deliverance* (verse 16). "He also (or, 'even this') shall be my salvation; for an hypocrite [as Job's friends charged him with being] shall not come before him." The fact of his appealing to God in the face of such peril, a proof of his innocence. "The foolish shall not stand in His presence" (Ps. v. 5). The righteous Judge would acquit him of the charges of his friends, and of any sin as the cause of his suffering. Even should death ensue, a deliverance awaited him beyond death. His innocence would be vindicated, which with him was salvation. The day would come when this would be done before an assembled universe (ch. xix. 25). *The believer's case always safe in God's hands* (2 Tim. i. 16.).

VI. Job requests his friends' attention to his pleading, and predicts his success (verse 17).

"Hear diligently my speech, and my declaration [in reference to my innocence] with your ears. Behold now, I have ordered my cause (—have already set in order my pleading as a general draws up his forces for battle) ; I know that I shall be justified" (—shall gain the cause and be pronounced righteous by my Judge). Job actually justified by God as he expected, though not till he had humbled himself and repented in dust and ashes (ch. xlii. 6). Observe—(1) *The boldness and assurance of a good conscience before a righteous tribunal.*—(2) Job's language *that of Christ himself, and of the believer trusting as a sinner in Christ's merits* (Is. l. 7—9; Rom. viii. 32—34). Job, in the circumstances, rightly trusted to his innocence and integrity as the ground of his justification by God. Men, as sinners, have not to plead their own righteousness as the ground of their acceptance, but that of the Surety provided for them by God Himself. "Who is he that condemneth ? It is Christ that died, yea rather that is risen again." Christ's name and title, *The Lord our righteousness* (Jer. xxiii. 6). This also the righteousness of Job, viewed as in common with others a sinner before God (ch. xl. 4; xlii. 6). Job upright in his life as a true servant of God, and so justified by *his own* righteousness before men ; Job a sinner in himself in the eye of the Divine law, and so justified by the righteousness of *his Surety* before God.

VII. Introduction to the pleading (verses 19—22).

1. *Challenges any opponent in the controversy* (verse 19). "Who is he that will plead with me ?" Defies any to shew that he is guilty of any crime deserving such unusual treatment. Similar challenge by God's righteous Servant (Is. l. 8); and by the Apostle in reference to believers (Rom. viii. 32).

2. *Expresses his intense desire to plead his cause before God, whatever the result.* "For now if I hold my tongue, I shall give up the ghost" (or, "for now [if he can make good his cause against me and prove me guilty] I will hold my tongue and die ").

3. *Begs only to be freed from restraint in pleading* (verse 20). "Only do not two things unto me, then will I not hide myself from thee." These two things specified—(1) The removal or lightening of his present suffering; "Withdraw thine hand far from me" (verse 21). (2) The withholding the overwhelming terror of his majesty; "and let not thy dread make me

afraid." The result of this request being granted,—"Then call thou (as plaintiff in the case), and I will answer (as defendant); or let me speak (as plaintiff), and answer thou me [the complaints that I have to make]." His wish either that God would accuse and give him an opportunity of answering for himself; or allow him to present his complaint as suffering without any known cause. No small presumption in the eyes of the friends for Job to wish either of these. The language only to be excused in the peculiar circumstances of the case. No sinner's part either to *complain against God*, or to *answer His charges*. Ultimately Job is taught to give up the place both of plaintiff and defendant. Observe—

1. Job's difficulties in pleading his cause were—God's *hand upon him*, and God's *dread over him.* God's hand easily made too heavy for any creature to bear. If so heavy on a *saint*, what must it be on a *sinner?* "If these things are done in the green tree, what shall be done in the dry?" If God's dread be overwhelming to a saint in a world of mercy, what will it be to the sinner in a world of doom? Good so to realise God's terror *now*, as to escape it *hereafter*.

2. The difficulties removed, Job would plead with God and not *hide himself from Him.* Natural for fallen men to seek to hide themselves from God. Adam's first act after the Fall was to sew fig-leaves together to *hide his own nakedness;* his second, to *hide himself* from God among the trees. Peter's language to Christ the natural expression of conscious guilt in presence of Divine majesty: Depart from me, for I am a sinful man, O Lord. Christ the true hiding-place of a sinner provided by God himself. Hidden by faith in the clefts of that Rock, the sinner can behold the majesty of God without dread.

VIII. Job pleads with God (verses 23—28).

1. *Asks to be shewn his sins which are the cause of his suffering* (verse 23). "How many are mine iniquities and my sins? Make me to know my transgression and my sin. Wherefore hidest thou thy face," &c. This not a confession of sin, but a desire to have it shown. Asked more in the spirit of self-justification than of humility. Job unconscious of such sin as to merit such suffering, yet willing to know it. First, as to the *number* of his sins, then ' any *particular transgression* that has entailed such chastisement. Three different kinds of offences indicated—(1) Iniquities, or perverse deviations from the Divine law; (2) Sins, or failures in duty; (3) Transgression, or the most heinous kind of sin, involving rebellion

and wilful breach of the law of God. Though not the cause of his sufferings, yet Job's offences immensely more numerous than he was aware of. Like Paul, had lived in all good conscience; yet secret unknown sins might still exist. David's acknowledgement—"Innumerable evils have compassed me about—mine iniquities are more than the hairs of my head" (Ps. xl. 12). God's testimony in regard to fallen man *before* the Flood, "Every imagination of the thought of his heart is only evil continually;" *after* the Flood, "The imagination of man's heart is evil from his youth" (Gen. vi. 5; viii. 21). Man's natural heart a poisonous upas tree and a corrupt spring. The fruit necessarily partakes of the nature of the tree; the streams, of that of the spring. Sin, in consequence of its effects on the soul, usually not known. Like the fish that discolours the water by its own secretion, and so escapes its pursuer. Important prayer (Ps. xix. 12; xxvi. 2; cxxxix. 23). Job ultimately made to know his transgression and his sin (ch. xlii. 6). *The discovery of the Divine glory is at the same time a discovery of our own sin.* The result of Job's trouble, as of all sanctified affliction. Knowledge of sin necessary to the knowledge of salvation. "The whole have no need of the physician." Sense of sin needful to sense of the blood that was shed for its remission.

2. *Pleads his present condition.* (1) As *forsaken by* God. "Wherefore hidest thou thy face, and holdest me for thine enemy?" (verse 24). This the most painful element in his sufferings. So with David (Ps. xiii. 1; xxii. 1), and with David's Lord (Matt. xxvii. 48). Implies previous enjoyment of His presence and favour (ch. xxix. 3—5). Only those who have known the sweetness of God's fellowship can realise the greatness of its loss. Intolerable to a child of God to be regarded and treated as an enemy. (2) As *feeble and afflicted.* "Wilt thou break a leaf driven to and fro? and wilt thou pursue the dry stubble?" Touching images of frailty and prostration—a leaf driven to and fro by the wind, and dry stubble, worthless and ready to take fire. Seemed unbecoming the Divine majesty to pursue so feeble a creature with so much severity. Job's sufferings already of some continuance. Had consisted in successive blows, increasing in severity, without mitigation or suspension.—*To the eye of sense God's dealings often unnatural and unlike Himself.* Hereafter seen to be all holy, and wise, and good, infinitely becoming His Divine Majesty and character. Winter with its gloom, as necessary and as much a part of nature's economy, as summer with its glow. "God is His own interpreter," &c.

Contrast with Job's pleading what the Saviour actually does (Ps. xlii. 3). 3. *Complains of the Divine treatment* (verses 26—29).—(1) *That God visited upon him the sins of his youth.* "Thou writest bitter things against me (—decreest bitter sufferings for me as the punishment of my offences), and makest me to possess (*Heb.* 'inherit') the iniquities of my youth (—to suffer the punishment of sins long passed, committed in the season of thoughtlessness, and then passed over)." Job entirely in the dark in regard to God's present dealings and the cause of his sufferings. *God's* part in them was to prove Job to be his faithful servant, in opposition to Satan's allegations. Believers unable to judge correctly of God's dealings from appearances. "Blind unbelief is sure to err," &c. Satan's object to get Job and every child of God to think as hardly of God as possible. God *might* visit the sins of youth on our riper years. Such sins deserving punishment, and requiring to be repented of in order to be forgiven. David remembered them, and besought *God* not to do so (Ps. xxv. 7). "Foolishness bound up in the heart of a child." The thoughts of man's heart evil from his youth. The natural effects of youthful sins sometimes experienced in maturer years. Job, conscious at least of youthful sins, supposes he must now be suffering the punishment of them. Yet Job's youth eminently virtuous and pious (ch. xxxi 1, 18). The sins of youth as well as of manhood atoned for by a Saviour's blood (Is. liii. 6). The bitterness of sin's punishment experienced by the Divine Surety on the cross (Matt. xxvii. 24).—(2) *That he was treated ignominiously as the vilest criminal* (ver. 27). "Thou puttest my feet also in the stocks." These a kind of clog, or fetter. Often a public, always a painful and ignominious punishment, and the severest restraint on personal liberty. Inflicted on Jeremiah in the gate, or most public place of the city

(Jer. xx. 2); and on Paul and Silas in the dungeon at Phillippi (Acts xvi. 24). Job's case appeared to him to resemble this. —"And lookest narrowly into all my paths" —either with the view of punishing, or of preventing escape. Job appeared to be watched as by a spy, or guarded as by a sentinel. Similar thought, ch. vii. 12, 20. His temptation common to believers. "Judge not the Lord by feeble sense." God's true character and dealings described by the prophet (Mic. vii. 18, 19).—"Thou settest a print upon the heels of my feet"— either—(*a*) as tracking his steps with a view to punishment; or (*b*) as marking him as a criminal or runaway slave with branded feet; or (*c*) as hemming in his path and forbidding escape. The flesh mistakes friends for foes. In the battle of Alma men fighting in the dark fired on their own countrymen. Satan's doings often mistaken for God's, and God mistaken for a foe.—(3) *That his lot was to pine away and perish* (verse 28). "And he as a rotten thing consumeth (or, 'and the same,' viz., the same unhappy culprit, meaning himself— a poetical and tragical change of the person, as better indicating his sense of his vile condition), as a garment that is moth-eaten." The humbling comparison of himself to worm-eaten wood, or to moth-eaten clothes, suggested by his bodily condition. The latter a common poetical figure for gradual but sure destruction. Applied to the body under disease (Ps. xxxix. 11); to men in general (Is. l. 9). The present verse closely connected with the following chapter, and forming a point of transition to it. Job's condition as frail and dying a plea with God for pity and forbearance. The plea remembered in regard to Israel (Ps. lxxviii. 39); in regard to men in general (Ps. ciii. 13, 14; Is. lvii. 16). God's mercy pities men's persons while his justice punishes their sins. Hence the gracious provision of a Substitute (Is. liii. 6).

CHAPTER XIV.

CONTINUATION OF JOB'S PLEADING WITH GOD.

I. **Pleads the common infirmity of human nature (verse 1—4).** Man, from the very nature of his birth, frail and mortal, suffering and sinful. "Born of a woman." Allusion to the sentence pronounced on Eve after the fall (Gen. iii. 16), "I will greatly multiply thy sorrow and thy conception; in sorrow shalt thou bring forth children." Like parent, like child. Such a birth a plea with the Almighty for lenience

and forbearance. Three evils resulting to humanity from that birth—

1. *Mortality.* "Of few days." Man ever since the fall has been short-lived. Jacob's testimony at the age of a hundred and thirty —"Few and evil have the days of the years of my life been" (Gen. xlvii. 9). The longest life short—(1) In comparison with eternity; (2) As compared with what it would have been but for the fall. Man's death the result

of sin. Probably the tree of life in the garden of Eden a symbol of man's immortality, and a means of effecting it. Death among the lower animals no argument against the doctrine that *man's* death is the wages of sin. As easy for God to make man's body immortal as to make it at all. If man reaching the age of Adam and Methuselah was short-lived, what is he now? Sad insanity, for the sake of this short span, to throw away a blissful eternity!

2. *Suffering.* "Full of trouble." Man's life on earth not merely sprinkled with trouble, but *saturated* with it. The first secue disclosed by Scripture after the Fall is,—Adam and Eve weeping tears of anguish over a son slaughtered by the hand of his brother. A representative event. Man's history, even under an economy of mercy and the operation of grace, a record of blood and tears. "Few and evil," the description of most men's lives. The "trouble" both inward and outward. Disquietude and unrest the natural man's daily experience. No peace to the wicked. Man's soul a sea continually agitated by the winds of passion. The name of external troubles "Legion." Bodily diseases a part of that death which is the wages of sin. Death itself a prominent element in the troubles of life. Life clouded by the fear and apprehension of it, in respect either to ourselves or our friends. Deep trouble through its inroads into the domestic or social circle. Man's inhumanity, unkindness, and wrong to his fellow-man. Reverses of fortune, poverty, want. Not least, the trouble superinduced by our own conduct. Suffering produced by sin as heat by fire. Trouble as man's lot on earth a fact of universal experience. "The world is an abode which if it make thee smile to-day, will make thee weep to-morrow" [*Hariri, an Arabian poet*].

Man's frailty and mortality set forth under two impressive figures:—

1. *A flower* (verse 2). "He cometh forth as a flower and is cut down." Man compared to a flower—(1) From its origin, the earth; (2) Its beauty; (3) Its delicate texture and construction, contrasted with the fruit; (4) Its frailty; (5) Its end. If allowed to grow, soon fades and falls off, but liable also to many casualties,—from the hand of men, the tooth of animals, the nipping frost, the mower's scythe. Man the goodliest flower framed by his Maker's hand. "Godlike, erect, with native honour clad." His goodliness as the flower of the field. Like the blossom, which opens, expands, reaches its perfection, fades, and then falls to its native earth. More frequently is prematurely "cut down." His life exposed to a thousand casualties. The flower however falls off only

to make way for the fruit. If prepared by grace, man dies only to ripen in a happier sphere.

2. *A shadow.* "He fleeth also as a shadow and continueth not." Time early measured by the shadow of a dial or a spear stuck in the ground. The shadow on the dial-plate never stands still. Glides on from hour to hour, from morning to noon, and from noon to night. The motion imperceptible, but constant and progressive. Neither stands still nor goes back. Only terminated by the setting of the sun or an unexpected cloud. So man's passage from the cradle to the grave. Hastens to the evening of death, which however often arrives unexpectedly before it is noon. The primæval sentence in continual execution,—"Dust thou art, and unto dust shalt thou return." The shadow an appropriate emblem also of the pleasures and pursuits of time, as empty and unsubstantial.—Lessons:—(1) To form a true estimate of the enjoyments and interests of time and eternity. (2) To improve our fleeting stay in this world to the preparation for a better. (3) To make a diligent use of present moments which alone are ours. (4) To stand always prepared for life's unexpected termination.

Human frailty employed by Job as a plea for leniency and forbearance (verse 3). "And dost thou open thine eyes upon (—pay rigid attention to) such an one (—one so frail, miserable, and short-lived)? and bringest me (or him) into judgment with thee" (—accusing and contending with him for his faults against thee)? The plea acknowledged by God (Ps. lxxviii. 39; ciii. 14; Is. lvii. 16; Gen. vi. 3). God however has opened His eyes on frail and suffering man, but differently from what Job intended. Has opened them in love and pity, so as to provide deliverance from man's wretched condition. So in regard to typical Israel (Exod. iii. 7, 8). God's eyes opened graciously on every humble and contrite soul (Is. lxvi. 2). On his covenant people, to watch over, defend, and bless them (Zech. xii. 4).

3. *Depravity,*—the third evil resulting to man from his birth (verse 4). "Who can bring a clean thing out of an unclean? Not one." From sinful parents can come only a sinful offspring. The plant must be according to the seed—the fruit according to the tree. God created Adam in His own likeness; Adam, after the Fall, begat children, not in God's likeness, but his own (Gen. v. 3). Men now shapen in iniquity and conceived in sin (Ps. li. 5). "In Adam all die,"—spiritually as well as physically and legally (1 Cor. xv. 22). The corruption of human nature in its root acknowledged by the heathen. "Nobody is born without vices,"

—the saying of a heathen poet. Man found everywhere and in all circumstances, corrupt and depraved. Savage and civilized partake of the same general character. Only to be accounted for by a common depraved nature. Children exhibit the same depravity as their parents. Deceit, envy, coveting, and self-will, common in early childhood. No outward restraint or appliances able to remove or overcome this innate depravity. No clean or holy thing ever brought forth out of man's sinful nature. "Out of the heart proceed evil thoughts," &c. "A corrupt tree cannot bring forth good fruit." Grapes not gathered from thorns. What is holy may proceed from a sinful *man*, but not from a sinful *nature*. God does not produce the fruits of the Spirit from man's old sinful nature, but from a new one imparted. Two distinct and opposite natures, the old man and the new, in a child of God, each producing its own proper fruits. The presence of the new makes the man a saint; that of the old a sinner. The believer is holy, and produces holy fruits in virtue of his new and holy nature; he is still sinful, and produces sinful fruits in virtue of his old and sinful one. Hence the Saviour's teaching: "Ye must be born again." The old nature crucified in a believer and destined to die; the new nature victorious even now, and ultimately alone in the field.

II. Pleads for removal or relaxation of his sufferings (verse 5—12).

His *prayer*, and the *grounds* of it.

1. *His prayer* (verse 6). "Turn from him" (or, "look away from him," *i.e.*, from Job himself), that he may rest (obtain relief from suffering, or rest in death), till he accomplish as an hireling his day" (or, 'that he may enjoy,' as far as a hireling may do so, ' his appointed period ' of labour, viz., the present life, or find the rest of evening after his toil, viz., in death). Human life already spoken of as "the days of a hireling" (ch. vii. 1);—(1) As a certain definite period; (2) As a period of toil and endurance. Job's day now felt to be especially oppressive. The burden and heat of the day for day-labourers in the East, especially severe (Matt. xx. 12). The rest of evening greatly longed for (ch. vii. 2). Job fluctuates between desire for alleviation of the burden, and for rest in the grave. So also in ch. vi. 8, 9; vii. 19; x. 20. *Times in a believer's experience when life seems especially burdensome.* The feeling of David (Ps. lv. 6); of Elijah (1 Kings, xix. 4); of Jonah (Jon. iv. 3, 8); of Jeremiah (Jer. ix. 2; xii. 5). Once the feeling of Jesus (Matt. xvii. 17). Christ at such times, as "a river of waters in a dry place, and the shadow of a great rock in a weary land," Believers not

tempted above what they are enabled to bear. In the day of the rough wind, the east wind stayed. Strength made equal to our day. "My grace is sufficient for thee."

2. *Grounds of the prayer* (verse v. 7—12). (1) *The time of our stay on earth fixed by God himself* (verse 5). "Seeing his days are determined, the number of his months are with thee, thou hast appointed his bounds that he cannot pass." Job troubled with no doubts on the subject of

Predestination.

That God appointed the bounds of man's life as certain with Job as that He made him at all. This belief held firmly by the Arabians to the present day. The doctrine of the Bible. Our time in God's hand. Man unable to add a cubit to his stature, an hour to his age. Consistent with the operation of second causes and natural laws. Means appointed along with the end. "Man's life no more governed by the Stoics blind fate than by the Epicurean's blind fortune" [*M. Henry*]. The fact pleaded by Job as a ground for the mitigation of his sufferings. The few short years allotted on earth may be graciously spared such excessive, accumulated, and continued affliction. It is still with God to say both how long and how severe our sufferings on earth shall be. Predestination perfectly consistent with

Prayer.

The Almighty not, like the God of the Stoics, bound by fate. May not change His *purpose*, but may alter His *procedure*. Changes in His outward procedure already in His secret purpose. The thread of man's life in God's hands, to lengthen or shorten it according to circumstances already foreseen. Hence full scope for the exercise of prayer. Prayer and its answers no interference with God's purposes. Not only *what* God does, but *how* He does it, already predetermined. *Believing prayer one of the means appointed with the end.* God builds up Zion at the "set time' to favour her, because He regards "the prayer of the destitute" (Ps. cii. 13—17). The duty and prevalence of prayer a fact as well of experience as of revelation. Prayer and its efficacy an instinct of human nature. One of the great moral laws under which God has placed His intelligent creatures. Man's inability to reconcile it with his philosophy no argument against it. *Man must pray ; and God is the hearer of prayer.*

(2.) *Our departure from this world final and irrevocable.* Man's case at death is—(i.) *contrasted* with that of a *felled tree* (verse 7). "For there is hope of a tree, if it be cut down, that it will sprout again, and that the tender branch (or shoot) thereof will not cease; though the root thereof wax old in the earth, and the stock thereof die (to all appearance) in the ground; yet through the scent of water (—its gentle contact, like an exhalation or an odour,) it will bud and bring forth boughs (*Heb.* 'a crop' of shoots) like a plant (or, 'as if it had been planted.') But man (even in his best estate— *Heb.* 'the strong man') dieth and wasteth away (or, ' is prostrated and gone'—loses all inward power of recovery or revival); yea, man (*Heb.*—man as sprung from the earth, '*Adam* ') giveth up the ghost and where is he?" (*i.e.*, is no more to be seen—a Biblical and Arab phrase).—(ii.) *Compared to water disappearing* by evaporation, absorption, or otherwise (verse 11). "As the waters fail from the sea (or lake,—the term applied to any considerable collection of water, Jer. li. 36; Is. xix. 5); and the flood (or winter-torrent) decayeth and drieth up (in summer); so man lieth down (in the grave) and riseth not ; till the heavens be no more they shall not awake, nor be raised out of their sleep." Man at death disappears for ever as a resident of this present world. No return to a mortal life. "The bourne whence no traveller returns." *That needs to be well done that can be done only once.* (See also ch. vii. 9, 10).

The question asked (verse 14)—"If a man shall die, shall he live again ?"—capable of a double answer. In regard to the present world, or the world in its present state, No ; in regard to a future resurrection, Yes. The fact of such resurrection, however, probably not, at least distinctly, in Job's mind. The doctrine of the

Resurrection

One of gradual development. Death viewed by most nations of antiquity as a "perpetual sleep." Revelation *assures* us of an awaking out of it (Dan. xii. 2 ; 1 Thess. iv. 14—17). That awaking at the Lord's appearing, when "the heavens shall pass away with a great noise" (2 Pet. iii. 7, 10, 11). New heavens and a new earth the promised abode of resurrection saints (2 Pet. iii. 13 ; Rev. xxi. 1). Resurrection only to follow the sin-atoning and death-destroying death on the cross. Hence the slight knowledge of it by Old Testament saints. The knowledge of it to be only according to the knowledge of that which was the foundation of it. Life and immortality brought to light by Christ Himself (2 Tim. i. 10). As in Adam all die, so only in Christ shall all be made alive. Christ rose as the first-fruits of them that slept. Christ the first-fruits; afterwards they that are Christ's at His

88

coming (1 Cor. xv. 20—23). Only faint and occasional glimpses of the resurrection obtained by Old Testament believers. David's hope expressed prophetically of the Messiah's resurrection, rather than personally of his own (Ps. xvi. 8; Acts ii. 25—31). The Lord's second appearing, and His people's resurrection as bound up with it, the blessed hope of New Testament believers. Vague and dim apprehension now exchanged for glorious certainty (2 Cor. v. 1 ; Phil. iii. 21).

State after death.

The question "Where is he ? (verse 10), solemn and important in relation to the *man*, viewed as possessing an immortal spirit. Only two states after death. Lazarus is carried into Abraham's bosom. The rich man lifts up his eyes in hell, being in torments. "The wicked is driven away in his wickedness." Where ? Judas went to "his own place." "The righteous hath hope in his death." The penitent thief was in Paradise, while his lifeless body was cast into a pit. Where was his companion who died in his sins ? Psalm ix. 17 gives the solemn answer. "Without holiness no man shall see the Lord."

III. Job desires a temporary concealment in the grave (verse 13).

"O that thou wouldst hide me in the grave until thy wrath be past (—the present affliction viewed as a token of that wrath); that thou wouldst appoint me a set time and remember me." Has doubts as to the possibility of this wish being accomplished. " If a man die, shall he live again ? " (verse 14).—Returns to his wish and states what would be the result of its being granted. "All the days of my appointed time (or warfare, as ch. vii. 1) will (or would) I wait till my change (dismission or renovation) come. Thou shalt (or shouldst) call and I will (or would) answer ; thou wilt (or wouldst) have a desire to the work of thine hands." A confused wish of Job's troubled spirit. Apparently inconsistent with his previous statements about man's irrevocable departure out of this world. Prayer, especially in deep affliction, often without much reflection. Even believers sometimes know not what they ask. Yet a great truth in his words, though but dimly apprehended by himself. Truths often uttered through the presence of the Spirit, when but imperfectly understood by the speaker (1 Pet. i. 12).

" To the imagination may be given
The type and shadow of an awful truth."

Much more when the human spirit is in intimate communion with the divine. God's saints actually hidden for a time in the grave and the spirit-world. The words of the prophet (Is. xxvi. 20), almost an echo of the patriarch's. A set time actually appointed to God's people for their recall from the grave. God remembers them there as he did Noah in the Ark (Gen. viii. 1). Their death precious in his sight. Their names engraven on the palms of his hands. Zion's wall's, though lying in ruins, continually before him (Is. xlix. 16). Living saints at the Lord's appearing not caught up till dead ones have been raised (1 Thess. iv. 15—17). The righteous, previous to the last and great tribulation, mostly taken away from the evil to come. Hidden in their chambers for a little moment till the indignation be overpast (Is. xxvi. 20). Observe—

1. Job's *faith and patience* (verse 14). "All the days of my appointed time will I wait till my change come. *Faith foresees* the change for the better, and *patience waits for* it. Three "*changes*" in a believer's experience—(1) When he is *born again*, and passes from spiritual death to life. (2) When he *falls asleep in Jesus* and enters the heavenly rest. (3) When he *rises from the grave* to be made in body and spirit entirely like Christ, and to be ever with the Lord. Probably the third of these vaguely and dimly indicated in Job's words. For this, as well as the change for the better at death, were his wish to be granted, he would patiently *wait*. Deliverance decreed for God's people from all trouble and from death itself. The *time* of that deliverance *in God's hands*. To be *patiently waited for*. Patient waiting the posture of believers in this world (Rom. viii. 23—25; 1 Thess. i. 10; Heb. x. 36). The vision is for an appointed time. The promise, Behold I come quickly. Blessed is he that waiteth. The change at a believer's death worth patient waiting for; much more the change at the Lord's appearing. At death we are *unclothed*, at the resurrection *clothed upon* (2 Cor. v. 2).

2. Job's *joyous anticipation*, should his wish be granted (verse 15). "Thou shalt call." No awaking from the sleep of death but at the Divine *call*. "Awake and sing, ye that dwell in dust" (Is. xxvi. 19). For the call, see also John v. 28; 1 Cor. xv. 52; 1 Thess. iv. 14—17. The call of the Bridegroom (Cant. ii. 10—13).—A ready response given by believers to the call. "And I will *answer*." The language of conscience innocence in the case of Job; of conscious acceptance " in the Beloved " in the case of every believer.—The *reason* of that Divine call—" Thou wilt have a desire to the *work of thine hands*." Believers especially the work of God's hands—(1) In *creation*. Man's

body a masterpiece of Divine skill directed by Divine benevolence.

" In their looks Divine
The image of their glorious Maker shone;
Truth, wisdom, sanctitude severe and pure."

(2) In *regeneration and sanctification*. Believers God's workmanship created in Christ Jesus (Eph. ii. 10). The expression frequent in Isaiah as applied to God's people (Is. xxix. 23; xlv. 11; lx. 21; lxi. 3). Believers a more costly work than all creation besides. Required the incarnation, suffering, and death of the Creator. The heavens the work of God's fingers, believers the work of God's hands (Ps. viii. 3). To this work of His hands God has a special *desire*. That desire one of—(1) Pity and benevolence; (2) Yearning affection; (3) Complacency and delight. The Father's desire is to them as His children; the Son's, as His Bride and the purchase of His blood; the Spirit's as His especial work. Faith unable, in the darkest time, to give up the idea of God's loving fatherhood. Looks through the gloomy passage of the grave, and sees more or less clearly a light shining at the farther end.

IV. Complains again of God's present severity (verse 16, 17). " For (or, 'but') now thou numberest my steps (taking strict account of all my actions); dost thou not watch over my sin (in order to punish it) ? My transgression is sealed up in a bag (as if so much treasure, that none may be lost or left unpunished, or as so much evidence preserved against me); and thou sewest up mine iniquity " (in order carefully to keep it for future punishment). A constant recurrence of God's present apparent severity. Remembered now, either as the reason for Job's wish for concealment in the grave (verse 13), or as the contrast of its fulfilment (' but now ' &c.). *Hard to get over present grievances*. All Job's sufferings viewed as the result of God's resolution to punish his every failure. Observe—(1) " *Faith and unbelief view God's character and dealings in an opposite light* ; (2) *A time of darkness and trouble unfavourable for a right judgment*. Job's present view of God's character and dealings entirely a mistaken one. His character is—" Slow to anger;" " Ready to forgive;" " Delighting in mercy." Sin, however, in order to its being forgiven, thus dealt with in the case of the Surety. The iniquities of all the redeemed laid upon Him. Strict account taken of sin by God in dealing with the Sin-bearer. No sin pardoned in the sinner without being punished in the Substitute. God just while justifying the ungodly. Job's view true in a dispensation of simple *law*. *Not* true in a dispensation of mercy and under the covenant of grace. Sad to live under a dispensation of mercy and not to avail oneself of its benefits. The worst of all cases, to have the guilt of a rejected Saviour added to all other transgressions.

V. Again bewails man's mortality and wretchedness (verse 18—22).

First by comparison with the mutability everywhere visible in Nature. (1) The *mountain and the rock*, that seem the firmest of all earthly objects. These, or at least portions of them, torn away from the rest by earthquakes or other agencies, fall and then lie mouldering and crumbling on the ground (verse 18). "And surely (or 'but') the mountain falling cometh to nought, and the rock is removed," &c. (2) *Stones*, the hardest of earthly materials, are worn away by the slow continual action of water (verse 19). "The waters wear the stones." (3) The very soil forming the loose surface of the earth, with the trees, grain, &c., that grow in it, is washed away by floods. "Thou washest away the things that grow out of the dust of the earth" (or, "the floods sweep away the dust," &c).

Man, a partaker of the general corruptibility and decay. "And (or, 'so') thou destroyest the hope of man" (—'wretched' man's hope and expectation of prolonging his life on the earth). Human mortality in keeping with the decay of all visible nature. Man ordinarily thinks of death as at a distance from him. "All men think all men mortal but themselves." The hope of evading the last enemy vain. The sentence has gone forth, Dust thou art, &c. (verse 20). "Thou prevailest for ever against him (—'always,' or, 'to complete victory'), and he passeth," (or, "he is gone,"—departs of this world). Man properly uses his endeavour to prolong his life. Battles against the sentence, "unto dust shalt thou return." In vain. The victory always with God who executes his own sentence. Three stages in this victory—(1) *Disease.* "Thou changest his countenance." Sickness alters the state of our frame, and the aspect of our face. Instead of the glow and plumpness of health comes the paleness and emaciation of disease. Job himself at the time an example of his own words. (2) *Death.* "Thou sendest him away." Death is God's dismission. "Return ye children of men." The world "a stage where every man must play his part." The time for his exit in God's hand. (3) *The disembodied state* in the

World of Spirits.

Represented by Job—

1. As a *state of ignorance of what takes place on earth*, especially as regards *surviving relatives* (verse 21). "His sons come to honour, and he knoweth it not; and they are brought low, but he perceiveth it not of them." Parents naturally very deeply interested in the prosperity or adversity of their children. In the spirit-world, ignorant of and unaffected by either. Absolute separation from all the living and the creatures of the present world. This however not necessarily to be regarded as a divine declaration of the real state of the case. Rather the utterance—(*a*) Of Job's own melancholy spirit at the time; (*b*) Of the views generally entertained on the subject at that early period. The knowledge possessed by the departed in reference to survivors still a mystery. Among "the spirits of the just," probably more of such knowledge than we are aware of. Joy among the angels of God over one repenting sinner. Naturally also among departed saints. Hence, still more, over a repenting relative. Such knowledge an obvious increase to their joy and praise. Angels constant attendants on believers in life, and their escort to paradise at death. Departed saints therefore probably made acquainted by angels, if not more directly, with the circumstances of converted relatives on earth. The mere worldly prosperity or adversity of surviving relatives, however, even if known, probably, as such, a matter of the utmost insignificance to departed saints.

2. As a *state of suffering and grief* (verse 22). "But his flesh upon him shall have pain, and his soul within him shall mourn" (or, "only his flesh shall have pain on account of himself, and his soul on account of himself shall mourn"). The dead man represented as occupied with his own concerns, not those of his surviving friends. His state not one of pleasure but of pain; his experience not one of joy but of grief. Spoken of man in general without reference to distinction of character. Also spoken according to the view then entertained of the state of departed spirits. That state one of anything but comfort or joy (see ch. x. 21, 22). The "flesh" and "soul" here viewed as making up the man, who is regarded as still conscious in the spirit-world. That consciousness, however, one only of discomfort. Hence, the desire for life so prevalent in Old Testament times. Almost any kind of life regarded as preferable to an abode in the world of spirits. Such views natural, apart from revelation. Even still the views of many living under the Gospel but ignorant of its truths. The experience of the body transferred to the departed spirit, as if partaking of it. The thing dreaded in death—"To lie

in cold abstraction and to rot." Views of the spirit-world entirely changed since the Advent of Him who is both the Life and the Light. Life and immortality brought by Him to light through the Gospel. The kingdom of heaven opened to all believers. The spirit-world now their Father's house—the better country—Paradise—the rest from labour—the Mount Zion—the place of Divine worship and communion—the heavenly Jerusalem—the general assembly and church of the first-born—the innumerable company of angels—the presence of Jesus, the Elder Brother and Mediator of the New Covenant. The views of Job more correctly applicable in reference to the unsaved dead. The rich man in hell (or Hades) lifted up his eyes, being in torment. Compared with the con-

dition of an unsaved soul in the world of spirits—

"The weariest and most loathed worldly life
That ache, age, penury and imprisonment
Can lay on Nature, is a paradise."

Lessons :—

1. The comparative insignificance of worldly prosperity or adversity in view of the eternal world.

2. The infinite importance of securing a place of happiness beyond the grave—(1) For ourselves ; (2) For our children and friends.

3. The value of the Gospel, and the duty of making ourselves acquainted with its precious contents.

4. The paramount necessity of a personal interest in Him who is the Way, the Truth, and the Life.

CHAPTER XV.

SECOND COURSE OF DIALOGUES.—SECOND SPEECH OF ELIPHAZ.

Eliphaz less gentle and courteous than in his former speech. Probably irritated at his little success with Job, who rejected his friend's counsel and still maintained his own uprightness. The hostility of the friends more pronounced as the dialogue proceeds.

I. **Eliphaz sharply reproves Job's speeches** (verses 2—13).

Censures—

1. Their *emptiness and vehemence* (verse 2). "Should a wise man (*Heb.*, 'the wise man') utter vain knowledge (*Heb.*, answer [with] knowledge of wind, or windy sentiments), and fill his belly (his mind or heart, John vii. 38) with the East wind,"—cherishing and uttering opinions which are not only empty as the wind, but injurious to himself and others ; like the parching, vehement east wind, scorching and drying up all vegetation. Such language as Job had employed, unbecoming, in the opinion of Eliphaz, the wise man that he had passed for. Job celebrated in his own country for wisdom as well as piety (ch. xxix. 8, 9, 21—23). "Should the wise man," &c., —probably a taunt. Men with a character for wisdom to be careful to speak and act consistently with it. A little folly in such men like the dead fly in the apothecary's perfume (Ecc. x. 1).

2. Their *verbiage and unprofitableness* (verse 3). "Should he reason with unprofitable talk, or with speeches," &c.,—as if Job's speeches were mere talk. A charge as ungenerous and unfeeling as it was untruthful and unjust. Job no mere talker, though his words not always wise. A Christian's speech to be with grace seasoned with salt, and good

to the use of edifying. The abundant talk of the lips tendeth to penury. In the multitude of words there wanteth not sin. Unprofitable talk the mark of an unregenerate heart.

3. Their *impiety and hurtful influence* (verse 4) "Yea thou casteth off fear (or, makest void the fear [of God as of no value], and restrainest (—lessenest or discouragest) prayer before God [as of no use]". Job's language viewed either as indicating want of reverence and piety in himself, or rather as tending to discourage it in others. The danger implied in Asaph's hasty conclusion : "Verily I have cleansed my heart in vain" (Ps. lxxiii. 13); or, in the language of the fool's heart : "There is no God" (Ps. xiv. 1). Observe—(1.) The *interests of religion greatly in the keeping of its professors* (2.) A believer in trouble to be careful so to speak as to bear a good testimony to religion before the world.

4. Their *wickedness and deceit* (verse 5). "Thy mouth uttereth thine iniquity (or, 'thine iniquity teacheth thy mouth,' viz. to utter such wickedness), and thou choosest the tongue of the crafty." Job's language viewed as the studied contrivance of a wicked heart. Out of the abundance of the heart the mouth speaketh. As a man is, so is his speech. When the heart restrains prayer the mouth puts forth peevishness. What piety appeared in Job's speeches uncharitably viewed by Eliphaz as only employed with the intent to deceive. His tongue that of the crafty, who "by good words and fair speeches deceive the hearts of the simple" (Rom. xvi. 18). No new thing

91

for an upright man to be charged with hypocrisy. God's testimony regarding Job the opposite to that of Eliphaz. Observe —(1.) *A small matter for men to speak ill if God speaks well of us*; (2.) Our speech and conversation to be with "*simplicity and godly sincerity*, not with fleshly wisdom, but *by the grace of God*" (2 Cor. i. 12).

The charge of Eliphaz untrue in both its senses. Job spoke rashly, but neither cast off the fear of God nor restrained prayer. His words not always wise, but neither tended to destroy religion nor discourage devotion. A godly man may sin *against* the commandments; it is the part of a wicked man to sin *away* the commandments themselves. The casting off of God's fear the cause of all evil. When the fear of God goes out, the practice of sin comes in. The fear of God the beginning of wisdom; the casting of it off, the abandonment to all wickedness. The fear of God the sum of all godliness; the casting of it off, the sum of all sinfulness. Sad not to possess the fear of God; still worse to cast it off. To be without it ourselves is bad; to destroy it in others still worse. The deepest brand of guilt on a man's brow is, not only to sin himself, but, like Jeroboam, to make others to sin also (1 Kings xiv. 16; xv. 30, 34; xvi. 2, 19, 26). Job's sin that he seemed more to complain against God than to pray to Him. Sad at any time to restrain prayer, still more in the time of affliction (Ps. l. 15; Is. xxvi. 16). Prayer a principal part of God's worship and of man's religion. A prayerless life the mark of a graceless heart. Prayer is restrained either —(1) From distaste for it; or (2) From disbelief in its efficacy; or (3) From disdain and self-sufficiency. To restrain prayer to God is to be a god to ourselves. Believing prayer opens the door of mercy and the windows of blessing; to restrain prayer is to shut both against us.

.5. Job's speeches reproved also for their *arrogance* and *pride* (verse 7). "Art thou the first man that was born, or wast thou made before the hills? Hast thou heard the secret (or, 'hast thou been a listener in the privy council') of God, and dost thou restrain wisdom to thyself? What knowest thou that we know not? What understandest thou which is not in us. With us are both the greyheaded and very aged men, much elder than thy father. Are the consolations of God small with thee (or, 'too small for thee,' or, 'of little account with thee')? Is there any secret thing with thee (or, 'and the word which dealeth gently with thee;' or, 'and our mild addresses to thee') ?" Job's ridicule of his friends' monopoly of wisdom retorted by Eliphaz upon himself. Grievous words stir up anger. Job had

ridiculed his friends as if they were the whole race ; is now ridiculed himself as if he were the first man that had been born. Wisdom rightly supposed to have been much greater in Adam than in his children, as made after the image of God himself. Similar language to that addressed here in ridicule to Job divinely applied to Christ as the wisdom of God (Prov. viii. 22—26). Hills spoken of as the firmest, and therefore supposed to be the most ancient, of earthly things. Said to be everlasting (Gen. xlix. 26; Heb. iii. 6). Eliphaz views his own and his friends' discourses as "the consolations of God," and angrily asks Job if these were too small for him, or if he held them of small account. Their discourses and consolations, however, rather adapted for an impenitent sinner than a tried suffering saint. Hence Job's low esteem of them (ch. xiii. 4, 12). Preachers and others to take care that what they present to mourners are in reality

The Consolations of God.

God the God of all comfort. Comforteth those that are cast down (2 Cor. i. 3, vii. 6). Comforts tenderly as a mother, effectually as a Creator, (Is. lxvi. 13, lxv. 18). Able to make either anything or nothing a comfort to us. Can multiply comforts as fast as the world multiplies crosses. His consolations viewed either as *spoken to us* or *wrought in us*. Are either good things *done for us* or *promised to us*. God comforts—(1) By His spirit; (2) By His word; (3) By His providence. His consolations include—(1) His purposes in trouble; (2) His promises of support and deliverance; (3) The benefits resulting from it; (4) The example of the saints and especially of the Son of God; (5) The fellowship of believers, and especially of Christ (Dan. iii. 25); (6) God Himself as our shield here and our portion hereafter; (7) His love as the origin of our trouble; (8) The glories of eternity as infinitely compensating for the troubles of time. Trouble itself a consolation to a child of God as the testimony of his Father's love. God's rod, like Jonathan's, brings honey on its point. "Thy rod and thy staff comfort me" (Ps. xxiii. 4). Observe—(1.) *The consolations of God are not small.* Are able to meet every case. Strong consolation (Heb. vi. 18). Exceeding great and precious promises (2 Pet. i. 4). The Scriptures written that through patience and comfort we might have hope. The plaster of God's Word able to cover the largest sore of a sin-stricken soul. God has great consolations for great sorrows. His consolations like Himself. Christ Himself the consolation of Israel. The Holy Ghost the comforter. The consolations of God are—(i.) True and solid; (ii.) Holy and satisfying; (iii.) Adequate and suitable; (iv.) Lasting and durable. (2) *The consolations of God are not to be accounted small.* No small sin to slight God's consolations, as either insufficient or unsuitable to our case. These, on the contrary, to be highly valued—(i.) On account of their origin—the love of God; (ii.) Their costliness—the purchase of a Saviour's blood; (iii.) Their efficacy—as able to meet our case; (iv.) Their freeness on God's part and their undeservedness on ours.

6. Job's speeches reproved also for their *passion and rebelliousness* (verse 12). "Why doth thine heart carry thee away, and what do thine eyes wink at (as indicating passion, pride, and evil purpose)? That thou turnest thy spirit against God, and lettest such words go out of thy mouth." Unfeeling and exaggerated questions. Neither Job's spirit nor his words to be always vindicated, but undeserving of such severe reproof. Reproof, when unjust and excessive, becomes cruelty instead of kindness. Tenderness a duty in dealing with a sinner, still more with a saint, and most of all with a sufferer. The language, and perhaps the looks of Job, at times indicative of unholy passion. The flesh even in a believer weak. The heat of the temper apt to carry away into hastiness of the tongue. Job at times too bold with God; yet his boldness that of a child, not that of an enemy. The spirit of an impenitent sinner is turned *against* God in trouble, that of a believer is turned *towards* Him. The latter the attitude of Job's spirit in his affliction (ch. xvi. 20).

II. **Eliphaz insists on man's depravity** (verse 14). "What is man (wretched fallen man, *Heb.*, ' *Enosh*'), that he should be clean? and he which is born of a woman, that he should be righteous? Behold, he putteth no trust in his saints (or angels,—*Heb.* 'holy ones'); yea, the heavens (literally, or their inhabitants) are not clean in his sight. How much more abominable and filthy is man (or, 'how much less [shall] abominable and filthy man [be clean in his sight]') which drinketh iniquity like water?" A clear and strong declaration of man's deep and universal depravity. The object to prove Job a sinner, and convict him of arrogance in maintaining his uprightness. The argument is—(1) *Unsound.* The premises true but the conclusion false. Man universally depraved, but Job not therefore a bad man or a hypocrite; otherwise Satan's allegation just,—no such thing as genuine religion in the world. Grace and holiness in the individual consistent with depravity in the race.

The object of redemption to renew fallen man to purity. Comparatively blameless morals and upright principles found even among the heathen. Examples; Socrates, Aristides the Just, Cyrus the Great. (2) *Useless.* Man's depravity admitted and maintained by Job as well as Eliphaz (ch. xiv. 4). Not absolute but relative purity claimed by Job. All but useless for a preacher to labour to prove what all his hearers fully admit. The passage valuable as a testimony to

The Depravity of Human Nature.

1. Declared in the *name* given to man here and elsewhere in the Hebrew Scriptures, "*Enosh*," — miserable and desperately diseased. Man's very nature morally diseased. Inward renovation necessary in order to purity and holiness. To cleanse and renew man's corrupt nature, the work of the Holy Spirit through the instrumentality of Gospel truth. "Now ye are clean through the word which I have spoken to you." The promise in the New Covenant: "I will sprinkle clean water upon you and ye shall be clean" (Ez. xxxvi. 25). David's prayer: "Create in me a clean heart." The object of Christ's death, to sanctify and cleanse the Church as with the washing of water by the word (Eph. v. 26). His prayer to the Father: "Sanctify them through thy truth; thy word is truth" (John xvii. 17). The believer in one sense "clean every whit" (John xiii. 10). Apart from grace none clean in God's sight. Sin stains man's best performances. His righteousnesses filthy rags (Is. lxiv. 6). Man only clean and holy as a member of Christ the Holy One, and in virtue of a new nature implanted in him by the Holy Ghost. At death, the last remains of the believer's sinful nature for ever gone. The leprous house taken down and rebuilt entirely free from the vile infection.

2. Man's depravity the result of his *birth*. Born naturally of a fallen woman, man's nature necessarily depraved. A clean thing not to be produced in the mere course of nature from an unclean (ch. xiv. 4). Man now shapen in iniquity in the womb, and conceived by his mother in sin (Ps. li. 5). Like mother, like child. One glorious and necessary exception. Christ "born of a woman," yet righteous and clean from His birth. The reason: "His conception by the immediate agency of the Holy Ghost (Luke i. 35). Man's Saviour must be Himself a man, yet absolutely clean from his birth. To be a man he must be "born of a woman;" to be clean his conception must be the immediate production of Divine power. No necessity for the figment of the immaculate

conception of the Saviour's mother. Mary a holy woman, not by nature but by grace. Her song that of a saved sinner (Luke i. 47).

3. Man's character given in three particulars—(1) *Abominable.* Something to be loathed. Sin the abominable thing that God hates. Makes every creature abominable in whom it prevails. Man, as depraved, cast out like Israel at his very birth, to the loathing of his person (Ezek. xvi, 5). No education, refinement, or accomplishment able to make an unrenewed man anything less than abominable in the sight of God. (2) *Filthy,*—the filthiness rather to the smell than the taste. The noisomeness of a corpse or of a sewer. The sourness of a fermenting mass. Sin is death and moral putrefaction. Makes a man in whom it reigns a living corpse. Not all the perfumes of Arabia able to sweeten an unrenewed soul. (3) *Drinking iniquity like water.* (i.) Man loves and delights in sin. (ii.) Thirsts for it and pursues it eagerly. (iii.) Expects and endeavours to satisfy himself by its commission. (iv.) Commits it as a thing necessary to his existence; can no more live without it than an ox can live without drinking water. (v.) Practises it habitually, as a horse must daily drink water. (vi.) Finds pleasure in its commission, but nothing that permanently satisfies him; thirsts again. (vii.) Commits it abundantly, not sipping but drinking it. (viii.) Goes to it naturally, as an animal goes naturally to drink water; sin natural to a depraved heart. (ix.) Commits it easily and without effort; sins on easy terms and small consideration; water a common drink. Observe, however, a *contrast* as well as a *resemblance* in the case:—(i.) Water a creature of God; sin a thing of the devil. (ii.) Water designed by God for the use of man and beast; sin strictly forbidden by Him. (iii.) Water necessary for man's existence; sin not only not necessary, but ruinous. (iv.) Water beneficial to the drinker of it; sin only hurtful and destructive.

III. Eliphaz proposes to convict Job from the Fathers (verse 17) &c.

"I will shew thee, hear me; and that which I have seen (—personally observed as well as heard from others) I will declare; which wise men have told from their fathers, and have not hid it. Unto whom alone the earth (or land) was given (for their residence and government,—in opposition to Job's statement in ch. ix, 24,) and no stranger passed among them" (or, "came among them," as a resident or invader). Traditional maxims of the ancients avowedly introduced by Eliphaz, as had already been done by Job

and the other speakers. These ancients the fathers of "wise men," who had handed down their moral sayings to their posterity. To this posterity belonged Eliphaz himself. Like Job, a contemporary of Serug and Reu, the son and grandson of Peleg, in whose days the earth was divided after the dispersion (Gen. x. 25). The ancients or fathers, therefore, probably Noah and his son Shem, or Noah's ancestors back to Adam. The "wise men," those to whom the land of Arabia was given as their residence, viz., the sons of Joktan, the younger son of Eber (Shem's grandson), and Peleg's brother, by whom Arabia was first populated (Gen. x. 25—30). One of these sons of Joktan named Jobab, supposed by some to be the same with Job. The boast of Eliphaz that among these "wise men" or sons of Joktan, "no stranger" or foreigner had ever been allowed to corrupt their religion and morals. The glory of the Arabs is their language, their sword, and their pure blood. The true religion often corrupted by the mixture of foreign nations. . Israel forbidden to make alliances with the nations around them lest they should "learn their ways." The saying of a heathen poet endorsed by Revelation, "Evil communications corrupt good manners." Arabia famed for its wise men. These handed down to posterity the moral and religious truth received in like manner from their fathers.—The true religion propagated by parents and others carefully instructing the rising generation in its truths. The obvious and sacred duty of all who possess it (Ps. xlviii. 13; lxxviii. 3, 4).

IV. Quotation from the Fathers in reference to the experience of the ungodly (verses 20—35).

Noble specimen of Oriental poetry. Sublime and tragical, and among the most ancient in the world. A description of unprincipled men whose only aim is the acquisition of wealth and power, stopping at no means to obtain it, and then abusing it to the oppression of their fellow-men. Applicable in every period of the world, but more particularly in its earlier ages, when, as before the flood, "the earth was filled with violence." The characters especially such as the "mighty men which were of old, men of renown" (Gen. vi. 4, 11—13). Men of the class of Cain, Nimrod and Pharaoh—impious and daring towards God, cruel and unjust towards their fellow-men. The application wrongfully intended for Job, in order to bring him to conviction and repentance. The only ground for the application in his circumstances, none whatever in his character and conduct. Job, once rich and prosperous, was now in great misery through successive blows of Divine providence. This sufficient ground with Eliphaz for its application. The doctrine intended by Eliphaz to be conveyed by it, as to the constant and exclusive attendance of misery upon wickedness in this world, repeatedly denied by Job (ch. xii. 6; xxi. 7), &c.

The description contains:—

1. The *character* of the persons intended. All sin deserving of punishment, but some sins more heinous in God's sight than others. The persons intended are described as— (1.) *Wicked* (verse 20). Men lawless and unprincipled, of wicked hearts and wicked lives. All men sinners, but by God's Providence and His renewing or restraining grace, all not *wicked* sinners.—(2.) *Violent oppressors* (verse 20). The distinctive character of these wicked men. Their wickedness manifested in their violent conduct and oppression of their fellow-men. Their object, power and wealth; their means of obtaining them, violence and wrong. Great warriors and conquerors. Ambitious chiefs and tyrants. Robbers on a large as well as a small scale. Particularly described by Zophar (ch. xx. 19). The character which Eliphaz afterwards directly ascribes to Job (ch. xxii. 6, 7, 9). A common character in those early ages, and in the barbarous and uncivilised state of a community.—(3.) *Daring and impious* (verse 25). "For he stretcheth out his hand against God and strengtheneth himself (or, 'plays the hero') against the Almighty; he runneth upon him (*viz.*, upon God,—rushes on Him with swiftness and fury, as Dan. viii. 6), even on his neck (like a fierce combatant, eager to grapple with his antagonist in close quarters; or, 'with his neck,' like a furious bull whose strength is in his neck and shoulders), upon (or with) the thick bosses of his bucklers" (like a band attacking with joined shields). The language of Pharaoh (Ex. v. 2); of Sennacherib (Is. xxxvi. 20); of the crucifiers of Christ (Acts iv. 25—27; Ps. ii. 1). Similar defiance of the Almighty exhibited by the Dragon and his angels (Rev. xii. 7). The character of obstinate and impenitent transgressors in general. Men "fight against God" while—(i.) Persevering in a course of sin; (ii.) Opposing God's cause or Gospel, His Church, or any of His people (Acts v. 39); (iii.) Contending for an object in opposition to His will, and by means which He forbids. Fearful stage in sin when men act as champions of hell against the God of heaven. —(4.) *Profligate and profane* (verse 34). "Hypocrites," or rather, profane and profligate men. Men who neither "fear God nor regard men." No reference intended by the term in the Old Testament to religious profession.—(5.) *Covetous and unjust* (verse 34).

Men given to "bribery." As rulers and judges, accepting gifts as the bribe for a favourable though unjust sentence. Men who wronged others by perverting justice in order to enrich themselves. Accepted gifts for the perpetration of wicked deeds.—(6.) *Plotters of mischief* (verse 35). "They conceive mischief and bring forth vanity" (*Margin*, "iniquity"). The same character described, Ps. xxxvi. 4; Prov. iv. 16. Sins against our neighbour chiefly intended. Those who do not fear God readily plot against men.—(7.) *Cunning and deceitful* (verse 35). "Their belly (mind or heart, but with reference to conception) prepareth (contrives or matures) deceit" (for *others* in order to their own gain, for *themselves* in their disappointment of it). Evil ends often attainable only by deceit. So Satan and our first parents; Haman and the Jews; Jezebel and Naboth's vineyard.

2. The *temporary prosperity* of the persons intended (verse 27). "Because he covereth (or, 'though he have covered') his face with fatness (see Ps. lxxiii. 7), and maketh collops of fat on his flanks" (or, "hath made fat on his loins"). Good living his object. His god his belly (Luke xvi. 19).—"And he inhabiteth desolate cities (or, 'and though he inhabited cities destroyed by him' and taken into his own possession,—conduct ascribed to Crassus the Roman general, and in houses which no man inhabiteth (—emptied of their proper inhabitants), which are ready to become heaps" (or, "are doomed to ruins")— reminding Job of his own calamity in the case of his children (ch. i. 19). Temporary success in sin to be followed by ultimate ruin. The wicked raised for a deeper fall. Iniquity often like a tree full of blossom, to be blighted by the frost or blasted by the lightning. Prosperous villainy one of the mysteries of Divine providence.

3. Their *subsequent misery*. Suffering corresponding with sin. This objected to by Job as to its universal occurrence in this life. The passage describes—(1.) The *inward experience* of the wicked in this life (verse 20, &c.). "The wicked man travaileth with pain (or, 'is inwardly tormented') all his days (lives a life of anxiety and fear); and the number of years hidden to the oppressor" (or, "and the number of years," or "the few years [which] are laid up for" him). The whole life of the oppressor comes to be full of anxiety and alarm under the goad of an evil conscience. Sin, like a corpse or a putrid ulcer, breeds worms.—"A dreadful sound (*Heb.* 'a voice of alarms,'—not one terror but many) is in his ears; in prosperity, the destroyer (God's avenging justice, or some hand of violence as the executioner of it) shall come upon him" (what actually takes

place, or what the voice of conscience inwardly threatens him with). The Avenging Furies of the heathen expressive of facts in the experience of the daring transgressor. The suddenness of the destruction intended, or the presence of these voices of terror in the midst of outward quiet and prosperity. The unexpectedness of calamity a serious aggravation of it. "When they shall say, Peace and safety," &c. (Verse 22).—"He believeth not that he shall return out of darkness (that he shall ever escape out of the misery that threatens or has already overtaken him,—the language sadly suggestive of Job's own case); and he is waited for of the sword" (actually or in his own apprehension). Besides present evils he anticipates future ones. The sword of Damocles hangs over his head at his most sumptuous feasts. His terrified imagination sees a dagger wherever he turns. Only a violent and bloody death is before his eyes. "Every one that findeth me shall slay me." Despair of good the greatest evil. A wicked man has neither ground nor heart to believe [*Caryl*]. Faith a shield against the fiery darts of the devil; unbelief a shield against the tender mercies of God. Faith makes evil good; unbelief makes good evil.—(Verse 23). "He wandereth abroad for bread, saying, Where is it?" He becomes like Cain, "a fugitive and a vagabond on the earth." Job's fall from affluence to poverty might seem to afford an example. The bread he has taken from others now fails himself. The wicked wander for bread when they are rich as well as when they are poor. The godly are content in every condition.—"He knoweth that the day of darkness is near at hand,"— has the inward conviction that a time of poverty and calamity will soon overtake him. Terrible certainty of a guilty conscience. The Furies brandish in his face their threatening whip. Conscience holds up the sentence of condemnation before his eyes. The experience which impelled Judas to the fatal tree. The certain apprehension of future and speedy perdition one principal cause of suicide. Such terrors aided, if not generated, by the Tempter, who now becomes the Tormentor. The Gospel of the grace of God, free and immediate forgiveness through the blood of the cross to the chief of sinners, the blessed and only remedy in such a case. The oil of pardoning mercy alone able to smooth that surging sea. Jesus the only Physician that can minister to that mind diseased. "Believe in the Lord Jesus Christ and thou shalt be saved," has already in multitudes "cleansed the bosom of that perilous grief which weighs upon the heart," and changed black despair into bright and joyous hope. "Fear not, only believe." (Verse 24).—"Trou-

ble and anguish (—multiplied and intensified distress, or, outward trouble and inward anguish) shall make him afraid." Again too much resemblance to Job's case (ch. vi. 4). Worse to fear evil than to feel it.—"They shall prevail against him" (or "hem him in"). Shall break his spirit or end his life. Shall scare him not only out of his comfort but out of his senses [*Caryl*].—"As a king (or general) ready to the battle." Trouble and anguish personified as a general in the midst of his troops, surrounding the enemy, rushing on to the attack and overpowering him. The evil-doer powerless to resist this attack of outward trouble and inward anguish. Troubles too great to bear, too thick to escape from. "My punishment is greater than I can bear." "The spirit of a man may sustain his infirmity, but a wounded spirit who can bear?" Such an experience often the result of long-rejected calls to repentance and offers of mercy (Prov. i. 24—30).

(2) The *outward visitation* of the wicked. (Verse 29). "He shall not be rich (or continue so,—shall not enjoy his ill-gotten wealth, which shall 'flow away on the day of wrath'), neither shall his substance continue, neither shall he prolong the perfection there of (or 'extend his possessions, flocks, &c.') upon the earth" (or in the land). Apparently another side-glance at Job's losses. Ill-gotten goods never lasting. Sinners earn wages to put them into a bag with holes. Earthly joys, like children's toys, easily broken and soon forgotten.—(Verse 30). "He shall not depart out of darkness"— shall not escape out of the trouble and misery that shall overtake him. Endless misery the just wages of unceasing sin. —"The flame (—lightning or the hot wind of the desert, emblems of the wrath of God) shall dry up his branches (—his prosperity, more especially his children; another sad cut for Job, ch. i. 16, 19); and by the breath of his mouth (—the anger of God, compared to a scorching or a scattering wind) shall he go away" (retreat as a worsted combatant, or be whirled away as chaff or stubble, Ps. i. 4). God's mere breath able to sweep away the sinner. Indicates also the suddenness of the destruction.—(Verse 32). "It (*viz.* his death) shall be accomplished (or, 'the recompense shall be fully paid'; or, 'he shall be cut off') before his time, and his branch shall not be green" (—his children shall not survive or prosper, or his prosperity shall not continue). The prosperous wicked compared, as in verse 30, to a flourishing tree. So ch. viii. 16, 17; Ps. xxxvii. 35.—(Verse 33). "He (the sinner under the figure of a tree, or God in his mysterious judgments) shall shake off his unripe grape as the vine, and shall cast

off his flower as the olive" (when smitten by the frost or a pestilential wind). His prosperity brought to a sudden and premature end. —(Verse 34). "For the congregation of hypocrites (—the wicked themselves and their families along with them) shall be desolate." Neither numbers nor combinations able to secure the ungodly against God's judgments. "Though hand join in hand &c." Wealth gathered by man's unrighteousness often scattered by God's wrath.—"And fire shall consume the tabernacles of bribery" (—the dwellings of corrupt and covetous judges). Divine judgments shall overthrow their families, if not their very dwellings, as in the mind of Eliphaz they had done in the case of Job's children (ch. i. 19). A literal exemplification in the case of the Cities of the Plain. Job cruelly made to see, as in a mirror, his own calamities, and, to intensify their bitterness, to see them as a judgment of God.

An apparent *warning* parenthetically introduced in the description by way of personal application (verse 31). "Let not him that is deceived trust in vanity (—in his riches, or in the iniquity which has procured them; or, let not him [any man] trust in the vanity by which he has been deceived): for vanity (probably used in another sense) shall be his recompense." A caution of general use, but especially intended for poor Job. The warning suggests the following lessons: —(1) All earthly possessions vanity, as unable to satisfy the soul, and sure to disappoint those who trust in them for happiness. The creature is vanity, both in its possession and its promises. Promises—(i.) Satisfaction; (ii.) Protection; (iii.) Continuance. Most vain to those who trust in it.—(2) Those possessions especially vain which have been dishonestly or violently obtained. "The getting of treasures by a lying tongue is a vanity tossed to and fro of them that seek death" (Prov. xxi. 6).—(3) The character of the ungodly to trust in vanity, in earthly possessions and pleasures which can-

not satisfy, and in sinful courses which only end in misery and ruin (Is. lii. 2.) Men must trust in something, either God or vanity.—(4) The property of sin to deceive (Rom. vii. 11). The deceitfulness of sin (Heb. iii. 13). Deceivableness of unrighteousness (2 Th. ii. 10). Sin deceives, as it promises—(i) Pleasure; (ii.) Profit; (iii.) Impunity. Sin promises all pleasure, and in the end robs of all peace.—(5) Men apt still to trust in that by which they have been already deceived (Prov. xxiii. 35).—(6) All unrenewed men deceived (Tit. iii. 3). He feedeth on ashes; a deceived heart hath turned him aside (Is. xliv. 20). Satan the deceiver of the nations (Rev. xx. 38). Men by nature, since the admission of Satan's first great deception, call evil good, and good evil; put darkness for light, and light for darkness; put bitter for sweet, and sweet for bitter (Is. v. 20).—(7) The recompense of trusting in vanity is vanity—emptiness, dissatisfaction, disappointment. In indulging in sin and sinful pleasures men embrace a cloud. Like the apples of Sodom, dust in the hand that grasps them instead of fruit. Beautiful soap-bubbles. Vanity pursued ends in vanity experienced.—(8) Sin in itself the recompense of sin. Vanity another name for sin. No greater punishment than to be given up to one's own lusts and passions (Rom. i. 26, 28). The commission of one sin often punished by being left to the commission of another. Great part of the misery of the lost the abandonment to the power of sinful lusts, without any means for their gratification. Their fire of sinful passions unquenchable, with no object any longer to act upon. To sow to the flesh is to reap corruption. He that is filthy shall, after death, be filthy still. Sowing the wind, men reap the whirlwind; wind, but more boisterous and destructive. Sin a serpent, which, sleeping for a time, awakes only to sting and torment the soul that harboured it.

CHAPTER XVI.

JOB'S SECOND REPLY TO ELIPHAZ.

I. Complaius of the want of sympathy on the part of his friends (verses 2–5).

1. *They gave him only verses from the ancients about the punishment of the wicked and the prosperity of the righteous, such as he was already familiar with.* (Verse 2).—"I have heard many such things." In this, and the manner in which they did it, they showed themselves "miserable" (*margin*, "trouble-some") comforters; (*Heb.* "comforters of

trouble or mischief"). Professing to come as comforters, they had turned out tormentors. Professed comfort may be only an exasperation of sorrow. No small sin to "talk to the grief of those whom God has wounded." In speaking to tried ones, we need a tender heart and a gentle tongue. Easy to irritate the wound instead of healing it. Words may either—

   " Scorch like drops of burning gall,
    Or soothe like honey-dew."

7

Deep distress and despondency not to be cured by moral and religious aphorisms. "To preach of patience is often the very means of stirring up all impatience " [*Maurice*]. The tongue of the wise nowhere more needed than in the house of sorrow. The two requisites for a "comforter" found in Solomon's virtuous woman: "She openeth her mouth with wisdom, and in her tongue is the law of kindness" (Prov. xxxi. 26).

Men are "miserable comforters "—(1) When they comfort others with error and falsehood—as with erroneous views of God, of His dealings, or of themselves; "daubing with untempered mortar;" healing the hurt of the mourner "slightly, saying peace, peace, when there is no peace;" (2) When they direct to improper means for relief—as drowning the remembrance of the trouble in the pleasures and pursuits of the world; (3) When they seek merely to divert the mourner's mind from the trouble, or persuade him to put away and forget his sorrow; (4) When they fail to point him to the true source of comfort—Christ as a Saviour and sympathizing Friend—the truths of the Gospel and of the Word of God. "The waters of Lethe will not change the nature of sorrow, but the blood of Christ will."

To be a true "comforter" we require— (1) To be able to sympathize with the troubled; (2) To understand, generally, the meaning and use of trouble. Trouble a part of our education for heaven, as well as for the right performance of our duties on earth, —to be accepted as a message from above—an angel of mercy sent by the God who is love; (3) To be acquainted ourselves with the truth with which we are to comfort others, and to have experienced in some degree the power of it on our own hearts; (4) To possess the spirit and imitate the conduct of Him whose mission on earth was to "comfort them that mourn;" (5) To speak truthfully and suitably to the case, while we present such views of God and His dealings as are fitted to impart light and comfort to the sad and sorrowing.

2. *Job's friends spoke as not realizing his sorrow.* They treated him either with unfeeling reproofs, or sometimes with fine speeches (verse 3). "Shall vain words (*Heb.* 'words of wind,'— airy, empty speeches) have an end?" The friends had all followed in the same unprofitable strain. Job returns the reproach of Eliphaz (ch. xv. 2). Too much of the spirit of angry retort in these discussions. The time and country of the speakers, however, to be remembered. The Gospel of Jesus teaches us to give the "soft answer that turneth away wrath."—"Or what emboldeneth (or exciteth) thee that

thou answerest?" No ground or need for continuing such speeches. Eliphaz had spoken as a man under excitement. The style and spirit of his second speech considerably different from that of his first. *Especially important for a comforter and instructor of others to exercise patience, and not to lose his temper.* No small part of wisdom to know how we "ought to answer every man." "Every man shall kiss his lips that giveth a right answer" (Prov. xxiv. 26). Job's friends found it easy to repeat commonplaces, and shake their head.—(Verse 4). "I also could speak as you do: if (or 'wouldthat') your soul were in my soul's stead, I could heap up words (—string sentences and verses together) against you, and shake mine head at you" (—either in condolence or solemn admonition). Easy for the whole to advise the sick. The great want in Job's friends a genuine sympathy. After the first oriental outburst of grief at their friend's calamity, all was cold, heartless, and even cruel. Selfishness the common sin of our fallen nature—

"The proud, the cold, untroubled heart of stone,
That never mused on sorrow but its own."

In Job's friends this coldness aggravated, if not generated, by false religious views and misinterpretations of Divine Providence. True religion softens the heart, and inclines it to kindness and compassion. A false religion generally the parent of cruelty.

Job expresses what his own conduct would be were they in his situation (verse 5). "I would strengthen you with my mouth, and the moving (or condolence) of my lips should assuage your grief" (—or perhaps, ironically, 'I could strengthen you with my *mouth*,' and give you lip-consolation as you give me, instead of the "hearty counsel " of a friend, Prov. xxvii. 9). Job's actual practice described. Acknowledged by Eliphaz himself to have been a comforter of many (ch. iv. 3, 4). His own testimony as to his manner of life in the time of his prosperity (ch. xxix. 25; xxxi. 18). His friends had dealt in words which had no weight or force (ch. vi. 25), and which only tended to exasperate his sorrow. *His* words, had their places been changed, would have strengthened and relieved them. Three objects to be aimed at in comforting those in trouble—(1) To strengthen them to bear their trouble; (2) To lighten their grief; (3) To lead them to the right improvement of their trial. The last, the object more especially aimed at by Elihu (ch. xxx. 15—30).

II. **Renews his sorrowful complaint regarding his condition (verse 6—16).**

His sorrow neither mitigated by speech

nor silence (verse 6). "Though I speak my grief is not assuaged; and though I forbear, what am I eased?" Natural for grief to find relief in words. The troubled spirit also often calmed by silent meditation. Job experienced neither. No relief found in the assertion of his innocence or utterance of his sorrow. He had spoken to God, to his friends, to himself, yet his grief remained. Had sat at first in silence many days, and had spent many silent hours since then. Still no ease to his trouble. A bad case that yields to no kind of treatment.

He ascribes his troubles to God (verse 7). "But now he hath made me weary" (—quite exhausted me, or laden me with trouble). Job's troubles accumulated and now of some continuance, with as yet no relief. The visit of his friends, instead of a balm, had proved a bitterness. All ascribed by Job to God. Good to eye God's hand in our troubles, whoever and whatever may be the instrument of it. No trial but of His sending. When Satan was labouring to "destroy" Job, it was only by God's permission and authority (ch. ii. 3). The part of a sanctified nature, to see God in every event of our lot, whether prosperous or adverse. So David—"Thou didst it" (Ps. xxxix. 9). "Let him curse, for the Lord hath bidden him" (2 Sam. xvi. 11).

He turns from man and addresses his complaint to God Himself. "Thou hast." One word spoken to God in our trouble better than a hundred to man. The invitation (Ps. vi. 15). The resolution (Ps. xlii. 8, 9). Tragic and touching description of Job's sorrows. Embraces—

1. *The loss of his family and alienation of his friends* (verse 7). "Thou hast made desolate all my company" (—overwhelmed in calamity all my family, and struck with astonishment all my friends). Difficult to forbear recurring to grievous visitations and present troubles. All Job's children removed by one fell swoop. His property gone. Himself a mass of loathsome ulcers. His wife and friends paralysed and alienated by his calamities. His very servants standing aloof from him (ch. xix. 13—19). A grievous aggravation of affliction when friends are alienated and stand a distance from us (Ps. xxxi. 11; xxxviii. 1; lxxxviii. 18). The experience of the Man of Sorrows foreshadowed in Job's (Matt. xxvi. 31, 34, 56).

2. *His wasted appearance construed by his friends into a token of guilt* (verse 8). "Thou hast filled me with wrinkles (or 'laid fast hold of me,' as a person arrested by the hand of justice), which [in the opinion of my friends] is a witness against me [that I am a guilty man]; and my leanness (—or 'liars,' or, ' my lie') rising up in me beareth

witness to my face." A marred and meagre visage may testify to our grief, but not to our guilt. Christ's visage marred more than any man's, and his form more than the sons of men (Is. lii. 14). *Our* guilt, not His own, and *our* sorrows carried by Him as our Surety, marred His visage and robbed His form of comeliness and beauty (Is. liii. 2, 4).

3. *The apprehension of Divine anger in His troubles* (verse 20). "He teareth me in his wrath who hateth me (*Heb.*, ' his wrath hath torn and violently opposed me'); he gnasheth upon me with his teeth: mine enemy sharpeneth his eyes upon me " (or, ' as my enemy he glares upon me with his eyes,'—looks on me with fierce, sparkling eyes, like an enraged lion, ready to pounce upon his prey.) The perverted view of God which Satan presents, and the flesh is ready to take under severe and protracted trouble. Sad that our best Friend should be viewed as a relentless foe,—that the God who is love, should be converted into a furious wild beast or a wrathful demon. Such a view on the part of Job Satan's especial object at present. His aim to bring him to curse God to His face. Satan but showed *himself* to Job, and sought to pass himself off for God. The bitterest ingredient in a believer's trials, when not love but anger is apprehended in them. To see love in a cross takes out all bitterness; to see wrath, adds poison to the dart. David's prayer—"Rebuke me, [but] not in thine anger, chasten me, [but] not in thy hot displeasure" (Ps. vi. 1).

4. *The bitter hostility of his friends* (verse 10). "They have gaped upon me with their mouth; they have smitten me upon the cheek reproachfully; they have gathered themselves together against me " (as conspirators, to effect my ruin; or, "they have attacked me with combined forces"). Terribly bitter cup when both God and man—especially our friends and professedly good men—seem to be turned against us. The cup given to Jesus as our Surety. The words of the first clause of the verse those of the Psalm which describes His experience on the cross (Ps. xxii. 13). His cheek literally smitten, according to the prophecy (Mic. v. 1; Matt. xxvi. 67; xxvii. 30; John xix. 3). Jews and Gentiles, rulers and people, were gathered together against Him (Acts iv. 27; (Ps. ii. 12). Man's combined opposition, joined to a frowning providence, no proof either of guilt or Divine displeasure. David's prayer: "Let them curse, but bless thou " (Ps. cix. 28).

5. *His apparent abandonment by God into the hands of wicked men* (verse 11). "God hath delivered me to the ungodly (*Heb.*, 'to an evil one'), and turned me

7—2*

over (or, 'thrown me down headlong') into the hands of the wicked." His case, in his own view, like that of a criminal delivered over to the executioners of justice ; or one cast into a gulf or dungeon, as the punishment of his crime. His friends appeared to him in the character, and as acting towards him the part, of wicked men. Job delivered by God into the hands of an "evil one" in a way that he was not then aware of. Possibly, however, some glimmering of the truth as to the immediate agent in his affliction. The doctrine of evil spirits, and of one prominent among them as their leader, not likely to have been unknown in Job's time. The tradition of man's temptation and fall widely spread and preserved in the line of Shem. No uncommon thing for a child of God to be for wise purposes left for a time in the hands of bad men and bad angels. Divine abandonment the bitterest ingredient in the Saviour's cup. The only thing that extorted a wail of sorrow from His lips (Matt. xxvii. 46). To be left in the hands of the wicked was itself a grievous affliction. "The tender mercies of the wicked are cruel." To appear to be abandoned by God at the same time a fearful aggravation. The Surety actually delivered into the hands of Satan to be tempted, and of wicked men to be put to death (Matt. iv. 1 ; Acts ii. 23).

6. *The sad and sudden reverse in his experience* (verse 12). "I was at ease (—in tranquillity and prosperity), but he hath broken me asunder (or, in pieces, thoroughly crushed and smashed me as an earthen vessel) ; he hath also taken me by my neck [as a wild beast does his prey] and shaken me to pieces (—or, dashed me as on the ground, or against a rock), and set me up for his mark" (—to shoot his arrows at, as Saracenic conquerors sometimes did with their captives, and as his own soldiers did with Sebastian, the martyr of Gaul). Great and sudden reverses among the sorest earthly trials. The remembrance of previous comfort and prosperity an embittering of present calamity and suffering. Once none more happy and prosperous than Job ; now none more afflicted and wretched. No greater contrast between past and present experience since Adam and Eve were driven out of Paradise. Labours for words to express the grievousness of the latter. Employs words of double form and intensified meaning. "Broken me asunder," "shaken me to pieces." No mere hurt, but utter destruction, like that of a glass or an earthen vessel dashed to the ground, and smashed into a thousand pieces, no more to be united. Children gone ; property lost ; wife alienated ; body covered from head to

100

foot with the most grievous and loathsome disease that ever afflicted fallen humanity ; mind harassed, depressed, distracted ; sleep taken away ; what sleep obtained made more wretched than the absence of it by horrifying dreams ; his sincerity and piety more than suspected by his friends, in consequence of his sufferings ; and his bruised spirit worried and irritated by their flippant and worldly arguments, to convince him that he must not be the man he had been taken to be, and that to be delivered from his troubles he must repent and seek God. And of all these overwhelming reverses, God Himself, whom he had diligently and faithfully served, the Author ! High and important object that for which God could do such violence to His nature in thus dealing with a faithful servant ! Transcendently glorious end in view, when He still more terribly bruised His faithful and well-beloved Son !

7. *A tragically sublime enlargement on his treatment at the Divine hand* (verse 13). "His archers (or 'his mighty ones,' perhaps 'his darts'—the many calamities with which God had visited and was still visiting him) compass me round about : he cleaveth my reins asunder (—attacks me in the most vital parts, and inflicts on me deadly wounds), and doth not spare : he poureth out my gall upon the ground" (—His strokes of the most fatal kind, leaving no hope of life). No pity shewn in dealing with His servant, but all kinds of severity inflicted. Sometimes God appears to lay aside His attribute of mercy, even in dealing with His own. So in visiting Jerusalem for her sins : "Thou hast not pitied" (Lam. iii. 43). Thus God "spared not his own Son."—(Verse 14). "He breaketh me with breach upon breach ;"—is continually dealing new blows, like a storming party attacking the walls of a fortress—is always inflicting new griefs. So David's complaint : "Deep calleth unto deep ; all thy waves and thy billows have gone over me,"—one after another in rapid succession " (Ps. lxii. 7). One severe trial often found almost sufficient to crush us. Ordinarily, "in the day of the rough wind," He "stayeth the east wind." Rarely, as with Job, are heavy strokes repeated, successive, and accumulated. Such, however, the experience of Jesus in the last hours of His earthly life. From the traitor's kiss to His dying cry upon the cross, "bruised and put to grief" by God, devils, and men ; smitten in soul and body with one wound after another, till at last reproach broke His heart, and He was brought to the dust of death. And all this, while standing in your place, reader, and mine.—" He runneth upon me like a giant," or, "as a warrior," sword in hand, with strength and fury. Appalling climax ! Terrible experience for a

child of God. Awful situation of an impenitent and Christless soul. "A fearful thing to fall into the hands of the living God." If these things be done in the green tree, what shall be done in the dry?

8. *The effect of this severity on the part of God* (verse 15). "I have sewed sackcloth upon my skin." Sackcloth, a garment of coarse cloth worn by mourners and penitents. Probably assumed by Job after the death of his children, and continued ever since. Worn next to the person, and now adhering to his skin through the purulent matter issuing from his ulcers. God's providence able very soon to change our silk into sackcloth. —"And defiled (or thrust) my horn in the dust,"—like a noble animal spent with fatigue or overpowered in conflict. Job now literally in the dust. His place still among the ashes. His condition one of the deepest misery. His experience that of sorrow and humiliation. The horn an emblem of strength and dignity. Job, as a prince or emir, naturally speaks of his "horn." Easy with God to bring the loftiest horn to the dust. Witness Haman, Nebuchadnezzar, Wolsey, Masaniello, the fisherman-saviour of Naples. Soon "high ambition lowly laid." (Verse 16).—"My face is foul (or red) with weeping." Job no stoic. His eye poured out tears to God (verse 20). Manly to weep from a sufficient cause. Jesus wept. It is only sin which makes men callous and insensible. True religion neither makes men stones nor stoics. "Scorn the proud man that is ashamed to weep."—"And on mine eyelids is the shadow of death." A speedy dissolution anticipated as the result of his calamities and disease. The dimness of death already appearing to him to settle on his eyes. Now viewed himself as a dying man (ch. xvii. 1.) Figuratively also, deep and continued sorrow clouded his eyes as with the dimness of death. The effect of grief and tears on the sight frequently complained of in the Psalms (Ps. vi. 7; xxxi. 9; xxxviii. 10. See, also, Sam. v. 17). Faustus, son of Vortigern, said to have wept himself blind for the abominations of his parents.

III. Re-asserts his innocence and integrity (verse 17).

"Not for any injustice (or, 'although,'— or, connecting with what follows,—'because there is not any violence') in mine hands; also my prayer is pure." Maintains that his sufferings were neither on account of wrong done to his neighbour or hypocrisy towards God. The two charges alleged or insinuated against him by his friends. The gist of their speeches to show that he must have made himself rich by oppression, or had abused his riches to the injury of his neigh-

bour, and that the justice of God now overtook him for his crimes. This conduct towards man necessarily implied that his profession of religion towards God had been false and hollow. Job maintains, like Paul, that he had exercised himself in having a conscience void of offence both towards God and towards man. "Prayer" here put for religion or religious duties in general—his duty towards God. A great part of religion consists in prayer or in communion with the Father of our spirits. Divine worship an approach of the soul to the mercy-seat. Job a man of prayer, contrary to the allegation of his friends (ch. xv. 4). A prayerless man is a man without religion and without God. Job speaks of

Prayer

as a matter of course, as a thing *natural* for a man. As natural for a man to pray as for an infant to utter cries to its mother. The natural instinct of a babe towards its earthly parent a picture of that in a human soul towards its heavenly one. Because *natural*, prayer is *universal*. Prayer to Deity in some form or other the language of man wherever found. The most degraded still sometimes prays, and pays respect to prayer when offered by another. Prayer *a thing of the spirit*, unconfined to time, or place, or form. In prayer, however, as in other things, the spirit seeks *outward expression*—in the lips, and the posture of the body, as bended knees, uplifted hands, &c. Prayer either public, solemn, formal, or private,—in the family, the closet, everywhere. "I will that men pray *everywhere*." Nehemiah prayed in the glittering banquet-hall while presenting, according to his office, the wine-cup to his royal master. Especial prominence given in the Bible to *united* prayer (Matt. xviii. 19; Acts xii. 5, 12). Prayer to be made for *others* as well as for ourselves. Job an intercessor (ch. i. 5; xlii. 10). *Patterns for prayer* given everywhere throughout the Scriptures. Especially found in "*the Lord's Prayer.*" The *first* part of this Divine form of devotion consists in three petitions for *God* himself—for God's glory, His kingdom, and His pleasure; the second part, in the remaining four, for *ourselves* and our *neighbour*. Of these four, the first is for *temporal* benefits; the second and third for *spiritual* ones; and the fourth and last, for *both combined*.

Job declares that his prayer was "*pure*." Prayer "pure" when offered with a sincere heart and pure conscience. More particularly—

1. When *not in hypocrisy* or "out of feigned lips"; when with the *heart* and not

101

merely the lip or outward posture (Is. xxix. 13; Matt. xv. 8).

2. When *not accompanied with the practice of sin.* The sacrifice of the wicked an abomination to the Lord (Prov. xv. 8; li. 27; xxviii. 9) "If I regard iniquity in my heart the Lord will not hear me" (Ps. lxvi. 17). Men to lift up "*holy* hands."

3. When *for right objects* and *from right motives.* "Ye ask and receive not, because ye ask amiss, that ye may consume it upon your lusts" (James iv. 3).

4. When *addressed to the only true God* (Ps. lxv. 2).

5. When presented *in a way according to His own will,* not through images or pictures, or with superstitious and humanly devised practices (Col. ii. xviii. 22).

6. When offered *with right disposition and feelings,* with benevolence and forgiveness of injuries. "Lifting up holy hands, without *wrath*" (1 Tim. ii. 8). "When ye stand praying, forgive" (Mark xi. 25).

7. When made *with humility through the one Mediator, and with faith in His atoning sacrifice.* "To this man will I look who is poor and of a contrite spirit" (Is. lxvi. 2). "There is one God and one Mediator between God and men, the man Christ Jesus." "No man cometh to the Father but by me" (1 Tim. ii. 5; John xiv. 6). Boldness given to enter into the holiest of all by the *blood* of Jesus (Heb. x. 19).

IV. Apostrophizes the earth in an impassioned prayer that his innocence may be made manifest (verse 18).

"O earth, cover not thou my blood, and let my cry have no place" (of concealment, or hindrance in its access to God'). Perhaps connected with the preceding: "Because I am innocent, let this be the case.'" Job, as an undeserving sufferer, regards himself as one whose blood is innocently shed. Probable reference to Abel's murder (Gen. iv. 10, 11). The narrative or document containing it well known to Job. The shedder of Job's blood either the immediate agent in his sufferings, or his friends who so cruelly persecuted him. People easily and often committed without actual shedding of blood. Parents often murdered by the unkindness of their children, and wives by the harsh treatment of their husbands. Words and looks kill as well as blows. Blood shed inwardly as well as outwardly,—shed where no eye sees it but God's.

Job's prayer heard. His innocence and his friends' unkindness at length revealed. No innocent blood always covered. "Murder will out" and be revenged. The blood of the slaughtered Huguenots visited on Charles IX.,

102

who died in a bloody sweat, crying: "What blood! what blood!"—and still visited in the wars and revolutions of France. A day coming when the earth shall "disclose her blood,"—the blood innocently shed on it and kept by it against a future day, and shall "no more cover her slain" (Is. xxvi. 21). Earth covers innocent blood till God uncovers and revenges it. Arabs say the dew never rests on a spot that has been wet with it. The innocent blood of the crucified One still speaks in heaven. Led to the sacking and burning of Jerusalem, with the slaughter and dispersion of its people. Is still visited on the outcast impenitent shedders of it. Speaks pardon and peace to all who, as guilty, take refuge in it as their only atonement and hope.

The "cry" of the helpless and oppressed never unheard. No place on earth able to hide it from God. Enters from the most humble and wretched hovel into the ears of the Lord of Sabaoth (James v. 4).

V. Job's consolation (verse 19, 20).

1. *In God's consciousness of his innocence* (verse 19). "Also now (—besides the testimony of my own consciousness; or, 'even now,' in the midst of these calamities and sufferings), behold (—strange as you may deem my assertion) my witness (—he who can and will bear testimony to my innocence) is in heaven, and my record (—the eye-witness of my upright life) is on high." Job's integrity already testified to by God in a way he was not aware of. The comfort of the righteous under oppression, that God is witness not only of their suffering, but of their integrity. God's great all-seeing eye the terror of the sinner, the comfort of the saint. The Eye-Witness in heaven will one day speak out on earth (Matt. xxv. 31–45). A grievous trial for a good man to lie under suspicion of hypocrisy, especially with good men. His comfort in the record on high,—the Eye-Witness unseen, but seeing all.

2. *In his constant tearful waiting upon God* (verse 20). "My friends scorn me (*Heb.,* 'my mockers are my friends'), but mine eye poureth out tears unto God." One of Job's great trials, that those who should have befriended and comforted him only mocked him, by dealing in wordy harangues and persuasions to repent in order to deliverance from his overwhelming troubles. His comfort in being able to turn from them to God. While his ear was stunned with their unfeeling reflections, his eye was pouring out tears to Him in whom· "the fatherless findeth mercy." A relief in trouble to be able to weep, much more in being able to weep to God. Tears wept to God do not scald, but cool. The misery of the world,

that they either do not weep in trouble, or do not weep to Him who is able both to pity and help them. Every tear wept to God put into His bottle. God's lachrymatory constantly filling with the tears of the sorrowful wept into His bosom. A day coming when each tear treasured up in it will sparkle as a gem in the mourner's crown. Prayers and tears the weapons of the saints. While the eye pours out tears to God, God pours in comfort and strength unto the soul. With God the eye pleads as effectually as the lips. The tearful eye an eloquent pleader when the tongue is unable to utter a word. Tears wept to God have a voice that He who sees them well understands. Those blessed troubles that open the sluices for tears to be poured out to God. Believers weep with their face to God, the world with their back to Him. Precious grace that enables a man to take his griefs and weep out his tears to God. The trouble that drives unbelievers farther from God is only driving a believer nearer to Him; as the wind that drives one mariner farther from home is wafting another nearer to it. The magnet, amid all the commotions of the earth, and sea, and sky, still keeps pointing to the north.

VI. His longing desire to have his case tried before God (verse 21).

"O that one might plead for a man with God, as a man pleadeth for his neighbour" (or, 'O that a man might plead,' or simply as expressing the subject of his prayer,—'that a man,—viz., himself,—might plead with God as a son of man with his neighbour'). Job's constant desire, from a consciousness of his integrity, to plead his cause with God (ch. ix.,19, 32—35). His aim not to establish his *sinlessness*, but his *sincerity*. His desire not to plead with God in reference to his personal acceptance with Him, but in reference to the particular matter and cause of his present sufferings. It is our happiness that we have not to plead our case with God as righteous persons, but as sinners. Even Job unable to answer God for one of a thousand charges he could bring against him (ch. ix., 3). It is the comfort of the Gospel—(1) That a sinner does not need to plead with God in order to establish his righteousness ; God justifies the *ungodly* who believe in His Son ; (2) That receiving Christ as a Saviour we have one who con-

stantly pleads for us. In Christ we have an Advocate who is God Himself while our Brother,—the Man who is Jehovah's Fellow (Zech. xiii. 7.) Our God-man Advocate pleads not our innocence, but His obedience unto death, as the ground of our justification. Exhibits before the Divine tribunal not our *tears*, but His own *blood*. Mentions in the plea not our works, but our faith in Himself.

The reason for Job's earnest desire (verse 22).—"When a few years are come (or 'for the years numbered to me,' or, 'my few years have come,' *i.e.*, to an end), then shall I go whence I shall not return." The apprehension of approaching death now always present with Job. His great desire that his cause might be tried and his innocence declared before he left this world. Elsewhere he comforts himself with the assurance that even if death should intervene, God would vindicate his character and manifest his innocence (ch. xix., 25—27). Natural to desire to see it done while living. Sad for a good man to die with a cloud of suspicion resting on his character.—Things which each ought to be earnest and diligent to have done before we go "whence we shall not return." (1) Our own acceptance with God made sure. (2) The salvation of our children secured. (3) Our family and affairs rightly ordered. (4) Peace and reconciliation sought with all men. (5) Duties towards our family, friends, and neighbours discharged. "Whatsoever thy hand findeth to do, do it with thy might" (Eccles. ix. 10).

Solemn enquiry: "When a few years are come," where shall I be, and what shall be my place and experience? Like Job, I shall be done with a present world. Its joys and sorrows, its cares and anxieties, will have ceased with me for ever. Shall I be enjoying a better state? Have I a house not made with hands, eternal in the heavens? Have I an interest in Christ, so as to be able to say : "To me to live is Christ, and to die is gain?" Do I know that God is the strength of my heart now, and that He shall be my portion for ever? That He will guide me with His counsel while here, and afterwards receive me to glory? While my body is mouldering in the grave, shall my spirit be mingling in the songs of saints and seraphim before the throne? Am I already washed in the blood of the Lamb?

CHAPTER XVII.

CONTINUATION OF JOB'S REPLY TO ELIPHAZ.

I. Bemoans his dying condition (verse 1).

"My breath is corrupt (or, 'my spirit or

vital energy is destroyed '), my days are extinct (or, extinguished, as a lamp or taper whose flame is expiring), the graves are

103

ready for me" (or, the place of graves, or chambers of the tomb, are destined for me, —*Heb.*, 'are for me,' or, 'are mine'). Job takes a calm but gloomy view of his condition. Now views himself always as a dying man. Speaks the language of deep despondency. Vital powers exhausted. Energy of spirit broken. The lamp of life all but extinguished. His only expected home the grave. This mentioned now—(1) As his reason for desiring to have his case speedily tried and his character vindicated; (2) In opposition to the flattering prospect held out by his friends as the result of his repentance. Observe—

1. *Good for us frequently to take a calm view of our condition as mortal and dying men.* Philip of Macedon kept a person for the sole purpose of daily reminding him of his mortality. Sad to be surprised by the summons of death, like the rich fool (Luke xii. 20). A good man, able, like Job, to chant his own dirge, both in the midst of life's joys and sorrows.

2. *True in reference to each what Job says of himself*—

"The graves are ready for me."

(1) Death is *appointed* to us. The lot of all but those who shall be living at the Lord's appearing. The sentence of death entailed on Adam's offspring as well as himself (Rom. v. 12). Death an enemy which all have to meet. No discharge in that war. The grave the home appointed for all living. Death a visitor whom no wealth can bribe, no power resist, no artifice elude.—(2) Death is *near* to us. "But a step between me and death." Death or the Lord's appearing not far from each of us. The grave probably much nearer both to reader and writer than to Job, when uttering these words. Job after this lived a hundred and forty years. Our entire life probably not more than half this amount. "Where is to-morrow? In another world. For numbers this is certain." Death probably much nearer to us than we think. Uses to be made of this fact : —(i.) To make careful preparation for death. While the body enters the grave the spirit enters the invisible and eternal world. Prepare to meet thy God.—(ii.). To make right use of time while it lasts. Much to be done, and but a short time to do it in (Eccles. ix. 10).—(iii.). To sit loose to the things of a present world. The world to be used, but not abused or used eagerly as if our all (1 Cor. vii. 29). "Why all this toil for triumphs of an hour?"—(iv.). To examine faithfully our views and prospects in regard to the grave. How do I regard it ? With comfort or with dread ? Is the

prospect of it a gloomy or a pleasant one ? To the believer to die is gain, because to depart is to be with Christ. To Him, the grave is only "a dark lattice letting in eternal day," the avenue

"To festive bowers,
Where nectars sparkle, angels minister,
And more than angels share."

Am I prepared for my final resting-place ? Are my accounts made straight with God ? Am I at peace with my Maker ? Are my sins cancelled with the blood of Jesus ?

II. Job complains of the conduct of his friends (verse 2).

"Are there not mockers (or mockings) with me ? Doth not mine eye continue (*Heb.*, remain all night) in their provocation ?" Cutting words and cruel reproaches not easily banished. What the eye sees and the ear hears by day, the thoughts dwell upon by night. Such, with Job, the unkind looks and bitter words of those who should now have been his comfort. These things now his "sorrowful meat" (ch. vi. 7). The conduct of his friends one great part of his affliction. "Man is to man the sorest, surest ill." Instead of sympathy to soothe his sufferings, Job had only scorn to aggravate them. Such painful experience, especially from friends, happily the lot of few sufferers. Yet that of the Man of sorrows standing in our room. Complained of by Him as one of his keenest trials (Ps. xxii. 7 ; Matt. xxvii. 39). "The contradiction of sinners against himself" mentioned as the burden of his sufferings (Heb. xii. 4). His heart broken by reproach (Ps. lxix. 20). In proportion to the sweetness of true friendship and sympathy in sorrow, is the bitterness of the want, and especially the *opposite*, of it. Friendship the "wine of life ;" unkind reproaches from professed friends, especially in trouble, distilled wormwood.

III. Earnestly beseeches God to grant a speedy trial of his case (verse 3).

"Lay down now (or, 'give a pledge, I pray thee' ; put me in a surety with thee (or, 'give,' or, 'be surety to me [in this controversy of mine] with thee,'—that thou wilt afford me a trial and act as a party); who is he that will strike hands with me ?" (or, 'who else is there that will,' &c.,—that is able to enter into the controversy? or, who is there, when such a pledge is given me by Thee, that will enter into the controversy with me ? I will challenge anyone to prove me a wicked dissembler). Always the great burden of Job's desire to have his case fairly tried. The result and evidence of his conscious integrity. The most painful part of his suffering, that he was treated as a wicked man, and, in consequence of that treatment, was regarded as such by his friends. A good man's name more precious to him than life. The cutting taunt of David's enemies, and those of David's antitype in trouble, where is now thy God? (Ps. xlii. 10; Matt. xlvii. 41—43). Christ esteemed by His enemies, "stricken, smitten by God, and afflicted," as a man under God's displeasure, and suffering for his sins (Is. liii. 4). For the consolation of anxious souls, God has given what Job desired, His promise and His oath (Heb. vi. 17, 18). These given, not that they shall have their case tried, but that, on accepting Christ as their substitute and righteousness, they shall be accepted as righteous with God, just as they are. God Himself a surety to such that no evil shall befal them (Ps. cxix 122). David's comfort that God had made with him an everlasting covenant (2 Sam. xxiii. 5). Christ provided by God as the surety of that covenant (Heb. vii. 22). The Divine pledge that on receiving Him, no good thing shall be witheld from us (Rom. viii. 32).—The reason for Job's request (ver. 4) "For thou hast hid their heart from understanding (withheld from his friends the wisdom and intelligence necessary to qualify them for giving a right judgment in his case, or to make them successful parties in the controversy; therefore shalt thou not exalt them" (as righteous judges, or as those who have had the better in the case). A two-fold ground of Job's request for a fair trial of his case by God Himself— (1) The incapacity of his friends to judge in the matter; (2) His consciousness of his innocence, and that in the controversy he will gain the cause. Job called to wage a double controversy— (1) As against God, in His appearing to afflict him as a wicked man; (2) As against his friends, in their charging him with being such.

Observe—
1. The highest "understanding" to judge correctly between right and wrong in principle and conduct, and rightly to interpret God's dealings and dispensations with men. No understanding as to moral and spiritual subjects, but as the gift of God. With God either to give or withhold this understanding (Matt. xi. 25). A measure of it given to all men (John i. 9). That measure capable of being increased or diminished. The increase or diminution according to the improvement made of it, and the means employed for increasing it. "To him that hath," &c. "He that walketh with wise men shall be wise."

—The want of a clear and correct moral judgment the consequence of sin. A dim perception and unsound judgment in moral and spiritual things one of the natural, as well as judicial, effects of transgression. The most upright, not the most learned, the most capable of forming a correct judgment on great moral questions. The secret of the Lord is with them that fear him. "A good understanding have all they that keep thy testimonies."

2. The true "exaltation" that which comes from God (Ps. lxxvi. 5—7; Dan. iv. 37). The possession and exercise of a sound moral judgment the ground of exaltation with God as of commendation with men (Prov. xii. 8). Prejudice and partiality in judging of an individual's state and character a serious ground of Divine displeasure. Harsh and uncharitable judgment of and conduct towards a faithful and suffering servant of His the object of His disapprobation. Hence—(1) The frequent denunciations in the Psalms in reference to David's enemies and persecutors; (2) The fearful judgments made to follow the Jewish nation for their treatment of God's righteous servant, their own Messiah. Job's friends not only not "exalted" by God, but deeply humbled and abased by Him in the end (ch. xlii. 7, 8). The enemies and persecutors of Christ and His cause ultimately clothed with shame (Ps. cxxxii). A bad cause only for a time apparently triumphant. "*Magna est veritas*," &c.

IV. A denunciation against treacherous and unfaithful friends (verse 5). "He that speaketh flattery to his friends (or the man who betrays his friends to [become a] spoil or prey; who deserts and betrays his friends from selfish considerations) the eyes of his children shall fail;" his sin is so grievous in the sight of God that it shall be visited not only on himself, but on his children. The treacherous and unfaithful conduct of Job's friends already the subject of his sorrowful complaint (ch. vi. 15—27). Observe—(1) *Treachery and unfaithfulness on the part of professed friends one of the most cutting trials with men, and the most condemning sins with God.* These concentrated in the conduct of Judas Iscariot. The frequent complaint of David, and the painful experience of David's antitype (Ps. xl. 9, lv. 12; John xiii. 18). (2) *Some sins more heinous in themselves and more disastrous in their consequences than others.* (3) *Sin in many cases entails its consequences on a man's children as well as on himself.* Gehazi's sin followed by the infliction of Naaman's leprosy on himself and his posterity for ever. On the other hand, the virtuous conduct of parents entails a blessing on their offsprings. So the faith of Abraham, the zeal of Phinehas, the piety of Obed-Edom. In the text, Job retorts upon his friends their cruel allusion to his children's calamity (ch. v. 4; viii. 4; xv. 30). Not only speaks according to the Old Testament platform, but announces a general law in God's moral government. The consequences of parents' sins upon their children often natural and in the ordinary course of Divine Providence; at the same time judicial, whatever may be the instrumentality or natural causes.

V. Returns to his own distressed condition.
His sufferings the cause of the suspicion resting upon his character. Mentions—
1. The *contempt* to which his circumstances exposed him (verse 6). "He (*i e.* God—frequently spoken of without being named) hath made me also a by-word (or proverb) of the people; and aforetime I was as a tabret" (or, "and I am become an object to spit before," or, "to spit at in the face"). Distressing contrast. Formerly the object of universal reverence and respect; now of public contempt and insult (ch. xxx. 10). To spit at or in the presence of another still a common mode of showing contempt among the Arabs. Mahommedans often thus exhibit their contempt of Christians. Trouble greatly aggravated by contrast with former prosperity. Contempt a bitter ingredient in a noble-minded man's cup of sorrow. A frequent subject of complaint in the Psalms (Ps. xxii. 6, 7; xxxv. 15, 16; lxix. 7, 11, 12, 19; cxxiii. 3, 4). The experience of the Man of Sorrows (Matt. xxvii. 28, 29, 41—44; Is. liii. 3). Jesus, like Job, spit upon by the rabble (Is. l. 6; Matt. xxvi. 67; xxvii. 30).
2. The *effect of grief upon his physical frame* (verse 7). "Mine eye also is dim by reason of sorrow, and all my members (or features) are as a shadow." The eye dimmed by weeping and nervous exhaustion. The emaciation consequent on protracted sorrow still more common. Grief preys on the whole frame. Digestive organs retarded in their operation; nutrition at a stand. Job's case (ch. xix. 20). David's complaint (Ps. xxii. 17). So the prophet representing the Jewish Church in its trouble (Ps. cii. 5; Sam. iv. 8). Job's trouble now of some continuance. The change in his appearance already such as to render him scarcely recognizable by his friends (ch. ii. 12). The Man of Sorrows, when little above thirty, spoken of as "not yet fifty years old" (John viii. 57). Job already a "by-word,"

or proverb, of suffering or sorrow. Probably regarded as an example of the justice of God overtaking a secret transgressor, and of the sudden overthrow of those who have made themselves rich. Similar experience of David as a type of the Messiah (Ps. lxix. 11). Job now for thousands of years a proverb of *patience*. His tears already gems. "Our sorrow the inverted image of our nobleness; perhaps, also, the measure of our sympathy" [*Carlyle*]. In Job three superlatives combined—nobleness of mind and character; trouble, with grief as its natural effect; patience, at least for a time, in enduring it.

VI. The contemplated effect of his sufferings on others.
This twofold—
1. *The encouragement of suffering innocence* (ver. 8). "Upright men shall be astonished at this [so aggravated is suffering in an innocent man, who yet maintains his integrity under it]; and the innocent [encouraged by my example] shall stir up himself against the hypocrite (or ungodly man)." Probably contemplates the effect, not merely of his suffering, but of the future public vindication of his character, at times confidently anticipated (ch. xix. 25—29; xxiii. 10). Hence, another reason for wishing a speedy decision of his case. Job's experience an encouragement to all suffering believers— (1) Not to be surprised if overtaken by signal affliction. God's dealings with His people often dark and mysterious. Suffering saints Asaph's perplexity (Ps. lxxiii. 10—15). (2) Not to wonder if subjected to misapprehension and suspicion even with good men. Job's antitype also an object of astonishment on account of unparalleled sufferings borne with unparalleled patience (Is. lii. 11; liii. 7). The support given to believers under suffering often an astonishment to themselves, as well as admiration to others. Astonishing trials bring astonishing consolations and deliverances. The anticipated result of Job's sufferings realized as long as there shall be suffering believers in the world. The encouragement of such one great object of the book. Job read by the early Church every year in Passion-week. The subject of frequent meditation with the Man of Sorrows—Job's great antitype. One means of building up his manhood and preparing him for patient suffering. Job the example of suffering patience especially for the Old Testament Church, as Jesus is for the New (Heb. xii. 2, 3. As the result of Job's sufferings, the pious should "stir up himself" against the profane, however prosperous in this world; not

against their persons, but their principles and practice. Saints to love the sinner but to hate and oppose his sin. Observe—(1) *The duty of believers to stir themselves up* (Is. lxiv. 7). Godliness requires energy and zeal for its maintenance and practice. This especially in times of persecution, of general backsliding and apostacy, or of prevailing lukewarmness and worldliness. No small matter to hold on against prosperous ungodliness. (2) *The effect of God's providential dealings with His church and people often very different from what is and might be expected.* God makes both the wrath of man and the sufferings of the saints—even their sins—to praise Him. The blood of the martyrs the seed of the Church. Hopeful's conversion due to Faithful's martyrdom. (3) *A mark of sincerity to take part with suffering piety.* The case of Nicodemus and Joseph of Arimathea. Believers at Rome waxed confident through Paul's bonds (Phil. i. 14).

2. *Encouragement to perseverance in Godliness* (verse 9). "The righteous also shall hold (or take firm hold) on his way, and he that is of clean hands shall be stronger and stronger." The example of perseverance in one an important means of promoting it in others. · God's wisdom and kindness in providing such an example as Job at so early a period of the world. Men more influenced by example than abstract reasoning or simple precept. The value of biography. Hence the large proportion of the Bible occupied with the life and history of individuals. Patient suffering a powerful sermon.

Perseverance in Holiness ·

The great duty of believers. Not without strenuous effort. Much to discourage and oppose. The current of the world and the flesh to swim against. Principalities and powers to be resisted. Many adversaries. The epistle to the Hebrews written to strengthen believers to hold on their way. Perseverance the test of sincerity (1 John, ii. 19). "The path of the just as the shining light, shining more and more unto the perfect day." Promised to believers (Phil. i. 6). The source of it, the power of God; the means, faith (1 Pet. i. 5). God's printing done with fast colours. God able to keep His people, and as willing as He is able. Christ both the Author and Finisher of our faith. Believers not of them that draw back unto perdition (Heb. x. 39; xii. 2). The godly, from Job's sufferings, not only to hold on their way, but to become "stronger and stronger" (Heb., "add strength"). Not only perseverance the duty and mark of believers, but

Growth.

Growth in holiness God's will—" Grow in grace." Provision made for it—"He giveth more grace." The object of Christ's advent that we "might have life, and have it more abundantly." Believers to be adding —"add to your faith virtue or courage, &c." "From strength to strength." Must either advance or retrograde. The character of those who grow—"He that is of clean hands." Clean hands the index and result of a clean heart. Hands only clean when washed by faith in the blood of cleansing. Growth necessary. New strength for new and sorer trials, new and harder duties, new and severer battles. Means of growth. —(1) Waiting on the Lord in prayer and otherwise (Is. xl. 30, 31). (2) Converse with the word of God, the food of the soul (1 Pet. ii. 2). (3) Faith in Christ as our strength and life (Heb. xii. 2). (4) Fellowship with God's faithful servants, and especially Christ himself (Prov. xiii. 20). (5) Contemplation of Christ's glory. His character, and His cross (2 Cor. iii. 18). (6) Exercise and improvement of the grace already given—"To him that hath, &c." (7) Discipline of Divine providence. Strength of religious principle heightened by suffering and trial. Tried grace is growing grace. The more Israel were afflicted in Egypt, "the more they grew."

VII. Job's dismission of his friends (verse 10).

"But as for you all (contrasting them with the upright innocent persons just mentioned), do ye return and come now (return again, *i.e.*, to the discussion—spoken ironically; or, return and depart, *i.e.*, to your own home)." The reason of this dismission of them twofold :—

1. The *want of wisdom they had manifested.* "For I do not find one wise man among you." Want of capacity shown for the office they had undertaken. Had all proved themselves "miserable comforters," "physicians of no value." Had either applied bad remedies or misapplied good ones. Observe—(1) *Men to hold an office no longer than they exhibit capacity for it.* Preachers listened to only as long as they are able to produce "words of truth and soberness." (2) *Great pretension to wisdom often only covers the want of it.* Shallow streams make greatest sound. (3) *Wisdom required in ministering to minds diseased.* "He that winneth souls," and he that rightly comforts mourners, "is wise." A "wise man," one who can "show out of a good conversation (or life) his works with meekness of wisdom " (James iii. 13). Two kinds of wisdom: one, "earthly, sensual,

devilish;" the other "from above,—pure, peaceable, gentle, full of mercy and good fruits." True wisdom is to know the truth and do it. To choose right ends, and seek them by right means. The wise man one who—(i.) Has understanding of God's character and ways, and is able to interpret them to others; (ii.) "knows both time and judgment;" "has understanding of the times;" and knows what both himself and others ought to do, and *does* it; (iii.) Faithfully and intelligently aims at the best interests of himself and his fellow men. True wisdom the gift of God, and to be asked in believing prayer (James i., 5, 6, 17; iii. 17). Christ made wisdom to those who are in Him (1 Cor. i. 30).

2. *The certainty and nearness of his own death which contradicted their promises of future prosperity* (verse 2). "My days (perhaps his *happy* ones) are past, my purposes are broken off, even the thoughts (*margin* 'possessions') of my 'heart' (the purposes and hopes which he had fondly cherished,—probably, according to Job's character, having reference more to the welfare of others than himself; these all dashed to the ground by his calamities and approaching death). Observe—(1) *The part of a good man to form plans of usefulness for his fellow man;* (2) *Necessary not to defer the execution of such plans.* Sickness, trouble, and death may intervene to prevent their accomplishment. "Whatsoever thy hand findeth to do, do it with thy might." (Eccles. ix. 10). Hence the folly and unreasonableness of the friends' counsel and promises. Their attempt that of those who (verse 12) "change (or make) the night into day" (talking of future prosperity in such dark and hopeless circumstances); the light is short because of darkness (or, they make "the light near in the very presence of darkness,"—talk of light when there is only darkness and death; the same idea repeated according to Hebrew parallelism). Like that in the Proverbs, under another figure,—"As vinegar upon nitre, so is he that singeth songs to a heavy heart" (Prov. xxv. 20). *Words in order to be useful must be spoken in season.*

Re-asserts the certainty and nearness of his end, to show the vanity of his friends' counsel (verse 13). "If I wait (indulge, hope, or expection), the grave is mine house (the only home I can look for, instead of the pleasant and prosperous habitation you hold out to me); "I have made my bed in darkness" (have already taken possession of the tomb as my abode, by spreading my couch in its darkness). (Verse 14)—"I have said to corruption (or 'the pit,' *i.e.*, of the grave), Thou art my father (as being now betrothed to death, and so made a

108

member of his family), and to the worm (that preys upon the lifeless corpse—an idea frequent in Arab poetry), Thou art my mother and sister" (as already allied to the sepulchral household). (Verse 15).—And where is now (or where is then) my hope (the hope you counsel me to entertain); as for my hope, who shall see it?" (such a hope would be soon quenched in death without any seeing its realization). (Verse 16)—"They (or it, viz., my hope) shall go down to the bars of the pit (to the gates or chambers of the grave), when our rest together is in the dust" (or, "it [or we] shall lie down together in the dust," my hopes should be buried with myself in the grave). Observe.—

1. *The grave viewed by a believer with calmness and with comfort.* To such, a home or resting place, where "the wicked cease from troubling and the weary are at rest." To a believer, death is "of all pain the period, not of joy."

"Death is the privilege of human nature,
And life without it were not worth the taking."

Relationship with the grave (i.) of an *endearing* kind. In a sense, our father, mother, and sister. Contains the dust of some of our dearest friends. A husband or a wife, a parent or a child; these give the grave a home-like aspect, and inspire a home-feeling believer's brethren and sisters, while heaven contains their spirits. (ii.) Of a *humbling* kind. Man himself a worm, sprung from the same ground. Worms the companions and sharers of his final resting place. Worms his future guests who shall feed upon himself.

2. *Man's duty to guard against delusion in the matter of his hope.* Good to ask with Job

What is my hope?

The hope of many, only such as to be buried with them in the same grave. Such the case if our hope is only of an earthly nature, or resting on a false foundation.

"Who builds on less than an immortal base,
Fond as he seems, condemns his joys to death."

Our hope may be either a cable or a cobweb; may either rest on solid rock or yielding sand. The believer's hope is—(i.) "a good hope," as having (a) a good *object*—the heavenly inheritance; (b) a good *foundation*,—Christ himself and his finished work. (ii.) A "*lively* hope," as one that shall survive the grave. Having Christ "as our hope," we plant our foot on the grave and sing our pæan over it: O grave where is thy victory? O death where is thy sting?

CHAPTER XVIII.

BILDAD'S SECOND SPEECH.

Bildad the bitterest and most hostile of the three friends. No speech as yet so insolent and provoking. Full of fiery scathing denunciation against—the wicked—intending, of course, its application to Job, without even the exhortation or promise to repentance.

I. His introduction. Contains only angry and vehement reproof. Reproves Job—

1. For his *loquacity and captiousness* (verse 2). "How long will it be ere ye make an end of words (or how long will ye lay snares for words?) mark (*Heb.* 'understand,' *i.e.*, consider, *viz.*, our arguments; perhaps, 'be temperate,' or 'speak clearly'), and afterwards we will speak" (or, "that afterwards we may speak"). Bildad's language and tone not only passionate but contemptuous. "How long will ye," &c., instead of "*thou.*" A great part of wisdom is to govern one's temper. "A fool's wrath is presently known; but a wise man keepeth it in till afterwards." "Better is he that ruleth his spirit than he that taketh a city." Yet a wise man, from the weakness of human nature, may allow himself to be surprised into angry and contemptuous words. True wisdom characterized by meekness and gentleness—"meekness of wisdom." The tongue and temper never more in need of a bridle than in a controversy. Easy to lose a religious spirit in a religious dispute. Christ, incarnate wisdom, a model in controversy—calm, patient, loving; always "meek and lowly;" reviled, without reviling again. Bildad impatient of Job's reproof and depreciatory remarks in reference to his and his friends' speeches. Represents Job as only catching at words; as like those Jews who "lay in wait for Jesus, seeking to catch something out of His mouth, and to entangle Him in His talk." Observe—(1) *Passion is seldom truthful.* (2) *Loss of temper generally proves weakness in argument.* Consciousness of truth gives calmness in dispute. To bully an opponent is to confess yourself beaten. (3) *Patience and courtesy always due to an adversary.*

2. For his *pride and contempt* (verse 3). "Wherefore are we counted as beasts (ignorant and brutish), and reputed vile in your sight?" Too much ground given in Job's language for Bildad's reproof. His spirit broken by trouble, and exasperated by

their unfeeling, unjust, and deceitful conduct, Job had treated his friends with too much severity and contempt. Bildad particularly stung by Job's contemptuous language in ch. xvii. 4, 10. Observe—(1) "*Grievous words*" to be avoided, as always *stirring up anger.* In controversy, hard things apt to be said, and to be made harder than they are. (2) *Man's moral as well as physical 'goodliness as the flower of the field.'* Job not always able to answer with the "meekness of wisdom," as in ch. ii. 10.

3. For his *passion* (verse 4). "He teareth himself (or, 'he that teareth himself,' or, 'thou that tearest thyself') in his anger." Job represented as a raging maniac. Probably too much foundation for the remark. Anger, according to a heathen sage, a short madness. Job's appearance and demeanour probably that of a man not only deeply distressed but greatly excited. "Oppression maketh a wise man mad." Arabs usually grave, solemn, unperturbed; yet capable of great excitement. Held highly discreditable for a good man to allow himself to be in a passion. Passion always injurious to the subject of it, both spiritually and physically. "He teareth *himself* in his anger;" *Heb.*, "he teareth *his soul.*" Wrathful dispositions, says a Greek poet, are justly most painful to the parties themselves. "Wrath killeth the foolish man" (ch. v. 2).

4. For his *self-conceit.* "Shall the earth be forsaken for thee? and shall the rock be removed out of his place?" More bitter words. Cruel and unfeeling as addressed to a crushed and afflicted man. Proverbial expressions with the Arabs in reproving pride and arrogance. Reference to Job's wish for a trial of his case by God, and his complaint of undue severity. Seemed as if he expected some special dispensation in his favour. The government of the world not to be abandoned for the sake of any individual's concerns. The Almighty not to go out of the way of his usual procedure to meet any man's wishes. The course of nature and the principles of the Divine government not to be arrested for any one's special accommodation. For any to think so implies vain conceit of his own importance. Yet Job's wish and complaint excusable. His circumstances peculiar. His treatment not in accordance with God's ordinary procedure, and with the consciousness of his own character. Bildad's questions founded in ignorance. Unnecessary

for God to neglect the government of the universe, or contravene the course of nature, in order to attend to the concerns of an individual. Such attention a part of that government. The fall of a sparrow, as well as of an empire, included in God's providence. Numbers the hairs of our head equally with the stars of the firmament. Man, in ignorance or forgetfulness, transfers his own weakness and limitation to God's Almightiness and infinity. The Divine government based on unchanging principles. Judgment and justice the habitation of God's throne. Impossible and unnecessary to depart from these principles to meet any particular case. "God is a rock—His work is perfect; a God of truth and without iniquity." God Himself, and the principles of His government, an immovable rock. His own unchangeableness, and that of His "immortal government," the foundation of His people's confidence.

II. Body of the Speech. Describes the experience and fate of the wicked (verse 5—20).

A favourite subject with these wise men in their dealing with Job. The object to terrify him into a penitent acknowledgment of guilt and supplication for forgiveness. The description meant to depict Job's circumstances, and so to suggest, if not prove, his guilt. This and those similar ones in ch. viii. 11—22, and ch. xv. 20—25, probably recitations from the ancients, or the productions of the inspired poet, the author of the book. Extemporary versification, however, a highly valued accomplishment among Arab poets and philosophers. The object of Satan in these horrifying descriptions to irritate Job to cast off his religion in despair, as of no use to him. The class described—that of hardened transgressors, secret or open, who had enriched themselves by oppression or abused their power to the injury of others —men who neither feared God nor regarded men. Job notoriously the reverse. Hence the mystery. The solution, according to the friends, in the secret iniquity of his heart and life. Job himself, conscious of his integrity, perplexed and distressed, and longing for a Divine explanation which should vindicate his character. Hence his occasional excitement and apparently extravagant language. Had to fight against appearances, manifest facts, and popular belief, or to confess himself a bad man. His outward and inward experience seldom, if ever, found except in notorious transgressors. Probably more frequent *then* than now. The following a highly-wrought picture, full of tragically sublime poetry. One image of horror followed by another still more terrific. The description that of a guilty man chased

by the avenging justice of God—the Furies of the Greeks. The elements in the description—

1. *Great reverse in circumstances* (verse 5). "Yea (notwithstanding your complaint; or 'also,' take another description of the fate of the ungodly), the light of the wicked shall be put out, and the spark (or flame) of his fire shall not shine." Perhaps more than a mere figure for the extinction of his prosperity and affluence. Probable allusion to the practice of rich Arabs kindling, towards evening, a fire in the neighbourhood of their dwelling, to invite and direct travellers to their hospitality. Such fires the glory of a wealthy Arab. Mark of the deepest adversity when no longer sustained. A frequent allusion in Arab poetry—

" Now by deepest want opprest;
Though once my hospitable light
Was blest by travellers at night."—
Hariri.

Job's fires of hospitality also now extinguished. (Verse 6).—"The light shall be dark in his tabernacle, and his candle (or lamp) shall be put out with him" (or "over him;" Arab houses and tents always having a lamp burning during the night, that of the principal apartment hanging from the ceiling or from the centre of the tent; hence the lamp a figure for prosperity and happiness, its extinction indicating utter desolation). Death and misfortune darken the dwelling. Job's present bitter experience. The experience of most at times. Only Jehovah himself an "an everlasting light." Is so to His people, even in the midst of trouble. "When I sit in darkness the Lord shall be a light unto me" (Mic. vii. 8).

2. *Removal of power and dignity* (verse 7). "The steps of His strength (his steps formerly strong, as of a man in full health, prosperity, and power) shall be straitened " (confined as of a man in chains or imprisonment, or suffering from personal affliction). Image taken from a noble lion caught in the toils, and now lying prostrate. Picture of the contrast between Job's former and present condition. For his former "steps" see ch. xxix. 6, 7. Now lying on an ash-heap. Steps of strength soon changed into the feebleness of disease. Plans the most likely to succeed often, in Divine providence, impeded and rendered abortive. The misfortune of the wicked referred to their own sin as the cause. "His own counsel shall cast him down." The lion caught in the toil when wandering about for prey. The wicked "snared in the work of their own hands." Pharaoh's counsel against Israel his own destruction. Cruel thrust at Job as a secret transgressor now caught in the midst of his ill-gotten gains.

3. *Sudden and accumulated calamity* (verse 8). "He is cast into a net by his own feet. (entangled with his feet in a net); he walketh upon a snare (walks unconsciously into a pit fall). The gin (or trap) shall take him by the heel, and the robber shall prevail against him (or, 'the snare lays hold upon him,' so that he is unable to escape). The snare (or cord) is laid (or hidden) in the ground for him, and a trap for him in the way." Image of a wild beast caught by the various strata-gems of the hunter. Men's calamities, especially those of the impenitent trans-gressor, often sudden. "As the fishes that are taken in an evil net, and as the birds that are caught in the snare, so are the sons of men snared in an evil time when it falleth suddenly upon them (Eccles. ix. 12; see also Luke xxi. 34—35, and Thess. v. 3). The worst troubles those which come un-foreseen. Job's actual circumstances. Over-taken by sudden calamities in the very hey-day of his prosperity. Variety of expression in the text to indicate the certainty and terribleness of the doom. "He who fleeth from the noise of the fear shall fall into the pit, and he that cometh up out of the midst of the pit shall be taken in the snare" (Is. xxiv. 17, 18).

5. *Inward terrors* (verse 11). "Terrors shall make him afraid on every side, and shall drive him to his feet." The terrors of an awakened and alarmed conscience among the consequences of persistent sin. Such terrors known in every land as overtaking the secret or notorious transgressors. "Who intent on evil ways will be able to defend his mind against the darts of conscience?" [*Sophocles*]. God's scourge in the sinner's own bosom. No rest or peace under its lashes. Attempts made to escape these "terrors," but in vain. All flight ineffectual except flight through the cross. The terrors of conscience only quenched in the atoning blood of Christ. Job distressed at present by the "terrors of God," but not those of an evil conscience (ch. vi. 4).

6. *Dreadful disease* (verse 12, 13). "His strength shall be hunger-bitten (famished; or, 'his disease shall be voracious'), and de-struction shall be ready at his side (or, 'pre-pared for his side,' or body,—ready to de-vour him). It shall devour the strength of his skin (the firm members of his body); even the first-born of death (one of the most dreadful of mortal diseases) shall devour his strength" (or, "prey upon his powerful limbs.") Disease, with its feebleness and emaciation, personified as the executioner of Divine vengeance—the hungry hound of justice. Disease the result of sin; and often inflicted as a chastisement on the good and a punishment on the bad. Herod, the per-secutor, seized and devoured by one of these dogs of vengeance in the midst of his pride and splendour (Acts xii. 21—23). Job's terrible disease also, a "first-born of death," to all appearance, and in the thought of his three friends, preying on him as a guilty transgressor. No creature, animate or inanimate, but may be made the instru-ment of Divine justice in punishing obstinate and impenitent offenders. Creatures, ani-mal or vegetable, invisible to the naked eye, often the cause of most dreadful diseases. Cholera and the plague among the "first-born of death."

7. *Utter want and desolation* (verse 14, 15). "His confidence (whatever he trusted in—wealth, power, family) shall be rooted out of his tabernacle (utterly, violently, and for ever removed, as a tree torn up by the roots), and it shall bring him to the king of terrors (or, 'terrors like a king shall urge him forward'). It (the terror or desola-tion) shall dwell in his tabernacle, because it is none of his; brimstone shall be scat-tered upon his habitation" (as that of a man lying under Divine wrath, or as a place doomed to a perpetual curse; made, like the Cities of the Plain, a monument of Divine vengeance). "The rich man's wealth is his strong city, and as an high wall in his own conceit (Prov. xviii. 11). This im-plied to have been Job's case. Expressly denied, however, by him (ch. xxxi. 24). Such confidence to be rooted out, as his now appeared to be. Chaldeans, Sabeans, and the fire of God had left only a single servant to carry the tale. Terror and deso-lation, like a victorious and relentless general, had marched him out of his strong city, to sit like a captive among the ashes. Observe—(1) "Riches profit not in the day of wrath." A man's house is his castle, but is unable to hold out against the judgments of God. Chaldeans and Sabeans only God's instruments in stripping a man of his ill-gotten wealth, and sending him out of a dwell-ing to which he has no just right. (2) Alas for him of whom it is to be said: "Lo, this is the man that made not God his strength, but trusted in the abundance of his riches " (Ps. lii. 7). The lightning that strikes down his cattle as truly God's messenger as the brimstone that was scattered on the houses of Sodom and Gomorrha. (2.) *Death emphatically a "king of terrors" to the impenitent.* The terrors of death only to be dissipated by faith in Him who "through death destroyed him that had the power of death, that is the devil; and delivered them, who through fear of death, were all their lifetime subject to bondage" (Heb. ii. 14, 15).

8. *Ruin of family and estate* (verse 16—19). "His roots shall be dried up beneath

(as under the influence of a mighty curse), and above his branch shall be cut off." His property and family alike annihilated by divine judgments. The narrative in Chap. i., a mournful commentary on this verse. Job's case apparently the doom of the wicked; destroyed "root and branch" (Mal. iv. 1). "He shall be driven from light into darkness (violently driven away out of life and luxury into death and despair), and chased out of the world (as a malefactor not fit to live). He shall neither have son nor nephew (or progeny) among his people, nor any remaining in his dwellings (either as relations to inherit his estate, or dependents who had been supported by his bounty). His remembrance shall perish from the earth (or the land), and he shall have no name in the street" (in the places of concourse in the city, or in the fields among shepherds and husbandmen). The great desire among the godless rich to make themselves a name, and perpetuate their memory and their family in the world. "They call their lands after their own names" (Ps. xlix. 11). But "the memory of the wicked shall rot." Only the righteous are worthy to be, and shall be, "held in everlasting remembrance." Job formerly the greatest man in the East, and his praise in everybody's mouth. Now likely soon to be forgotten, and his name never to be mentioned but with a shudder. So his friends thought. But Job was not a wicked man, and a different fate awaited him. His patience and piety have diffused a fragrance throughout the world. His name one of the brightest constellations in the firmament of Holy Scripture.

9. *An astonishment and horror to contempories and posterity* (verse 20). "They that come after him (succeeding generations, or 'those in western regions') shall be astonished at his day (his history, and the awful fate that overtook him), as they that went before (his contempories, or 'those in eastern regions'), were affrighted." Men in opposite quarters of the world, and even future generations should be struck with horror at his secret or open wickedness, and the terrible doom that followed it. Sufficiently harrowing to poor Job, who might see his present experience pourtrayed in the description. His calamities already a cause of astonishment and horror, as they have been in all ages—(1) For their terribleness and extent; (2) Their unlikeliness to happen to such a man; (3) Their suddenness; (4) The rapidity with which they followed each other; (5) Their singularity and unusualness; (6) Their contrast with his former prosperity; (7) The mark they bore of the Divine anger, notwithstanding his pious and upright character. Job already a byword by his own confession. Awful prospect of

what would be the case hereafter, unless God vindicated his character in time. Oppression in all this description sufficient to drive a wise man mad. Observe—(i.) Satan terribly skilful in the means he employs to allure a man to his ruin, or good him to despair. (ii.) Blessed proof of the reality of religion, that Job, notwithstanding all this, still held fast his integrity. (iii.) God's thoughts in regard to his people not as man's thoughts. Job's sufferings have thrown around his name a halo of imperishable glory, while man thought they would only surround it with horror.

III. Conclusion of the speech.

Bildad clenches the terrible description with an emphatic application, by which Job was to appropriate it to himself, or at least to take warning from it. "Surely such are the dwellings of the wicked, and this is the place of him that knoweth not God." This with Job's desolate dwelling before his eyes! Not always true, however, in this life. Bad men not always haunted with terrors and tracked with misfortunes in this world. All the worse, however, if the vengeance is deferred to another. Awful picture presented in this description, of the experience awaiting the impenitent transgressor in a future state. The New Testament, as well as the Old, declares that "God is not mocked; for whatsoever a man soweth, that shall he also reap." Righteous vengeance to overtake all that "know not God, and obey not the Gospel of his Son Jesus Christ." To sin wilfully after receiving the knowledge of the truth is to bring down a fiery indignation which shall devour the adversaries.

Bildad's vehemence, however, overshot itself. His closing sentence such as unintentionally to bring consolation rather than despair. Conscience could whisper,—Thou art *not* the man. Job neither wicked nor one who knew not God. This certain to himself, though perhaps more than doubtful to his vehement assailant. Observe:—(1) *Certainty as to our character and standing needful to bear up against Satan's terrible blasts.* The scathing storm of Bildad's fiery denunciations keenly felt, but Job conscious he was a child and servant of God. (2) *Blessed to be able, amidst Satanic buffetings, still to cling to God as a Father.* (3) *The believer safe even in the pelting of the most pitiless storm.* The righteous in Christ is an 'everlasting foundation,' which floods of temptations and hellish assaults are unable to sweep away. The name of the Lord is a strong tower; the righteous runneth into it, and is safe. That name blessedly known to Job (ch. xix. 25). Is it so to the reader?

CHAPTER XIX.

JOB'S REPLY.   BILDAD'S SECOND SPEECH.

This chapter the crowning part of the controversy. Both in form and in fact the centre of the whole book. Like the eighth chapter of the Epistle to the Romans, the jewel in the ring. Job's faith soars like an eagle through clouds and tempests into the open heaven, and gazes for a few moments on the sun. The culmination of all the preceding conflict. What follows of a considerably different character. Job afterwards descends again into the arena, but much more tranquillised in spirit.

I. **His complaint of his friends' continued reproaches and unkind treatment.**
Their treatment of him was—1. *Distressing* (verse 2). How long will ye vex my soul, and break me in pieces ('bruise or pound me as in a mortar') with words (unkind and reproachful words, or with speeches and recitations which contain only words instead of arguments)?" The bruising of Job's sorrowful spirit the natural effect of his friends' speeches; especially of their long-drawn and highly-coloured quotations about the fate of the wicked. Job put down in them for a wicked man, suffering the righteous consequence of his sins, and threatened with still more dreadful ones. Bruised in soul by his friends' words, as in body by Satan's blows. His internal afflictions thus made to rival his external ones. More grievously robbed by his friends than by either Chaldeans or Sabeans. Worse to be robbed of our peace and good name than of our property. "Who steals my purse steals trash." The experience of David, or whoever wrote Psalm cxix: "Bands of the wicked robbed me" (Ps. cxix. 61). Reproach the bitterest of Christ's sufferings, next to the hiding of His Father's face (Ps. lxix. 20). Job's affliction reaches its height in this chapter, as also his faith and his consolation. Observe—(1.) *Truth misapplied as mischevious as error.* (2.) *A sin not to soothe affliction; a still greater one to aggravate it.* A high offence in God's sight to "talk to the grief of those whom God has wounded" (Ps. lxix. 26). The part of the wicked to "help forward the affliction" of God's suffering people (Zech. i. 15).
2. *Persistent* (verse 3). "These ten (many) times have ye reproached me." Each of the three friends had now attacked him, and two of them a second time. Their

speeches all partaking of the same reproachful character   Their harshness and vehemence only increased as they advanced. The complaint of David as typical of the Messiah, "Reproach hath broken mine heart" (Ps. lxix. 20).
3. *Shameless.* "Ye are not ashamed." A sin to act harshly to any; a shame to act harshly to the afflicted; still more shameful when the afflicted one is a friend. An aggravation of any sin when it is committed without shame.
4. Their treatment was *cruel.* "Ye make yourselves strange to me," *margin,* "harden yourselves against me"; or, "treat me cruelly;" or, "stun me" [with your reproaches]. Unfeeling conduct towards a friend held base even among the heathen. The light of nature teaches that "he who hath friends, must show himself friendly." The effect of false religious views to render men cruel and unfeeling towards others. Religious persecutions especially malignant. True religion a religion of gentleness and love. The more of it, the more gentle and loving. The more of a false religion, the more cruel and unfeeling. Herod put one or two of Christ's disciples to death because it pleased the Jews: Saul, with more religion, kept "breathing out threatenings and slaughter against them" (Acts xii. 1—3; ix. 1).

II. **He wards off their reproaches.** Does so with three considerations—
1. *That he suffers, alone, the effect of his error, if he has committed any* (verse 4). "And be it indeed that I have erred ('gone astray' from God and His commandments), mine error (in the consequences of it) remaineth with myself." *Sufficient to a man to suffer the effect of his error, without his having to bear the additional pain of reproach.* The reproach of friends often harder to bear than the violence of enemies.
2. *That his offence, if committed, was an unconscious one.* "Mine error." Marked difference made in the law between sins committed presumptuously or deliberately and those committed in error or ignorance. Job's among the latter. Such found in the best, "Who can understand his errors?" Yet even then calling for humiliation, and requiring the blood of atonement. One object of affliction to bring sins of ignorance to

our consciousness in order to their confession. Many, perhaps most, of our sins, like letters, written with invisible ink, requiring the fire to bring them to view; or, like the characters traced with phosphorous, only made visible in the dark chamber of trouble. Cleansing to be sought "from secret faults" (Ps. xix. 12).

3. *That his afflictions were from the hand of God* (verse 5). "If, indeed, ye will magnify yourselves against me, and plead against me, my reproach (make my calamities which you reproach me with an argument to prove my guilt; or, prove to me my reproach, that I am guilty and suffer deservedly), know now (on the contrary, or, as a thing I fully admit, but which ought to move your pity), that God hath overthrown me (hath thrust me down and brought me low, doing it of His own free will and pleasure, without reference to any guilt of mine as the cause), and hath compassed me with His net," (as a hunter the animal that he wishes to take). Bildad had said the wicked are entangled in a net: Job admits he was taken in a net; but that net was God's. Observe:—(1.) *A Godly man sees and acknowledges God in his troubles, as well as in his triumphs.* In the friend's view, as well as Job's, his afflictions from God; the difference, that in theirs, they were *retributive ;* in his, arbitrary and mysterious. This pleaded by Job as a reason for their pity and more gentle treatment. Enough for *God* to lay on His hand, without man adding his also.—(2.) *That our afflictions are from God may be either an alleviation or an aggravation.* An *alleviation*, when there is faith in His Fatherly love; an *aggravation*, when there is only apprehension of His wrath. The hand of a loving Father seen in our trouble takes away its sting; the apprehension of His anger exasperates the wound. —(3.) *Sin, and not suffering, is itself a "reproach."* Suffering no reproach, but as the effect of sin. "Sin, a reproach to any people."

4. *That he can obtain no redress from God* (verse 7). "Behold, I cry out of wrong (of violence done to me in these afflictions sent without any guiltiness as the cause), but I am not heard: I cry aloud (from intensity of suffering and earnestness to be heard), but there is no judgment" (no impartial trial afforded of my case, and no redress of my wrongs). One of the hardest things spoken by Job in regard to God. Seemed to charge God foolishly. Even Moses, the meekest man on earth, "spake unadvisedly with his lips." One of the sayings for which Job was at last reproved by God, and for which he humbled himself in dust and ashes. Yet the language in a sense true, though

114

both rash and irreverent. According to God's own testimony, Job was "destroyed without cause" (ch. ii. 3). Job correct as to the fact itself ; *not* correct as to the conduct he ascribes to God in the matter. God might have, as He actually had, the holiest, kindest, wisest, best reasons for treating, or allowing others to treat, him as He did. But to ascribe wrong or violence to his Creator was only the suggestion of his adversary, and enough to bring Job, as it did afterwards bring him, to the dust. Job's language sinfully presents God in the view of the unjust judge in the parable. Observe —(1.) *God's outward dealings not always the criterion of His character or His heart.* Seems at times to wink at the sins of His enemies and to disregard the cry of His friends. May, however, bear long with His people, but in the end will avenge them. Their part to believe this, and still to cry and wait on (Luke xviii. 1—8). (2.) *God's silence to His people's cry one of their greatest trials.* Experienced by David and by David's Antitype (Ps. xxii. 1, 2).

III. Enlarges on God's severe treatment of him (verse 8—19). Specifies—

1. *His bringing him into inextricable straits* (verse 8). "He hath fenced up my way that I cannot pass, and he hath set darkness in my paths." Describes his troubles—(1) Externally ; as of the nature of an impassable fence. By the character of his disease, excluded from society and confined to his ash-heap. His disease an incurable one. All his troubles apparently irremediable. (2) Internally ; his mind full of darkness and confusion. Saw no way of escape. Acknowledges that "the steps of his strength" were "straitened," but straitened by *God*, for what cause he knew not. Observe—One usual way in which God afflicts and tries His people is to bring them into straits, out of which they can find no escape. Hedges up their way that they cannot find their paths (Hos. ii. 6; Lam. iii. 7; Ps. lxxxviii. 8). Thus shuts them up to Himself—(i.) to humble submission to Him ; (ii.) to entire dependence upon Him.

2. *His so deeply humbling and abasing him* (verse 9). "He has stripped me of my glory, and taken the crown from my head." Similar complaint in ch. xvi. 15. The change in his circumstances here ascribed directly to God. The Chaldeans and Sabeans, the fire and the whirlwind, and finally, the loathsome leprosy itself, only God's instruments. Observe— (1) *The part of faith and piety, to view all our adversities, whatever the instruments, as coming from God himself* (Ps. lxvi. 11, 12; lxxi. 20). (2) *All earthly "glory," such as a man can be stripped of by Divine Providence,—*

children, friends, wealth, fame, influence, rank. That only the true "glory" of which a man cannot be stripped, even by death itself. God himself the believer's unfading glory (Isaiah xl. 19). (3) *The brightest earthly crown such as may, like Job's, be suddenly laid in the dust.* The poorest believer the heir of "a crown that fadeth not away" (1 Pet. v. 4). A man's crown, whatever is his ornament and honour. For Job's earthly crown, read ch. xxix.

3. *His utterly extirpating him and blighting his hopes* (verse 10). "He hath destroyed me ('plucked me up') on every side, and I am gone; and mine hope he hath removed like a tree." The figure that of a tree thoroughly torn up by the roots. Job's case, both in regard to person and progeny, property and position. All his expectation of comfort, prosperity, and usefulness hopelessly blasted. For his hope, see chap. xxix. 18. The frustration of his hopes, a part of his trial (chap. xiv. 19; xvii. 11). Hard to give up our hopes and see our expectations blasted. All earthly hopes liable to disappointment. Job's previous condition and character such as might warrant such hopes, if any could.

4. *His treating him as an enemy* (verse 11). "He hath also kindled his wrath against me, and he counteth me unto him as one of his enemies." Job had lived, like Abraham, as the "friend of God;" had experienced his friendship and familiarity (chap. xxix. 4, 5); had, like Enoch, "walked with God," and sought to please Him (chap. vi. 10). Intensely trying to oe now treated by Him as an enemy (chap. xiii. 24). Yet God's secret testimony of him: "My servant Job." The same borne openly at the close of the trial. Observe—(1) *Love and hatred, on the part of God, and His estimate of individuals, not known from His dealings with men in this world* (Eccles. ix. 1). (2) *Apprehended wrath on the part of God, the believer's greatest trial.*

5. *His appearing to employ His creatures for his destruction* (verse 12). "His troops (His creatures whom He employs as a general does his troops) come together (as if summoned from different quarters to the siege), and raise up their way against me, and encamp round about my tabernacle." The Sabeans and Chaldeans, lightning and whirlwind, hostile friends and neighbours, good and bad angels, all viewed as God's armies, employed by Him for his destruction. All nature, animate and inanimate, rational and irrational, visible and invisible, capable of being employed as His forces, either for mercy or judgment. The Roman troops besieging Jerusalem spoken of as God's armies (Matt. xxii. 7). So the swarms of locusts devastating Judæa (Joel ii. 25). Creation but "a

reservoir of means" made ready for the Creator's use. Man being in rebellion against God,

"The very elements, though each be meant
The minister of man to serve his wants,
Conspire against him."

Holy angels especially God's troops (Ps. ciii. 21). These pitch their tent around God's servants for their protection (Ps. xxxiv. 7; xci. 10, 11). Appeared now to do so around Job's tabernacle for his destruction. "Blind unbelief is sure to err," &c. Job's affliction now apparently chronic. The ministers of destruction had not only raised up their way, as troops advancing to the siege, but had sat down around the beleaguered fortress.

6. *His alienating from him his friends, domestics, and others* (verses 13—15). "He hath put my brethren far from me, and mine acquaintance are verily estranged from me. My kinsfolk have failed (ceased from their kind offices as such), and my familiar friends have forgotten me. They that dwell in my house (servants and dependents, or strangers partaking, according to Arab custom, of his hospitality and protection, ch. xxxi. 17, 18), and my maids (from whose sex more tenderness and respect might have been expected) count me for a stranger. I am an alien in their sight,"—instead of being regarded as the master in my own dwelling. A painful aggravation of adversity and affliction when relations are more kin than kind. Job enlarges on this distressing change in his domestic and social relations (verse 16). "I called my servant and he gave me no answer (thus treating me not only with disrespect but contempt): I entreated him (instead of commanding him, as a master) with my mouth" (with my own mouth instead of another's, or with a loud call instead of a mere whisper; or rather, instead of summoning him with my hands,—servants in the East being summoned, not by the voice, but by clapping the hands). A still greater trial, however, than this humiliation in his own house, was his (verse 17). "My breath (or my spirit) is strange (odious and disgusting) to my wife (causing her to withdraw from all nearness to me and intercourse with me), though I entreated for the children's sake of mine own body" (or, 'and I stink in the nostrils of the children of my womb; *i.e.* of the womb that bare me, viz. my own brothers and sisters; or the children of my own body —either grandchildren, or the children of my concubines; or, 'my prayer is loathsome to the children,' &c.). The contemptuous treatment extended beyond his own house (verse 18). "Yea, young children (possibly those of his slaves or domestics, or according

to *margin*, 'the wicked,' the idle rabble, drawn from such curiosity to such a spectacle of misfortune and disease) despise me; I arose (or 'I rise' or 'stand up' to speak, treating them with courtesy and respect, or commanding them away), and they spake against me." Sad contrast with his former treatment (chap. xxix. 8—10, 21—23). One of the greatest indignities in the East to be treated by young persons and inferiors with disrespect. Deference to seniors and superiors a prominent feature in Oriental manners. Verse 19.—"All my inward friends (*Heb.*'the men of my secret,' my most intimate and confidential friends) abhorred me; and they whom I loved are turned against me." Job's treatment by his three friends a specimen of this part of his affliction, and probably now alluded to. Their feeling, instead of sympathy, one of abhorrence. Their abhorrence from—(1) His loathsome disease; (2) The appearance of his being treated as a wicked man and a hypocrite, whom Divine justice was only now overtaking and bringing his secret wickedness to light. A duty suggested by the light of Nature to withdraw from such. This treatment one of Job's keenest sufferings. The bitter complaint of David and of David's Antitype, Messiah. (Ps. xli. 9; lv. 13, 14, 20). This treatment, like his other trials, ascribed by the patriarch to God. So with David—"Lover and friend hast thou put far from me" (Ps. xxxviii. 11; xxxi. 11; lxix. 8). "The Lord hath said unto him, Curse David" (2 Sam. xvi. 10). Observe—

1. The sinful and undutiful conduct of men to be ascribed to God only as secretly permitted, and for wise and holy ends providentially appointed, but neither as commanded nor instigated by Him. So Joseph's treatment by his brethren, and the Crucifixion of Jesus by the Jews.

2. The bonds of affection and friendship in God's hands. These He has but to loose and friends turn foes. The social as well as physical system under His control, and dependent on His will.

3. Satan a willing and powerful agent in producing evil as soon as he obtains permission. His part that of the tale-bearer, to "separate chief friends," and "sow discord among brethren." His name Diabolus, or Devil, "the slanderer," indicative of his character and employment.

4. Evil latent in every heart, and only requiring the removal of restraints in order to its breaking forth. These restraints in God's hand, who makes the wrath of man to praise Him, while the "remainder" of that wrath He restrains (Ps. lxxvi. 10).

5. Civil and domestic concord, and the dutiful conduct of subjects and inferiors, due to God's overruling Providence. The

116

sins of rulers and heads of families often punished by the removal of Providential restraints, and the abandonment of the heart of subjects and children to its own corruption. Hence insubordination, alienation, disobedience, discord. On the other hand, "when a man's ways please the Lord, he maketh even his enemies to be at peace with him" (Prov. xvi. 7).

6. Job, in these verses, a manifest type of God's Righteous Servant, the Messiah, in His last sufferings. (Read Matthew xxvi. and xxvii.)

IV. Touching appeal to his friends (verses 20—22).

1. *Describes his reduced condition* (verse 20). "My bone cleaveth to my skin and to my flesh (or 'as to my flesh,'—his flesh gone, and his bones adhering to and appearing through his skin); and I am escaped with the skin of my teeth" (with only the skin about the teeth and gums left free from ulcers,—proverbial expression denoting extreme emaciation and peril of life). Satan goes the utmost length of his permission (ch. ii. 6). Job's emaciation already alluded to (ch. xvi. 8). The result partly of his disease, partly of his continued grief. Man's beauty soon made to consume away under God's rebukes (Ps. xxxix. 11).

2. *Entreats the pity of his friends* (verse 21). "Have pity upon me, have pity upon me, O ye my friends; for the hand of God hath touched me." Job's spirit calmer and more humble. The heart a flinty rock that could resist his appeal. Yet resisted by his friends. Left to himself man has "no flesh" in his obdurate heart." Pity no less his duty, and the want of it his sin (ch. vi. 14). Job's appeals for pity on the ground—(1) Of *their relation to him as his* "*friends.*" Natural for a man in trouble to cast himself on the sympathy of his friends. Even an enemy will pity in deep distress. A brother born for adversity. Men bearing the name and profession of friends to be careful to act as such (Prov. xviii. 24). Jesus the "Friend of sinners" (Matt. xi. 19); a Friend that sticketh closer than a brother (Prov. xviii. 24). Appropriated by believers as *their* Friend (Cant. v. 16). Touched with the feeling of our infirmities (Heb. iv. 15). Precious privilege to possess a true and tried friend. Such to be grappled to our soul "with hooks of steel."

" Poor is the friendless master of a world ;
A world in purchase for a friend is gain."

(2) On the ground of *his great affliction*. "The hand of God hath touched me." When God smites, man should pity, not reproach. The heavier the blow, the more tender the

sympathy. Observe—*All Job's afflictions but the touch of God's hand.* That touch all that Satan craved. Able in a moment to turn our joy into sorrow, our comeliness into corruption. Can in a few days strip us of our property, bereave us of our children, alienate our friends, deprive us of our health, and render us an object of loathing to all who see us. "A fearful thing to fall into the hands of the living God."

3. *Deprecates their severity* (verse 22). "Why do ye persecute me as God (adding your groundless severity to His), and are not satisfied with my flesh" (which you see mangled and consumed, but will add your reproaches and thus lacerate my spirit as well). Appeals to conscience and humanity as well as to friendship and pity. God's apparent severity towards any of His creatures no reason for man's severity to his suffering fellow-creature. In all circumstances God makes humanity man's duty. "To love mercy" one of the three grand requirements on the part of man (Micah vi. 8). Mercy "twice blessed." Neither man's sins nor God's strokes intended to turn the "milk of human kindness" into gall. The more God wounds in His Providence, the more man's duty to heal with his pity, his prayers, and if need be, his purse. Christ's parable of the Good Samaritan to be the Christian's practice as it was His own.

V. An impassioned wish (verses 23, 24). "O that my words were now written! Oh that they were printed in a book (or public register)! That they were graven with an iron pen and lead in the rock for ever!" Observe—

1. Reference made to the various modes of writing then practiced—(1) On linen or papyrus; (2) On leaden tablets; (3) On rocks or stone pillars, the characters formed with an iron graver and filled up with lead for greater preservation and distinctness. Papyrus rolls still exist from the remotest age of the Pharaohs. Such mode of writing common in the age of Cheops, the founder of the Great Pyramid, 2000 years before Christ. Montfaucon, in 1699, purchased a book in Rome entirely of lead. Wady Mokatteb, along the route of the Israelites in the Desert, full of inscriptions cut in the rocks. At Hisn Ghorab, on the shores of South Arabia, on a high rock terrace, is a large inscription of ten lines in Himyaritic characters, the letters four inches long by one-third of an inch broad, and one-tenth deep, cut in notches, and having apparently been "graven with an iron pen." The inscription is made on a very light grey or lead-coloured stone, a vein of the quarry coming out on the face of the cliff. It is as follows: "We believed in

the miracle-mystery, and in the resurrection-mystery, and in the nostril-mystery." The name of *Aws* at the foot of the inscription indicates it to be a relic of the long-lost tribe of Ad, the son of Aws or Uz, the son of Aram and grandson of Shem, and connects it closely with the country in which Job lived.—(*Sermons in Stones*).

2. Reference to writing as already well known. Practised long anterior to the time of Moses. Originally in hieroglyphics; then in letters formed from these. Three kinds of writing practised among the ancient Egyptians—the hieroglyphic, the hieratic (used by the priests), and the demotic, used by the people. Printing originally by carving in stone. Printing by blocks long practised in China. Printing by types only invented in 1440 A.D.; the art begun at Haarlem, in Holland, and perfected at Mainz, in Germany. The first printed book, with a date, a Psalter printed by John Faust in 1457. The first printed Bible with a date, produced by the same person, in 1460.

3. Job's spirit elevated to a high pitch of sublimity and faith. Looks into the future with calmness and triumph. His language that of conscious integrity, and of certainty as to his ultimate vindication. Desires the perpetuation of his words to all generations. His words either those in which he had already declared his innocence, or those in which he was about to declare the certainty of his faith in his Divine Redeemer and Vindicator. Wished to tell out his confidence and confession of Him, without the fear of having a single word to efface.

4. Job's wish fulfilled to an extent undreamt of at the time. His words written in the imperishable records of Holy Scripture. Printed by the British and Foreign Bible Society fifty millions of times in more than a hundred languages, and spread over all the earth, during the last seventy years. The last language in which they have been printed, viz., in this present year 1875, by the Pilgrim-Mission Printing Press at St. Chrischona, near Bâle, is the Amharic, the modern Ethiopic or Abyssinian, nearly related to the language which Job spoke. The Himyaritic, already mentioned, is closely allied to the Ethiopic and Hebrew; and the Amharic has chiefly helped to interpret it. May contain the remains of the language of the earlier races of Arabia, as the Adites and Amalekites, and is considered a form of Arabic which preceded the Ishmaelitic, the Kufic, and of course the ordinary Arabic of the Koran. Hmyar, from whom it has its name, was a grandson of Kahtan or Joktan, the brother of Peleg; and from him were all the princes descended who reigned in Yemen or Arabia

Felix, till the time of Mahomed. His father Yarab is said to have been the inventor of the Arabic language and the progenitor of all the Arabs of Yemen. Abyssinia, whose language is the Amharic, is called by the natives Habesh, or 'mixture,' from the united descendants of Shem and Ham who peopled it, Ham having probably fled at once from his father's presence across the Desert into Egypt, his posterity multiplying in the valley of the Nile and in Abyssinia.

All our words graven as in a rock for ever as a testimony either for us or against us. By our words, as well as by our deeds, we shall be justified or condemned at the final assize (Matt. xii. 36, 37 ; Jude 15).

VI. Job's triumphant testimony and joyful assurance (verses 25—27). "For I know (Heb. 'And,'—'even, or also, I know,') that my Redeemer liveth (or, 'is living,' or 'is the living One '), and that He shall stand at the latter day upon the earth (or, that He at last,—hereafter, or as the last One,—shall arise upon the dust or earth,—or 'shalt stand over the grave,' viz., my dust, or the dust of the grave, or mankind) ; and though after my skin worms destroy this body (or, 'and after my skin shall be mangled thus; or, 'even this,' pointing to it), yet in my flesh (Heb. 'out of my flesh,' i.e., as my habitation or point of vision,—or, 'without my flesh,' i.e., in a disembodied state) shall I see God; whom I (emphatic, 'Even I myself' shall see for myself—to my advantage, on my side, or as my own), and mine eyes shall behold and not another (or, 'not estranged' as he now appears to be); though my reins be consumed within me" (Heb. "my reins,—without 'though'—are consumed in my bosom," viz., either from disease, or, as margin, with desire for that day). One of the most remarkable and magnificent passages in the Bible. Observe —(1) the solemnity with which in the previous verses it has been introduced ; (2) The place which it holds in the Book as the climax in Job's speeches. Job's faith here rises to its loftiest triumph. The words uttered when, to outward sense, all was cheerless despair. A glorious example of Christian faith. Job's faith "the substance of (or what gives reality to) things hoped for, the evidence (or certain conviction) of things not seen" (Heb. xi. 1). Believes what it sees not. Hopes even against hope, or contrary to all appearances against it. His faith and hope the cordial in his trouble. All calumny and suffering easily borne in the certain possession of a personal Redeemer and the assured hope of a blessed deliverance. The passage early incorporated in the Church's burial service, as the expression of

her faith and hope of a glorious resurrection. The opening words—

" I know that my Redeemer liveth,"

Among the most memorable sayings of Scripture. Worthy to be written in gems and gold. Perhaps more familiar to Christians than any other text either in the Old or New Testament. Repeated over the open sepulchre for hundreds of years, proclaiming death a conquered foe, and the grave rifled of its spoils. A cheering and joyous light to millions in the dark valley of trouble and of death itself. Job amply compensated for all his suffering in being made thereby the author of these blessed and imperishable words. Consider under the passage—

1. The assured knowledge which Job asserts: "I know." The language of absolute certainty. The thing no mere guess, or conjecture, or vague hope. No hesitation or doubt about the matter. Known by Job as certainly as that the sun was shining in the heavens. His faith neither to be shaken by his terrible losses, nor his wife's reproaches, nor his friends' suspicions and accusations. Like the life-boat, which buried for a few moments in the surging billows, comes again to the surface. Christian faith is certain knowledge (Heb. ii. 1).

Job glories in his knowledge. I know. The "I" emphatic. I, who am so reduced in body and in circumstances, so despised, so wretched, so loathsome. I, who am standing on the very brink of the grave. I know, whatever you may do, and whatever your unfavourable opinion concerning me. I know it, as my unspeakable comfort and my glorious privilege. The believer's knowledge of Christ something to glory in. "I know whom I have believed."

The grounds and sources of this assurance. Both internal and external. Internally—(1) Divine enlightenment. All true and saving knowledge of God as our Redeemer the result of Divine teaching (Is. liv. 13). "No man knoweth the Son but the Father; neither knoweth any man the Father, save the Son, and he to whomsoever the Son will reveal him." "Blessed art thou, Simon Bar-jonas; for flesh and blood hath not revealed this [knowledge of me] unto thee, but my Father who is in heaven." "It pleased God to reveal his Son in me." "We know that the Son of God is come, and hath given us an understanding, that we may know him that is true" (Matt. xi. 27; xvi. 17; Gal. i. 15, 16; 1 John iv. 20). (2) Previous personal acquaintance with God, experience of His grace, and habitual walking with Him (Hos. vi. 3).—Externally: (1) The original promise in Eden. That promise one of a

Redeemer who should avenge on the serpent, the devil, the injuries he had inflicted on the human race, to be claimed therefore by Job as his Redeemer. This promise the germ of all redemption acts and offices performed by Jehovah towards mankind. Handed down from father to son and extended through the world. Found in various tribes and nations in a distorted form. Preserved pure in the line of Shem. The Fall through the Serpent represented on the temple of Osiris at Phyle, in Upper Egypt. The resurrection exhibited on the tomb of Mycerinus in one of the Pyramids four thousand years ago. (2) Enoch's prophecy, preserved by tradition and quoted by Jude in his epistle (verses 14, 15). (3) Enoch's translation to heaven before the Flood. (4) The preservation of Noah and his family in the Ark. (5) The continually offered sacrifices, which told of a Redeemer who by death should destroy him that had the power of death (Heb. ii. 14). Observe—(1) Job's certainty as to a living Redeemer in that early age more than 2000 years before his appearance on the earth, a solemn witness against all unbelief in our own, nearly 2000 years after it. (2) Job's happiness and comfort in the knowledge of a personal Redeemer *before* he came, rather to be exceeded by our own so long *after* he has done so. (3) The sweetest and surest knowledge of God as in Christ our own gracious Redeemer obtained in the time of trouble and affliction. At eventide light.

2. *The contents of Job's knowledge, or the thing asserted to be known.* Has reference— (1). To *God.* "I know that my Redeemer liveth," &c. Regarding God, he knew— (i.) That He was *his Redeemer.* The name (*Heb.* Goel), applied—(a) To the *kinsman,* whose duty under the law, was, as next-of-kin, to redeem a captive or enslaved relative; to buy back his sold or forfeited inheritance; to marry his childless widow if unmarried himself; and to avenge his innocent blood. The institution recognised and established in the Mosaic law, but doubtless in existence long before. Still existing more or less in the East. Like others under the law, typical of the Messiah and His redemption-work. The name applied—(b) To God as the Redeemer and Deliverer of His people, especially of Israel from Egyptian bondage and Babylonian captivity. Peculiarly applied —(c) To God the Son, who, as the promised Deliverer of the human race, should become incarnate as the woman's seed, and through His own death bruise the Serpent's head. The name not expressly applied to Him in the New Testament, but the thing every where. (See Rom. iii. 24; Eph. i. 7; Gal. iii. 13; iv. 5; Titus ii. 14; Heb. ix. 12; Rev. v. 9). The name proper to a kinsman.

Under the law, only such had the right to redeem. Pointed to the fact that He who was to be man's Redeemer was to be also his Brother. The human kinsmanship of the Divine Redeemer, a subject of express prophecy: "Awake, O sword, against my shepherd, against the *man that is my fellow*" (Zech. xiii. 7). Such kinmanship ascribed to Him by the Apostle as necessary for His undertaking. "Forasmuch as the children were partakers of flesh and blood, he likewise himself also took part of the same, that through death he might destroy him that had the power of death, and deliver them," &c. (Heb. ii. 14). God the Son the Author of all redeeming acts towards Israel. (Ps. lxviii. 17, 18, compared with Eph. iv. 8—10).

God the Son regarded by Job more or less distinctly as his Redeemer, in—(a) Delivering him from troubles (so Jacob, Gen. xlviii. 16); (b) Vindicating his character and avenging his wrongs; (c) Delivering him from death and the grave; (d) Delivering him from the hand of the great adversary, the devil. His words uttered under a deep sense of his wants and necessities. His spirit at the time more than ordinarily elevated and illuminated. His language, perhaps, primarily referring to the divine vindication of his character, but extending much beyond it. Appears to triumph over death and the grave, of which he had the nearest prospect. The language only understood in its fullest sense in New Testament times. Words uttered by the prophets with a meaning not fully apprehended at the time by themselves (1 Pet. i. 10—12). Redemption the term most generally employed in the New Testament to designate the Saviour's work. Viewed as redemption from the curse or condemning sentence of the Divine law (Gal. iii. 13); the power of Satan, who had acquired a right over us through that sentence (Heb. ii. 14); death and hell, as the punishment awarded by the Divine law to transgression (Cor. xv. 56, 57); and very specially from sin itself (Tit. ii. 14; 1 Pet. i. 18, 19; Eph. v, 25—27; Matt. i. 21). Israel's national and external redemption typical of that of mankind as sinners, by Jesus Christ. The great redemption by the Son of God effected—(1) By purchase; (2) By power. The price of human redemption the blood of Christ, His substituted suffering and death. The power employed in it that of the Holy Ghost, sent in virtue of the price paid upon the Cross. His power required— (1) In quickening the soul to a new spiritual life; (2) Preserving and perfecting it in the image of God.

Job declares his *personal interest* in the Redeemer: "*My* Redeemer." The language —(1) Of appropriation; (2) Of faith; (3)

Of choice; (4) Of love; (5) Of knowledge and past experience; (6) Of satisfaction. Something to say *the* Redeemer; more to say *our* Redeemer; most and best to say *my* Redeemer. Devils able to say the first; unsaved men the second; only saved believers the last. '*My*' the word that links the lost sinner to the dying Saviour. I may well rejoice that Christ is *a* Redeemer; immensely more that He is *my* Redeemer. This little word, like the honey on the point of Jonathan's staff, enlightens the eyes and puts strength into the soul. Inexpressibly more sweetness and satisfaction in two such words as "My God," &c., than in all the pleasures of the world since its creation [*John Brown of Haddington*]. His last words were: "My Christ." *My* does not engross the Redeemer, but claims its share in Him with others. Faith's first act is to believe Christ to be *a* Redeemer; the second to take Him as *my* Redeemer. The privilege as well as duty of each human soul thus to appropriate Christ as his Redeemer. The world's as well as Israel's sin and condemnation *not* to do so. "He came unto His own, and His own received Him not; but to as many as received Him, to them gave He power to become the sons of God" (John i. 11, 12).

(ii.). Job asserts that this, his Redeemer, was *living,* or "the living One." "My Redeemer *liveth.*" The Redeemer thus viewed as—(*a*) *Personally living.* (*b*) *Continuing to exist beyond the bounds of time.* Able, therefore, to redeem him from death and the grave. Lived to vindicate His character after his body had mingled with the dust. Able to save to the uttermost, or to the end. (*c*) *The Mighty One.* Life the expression of strength and power. "Mine enemies are *lively,* and they are *strong.*" Job's Redeemer and our's possessed of all power in heaven and earth. "Has power over all flesh to give eternal life to as many as the Father hath given Him" (John xvii. 3). (*d*) *The Author and Giver of life.* Having life in Himself and able to communicate it to others. The living and life-giving Redeemer set over against Job's state as dying, or virtually dead. The epithet one proper to God. Called "the living God;" He that "liveth for ever and ever." Appropriated by Christ: "I am He that liveth and was dead, and am alive for evermore." Christ the Resurrection and the Life. The Way, the Truth, and Life. The true God and eternal life (Rev. i. 18; John ii. 25; xiv. 16; 1 John v. 20). A living and life-giving Redeemer our comfort in a dying body in a dying world, and with the remains of death in our soul. Christ, as our Redeemer, lives—(*a*) To plead our cause in heaven (Heb. vii. 25); (*b*) To send down supplies of needed grace (2 Cor. xii. 9); (*c*) To prepare a

120

place for us in Paradise (John xiv. 2); (*d*) To attend to all our concerns (Heb. iv. 14—16); (*e*) To overcome all our enemies; (*f*) To deliver us out of all our troubles; (*g*) To give victory over temptation and sin; (*h*) To make us partakers of his life; (*i*) To receive us to Himself; (*j*) To come again in glory. Christ as an ever-living Redeemer, the hope and trust of the believer. That our Redeemer lives, an antidote against the fear of man, of troubles, of death, of judgment (Isa. li. 12, 13; xliii. 2, 3; Rev. i. 17, 18). Our case safe in the hands of a living Redeemer. Enough for a dying saint that his Redeemer lives. One at least whom death cannot remove from us. His life a pledge of His people's (John xiv. 19).

(iii.) *That He should "stand (or rise up) at the last day (or 'as the last one') upon (or over) the earth."* Job elevated by the Holy Spirit to the place and office of a prophet. The book a part of those Scriptures which "testify" of Christ, and out of which Christ expounded to the disciples the things concerning Himself. The testimony of Jesus is the spirit of prophecy. The prophets testified beforehand the sufferings of Christ, and the glory that should follow (1 Pet. i. 11). The testimony of Moses and the prophets that Christ should suffer, and should be the first that should rise from the dead (Acts xxvi. 22, 23). Job's present language a prophecy, as well as the expression of his faith and assurance. Declares—(1) That God as his Redeemer *would one day appear on behalf of his suffering servant.* "Standing" or "rising up" the Scripture expression for a Divine appearance as the deliverer and avenger of His people (Ps. vii. 6; x. 12; xii. 5; Isa. xxxiii. 10). (2) That he *would appear on or over the earth.* Appears to be a double prophecy, viz., of the Redeemer's incarnation and His coming to judgment. These often united in the prophets, being, as here, viewed together as one event. The first necessary to the second, the second the compliment of the first. His coming to suffer necessary in order to His coming to reign. His second coming completes what His first began. Christ called by the apostle, speaking of the resurrection of the dead, the last Adam, or second Man, as apparently here, the last or latter One (1 Cor. xv. 21, 22, 45, 47). The first Adam brought man's body to the dust; and second comes to raise it from it. Observe—(1) Faith comforts by turning the sufferer's eye from God's *present* dealings with him to his *future* ones. (2) The consolation of the Church is—(i.) That Christ has suffered for our sins, the Just One in the room of the unjust; (ii.) That he has risen as the first-fruits of them that

slept; (iii.) That to them that look for Him
He will appear the second time without sin
unto salvation; (iv.) That them that sleep
in Jesus God will bring with Him (1 Pet.
iii. 18; 1 Cor. xv. 20, 23; Heb. ix. 28;
1 Thess. iv. 14).—The knowledge asserted
by Job has reference also—
(2) To *himself* (verse 27). "And though
after my skin, &c., yet in my flesh shall I
see God; whom I shall see for myself," &c.
The centre of his faith and hope, not only
that his Redeemer lives, and should one
day appear, but that as the result of it he
should

See God.

Two ways of seeing God—(i.) Mentally and
spiritually; (ii.) Physically and corporeally.
God seen—(i.) In His character and works;
(ii.) In His person. The former only our
privilege here, while in the body; the latter,
hereafter, out of the body and after the
resurrection. God seen in His Person in
His Son Jesus Christ. "He that hath seen
Me hath seen the Father." In Christ is seen
"all the fulness of the Godhead bodily."
Isaiah, in vision, beheld the Lord (Jehovah)
sitting on His throne in the temple (Is. vi.
1). He beheld the "glory" of Christ (John
xii. 41). As distinct from the glorified
Redeemer, at the right hand of the Father,
Stephen beheld "the glory of God" (Acts
vii. 55). In heaven the angels always behold
"the face" of the Father (Matt. xviii. 10).
The vision of God, anticipated by Job, generally understood to be a corporeal one in
His restored body. Appears to emphasize it
in this view—" Whom mine eyes shall behold." Christ, at His second appearing, the
object of bodily vision. "Every eye shall
see him, and they also that pierced him."
The prospect re-asserted and dwelt upon
from its sweetness and certainty. I shall
see God—see Him for myself—mine eyes
shall behold Him. Contrasted with his present experience,—unable to perceive God.
God hiding Himself from him, his greatest
trial (ch. xiii. 24; ix. 11; xxiii. 8, 9).
Observe—(i.) The vision of God the blessedness of the glorified (Ps. xvii. 15; Matt. v. 8;
1 John iii. 2; Rev. xxii. 4). Implies—(1)
A much higher and clearer knowledge of
God (1 Cor. xiii. 9—12). (2) Enjoyment
of immediate and uninterrupted fellowship
with Him. (3) More blissful consciousness of
His favour and love. (4) Fuller understanding of His providential dealings here.
—(ii.) The nature of faith to believe that
though God now hides His face, yet we shall
again behold it (Micah vii. 8; Hab. iii. 17—
19). Faith trusts in the dark and hopes
for what it sees not.—(iii.) Joyful anticipation of seeing God the peculiar privilege of a

believer. Implies—(1) A conscious state
of peace and reconciliation with God. (2)
A renewed nature, capable of delighting in
God and in His fellowship. (3) Purity of
heart, and conscious integrity of character.
Only the pure in heart capable of seeing
God (Matt. v. 8). Evil cannot dwell with
Him. A hypocrite shall not come before
Him. To see God's face, coupled with serving
Him, the blessedness of the glorified (Rev.
xxii. 4). The sight of God and the Lamb at
His second appearing, the world's greatest
dread (Rev. vi. 15—17). The comfort of
believers that when God shall appear, it will
be "for them," as their Friend and Redeemer, for their full and everlasting salvation (Heb. ix. 28).
The appearing of his Redeemer, and the
future sight of God as his friend, the object of Job's intense longing. "My reins
are consumed in my bosom"—with desire
for that day (*margin*). Contrasted with the
object of desire held forth by his three
friends—health and prosperity in this life.
The salvation of God, perfected at the
Saviour's second appearing, the Church's
desire both in the Old and New Testament.
Jacob's experience: "I have waited for thy
salvation, O Lord." David's: "My flesh
shall rest in hope, for thou wilt not leave my
soul in hell" (wilt not leave me in the grave).
"I shall be satisfied when I awake in thy
likeness." Isaiah, and the Church in his
day: "With my soul have I desired thee in
the night;" the answer: "Thy dead men shall
live, together with my dead body shall they
arise. Awake and sing ye that dwell in dust;
for thy dew is as the dew of herbs, and the
earth shall cast out the dead" (Is. xxvi 9,
19). The last words of the spouse in the
Song: "Make haste, my beloved, and be
like a roe or a young hart upon the mountain
of spices." Christ's glorious appearing the
blessed hope and desire of the early Christians, exposed as they were to death and all
kinds of suffering for the truth's sake. "The
Spirit and the Bride said, Come—the Spirit
in the Bride" (Rev. xxii. 17; Rom. viii. 23).
In reply to the promise: "Behold, I come
quickly;" the Church's last recorded prayer
is: "Even so, come, Lord Jesus." The cry
of the souls under the altar: "How long, O
Lord, wilt thou not avenge our blood on the
earth."
The Lord's second appearing, and the
resurrection consequent on it, to be desired
and longed for, as—(1) The time of full redemption and salvation in body and soul to
believers themselves; (2) The same to their
brethren in Christ, whether living or long
departed; (3) The time of deliverance to
the whole creation from the bondage of corruption entailed upon them by man's sin;

(4) The time when Christ shall be manifested in glory, and the kingdom of God shall fully come; (5) The period for the creation of the new heavens and the new earth, wherein dwelleth righteousness (Rom. viii. 19—23; 1 Thess. iv. 16, 17; 2 Thess. i. 10; 2 Tim. iv. 1; 2 Pet. iii. 12, 13).

" He whose car the winds are, and the clouds
The dust that waits upon his sultry march,
When sin hath moved him, and his wrath is hot,
Shall visit earth in mercy; shall descend
Propitious in his chariot paved with love;
And what his storms have blasted and defaced
For man's revolt, shall with a smile repair.
Come then, and, added to thy many crowns,
Receive yet one, the crown of all the earth,
Thou who alone art worthy!"

VII. Addresses remonstrance and warning to his friends (verse 28, 29).
1. The *Remonstrance* (verse 28). "But ye should say (or, 'because ye say') why persecute we him? (or, 'how shall we persecute him,') seeing the root of the matter is found in me," (*margin* "and what root of matter is found in me?"—or, "and how shall we find a ground of accusation" [*Heb.* 'the root of a word or thing'] against him?) The great offence of Job's friends their persecution of a suffering brother. Their desire and aim to prove him a wicked man and deserving the calamities sent upon him. Sought therefore to find ground of accusation against him. Hence Job's name: "the persecuted one." In this, as in other things, a type of Christ. Job's friends the representatives of the Scribes and Pharisees, priests and elders of the Jews (Matt. xii. 13; Luke xi. 54; John viii. 6).

Persecution

Bequeathed to all Christ's members (John xv. 20; 2 Tim. iii. 12). Its endurance by the Church a characteristic of the reign of Antichrist (Rev. xi. 2—5; xii. 11—17). Satan the great persecutor. Persecution in accordance with the original promise of a Saviour (Gen. iii. 15). May be either bloody or unbloody—from the openly profane or the professedly godly. Petty persecution in the family or the workshop often as trying as that of the dungeon and the scaffold. Almost one continued persecution of the Church from Jews and Pagans during the first three hundred years of its existence. The Church nursed in blood. That blood made the means of its increase. Like Israel in Egypt (Ex. i. 12). Ten great persecutions enumerated before the establishment of Christianity as the religion of the Roman

Empire. Persecution frequently that of one part of the professing Church by another. The dominant section often a persecutor of the rest. The spirit and ground of persecution—(1) Enmity to the truth; (2) Desire for supremacy; (3) Intolerance of opposition; (4) Blind and misguided zeal (Gal. iv. 29; 3 John ix. 10; John xvi. 2, 3). Babylon the great, the mother of harlots, the mystical seven-hilled city, drunk with the blood of the saints (Rev. xvii. 6). Note in Rhemish Testament on this passage (Rev. xvii. 6),—"Their blood," viz., that of heretics, "is not called the blood of saints, no more than the blood of thieves, mankillers, and other malefactors; for the shedding of which by order of justice, no commonwealth shall answer." More blood shed in Christian persecutions than in Pagan ones. A long blood-stained history of Inquisitions, Crusades, Massacres, and Star-chambers. Between the twelfth and eighteenth centuries, about a million of non-conforming Albigenses and Waldenses put to death by armies sent for that purpose with the Pope's blessing and the promise of eternal salvation. Nearly a million more suffered death on the same grounds, within fifty years after the institution of the order of the Jesuits in 1540. In the Netherlands, the Duke of Alva boasted that thirty-six thousand heretics had been put to death by the common executioner. Within thirty days from the Massacre of St. Bartholomew's day (1572), thirty thousand at least calculated to have been butchered in Paris and throughout France. Public thanks ordered by the Pope to be given in one of the churches at Rome, and a medal to be struck for its commemoration.

2. *The threatening* (verse 29). "Be ye afraid of the sword; for wrath (such as you manifest against me) bringeth the punishments of the sword (or, 'is one of the iniquities [deserving and meeting with the punishment] of the sword'), that ye may know that there is a judgment." The sword the symbol of justice, here the justice of God (Rom. xiii. 4; Deut. xxiii. 41). An invisible avenger takes the part of the persecuted and oppressed. Persecutors especially threatened in the New Testament. Christ's second appearing especially terrible to such as smite their fellow servants (Matt. xxiv. 49). A righteous thing with God to recompense tribulation to them that trouble His people (2 Thess. i. 6—10). The judgments of the last days especially inflicted on the persecutors of the saints (Rev. xviii. 6, 24). Observe :—(1) *Persecution a hard and terrible enterprise.* Pagan persecutors noted as having generally died by horrible deaths. Charles IX., who authorized the Parisian massacre of 1572, died in despair in a bloody

sweat. Christ's words to Saul addressed to all persecutors: "It is hard for thee to kick against the pricks." (2) *The part of charity and piety to seek to turn persecutors from their sin, and so avert their doom.* (3) *Anger against the servants of God, though shewn only in words, viewed by God as a sin equivalent to murder.* The sin of Job's friends. Hence to be atoned for by sacrifice at the close of the controversy. (4) *Men not secured from Divine judgment by a religious profession.* (5) *The treatment given to Christ's servants and brethren one great criterion by which men will hereafter be judged* (Matt. xxv. 34—46). (6) *The comfort of God's people that they can appeal from man's judgment to God's.* (7) *A day coming when*

men's character and doings will be clearly revealed (Mal. iii. 18). Men to be "brought out in their blacks and whites" [*S. Rutherford*]. (8) *A day of judgment terribly certain.* (i.) From the *testimony of Scripture.* The first recorded inspired declaration such a testimony (Jude xiv. 15). Enoch's prophecy doubtless known to Job. Such testimony greatly accumulated since then (Eccles. ii. 9; xii. 14; Matt. xii. 36; Acts ii. 30, 31; Rom. ii. 16; xiv. 10, 12; 1 Cor. iv. 5; 2 Cor. v. 10. (ii.) From the *universal voice of conscience.* (iii.) From *God's providential dealings in the world.* Sin punished here so far as to shew that God marks and punishes it; left unpunished, so far as to shew that "there is a judgment" to come.

CHAPTER XX.

ZOPHAR'S SECOND SPEECH.

Produces nothing new; much more outspoken than before. Enlarges on the miseries overtaking the wicked, insinuating that Job was such. His argument,—like in condition, like in character.

I. The introduction to the speech.

His reason for speaking again, viz., Job's charges of cruelty and unkindness, and his denunciation of Divine wrath against them on account of it (verse 2). "Therefore (because of thy charges and denunciations), do my thoughts (cogitations as to what I ought to do) cause me to answer, and for this I make haste (*margin*, 'my haste' [or earnestness] is in me). I have heard the check of my reproach (reproof that is a reproach to me), and the spirit of my understanding (my spirit which has intelligence regarding the subject in question) causeth me to answer." Observe—

1. *The part of a wise man not to speak without sufficient reason.* Zophar had a reason for speaking, but not a correct one. Job's charges and denunciations were true and just.

2. *Pride ill brooks reproof.* Men seldom willing to take the reproach which they give to others. "Judge not, that ye be not judged."

3. *Right to think well before uttering one's sentiments on more serious subjects.* Better that our *thoughts* cause us to answer than our feelings.

4. *Insensibility no part of piety.* Zophar *felt* as well as thought. Spoke from ardour as well as reflection. Good to be zealously affected in a good thing. What is not spoken earnestly may as well remain unspoken.

5. *Earnestness to be grounded on just considerations.* Thought to lead, feeling to

follow. "While I was musing the fire burned." Zophar's feeling called "haste." Often too much haste both in our feeling and our words. With less haste in Zophar's spirit, there had been more humanity in his speech. "He that hasteth with his feet sinneth." Not less he that hasteth with his tongue. "Be not rash with thy mouth." "Slow to speak, swift to hear." What is spoken in haste, frequently not according to truth. Hasty words make matter for repentance. Hastily spoken not always hastily forgotten. Hasty words often make deep wounds. "The hasty to speak the slowest to learn" (Prov. xxix. 20).

6. *A spirit of intelligence to be prized and cultivated.* Natural understanding the gift of God, but may either be fed or famished. The best way to a good understanding is a good life. "An honest man has half as much more brains as he needs." "A good understanding have all they that keep His commandments." Christ made "wisdom" to those who are in Him, as well as righteousness and sanctification (1 Cor. i. 30). Wisdom given to believing prayer (James i. 5, 6). To have a good understanding one needs to keep both eyes and ears open. A spirit of intelligence necessary to a good answer. A light needful for entering a dark chamber. Safe not to speak on a subject till you are conscious of understanding it.

II. The speech itself.

The gist of it—Job must be a wicked man. The reasoning—Wicked men are miserable, either now or afterwards; Job is very miserable; therefore Job is a wicked man. The question: Are *only* wicked men miserable in this life? Job maintains that the wicked are not always nor alone miserable; that

" time and chance come alike to all."
Zophar's second speech another example of
lofty Oriental poetry. Contains solemn and
weighty truths, quoted and verified to. this
day. His opening statement such (verse 5).
" The triumphing (or song) of the wicked is
short (*Heb.*, from near; like water taken from
the surface instead of a deep well, therefore
ending quickly and abruptly); the joy of the
hypocrite (or profane) is but for a moment."
The allusion to Job's case too obvious. The
statement true, but not always in the sense
of Zophar. The joy of the wicked short-
lived. May last through life, but not beyond
it. The pleasure of sin but for a season.
The joy of the ungodly short, as—(1) It has
no solid foundation—built only on earthly
things that perish with the using; (2) Is
based upon a falsehood, viz., that sin and the
creature are able to give happiness; (3)
Can only exist in the present life. Creature-
enjoyment no longer-lived than the creature
itself. Sin in its own nature opposed to
lasting enjoyment. Divine justice engaged
to terminate it in this life. Sin a tree with
branches enough, but no root; with plenty
of blossom, but no fruit. Observe—1. *The
longest life but "for a moment."* (1) In comparison with eternity; (2) In the view of the
individual himself towards its close. Sad,
for the pleasure of a moment to throw away
the joys of an endless life.—2. *The joy of the
hypocrite or profane "but for a moment."*—
(1) As confined to this life; (2) In comparison with the joy of the righteous, which
is lasting. The joy of a false religion, or of
a mere external profession and shallow experience of the true, a lamp that goes out
from want of oil.—Zophar refers to all past
history for confirmation (verse 4). " Knowest thou not this of old," &c. The history
of the past most useful when serving as a
guide to the present. History full of examples of the

Short-lived prosperity of sin.

The memory of the Flood and its terrible
lessons still fresh in the days of Zophar.
The truth solemn and salutary, but Zophar's
application of it cruel and unjust. His
statements, too, require a wider field of
vision than the present world.
1. *The prosperous ungodly sooner or later
overthrown with contempt and infamy* (verse
6). " Though his excellency (loftiness or
exaltation) mount up to the heavens, and
his head reach unto the clouds (though he
attain the highest pitch of earthly prosperity
and grandeur), yet he shall perish for ever
like his own dung (cast away with contempt
and abhorrence); or, according to some, ' in
the midst of his splendour'); they that have

seen him (beholding with admiration ·his
prosperity) shall say, ' Where is he?' Obvious allusion to Job's former dignity and
prosperity. Prosperous wickedness is—(1)
One of the mysteries of Providence; (2) One
of the trials of good men; (3) One of the
proofs of a future judgment. The perplexity
of Asaph till he " went into the sanctuary of
God," and understood the end (Ps. lxxiii. 17).
No man to be called happy till the end of his
life, a maxim of the ancient heathen. Revelation adds, Nor till *after* the end of it.
Christ lifts the curtain and shows what is
beyond. Humbling contrast with former
haughtiness and magnificence implied in
Zophar's simile (so Ps. lxxxiii. 10). Contempt and infamy attach to wickedness,
however prosperous. A day coming when
God's despisers shall be an abhorring to all
flesh (Is. lxvi. 24).
2. *The prosperous ungodly vanish from
sight and memory* (verse 8). " He shall fly
away as a dream, and shall not be found;
yea, he shall be chased away as a vision of
the night. The eye also which saw him
(looked on him with admiration) shall see
him no more, &c." The life of the ungodly
especially a dream, as—(1) Without solidity
and reality; (2) As quickly terminating;
(3) As soon forgotten. No trace left that
men care to cherish. No pleasing and profitable " footprints on the sands of time.'
Good men only the truly " great" who
" remind us we can make our lives sublime."
" The memory of the wicked shall rot."
Associated with nothing excellent, noble, or
benevolent. The presence of bad great men
on earth a nightmare, which men would fain
" chase away " and then forget. Seen especially in the case of tyrants, ambitious and
unprincipled rulers, men climbing to power
by forbidden ways and employing it for evil
ends.
3. *Their children affected by their sin*
(verse 10). " His children shall seek to
please the poor (to propitiate the poor, whom
their father oppressed or defrauded; or,
shall be so reduced as to court the favour
even of the poor; *margin*, ' the poor shall
oppress his children'; *Coverdale*—' his children shall go a begging'); and his hand (or,
" their hands ") shall restore their goods "
(the goods of which their father had plundered them). Observe—(1) *An inheritance of trouble bequeathed by the ungodly to
their offspring.* In the Providence of God,
the effects of a man's oppression made to
extend to his children. The child often
reaps what the father sows, good or bad.
(2) *Ill-gotten wealth, sooner or later, proves
ill-gotten woe.* Restitution of unjust gains
follows either in a man's own life-time or his
children's. Made voluntarily, the curse is

averted both from himself and them. Zaccheus the publican (Luke xix. 1, &c). The reference here to the rich man's children cruel towards Job, still mourning the loss of his seven sons and three daughters.

4. *Effects of their sin entailed on their own person* (verse 11). "His bones are full of the sins of his youth (or of his secret sins, or of youthful vigour), which shall lie down with him in the dust." Apparent allusion to Job's diseased body. Observe—(1) *Bodily disease often the result of by-gone excesses.* Age often made to inherit the sins of youth (ch. xiii. 26). Hence David's prayer (Ps. xxv. 7). Seeds of disease sown in sinful indulgences. The drunkard carries the effects of his cups to the grave. Secret sins often followed by open sufferings. A cruel insinuation on the part of Zophar that this was Job's case. (2) The sinner often smitten with disease and death in the midst of prosperity and apparent strength. Herod at Cesarea (Acts xii. 21—23). (3) *Sad when a man's sins lie down with him in the dust.* Certain, if not prevented by repentance, faith, and forgiveness. To lie down with him in the dust is to continue his companions for ever (Rev. xxii. 11). Separation from our sins either now or never.

5. *Terrible misery after temporary enjoyment* (verse 12—14). "Though wickedness (especially in the acquisition and enjoyment of ill-gotten wealth), be sweet in his mouth; though he hide it under his tongue (either for secrecy or continued enjoyment); though he spare it and forsake it not; but keep it still within his mouth: yet his meat in his bowels is turned; it is the gall of asps (the most deadly poison) within him." Sin sweet to the unrenewed heart. Stolen waters sweet. Such sweetness short-lived. Honey in the mouth becomes gall in the bowels. Sin in itself a deadly poison. Death itself, and death its wages. David's sweet sin with Bathsheba broke his bones. The blood of Urijah brought blood into his house. The effect of sinful enjoyment is to "mourn at the last" (Prov. v. 11—14). Poison no less deadly became sweet to the taste. The sweetest things often the sourest afterwards.

6. *Forced surrender of acquired wealth* (verse 15). "He hath swallowed down riches, and he shall vomit them up again; God shall cast them out of his belly." Apparently Job's case. Riches eagerly pursued, abundantly obtained, and fondly enjoyed, to be sooner or later unwillingly surrendered. The worldling and his wealth part company, if not before, yet on a dying bed. The glutton compelled to vomit up his dainty morsels. "Thou fool, this night thy soul shall be required of thee." The

sumptuous table then gladly exchanged for a drop of water. The worldling unable to keep his wealth a moment beyond God's pleasure. A thousand means at His disposal of making him quit his grasp on this side of death. The failure of a bank, the fall of a mercantile house, the explosion of some promising speculation, sufficient for the purpose. "But even now worth this, and now worth nothing!"

7. *Death in some distressing form and circumstances* (verse 16). "He shall suck the poison of asps (the most deadly one); the viper's tongue (put out when about to bite), shall slay him." All animate and inanimate nature only instruments for the execution of God's purposes, whether of judgment or of mercy. The effect of the intoxicating cup, that at last it bites like a serpent and stings like an adder (Prov. xxiii. 32). To suck the pleasures of sin now is to suck the poison of asps hereafter. The Bible draws aside the veil and reveals man's tempter become his tormenter (Luke xvi. 19—26).

8. *Bitter disappointment and exclusion from future happiness* (verse 17). "He shall not see the rivers, the floods, the brooks of honey and butter." A blessedness even in this life, of which the worldling deprives himself. Still more in the life to come. The river of life, the wine of the kingdom, the fruits of paradise, the joys at God's right hand, the pleasures for evermore, all forfeited for the momentary pleasures of sin. To the cry at the closed gates: "Lord, Lord, open unto us," the only response: "Depart from me, I never know you."

9. *No real enjoyment of his riches even here* (verse 18). "That which he laboured for shall he restore, and shall not swallow it down (or enjoy it); according to his substance shall the restitution be, and he shall not rejoice therein." Riches gathered often become riches scattered. To obtain wealth one thing, to enjoy it another. Great gains not always great gain. Man *gets*, God *gives*. Ill-gotten, ill-gone, [*Latin Proverb*]. Wealth often the parent of woe. A canker in a sinner's gold (James v. 3). Wages earned without God only put into a bag with holes. The world a lie, especially to those who trust in it. Money outside the heart a blessing, inside of it a curse.

10. *A troubled conscience* (verses 19, 20). "Because he hath oppressed and hath forsaken the poor; because he hath violently taken away an house which he builded not (obtaining it by fraud instead of honest industry); surely he shall not feel quietness in his belly (his mind or conscience), he shall not save of that which he desired" (or, shall not escape with his coveted but ill-

gotten wealth). Another cruel and unjust allusion to Job. The charge of oppression afterwards directly made by Eliphaz (ch. xxii. 5—9). Taken generally, the statement true. Ill-gained wealth, like the hoarded manna, breeds worms; the worm of an accusing conscience. The rust of dishonest gain eats into the flesh like fire (James v. 3). A house built by oppression gives a voice to its stones and timber (Hab. ii. 9—11). A quiet conscience better than a well-filled coffer. Naboth's coveted vineyard a curse both to Ahab and his wife (1 Kings xxi. 1—19).

11. *Loss of property and of children* (verse 21). There shall none of his meat be left (*margin*, "there shall none be left for his meat"); therefore shall no man look for his goods." A cutting sentence for impoverished and bereaved Job. Job's full house now an empty one. His goods gone, and none to inherit the miserable remnant. The richest man in Uz now penniless. The man with ten adult children now without even one. Able lately to leave an ample inheritance to his children, now without either estate or sons to inherit it. One of the world's vanities the desire to enrich one's heirs. God and man often robbed while living to leave larger sums when dead. A worldly man's great affliction to lose the heir of his, hoarded wealth. The rich worldling often compelled to leave his riches to those for whom he cares not, and who care not for him.

12. *Perplexity and trouble in the midst of his riches* (verse 22). "In the fulness of his sufficiency he shall be in straits: every hand of the wicked (or of the mischievous; every kind of mischief; or every blow that comes upon the wretched) shall come upon him." A sad and cutting remembrancer to Job of his various calamities and the quarter from which some of them had come. God, in His providence, visits the prosperous wicked with sudden and unexpected manifestations of His anger (verse 23) "When he is about to fill his belly (or, 'there shall be wherewith to fill his belly') God shall cast the fury of His wrath upon him, and shall rain it upon him (as literally on Sodom and Gomorrha; also implying the vehemence and abundance of the judgments) while he is eating" (in the midst of his enjoyment; or, "as his food"). A bitter sarcasm. The worldling sits down to his sumptuous table, but the wrath of God shall be his dish. Vengeance shall be his viand. He shall be fed with fury for his food. Case of the rich fool (Luke xii. 16—20). Experienced by Israel in the wilderness (Num. xi. 33; Ps. lxxviii. 30, 31. Appeared to have been realised in Job. Overtaken by apparent

judgments in the midst of his prosperity. Fire rained on his cattle as on the cities of the Plain (ch. i. 16; Gen. xix. 24). Fiery rain instead of refreshing showers an awful sign of judgment (Ps. l. 3).

13. *Inability to effect escape* (verse 24). "He shall flee from the iron weapon (the weapon employed in close combat,—visible judgments),—and the bow (discharging its arrows from a distance,—invisible judgments) of steel (*Heb.* of brass; therefore with all the more force) shall strike him through." Seeking to escape from one evil he falls into another. Fleeing from the pit he falls into the snare. God at no loss for means to punish the ungodly. Vain attempt to escape when God purposes to destroy. The only place of refuge for a sinner the wounds of Jesus opened to satisfy justice for his sins. Submission to God and faith in His Son the only but certain safety for the guilty.

14. *Rapid and effectual execution of God's purposes of vengeance* (verse 25). "It is drawn (viz., the arrow or the sword with which to punish the ungodly), and cometh out of the body (having passed through it); yea, the glittering sword (of Divine vengeance, Deut. xxxii. 41; Ez. xxi. 9, 10) cometh out of his gall (or gall-bladder, having thus inflicted a deadly wound): terrors are upon him" (the terror of death which now stares him in the face, and the terrors of judgment immediately to follow). The language rapid, elliptical, and in the past and present tense, to indicate the suddenness and certainty of the blow. A fearful thing to fall into the hands of the living God. How shall we escape if we neglect the great salvation? (Verse 16.—"All darkness (all kinds of calamity, or accumulated misery) shall be hid in his secret places," (hid amongst his choicest treasures, or secretly laid up for him in places where he expected safety). Observe—(1) *God's judgments find the sinner in his most secret and secure retreat.* "When they shall say, peace and safety, then sudden destruction cometh upon them." (2) *Among a sinner's most valuable possessions lies a hidden curse.* "A fire not blown (requiring no blowing, or not kindled by man, viz., the 'fire of God' or lightning, as ch. i. 16) shall consume him." Terrible word for poor Job, who had seen his sheep and the shepherds consumed in this very way. A similar judgment on the household of Korah, &c. (Num. xvi. 35. "It shall go ill with him that is left (or, 'it shall consume' what is left) in his tabernacle." Words cruelly telling in the case of Job. The fire of God had left but one shepherd to tell the tale of the disaster. Stroke after stroke had fallen on his property

and household, till all were consumed but his wife and three servants. Job, if any, seemed marked out by Divine judgments as a secret and guilty transgressor. Terrible trial for faith. "Who may stand in thy sight when once thou art angry?" (Ps. lxxvi. 7).

15. *Secret sins discovered* (verse 27). "The heavens shall reveal his iniquity; and the earth shall rise up against him." Apparently verified in Job's case. The lightning from *heaven*, and the Chaldean and Sabean marauders, with the whirlwind of the desert, from the *earth*, seemed to proclaim him a wicked man, whom vengeance was at length overtaking (Acts xxviii. 4). Observe—(1) *Animate and inanimate creation made at God's pleasure to conspire against his enemies.* (2) *Iniquity, however secretly committed, sooner or later revealed.* No darkness or shadow of death where the workers of iniquity may hide either themselves or their sins. Secret iniquity not only open to God's view, but one day to be so to that of the universe. Hypocrisy only *now* "the only evil that walks invisible, except to God alone."' No cloak of religion able to hide sin from God, or by-and-by, from our neighbour either. Terrible exposure awaiting secret evil-doers. (3) *Our sins either to be found out now by ourselves and brought to the throne of grace to be pardoned, or to be found out hereafter by God, and brought to the throne of judgment to be punished.*

16. *Destruction of all belongings in a day of wrath* (verse 28). "The increase (progeny, or natural products) of his house shall depart, and his goods shall flow away (be swept away as by a torrent, suddenly and irrecoverably) in the day of his wrath." Sad verification of this apparently afforded in the case of Job. The whole progeny of his house, with all his goods, swept away as by an inundation. A day of wrath now surely overtaking this prince of Uz. Difficult for him and his friends to believe otherwise. To the latter the thing was clear. To Job it *seemed* so; but if actual *wrath*, it was *undeserved*. Job's error in sometimes inclining to the latter alternative. His *apparent* "day of

wrath" was, in reality, a day of love. Observe—(1) *The province of faith to believe against all appearances.* "Behind a frowning providence," &c. (2) *Easy with God to sweep away all the increase of a man's house.* (3) *A day of wrath coming, in which all earthly possessions will flow away.* "The earth and the works therein shall be burned up" (2 Pet. iii. 10).

III. The summing-up (verse 29). "This is the portion of a wicked man from God, and the heritage appointed unto him by God" (*Heb.*, the heritage of the decree of the Mighty One; decreed by Him who is Almighty, therefore irresistible). Similar language in Ps. xi. 6. The conclusion apparently unavoidable in relation to Job. The portion of a wicked man manifestly meted out to him. If Job is not such a man, all our notions of the Divine government in this world are upset—the rock is "removed out of his place." Strong faith and a sound conscience required by Job to believe that God would yet clear his character. The statement of Zophar both true and untrue. Viewed in relation to this life, not always true. Viewed in relation to the next, far short of the fact. A more terrible portion awaits the impenitent in another world. The harrowing things mentioned by Zophar only a foreshadowing and prelude to the sinner's future doom. Wrath rarely exhibited in this world, because reserved for the next. Days of wrath here sent as specimens and warnings of that which is to come.

"That day of wrath, that dreadful day,
  When heaven and earth shall pass away.
What power shall be the sinner's stay?
How shall ye meet that dreadful day?
Jesus, be Thou my spirit's stay,
Though heaven and earth shall pass away."

Observe—(1) *A sinner's portion not what he wishes, but what God appoints.* (2) His portion a *heritage*—(i.) As contrasted with his earthly possessions and enjoyments; (ii.) As certain to find him as its *heir*; (3) *Solemn contrast between this portion and that of the believer in Jesus* (Ps. xvi. 56; 1 Pet. i. 3).

CHAPTER XXI.

JOB'S REPLY TO ZOPHAR'S SECOND SPEECH.

The ungodly, instead of experiencing the miseries indicated by Zophar, often, perhaps generally, enjoy continued ease and prosperity in this life.

I. Introduction (verse 2—6).
1. *Bespeaks earnest attention* (verse 2).

"Hear diligently my speech." Men of wisdom and experience, especially pious sufferers, worthy to be seriously listened to. Solemn and weighty truths to be heard with corresponding attention. *Heb.*, "Hear, hear.' Serious matters call for double or diligent hearing. Deep attention to be given to

127

truths concerning God's mysterious providence, still more to those regarding a provided Saviour and the great salvation (Heb. ii. 1). An aggravated sin when God stretches out His hand and no man regards it (Prov. i. 24).

A reason given for such attention: "And let this be (or, 'and this shall be') your consolations." Allusion to Zophar's boasted consolations (ch. xv. 11). Sometimes mourners more relieved by our listening to *their* sentiments than by uttering our own. Better to be silent in the presence of the afflicted than to dispute or censure. Consolation due to sufferers from their friends. A brother born for adversity. Professed comforters may become real tormentors.

2. *Solicits patience* (verse 3). "Suffer me that I may speak." Patience especially due to sufferers. Persons who speak much themselves generally most impatient of others. The Scripture rule—"Swift to hear, slow to speak."—"And after that I have spoken, mock on." A troubled spirit often eased by utterance. Sad when those who ought to be comforters in our affliction become mockers (ch. xvii. 2). One of Job's greatest trials to be mocked by his friends (ch. xii. 4). As much patience required to endure mockings as scourgings (Heb. xi. 36).

3. *Justifies his displeasure* (verse 4). "As for me, is my complaint to man? And if it were so, why should not my spirit be troubled?" (*margin*, "shortened;" same word rendered "discouraged," Num. xxi. 5; "grieved," Jud. x. 16; "vexed," Jud. xvi. 16; "straitened," Mic. ii. 7; "hasty," Prov. xiv. 29; "anguish," Exod. vi. 9). Sorrow contracts the heart as joy enlarges it (Ps. cxix. 32). The flesh is soon angry, while grace is long suffering. Job complains not to man, but to God, as the author of his troubles. His complaint both *of* God and *to* God; the former the complaint of the *flesh*, the latter that of the spirit. Grace teaches to look away from instruments and second causes to God Himself. So David (2 Sam. xvi. 10).

Job justifies his displeasure on the ground that God dealt so hardly with him. His language too much that of the prophet at Nineveh and Elijah under the juniper-tree. The flesh always much in all alike. Thinks that under severe trouble we "do well to be angry." Grace enables us to kiss the rod that smites us, and to say, "Abba, Father; not my will, but Thine be done." Jesus rather than Job our pattern in affliction. Our privilege in Christ to be strengthened with all might, according to God's glorious power, unto all patience and long-suffering with joyfulness (Col. i. 11).

4. *Invites solemn attention to the astounding fact of suffering saints and prosperous sinners* (verse 5). "Mark me and be astonished, and lay your hand upon your mouth" [in silent awe and wonder]. God's dealings in Providence to be regarded with reverence and awe. Habakkuk's experience (Hab. iii. 16); David's (Ps. cxix. 120). The sufferings of saints and prosperity of sinners a subject mysterious and inscrutable till read in the light of inspired Scripture (Ps. xiii. 17). Anomalies in God's government awaiting the explanations of eternity.

Expresses his own feelings in reference to this mysterious fact and its influence upon himself (verse 6). "Even when I remember I am afraid, and trembling taketh hold on my flesh." Our own experience, as well as that of others, often to be remembered with trembling (Lam. iii. 19, 20). The part of grace not only to tremble at God's *word*, but God's *works* (Is. lxvi. 2). The speaker to be duly affected himself by the truths he addresses to others. Must weep himself if he would have his hearers weep.

II. Problem proposed. Commences with a question implying an undoubted fact (verse 7).

"Wherefore do the wicked live (or, enjoy life), become old, yea mighty in power" (or wealth). Three facts implied regarding the ungodly in this life:—1. They "live;" are permitted to continue in life and to enjoy it. 2. In many instances "become old;" ordinarily viewed as an element of prosperity and a mark of Divine favour. The hoary head not always found in the way of righteousness. 3. "Become mighty in power" and substance; enjoy great worldly prosperity (Ps. lxxiii. 12). Such facts hardly to be expected under the government of a righteous God. The perplexity and almost despair of Asaph (Ps. lxxiii. 2—13). The 73rd Psalm a commentary on this chapter of Job. Such facts suggest inquiry as to the cause. Scripture furnishes the reply. (See Rom. ii. 4; 1 Tim. i. 16; Ps. lxxiii. 18; Ecc. viii. 11—13; Luke ii. 35, &c.; Ps. xvi. 4; Rom. ix. 22). The present not the only state of man's existence. This life a state of probation and discipline, not of retribution. The present a time of forbearance and mercy; God waiting for the sinner's repentance in order to be gracious to him. God's goodness intended to lead to repentance. The ungodly spared in order to have time for repentance; "the long-suffering of God is salvation;" not willing that any should perish (2 Peter iii. 9—15). Their prosperity an exercise for the faith of the godly. A standing evidence of a time of future retribution. A monument to the glory of the Divine patience and long-suffering. Renders the impenitence of men inexcusable and justifies all their future punishment. Demonstrates the inferiority of earthly to heavenly blessings.

III. Description of the prosperity of the ungodly (verses 8—13).

1. In relation to their *children* (verse 8). "Their seed is established in their sight with them, and their offspring before their eyes." Their children obtain a firm and prosperous position in the world, and that while they themselves still live to see and enjoy it. Important elements in a man's earthly felicity: —(1) To have a numerous offspring; (2) To see his children prosperous and established in the world; (3) To have them continuing to live with or near him; (4) To live to see and rejoice in their earthly prosperity and happiness. Some of these elements formerly enjoyed by Job, though no longer so. The happiness of the ungodly, in relation to their children, again touched upon under another aspect in verse 11. "They send forth their little ones (out of doors, under a guardian or guide), and their children dance" (frisk sportively as lambs in the pasture). Pleasing picture of domestic happiness and prosperity. The children viewed as still young and under their parents' guardianship. Healthy, happy, frolicking children a pleasant spectacle, especially to parents' eyes. A large ingredient in the cup of earthly bliss. Homes lighted up with children's innocent hilarities the gift of a gracious God.

2. *Domestic security and freedom from affliction and trouble* (verse 9). "Their houses are safe from fear (of any hostile attack or elemental violence), neither is the rod of God upon them." The contrast to the case of Job and his children. Sons experience chastisement from which slaves are exempt. Freedom from afflictions and trials no mark of a child of God. The ungodly "have no changes, therefore they fear not God" (Ps. lv. 19). Ill sign for a man when God will not spend a rod upon him [*Brookes*].

3. *Success in business and freedom from worldly losses* (verse 10). "Their bull gendereth and faileth not; their cow calveth and casteth not her calf" (by an untimely birth). Matters in which human skill and industry seem to have but little to do. As if a blessing rested on all the work of their hands, and on all their belongings. Their very cattle prosperous and fruitful. People in everything fortunate, and, as the world say, lucky.

4. *Enjoyment of music and festivity* (verse 12). "They take (or 'lift up' [their voice] to) the timbrel and harp, and rejoice at (or, trip merrily to) the sound of the organ" (or

pipe—musical instruments of greatest antiquity [Gen. iv. 21; xxxi. 27]; the "organ" with us a comparatively modern invention). The life of the persons in question one, to a large extent, of festivity and enjoyment. Their dwellings abundantly enlivened with the sound of music, vocal and instrumental. The ungodly no strangers to the hilarity of music and dancing. "The harp and viol, the tabret and pipe, are in their feasts, while they regard not the work of the Lord" (Is. v. 12). "They chant to the sound of the viol and invent to themselves instruments of music like David, but are not grieved for the affliction of Joseph" (Amos vi. 5, 6). Musical instruments an invention of the descendants of Cain (Gen. iv. 21). Yet

Music

one of God's choicest earthly blessings. Its influence beneficial on the individual and the household. Its effects on man's nature manifold and important. Rests fatigue. Relieves pain. Subdues passion. Soothes suffering. Mitigates sorrow. Allays nervous irritation. Resists melancholy. Saul's evil spirit yielded to the sweet sounds of David's harp (1 Sam. xvi. 23). Inspires courage and inspirits the brave. The rousing strains of Highland bagpipes helped to win the day at Waterloo. Music powerful in the conflict of life. A means of moral culture. Assists devotion. Calms and elevates the mind for the communication and reception of Divine truth. The prophet calls first for the aid of a minstrel (2 Kings iii. 15). Music a Divine art and heavenly employment. Heaven filled with music. Something of divinity in music more than the ear discovers [*Sir T. Browne*]. The beneficial effect of soft and sweet sounds, especially of sacred music, upon the sick, an acknowledged fact. Music "whispered to the weary spirit" sometimes the only sound to be endured by the sick and sorrowful. Music to be consecrated to the glory of its Divine Author. "A table without music little better than a manger" [*Epictetus*]. Especially true of the song of praise and thanksgiving. Music, like other Divine gifts, often desecrated to the service of the god of this world. The Enemy's object to make a sinful and worldly life as agreeable as possible. Helps men to forget death and a judgment to come in the sweet sounds of earthly music. Nero played on his harp while gazing on Rome in flames, the probable effect of his own wickedness.

5. *A joyous life and an easy and painless death.* Verse 13.—"They spend their days in wealth (prosperity or pleasure), and in a moment go down to the grave" (without

9

His penitent and praying children ; God, apart from Christ, a consuming fire to devour His impenitent and prayerless adversaries. A sinner's blessedness to meet with God as, in Christ, reconciled and reconciling the World to Himself.

V. Job's protest against a life of prosperous ungodliness (verse 16).

"Lo, their good is not in their hand : the counsel of the wicked is far from me." Observe—

1. *Worldly prosperity and earthly blessings not less a good because abused*—a good, though not the chief good. The part of sin—(1) to pervert what is good in itself into an evil ; (2) To make a *temporal* good the chief good instead of an eternal one. 2. *The good enjoyed by the ungodly neither a satisfying nor a lasting one* ; "their good is not in their hand,"—a thing neither to be grasped nor retained. Mighty difference between the good of the believer and the worldling. The one substance, the other shadow ; the one lasting and eternal, the other momentary and perishing. The ungodly unable to retain their prosperity and happiness a moment beyond God's pleasure. A thousand accidents able to rob them of it at any moment. No real good in their hand, and still less in their hope. 3. *Care to be taken not to be influenced by the prosperity of the godless and worldly*. (1) By consideration of the truth and reality of their case ; their prosperity only temporary, and their happiness unreal ; "their good not in their hand ;" (2) By steadfast repudiation of their principles and life. "The counsel of the wicked is far from me." Consider, in regard to—

The counsel of the wicked,

First : *what it is*. The principles upon which they act and by which their life is governed. These are—(1) To make the enjoyment of the present life their chief good,—their first if not their only aim—take care for this life, and let the next take care of itself. (2) To gain that enjoyment in any way they can with safety :—if honestly, well ; if not, in any way you can. (3) To depend on their own endeavours for what they desire, instead of God :—" Mine own hand hath gotten me this wealth." (4) To ignore God and eternity, heaven and hell, either as having no existence or no relation to themselves. The worldling's creed—no reality but what is visible or cognizable by themselves. The seen and sensible only substance, all else shadow and moonshine. (5) To despise the provision of a Saviour. Not this man, but Barabbas ; (6) To care for one's self and immediate connections, and leave others to do the same. Attend to number one.

Second : Job's *conduct in regard to this counsel*. "The counsel of the wicked is far from me." The principles and practice of the ungodly, not only to be put away, but *far* away from us. Safest to stand at the greatest distance from sin. Joseph kept far from it, and had God's blessing in the dungeon. David went near it and got broken bones. Sin an infectious plague ; therefore not to be approached. The surest way not to walk in the counsel of the wicked is to keep far from it. "Enter not into the path of the wicked ; avoid it, pass not by it, turn from it and pass away." Occasions of sin to be avoided as well as sin itself. The harlot's door to be avoided. He who carries gunpowder must keep far away from sparks. God only keeps from acts of sin those who keep from occasions of it. Look not intently on what you may not love entirely. (*Brookes*.) The counsel of the wicked to be put far from us—(1) In our *judgment*. To be viewed in its real character. Condemned and repudiated as what it really is—wicked, abominable, destructive. (2) In our *will and purpose*. Our language to be, what have I to do with idols ? (Hos. xiv. 8). To choose with Mary the good part. To say with David : "Depart from me, ye evil-doers ; for I will keep the commandments of my God." "I have sworn, and I will perform it, that I will keep thy righteous judgments " (Ps. cxix. 106, 115). So Daniel "purposed in his heart that he would not defile himself with the king's meat " (Dan. i. 8). (3) In our *practice*. Purpose to become practice. The man only blessed who "*walketh* not in the counsel of the ungodly " (Ps. i. 1). Our life to be governed by opposite principles.

Third : *why* is the counsel of the ungodly to be put far from us ? From its character and issues. The principles of the ungodly and worldly are—(1) *Foolish and unreasonable*. Only the fool says in his heart, no God. Absurd only to believe what we see. Madness to prefer the enjoyment of a day to that of a life-time ; the enjoyment of a short life-time to that of an endless eternity. The part of a fool to make careful provision for the body and neglect the soul which shall eternally survive it. (2) *Wicked*. Intensely wicked to ignore and repudiate the God that made, preserves, and every moment sustains us ; a God possessed of every excellence—the Author of our Being and our Well-being. (3) *Destructive*. Certain and endless ruin the result of a sinful and worldly life,—of despising God and rejecting His Son, Jesus Christ. "All they that hate me love death." What is sown here is reaped hereafter (Gal. vi. 7, 8 ; Ps. xvi. 4 ; Is. l. 11 ; Rom. iii. 16 ; vi. 21, 23 ; John viii. 21, 24).

Fourth : *How* is the counsel of the wicked

to be put far away from us? Not easily. The counsel of the wicked is—(1) *Natural to a depraved heart.* The carnal mind enmity against God. To follow the counsel of the wicked is to swim with the stream. (2) *Popular.* The way of the multitude. To put it far away is to be singular. Not always easy to come out and be separate. (3) *Pleasing to the flesh.* Sin wears a serpent's skin. The forbidden fruit pleasing to the eye, and sweet to the taste. The principles and practice of the wicked and worldly only to be put far away from us—(1) *By a change of heart.* A corrupt tree only brings forth evil fruit. "Out of the heart proceed evil thoughts," &c. "Ye must be born again." Except a man be born of water and of the Spirit, he cannot see the kingdom of God. (2) *By acceptance of the offered Saviour and reliance on His grace.* In looking to Him who died for our sin we are delivered from its power, and receive strength to overcome it. The cross of Christ our only deliverance from the counsel of the ungodly (Gal. vi. 14). (3) *By the due use of means.* (i.) *Prayer.* Spiritual strength given to waiting upon God and in answer to prayer (Is. xl. 22—31; Ezek. xxxvi. 25—27, 37). (ii.) *Reading* and *meditation* in the *Scriptures* (Ps. xvii. 4; cxix. 11; John xv. 3; xviii. 17). (iii.) Contemplation of the Saviour's *character* and *cross* (2 Cor. iii. 18; Gal. vi. 14). (iv.) Consideration of the *character* and *consequences* of *sin.*

Job's practical renunciation of the counsel of the ungodly already a fact. Resolution is to become reality. The future to be translated into the present,—"Let it be" to become "it is."

VI. The final misery of the ungodly, notwithstanding present prosperity (verse 17). "How oft is the candle of the wicked put out." May be read either as a question implying the rarity of the case, or as an exclamation implying its frequency. The "candle," or prosperity, of the wicked, extinguished by death, though frequently before it. Job's main assertion, that the wicked often live, become old, and die in prosperity and ease. Yet their end destruction not the less. Asaph stumbled at the prosperity of the wicked till he went into the sanctuary and understood their end (Ps. lxxiii. 17).—"How oft cometh their destruction upon them." Not always, nor even usually, visited with signal judgment and a miserable death. Occasional cases as warnings, and as indications of a future judgment. Examples: the Deluge; destruction of Sodom and Gomorrha; Haman; Saul, Herod.—"God distributeth sorrows in His anger. Observe—1. *Continuance of outward*

prosperity consistent with secret wrath. The abuse of Divine gifts the greatest provocation of Divine anger. God's wrath certain against ungodliness, however long its manifestation may be withheld. God angry with the wicked every day. Wrath treasured up against the day of wrath. (2) The *sorrows of the ungodly often sent in anger; those of the godly always in love.* Those the most terrible sorrows that are distributed in God's anger. (3) *Sorrows distributed by God as well as mercies.* All sorrows distributed by a Divine hand; only, some distributed in anger, others in love. Trouble not from the dust. Wisely meted out, whether in mercy or in judgment. The cup mingled and measured, and sooner or later put into the hand of each. The cup of sorrow held out to a believer by a Father's hand, to be exchanged ere long for the cup of joy. To be put at last into the hand of the ungodly (Is. li. 22 23; Luke xvi. 25). (4) *Terrible end of the wicked after a life of prosperity and pleasure* (verse 18). "They are as stubble before the wind, and as chaff that the storm carrieth away, (margin, "stealeth away," rapidly and unexpectedly as a thief in the night, Matt. xxiv. 43; 1 Thess. v. 2; 2 Peter iii. 10; Rev. xvi. 15). Frequent comparison of the ungodly to the fragments of straw and the chaff separated from the wheat on the open threshing-floor, exposed to the wind on a lofty situation, and thus carried violently, suddenly, and rapidly away by it, while the wheat is left for the garner (Ps. i. 4; Is. xxix. 5; Hos. xiii. 3). Indicates—(1) God's long-continued but exhausted patience; (2) The worthlessness of the ungodly; (3) Their final separation from the godly; (4) Their utter and irremediable destruction.

VII. A sinful life often punished in its consequences on the sinner's children (verse 19). "God layeth up his iniquity (or the punishment of it) for his children; he rewardeth him and he shall know (or feel) it. His eyes shall see his destruction (implying more than mere destruction itself; he shall have full and bitter experience of it; or shall see it approaching and yet be unable to escape from it), and he shall drink of the wrath of the Almighty [as before he drank iniquity, which is the cause of it]. For what pleasure hath he in his house after him, when the number of his months is cut off in the midst?" Perhaps an objection to his statement here anticipated and answered. If God does not punish the ungodly man in this life, yet, say the three friends, He punishes him in his children after him. But, replies Job, the punishment ought to be inflicted on himself; and he, not his children, ought, according to your principles, to feel it. His eyes ought to see his own destruction. For what has he to do with his family after him when he his dead? Observe—(1) *An undeniable truth that a man's sins often entail their consequences on his children.* Embodied in the second commandment (Ex. xx. 5). Temporal consequences often entailed apart from sins in the children. The parents' sins frequently inherited by the children, and their consequences along with them. A man in some degree punished in the person of his children. His children closely bound up with him as part of himself. A natural desire that it should be well with them after his death. His children's suffering after his death an aggravation of his own. (2) *Sin, however, mainly punished in the person himself who commits it.* Hence, that punishment not always inflicted in this life, as Zophar and his friends maintained. No less certainly however in the next, as maintained by Job.

VIII. Assertion of God's infinite wisdom and knowledge (verse 22). "Shall any teach God knowledge? Seeing he judgeth those that are high." God, unable to receive any accession to His wisdom or knowledge from the most intelligent of His creatures. The highest intelligences under His government and control. God universally acknowledged as the Judge and Ruler of heaven and earth (Gen. xviii. 25). Angels, devils, and men of every rank, under His sway and jurisdiction. Hell and destruction naked and open before Him. The hearts and counsels of men and angels exposed to His view. The expulsion of fallen angels an example of His judging "those that are high." The judge of angels not to be directed by puny men (Rom. xi. 34; 1 Cor. ii. 16). He who judges angels needs no instruction how to deal with men. Hence—(1) The case of each safe in his hands; (2) No room for questioning or cavilling on the part of any of His creatures in reference to His providential dealings with them.

IX. Sovereignty and inscrutableness of Divine Providence. Men variously dealt with both in life and death without apparent reference to character and desert (verse 23). "One dieth in his full strength [with unimpaired health and vigour], being wholly at ease and quiet [in the hey-day of prosperity]. His breasts (*margin*, 'milk pails') are full of milk (or, his vessels, intestines, or sides are full of fat), and his bones are moistened with marrow. And another dieth in the bitterness of his soul (with an experience the opposite of the former), grief and pain pursuing him to the end), and never catch with pleasure" (or, "never enjoys

pleasure,"—a sufferer during his whole life) Varieties everywhere in men's experience, both in life and in death. These varieties often and generally due rather to the sovereignty of the Divine Disposer than to the character and merits of individuals. Love and hatred not to be discovered by the external events in our lot. One event to all (Ecc. ix. 2).—Death equally the end of all (verse 25). "They shall lie down alike in the dust, and the worms shall cover them," Lessons from this universality of death:— (1) *Contentment with one's lot.* External differences only for a short period of this present life. These assigned now in infinite wisdom, and all forgotten in the grave. (2) *Humility.* The dust our final resting-place. Worms by-and-by our principal covering; (3) *Necessity of immediate preparation and constant readiness for death.* Nothing more certain than death, and more uncertain than the time and circumstances. The grave a resting-place for the body; the soul, immortal and immaterial, has its dwelling elsewhere. Its place in the spirit-world according to its character and deeds in this. After death the judgment (Matt. xxv. 31—46; Rom. ii. 6—10). In the eternal world the rich and poor often change places. Lazarus comforted, Dives tormented (Luke xvi. 25).

X. Job's remonstrance with his friends on their erroneous and uncharitable views (verses 27—30). 1. *Exposes their secret cogitations regarding him* (verse 27). "Behold I know your thoughts, and the devises which ye wrongfully imagine against me. For ye say [within yourselves], where is the house of the prince (the rich or munificent chief — alluding to Job himself, whose house was now desolate, and that of his eldest son in ruins)? and where are the dwelling-places of the wicked?" (*margin*, "the tent of the tabernacles;" *Heb.*, the tent of the dwelling-places; either that of the rich chief in the midst of those of his household and clan, [chap. xxv. 29] or his house as divided into various apartments). The secret surmise of Job's friends that the desolation of his own house, and that of his son, was a Divine retribution. From this desolation they injuriously conclude they had been wicked men. The errors of the Jews in Christ's day, in reference to the slaughtered Galilæans and the disaster in Siloam (Luke xiii. 1—5). That of the Melitians, in regard to Paul and the viper which fastened on his hand (Acts xxviii. 4). 2. *Refers them to the testimony of men of travel and observation* (verse 29). "Have ye not asked them that go by the way? and do ye not know their tokens?" (or, "acknowledge their testimonies,"—the examples met with in their travels, and related by them to others, or their written communications, which are proofs of what I now advance). In the early ages of the world, and still to a great extent in the East, most of the information as to events in other lands obtained by travellers. That information, however, probably to some extent committed early to letters, here called "tokens,"—signs or marks (Gen. iv. 15). Moses directed by God to write the song he delivered before his death, as well as the law of commandments (Deut. xxxi. 19 —24). Letters among the earliest inventions. Probably at first hieroglyphics, or figures of animate or inanimate objects. (See ch. xix. 23, 24).

3. *Testimony of travellers in relation to the wicked* (verse 30). "That the wicked is reserved to the day of destruction (spared often and long in this world, even in the midst of calamities that overtake others, though sure to be punished in the next, if not ultimately in this, as in the case of Pharaoh)? they shall be brought forth to the day of wrath" (or, "they are led [as in a pompous procession] to the day of wrath," which sooner or later overtakes them; or, "they are led [in safety] in the day of wrath" which comes upon the community; *margin*, the day of *wraths*—great or accumulated wrath, as Rev. vi. 17). Job's first position—God destroys, by external calamities, the righteous and the wicked indiscriminately (ch. ix. 22, 23). His second—The wicked are often spared in the midst of such calamities,—spared in ease and prosperity,—and spared long. Rests his assertions on facts. These facts not invalidated by occasional examples of the contrary. These in perfect harmony with, and even when rightly viewed, a confirmation of, a future retribution. Every day of wrath in this world points its finger to a still greater one in the next.

XI. Returns to the prosperity and power of the wicked as following them even to the grave.

The ungodly often so powerful as to escape all reproof and punishment for their crimes in this world (verse 31). "Who shall declare his way to his face? and who shall repay him what he hath done?" None bold enough for the one, or powerful enough for the other. The case of John the Baptist in relation to Herod the Tetrarch, a rare one, especially in those early times. Verse 32.—"Yet shall he (or 'even this man') be brought (conveyed in pomp and honour) to the grave. *Margin*, 'graves,' the place of graves; or the sepulchral grot, with its various apartments and numerous niches for the dead;

or an eminent and magnificent grave—a large and splendid mausoleum, perhaps a pyramid); and shall remain in the tomb," (*Margin*, "shall watch in the heap;" shall appear still to live at his tomb, as embalmed and preserved from corruption, or as represented by his statue or other memorial; or "watch shall be kept [by others] at his tomb," to preserve it and do him honour). Honour not only attends him in life, but follows him to the tomb both in and after his death. So "the rich man died and was buried," *i.e.* had a large and splendid funeral; nothing said of the burial of Lazarus (Luke xvi. 22). The pompous funeral of the wicked also a noticeable object in the days of the royal preacher (Ecc. viii. 10). Verse 33.—"The clods of the valley shall be sweet unto him." Buried, like great men, at the foot of a mountain where the winter stream keeps moist the sods that cover him. He has a pleasant resting-place for his remains, and the sod lies softly upon him. Apparently as enviable in his death as he had been in his life. Himself still supposed to enjoy in the spirit-world the honour done to his earthly remains, and the agreeable circumstances which attend them. Pleasing delusion of the imagination! The experience of the rich man in hell (Hades or the spirit-world) the opposite of that suggested by his costly funeral and beautifully adorned grave.—"And every man shall draw after him as there are innumerable before him." His death no solitary case. Death the common lot of fallen humanity, without respect to character or conduct. The wicked abundantly accompanied in the spirit-world. Company however no alleviation. The second desire of the rich man in Hades, that his five brethren might not come also to that place of torment (Luke xvi. 28). The presence of others rather an aggravation than a relief.

XII. Conclusion (verse 34). The friend's

consolation vain because grounded on false principles. "How then comfort ye me in vain, seeing that in your answers there remaineth falsehood" (*Margin*, "transgressions," opposition to the truth, or, malice and evil intent). Consolation, to be of any value, to be grounded on right principles. Must be—(1) *True*, in the *matter*; according to the Word of God, the only infallible standard. (2) *Suitable* in its *application*; adapted to the circumstances of the case, and of the individual addressed. Truth misapplied becomes error. (3) *Loving*, in its *manner*—truth spoken in love. Truth, spoken harshly and uncharitably, irritates rather than heals the wounded spirit. "Falsehood" in the answers and arguments of Job's friends, inasmuch as they maintained—(1) That God acts, in His government of the world, in a way which He does not; uniformly visiting the sins of the ungodly upon them in the present life, and rewarding the godly with worldly prosperity and ease. (2) That, according to these principles, those who are great sufferers must be great sinners. (3) That the only way to be delivered from such suffering, and to enjoy such prosperity, is by acknowledgment of sin and a turning from it to God,—to be with that view immediately made by the sufferer, and therefore by Job himself. *Malice* or evil intent in their answers; their aim being to make Job a grievous transgressor in the sight of God, and one who was suffering justly the punishment of his sins—the "devices the wrongfully imagined against him" (ch. xxi.). Their offence not only against truth but charity.

CHAPTER XXII.

THIRD SPEECH OF ELIPHAZ THE TEMANITE.

Remonstrates with Job on his self-righteousness, and plainly charges him with grievous transgressions as the cause of his present sufferings ; concludes with promises of prosperity and blessing on his repentance.

I. Reproves his apparent pride and self-righteousness (verse 2—4) God laid under no obligation by his piety. "Can a man be profitable unto God as he that is wise is profitable to himself? (or, when he by acting wisely profits himself; *Margin*, 'if he may be profitable, does his good success depend on himself?') Is it any pleasure to the Almighty that thou act righteous? or is it gain to Him that thou makest thy ways perfect? Will he reprove thee for fear of thee (lest He suffer injury and loss by thy conduct)? Will He enter with thee into judgment (to recover His right as an injured person)?" Observe—

1. *God under no obligation to treat men better than He does.* God no man's debtor. A secret feeling at the bottom of men's complaint against His providential dealings, as if they were wronged by Him and had a right to expect better treatment. On the contrary, all treated infinitely better than they deserve. All good in men is from God, not themselves. Men come infinitely short of rendering to God what He has a right to as their Creator, Preserver, and constant Benefactor.

2. *God's glory and happiness independent of man's conduct.* God no loser by men's want of religion, nor gainer by their practice of it (Ps. xvi. 2). God reproves men not from *fear* of them, but from *love* to them (Rev. iii. 19). Men never too bad for Him to love them, nor too great for Him to fear them. God neither rebukes the good from unkindness, nor the great from fear. Still true—(1) That men may, through grace, promote God's glory and advance His kingdom in the world; (2) That He has pleasure in holy men and in their holy lives (Ps. cxlvii. 11 ; Prov. xi. 20); (3) That men have it

in their power to render to God His rightful claim, or to rob Him of what is His (Mal. iii. 8). This the grievous sin not only of the Jews, but of men in general (Matt. xxi. 34, 41).

3. *True wisdom always profitable to the possessor of it.* That wisdom the fear of God and a life of godliness. Wisdom the knowledge, choice, and pursuit of the best end by the best means. Here equivalent to being "righteous," or "making one's ways perfect" or upright. Profitable in regard both to body and soul, time and eternity. Godliness with contentment great gain (1 Tim. vi. 6). The gains of religion infinitely greater than its losses. Wisdom's ways pleasantness and peace. Length of days in her right hand, in her left riches and honour. Godliness profitableness unto all things (1 Tim. iv. 8). No good which is not gained by it ; nothing lost by it which we are not the better by losing.

II. Charges Job with multiplied and grievous transgressions (verse 5—9).

1. *In general terms* (verse 5). "Is not thy wickedness great and thine iniquities infinite?" True, more or less, of all men, Job included. Not however in the sense of Eliphaz. According to Eliphaz, Job's wickedness great in comparison with that of other men, and with his own. The thought that of the Pharisee in the temple.—Great and multiplied transgressions humbly acknowledged by the best (Ps. xxv. 11 ; xl. 12 ; Ezra ix. 61). The certain result of a fallen and corrupt nature (Matt. xv. 19 ; Gen. vi. 5 ; viii. 21). Corrupt streams constantly flow from a corrupt spring. Yet along with this, in Job and in all good men, a nature opposed to evil. Hence—(1) the evil resisted, held in check, weakened, and more or less overcome ; (2) Good, though imperfectly, yet with more or less uniformity performed. Truly good men, in virtue of a two-fold nature, both saints and sinners. The former *with* their will, the latter *against*

it. Good men do good, but not all they would, or any *as* they would. Do evil, but not all they otherwise would, nor would they do any (Gal. v. 17). Observe—(i.) *All wickedness great*, as committed—(*a*) Against a great God; (*b*) Against great obligations to the contrary; (*c*) With comparatively little inducement to commit it; (*d*) With great evil as the result both to ourselves and others. (ii.) *The wickedness of some greater than that of others*; as committed—(*a*) With greater boldness; (*b*) Under great obligations to the contrary; (*c*) With greater knowledge and means of resistance; (*d*) With less temptation to the commission of it. (iii.) *Men's iniquities infinite*—as (*a*) Against an infinite God; (*b*) Against infinite obligations to the contrary; (*c*) Numberless; (*d*) Incessant during life; (*e*) But for Divine grace, continuing to be committed throughout eternity; (*f*) Attended with infinitely disastrous results. Sins committed against infinite majesty and goodness have in them an infinite malignity and greatness.

2. *Charges him with specific crimes* (verse 6—9.) (1) *Cruelty and wrong* (verse 6). "Thou hast taken a pledge from the poor for nought,"—unjustly, when nothing, or next to nothing, was due;—taking his garment from him for that purpose without restoring it to him by sunset, as afterwards required by the law (Ex. xxii. 26—27), and as was always the part of a right-minded man,—the poor man's garment by day being also his covering by night. Sometimes the bed itself taken as a pledge by rapacious and unfeeling creditors (Prov. xxii. 27). The sin of not restoring the pledge spoken of as not uncommon among the Jews in the days of the prophets (Ezek. xviii. 12; Amos. i. 8). This alleged sin of Job's marked by Eliphaz as particularly heinous from its being committed against a "brother." The "brother" not necessarily a relative, or even a countryman. All men brethren. All wrong done to our fellowmen done to our "brother." "Sirs, ye are brethren,"—a powerful reason for not wronging one another (Acts. vii. 26; Exod. ii. 11), &c. — The charge enlarged upon. "Thou hast stripped the naked (the poor and poorly clad) of their clothing,"—the large upper garment, or Arab hyke, worn as a garment by day and serving as a covering to sleep in at night. Among the articles taken and kept by rapacious and hard-hearted creditors. This charge the very opposite of Job's character (ch. xxix. 12—17; xxxi. 19, 20). (2) *Want of kindness and charity to the poor and needy* (verse 7.) "Thou hast not given water to the weary to drink, and thou hast witholden bread from the hungry." Acts of kindness and hospitality particularly required in the

East, and especially at that early period: no inns for travellers; people often poor; travelling generally performed on foot; climate hot and creating thirst; water often scarce and always precious; inhabitants often plundered by marauders, and forced to wander from house and home by invaders. Hence duties of hospitality held peculiarly sacred among Orientals, especially in Arabia (Gen. xviii, 4. 5; xix. 2; xxi. 14, 15; xxviii. 11; Ex. ii. 15). Fountains even in cities often bequeathed by wealthy Arabs for the free use of the poor, as well as money to provide persons to dispense it gratuitously in the streets. Job's actual conduct the reverse of that here ascribed to him (ch. xxxi. 17, 32). (3) *Partiality to the rich* (verse 8). "But as for the mighty man, he had the earth (or land), and the honourable man dwelt in it." Reference probably intended to Job's judicial conduct as an Arab chief, emir, or prince. The charge that of neglecting and wronging the poor, while the rich and mighty were favoured. The former expelled from their homes and inheritances to make room for the latter. Violence and wrong on the part of the great connived at. Partiality to the rich a grievous offence in the sight of God (Prov. xxviii. 21). Especially on the part of judges and magistrates (Lev. xix. 15). Condemned as existing in early Christian churches (James ii. 1—9). To feast the rich and neglect to feed the poor, the opposite of Christ's rule (Luke xiv. 12—14). The peculiar temptation of the rich. (4) *Neglect and oppression of the widow and fatherless* (verse 9). "Thou hast sent the widows away empty, and the arms of the fatherless have been broken,"—their support and means of subsistence taken from them, either by Job himself, or by others with his connivance. His alleged conduct either as that of a rich and powerful man in private life, or of a judge and magistrate, such as Job actually was (ch. xxix. 7—17. The conduct here ascribed to him that of the unjust judge in the Parable (Luke xviii. 2—5). The opposite of Job's real conduct (ch. xxi. 12—17; xxxi. 17,18, 21). The offence laid to his charge one of the most aggravated. Neglect of the cause of an injured person a grievous offence on the part of the judge or magistrate; still more so when the cause is that of those who are bereft of their natural defenders and unable to defend themselves. To injure any a sin in the sight of God; an aggravated sin to injure the widow and the fatherless. Widows and fatherless children entitled to pity; still more to justice. Not to assist such, a sin; a still greater one to injure them. The widow and fatherless especially cared for by God (Ps. lxviii. 5).

The same required by Him of others, both under the law (Exod. xxii. 22) and under the Gospel (James. i. 27).

These charges exhibit—(1) The wrong done to Job by his friends; (2) The trial thus endured by himself. The open expression of what had been their secret thoughts from the first of their visit (ch. xxi. 27). False charges both a grievous wrong against men and a heinous sin against God. An aggravation when, as in this case, laid against a good man and a friend.

The multiplicity and magnitude of Job's offences only inferred by Eliphaz from his extraordinary sufferings. His false and uncharitable charges the result of a false philosophy and mistaken views of the Divine government. Errors in religion no less condemnable in themselves or injurious in their consequences from being sincerely held and earnestly defended. Christ's followers often put to cruel deaths under the impression of doing God service (John xvi. 2). No new thing for God's faithful servants to have things laid to their charge, of which they not only are innocent, but which they utterly abhor. Innocence itself no security against false and abominable charges. Christ put to death under a charge of blasphemy. Stigmatized as a drunkard and a glutton, a deceiver of the people and exciter of sedition.

III. Imputes Job's calamities directly to his sins (verse 9). "Therefore snares are round about thee, and sudden fear troubleth thee; or darkness that thou canst not see [any way of escape] and abundance of waters (—overwhelming troubles) cover thee." Refers—(1) To his sudden and multiplied calamities; (2) To his inward darkness and distress; (3) To his perplexity and confusion of mind, both as to the cause of his troubles and any way of escape out of them. Fear and consternation the natural result of great, unlooked for, and successive calamities. Job's present experience. His case an apparent contravention of the promise: "He shall not be afraid of evil tidings (Ps. cxii. 7). Calmness and fearlessness in reference to calamity and trouble the believer's duty and privilege (Phil. iv. 67). Christ in the midst of the storm: "It is I, be not afraid." —Job's great troubles, according to Eliphaz, due to great sins. No sins likely to be more severely visited than those falsely charged upon him—unmercifulness to and oppression of the poor and needy. He shall have judgment without mercy that hath shewed no mercy (James ii. 13). No louder cry than that of wrong done to the widow, the fatherless, and the poor (James v. 4).

IV. Charges Job with infidel principles (verses 11—14). "Is not God in the height of heaven? And behold the height of the stars how high they are!" As spoken by Eliphaz himself, expresses the Divine supremacy over all—even the highest created beings—and the ability of God to take full cognizance of the affairs of men. As possibly ascribed by him to Job expressed the supposed distance of God from this lower world, and the consequent unlikelihood of his taking any notice of human affairs. "And ('yet' or 'therefore') thou sayest [in effect, if not in so many words]. How (*Margin*, what) doth God know? Can he judge (—rule in the affairs of men) through the thick cloud? Thick clouds are a covering to him that He seeth not; and He walketh in the circuit of heaven." The sentiment here falsely ascribed to Job that of a heart blinded by sin and alienated from God,—God too far off and too much occupied with higher things than to care for or take cognizance of human affairs (Ps. x. 11; lxxiii. 11). Finite man thinks of God as finite and imperfect like himself. Perhaps in this case the wish the father to the thought. The fool hath said in his *heart*, "There is no God"— to take cognizance of earthly things (Ps. xiv. 1). God's omnipresence and omniscience little realized because little loved. Hence—(1) Indulgence in a course of sin and oppression such as is here falsely ascribed to Job; (2) Murmuring under trouble and oppression as if God took no heed either of man's doings or sufferings. Even a child of God, under deep and accumulated afflictions, tempted with such unbelieving and God-dishonouring thoughts. Faith in God's omnipresence, omniscience, and all-superintending Providence, our comfort in trouble and our guard in temptation. The worst sentiments often falsely ascribed to the children of God. "Blessed are ye when man shall say all manner of evil against you for my sake" (Matt. v. 11).

The immense height or distance of the stars impressive even to ordinary observers. That distance, however, probably much greater than could be dreamt of in the days of Eliphaz. The nearest fixed star thousands of millions of miles distant. Millions of stars thousands of times more distant still. The Milky Way, "powdered with stars," an immense cluster of stars too distant to be distinguished as such by the naked eye. Stars so distant that their light travelling at the same rate as that of the sun only reaches us so as to render them visible after thousands of years. A false and foolish conclusion that because God is present with and governs those distant worlds or suns, he cannot be supposed to superintend or care for the affairs of this minor planet. God necessarily equally present in, and equally cognisant of, every part of his boundless dominions. The most distant and the most minute of His creatures equally and at once observed by His eye and supported by His hand. The same omniscience that numbers the stars numbers also the hairs of our head. Divinely enlightened reason sees everywhere

> "The unambiguous footsteps of the God
> Who gives its lustre to an insect's wing,
> And wheels His throne upon the rolling
>   worlds."

Universal government no burden to an infinite God. An animalcule shares His attention with a sun, a worm with a seraph. God higher than the highest star, yet nearer to both reader and writer than his nearest friend. Hence :—

1. God infinitely glorious and worthy of all adoration. "The heavens declare the glory of God" (Ps. xix. 1).

2. Submission to God in all circumstances the creature's duty.

3. Trust in God, under the severest trials, the believer's privilege.

4. Awful infidelity of the heart to ignore God and expel Him from His own world.

5. Dreadful nature of sin that despises and rebels against a God at once so infinitely great and good.

V. Adduces as a warning to Job the example of the antediluvian world (verse 15—20). "Hast thou marked the old way which wicked men have trodden? Which were cut down out of time (or prematurely), whose foundation was overflown with a flood (*Margin*, 'a flood was poured upon their foundations;' or, 'a river poured forth was their foundation,' *i.e.*, their dwelling which seemed most secure, or all they trusted in); which said unto God, Depart from us, and what can the Almighty do for them (or, 'for us,' or 'to us')? Yet he filled their houses with good things : but the counsel of the wicked is far from me (either the protest of Eliphaz himself against the principles and practice of those antediluvian sinners, and others like them, or perhaps the words of Job repeated in irony). The righteous see it (viz., the destruction of the ungodly) and are glad, and the innocent laugh them to scorn (Ps. lii. 6; lviii. 10, 11). Whereas our substance is not cut down (or, 'verily our adversary is destroyed'); but (or 'and') the remnant of them (*Margin*, 'their excellency') the fire devoureth." Possible allusion to the destruction of the cities of the Plain, with a cruel side-glance at Job's own losses and the occasion of one of them. Observe :—

1. Some dealt with by God in judgment for the warning of others (2 Pet. ii. 6).

2. Sin an "old way," older than the world itself, trodden by the angels that fell, and then by the world before the Flood (Gen. vi. 5.)

3. A course of sin sooner or later ends in suffering. Sin, though an old and well-trodden way, as dangerous and disastrous as ever (Rom. vi. 23).

4. The conduct of sinners and its fatal consequences to be carefully "marked" and avoided.

5. The firmest earthly possession easily swept away by the judgments of God; "whose foundation," &c.

6. Dislike of God the essence of sin and the root of a sinful life; "Which said unto God, Depart from us."

7. God and sin unable to dwell together at peace in the same heart.

8. The unrenewed heart unable to get God far enough; the renewed one unable to get Him near enough.

9. The baseness and blindness of sin. Like the man who turns his best friend and benefactor out of doors.

10. The ungodly often the most prosperous in this world. "He filled their houses," &c.

11. The part of the impenitent to despise God's goodness as well as defy His power (Rom. ii. 4).

12. God's multiplied favours a fearful aggravation of a sinful life. "Yet He filled their houses," &c. Sad when a house full of good things is not accompanied with a heart full of grace.

13. A constant protest to be entered against an ungodly life, however prosperous. The "counsel of the wicked," however fair and flattering, to be kept far from us.

14. Prosperous wickedness and suffering piety only for a time. A day cometh when the tables will be turned. "Blessed are ye that weep now, for ye shall laugh; woe unto you that laugh now, for ye shall mourn and weep" (Luke vi. 21—25). Abraham's— "Son, remember" (Luke xvi. 25).

15. The righteous glad, not at the sinner's calamity itself, but at the holiness and justice of God appearing in it. The Creator's character dearer to holy men and angels than the creature's comfort.

16. Proud and presumptuous sinners at last put to shame (Dan. xii. 2).

17. Happy when we can truly rank ourselves with the godly. "Whereas *our* substance," &c., *i.e.* that of the righteous; or, "Truly *our* adversary," &c. God's saints regard His adversaries as their own.

VI. Exhorts to repentance and piety (verse 21—23).

1. *Exhortation to submission and reconciliation with God* (verse 21). "Acquaint now

thyself (or, 'Submit thyself, and cultivate friendship and fellowship') with Him, and be at peace; thereby good shall come unto thee" (or, "thine increase shall be good "). Precious exhortation, but unjustly addressed to Job, as if still estranged from God. Contains :

First, the *Exhortation proper.* Two parts. Part *First.*

" Acquaint thyself with God."

Acquaintance or friendship with God our first duty and highest interest. Implies— (1) *Knowledge of God.* Knowledge necessary to acquaintanceship. To have friendship with God we must know Him,—as far as He is pleased to reveal Himself, and as far as creatures can know Him, in His nature, His attributes and His relations. God to be known as a Spirit, and as a Unity in Three Persons,—Father, Son, and Holy Spirit. To be known as infinite, eternal, and unchanging; as omnipresent, omniscient, and omnipotent; as holy, just, wise, and good. To be known as our Creator, Preserver, Governor, and through the incarnation, obedience, and death of His Son, our Redeemer. To be known in part from His works, but most from His Word. Only rightly and savingly known through the inward illumination and revelation of His Holy Spirit. To be known as revealed in His Son Jesus Christ (John xiv. 9). Power given to Christ by the Father to communicate the saving knowledge of Himself to men (Matt. xi. 27; John xvii. 2, 3). The Son's mission to reveal the Father (John i. 18). Knowledge of God to be obtained—(i.) Through *attention to and faith in the Word that reveals Him.* The Scriptures testify of Christ; therefore to be searched (John v. 39). (ii.) Through *earnest prayer for Divine illumination and teaching* (Prov. ii. 3—5). Wisdom, including the true knowledge of God, given by God Himself in answer to believing prayer (James i. 4). (iii.) Through *application to and acceptance of Christ as a Saviour.* One part of His work as a Saviour, to teach, enlighten, and communicate the saving knowledge of God (Matt. ii. 27—29; John xvii. 2, 3). Christ Himself made wisdom to those who receive and trust in Him (1 Cor. i. 30).—(2) *Submission to God.* Submission to God the first duty of a creature. Necessary to acquaintance and friendly intercourse with God. God's gracious regard directed to the humble and submissive (Isa. lxvi. 2). Submission the first lesson in the school of Christ, and the first step to the enjoyment of the Divine favour and friendship (Matt. xi. 27—29).— (3) *Reconciliation with God.* Man, through sin, in a state of enmity with God. As a

138

transgressor of His law, is under condemnation. Sin to be forgiven, and man reconciled to God before any enjoyment of acquaintanceship or friendly intercourse. Reconciliation with God the object of the Son's incarnation and vicarious death. Sin a separating element between God and His creatures. The sword of justice between God and the sinner. To be sheathed before any friendly fellowship can exist. Only sheathed when satisfaction has been made to law and justice for transgression. To be first stained with the blood of a substitute. Hence the oblation of sacrifices. Christ the only true Sacrifice and Substitute. Men reconciled to God by His blood (Eph. ii. 13—16; Col. i. 21, 22; Rom. v. 10).—(4) *Conformity to God's will and character.* Agreement in spirit and principles necessary to friendship and fellowship (Amos iii. 3). Conformity to God's will and ways a creature's highest duty and interest. Without it man's spirit a troubled sea that cannot rest.—(5) *Friendly walk and fellowship with God.* The end of all the preceding. The highest happiness of a creature. Our privilege in this life, our blessedness in the next (Rev. iii. 4). The testimony borne to Enoch and Noah before the Flood: they "walked with God." The third duty required of man (Mic. vi. 8). Abraham the friend of God. God's friendship and fellowship man's highest happiness in Paradise (Gen. ii. 8). Lost by the Fall, but restored in Christ (John xiv. 23). The secret of happiness in a suffering world and of contentment in every lot. He cannot be unhappy who has the Almighty for his friend. Observe—(i.) *Our honour to be made capable of acquaintance and fellowship with God.* Heaven, its endless enjoyment; hell, its irrecoverable loss. (ii.) *Ever increasing acquaintance with God, in and through Jesus Christ, our precious privilege.*

Second part of exhortation :

"Be at peace."

Peace the sweetest word in any language. Includes all good. God's best gift. God the God of peace. True peace the "peace of God." Peace on earth the object and result of the Saviour's incarnation (Luke ii. 14). Peace the purchase of His blood. Christ Himself our peace. His title 'the Prince of Peace.' Peace His legacy and gift to His followers. Imparts His own peace (John xiv. 27). Gives it not in word as a mere salutation, but in reality and experience. Peace either external or internal. The former precious; the latter still more so. In this world, the believers enjoy the latter without the former (John xvi. 33). In the next, they enjoy both. Acquaintance with God the only way to peace. The world without peace because without God. Sometimes an external peace enjoyed without the internal. True peace only to be found in Him who is our peace. No peace without pardon, no pardon without Christ. Peace with God before peace in ourselves. Peace offered by God through the death of His Son. The Gospel an ambassage of peace from the King of kings. God in Christ reconciling the world to Himself, and now beseeching men to be reconciled to Him (2 Cor. v. 19—21). Peace with God the immediate result of crediting the message and accepting the offer (Rom. v. 1). Followed by internal peace (Phil. iv. 6, 7). Preserved by trust in Christ, and obedience as its fruit. Christ trusted in, as our Surety and Substitute, our peace as sinners; Christ followed as our Master and Pattern, our peace as saints.

Second. The *Promise* attached to the exhortation proper: "Thereby good shall come unto thee." Peace with God brings every blessing in its train (Rom. v. 1), &c. No good withheld "from them that walk uprightly," as His reconciled and obedient children (Ps. lxxxiv. 11). All things made to work together for good to them that love God (Rom. viii. 28). Afflictions and trials converted into blessings (Heb. xii. 11). To the submissive and believing, good comes in this life; still more in the life to come, Present good to believers only a foretaste of the future. Suffering with Christ here, glorified with Him hereafter. Death separates them from all evil, and introduces them into all good. Peace on earth crowned with glory in heaven.

2. Exhortation to a *cordial acceptance of and attention to Divine teaching and admonition* (verse 22). "Receive, I pray thee, the law at His mouth, and lay up His words in thine heart." The enjoyment of peace to be followed by a life of purity. Friendship with God inseparable from obedience to Him. Christ's yoke accepted with rest imparted (Matt. xi. 28, 29). The rest continued as the yoke is carried. Mary at peace sits down at the Master's feet and hears His words. God a King as well as a Father and Friend. Christ a Master as well as a Saviour. With Christ, the law given as a directory of conduct, not as a covenant of life. At first given with —"Do this and live;" now given with,—"Live and do this." Our happiness, that the law is to be received at the hands of Him who has Himself fulfilled its commands and endured its curse as our Surety. The same pierced hands that purchased peace for our enjoyment, presents the law for our obedience. The peace of the Gospel preserved by obedience to the law. The law from God's "mouth,"—spoken and given by Himself. At first given to man at his

creation; afterwards on various occasions, and in different ways. God spake to the fathers at sundry times and in divers manners (Heb. i. 1). The "law" here probably equivalent to "His words" in the next clause. The directory not only of our conduct but of our faith. Taken in a general sense as including both law and Gospel, precept and promise. —*God's Law,* not our own will or reason, or the maxims and customs of the world to be the guide of our practice and opinions. —God's law to be "received,"—(1) By reverent attention; (2) Thankful receptance; (3) Cordial faith; (4) Cheerful obedience; (5) Humble submission. To be not merely read but "received." God's law one of His most precious gifts (Hos. viii. 12; Ps. cxlvi. 19, 20). His law, properly so called, as much a gift as his Gospel.

God's "words" to be "laid up in our heart,"—for remembrance, meditation, and use. To be laid up as our most precious treasure. To be laid up, not in our chest or our chamber, but in our heart. To be hidden in the heart that we may not sin (Ps. cxix. 11). So treasured by Christ, and ready for use in the hour of temptation (Ps. xl. 8; Matt. iv. 4). To be laid up in the heart,— (1) By deep attention; (2) Frequent reading or hearing; (3) Serious reflection. Not only to be learned but "laid up." The mark of a loving child to prize, ponder, and preserve the words of an absent parent. God's words laid up *for* us in the Scripture, and to be laid up *by* us in our heart. Worthy to be so laid up as our choicest treasure (Ps. xix. 10). God's words both words of promise and precept, wooing, and warning. Given both for direction and comfort. Found both in the Old and New Testaments.

VII. Holds forth various promises with conditions (verse 23—30).

"If thou return to the Almighty, thou shalt be built up (more especially in a family, with a new and numerous race of children); thou shalt (rather, 'if thou shalt') put away iniquity (or wrong doing) far from thy tabernacles (plural,—Job addressed as a chief or emir); then shalt thou lay up gold as the dust (or, as *Margin,* 'and lay the precious metals on the dust,' as things of no value and only to be trodden on), and the gold of Ophir (a place in Arabia distinguished for its gold) as (or 'on') the stones of the brooks; then shall the Almighty be thy defence (*Margin,* 'thy gold'), and thou shalt have plenty of silver (or, 'and [he shall be] treasures of silver unto thee'). For (or 'yea,'—a still greater blessing) thou shalt have thy delight in the Almighty, and shall lift up thy face unto God. Thou shalt make thy prayer unto him (as incense), and he shall hear thee, and thou shalt perform thy vows [on thy prayer being answered]. Thou shalt also decree (or purpose) a thing and it shall be established unto thee, and the light [of prosperity and the Divine blessing] shall shine upon thy ways. When men are cast down (or 'shall cast [thee] down'; or, 'shall humble themselves'), then thou shalt say [in confident assurance], there is (or 'shall be') lifting up; and he shall save the humble person. He (*i.e.* God) shall deliver the island (or 'the country' or 'dwelling') of the innocent (or, 'He shall deliver him that is not innocent', viz., at thy intercession), and it is delivered (or, 'he shall be delivered') by the pureness of thy hands." Three conditions—

1. *Returning to God.* "If thou return to the Almighty,—return home to Him as a prodigal to his father, so as again to be united to him and to the family,—return to Him in submission, obedience and love. Job unjustly regarded as having forsaken God and cast off his fear (ch. xv. 4.) Always true that the first step to a sinner's happiness is returning to God: "I will arise and go to my Father." All we like sheep have gone astray. God's constant call to the unconverted: Turn ye, turn ye; for why will ye die? "*To* the Almighty." "*To*" emphatic, even or quite to Him; not only in good inclinations and beginnings, but fully and thoroughly. "He arose and went to His Father." Not enough to *turn from sin*, but to *return to God* (Jer. iv. 1; Hos. vii. 16). Christ the way back to the Father (John xiv. 6). Returning to God a necessary condition of God returning to us (Mal. iii. 7). Important prayer (Jer. xxxi. 18).

2. *Putting iniquity far from us and from our dwelling.* "Thou shalt put iniquity far from thy tabernacles." No true returning to God without turning from sin. God and sin at opposite poles; the face to the one, the back to the other. No friendship with God without a falling out with sin. Sin the abominable thing which God hates (Jer. xliv. 4).—To be put away not only from ourselves but from our *dwelling*. A man responsible for what is done in his house. David's resolution (Ps. ci. 3—7). Joshua's (Josh. xxiv. 15). Much of a man's sin committed in his own house. A man to purify his house as well as his heart. Job's piety seen in his care about his children's conduct as well as his own (ch. i. 6).—Iniquity not only to be put away but *far* away (ch. xxi. 16).—Sin represented here as "*iniquity.*" Sin many-sided. Here especially its relation to our neighbour. Injustice, oppression, wrong, retention of dishonest gain, inconsistent with the enjoyment of the Divine favour and blessing.

3. *Ceasing to love and trust in riches.* "Lay gold on the dust," (*Margin*). The heart to be withdrawn from covetousness. Love to the world incompatible with love to God. Trust in riches, heart idolatry. No man able to serve two masters. God not to be served with a divided heart (Hos. x. 2). Trust in riches the worship of Mammon. Solemnly repudiated by Job (ch. xxxi. 24, 25).

Promises.

1. *Upbuilding* (verse 23). "Thou shalt built up." God, who pulls down, able also to build up. Allusion to Job's calamities, both as to fortune and family. Building up both external and internal. Here probably rather the former; temporal prosperity, and more especially in relation to offspring. Upbuilding in spiritual blessing, and soul-prosperity the New Testament promise (Acts ix. 31). Implies growth in grace, comfort, spiritual strength. Upbuilding in Christ (Col. ii. 7); in faith (Jude 20); in love (Eph. iv. 16). Spiritual growth dependent on consistent walk (Is. lviii. 9—12).

2. *Enjoyment of God as our portion and defence* (verse 25). "The Almighty shall be thy defence" (or treasure). The believer's place of defence is the munition of rocks. Underneath are the everlasting arms. God Himself the portion of His people (Deut. xxii. 9; Ps. xvi. 5). He is safe who has the Almighty for his defence, and rich who has God for his treasure.

> "Give what Thou canst, without Thee we
> are poor;
> And with Thee rich, take what Thou wilt
> away."

3. *Delight in God* (verse 26). "Thou shalt have thy delight in the Almighty." God the fountain of joy and ocean of delights. more than enough in Him to fill all hearts with pleasure. God a sun to gladden, while a shield to guard. Giving up the unsatisfying short-lived pleasures of sin, we receive those which are perfect and enduring. Only a penitent and renewed heart capable of delighting in the Almighty. The pure in heart see God (Matt. v. 8).

4. *Access to, and confidence in, God as a reconciled Father* (verse 26). "Thou shalt lift up thy face unto God." Implies conscious acceptance, delight, and confidence. The experience of one conscious of forgiveness and acceptance "in the Beloved." The face "lifted up" in prayer and communion with God. The spirit of adoption, crying, Abba, Father. Boldness of access to a father the privilege of a child. The believer's privilege in relation to God (Eph. iii. 12). Enjoyed in Christ. Boldness to enter into the holiest of all by the blood of

Jesus (Heb. x. 19). Believers to come boldly to the throne of grace, having Jesus there as their High Priest (Heb. iv. 16). Confidence towards God connected with consciousness of obeying Him (1 John iii. 21, 22). Abiding in Christ now gives confidence before Him at His appearing hereafter (1 John ii. 28). A loving heart gives boldness in the day of judgment (1 John iv. 18).

5. *The spirit of prayer and acceptance of our petitions* (verse 27). "Thou shalt make thy prayer to him, and he shall hear thee." Ability to pray, and to pray with acceptance, the gift of God. Children, not slaves, free to bring their requests to the master. The spirit of prayer connected with a state of acceptance. Answers to prayer given to believers along with the spirit of prayer (1 John v. 14—16). Answers to prayer the privilege of the upright (Ps. lxvi. 18; xv. 8). The Lord fulfils the desire of them that fear Him (Ps. cxlv. 6). Prayer as incense, from the Saviour's merits and the Spirit's grace (Ps. cxli. 2; Rev. viii. 3, 4). Answered for the sake of the Elder Brother (John xvi. 23). God never weary of blessing His people, because never weary of loving His Son. Universal promise made to prayer offered believingly in the Saviour's name (John xv. 7; 1 John v. 15; Mark xi. 24).

6. *The grace of thanksgiving with answers to prayer* (verse 27). "And thou shalt perform thy vows." Grace to render thanks for mercies received no less a mercy than the mercies themselves. Thanksgiving both our duty and our privilege. When God graciously fulfils our prayers we ought faithfully to fulfil our vows. Thanksgiving for answers to prayer and performance of vows practised by the heathen themselves (Jonah i. 16).

7. *Success in undertakings* (verse 28). "Thou shalt also decree a thing, and it shall be established unto thee, and the light shall shine upon thy ways." Prosperity and success in our undertakings dependent upon God (Rom. i. 8). Promised to the confiding and con-

sistent believer (2 Chron. xv. 20 ; Ps. i. 3; xxxvii. 5). Promised to Joshua (Josh i. 8). Afforded to Joseph (Gen. xxxix. 3, 23); and to Daniel (Dan. vi. 28). The prayer of Abraham's servant (Gen. xxiv. 12); and of Nehemiah (Neh. i. 11).

8. *Comfort, hope, and deliverance in time of trouble and depression* (verse 29). "When men are cast down (or, 'when they shall cast thee down,' or, 'when thou art depressed') then thou shalt say [to thyself, or to others], there is (or, 'shall be') lifting up ; and he shall save the humble person." Comfort and confidence of help and deliverance in time of common as well as personal danger and depression, with encouragement to others. Realized by Paul in the ship (Acts xxvii. 21—25. The Lord a light to His people in time of darkness (Micah vii. 8). Confidence, joy, and hope, in seasons of trouble and adversity, the fruit of faith and obedience (Hab. iii. 17—19). Job's own experience at times (ch. xxiii. 10).

8. *Usefulness to others* (verse 30). "He shall deliver the island (country or dwelling) of the innocent (or, "shall deliver Him that is not innocent, *i.e.*, that is guilty); and it (or he) is delivered by the pureness of thy hands." God honours His faithful and confiding people by not only blessing themselves, but making them blessings to others. So Abraham, Joseph, Daniel, Paul. Not only makes them grow themselves, but brings others to sit under their shadow (Hosea xiv. 6, 7). Saves them, and gives them to share with Himself the joy of saving others (James v. 23; Jude 23; 1 Tim. iv. 16). The accepted and faithful believer's prayers made efficacious even for the ungodly (1 John v. 16). So Abraham's would have been in the care of Sodom (Gen. xviii. 24). A community, company, or family, often saved for the sake of the godly in it (Acts xxvii. 24). Pureness of hands, both in practice and prayer, necessary to real usefulness to others. The promises in the text realized in Job's case in a way not anticipated by Eliphaz (ch. xlii. 7—9). A praying man a public good.

CHAPTER XXIII.

JOB'S THIRD REPLY TO ELIPHAZ.

Ceases directly to address his friends. His present speech rather a soliloquy. Takes no notice of the charges laid against him by Eliphaz. Laments the want of access to God in order to plead his cause before Him. Expresses his consciousness of integrity and obedience to the Divine will, as well as his solemn awe at the absolute sovereignty of

God, and the mysterious character of His dealings with him.

I. Complains of the continuance of his troubles and the view still taken of his conduct under it (verse 2). "Even to-day [after all I have already suffered] is my complaint bitter (or, 'even to-day [after

141

all I have asserted of my innocence] is my speech [regarded as] rebellion '); my stroke is heavier than my groaning " (or, is [viewed as] heavy on account of my groaning). Expresses either his own sorrowful experience, or the views of his friends regarding it. His troubles now of some weeks, or perhaps months, continuance. No relief as yet either to his mental distress or physical disease. Observe—

1. *Protracted trouble worst to endure.* The spirit worn out and exhausted by continued suffering. David's complaint—"Day and night thy hand was heavy upon me" (Ps. iii. 24). The misery of the lost that time brings no change. Eternity the only lane that has no turning. As the tree falls, so it lies.

2. An aggravation of trouble when complaint is construed into rebellion. Job's complaint perhaps not always entirely free from it. His spirit not always what it was in ch. i. and ii. To complain under such sufferings only human. Bitterness of complaint not always rebelliousness of spirit. Bitter complaint consistent with meekness and submission. A bitter cry heard on the cross from the lips of the only spotless sufferer (Matt. xxvii. 46). Job alone conscious of the depth of his distress. The heart knoweth its own bitterness.

3. Grace forbids not to groan under trouble, but puts a bridle upon the lips. Job's groanings frequent but restrained. He is a conqueror, not who never groans under protracted trouble, but who holds out patiently to the end. Terrible conflict sometimes to be maintained—(1) Against suffering; (2) Against sin; (3) Against suffering and sinning at the same time.

II. **Longs for free access to God** (verse 3). "O that I knew where I might find him, that I might come even to his seat. I would order my cause before him, I would fill my mouth with arguments [in proving myself an innocent sufferer]; I would know [without fear of the result] the words which he would answer me, and understand what he would say unto me" [in answer to my arguments, and in reference to my character and the cause of my suffering]. Perhaps his answer to the exhortation of Eliphaz (ch. xxii. 21). God so familiar to Job's thoughts as to be spoken of without being named. His life, like Enoch's, a walking with God. Observe—

1. *No uncommon thing for one who walks with God to be at times without free access to Him.* God, for wise purposes, hides Himself at times even from His own (Jer. xiv. 8). No finding God but as He reveals Himself. Want of access in time of trouble a special trial of faith and patience.

2. *Access to God the privilege of believers.* A time for finding God (Ps. xxxii. 6; Is. lv. 6). The contrary implied (Prov. i. 24—29). God found nowhere but in Christ. Christ the way to the Father (John xiv. 6). Free access to God for sinners through Him and His shed blood (Heb. iv. 15, 16; x. 19—22. The Holy Spirit given to believers in order to their free access and approach to God through Christ (Eph. ii. 18). The spirit of grace and of supplication (Zech. x. 12); of adoption, crying: Abba Father (Gal. iv. 6). Helps infirmities of the saints, making inward intercession for them with groanings which cannot be uttered (Rom. viii. 26).

3. *God not always found immediately* (Prov. viii. 34, 35; Luke xviii. 17). Yet always found where there is earnestness, humility, and faith in seeking Him (Is. xlv. 9; Jer. xxix. 13). In the time of Job, the way to God through Christ still comparatively obscure, and the Holy Spirit, as the Spirit of supplication and adoption, still comparatively withheld. God found the sooner the more we are humbled under a sense of sin and unworthiness. Job's desire still rather to have access to God as a righteous man, in order to have his innocence affirmed, than as a sinner to have his sins forgiven. God reveals Himself to the humble and contrite, not the self-righteous (Is. lxvi. 2; Luke xviii. 10—14).

Job still persuaded of God's favourable regard (verse 6). "Will he plead against me (overawe me or put me down) with his great power [as unable to prevail by words]? No, but he would put strength in me" (enabling me to plead my cause successfully; or, "he would give heed to me," affording a gracious and impartial hearing to my case). God the opposite of the Unjust Judge in the Parable. Not only hearkens to our pleading but gives strength to plead. So the Divine angel wrestling with Jacob at Penuel (Gen. xxxii. 24—30).

His confidence as to the result (verse 7). "There (in such a case—on being admitted to His tribunal) the righteous might dispute with him (the innocent man—referring to himself—might freely plead his cause); so should I be delivered for ever (come off victorious) from my judge." (1) *God's throne at once one of justice and grace.* (2) *The comfort of true and tried believers that they shall obtain a favourable verdict from God.* Believers have—(i.) The testimony of a good conscience; (ii.) The consciousness of a personal interest in Christ as their Surety and Advocate with the Father (1 John iii. 21; ii. 1). The believer not absolutely righteous in himself, but in Christ the Righteous One his Head and Representative (Rom. v. 14; 2 Cor. v. 21). The confidence of Messiah. as God's righteous servant transferred to His believing members (Is. l. 5—9; Rom. viii. 32—34). (3) *A small matter that man condemns if God approves* (1 Cor. iv. 3).

III. Laments his inability to find God as he desired (verse 8). "Behold, I go forward (or, 'to the east') but he is not there; and backward (or, 'to the west'), but I cannot perceive him; on the left hand (or, on the north) where he doth work (the north being the more populous part of the world, the region of stars and constellations and the birthplace of storms and tempests), but I cannot behold him; he hideth himself on the right hand (or, on the south, where all is solitude and waste), but I cannot see him." Observe—

1. *A believer, while in darkness and trouble, makes continual attempts to find God* (Song iii. 2). Nothing satisfies a living soul but God Himself (Ps. lxiii. 1, 2).

2. *God found anywhere with humility, earnestness, and faith; without them, nowhere.* Found neither in solitude nor society unless He graciously reveals Himself in Christ through the Spirit. God's absolute presence everywhere; His gracious manifested presence only as He is pleased to afford it. The latter promised to faithful believers (John xiv. 21—23). God's dealings with men in Providence with a view to their seeking Him, feeling after Him, and finding Him (Acts xvii. 26, 27).

3. *God often graciously near us when we are without sense or consciousness of His presence.* Job's case now like that of Hagar in the Wilderness (Gen. xvi. 13; xxi. 19).

4. *Prayer answered at the best time and in the best way.* Job's desire ultimately granted after Elihu's speech had prepard him for it. Then no longer has a case to plead, but conscious of personal unworthiness and the Divine perfection, is able to leave it entirely in the Lord's hands. Our own spirit generally the greatest hindrance to our prayers being answered.

5. *God's manifested and enjoyed presence the greatest happiness.* Happy when everything in nature, sunrise and sunset, storm and calm, "prompts with remembrance of a present God."

"His presence who made all so fair, perceived,
Makes all still fairer."

IV. Comforts himself with the thought of the Divine omniscience and the assurance of ultimate triumph (verse 10). "But he knoweth the way that I take (*Margin:* 'that is with me,'—all my experience and conduct in this affliction, as well as all my previous course of life); when he

hath tried me [sufficiently by these troubles; or, simply, 'he hath tried me, viz., by these present sufferings], I shall come forth, out of this furnace of affliction, or out of this probation to which I am now subjected] as gold" [comes out of the fire that tries and purifies it, refined from the dross of remaining corruption, and freed from all charges and suspicions as to my character and conduct]. Observe—

1. *The mark of an upright believer to rejoice that God is acquainted with all his ways.*

2. *A believer's comfort under affliction and reproach, to know that God is perfectly acquainted both with his character and experience.* If in trouble we cannot see God, it should be our comfort that God sees us, and knows all about us. Hagar's happy discovery in the wilderness: "Thou God seest me" (Gen. xvi. 13).

3. *Our great comfort, when reproached by men, to know that our conduct is approved by God.* Our main concern, therefore, ought to be to obtain that approval. "Let them curse, but bless Thou" (Ps. cxix. 28).

4. *God tries and proves all his children* (Ps. xi. 5; Jer. xx. 12). The desire of a sound believer to be tried by God (Ps. xvii. 3; xxvi. 2; cxxxix. 23). A believer's trials and afflictions often only the divinely intended means of proving his principles and faith (1 Pet. i. 7; James i. 12; Deut. viii. 2).

5. *The result of a true believer's trials certain.* This result threefold: (1) The justification of his faith; (2) The confirmation of his hope; (3) The purification of his love (Rom. v. 4, &c.; Is. xxvii. 9; Heb. xii. 10, 11; Dan. xii. 10).

6. *Genuine believers like gold.* (1) Precious (Lam. iv. 2; Is. xliii. 4); (2) Rare (Matt. vii. 14; Luke xii. 32); (3) Usually found mixed with earth and dross (Is. i. 25); (4) Subjected to the fire of purification (Zech. xiii. 9); 1 Pet. i. 7; (5) Able to endure the fire (1 Cor. iii. 12; (6) Ultimately made perfectly pure (Is. i. 25).

V. Declares the ground of his assurance (verse 11, 12). That ground the consciousness of his character and conduct (1 John iii. 21). Job conscious of—

1. *Persevering obedience to God's will* (verse 11). "My foot hath held his steps (followed faithfully and perseveringly the steps he prescribed to me, and which were pleasing in his sight); his ways have I kept, and not declined: neither have I gone back from the commandments of his lips." God's steps not only prescribed by Him, but trodden by Himself. "Be ye followers of God, as dear children." "Be ye holy, for I am holy." "Be merciful, as your heavenly Father is merciful" (Eph. v. 1; 1 Pet. i. 16.

Luke vi. 36). Especially trodden by God manifest in the flesh (John xiii. 15; Eph. v. 2; Phil. ii. 5; 1 Pet. ii. 21; 1 John ii. 6). Those steps marked in the Scriptures (1 Thess. iv. 2). Observe—(1) *The proof of sincerity not merely to put our feet in God's steps, but to keep them there;* not only to enter upon God's way, but not to decline or turn aside from it. (2) *God's way to be kept, not our own;* (3) *Many temptations to decline from God's way.* These are—(i.) From the world; (ii.) From our own heart. Sometimes the frowns of the world, sometimes its smiles, prove temptations. Hence Agur's prayer (Prov. xxx. 8, 9). (4) *Possible for a man to keep God's way, and not decline from it.* True generally, though not absolutely. "Not a just man on earth that doeth good and sinneth not." "If we say we have no sin we deceive ourselves" (Prov. vii. 20; 1 John i. 8). In a general sense, possible with Paul to live in all good conscience before God (Acts xxiii. 1). So David, as typical of Christ (Ps. xviii. 21—23); Hezekiah (2 Kings xviii. 6; xx. 3); Josiah (2 Kings xxii. 2; xxiii. 25); the writer of Psalm cxix. (Daniel?) (Ps. cxix. 22, 31, 51, 55, 56). God's Word given and to be attended to for this purpose (Josh. i. 7, 8; Ps. cxix. 11). Requires—(i.) Reflection (Prov. iv. 26; Ps. cxix. 59; (ii.) Resolution (Ps. cxix. 106); (iii.) Courage; (iv.) Watchfulness; (v.) Dependence on Divine strength; (vi.) Prayer. (5) *Job in the Old, an example to believers in the New Testament dispensation.* Much more light and grace vouchsafed in the latter than in the former. The Gospel dispensation especially the dispensation of the Spirit (2 Cor. iii. 8—11). Hence a still higher and holier life to be expected. Believers to be "filled with the Spirit" (Eph. v. 18).

2. *High esteem for the words of God* (verse 12). "I have esteemed (*Hebrew*: 'hidden, or treasured up') the words of His mouth more than my necessary food" (*Margin:* "My appointed portion;" or, "than my own purpose," when these have come in collision). Words from God's mouth known in all ages. God, at sundry times and in divers manners, spake in time past to the fathers (Heb. i. 1). The words of God's mouth treasured up in the Scriptures of truth (Deut. xxxi. 19, 22, 24; Is. xxx. 8; Hab. ii. 2). Spoken and preserved as the rule of faith and practice. To be—(1) Highly esteemed as our most precious treasure; (2) Chosen and adopted as the only rule of our faith and practice; (3) Carefully treasured up in memory and heart; (4) Held fast and persevered in.

Reasons for highly esteeming God's Word. (1) Its *source,*—God Himself; (2) Its *nature*

and *character*—(i.) Pure; (ii.) True; (iii.) Efficacious. (3) Its *tendency* and *end.* The Word of God is—(i.) A means of convincing of sin and error (Ps. xix. 11; Heb. iv. 12); (ii.) A means of conversion (Ps. xix. 7); (iii.) The Holy Spirit's instrument in regeneration (James i. 18); 1 Pet. i. 23); (iv.) Means of spiritual enlightenment (Ps. xix. 8; cxix. 130); (v.) Directory as to duty and the way of salvation (2 Tim. iii. 16; John v. 30); (vi.) Means of spiritual comfort, refreshment, and delight (Ps. cxix. 50, 54, 111; xix. 8, 10; Jer. xv. 16; (vii.) Means of sanctification (John xv. 3; xvii. 17; 2 Cor. iii. 18); (viii.) Means of spiritual fruitfulness (John xv. 7, 8); (ix.) Means of perfecting Christian character (2 Tim. iii. 17); (x.) Means of preparing for usefulness (2 Tim. iii. 17).

Evidences of highly esteeming God's Word —(i.) When it is attentively read or heard (Prov. viii. 34; John v. 39; (ii.) When seriously and frequently pondered (Luke ii. 19); (iii.) When carefully treasured up in the memory (Ps. cxix. 11); (iv.) When preferred to earthly comforts, possessions, liberty, even life itself; (v.) When our own views, purposes, and practices are given up because in opposition to its teachings; (vi.) When suffering and loss are preferred to the violation of its precepts.

Examples of such esteem: David (Ps. xix. 10; cxix. 97); Jeremiah (xv. 16); Daniel (Dan. vi. 5, 10); Mary (Luke x. 39—42). "I had rather be without meat, drink, light, everything than Matt xi. 28." —*Selnecccer.* "I would not for all the world that John xvii. 24 had been left out of the Bible."—*Baxter.* "My soul hath found inexpressibly more sweetness and satisfaction in a single line of the Bible, than in all the pleasures found in the things of the world, since the creation, could equal,"—*John Brown of Haddington.* "I would not live in Paradise *without* the Word, and could live in hell *with* it.—*Luther.*

God's Word to be esteemed more than our "necessary food," His Word the food of the soul, and necessary unto health and vigour (1 Pet. ii. 2). The spiritual part of our nature of greater consequence than the material. Man's life not sustained by bread alone, but by every word of God (Matt. v. 4; Deut. viii. 3). God's favour better than life. Spiritual refreshment sweeter and more valuable than corporeal. Better for the soul to be satisfied from God's Word than for the body to be satisfied from the best spread table. "The flesh profiteth nothing; the words that I speak unto you, they are spirit and they are life" (John vi. 63). Man's soul can no more dispense with spiritual than the body with material food. A famine of the

Word of God a much greater calamity than a famine of bread (Am. viii. 11).

VI. Recals with awe the unchangeableness and absolute sovereignty of God (verse 13). "But he is of one mind (or, 'truly He is one,' the only Supreme Ruler and Potentate; or, 'He is one and the same' [in purpose], *i.e.* unchangeable; or, when he is [set] on any one [object or purpose]) who can turn Him? and what his soul desireth, even that he , doeth. And he performeth the thing that is appointed for me; and many such things (either such sovereign and mysterious purposes and proceedings in relation to His creatures, or such severe dealings in relation to Job himself), are with Him. Therefore am I troubled at His presence [in my thoughts, or at His dealings with me]; when I consider [His majesty, power, and sovereignty], I am afraid of Him." Observe—

1. *God the only Potentate or supreme Ruler of the universe* (1 Tim. vi. 15). Rules and works according to His will. None able to influence, restrain, check, or counteract His procedure.

2. *God unchangeable in His purposes.* Ever like Himself. The same yesterday, to-day, and for ever. Free from the inconstancy and variableness adhering to creatures. The Father of lights, without variableness or shadow of turning (James i. 17). Is of one mind, character, and purpose. Hence our safety and comfort. "I am the Lord; I change not, therefore ye sons of Jacob are not consumed" (Mal. iii. 6). God neither fickle in Himself, nor capable of being influenced by persons or events so as to change His purpose. The history of the universe eternally planned and mapped out by His infinite mind, in full harmony with the freedom of the creature's will and the operation of second causes, which are included in it. Eternity, with all its actualities and possibilities, every moment open to His all-seeing view. His being one eternal NOW. Unnecessary and impossible for a Being, omniscient and omnipotent, all-holy, all-wise, and all-good, to change His purpose. Such change at any time only apparent. Ascribed to Him in condescension to our capacity. A change in His external procedure no change in His eternal plan.

3. *God irresistible in His purposes.* "I will work, and who shall let it" (Is. xliii. 13). God as irresistible in His power as He is immutable in His purpose. Nothing too hard for the Lord. For creatures to resist His will is for thorns and briars to oppose a consuming fire. God as able to execute, as He is wise to construct, His plan. The creature's safety, happiness,

and success, in falling in with the Creator's will.

6. *God's purposes extend to all His creatures.* No creature so insignificant but has his lot "appointed" for him. Nothing in the universe left to chance. The fall of a sparrow under His goverance as truly as the wreck of a world. Nothing either too minute or too vast for an infinite mind to direct or an almighty hand to control. Creatures and events linked with each other in His purpose throughout the universe, the chain extending from one eternity to another. The combination of a thousand events necessary to raise Joseph to his designed elevation, in order, among many other things, "to save much people alive" (Gen. l. 20).

5. *God's Being, Purposes, and Providence such as to beget deep reverential awe.* Too deep and mysterious for man's faculties to fathom or comprehend. The constant nearness of such a Being to us, our intimate relation to, and absolute dependence upon, Him, overwhelming. Our comfort that He is at once infinitely wise and holy, and just and good. The interests of all His creatures safe in His hands. Only disobedience and rebellion can interfere with the creature's happiness. God revealed in the Gospel in the most amiable possible light as love itself, and as giving the most unequivocal evidence of His character as such, in assuming our nature, obeying His own law, and enduring the utmost penalty of our disobedience, in order to our eternal redemption (1 John iii. 16 ; iv. 8—10).

6. *Fear the natural effect of thoughts of God viewed apart from Christ and His work of redemption.* Man inwardly and secretly conscious of sin and alienation from God. Fear, Peter's first feeling on the apprehension of Christ's Divine character, "Depart from me ; for I am a sinful man, O Lord" (Luke v. 8).

VII. Returns to his own particular case (verse 16). "For God maketh my heart soft [with fear and dismay (Josh. ii. 11)], and the Almighty troubleth (or 'confoundeth') me [by His mysterious and apparently cruel procedure]: because I was not cut off [by death] before the darkness [of these calamities came], neither hath he covered the darkness (*Heb.* 'thick darkness' of such accumulated trouble) from my eyes" [by hiding me in the tomb]. Observe—

1. *God able by His providence to make the stoutest heart soft with fear.* Able also by His grace to make the hardest heart soft with penitence and love. Often makes the softness of fear from the iron rod of the law a precursor and preparative to the soft-

ness of love from the golden sceptre of the Gospel.

2. *God able to trouble and confound the wisest and most daring by His mysterious and righteous dealings* (Exod. xiv. 24; viii. 19).

3. *God's dealings with ourselves often such as we are unable to comprehend.*

4. *A mystery that a benevolent and Almighty Being brings men into the world who are destined to suffer.* But—(1) No suffering which is not in some way the consequence of sinning. (2) All things made by God for Himself and for His own glory. In a way unknown to us, every creature made to contribute to the end of its creation. Perhaps God's highest glory hereafter from those who suffer most here. God's grace often greatly glorified by patient suffering even in this life. A patient, submissive, and thankful sufferer

here probably one of the brightest jewels in the cabinet of God hereafter. (3) Suffering the appointed path to glory (Acts xiv. 22; Rom. viii. 17). Probably the greatest sufferer in time the loudest singer in eternity. The crown of thorns preparatory to the crown of glory. As with the Head, so with the members (Luke xxiv. 26; Rom. viii. 17). (4) The sufferings of one made to contribute to the benefit of another. Paul's testimony in reference to himself, applicable to believers in general (Col. i. 24). The members thus made to share with the Head. Probably the happiness, moral excellence, and mutual love of redeemed men greatly increased by such a Divine arrangement. (5) The wisdom and the love of God in bringing Job into the world where he had so much to suffer, long ago made manifest both to himself and others.

CHAPTER XXIV.

CONTINUATION OF JOB'S REPLY TO ELIPHAZ.

Prosecutes his own view of the Divine government. Enlarges on the crimes of one part of men and the sufferings of another as the consequences of them, to shew that judgment is not executed on the ungodly in this world, and that men often suffer without anything in their own conduct to deserve it. The ungodly, however, not left unpunished; and their prosperity and power only for a time.

I. **Proposes a question for solution in reference to the Divine government** (verse 1). "Why, seeing times are not hidden from the Almighty, do they that know him not see his days?" Or, "Why are not [stated] times [of judgment] laid up (or kept) by the Almighty, and [why do] they that know Him not see His days" [of inflicting punishment on the ungodly?] The question takes the fact for granted and asks the reason of it. The fact supposed—

1. That *stated times of judgment, or Divine court-days, for trying men's actions are manifestly not held.* Men not brought before a Divine tribunal in this life. The great assizes yet to come. Such a day appointed (Acts xvii. 31; x. 42; Rom. ii. 16; xiv. 10; Rev. xx. 12). Men only registered now for judgment and public trial on that day. Sins in this life apparently winked at by God (Ps. l. 21). Sentence against an evil work not speedily executed. The fact sometimes staggering to the godly, especially in earlier times. Remains as a trial for faith and patience. Abused by the ungodly to impenitence and licentiousness.

2. *Times for the visible infliction of punishment on the wicked not seen by the godly in this life.* For the most part sin suffered by God to pass with impunity as to this world. The fact noted by Job (ch. xxi 7); by Asaph (Ps. lxxiii. 5); by David (Ps. l. 21); by Solomon (Ecc. viii. 11); by Jeremiah (Jer. xii. 1); by Habakkuk, (Hab. i. 13, 16). Visible judgments rare. Such examples—the deluge; destruction of Sodom, &c.; Herod's death (Acts xii. 23). According to the views of Eliphaz and his two friends, such cases should have been of frequent occurrence.

From the text observe—

1. *Times, in the sense of events, not hidden from the Almighty.* All actions, bad and good, naked and open before Him. Sin, though not *punished*, not the less *perceived*. "Thou God seest me," a truth both for the godly and the ungodly.

2. *Times for the accomplishment of future events not hidden from God.* The future as truly as the present under His perfect inspection. The times and seasons reserved in His own power (Acts i. 15). Though unknown to us, not the less certain to Him (Acts xv. 18.)

3. *Sufficient to describe the godly as "those that know God."* Such knowledge one of— (1) Certainty (1 John iv. 16); (2) Divine communication (John xvii. 2, 3); (Matt. xi. 27); (3) Experience (1 Pet. ii. 3); (4) Regard and love, as Ps. i. 6; (5) Acquaintance and fellowship (Job xxii. 21; Gen. v., 24, vi. 9). As the result of such knowledge the righteous trust in God as a Father (Ps.

ix. 10). Not to know God the characteristic of the ungodly (1 Thess. iv. 5; 2 Thess. i. 8). Godly men the friends of God. Abraham's title of nobility shared by each of them. (Compare James ii. 3; Is. xli. 8, with Luke xii. 4; John xv. 14, 15).

4. *God's friends made acquainted with His purposes and procedure in the world* (Gen. xvii. 17; Ps. xxv. 4; Am. iii. 7; John xv. 15). The characteristic of the ungodly, that they "regard not the works of the Lord nor consider the operation of His hands" (Ps. xxviii. 5; Is. v. 12). Wisdom given to the children of God to discern and know the times (Luke xii. 56; 1 Thess. v. 1—4; Rom. xiii. 11). Times and seasons, however, while still future, reserved in the Lord's own knowledge, except in so far as He is pleased to communicate them (Acts i. 7; Matt. xxiv. 36; Rev. i. 1).

II. Describes the conduct of various classes of men in relation to their fellows, with its consequences (verses 2—8).

First: Their *conduct* (verses 2—4).

1. *Fraud, theft,* and *violence* (verse 2). Exhibited in—

(1.) *Removing "landmarks."* Placing farther back the stones erected to distinguish their own fields from their neighbour's,—common in Eastern and other countries where hedges are not frequent; and doing this for the purposes of fraudulently enlarging their own estate at the expense of their neighbour's. Expressly forbidden in the law of Moses (Deut. xix. 14). Persons guilty of it pronounced accursed (Deut. xxvii. 14). Found in the days of Hosea (Hos. v. 10).

(2.) *Stealing sheep and feeding them as if their own* (verse 2). "They violently take away (or steal) flocks and feed thereof (*margin*, 'feed them')." Job's own experience in reference to his oxen, asses, and camels (ch. i. 14, 15, 17). Pasturing the stolen sheep an aggravation of the crime. Indicated boldness and perseverance in sin. The practice common among the Bedouins. Marks an uncivilized state of society. Practised even in Scotland in the last century in regard to larger cattle. Observe— (i.) The character of sin to sear and deaden the conscience; (ii.) The ungodly often apparently permitted to enjoy the fruit of their sin.

2. *Cruelty and hardheartedness* (verse 3).

(1.) In reference to the *fatherless.* "They drive away the ass of the fatherless" (in order to appropriate it to themselves, probably on some pretended claim, perhaps, as in the next clause, as a pledge or pawn for some loan or debt). The one ass of the fatherless his means of subsistence. The fatherless not only poor, but without any to defend them from such oppression. An ass still the means of subsistence to fatherless and poor children in the East, being used both for riding and carrying burdens.

(2) In reference to the *widow.* "Take the widow's ox for a pledge,"—taking it in pawn for the loan of a trifling sum, and keeping it in their possession. An aggravated cruelty, the ox being the only means of her subsistence by ploughing her little plot of ground and yielding her milk. The widow herself an object of sympathy, her poverty having necessitated her to ask a loan or incur a debt with her hard-hearted neighbour. The sin expressly forbidden by the law (Ex. xxii. 26, 27; Deut. xxiv. 6, 10. "No flesh in man's obdurate heart."

3. *Insolence and oppression of the poor* (verse 4). "They turn the needy out of the way,"—acting towards them with overbearing violence; compelling them by their cruelty and oppression to abandon the highways and frequented parts of the country, and thus preventing them from following their ordinary pursuits; perhaps removing them in order to take possession of their little fields; or forbidding them the highway for their ox or their ass. The "clearances" of modern times. A sin not to aid the poor; still more to expel them from the neighbourhood as burdens and nuisances. The poor never to cease out of the land (Deut. xv. 11). Left as objects for the exercise of kindness and benevolence (Matt. xxvi. 11. To oppress the poor is to reproach their Maker.

Second: The *consequence* of this oppression (verse 4). "The poor of the earth (or land) hide themselves together;" disappearing as unable to endure the oppression or resist their oppressors. "When the wicked rise [in power], men hide themselves" (Prov. xxviii. 20). Forced by oppression into solitudes where they congregate and enjoy comparative safety. The godly under persecution thus often made to wander in deserts and mountains, and in dens and caves of the earth (Heb. xi. 38). The case of Elijah and other servants of God in the days of Ahab and Jezebel (1 Kings xvii., 3, xviii. 13). The pilgrim fathers of England and the Huguenots of France. Bedouins and others in the East often obliged to seek refuge in the desert from the oppressions of tyrannical governors. Their life in such circumstances made one of privation and suffering (verse 5). "Behold, as wild asses in the desert [instead of their own fields as formerly], go they forth to their work, rising betimes [before the excessive heat] for a prey (or to obtain food); the wilderness yieldeth food [a scanty and miserable subsistence] for them and for their children" (whole families being thus driven forth from their homes and from society). The wild ass a "solitary, timorous animal, whose only defence is its heels." The reference here rather to their solitude and fear than to savage wildness. A barbarous and uncivilized state, however, the likely consequence of the treatment they receive (Gen. xvi. 12, xxi. 20).—(Verse 6). They reap every one [by himself] his corn (*margin*, "mingled corn or dredge," a mixture of grain ordinarily used as fodder for cattle, and so generally translated, as in Is. xxx. 24, in the field (or perhaps, 'they reap [as hired or forced labourers] every one in a field which is not his own'); and they gather the vintage of the wicked (to obtain as hirelings a subsistence for their families; the proprietors of the vineyards characterized as wicked from their cruelty and oppression of the poor, but in time of vintage, glad to obtain their aid in gathering the grapes; or possibly obliged to render forced labour so common in the east). They cause the naked (the poor and poorly clad) to lodge (or 'pass the night') without clothing [having taken to pledge their upper garment, usually serving also as a covering by night] (Deut. xxiv. 13), that they have no covering in the cold (the nights in eastern countries being often as cold as the days are hot) (Gen. xxxi 40). They are wet (or drenched) with the showers (or heavy driving rains) of the mountains (where, as travellers often experience, such storms of wind and rain are common), and embrace the rock (clinging to some cave or hollow in its side) for want of a shelter."

The picture presented in the eighth verse suggests—

The True Rock and its Shelter.

1. *As sinners men are by nature in the condition of the persons here referred to,—exposed to a storm.* That storm God's righteous anger on account of sin. The wrath of God revealed from heaven against all ungodliness and unrighteousness of men (Rom. i. 18; Col. iii. 6). "Wrath to come" awaiting the unsaved sinner. The day of judgment the great day of Divine wrath—the wrath of the Lamb (Rev. vi. 16, 17). That wrath compared to a storm. "On the wicked God shall rain snares (*Margin*, 'burning coals'), fire and brimstone, and an horrible tempest" (Ps. xi. 6). No storm on earth ever equal to it. (i.) Other storms affect only the body, this the soul; (ii.) Others endure but for a short time, this for ever; (iii.) Others may have peace within; this fills with anguish and despair.

Felt at times in the sinner's conscience even in this life. Even then intolerable. Escape from it in this life possible. Hereafter rocks and mountains invoked in vain for shelter. Exposure to the storm wherever sin is still unpardoned. Though now unfelt, yet even ready to burst upon the Christless soul. The case of men universally. Men by nature children of wrath, even as others (Eph. ii. 3.).

2. *Men in themselves are without a shelter.* Have no means of averting or screening themselves from deserved wrath. Wealth unable to purchase a shelter from it. Power unable to; command one. Science unable to contrive one. Good works unable to merit one. Our own works like Adam and Eve's fig-leaved aprons. Monarch and mendicant equally powerless to screen themselves from this storm. No shelter without satisfaction to the demands of a righteous law. The required shelter to be strong enough to resist the brunt of the storm. Able to stand between the sinner and the storm that must otherwise beat on his defenceless head.

3. *Such a shelter provided in Christ.* Christ, given by God the Father for that purpose, came into the world to save sinners from the storm. Promised as an hiding-place from the wind and a covert from the tempest (Is. xxxii. 2). Fitted to be such a shelter. God manifest in the flesh. As man, Christ has done and suffered in our stead what the law of God demands in the way of obedience and penalty. As God in our nature, He is able to stand as a substitute for us, and to give infinite value to His obedience and suffering in our stead. Provided for us in pure love on the part of God (John iii. 16). God's will that all should flee to and find shelter in this rock. Christ as a rock—(1.) *Affords perfect safety to the soul that trusts in Him.* A rock is strong, firm, impenetrable. None ever trusted in Him and perished; (2) *Never changes.* A rock the most abiding and unchanging object in nature. Christ the Rock of Ages—the everlasting Rock. The same yesterday, to-day, and for ever. (3) *Is sufficient to receive and shelter all who betake themselves to Him.* Rocky caverns in Judæa, as the cave of Adullam, large enough to contain thousands of men. Room in Christ for millions at once. Millions sheltered in this Rock already, and yet there is room. (4) *Is comfortable and well replenished.* Caverns sometimes found already furnished with necessary articles left there by previous occupants; the contrary, however, being generally the case. In Christ, all things provided needful for comfort and well-being, both here and hereafter. Christ made of God to those

who are in Him, both wisdom, and righteousness, and sanctification, and redemption (1 Cor. i. 30). The world, life, death, all things, ours when we are Christ's. All fulness in Him, out of which we may receive even grace upon grace. All our needs supplied. In the world tribulation, but in Him peace. Grace found in Him sufficient for daily duty, daily temptation, daily trial. (5) *Is accessible to all.* Stands open and free. Its entrance obstructed by no formidable barrier. No steep and rugged height to climb in order to reach it. Accessible even to a child. Entered not by toil or merit, but by *faith*,—believing God's testimony true concerning it, and so trusting in it. Over its portal stand the words: Believe in the Lord Jesus Christ and thou shalt be saved. (6) *All are welcome to its shelter.* Entrance without money and without price. No qualification required but sense of need, desire for shelter, and belief in its sufficiency. "A guilty, helpless sinner desiring shelter," a sufficient passport. All classes without distinction invited to enter and be safe.

4. *This Rock is to be "embraced."* A rock of no use for shelter but as it is fled to, entered, and clung to. Christ is for personal acceptance, appropriation, and trust. The ark, when made, to be entered by Noah and his family. Not enough to hear of the rock, look at it, understand about it, or be near it. Must be entered and "embraced." "Found *in* Christ" gives safety, not found *near* Him. No time to be lost in entering this Rock. Too late when the storm descends. "Behold, *now* is the accepted time! behold *now* is the day of salvation!"

Important question. Where am I? In the Rock? or still exposed to the storm? If the former, then "let the inhabitant of the Rock sing," and praise aloud the God of his salvation (Is. xlii. 11). If the latter is still the case, the call is, Come in *now.* The door still open. Still room. Delay not. Why remain outside exposed to the storm? Death hastens. The door will soon be shut. Entrance may within another hour be impossible. Then no shelter from the storm for evermore. "To-day if ye will hear his voice, harden not your heart."

III. **Proceeds further to describe the cruelty and oppression of the ungodly rich, and their apparent impunity** (verse 9). "They pluck the fatherless from the breast (infants whose fathers are already dead, and whom these men snatch from the widowed mother's breast to make their own, as pledges or in payment of some real or pretended debt), and take a pledge of the poor (either the poor man himself to be their

bondslave till the debt is paid, as Lev. xxv. 39; Matt. xviii. 25; or his *garment*, as ch. xxii. 6). They cause him (the poor whose garment they have taken in pawn) to go naked, without clothing, and they take away the sheaf from the hungry (the handful of corn they have plucked to satisfy their hunger, or the gleanings of the harvest field, which were usually regarded, and were afterwards by the law of Moses expressly appointed, as the perquisite of the poor, Lev. xix 9); which make oil within their walls (for the benefit of these rich oppressors; or 'who toil at noontide in their vineyards' as hired, or rather as forced, labourers), and tread their wine-presses and suffer thirst" (not being permitted to allay their thirst with the juice of the grapes they were laboriously expressing.)

"Slaves in the midst of nature's bounty curst,
And in the loaden vineyard suffer thirst."
Addison's Letters from Italy.

Cruelty and oppression not confined to the country (verse 12). "Men (or 'the dying') groan [under injuries and oppressions] from the city [where justice is wont to be exercised, and where fear might be supposed to restrain evil-doers), and the soul of the wounded—[not only having their spirits but their very life crushed out of them by oppression] crieth out [to God and men for help, or to God for vengeance]: yet God layeth not folly to them"—(apparently lays it not to their charge, or appears to give no heed to it; or, "does nothing absurd" or unbecoming His Divine character in permitting such things; or, according to another way of reading the word here rendered "folly," "pays no attention to their prayer," viz., that of these suffering and oppressed ones). The frequent complaint in the Psalms that the wicked oppress the godly poor with impunity, while God appears to take no notice either of the crimes of the one party or the sufferings of the other (Ps. x. 1—14; xxxv. 17; xlii. 9; xliv. 23, 24). Observe—

1. *Crimes committed and cruelty perpetrated while God keeps silence* (Ps. l. 21). Sentence against an evil work not often speedily executed (Ecc. viii. 11). Yet forbearance no acquitance.

2. *The effect of sin to harden the heart and deaden the feelings of humanity.*

3. *Loss of power or gain stops at no crime or cruelty to attain its object.*

4. *Sin assimilates men to Satan, the "murderer from the beginning."*

5. *Great sufferings often superinduced by other men's sins* (verse 12).

6. *The cry of oppressed ones terrible for the oppressor* (James v. 4).

149

7. *City as well as country the theatre of the oppressions of some and the sufferings of others* (verse 12). Solemn warning in this verse for such cities as London. Eternity alone will reveal how many lives have been crushed out of men and women by oppressive labour and scanty remuneration.

IV. Describes other classes of wicked men,—*those who practise sin in secrecy and under the cover of darkness* (verse 13). "They (or 'these,' as distinguished from the former) are of those that rebel against the light (hating and shunning it as unfavourable to their wicked deeds, John iii. 19, 20); they know not the ways thereof, nor abide in the paths thereof" (prefer darkness to light, and night to day, for the perpetration of their crimes). The first of these classes, the *Murderer* (verse 14). "The murderer rising with the light (at earliest dawn) killeth the poor and needy [as unable to resist him and his demands], and in the night is as a thief" (or, "acts the thief"). In the East, murders are committed at early dawn, the most favourable part of the day both for travelling and work, while thieves or housebreakers practise their crimes during the night.—The *second* class, the *Adulterer* (verse 15). "The eye also of the adulterer waiteth for the twilight (the evening or night, as more favourable for his purpose, Prov. vii. 9, saying, No eye shall see me, and disguiseth (muffles up or puts a mask on) his face. In the dark they (the two classes already mentioned, or perhaps a *third*, *Burglars* or Housebreakers) dig through houses (insinuating themselves, like the adulterer, or literally, digging an entrance for themselves, like the housebreaker, through the mud walls of the houses) which they had marked for themselves (or 'having shut themselves up') in the daytime; they know not the light (—hate and shun it). For the morning is to them even as the shadow of death (as hateful and as feared, as discovering and detecting their evil deeds (Eph. v. 13); or, the shadow of death is to them as morning,—darkness is as desirable and delightful to them as morning is to others); if one know them (or discover them, or 'when one can recognize, people,' *i.e.*, in the light of the morning), they are in the terrors of the shadows of death" (or, "it is the terrors of, &c., to them"; or, "the terrors, &c., are upon them.") Observe—

1. *The character of sin, that loves the darkness for its commission.* A reptile that loves the darkness of caves and dungeons. A work of darkness, to be practised only out of observation, and in the ignorance of God and truth. A testimony to the value

150

and excellence of godliness, that it does not fear the light (John iii. 21).

2. *Sin opposed to the light of truth as well as to the light of day.* Hence hatred to the truth, which both exposes and opposes sin. The great condemnation, to have the light and yet hate and avoid it (John iii. 20). The sin of Christless persons in a Christian land, neighbourhood, or family.

3. *A sovereign authority in light to keep men from evil deeds.*

4. *The present in many places a time of light; hence corresponding responsibility.*

5. *Murder a common crime where not restrained by fear* (verse 14). "Feet swift to shed blood," part of the inspired description of fallen humanity (Rom. iii. 15).

6. *Sin aggravated when committed with purpose and deliberation* (verse 15).

7. *The ungodly, when not committing iniquity, often plotting it.*

8. *Sin committed in forgetfulness of God.* "No eye seeth me."

9. *The wicked often tortured between lust and fear.* Raging lust before commission; deadly fear of detection in and after it.

10. *Pleasures of sin dearly bought.* The terrors of the shadow of death sooner or later the consequence of it. The ways of transgressors hard.

V. Describes the experience of the wicked (verse 18). "He is swift as the waters (or, 'light on the face of the waters;' carried away by Divine vengeance as the foam or other light substance on the surface of the stream; or, gradually and quietly, though swiftly, borne along to the grave where he finally disappears); their portion (or estate) is cursed (—ultimately abandoned to desolation) in the earth (or land): he beholdeth not the way of the vineyards (—is cut off ultimately from his former haunts, pleasures, and pursuits, 'from the cheerful ways of men'). Drought and heat [in summer] consume the snow waters (—gradually dry up the torrents and mountain streams formed by the melted snow (ch. vi. 15, 18); so doth the grave (—death and the invisible world, which sooner or later swallow up and cause to disappear from the earth) those that have sinned [in the gross and open way already, and yet to be, described]. The womb (even the mother that bare him) shall forget him (so worthless his character, and utterly abandoned by, and cut off from, friends and relatives): the worm shall feed sweetly upon him (or 'shall he sweet to him,' his only companion now, ch. xxi. 33); he shall be no more remembered [having done nothing to cause his memory to be cherished, but the contrary (Prov. x. 7)]: and wickedness (or the wicked man) shall be broken as a tree" [useless and already decayed]. Observe—

1. *The character of the selfish and ungodly, however rich, a worthless one.* The sinner in his best and most prosperous state light as foam on the surface of the stream.

2. *All the sinner's earthly enjoyments speedily brought to an end.* Slowly or suddenly, the grave terminates his pleasures and pursuits (verse 19). The pleasures of sin but for a season.

3. *The grave only formidable to those who have led a sinful life, and die without renewal of heart and removal of guilt.*

4. *Humbling contrast between the grave and its wormy inhabitants, and the sinful indulgences and worldly pomp of a godless and prosperous life.* The rich man in the Gospel lifts up his eyes in hell, and craves, not for deliverance, but a drop of water to cool his burning tongue.

5. *Sin soon covers men's names with oblivion, and makes even their nearest relations to forget them* (verse 20). "The righteous is held in everlasting remembrance, but the memory of the wicked shall rot" (Prov. x. 7).

VI. Returns to the character and ways of the ungodly as meriting the punishment already mentioned (verses 21—24). "He evil entreateth the barren that beareth not (thus adding affliction to the afflicted, barrenness being held a reproach and at the same time leaving the widow without natural defenders), and doeth not good to the widow (not only withholding the sympathy and succour which her circumstances claim, but acting towards her in a way the very reverse). He draweth also the mighty with his power (attaching him to his interests for the purpose of oppressing others); he riseth up (for the purpose of completing his wicked designs; or, he rises to power), and no man is sure of life (so formidable his power and so regardless of right). Though it be given him to be in safety (by God himself, who bears long with him instead of punishing him at once in the midst of his wickedness), whereon he resteth (living at ease and in security in consequence of this forbearance); yet his (viz., God's) eyes are upon their ways (though now keeping silence and apparently winking at his evil deeds). They are exalted for a little while but are gone (*Heb.* and *Marg.* ' and are not,' are no more, but disappear from the stage), and (are) brought low (by death which terminates at once their power and their pride); they are taken out of the way as all others (even the meanest whom they have oppressed), and cut off as the tops of the ears of corn." Observe—

1. *Injury done to a fellow creature a sin marked by God; that sin aggravated when the* injury is done to one already in any way *afflicted* (verse 21). The afflicted, destitute and reproached, have already claims on our sympathy and succour.

2. *A sin in the sight of God, not only to injure the afflicted and destitute, but even to withhold our sympathy and aid.* Not to do the good in our power, a sin as well as to do evil (Prov. iii. 27; xxiv. 11, 12). Neglect of the fifth commandment a sin as truly as the transgression of the sixth. Sins of omission discover the character and bring condemnation as truly as those of commission. The sins produced at last day for judgment, especially the latter (Matt. xxv. 42—45.) Pure and undefiled religion before God, to visit the fatherless and widows in their affliction (James i. 27).

3. *A high aggravation of sin when we not only do wrong ourselves, but endeavour by our influence to draw others into the same practice* (verse 22). Ahab specially branded in the Bible as not only having sinned himself, but also "made Israel to sin." The character of the ungodly not only to sin themselves but to draw others into participation in their sin (Prov. i. 10—14).

4. *An aggravated sin to abuse God's goodness and forbearance to the practice of evil* (verse 23). God's goodness intended, on the contrary, to lead to repentance (Rom. ii. 4). Sin persevered in on the calculation that "to-morrow shall be as this day and much more abundant" (Is. lvi. 12).

5. *Sin, though passed over for the present, yet marked for future visitation, if not prevented by timely repentance* (verse 23). Sentence against an evil work not speedily executed. The sinner allowed to do evil a hundred times (Ex. viii. 11, 12). Yet God's eyes are upon men's ways.

6. *The power and pride of the ungodly but of short continuance* (verse 24).

7. *Sinners often cut off when their prosperity has reached its highest pitch, like the "tops of the ears of corn."*

8. *Men spared to ripen either for mercy or judgment.*

VII. Challenges contradiction or refutation (verse 25). "If it be not so now [that the case is as I represented it], who will make me a liar (or prove me in error), and make my speech nothing worth?" Job's position that of Asaph (Ps. lxxiii.), that the ungodly often live long and prosper in this world, and are without any "bands in their death," though ultimately brought to judgment. His position assailed by his friends as derogatory to God's righteousness as the Governor of the world, and as savouring of infidelity. In Job's view, his position unaffected by their speeches and arguments. Observe :—

1. *Our duty to see that the views we hold in regard to God and His moral government rest on solid grounds.*

2. *Our duty in regard to subjects upon which there is room for doubt, to be open to conviction and argument on the opposite side.*

3. *Our views on all religious subjects to be brought to the touchstone of reason and Scripture.* Truth able to bear testing.

CHAPTER XXV.

THIRD SPEECH OF BILDAD THE SHUHITE.

His speech either a very abortive one, or it includes, as some think, the following chapter from the fifth verse to the end, the first four verses of that chapter probably belonging to the next one, but, by the mistake of transcribers, placed at the beginning of this.

The object of the speech to show Job's presumption in thinking himself righteous before God, and in wishing to debate his cause with Him as an innocent sufferer.

With this view he sets forth the character and attributes of God. Appears to charge Job, though only by implication, with rebellion against the Divine Majesty, and to wish to overwhelm him with a view of the Divine power and holiness.

The speech true in its statements, just in its sentiments, sublime in its poetry. The argument employed in it solid, and similar to that ultimately used by Jehovah Himself to silence Job. The speech wanting in appropriateness to the case in hand, and in sympathy with the party addressed.

I. **Bildad briefly descants on the attributes of God.**

1. *His sovereignty* (verse 2). "*Dominion* and fear are with him." God not named. With Him whom thou challengest. Him emphatic. With Him and no other. God "the great and only Potentate." The Supreme Ruler in heaven, earth, and hell. Therefore not to be resisted with impunity. As the supreme universal Ruler, God must be righteous in all His works. Therefore wicked, as well as ruinous, to oppose Him. God's attribute of sovereignty frequently insisted on in the Scriptures. Examples: Ps. ciii. 19; Is. xlv. 9; Dan. iv. 25, 34, 35. Fitted—(1) To silence murmurings under affliction and trial.—(2) To pacify and rest the soul under dark dispensations and mysterious providences. "Shall not the judge of all the earth do right?"—(3) To comfort the heart depressed by a view of abounding sin and misery, and of the apparent triumph of iniquity in the world. God, as Sovereign Ruler, able to make the wrath of man to praise Him, and to restrain the remainder of that wrath. Suffering only the discipline

employed, or the punishment inflicted, by the Supreme Governor. Hell his prison-house for rebellious and impenitent subjects. His sovereignty consistent with the permission of rebellion and evil in His dominions. Will one day bring all things into full subjection.

2. *Terrible majesty.* "Dominion and fear are with him." "With God is terrible majesty" (ch. xxxvii. 22). God's majesty fitted to awaken fear. All the earth to stand in awe of Him. "Who shall not fear Thee?" —the song in heaven (Rev. xv. 4). "God greatly to be feared even in the assembly of his saints" (Ps. lxxxix. 7). Seraphim cover their faces with their wings before Him (Is. vi. 2). The posts of the temple-doors and the granite mass of Sinai shook at His presence (Is. vi. 4; Ps. lxviii. 8). John, in Patmos, from fear fell at His feet as dead (Rev. i. 17). Sin especially makes men afraid of God. "Depart from me, for I am a sinful man, O Lord" (Luke v. 8).—As a consequence of God's sovereignty and Divine majesty, He preserves harmony among the highest classes of His creatures. "He maketh peace in His high places."—(1) Among the *angels*, His higher intelligent creatures (Ps. ciii. 20). God's will done perfectly in heaven. No rebellious thought, word, or action found there. All loving, reverential submission to, and acquiescence in, the Divine will. Rebellion once permitted to enter, but immediately subdued and expelled for ever. Heaven a place of peace and harmony, order and tranquillity, safety and felicity. No hostile attempts suffered to be made upon its inhabitants from without; no disturbance or disquiet to arise within.—(2) Among the *heavenly bodies.* These preserved by the Supreme Ruler in their respective orbits. No collision or injurious disturbance permitted from each other. "Music of the spheres," an idea as true as it is beautiful.—Inferences: (1) *If peace prevails in His high places, it should also do so in His lower ones*—the earth and its inhabitants. Monstrous for man to be in rebellion against His Creator.—(2) *If God makes peace in His high places, He will also make it in His lower ones.* God's will to be done on earth as it is in heaven. To make

peace on earth, the object of His Son's mission into the world. "On earth peace" (Luke ii. 14).—(3) *God the great peacemaker.* His nature peace. True peace the peace of God. All true peace from Him. The God of peace. The author not of confusion, but of peace, order, and concord (1 Cor. xiv. 33).—(4) *No rebellion which God is not able to quell.* The continuance of rebellion on earth not the result of God's weakness or indifference, but of His patience, compassion, and wisdom. The long-suffering of God is salvation. Not willing that any should perish, but that all should come to repentance (2 Pet. iii. 9, 15). He who makes peace in His places, is *able* to make it also in His lower ones.—(5) *God's rule an efficient one.* He not only wishes, but *makes* peace. Our great comfort. Man's efforts to make peace in the world, in a country, in a family, in himself, ineffectual. God able to subdue all things to Himself, and so to make peace. He maketh wars to cease unto the ends of the earth (Ps. xlvi. 9). Shall speak peace to the heathen (Zech. ix. 10). Commands peace to raging winds and threatening waves. Speaks peace to the troubled soul: "Be of good comfort; thy sins are forgiven thee: go in peace."

3. *His power and greatness* (ver. 3). "Is there any number of his armies?" These armies are—(1) *Angels* (Ps. ciii. 21). These innumerable (Ps. lxviii. 17; Rev. v. 11; Dan. vii. 10). Angels of light doubtless much more numerous than those of darkness. Yet of these a legion, or some thousands, found in one single person (Mark v. 9, 13). Milton rightly sings—

"Millions of spiritual creatures walk the earth Unseen, both when we wake and when we sleep."

The inhabitants of this earth probably only as a drop in the ocean compared with the "innumerable company of angels."—(2) *Heavenly bodies* (Is. xl. 26). These to us literally innumerable. Vastly more numerous than could be dreamt of by Bildad at that time. Only a very few of these visible to the naked eye. An immense multitude of dense clusters of stars apparently scattered throughout all space. These clusters like so many vast armies. The whole aggregate of these starry worlds a mighty host drawn up in endless battalions, probably only visible at once to the eye of the Almighty. Our Galaxy, or Milky Way, one of those immense clusters of stars or suns, with nearly thirty times as many towards the centre as near the extremities,—being rather a succession of irregular masses, more or less connected by isthmuses or bridges of orbs,

stretching from the one to the other, in any one of which the number of stars is past reckoning. Yet this immense cluster, or combination of clusters, with its stars scattered by millions like glittering dust, is only one of these numerous "armies" that compose the celestial host. Upwards of two thousand of these nebulous clusters discovered in the northern, and more than one thousand in the southern heavens, which, by powerful telescopes, have been resolved into innumerable stars.—(3) *All creatures employed in serving God and ministering to His will.* So locusts, &c., spoken of as Jehovah's "great army" (Joel ii. 25). The army of the Medes and Persians His weapons against Babylon (Is. xiii. 5; Jer. l. 14). "Fire and hail, snow and vapour, stormy wind fulfilling his word," included among his armies (Ps. cxlviii. 8; Job xxxviii. 22, 23). All nature His servants when "the Lord of hosts mustereth his host of the battle" (Is. xiii. 4).

"What is creation less
Than a capacious reservoir of means
Formed for His use, and ready at His will?"

4. *His goodness and beneficence.* "On whom doth not his light arise." His light is: (1) Literally and physically the light of *the sun in the heavens.* "His going forth is from the end of the earth, and his circuit unto the ends of it: nothing hid from the heat thereof" (Ps. xix. 6). "He maketh his sun to shine on the evil and on the good." All lands, classes, characters, individuals, partakers of the precious benefit. Its preciousness only fully realized by those who have long felt its want—surrounded by "clouds instead, and ever-during dark."— (2) Figuratively, *His favour and providential goodness.* This universal. "The Lord is good to all, and His tender mercies are over all His works." "He is kind unto the unthankful and to the evil" (Luke vi. 35). "The Lord loveth the stranger in giving him food and raiment" (Deut. x. 18). He sendeth rain both on the just and on the unjust. "Giveth rain from heaven, and fruitful seasons, filling our hearts with food and gladness" (Acts xvi. 17). God the Father of lights, from whom cometh down every good gift and every perfect gift (James i. 17).—(3). "The light of *truth and saving knowledge*" (2 Cor. iv. 16). That light designed for all men. Christ the Light and the Saviour of the world. The true Light which lighteth every man that cometh into the world (John i. 9). A light to lighten the Gentiles. His birth glad tidings of great joy, which should be to all people. His commission to His disciples, Go ye unto all the world, and preach the Gospel to every crea-

ture. In Paul's time that Gospel had already come into all the known world (Col. i. 6). Christ lifted up to draw all men unto Him. The duty of the Church everywhere to hold forth this light (Phil. ii. 15, 16). Though the light may arise on all, men may wilfully shut it out, or not care to come forth and enjoy it. Unbelief closes the shutters against the light of life. Men may love darkness rather than light, their deeds being evil. No argument against the unversality of light that some men are blind, or shut up in prison, or refuse to enjoy its beams. The condemnation of many that light is come into the world (John iii. 19).

5. *His purity and holiness.*—Verse 5. "Behold, even to the moon, and it shineth not; yea, the stars are not pure in his sight." The moon and stars probably visible at the time, the dialogue being held in the soft moonlight of a tranquil evening in Arabia. Moon and stars apparently the fairest and purest objects in the visible creation. Yet even these impure in the view of and in comparison with God. The moon loses its brightness when seen beside Him, as the stars pale before the rising sun. *All, even the purest creatures, impure in comparison with God.* Seraphim cover their faces and their feet with their wings while standing before Him. Their adoring exclamation one to another : "Holy, holy, holy, is the Lord of Hosts" (Is. vi. 3). The song of glorified Saints : " Who shall not fear Thee, O Lord? for thou only are holy" (Rev. xv. 4). Isaiah, in the view of Jehovah's glory in the temple, exclaims : "Woe is me ! for I am undone ; for I am a man of unclean lips, and dwell among a people of unclean lips" (Is. vi. 5). Imperfection and variableness inherent in every creature. Spots on the sun and dark shadows on the surface of the moon. Absolute purity and perfection alone in God. The slightest shade of evil or imperfection infinitely removed from His spotlessly holy nature. All sin His perfect and unchangeable abhorrence. The lustre of stars and the holiness of angels only a faint reflection from His own.

II. Bildad's Inference (verse 4—6).

1. *From God's perfections in themselves.* Verse 4.—"How then can man (*Hebrew,* 'weak, miserable man,'—*enosh*) be justified (*Heb.*, 'just' or righteous) with God ? Or How can he be clean that is born of a woman ?" If God be such, how can man be righteous "*with Him?*" (1) In comparison with Him; (2) In His sight; (3) In controversy with Him as a party ; (4) Before His tribunal as a judge.

Bildad's inference intended to have pecial reference to Job. Founded on man's

154

character as a creature, — poor, weak, miserable, liable to suffering, disease, and, death. The reference rather to his physical than to his moral character. The latter however bound up with the former. Both the result of the Fall in Eden. Bildad infers man's impurity from his physical infirmity as a creature. Man in his best estate necessarily impure in comparison with God. His moral impurity, however, not from his being a *creature*, but a *fallen creature.* "God made man upright." Adam created in God's image and after God's likeness. As he left His Creator's hands, pronounced by Himself "very good." A suffering and a sinful state the twin effect of the first disobedience. "By one man sin entered the world, and death by sin." "By one man's disobedience many were made sinners" (Rom. v. 12, 19). Only by the grace of God and the obedience of a second Adam can man now be righteous. The righteousness in which a man can now stand that of one who is both God and man,—one "born of a woman" like other men, and yet, unlike other men, begotten by the Father, and conceived in a virgin's womb by the power of the Holy Ghost. *The man Christ Jesus the specimen of a righteous man without sin.* All believers viewed as righteous in Him. Made also partakers of His holy nature and character. The Gospel of the Grace of God gives the only answer to Bildad's question, How can man be just with God? The answer, By union with the God-man Christ Jesus, effected through faith in him by the operation of the Holy Ghost. A man is now righteous with God, *legally,* through the imputation of Christ's righteousness *to* him ; pure in God's sight, *morally,* through the regenerating power of the Holy Ghost *in* him. Viewed in Christ, God sees "no iniquity in Jacob." Washed by faith in the blood of the Lamb we are made "whiter than the snow." "Thou art all fair, my love; there is no spot in thee (Cant. iv. 7). Man, as "born of a woman," is unclean; as born again of God, is or shall be pure as God is pure (1 John iii. 2, 3).

2. *From the impurity in God's sight belonging to the purest creatures.* Verse 6—"How much less [pure in his sight is] man that is a worm (or maggot, the product of putridity), and the son of man who is a [crawling] worm (kindred terms used to denote the lowest state of degradation as well as weakness and defilement)." If the purest creatures are not clean in God's sight, how then can man be so? Man made lower than the angels (Ps. viii. 5). A worm—(1) In his place as a creature. (2) In his character as a sinner.

Bildad's second question also answered by the Gospel. *Man, though a worm, can be clean in God's sight.* Christ, the Holy One of God, a worm, as a partaker of our weak humanity. Believers made one with Him are partakers of His pure and holy nature. The Son of God became a worm with man, to make worms sons of God with Himself. Every believer now possessed of a higher and holier nature than that of angels—the nature of the Son of God (Gal. ii. 20; Eph. v. 30; 2 Pet. i. 4). The word of Christ, received by faith, the instrument in producing this purity (John xv. 3; xvii. 17; Eph. v. 26; 1 Pet. i. 22).

CHAPTER XXVI.

JOB'S REPLY TO BILDAD.

Job, more alive to Bildad's want of sympathy than to the excellence of his sentiments in regard to the Divine perfections, speaks somewhat petulantly,—certainly with irony and sarcasm. Job not yet humbled. He hears of God "by the hearing of the ear," but as yet his eye does not see him (ch. xlii. 5). Mere verbal representations, even of the truth, not sufficient to humble and pacify the soul. God must reveal Himself.

Uncertain whether the larger portion of this chapter, *viz.*, from verse 5 to the end, does not properly belong to the preceding one as part of Bildad's speech. Viewed as belonging to Job, its object would be to show that Job could as easily, and more comprehensively, descant on the Divine perfections as Bildad himself. The sentiments contained in the portion not affected by the question as to the speaker.

I. Job's ironical and indignant reflection on Bildad's speech (verses 2—4).

1. *Its want of sympathy and succour.* Verse 2—"How hast thou helped him that is without power! How savest thou the arm that hath no strength!" Means himself,—either seriously, as really without power and strength; or ironically, being so in the esteem of Bildad and his friends. Bildad's speech contained nothing calculated to support Job in his deep prostration. Its object rather to convict him of pride and self-righteousness, and to overwhelm him with a view of the Divine perfections. Job needed comfort and support, and found none. So with his great antitype (Matt. xxvi. 40). Observe— (1) *Our duty to succour by our words those who are in trouble and distress, and to support those who are weak and ready to fall.* Words sometimes more effectual than deeds in helping those who are "without strength." Job's own practice in his better days (ch. iv. 3, 4). All the more painfully sensible of the want of it in his friends. (2) *Ministers and preachers to be careful in their ministrations and addresses to come up to their profession.* One great part of a minister's duty to support the weak, comfort the feeble-minded, and strengthen the tempted (Acts xx. 35; 1

Thess. ii. 7; v. 14; Heb. xii. 12). Peter required, when converted after his fall, to strengthen his brethren (Luke xxii. 32). The duty best discharged by those who have realized their own weakness and need of support. According to Luther, temptation one of the three things that make a preacher. Christ Himself able to succour them that are tempted, having been tempted Himself.

2. *Its want of suitable counsel.* Verse 3 —"How hath thou counselled him that hath no wisdom!" Still refers to himself. Addressed by Bildad as if ignorant of the Divine perfections. Bildad's speech as void of counsel as of sympathy. Counsel never more needed than when in spiritual darkness and affliction. One of the blessings of true friendship. "Ointment and perfume rejoice the heart; so doth the sweetness of a man's friend by hearty counsel" (Prov. xxvii. 9). One of the offices of Jesus, as the Saviour of men and Head of His Church, to give counsel. Therefore possessed of "the spirit of counsel and might" (Isa. xi. 2). One of His titles, "The Counsellor" (Isa. ix. 6). One of the believer's privileges to enjoy such counsel (Ps. xvi. 7). Observe—(1) *The part of ministers, preachers, and Christians in general, to counsel erring, perplexed, and troubled souls.* (i.) Men *out of Christ* constantly in need of right and loving counsel. Christ counsels such to buy of Him gold tried in the fire, &c. (Rev. iii. 17, 18). Preachers and believers to do the same. (ii.) *Anxious souls* in need of sound counsel. The question to be wisely answered: "Sirs, what must I do to be saved? Men and brethren, what shall we do?" (iii.) *Believers themselves* often in circumstances requiring judicious spiritual counsel.—(2) Ministers and others to seek to be well qualified to give true spiritual counsel both to perplexed believers and to anxious inquirers. The tongue of the spiritually-learned needed "to speak a word in season to him that is weary" (Isa. l. 4).

3. *Its defectiveness in regard to the matter in hand.* "How hast thou plentifully declared the thing as it is" ("the real truth," or "sound wisdom," as ch. xi. 6; Prov. viii. 14). Bildad had declared the truth, but not

155

the whole truth, nor yet, in Job's view at least, the seasonable truth. Job did not require to be instructed by Bildad about the Divine perfections. It was one thing for these to be set forth by Bildad, and another for them to be exhibited by God Himself, as was afterwards done. Observe — (1) Not only is *truth* to be spoken in addressing men on Divine things, but the *whole* truth, and especially *seasonable* truth. (2) Words and high-sounding descriptions, however true, not suited to carry conviction to the hearts of hearers. General declamations about the Divine perfections not such as to meet the case either of the careless or the concerned. (3) *Preachers to be careful to give just representations of Divine things, and such as are adapted to meet the case of the hearers.* The pulpit not the place to indulge one's taste for elegant composition, learned research, metaphysical subtleties, or poetic description. Pompous common-places and flights of rhetoric only famish the hearers, and render the preacher himself ridiculous. A Nero fiddled while Rome was burning. Paul an example to preachers: would rather speak five words in the Church that he might teach others also, "than ten thousand words in an unknown tongue" (1 Cor. xiv. 19).

4. *Its conceit.* Verse 4.—" To whom hast thou uttered words? (verses or set phrases)." Bildad's speech ridiculed by Job as rather mere words or set phrases; light-sounding diction, rather than plain homely truth suited to the occasion. Probably more of the traditional poetry of the country, which he pompously repeats to a man crushed under a weight of sorrow. Had treated Job as an ignorant and godless man. Had set himself forth as his teacher in regard to the Divine character and works. Had spoken as immensely Job's superior both in piety and knowledge. *Conceit one of the most repulsive and contemptible things in a preacher.* Modesty in regard to himself, and due respect for his hearers, to be exhibited by every teacher of Divine truth. Paul's example: " I speak as unto wise men ; judge ye what I say." " I am persuaded of you, my brethren, that ye are filled with all knowledge, able also to admonish one another; nevertheless I have written to you in some sort, as putting you in mind " (1 Cor. x. 15; Rom. xv. 14, 15). Peter's " I put you in remembrance of these things, though ye know them, and be established in the present truth. I stir up your pure minds by way of remembrance " (2 Pet. i. 12, ii. 1).

5. *Its want of originality and divine unction.* " Whose spirit (breath, or inspiration) came from thee.' Job ridicules Bildad's speech as either an echo of those of his brothers, or a string of trite maxims of

the sages; at the most, the effusion of his own spirit, not that of the spirit of God. Says nothing against the sentiments themselves. However uttered by Bildad, they are recorded by the Spirit of God for our instruction. Observe — (1) Preachers to beware of giving other men's productions as their own. If other men's sermons are read or repeated, it should be acknowledged. (2) Preachers not to be mere imitators or retailers of other men's sentiments. (3) A preacher to speak from his own heart, if he would reach the hearts of his hearers. (4) Preachers to give to their hearers not merely the effusion of their own spirit, but what they have received from the Spirit of God. Five plain words uttered from the heart by the inspiration of the Holy Spirit worth more than five thousand of the most polished sentences, whether borrowed from others or the product of our own talent and study. The preacher who would win souls or edify believers, while not neglecting study and preparation, to be mainly concerned to receive his messages from God in answer to prayer, and to have the Spirit of God in the delivery of them. Two things to be sought by every preacher—a Divine unction *in* his discourses, and a Divine energy *with* them.

Stray hints for preachers :—

He who desires, according to Paul, to be apt to teach, must first himself be taught of God.—*Erasmus.*

Those are the best preachers to the common people who teach with the simplicity of a child.—*Luther.*

Let your discourses be neither absolutely without ornament, nor indecently clothed with it.—*Augustine.*

It requires all our learning to make things plain.—*Archbishop Usher.*

Preachers are to feed the people, not with gay tulips and useless daffodils, but with the bread of life, and medicinal plants springing from the margin of the fountain of salvation.—*Jeremy Taylor.*

Very fine, sir—very fine ; but people can't live upon flowers.—*Robert Hall.*

I had rather be fully understood by ten, than be admired by ten thousand.—*Dr. John Edwards.*

Aim at pricking the heart, not at stroking the skin.—*Jerome.*

Here lies the secret [of the actor's greater power in moving an audience than the preacher's]: you deliver your truths as if they were fictions ; we deliver our fictions as if they were truths.—*Garrick.*

The prayer of an old writer: "Lord, let me never be guilty, by painting the windows, of hindering the light of thy glorious Gospel from shining powerfully into men's hearts."

Leigh Richmond's dying message to his son : "Tell him, his father learnt his most valuable lessons for the ministry, and his most useful experience, in the poor man's cottage."

"I'll preach as though I ne'er shall preach again,
And as a dying man to dying men."
Richard Baxter.

II. Descants more largely on the Divine perfections and works both in creation and providence (verse 5—13).

1. *His sovereignty over the dead and the invisible world.* Verse 5—"Dead things are formed from under the waters, and the inhabitants thereof" (or, 'the dead groan from beneath the waters, and the inhabitants thereof'). Bildad had represented God as exercising sovereign dominion in his high places (verse xxv. 2). Here Job (if not Bildad himself) apparently shows that sovereignty extending to the lower world or place of the dead. The "dead," or shades of the departed, perhaps more especially the wicked dead, and in particular the giants or mighty ones before the flood (Gen. vi. 4). These represented as groaning or trembling from beneath, under the mighty hand of God upon them. The "waters" probably the "deep" or abyss (Luke viii. 31; Rom. x. 7), supposed by Jewish rabbis to be lower than the earth; the place of the dead (Rom. x. 7), and the prepared abode of the fallen angels from which they recoil with horror (Luke viii. 31). Perhaps the "fountains of the great deep," broken up at the time of the Deluge (Gen. viii. 11), and the "water under the earth" (Exod. xx. 4). Possibly what shall afterwards constitute the "lake that burneth with fire and brimstone" (Rev. xx. 10, 14, 15; xxi. 8).

The language of the text according to the Old Testament view of the state of the dead in general. According to it the spirits of the departed still in conscious existence. That existence, however, one rather of pain and privation than of enjoyment. The place of the disembodied spirits represented as one of darkness (chap. x. 21, 22); Ps. lxxxviii. 12), and of pain (ch. xiv. 22). Hence the great shrinking from death on the part of Old Testament saints (Ps. xxx. 8, 9; lxxxviii. 9—12; Isa. xxxviii. 10—12, 17, 18). Yet Enoch and Elijah both taken to be with God. Abraham and Moses in a state of blessedness (Luke ix. 30, 31; xvi. 23). Lazarus comforted in the world of spirits, while Dives was tormented (Luke xvi. 25). The doctrine of the state of the dead only gradually developed.

Its full exhibition reserved for the advent of the Messiah (2 Tim. i. 10). Possibly a change made in the state of departed saints after his resurrection (Matt. xxvii. 52, 53). Perhaps, in more senses than one, Christ, after overcoming "the sharpness of death, opened the kingdom of heaven to all believers."—(1) A separate state of conscious existence after death not only the doctrine of the Bible, but the general sense of mankind. Consistent with reason. Mind not necessarily dependent on matter or any material organization. (2) The state of the departed ungodly one of pain and trembling—"wailing and gnashing of teeth." The consciousness of God's power exercised in the invisible world only an increase to their suffering.

2. *God's perfect cognizance of the invisible world.* (Verse 6)—"Hell is naked before him, and destruction hath no covering." "Hell" (*Hebrew,* "Sheol;" *Greek,* "Hades") used in Scripture to denote—(1) The grave, or receptacle for the dead body. (2) The invisible world, or place of departed spirits in general, without respect to character or experience. The latter supposed by the Jews to be a vast cavern far in the interior of the earth. Probably the prison mentioned by Peter as enclosing the spirits of the disobedient Antediluvians (1 Peter iii. 19, 20). May include both prison and paradise. The place into which the disembodied spirit of the Saviour went, in order to satisfy the law of death as other men. Yet his spirit on the same day in Paradise (Luke xxiii. 43). The clause in the so-called Apostles' Creed, "he descended into hell," not found in the early Roman or Oriental creeds. First used as a part of the Creed by the Church of Aquileia, not quite 400 years after Christ. See *Pearson* on the Creed, Art. v. "Destruction" (*Hebrew,* "Abaddon," the name given to the Angel of the Bottomless Pit (Rev. ix. 11), like "hell," the place of the dead or of departed spirits, its inhabitants being "lost" to human view; perhaps more especially the place of lost men and angels. "Hell" and "destruction," as synonymous terms denoting the invisible world or place of the dead, found together also in Prov. xv. 11; xxvii. 20; perhaps another hint as to the period of the composition of the book. "Hell" and "death" mentioned together in Rev. i. 18; xx. 13, 14. Their keys in the hand of Jesus as Lord of the invisible world (Rev. i. 18.)—(1) Believers need have no fear in entering the invisible world. Christ their Saviour and Elder Brother has been there before them, and now holds the keys. (2) The grave with its countless dust, as well as the invisible world with its innumerable inhabitants, all open to the view of the

157

Almighty. The dust of His saints precious in his sight and cannot be lost (Ps. cxvi. 15). (3) The most secret depths of earth and sea, with their countless objects and inhabitants, open to the same omniscient eye. Not an animalcule or infusiorium, thousands of which are contained in a single drop of water, but is the object of His inspection and care. (4) "Hell and destruction are before the Lord; how much more the hearts of the children of men." There is no darkness or shadow of death where the workers of iniquity may hide themselves" (Prov. xv. 11; Job xxxiv. 22).

3. *His power and wisdom in the works of Creation and Providence* (verses 7—13). (1) *In giving the earth and heavenly bodies their present situation, and suspending them in empty space.* Verse 7—"He stretcheth (or stretched) out [as a canopy] the north (or northern celestial hemisphere, the only part visible to Job and his friends, and here put for the heavens in general) over the empty place, and hangeth (or hung) the earth upon nothing." The former clause according to *appearance*, and the old opinion that the heavens formed an immense arch, or vault, stretching over the earth. The latter philosophically true, and a remarkable anticipation of the Newtonian theory of gravitation. The earth and planets suspended in empty space, and preserved in their orbit by the operation of two opposite forces, one (the *centripetal*) which attracts them to the sun, or centre of the system, the other (the *centrifugal*) which, in consequence of the rotatory motion given them, keeps them moving on in a circle or ellipse round the sun, instead of being drawn absolutely to it. The spherical form of the earth thus also indicated. "Earth self-balanced on her centre hung." (2) *In forming the clouds and preserving the watery particles collected in them.* Verse 8—"He bindeth up the waters (or watery vapours) in his thick clouds, and the cloud is not rent under them." Probably an allusion to the second day's work of creation —the formation of the firmament, or atmosphere, for the separation of the waters beneath from those above, and collecting the latter in clouds, and preserving them in their place. An obvious manifestation of Divine wisdom, power, and goodness. The provision made for the earth's fertility. Reservoirs of water kept far above the earth in clouds by the operation of natural laws. These clouds so constituted that, notwithstanding the quantity of water contained in them, they do not burst and discharge their contents in one vast destructive deluge. Their contents made on the contrary to fall in such gentle and temporary showers as to meet the earth's requirements. Such discharge made to result

from a change in the temperature, or the influence of electricity. The clouds on one special occasion "rent under" their contents, when the "windows of heaven were opened" to deluge a disobedient world. A partial "rending" in extraordinarily heavy and deluging rains. (3) *In so collecting dense clouds as to darken the sky with them.* Verse 9—"He holdeth back the face of his throne, and spreadeth his cloud upon it." The sky, or heaven, viewed as God's throne (Matt. v. 34; Isa. lxvi. 1). Concealed by Him from time to time by a curtain of dark clouds. These clouds of His own formation, from the watery particles exhaled by the sun's heat from the earth and sea, and directed by currents of air into one locality. Clouds serve various and important purposes :—(i.) In irrigating the ground. (ii.) In moderating the heat. (iii.) In beautifying the sky. The beauty of the sky, especially at sunset, thus made to vie with that of the earth. Observe — *God himself invisible, though His agency is everywhere seen and felt.* His throne still there, though He spread a cloud over it. God to be trusted and to be believed in when we cannot see Him. (4) *In appointing the alternation of light and darkness, and the vicissitude of day and night.* Verse 10—"He hath compassed the waters with bounds, until the day and night come to an end" (or, "He hath drawn a circular boundary upon the waters with exact proportion of light and darkness ;" or, "even to the limit of light with darkness," *i. e.,* where the light ceases and darkness begins ;— *Margin,* "until the end of light with darkness"). Apparent allusion to the first day's work at the creation—the dividing the light from the darkness, and appointing the alternation of day and night (Gen. i. 3—5). The "bound" here mentioned probably the horizon. The earth popularly supposed to be a plane bounded by the "waters" of the ocean on which the vault of heaven appears to rest and to form a circular boundary,— the place where light ends, and darkness commences. The sun supposed to move from the eastern to the western boundary, where it disappears till the following morning. The description in the text, like others in the Bible, given popularly, according to appearance. The earth's diurnal rotation on its axis not then generally known. No object of the Bible to teach the facts that progressive science was in due time to discover. The language of the Bible popular, not scientific or philosophical. The horizon an apparent boundary between light and darkness. That boundary a part of God's work in creation and providence. Science only informs us *how.*

The alternation of light and darkness, day

and night, one of the most conspicuous and beneficial arrangements of the Divine Creator. Among its benefits are—(i.) An agreeable variety instead of the uniform sameness even of constant day. "The sweet approach of even and morn," the joyous thrill of sunrise, and the gorgeous beauty of sunset, due to this alternation. (ii.) Suitable seasons afforded for the varied requirements of men and other animals. Night and darkness suitable to man for rest, as daytime and light are for labour. The darkness of night necessary for predaceous animals obtaining their food. (iii.) Evening valuable as tranquillizing the mind, inviting to sober meditation and reflection, and affording opportunity for domestic and social enjoyment. Eventide the season chosen by Isaac for meditation in the fields (Gen. xxiv. 63).

"Eve following eve,
Dear tranquil time, when the sweet sense of home
Is sweetest! Moments for their own sake hail'd!"

(iv.) The earth kept cool and moistened with dew through the same wise and beneficent provision. (v.) Plants and animals mutually benefited by the interchange of light and darkness. "In the various processes of combustion, and by the respiration of animals, a large amount of the oxygen of the atmosphere, or its vital part, is withdrawn, and, united with carbon, is returned as carbonic acid—an ingredient deleterious to animal life. But this deteriorating process is counteracted, at least to a certain extent, by the vegetable tribes. The same luminous influence which serves to generate chromule (the green matter in plants), likewise aids the plant in decomposing the carbonic acid which has been absorbed; appropriating the carbon to the construction of the ligneous tissue, and returning the pure oxygen to the atmosphere, it fits it again for the purposes of respiration. Animals may therefore be viewed as preparing food for plants by the air which they vitiate; while plants, on the other hand, by their action under the influence of light, appropriate to themselves nourishment, and restore the air to its normal state."—*Professor Fleming's Temperature of the Seasons.* (6) The starry sky, with its entrancing beauty and elevating lessons, thus alone made visible. To the alternation of light and darkness—day and night—we owe the poet's magnificent description of Evening :—

"Now came still evening on, and twilight gray
Had in her sober livery all things clad.
Silence was pleased. Now glow'd the firmament
With living sapphires: Hesperus, that led

The starry host, rode brightest, 'till the moon,
Rising in clouded majesty, at length
Apparent queen, unveil'd her peerless light,
And o'er the dark her silver mantle threw."

God to be adored as the author of this beneficent interchange of light and darkness. "Thou makest the outgoings of the morning and the evening to rejoice." "The day is thine; the night also is thine: thou hast prepared the light and the sun." "Thou makest darkness, and it is night, wherein all the beasts of the forest do creep forth" (Ps. lxv. 8; lxxiv. 16; civ. 20).—(5) *In exciting storms and disturbances in the earth and air.* Verse 11—"The pillars of heaven tremble, and are astonished at his reproof." The visible heavens viewed as a magnificent edifice supported on columns. These imaginary pillars personified, and poetically represented as in some tremendous commotion of the earth or elements standing aghast at the apparent reproof of their Creator. That reproof supposed to be directed either against themselves or mankind. So the sea said to be dried up at His rebuke (Ps. cvi. 9; Nahum i. 4). The raging wind and waves literally rebuked by the Saviour, and hushed into a calm (Matt. viii. 26). Storms and earthquakes among the most striking incidents in nature. Especially awful and sublime in hot climates and mountainous regions. Naturally strike the mind as indications or suggestions of Divine displeasure. Strictly due to the Divine will, and, though effected through the agency of natural laws, a part of His providential government. Serve various and important purposes—(i.) Morally: as—(*a*) Reminding us of the existence, attributes, and agency of a Divine Ruler and Judge. Few persons fail, during a tremendous thunderstorm, to think of a Supreme Being. (*b*) Tending to produce elevating and reverential thoughts of God. One of the sublimest descriptions of a thunderstorm, with its effects both physically and morally, found in Ps. xxix. 3—10. (*c*) Suggesting the instability of earthly things and the danger to which human life is exposed, with the importance of securing the favour of God and the assurance of a better world. (*d*) Tending to elevate the mind and strengthen the character by bringing it in contact with the sublime and terrible in Nature.—(ii.) Physically: as—(*a*) Purifying the atmosphere. (*b*) Tending to the greater irrigation of the earth. (*c*) Aiding in the processes of vegetation.—(6) *In His power over the ocean is exciting and stilling its waves.* Verse 12—"He divideth (or cleaveth) the sea with his power; and by his understanding he smiteth through the proud " (or "stilleth its pride"—*Hebrew*, "Rahab").

The sea, so uncontrollable by man, entirely subject to the will and power of God. Already literally divided, so as to form a pathway in the midst of its waters (Exod. xiv. 21, 22; Is. li. 10—15). Ordinarily divided and cleft by storms and tempests. By the same Divine power, its towering billows and yawning chasms made to disappear, and the storm changed into a calm (Ps. lxv. 7; cvii. 29). Done by Christ (Matt. viii. 26). Observe — *Power* more conspicuous in exciting the storm at sea; *understanding*, in quelling it. The latter frequently in answer to prayer (Ps. cvii. 28, 29; Matt. viii. 25, 26). Prayer in such circumstances the voice of nature (Jonah i. 5, 6).—(7) *In making the sky bright and serene by day and studding it with stars by night.* Verse 13—"By his spirit (or 'breath,' his power or command; or perhaps the Third Person in the Godhead, also engaged in creation, *Gen.* i. 2) he hath garnished the heavens (or, 'the heavens are brightness or beauty,' *i.e.* bright and beautiful); and his hand hath formed (possibly 'wounded,' or 'slain') the crooked (gliding or darting) serpent" (perhaps the Zodiac, with its twelve signs or constellations, anciently represented as a serpent with its tail in its mouth; or, more probably, a northern constellation, called Draco, or the Dragon, the description being taken from the living serpent). Apparent allusion to the fourth day's work in creation (Gen. i. 14—16). The bright clear heaven lighted up with sunshine, a beautiful object, especially as succeeding a storm or the darkness of night. Still more beautiful is the nocturnal sky, spangled with stars. Affords an impressive exhibition of Divine power (Is. xl. 26). The stars countless in number. In themselves, probably so many suns and centres of systems like our own. Those forming any of the constellations millions of miles apart from each other. A nebula or white fleecy speck in the belt of Orion, resolved by the telescope into a mass of stars at incalculable distances from us and from each other. Stars early grouped, for convenience, into imaginary figures of men, animals, &c.

Some terms and ideas in the preceding verse also brought together in Is. li. 9; xxvii. 1; Ps. lxxxix. 10. Rahab here rendered "proud," or "pride;" used also as a proper name for Egypt, while Pharaoh is symbolized by the dragon or leviathan—the crocodile of the Nile.—Operations in the natural world analogous to those in the social and moral. The natural world itself a mirror of the spiritual. The towering billows of the ocean a picture of the swelling pride of God's enemies, as exemplified in Egypt and her hosts at the time of the exodus (Ps. xv. 7). Monsters of the land

and sea symbolical of cruel and injurious men, as well as of Satan and his infernal legions. The power that quells the one employed in subduing the other. A reference in the text supposed by some to the exodus, and also to Gen. iii. 15.

III. Reflection on the greatness of the Almighty's works. Verse 14—"Lo, these are parts (outlines or extremities) of his ways; but how little a portion (or, 'what a mere whisper') is heard of him (or of what is 'in Him'—His being and perfections); but the thunder (or full manifestation) of his power who can understand?" The stupendous works and operations of His hands which are visible to us only a small part—the mere outline or extremities—of the whole. What we see and hear of in relation to God and His works, as compared with the fulness of His power, only a mere whisper in comparison with the mighty thunder. Observe—

1. *Much more to be known of God and His works than is possible for us to know in our present state.* Yet all His visible ordinary operations would be regarded as miracles, if not seen daily.

2. *A sound and deep theology grounded on this verse.* Man's knowledge confined to parts only of God's ways. The extremities or forthgoings of His administration on earth only visible. The springs, principles, and anterior steps above and out of man's sight.—*Dr. Chalmers.* The humbling acknowledgment of those who have penetrated farthest into the mysteries of nature. "The phenomena of matter and force lie within our intellectual range. . . . But behind and above, and around all, the real mystery of the universe remains unsolved."—*Professor Tyndall, Lecture to Working Men at the Dundee British Association Meeting,* Sept., 1867. "Alike in the external and the internal worlds, the man of science sees himself in the midst of perpetual changes, of which he can discover neither the beginning nor the end. In all directions his investigations eventually bring him face to face with an insoluble enigma; and he ever more clearly perceives it to be an insoluble enigma.—*Herbert Spencer's First Principles.* "All our science is but an investigation of the mode in which the Creator acts; its highest laws are but expressions of the mode in which he manifests His agency to us. And when the physiologist is inclined to dwell unduly upon his capacity for penetrating the secrets of nature, it may be salutary for him to reflect that, even should he succeed in placing his department of study on a level with those physical sciences in which the most complete knowledge of

causation (using that term in the sense of 'unconditional sequence') has been acquired, and in which the highest generalizations have been attained, he is still as far as ever from being able to comprehend that power which is the efficient cause alike of the simplest and most minute, and of the most complicated and most majestic, in the universe,"—*W. B. Carpenter, General and Comparative Physiology.*

3. *A glorious increase of knowledge awaiting the believer in another world.* There we shall know even as we are known (1 Cor. xiii. 12). From this ever-enlarging enlightenment the proud unbeliever, however scientific and philosophical now unhappily, cuts himself off. To him the future will be a world of darkness, not of light.

4. *Exertions of Divine power yet to be displayed even in connection with this earth far beyond what has been already witnessed.* What the Bible declares, observation confirms, sound reason assents to, and what every genuine Christian cordially believes, of a resurrection of the dead, is only an example of such power (Matt. xxii. 26; Eph. i. 19, 20). Resurrection a miracle; but even such a miracle only something of "the thunder of His power." Why thought incredible with a Being who is Almighty (Acts xxvi. 8)?

5. *The lower exertions of God's power in the universe beyond man's comprehension; how much the higher?* In the presence of Divine declarations, the part of sound *philosophy*, as well of true *piety*, is to *believe* and *adore.*

CHAPTER XXVII.

JOB'S REPLY TO THE FRIENDS IN GENERAL.

Job now alone in the field. Zophar, who should have followed Bildad, and to whom Job had given opportunity to speak, has apparently nothing to say. Job, therefore, after a pause, resumes his discourse, but in a different tone. Speaks more calmly, and even more solemnly. Declares, even with an appeal to the Almighty, that, notwithstanding all he still suffers at the hand of God, and however God seems to treat him as a guilty person, he is resolved, as a sincere and upright man, to maintain the integrity of his past life, and not, for the sake of bettering his condition, as his friends would persuade him, admit hypocritically the justice of their reasoning and of their charges against him. Declares His utter abhorrence of all ungodliness, oppression, and hypocrisy, and maintains, along with the friends, that however wickedness may appear for a time to prosper, it is certain, sooner or later, to end in misery and ruin.

Job represented (verse 1) as again "taking up his parable," or "proverb"—a weighty, sententious discourse or saying, such as uttered by sages and prophets (Numb. xxiii. 7; xxiv. 3—15; Ps. xlix. 4; lxxviii. 2; Prov. i. 16; xxvi. 7). In the New Testament used in the sense of extended similitude. The latter part of the chapter, from verse 11 to the end, from its connection and position, one of the most perplexing portions of the book.

I. **Job's resolution to maintain his innocence.** Verse 26.—"As God liveth, who hath taken away my judgment (has for some mysterious purpose, dealt with me contrary to the justice of my cause and the

uprightness of my character, and who still refrains from declaring my innocence, or affording me an opportunity of pleading my cause before Him), and the Almighty who hath vexed (or 'embittered') my soul (with such severe afflictions); all the while my breath is in me, and the Spirit of God is in my nostrils (so long as I have life continued to me; apparent allusion to Gen. ii. 7), my lips shall not speak wickedness nor my tongue utter deceit (in falsely and contrary to my conscience admitting myself to have been a secret and guilty transgressor). God forbid that I should justify you (in your erroneous reasoning, and your consequent charges against me, by acknowledging myself a wicked man); my heart shall not reproach me, so long as I live" (or, "doth not and shall not reproach me for any of my days," as having at any time lived in the practice of secret ungodliness, or for now denying the truth concerning myself).

Job now speaks as victor in the controversy. More solemnly than ever declares his purpose to maintain his innocence, notwithstanding his present treatment. Gives his asseveration the form of an oath—"As God liveth." Here, therefore, the controversy proper between him and his three friends takes end. *Lawful in certain circumstances to appeal to God for the truth of what we affirm, and to confirm a holy righteous resolution by a solemn oath.* So Luther, at the Diet of Worms: "Here I stand; I can do nothing else; so God help me." "An oath for confirmation is an end of all strife."

Job an illustrious example of a man suffering innocently, yet resolutely refusing to utter a single word contrary to his conscience. Thus confirms the testimony given of him by God Himself. Satan thus defeated and shown to be a lying slanderer in asserting that, if only sufficiently afflicted, Job would renounce his religion—would "curse God to his face." Job thus eminently belonging to "the noble army of martyrs." Would rather still underlie the false accusations of his friends, and suffer as an apparently wicked man the severities of his present distressing condition, than speak or act contrary to the dictates of his conscience, or deny what he knew to be true. Observe—

1. A truly good man will be driven by no sufferings, threatened or endured, absolutely to renounce his religion. Through the weakness of the flesh, extreme torture may force out a recantation, which by the strength of grace will speedily be withdrawn. Cranmer an example—holding over the flames the hand that signed the recantation, and exclaiming: "That unworthy hand!" "Torture me if you will; but whatever the weakness of my nature may force me in my suffering to confess contrary to the truth of Christ, I will recall as soon as the torture is withdrawn."—*An Early Female Martyr to her Persecutors.* The spirit of the martyrs expressed in the language of the three godly youths in Babylon (Dan. iii. 16—18).

2. The part of true piety to wait God's own time for declaring our innocence, and to take up hasty measures for clearing our character or avoiding suffering and reproach. "Fret not thyself in any wise to do evil. Commit thy way to the Lord; trust also in him, and he shall bring it to pass; and he shall bring forth thy righteousness as the light, and thy judgment as the noon-day" (Ps. xxxvii. 5—8).

3. Lawful in certain circumstances strongly to declare the sincerity of our character and the integrity of our life. So Paul before the Sanhedrim: "Men and brethren, I have lived in all good conscience before God until this day" (Acts xxiii. 1). Our own uprightness to be maintained on such occasions, as due—(1) To God. (2) To our neighbour. (3) To ourselves. Our own righteousness of life valuable—(1) As a fruit of Divine grace and the work of God's Spirit in our hearts. (2) As the evidence of our reconciliation and sonship to God. (3) As an example to our fellow-men. Worthless as the ground of our justification before God. A twofold righteousness belonging to the believer—an imputed, and an inherent or personal one. The latter to be maintained for our justification before men; the former for our justification before God; *viz.,* the righteousness of the man Christ Jesus, our Head and Representative, "the Lord our righteousness" (Is. xlv. 24,

25; Jer. xxiii. 6; Acts xiii. 39; Rom. iii. 20—24). Imputed righteousness to be held fast by a steadfast faith; personal righteousness by holy resolution, dependence on Divine grace, and, if need be, a fearless declaration.

4. Believers so to live that their hearts may not condemn them. "If our hearts condemn us not, then have we confidence toward God" (1 John iii. 21).

5. Job in his suffering from false charges, and in the maintenance of his integrity under them, a type of the Messiah (Isa liii. 8; Acts viii. 33; Isa. l. 5—9).

II. **Declares his abhorrence of ungodliness, and his assurance of being one day justified.** Verse 7.—"Let mine enemy be as the wicked (or 'mine enemy shall be &c.'), and he that riseth up against me as the unrighteous." May be viewed either as in the form of a wish or of a declaration. As the former—strongly expresses his abhorrence of ungodliness. A godless character the worst thing he could wish to his enemy. Thus a form of the assertion of his integrity, without implying any evil wish against his enemies. As the latter—expresses the conviction that the day would come when those who now opposed him would appear to be the guilty party. This conviction ultimately realized, ch. xlii. 7, 8. Observe—

1. Abhorrence of ungodliness to be deeply cherished, and on all due occasions to be boldly declared.

2. Sin to be regarded and avoided as the greatest evil, both to ourselves and others.

3. Certain that God's faithful servants will not always underlie false charges (Isa. lxvi. 5; Rev. iii. 9). A day at hand when "all shall be brought out in their blacks and whites."—*S. Rutherford.*

4. A good man to be careful that his enemies are only the ungodly. A faithful follower of Jesus likely, sooner or later, to have the ungodly for his enemies and calumniators. A woe pronounced on the disciples when all men shall speak well of them; a blessing, when men shall revile them, and speak all manner of evil against them, falsely, for their Master's sake. Christ Himself hated by the world, because He testified of it that its deeds are evil. His followers to imitate His example and partake of His experience (John vii. 7; xv. 18—21; Matt. x. 24, 25).

III. **Gives his reasons for his abhorrence of ungodliness and hypocrisy, as well as a proof that his was not such a character (verses 8—10) Four things not found in a hypocrite or godless person, but which Job possessed—(1) A good hope. (2) A hearing with God. (3) A holy joy in God Himself. (4) A heart always to pray.

1. *The hope of the ungodly, however prosperous in this world, doomed to disappointment.* Verse 8.—"For what is the hope of the hypocrite (or godless person), though he have gained (or, 'when God cuts him off,' as in ch. vi. 9; Is. xxxviii. 12), when God takes away (or draws forth) his soul?" The hope of the prosperous hypocrite doomed to perish. Riches profit not in the day of wrath. The sinner may live to do evil "a hundred times," but must, if impenitent, perish in the end. The rich fool in the Gospel cut off in the midst of his prosperity, and in the height of his hope. Dives taken from his sumptuous table, to cry in hell for a drop of water to cool his tongue. The Saviour's problem for a worldly man,— What shall a man be profited if he shall gain the whole world and lose his own soul? (Matt. xvi. 26). Solon's maxim not far from the truth,—Call no man happy till his death. Observe—(1) Our course of life to be constantly viewed in the light of *eternity* and a *dying* bed.

"Thrones will then be toys,
And earth and skies seem dust upon the scales."

(2) A man is happy according to his *character* rather than his condition. (3) The text an emphatic *testimony to a future life.* But for this, the case of the prosperous wicked might have the best of it. If in this life only we have hope in Christ, then are we of all men most miserable (1 Cor. xv. 19). (4) A prosperous life often suddenly cut short by the stroke of death. Life in God's hands. The thread cut off at His pleasure. (5) The soul of the ungodly man *forced* to quit the body; that of the godly gladly departs from it. The wicked is driven away in his death. Body and soul must part; the question is, how? (6) That hope only worth having that *looks beyond the grave.* "He builds too low that builds beneath the skies." (7) The gain of the world a poor compensation for the loss of the soul. (8) Awful condition for a man to be suddenly called into eternity in the midst of his earthly enjoyments, and *unprepared.*

"How shocking must thy summons be, O death,
To him who is at ease in his possessions!
Who, counting on long years of pleasure here,
Is quite unfurnish'd for that world to come."

(9) Gold able to procure entrance anywhere but into the kingdom of God. (10) True wisdom to ask, What is my hope in the event of a sudden death? Reader, what is yours? Only *faith* in Christ's blood and righteousness, confirmed by a life of *love* towards God and men, the only sure foundation of a good hope. Christ our hope. Such hope the anchor of the soul amid the storms of life and "the swellings of Jordan."

2. *The prayer of the ungodly unheard in the time of trouble.* Verse 9—"Will God hear his cry, when trouble cometh upon him?" Two questions implied—(1) Will the ungodly pray in time of trouble? (2) Will God hear him if he does? A heart to pray not always found in time of trouble. The spirit to pray a gift from God. *A prayerless life often followed by a prayerless death.* Prayer, even if offered, in time of trouble not always heard (Prov. i. 24—28; Is. i. 15). Acceptable prayer implies both repentance and faith. Both wanting in the prayer of the ungodly and the hypocrite. An acceptable time when God may be found and prayer heard;—and the *contrary.* A time when knocking at mercy's gate will be followed by no opening (Matt. xxv. 11, 12). He who will not pray when he might, perhaps cannot pray when he would, or is unheard when he does. To shut the door of our heart in God's face, is the way to have the door of his heaven shut in ours. Observe—(1) *A time of trouble sure sooner or later to come upon each one.* (2) *To pray in the time of trouble the language of nature.* So the heathen sailors in the ship with Jonah (Jon. i. 5, 6). In ordinary circumstances the Athenians prayed to their false deities, but in public distress to "the unknown God." (3) *The ungodly either not able to pray in time of trouble, or not heard if they do.* (4) *The mark of a hypocrite to pray only when trouble comes upon him.*

3. *The ungodly has no delight in God.* (Verse 10)—"Will he delight himself in the Almighty?" The ungodly would have God's gifts, but not Himself; the godly would rather have God than His gifts. A mark of grace to delight oneself in God. An unholy heart unable to delight in a holy God.

Delight in God.

(1) *A leading part in true piety.* God desires not that we serve Him as a slave, but that we delight in Him as a child.

(2) *God Himself the chief good to an intelligent creature.* Everything in Him for such a creature to delight in. The source and centre of all good. "Of all Thy gifts Thyself the crown." All the beauty, loveliness, and sweetness in the creature, in comparison with what is in God, only a drop compared with the ocean. Not to delight in God is either not to know Him or to be

under the power of a nature that hates Him.
They that know Him not only trust but
delight in Him. The greatest misery, as
well as sin, of an intelligent creature, not to
delight in God. Not to delight in God is
either to be ignorant of Him, or to declare
that we see nothing in Him to delight in. If
God, only *as God*, is such as to be supremely
delighted in by unfallen intelligent creatures,
much more is He, as a God in Christ, to be
delighted in by fallen ones.

(3) *God the delight of heaven.* Hence no
unregenerate or unholy person able to enter,
or find enjoyment there if he could. To delight in God hereafter, we must first learn to
delight in Him here.

(4) *Delight in the creature only right when
we first delight supremely in God.* Delight
in the creature instead of God, not only
idolatry but insult.

(5) *A sinner's greatest delight often his
greatest sin.* The greater the delight in the
creature to the rejection of God, the deeper
the idolatry and the fouler the insult.

(6) *A man's character proclaimed by what
he delights in.* The sow delights in the mire,
the crow in carrion, the cock in the dunghill,
and the worm in corruption. The delight of
the holy, in God; that of the unholy, in the
creature. Important question—*What do
I delight in?* God, or the creature?

(7) *Delight in God not affected by outward
circumstances.* Often highest when outward
circumstances are lowest.

(8) *The mark of a godly man, that, when in
deepest affliction, he can delight himself in
God.* Job's case. Here apparently appealed to by Him as a proof of the sincerity
of his piety.

4. *The prayers of the ungodly are only
casual and temporary.* "Will he always call
upon God?"

Persevering Prayer.

1. The ungodly man prays in *sickness and
trouble*, but not in health and prosperity.
Fitful prayers like smoke driven aside by the
wind and never reaching the clouds. Answers to prayer often withheld to prove its
faith and sincerity. Some pray only in the
sunshine, others only in the storm; the
believer prays *always*.

2. The ungodly man's prayers *not persevered in*. Prayer, wanting the wings of
faith, soon tires and comes to the ground.
Prayer proves its sincerity by its continuance.
Fallen nature prays; but only grace prays
always. The hypocrite and unbeliever draws
in his hand if not immediately filled. Many
lose their prayers by not drawing the bow
sufficiently for the discharge of the arrow.
Successful prayer a bolt shot up into

heaven. The believer stands knocking at
God's door, and waiting His own time of
opening. Christ taught His disciples always
to pray, and not "to faint" (Luke xviii. 1).
Answers only promised to persevering
prayer. He who prays successfully finds
enjoyment in the exercise which brings
him back to it. A man's religion which
is only by fits and starts wants the stamp
of divinity. Prayer, without perseverance,
not current at the gate of heaven.

Job able to stand both tests. Prayed
both in prosperity and adversity, and *persevered* in his prayers.

**IV. Declares his faith in the recti-
tude of the Divine government.**

1. Speak as one *conscious of greater illumination than his pretentious friends.* Verse
11.—"I will teach you by the hand of God
(or, concerning God's dealings with men;
and what is with the almighty (His purposes
and procedure in regard to evil doers) I will
not conceal." Observe — *Light given in
order to be communicated.* A good man constituted by God himself a teacher of others.
Made a light in the world to hold forth the
word of life (Phil. ii. 15, 16). Truth not to
be concealed from selfish love of ease or
slavish fear of consequences.

2. Yet appeals to their own observation,
and professes only to communicate facts
with which they themselves were already
acquainted. Verse 12. — "Behold, all ye
yourselves have seen it." His friends had
already referred to the facts, but failed to
make a right application of them. Their
error not in respect to the *facts*, but the *use*
of them; not in asserting that hypocrites
and oppressors sooner or later suffer the
punishment of their sins, but that Job, who
was now suffering apparently at the hand of
God, must be one of them. Job asserts the
fact, but denies the inference. Maintains
that all oppressors and bad men, sooner
or later, suffer; but denies—(1) That therefore all oppressors and bad men suffer in
this life. (2) That all that suffer are oppressors and bad men. Observe — (1)
*Hearers themselves to be often appealed to
for the truth of what is asserted.* Appeals
to the hearers' own observation and experience often the most convincing argument.
Hearers frequently do not so much require
the knowledge of truths or facts, as the *right
use and application of them.* (2) The dealings of Divine Providence open to men's
view, and calling for observation and reflection.

3. *Hence reproves them for their vain and
useless arguments.* "Why then are ye thus
altogether vain?" (or "babble forth such
vanities"?) Their vanity—(1) In address-

ing Job as if ignorant of, or absolutely denying, the facts they so much insisted on in regard to the fate of the ungodly. (2) In erroneously arguing from those facts that Job, who suffered so much, must be a bad man. That Job could maintain the facts as decidedly as themselves, a proof—(1) That he was not the wicked man they had represented him to be. (2) That he needed not their instruction on the subject. (3) That they had only been vainly insisting on things which he himself admitted. (4) That they had been one-sided in their views and representations. They had, therefore, poured forth their eloquence, whether original or second-hand, only "as one that beateth the air." (1) Preachers to see that in their discourses they are aiming at a right object, and employing right arguments in support of it. (2) Preachers not to dwell on known and admitted truths without shewing the right use and application of them. Not enough to repeat that all who believe and come to Christ will be saved, but to endeavour to shew *what it is* to believe and come to Him, and *how* people may do so. Not sufficient to insist that Christ died for sinners, but to show how a man obtains a saving interest in His death.

V. Describes the lot of oppressors and of the prosperous ungodly. Verse 13.— "This is the portion of wicked men with God, and the heritage of oppressors which they shall receive of the Almighty." Seems to take up the language of Zophar (ch. xx. 29). Observe — (1) Faith and piety look to the end. (2) Each man's destiny faithfully meted out by the Almighty according to his character and conduct. (3). The main question for a man—what shall I receive at the hands of the Almighty? Man kills the body; but the soul still in God's hands. The lot of the ungodly described in reference to—

1. Their *children.* Verse 14.—"If his children be multiplied (or become great—a mark of propriety), it is for the sword (or they are doomed to the sword—shall fall in the siege or battle as threatened, Hos. ix. 13), and his offspring shall not be satisfied with bread." Misery often entailed on children by their parents' sin, an acknowledged fact. "The seed of evil doers shall never be renowned"—a standing maxim. Children usually serve themselves heirs of their parents' sufferings by practising their parents' sins. Effects of the sins of parents often in this world more visible in the children than in themselves. Proof of a judgment to come and a future life. Effects from parents' sins, suffered by children in this life, may be overruled by a gracious Providence for their

benefit in the next. Contrast the text with what is stated of the children of the godly (Ps. xxxvii. 25, 26). Job's children neither perished by the sword nor suffered want of bread. Verse 15.—"Those that remain of him (escaping the sword) shall be buried in death (immediately on their death as in a time of pestilence, or buried by the pestilence as the cause of their death); and his (or their) widows shall not weep" (as in an ordinary case of burial, the want of such funeral lamentation being with Orientals a grievous misfortune—"the burial of an ass," Jer. xxii. 18, 19).

2. Their *possessions.* Verse 16.—"Though he heap up silver as the dust, and prepare raiment (another form of Oriental riches) as the clay; He may prepare it, but the just shall put it on, and the innocent shall divide the silver." The answer to the question put to the rich fool: "Then whose shall those things be which thou hast provided?" (Luke xii. 20). The sinner's wages earned to be put into a bag with holes. Himself often snatched away by death when expecting to enjoy his acquired possessions. In the Providence of God a good man often made to reap the benefit of a bad man's gains. Insecurity and transitoriness the characteristics of the prosperous sinner's earthly goods. Verse 18.—"He buildeth his house as the moth (which is easily shaken out of the garment where it has made its nest, and which often devours its own house), and as a booth (or hut) which the keeper [of a vineyard] maketh" (intended only to last for the season, and to be taken down as soon the fruit is gathered).

3. His *person.* He is often—(1) *Carried off by a sudden and unexpected death.* Verse 19.—"The rich man shall lie down [at night on his bed of rest], but he shall not be gathered (or, according to another reading, ' he shall not do so any more,'—he lies down for the last time); he openeth his eyes (or, as quickly as 'one opens one's eyes '—in the twinkling of an eye) and he is not " (is no more in this world, having been carried often by a sudden death during the night). Exemplified in the rich fool of Gospel, and perhaps forming the foundation of the Saviour's illustration: "This night thy soul shall be required of thee" (Luke xii. 20). (2) *Seized with sudden fear of approaching judgment.* Verse 20.—"Terrors take hold on him as waters (suddenly overwhelming him like a mountain-torrent rushing down with widespread ruin) ; a tempest stealeth him away in the night (some judgment carrying him away like a sudden tornado, never dreaming of such an event). The east wind (the most vehement and destructive in Oriental countries) carrieth him away, and

he departeth (no more to be seen), and as a storm hurleth him out of his place (his fancied paradise, where he expected to remain, and long enjoy his accumulated wealth. (3) *Visited with calamity from which he is unable to escape.* Verse 22.—"For God shall cast [His judgments] upon him, and not spare; he would fain flee out of His hand." Unsparing sin prepares for unsparing judgment. Escape often sought only when too late. "The prudent foreseeth the evil and hideth himself; the foolish passeth on and is punished." "A fearful thing to fall into the hands of the living God." (4) *Made the object of execration and abhorrence to his fellow-men.* Verse 23.— "Men shall clap their hands at him (in abhorrence of his character and joy at his fall), and shall hiss him out of his place" (as an object of execration and a nuisance to society). The most prosperous evil-doer made one day "an abhorrence to all flesh." Some to leave their graves unto everlasting life; some "to shame and everlasting contempt" (Dan. xii. 2; Isa. lxvi. 24). Observe— (i.) Power of faith and a good conscience to enable a man, while deeply suffering both outwardly and inwardly, calmly to contemplate and boldly to declare the consequences of a life of sin. (ii.) A godly man, however tried and afflicted, takes the part of God against evil-doers, however prosperous in this world. (iii.) Terrible consequences, sooner or later, to a life of worldliness and ungodliness. (iv.) The tinsel of worldly prosperity to be one day stripped off from the godless possessor of it. (v.) Awful madness to peril the destinies of eternity for the momentary pleasures of time.

CHAPTER XXVIII.

JOB'S DESCANT ON TRUE WISDOM.

The place occupied by this chapter one peculiar to itself. Its connection with the preceding or succeeding portions of the book by no means obvious. Appears scarcely to form a part of the dialogue. Seems, as it stands before us, to have been delivered by Job during a lull in the controversy. Forms a poetical descant on the praises of true wisdom. Job left alone in the field, and now in a much calmer mood, in circumstances to enter on such a subject. Perhaps led to it by what he had stated in the preceding chapter in regard to the wicked, as well as by his own affliction and the inability of his friends and himself to account for it. Strongly expresses his approbation of true piety, and so affirms his own character. Himself an exemplification of his own definition of true wisdom. That definition the character secretly given him by God, and which Job was resolved at all hazards to hold fast. The section thus appears to be introduced by the author to give prominence to Job's real character. Probably indicates the author's design in the book to give an exhibition of the nature of true wisdom. Has a special importance in connecting the book with other parts of Scripture, especially with the writings of David and Solomon, and the wise men of that period (1 Kings iv. 30, 31), and, in the New Testament, with those especially of Paul and James (1 Cor. xiii. ; James i. 3). Its similarity to passages in the Proverbs at once obvious, especially to chapters i., iii, viii. The last verse of the section, which gives the key of the whole, almost an echo of Ps. cxi. 10 ; Prov. i. 7; and Prov. ix. 10. Perhaps an indication thus afforded of the period of the composition of the book, as one when the attention of thoughtful pious men was especially directed to the subject of true wisdom. The section exhibits—(1) The inability of man, by his own unaided powers, either to discover or acquire true wisdom. (2) The supreme excellence of that wisdom. (3) Its origin and discovery with God Himself, the Creator of all things. (4) Its nature, as consisting of true piety—the fear of God and the consequent departing from all evil. This chapter, the oldest and finest piece of natural history in the world (*Adam Clarke*). Indicates Job to have lived in a period of considerable advancement in civilization.— *Barnes.*

True Wisdom.

I. Man unable, by his own unaided powers, either to discover or acquire it. Wisdom not to be discovered or obtained like metals or gems. These hid in the bowels of the earth, but discovered and obtained by human art and industry. (Verse 1)—"Surely (or, 'for indeed' the speaker being about to show the rarity and excellence of true wisdom as contrasted with what he had said of the prosperous ungodly) there is a vein (or 'outlet,' *Margin,* 'mine') for the silver, and a place for gold where they fine it "? (or, "which they smelt," to render it fit for the purposes of life). Gold formerly found in Arabia. Abundant in Judæa in the time of Solomon (1 Kings x. 12, 14, 15). The art of extracting and refining it learned at an early period of the world. Mortals soon became metalleries. *Trapp.* The discovery and earliest manufacture of metals apparently ascribed to the descendants of Cain (Gen. iv. 22). The search for gold and silver poetically ascribed by Milton to the suggestion of Mammon, a fallen angel whose name denotes "riches:"

"By him first
Men also, and by his suggestion taught,
Ransack'd the centre, and with impious hands
Rifled the bowels of their mother earth,
For treasures better hid."

According to Pliny, gold first found by Cadmus, the Phœnician. According to Herodotus, first coined into money by the Syrians. Verse 2.—"Iron is taken out of the earth, and brass (or 'copper') is molten out of [and so separated from] the stone. He (the miner or metallurgist, in searching for and producing these metals from the earth) setteth an end to darkness [by sinking shafts, and, with the aid of torches, exploring mines], and searcheth out all perfection (or, 'searcheth out with the utmost thoroughness') the stones of darkness (lying hid beneath the earth's surface), and the shadow of death" (or places of deepest darkness). Tubal-Cain, probably identical with the Vulcan of Greek and Roman mythology, represented by Moses as the first artificer in brass and iron (Gen. iv. 22). The Chalybes, or Cyclops, said by Pliny to be the discoverers and earliest workers of these metals. Brass and iron said by Moses to be found in the rocky mountains of Palestine (Deut. viii. 9). Iron appointed by Lycurgus to be used by the Spartans for money instead of gold, to prevent its accumulation. Verse 4.—"The flood breaketh out from the inhabitant (or, 'he' [the miner] openeth a channel or shaft away from the habitations of men,—or, 'from the foot of the mountain'); even the waters forgotten of the foot (or, 'the men forgotten of the foot,' *i.e.*, descending to places in the mine untrodden by human or any other feet,—nothing in the Hebrew text either for waters or men): they are dried up, they are gone away from men (or, 'they [the miners] are suspended,' *viz.*, by ropes from the mouth of the mine; 'they swing away from men' [who remain above on the surface]). As for the earth, out of it cometh bread (or bread-corn), and under it (or 'underneath,' or 'its lower parts') is turned up as it were fire (combustible materials, as sulphur, bitumen, naphtha, coal (Gen. xiv. 10); or perhaps precious stones glowing like fire (Ezek. xxviii. 14). Note—Underground warmth, boiling springs, and red-hot mud, are believed to prove that fire still exists within the globe.—"The stones of it are the place (or bed) of sapphires, and it hath [belonging to it] the dust of gold" ('clods or lumps of

gold'—*Margin*, 'gold ore'). There is (or 'it is,' *viz.* the mine) a path which no fowl [however keen-sighted] knoweth, and which the vulture's eye hath not seen. The lion's whelps (or, 'the proud wild beasts,' in their search for prey) have not trodden it, nor the fierce lion passed by it" [being deep below the surface of the earth]. Yet even there man's skill and enterprise find a way. Verse 9.—"He [the miner] putteth forth his hand upon the rock (*Heb.*, 'the flinty rock,' *viz.* with a view to its excavation); he overturneth the mountains by the roots [by means of wedges and hammers, acid liquids, or, as in more modern times, by gunpowder—overcoming every obstacle that stands in his way]. He cutteth out rivers (or 'channels') among the rocks [in searching for the precious metals or still more precious gems]; and his eye [with the aid of torches] seeth every precious thing [whether metal or gem, contained in those dark recesses]. He bindeth the floods from overflowing (stops or dams up the water to prevent them from trickling and overflowing the mine); and the thing that is hid (the metals or gems he is in quest of) bringeth he forth to light." Observe—

1. *The remarkable provision of Divine goodness and wisdom in making the earth itself a storehouse of substances that should contribute so largely to the comfort, gratification, and improvement of the human race.* For example, iron and coal, not to speak of gold, silver, and precious stones. Beds of coal, many feet thick, and extending over an area of many hundreds of miles, stored up far below the earth's surface. These beds the remains of ancient forests, and the result of changes on what was the earth's surface many thousand years ago. Iron, so important for man's use and progress in the arts of civilized life, largely embedded in rocks, slowly formed thousands of years before man was upon the earth. Remarkable, too, that as these beds of iron-stone required fire both for the extraction and working of the metal, they are generally found in close proximity to beds of coal, as well as to sulphur which facilitates its production.

2. *Man's art and industry necessary to the acquisition and use of those materials which God has stored up in the earth for his benefit.* Man intended for work, and so to be a kind of fellow-worker with his Creator. The materials provided for him by God, but, in order to his enjoyment and use of them, requiring to be discovered, obtained, and elaborated by himself through the intellect with which God has endowed him. Man not only to exercise his art and industry on the productions of the earth's surface in order to obtain his daily food, but also on what lies

beneath it for the purposes of civilized life. In the one case, as well as the other, man must eat his bread in the sweat of his brow.

3. *Remarkable adaptation between the productions and contents of the earth, and the faculties given to man for their discovery and use.* Faculties bestowed on man to fit him for subduing the earth and turning its treasures to his advantage. The art and industry of the miner and metallurgist from the same Creator as the minerals on which he works. The ant operates on his little hill; the bee on its comb; the beaver on his dam; man on the earth itself, with all that it contains. "His God doth instruct him to discretion, and doth teach him" (Isaiah xxviii. 26). Human intelligence and skill a faint reflection of that wisdom with which God made the world, and part of that Divine image in which man was created. "This also cometh forth from the Lord of hosts, who is wonderful in counsel and excellent in working" (Isaiah xxviii. 29).

4. *Man's industry in searching for the precious metals an example of the earnestness and perseverance with which he should seek for the better and more enduring riches.* Treasures exist for man, compared with which all earthly possessions are but as the dust of the balance. Heavenly wisdom, in which are durable riches and unending happiness, to be sought for as silver, and to be searched for as for hid treasures (Prov. ii. 4). The earnestness of the miner, with much less toil, under the direction afforded by the Gospel, sufficient to put a man in speedy possession of gold which no thief can steal, and of which not even death itself can deprive him. Eternal riches close at hand wherever the Gospel is revealed, and awaiting only the humble and earnest seeker (Rev. iii. 18; Matt. xiii. 44).

II. **The supreme value and excellence of true wisdom.** Verses 12—19.— "But where shall wisdom be found? and where is the place of understanding [where it may be found like gold and silver]? Man knoweth not the price thereof, neither is it found in the land of the living (not only not to be discovered by the highest human intellect, but not to be purchased with anything on earth). The depth (or abyss—waters under the earth—perhaps the ocean with its 'deep unfathomed caves') saith, It is not in me; and the sea (waters on the earth's surface) saith, It is not with me (nothing in either one or the other able either to discover it to man or afford him a price to buy it with). Note—The ocean's bed covered for hundreds of miles with beautiful seaweeds, and with submarine forests and jungles thronged with living beings. "It cannot be gotten for gold (the

most precious and pure, 1 Kings vi. 20, 21): neither shall silver be weighed (as in ancient times, Gen. xxiii. 16) for the price thereof. It cannot be valued with the gold of Ophir (stamped gold, or the golden wedge or ingot from the place most distinguished for its production), with the precious onyx, or the sapphire. The gold and the crystal (or vases of crystal and gold) cannot equal it; and the exchange (or barter of it, according to the ancient mode of traffic) shall not be for jewels of fine gold (vessels or ornaments of pure and massive gold, such as have been recently discovered in the coffin of an Egyptian princess living in the time of Joseph, nearly four thousand years ago). No mention shall be made of coral (some costly gem or natural production—long uncertain what), or of pearls (always held in highest esteem among men, Matt. xiii. 45, 46); for the price of wisdom is above rubies. The topaz of Ethiopia shall not equal it; neither shall it be valued with pure gold." Gold so abundant in Job's time and country, and so variously employed, that five kinds or forms of it are mentioned in these few verses.

Similar language to that of the text in reference to the excellence and preciousness of true wisdom, found in Prov. iii. 13—15; iv. 7; viii. 10, 11, 18, 19. That exhibited in various particulars by Solomon in the Book of Proverbs, which is only asserted by the author of Job. (Compare Prov. iii. 16—18; iv. 5—9; viii. 20, 21, 35). The superiority of Divine wisdom or true piety over all earthly treasures evinced—

1. In its *intrinsic excellence.* Other treasures only material, and of the earth; this spiritual—a thing of the soul—as much excelling material treasures as spirit excels matter, and as moral and spiritual beauty excels material. Gems and gold adorn the body, wisdom and piety the soul. Those beautiful and attractive to the eye of sense; these to the spiritual eye, both of God, angels, and holy men. True wisdom, or the fear of God, assimilates us to God Himself, the source and model of wisdom, "the only wise God." That which mainly constitutes the Divine image in us (Prov. iii. 19, 20; viii. 22—31; Col. iii. 10). Allies us to all holy beings, the unfallen intelligences of heaven. Is to man what creative and providential wisdom is to God. Prepares us for correct, satisfying, and ever-increasing knowledge of God and of His ways and works. Purifies the heart, sanctifies the will, and enlightens the understanding.

2. In its *ability to afford true and solid happiness.* Other treasures only gratify the senses, or furnish the means of gratifying them. This gives peace and satisfaction to the soul. Other things unable to repel

sickness and trouble, or to give solace under them. This acts like oil on the troubled waters. Divine wisdom like the voice of Jesus to the winds and waves: Peace be still. Her ways pleasantness and her paths peace. Delivers from the disturbing and destructive tyranny of the passions. Secures enjoyment of the Divine favour, which is life. Wisdom is a tree of life to every one who lays hold of her. Gives health to the soul, and even contributes to that of the body. Profitable to all things, having the promise both of the life that now is, and of that which is to come.

3. In its *endless durability.* All earthly treasures perishable. Gold and gems soon cease to delight. At most only follow us to the grave. Unable, except as rightly used, to further our interests or promote our happiness in another world. Wisdom or true piety not only accompanies its possessor to the grave, but beyond it. The greatest of the noble triad—faith, hope, and charity. Faith ultimately changed into sight, and hope into enjoyment; charity or love, another name for wisdom, lives on and never dies. A cut rather than a comfort in the words of Abraham and Dives—"Son, remember that thou in thy lifetime receivedst thy good things." Sad when our good things must end with our life. The excellence of heavenly wisdom that it not only gives solid peace here, but prepares us for eternal joy hereafter. Wisdom not only accompanies her children through the chilly waves of death, but takes them by the hand on the other side, and introduces them into the presence of God and the Lamb, who is wisdom itself. True wisdom, like its Author and Archetype, everlasting.

III. God Himself the author and revealer of true wisdom (verses 20—28). "Whence then cometh wisdom? and where is the place of understanding? Seeing it is hid from the eyes of all living (or of every beast or animal), and kept close from the fowls of the air (referring to verses 7 and 8). Destruction and death (the regions of the dead or under-world, or those inhabiting it) say, We have heard the fame thereof with our ears" (only *heard* of it, as neither possessing it themselves nor able to communicate it to others, but as if approaching nearer to the knowledge of it, men often having their eyes opened only when it is too late, and regretting the loss of past opportunities for obtaining the knowledge and possession of true wisdom, Prov. v. 11—14). Observe—(1) *That of which earlier generations only heard the report, now clearly revealed.* (2) *Sad to be only hearing the fame of a good thing which can make us happy, and to*

be unable to obtain it. The case of the lost in another world; happily not the case in this. The rich man in hell "*saw* Abraham *afar off*, and Lazarus in his bosom," but was unable to reach him. Verse 23.— " God understandeth the way thereof (how it is to be obtained), and He knoweth the place thereof (where it is to be found and in what it consists). For He looketh to the ends of the earth, and seeth under the whole heaven" (penetrating the universe with one glance of His omniscient eye; therefore able to instruct man as to true wisdom,—what is his highest interest, and the way to secure it). God, however, not only omniscient and surveying all things, but the all-wise creator and disposer of universal nature, and as such the fountain and model of wisdom to His intelligent creatures. For the same thought see Prov. iii. 13—20; viii. 11—29. Divine wisdom displayed in establishing the universe with all its mysterious laws and forces, assigning to each department of nature its bounds and operations. Verse 25.—" To make (while making or about to make) the weight for the winds (giving due weight to the atmospheric air when at rest—fifteen pounds of it pressing on every square inch of the earth's surface—as well as proper momentum to it when in motion in the form of wind, through the earth's motion on its axis, and more especially through the rarefaction of some parts of it by the sun's heat, and the rushing in of colder parts to take their place; so as to be not only not hurtful and destructive to the earth's inhabitants, but in many respects highly beneficial to them); and He weigheth the waters by measure" (having at creation assigned their respective quantities to land and water, so that there should be sufficient of the latter for the irrigation of the former, as also to the waters on the earth, and those suspended in the atmosphere, whether as clouds or invisible vapour). Observe—(1) *All things in nature arranged in exact measure and proportion,* of which chemistry affords an interesting example. (2) *As winds and waters, so also trials and afflictions are measured* (Isa. xxvii. 8). Verse 26.—" When he made a decree for the rain (constituting those natural laws by which it should be formed from the vapour exhaled from land and sea, and should descend in showers according to the earth's requirements), and a way for the lightning of the thunder (or the lightning which precedes the thunder; how it should be produced as the electric flash which proceeds from the clouds, when, to restore the equilibrium, the superabundant electricity discharges itself in passing from one cloud to another, causing the thunder to follow it, as the report of a gun follows the flash, by the particles of the rent atmosphere suddenly striking together again —electricity, of which that flash is the expression, being one of the most mysterious forces in nature). Then (even when at the creation He prescribed the laws by which external nature was to be governed) did he see it (contemplate this wisdom in its excellence and suitability for man's welfare and happiness), and declare it (*Margin,* 'number it,' as carefully considering its nature and results,—take an exact survey of it, noting it as it were in a book for future communication); he prepared it (set it before him for contemplation, or established it as what should constitute man's true wisdom), yea, and searched it out (examined it fully in all its properties and bearings,—actions ascribed to God in condescension to our capacity, in order to indicate the excellence and importance of the thing spoken of). And unto man [as that work of His hands in whom the image of His own essential wisdom was to be reflected] he said [on the day of his creation, either speaking by an external voice or writing it internally on his conscience, in order that he might know wherein his true interest lay, and what was the true wisdom for him as a moral and intelligent creature], Behold, the fear of the Lord [not the proud self-sufficient scrutiny, or even the mere intellectual study, of the Divine operations, whether in creation or providence], that is wisdom [the wisdom for him, as a finite but moral and intelligent creature]; and to depart from evil [not the knowledge or examination of my secret purposes in dealing thus or thus with any of my creatures] is understanding" [that fear of the Lord and departing from evil being at the same time the best way by which he will come to know and understand why I act as I do in my providential dispensations]. This emphatic, cardinal, and ever-outstanding statement introduced with a "Behold," as indicating—(1) The importance of it. (2) The unlikeness of it to what proud man might himself have conceived. (3) The backwardness of man to believe, learn, and embrace it. Observe—

1. *All nature under laws prescribed by God Himself.* Nature itself God's work. The universe, with all its laws, only the material expression of His being and attributes. Every part formed and placed by Him in exact fitness to each other, and to the whole. Those laws established by Him at the first in infinite wisdom, and preserved in their operation according to His own will and for His own purposes. God's kingdom a kingdom of settled law; not of chance or caprice. Hence the comfort and confidence of His intelligent creatures. Men not afflicted capriciously, but in wisdom. The execution as well as constitution of natural laws with God Himself, who may suspend or contravene them for His own purposes as He pleases.

2. *Man enabled to penetrate far into the secrets of nature and the facts of the universe, but unable of himself to discover true wisdom.* The greatest philosophers of antiquity in the dark in regard to it. Professing themselves wise, they became fools. Man, like the mole, does all his works underground (*Epiphanius*). Homer called all-wise, and said to know all things human. Aristotle, for his soaring wisdom, called an eagle fallen from the clouds. Yet the greatest of Grecian sages professed they wanted other lights, and took it for granted the time would come when God would impart a further revelation of His will to mankind.

" The first and wisest of them all (Socrates) profess'd
To know this only, that he nothing knew;
The next (Plato) to fabling fell and smooth conceits;
A third sort (Pyrrho) doubted all things, though plain sense;
Others (Aristotle) in virtue placed felicity,
But virtue joined with riches and long life;
In corporal pleasures he (Epicurus), and careless ease;
The Stoic last, in philosophic pride,
By him called virtue; and his virtuous man,
Wise, perfect in himself, and all possessing,
Equal to God, oft shames not to prefer,
As fearing God nor man."
Paradise Regained, Book iv.

Jerome said to have known all that was knowable, yet one of the most devoted students of revelation. The greatest philosophers in our own or any other country, as Newton, Faraday, and Brewster, have loved to sit with the humility of a child at the feet of Jesus, to learn wisdom out of the Scriptures of truth.

3. *God alone able to inform man as to his true interests.* One of the great problems among the sages of antiquity, wherein lies man's chief good. A question naturally occurring to thinking men. God answers it for man: "He hath shewed thee, O man, what is good" (Micah vi. 8). As great diversity of opinion among ancient sages about wisdom as about the chief good. With those of Chaldæa, it was the study of the starry firmament and its interpretation as declarative of the events of Providence; with those of Arabia, that of the designs of God in His dealings with men and the whole system of the Divine government; with those of Egypt, the origin of the universe; with those of Greece and Rome, the nature of the Deity, with the problems of their own

existence and of the universe around them. Such speculations, apart from revealed truth, represented by Milton as the employment, perhaps in part the punishment, of some of the fallen angels.

"Others apart sat on a hill retired.
    In thoughts more elevate, and reason'd high
Of Providence, foreknowledge, will, and fate;
Fix'd fate, free-will, foreknowledge absolute;
And found no end, in wandering mazes lost.
Of good and evil much they argued then,
Of happiness and final misery,
Passion and apathy, and glory and shame;
Vain wisdom all, and false philosophy."

In opposition to all this, God Himself declares what is the true wisdom for man,—the fear of the Lord, and as its consequence, to depart from evil. This prescribed by God to man in the exercise of His own infinite wisdom as Creator and Governor of the universe. Made the law for man by Him who gave laws to universal nature, and at the time that He did so. A wisdom that is "earthly, sensual, devilish." True wisdom from above,—the gift of "the Father of lights." "The law (or revealed will) of the Lord maketh wise the simple." The Scriptures able to make men "wise unto salvation." The Gospel of Christ "the hidden wisdom." Christ Himself the "wisdom of God" and the "light of the world." Whoever follows Him "shall not walk in darkness, but shall have the light of life." Christ the teacher come from God. Anoints with eye-salve the eyes of the spiritually blind, "that they may see." Gives "the unction of the Holy One," that we know all things. Nature, in all its departments, tells of a God, but not how to obtain His favour and forgiveness. Christ reveals both in His Word. Himself, as the Son of God, eternal wisdom; as the Son of Man, incarnate wisdom; and "of God is made wisdom" to all who are "in Him" (1 Cor. i. 24, 30; Prov. viii. 12—36).

IV. The nature of true wisdom.
Verse 28.—"The fear of the Lord, that is wisdom; and to depart from evil is understanding." The gold and the silver, the sapphire and the ruby, have their place in the bowels of the earth. Wisdom has *its* place in the "fear of the Lord" and the "departing from evil." The one the root, the other the stem and the branches. The former the spring, the latter the streams issuing from it.

1. *The "fear of the Lord"* (*Heb.* 'Adonai,' denoting 'lord' or 'governor,'—usually applied to the Messiah, and by the Jews substituted for Jehovah) *the first part of true wisdom.* That fear not a slavish, but a filial one. A reverential feeling and conduct as much allied to love as fear. The fear rather of a child in regard to a beloved parent, than of a slave in regard to a dreaded master. When genuine, always combined, if not identical, with love. Love as directed to a superior, especially to the Supreme Being. A feeling and deportment due from an intelligent creature to his Creator—a being at once of unbounded goodness, infinite excellence, supreme majesty, and almighty power. A fear that shudders at offending, not so much from the dread of punishment as from an inward consciousness of, and love to, what is right. A principle originally implanted in man as the law of his being. Obedience to it his wisdom and interest. The violation of it his ruin. Actually violated and cast off at the Fall. Now universally violated by fallen humanity. Its violation the cause of all the misery in the world. Its observance the harmony of the soul, the harmony of man with man, and the harmony of man with his Maker. May be re-implanted in man's breast. Its re-implanting the object of the Saviour's mission, and the effect of the Holy Spirit's grace in the soul (Jer. xxxii. 40).

2. *To "depart from evil" the second part of true wisdom.* Moral evil, or sin, that abominable thing which the Lord hates (Jer. xliv. 4). To be departed from—(1) As contrary to the nature and will of our Creator. (2) As opposed to our own interest and happiness. All sin the opposite of God's character which is goodness, purity, and holiness. Moral evil the necessary source of all physical and social evil. The fear of the Lord necessarily evinced by, and conducting to, a departure from evil. The two combined constitute the perfect man. Job's own character (ch. i. 1, 8). Evil to be departed from—(1) Earnestly. (2) Entirely. (3) Perseveringly. (4) At all hazards. Moral evil both internal and external—both in heart and life. Both to be equally departed from. Departure from evil necessarily connected with the practice of good. The only way for a fallen man to depart from evil is by the implantation of a new nature through the operation of God's Spirit in the heart. Hence the promise (Jer. xxiv. 7; xxxii. 39; Ezek. xi. 19; xxxvi. 26, 27).

3. *The fear of God or true religion the wisdom of man.* Wisdom the choice of the best end, and employment of the best means for attaining it. True religion both aims at and secures glory to God and our own best interests. Seeks and secures the chief end

for which man was made—to glorify God and enjoy Him for ever. The only means of man's happiness, either here or hereafter. Godliness favourable both to his physical and spiritual, temporal and eternal, welfare. Has the promise both of the life that now is, and of that which is to come. The way to make the best of both worlds. Gives much in the hand, more in the hope. Is in harmony with man's moral nature given him by his Creator. The foundation of personal and domestic, social and civil, peace. Fits for the enjoyment of the Divine fellowship—man's highest happiness. Smooths the pillow of death. Prepares for a happy eternity beyond the grave. Preserves him from many troubles, and enables him calmly to meet and patiently to endure those that are unavoidable. Allies him with the noblest and choicest of God's intelligent creatures. Opens to him an ever-brightening path of excellence and delight. Renders him a blessing to others and a fellow-worker with God.

4. *Lay testimonies from Statesmen, Philosophers, and Poets, to the value of true religion in promoting men's best interests.*

"That *summum bonum* which is only able to make thee happy, as well as in thy death as in thy life; I mean the true knowledge and worship of thy Creator and Redeemer, without which all other things are vain and miserable."—*Lord Burleigh to his Son.*

"I have lived to see five sovereigns, and have been privy councillor to four of them; I have seen the most remarkable things in foreign parts, and have been present at most state transactions for the last thirty years; and I have learned, after so many years' experience, that seriousness is the greatest wisdom, temperance the best physic, and a good conscience the best estate."—*Sir John Mason: died* 1566.

"Love my memory, cherish my friends, but, above all, govern your will and affections by the will and Word of your Creator; in me beholding the end of this world with all her vanities."—*Sir Philip Sidney to his Brother,* 1586.

"Love God, and begin betimes. In Him you shall find everlasting and endless comfort; when you have travelled and wearied yourself with all sorts of worldly cogitations, you shall sit down by sorrow in the end."—*Sir Walter Raleigh to his Wife, before his execution,* 1618.

"Living in an age of extraordinary events and revolutions, I have learned from thence this truth, which I desire might thus be communicated to posterity: that all is vanity which is not honest, and that there is no solid wisdom but in real piety."—*John Evelyn—Epitaph by Himself,* 1706.

"Depend upon this truth, that every man is the worse looked upon, and the less trusted, for being thought to have no religion, in spite of all the pompous, specious epithets he may assume, of *esprits forts*, free-thinker, or moral philosopher; and a wise atheist, if such thing there is, would, for his own interest and character in this world, pretend to some religion."—*Lord Chesterfield—Letters to his Son.*

"Philosophy may infuse stubbornness, but religion only can give patience."—*Dr. S. Johnson.*

"Hold fast, therefore, by this sheet anchor of happiness, religion. You will often want it in the times of most danger—the storms and tempests of life. Cherish true religion as preciously as you would fly with abhorrence and contempt from superstition and enthusiasm. The first is the perfection and glory of human nature; the two last the depravation and disgrace of it. Remember, the essence of religion is a heart void of offence towards God and man; not subtle, speculative opinions, but an active vital principle of faith."—*Lord Chatham—Letters to his Nephew.*

"To religion, then, we must hold in every circumstance of life for our truest comforts; for, if we are already happy, it is a pleasure to think that we can make that happiness unending; and if we are miserable, it is very consoling to think there is a place of rest. Thus, to the fortunate, religion holds out a continuance of bliss; to the wretched, a change from pain."—*Oliver Goldsmith.*

"We know, and, what is better, we feel inwardly, that religion is the basis of civil society, and the source of all good and of all comfort."—*Edmund Burke, on the French Revolution.*

"With all my follies of youth, and, I fear, a few vices of manhood, still I congratulate myself as having had, in early days, religion strongly impressed on my mind. . . . I look on the man who is firmly persuaded of infinite wisdom and goodness, superintending and directing every circumstance that can happen in his lot, I felicitate such a man as having a solid foundation for his mutual enjoyment, a firm prop and sure stay in the hour of difficulty, trouble, and distress; and a never-failing anchor of hope when he looks beyond the grave."—*Robert Burns.*

"Where there is most love of God, there will be the truest and most enlarged philanthropy. No other foundation is secure. There is no other means whereby nations can be reformed, than that by which alone individuals can be regenerated. . . . While men are subject to disease, infirmity, affliction, and death, the good never will exist without the hopes of religion; the wicked never without its fears."—*Southey.*

" I envy no quality of the mind or intellect in others; not genius, wit, or fancy. But if I could choose what would be most delightful, and I believe most useful to me, I should prefer a firm religious belief to every other blessing. For it makes life a discipline of goodness, creates new hopes when all earthly hopes vanish, and throws over the decay and the destruction of existence, the most gorgeous of all rights; awakens life even in death; and from corruption and decay calls up beauty and divinity; makes an instrument of torture and of shame the ladder of ascent to paradise."—*Sir Humphrey Davy.*

CHAPTER XXIX.

JOB'S RETROSPECT.

Takes a calm retrospective view of his past experience and life. Thus disproves the suspicions and accusations of his friends, and shows that his complaints were sufficiently well-grounded. The character secretly given him by God thus affirmed out of his own mouth. Does this not from a feeling of vanity and pride, but, like Paul, as compelled to it, for self-vindication. Probably resumes his speech (verse 1, "continued his parable") after pausing for a reply which was not forthcoming.

Commences in a tone of lamentation as he looks back upon his former happiness and prosperity, now apparently for ever fled. Verse 2.—"O that I were," &c. Natural to look back with regret from a state of protracted suffering and depression to one of happiness and comfort, and to long, however vainly, for its return. The believer, in a state of spiritual darkness under the loss of God's sensible presence, often unable to refrain from similar language. "How sweet the hours I once enjoyed." &c. *Better and safer to long for the return of spiritual than of temporal prosperity and comfort.*

I. Job's past happiness (verses 2–11). Embraced—

1. *His enjoyment of the Divine favour and fellowship.* Verse 2—4.—"O that I were as in months past, as in the days when God preserved me! when His candle (or lamp—symbol of favour and blessing, chap. xviii. 6; Psa. xviii. 28; cxxxii. 17) shined upon (or over) my head (the lamp in Arab tents and dwellings being usually suspended from the top or ceiling, and kept burning all night), and when by his light I walked through darkness" (by his protection and guidance escaping dangers, and overcoming difficulties and trials—like the caravans travelling through the desert by night with lights burning in their front). Note—*All a believer's present comfort and blessing only candle-light compared with the future.*—"As I was in the days of my youth (or full prosperity; *Heb.*, 'My autumn,' the time of ripe fruits; the reference to his circumstances rather than to his age), when the secret (or intimate friendship) of God was upon (or in) my tabernacle; when the Almighty was yet with me " (present with me, or on my side; or, "when my vigour," &c., the clause in this case belonging rather to the next head). Observe—(1) *No blessing so great or enjoyment so sweet, as that of communion with God and the friendship of our Maker.* These placed by Job at the head of his list of mercies and the retrospect of his happiness. The madness of the world seen in neglecting and despising this. True wisdom in making the enjoyment of it our first concern. Its re-enjoyment by man the object of Christ's mission into the world. (2). *The favour of God the fountain of all real blessing and true happiness.* "The blessing of the Lord maketh rich," &c. (3) *Intimate fellowship and personal friendship with God to be enjoyed in this life.* Abraham the friend of God. "Shall I hide from Abraham that thing which I do?" (Gen. xviii. 17). Henceforth I call you not servants but friends; for all things that I have heard of my Father, I have made known unto you" (John xv. 15). "The Lord God will do nothing; but he revealeth his secret unto his servants the prophets" (Amos iii. 7). "The secret of the Lord is with them that fear him, and he will show them his covenant" (Psa. xxv. 14, Prov. iii. 32). (4) *God's presence and favour sweeten every blessing.*

" Happy who walks with Him! Whom what he finds
Of flavour or of scent in fruit or flower,
Or what he views of beautiful or grand
In nature, from the broad majestic oak
To the green blade that twinkles in the sun,
Prompts with remembrance of a present God.
His presence who made all so fair, perceiv'd,
Makes all still fairer. As with Him no scene
Is dreary, so with Him all seasons please."

2. *His enjoyment of outward mercies* (verses 5—11). These were—(1) *Domestic comfort.* Verse 5.—" When my children (perhaps including servants) were about me." Job's

children now dead, and his servants partly killed (ch. i. 15, 17), and partly fleeing from him in his affliction (chap. xix. 15, 16). Job's home once a snug and well-feathered nest, with an abundant brood of happy young ones in it (verse 18). Mentions his family before his fortune. A happy home a greater treasure than a wide domain. A healthy and happy family one of the greatest of earthly comforts. A home, when what it ought to be—the sweetner of life. Mercifully preserved to man after the Fall. Domestic happiness impaired by sin. Restored by grace. Realized in the enjoyment of God's favour and blessing in Christ (Psa. cxvii. 15). Job's home a happy one, because a holy one (chap. i. 5). "Blest, that home where God is felt."—(2) *Outward prosperity.* Verses 6, 19, 20.—"When I washed my steps with butter (cream, or thick milk), and the rock poured me out rivers of oil" (*Heb.* "poured out, &c., with me," *i.e.,* alongside of me, wherever I went—like the rock that followed Israel with its refreshing stream all through the desert). Abundance of milk and oil Oriental emblems of plenty (Deut. xxxii. 13, 14). Canaan a land flowing with milk and honey. Rocky land, as in Arabia and Syria, most favourable for the cultivation of the olive. Oil a great part of Oriental produce. Verse 19 —"My root was spread out by the waters (imbibing their moisture, as Psalm i. 3) and the dew (abundant in the East, and compensating for the scarcity of rain) lay all night upon my branch (or crops,—thus nourished both above and beneath the soil). My glory (reputation for wisdom, piety and justice; or simply, my prosperous estate) was no in me (*Heb.,* 'with me,' always new, like a flourishing evergreen), and my bow was renewed in my hand" (my strength always renewing itself after exhaustion, and acquiring fresh vigour (Is. xl. 31), as a bow, after shooting its arrow, returns to its former position and strength). — Observe — (1) Job's riches ascribed by him to God's blessing. The lamp of God's favour was over his head before the rocks poured out oil at his feet. "The blessing of the Lord, it maketh rich." "The Lord giveth thee power to get wealth." (2) Riches a blessing when *from* God, *with* God, and *to* God. "When rich I enjoyed God in all; now when poor, I enjoy all in God." 3. *Public honour I respect.* Verses 7–11, 21—25—"When I went out—(from his residence which was probably in the country) to the gate through the city (or 'up to the city,'—Oriental cities being usually on an eminence, and the city-gate the place of justice, deliberation and business, Ruth iv. 12; Prov. xxxi. 23); when I prepared my seat—(sending his servant before with his

cushion, according to Oriental manners, to spread it for him) in the street (or broad open space in front of the gate, used both for court and market, such as is found in the remains of Persepolis and Nineveh, and still exists in eastern cities). The young men (in the forum or market-place) saw me and hid themselves (from modesty and reverence retiring back out of immediate sight); the aged men (the elders of the city composing the court or senate—Ruth 2; Prov. xxxi 23) arose and stood up (from respect, as to one of superior wisdom and standing). The princes (sheikhs, or chiefs of their tribes) refrained talking, and laid their hand on their mouth (a token of silence and expression of the greatest deference). The nobles (men of wealth and position in the country) held their peace, and their tongue cleaved to the roof of their mouth. When the ear heard me [while addressing the assembly], then it blessed me—(pronounced him blessed for the wisdom, justice, and benevolence that shone in his speech); when the eye saw me, it gave witness to me [as the friend and benefactor of my country and my race]. Verse 21—"Unto me men gave ear (listening to my opinion or counsel) and waited; and kept silence at my counsel (having nothing either to add, correct, or gainsay). After my words they spake not again (not even replying, much less contradicting,—satisfied with the wisdom of what had been advanced); and my speech dropped upon them (as the dew, easy-flowing, pleasant and beneficial, Deut. xxxii. 2). And they waited for me as [the parched earth waits] for the rain; and they opened their mouth wide as [the earth does] for the latter rain" (the rain in those eastern countries falling at two seasons in the year; the former rain in September or October, the latter rain in February or March). Note— Salutary instruction frequently represented in Scripture and Oriental poetry under the figure of rain and dew. Copious rain or dew the Egyptian hieroglyphic for learning and instruction. Ver. 24—"If I laughed (or smiled) on them (relaxing my gravity, and showing a token of pleasure or recognition), they believed it not (as too great an honour; or, 'did not thereby become bold and familiar'); and the light (smile or serenity) of my countenance they cast not down—(grieving or displeasing him by their undutiful or disrespectful behaviour). I chose out their way (as their counsellor and guide; or, '[If] I joined their society'), and sat chief (occupied the first place, and presided in all their public deliberations), and dwelt [in my settled residence] as a king (or, 'a very king') in the army (or 'troop,' in whom his presence inspires life and courage, and to whom his word is law), as one that comforteth the mourners" [who hang upon his lips, and drink in his every word]. Observe—(1) *Goodness often the shortest as well as the safest way to greatness.* God's standing promise,—"Them that honour me 1 will honour" (1 Sam. ii. 30). In wisdom's left hand—only her *left* hand—are riches and honour. (2) *A good man sure, sooner or later, to gain the esteem and confidence of his fellows.* A wise head, a warm heart, and a willing hand likely to secure love and respect. Christ's promise,—"He that believeth on me, out of him shall flow rivers of living water" (John vii. 37). Job, from his piety, benevolence, and wisdom, both the darling and the oracle of his country. (3) A man's noblest ambition—(i.) To excel others in virtue, piety, and benevolence. (ii.) To act as the counsellor and guide of his fellows. (iii.) To comfort the mourners while commanding the multitude.

II. Job's character (verses 11—17). His reputation not without just grounds. The fruit not of his riches or power, but of his benevolent and upright character. 1. *His benevolence and compassion as a private individual.* Verses 11, 13, 15, 16.—" Because I delivered the poor that cried [under suffering or oppression], and the fatherless, and him that had none to help him. The blessing of him that was ready to perish [from want or oppression] came upon me [as his deliverer], and I caused the widow's heart to sing for joy (by comforting, relieving, or delivering her). I was eyes to the blind (as an instructor, counsellor, and guide to the ignorant, inexperienced, and erring, and feet was I to the lame (doing for the weak, infirm, and helpless, what they were unable to do for themselves). I was a father to the poor (counselling, defending, and providing for them) ; and the cause which I knew not (or, ' the cause of those I knew not,' *i.e.,* of the stranger), I searched out (or into, in order to his relief and defence—doing this as well in the capacity of a private individual as of a magistrate or judge). Observe—(1) Job's religion not one of mere contemplation, still less one of mere profession or outward observance. His the "pure and undefiled religion before God the Father—to visit the fatherless and the widows in their affliction, and to keep himself unspotted from the world" (James ii. 27). (2) Job's character an exemplification of "the wisdom that is from above—first pure, then peaceable, gentle, full of mercy and of good fruits." (3) In Job, the fear of God evinced by active love to man. To be so always.

" First daughter to the love of God
Is charity to man."

" He that loveth not his brother whom he hath seen, how can he love God whom he hath not seen ?" (1 John iv. 20). (4) The nature of that love which the law requires, and which verifies a man's religion. A love not in word or in tongue, but in deed and in truth (1 John iii. 18). True charity is kind and seeketh not her own (1 Cor. xiii. 4, 5). (5) Job's faith, like Abraham's, made perfect by his works (James ii. 22). (6) Wealth and high position no hindrance to the exercise of compassion and benevolence. Should rather be a help to it.

2. *His faithfulness and justice as a magistrate.* Verses 13, 14.—"The cause which I knew not I searched out (careful—(1) that before giving sentence, he thoroughly understood the case ; (2) That none, even the stranger, should have his case neglected). I put on righteousness—(practising it in his daily conduct, and especially as a magistrate and judge), and it clothed me (or, ' put on me,'—wholly filled me, made me righteous, —both without and within). My judgment (or upright dealing) was [to me] as a robe and a diadem " (or turban, worn as a head-dress by kings and nobles, Is. lxii. 3 ; the high priest, Zech. iii. 5 ; and even by Jewish ladies of fashion in the days of Isaiah, Is. iii. 20; the flowing robe and turban still the prominent articles of a wealthy Arab's dress). Job's character as a magistrate the opposite of that ascribed to him by Eliphaz (chap. xxii. 5—9). Job not less just than generous. Observe—(1) Justice and benevolence the brightest ornament either of public or private life. Wisdom an ornament of grace and a crown of glory to all her possessors. Knowledge is a youth's diadem—*Arab Proverb.* (2) Uprightness of character and life to be worn as our dress; cleaving to us and accompanying us at all times and in all places. To be our *habit* in both senses of the word. Patent to the eyes of the world like our outer garments. (3) Upright conduct to be regarded as our honour. To be neither ostentatiously paraded nor pusillanimously ashamed of. (4) A better righteousness than our own given us in Christ as our ground of confidence before God (Rom. iv. 2—6; Gal. vi. 14; Phil. iii. 7—9).

3. *His boldness in opposing the wicked and oppressive.* Verse 17.—Perhaps also belonging to his character as a magistrate. " I broke the jaws (or jaw-teeth) of the wicked (especially the rich and powerful oppressor, often represented as a beast of prey, chap. iv. 10), and plucked the spoil out of his teeth." The opposite of the unjust judge in the Gospel (Luke xviii. 3, 4). Observe

—(1) A truly good man a comfort to the oppressed and a terror to the oppressor. "They that forsake the law praise the wicked, but such as keep the law contend with him" (Prov. xxviii. 4). (2) A good man not deterred from duty by the fear of consequences. Job did good and executed justice at the risk—i. Of being unpopular with the great. ii. Of incurring personal danger. iii. Of much trouble to himself.

III. Job's anticipation. Verse 18.—

Perhaps continued to the end of the chapter. "Then I said [within myself, while reflecting upon my prosperity and character], I shall die in my nest (in comfort and security, neither by a violent nor untimely, but a natural and peaceful death); I shall multiply my days as the sand" (or, according to another reading, "as the Phœnix"—a fabulous bird, said to spring from a nest of myrrh made by the parent bird before his death, living to the age of a thousand years, and coming from Arabia to Egypt once in five hundred years, and then burning his father,—a hieroglyphical mode with the Egyptians of representing a particular chronological era or cycle). Natural in Job's circumstances to cherish bright anticipations of the future. The tendency of continued prosperity and honour to beguile into false security and confidence. David's error (Ps. xxx. 6, 7). Job's anticipations to be soon apparently blasted. Yet in the end abundantly realized (chap. xlii. 16). Observe—

1. A good old age, and a comfortable death in the bosom of one's family and home, among the appointments of a favouring Providence. The opposite threatened as a punishment (Is. xxii. 17, 18; Jer. xxii. 18, 19). These, however, not proofs of pardoning mercy, nor necessarily belonging to the children of God. Ishmael, out of the covenant, dies in the midst of all his brethren; Moses, in it, dies alone on a solitary mountain (Gen. xxv. 18; Deut. xxxii. 49, 50). Best to have the circumstances of our death as well as of our life chosen for us by our heavenly Father. The everlasting covenant of God's grace in Christ the softest and safest nest in which either to live or die (2 Sam. xxiii. 5). (2) To multiply our days a blessing; to make right use of them a greater. Days often multiplied only to multiply shame and sorrow (Is. li. 11). The longest life, if ill-spent, is short; the shortest, if well-spent, is long. Life not to be measured by the number of its days, but by the character of its deeds. (3) Job's anticipation, a long life and a comfortable death; that of the believer under the Gospel dispensation, an

eternal blessedness reserved for him in heaven (2 Cor. iv. 18).

IV. Lessons suggested by the retrospect as a whole.

1. *Evidence of the statement that "the fear of the Lord is wisdom."* Job's piety the fountain both of his happiness and honour. None ever exhibited more of the former or enjoyed more of the latter. His life and experience a verification of the truth that "length of days is in wisdom's right hand, and in her left hand riches and honour" (Prov. iii. 16).

2. *Proof that true piety towards God is accompanied with the purest morality and love to men.* Job as much distinguished for the one as the other. The fear and love of God the only and sure guarantee of faithfulness and love to men. True piety the natural fountain both of a pure morality and a disinterested benevolence. Integrity of life and love to our neighbour only branches of that tree whose root is the love of God. Love to God the first table of the Decalogue; love to man the second. The two twin sisters of the same parent, the nature and image of God who is love. He who loves and fears God cannot be regardless of God's will or God's offspring.

3. *An example afforded of what grace can effect in restoring and renewing fallen humanity.* Job a specimen of the power of that grace of God which teaches us to "deny ungodliness, and worldly lusts, and to live soberly, righteously, and godly in this present world." His virtues not the product of fallen nature but of renewing grace. Though in the older dispensation and before the full effusion of the Holy Spirit, his character and life the fruits of that Spirit, viz., love, joy, peace, long-suffering, gentleness, goodness, faith (Gal. v. 17). Exhibits the features of the new man created in the believer by the Holy Ghost after the image of God. The object and effect of Divine grace to produce the lineaments of Christ, the perfect man in the renewed soul. The polluted but believing Corinthians not only justified but washed and sanctified (1 Cor. vi. 11). The converted cannibals of Fiji risk health and life to communicate their blessings to the cannibals of New Guinea.

4. *A pattern for Christians both in public and private life.* Job's daily life a scattering of seeds of kindness. Might have sat for the picture of the Good Samaritan. Job's goodness, if not his greatness, within every one's reach. The poor always with us. No large estate required in order to be "eyes to the blind, feet to the lame, and a father to the poor." A kind word or a trifling gift

often able to make the widow's heart sing for joy. More grace provided and attainable for the exercise of Job's virtues in the Christian dispensation than in that under which the patriarch himself lived. The follower of Jesus both required and enabled to practise every virtue and every praise that adorned Job's character (Phil. iv. 8).

5. *The retrospect of a holy and useful life a source of pure and elevated comfort in sickness and adversity.* Job's comfort in his afflictions not in looking back on his wealth and honours, but on the way he employed them. The seeds of scattered kindness in the time of health and prosperity often bear their fruit in this life in the season of trouble and adversity. Friends made of the "Mammon of unrighteousness," both for time and eternity (Luke xvi. 9). A man may be richer in the retrospect of the manner in which he spent his money than others who selfishly hoard it are in its continued possession.

6. *Example of the uncertainty of earthly comforts and riches.* None ever enjoyed more of these than Job, and none ever more thoroughly stripped of them. The comfortable nest in which he hoped to end his days now rifled and torn in pieces, and himself sitting, a loathsome leper, on an ash-heap. Boast not thyself of to-morrow. Madness to pursue a fleeting and neglect an enduring substance. Means and opportunities of doing good to be faithfully employed while they last. Riches not for ever, nor the crown to all generations.

7. *The experience of believers in respect to the sensible enjoyment of the Divine presence and fellowship liable to fluctuation.* Not only Job's outward and temporal but his inward and spiritual comfort now in an eclipse. The sin of God's countenance may for wise reasons be hidden behind a cloud. No proof of God's anger that His favour is not sensibly enjoyed. The shining of the sun to be *believed*, though not *seen*. The path of a believer through the world like that of the moon among sailing clouds. Darkness and light the experience of a believer till he reaches the land where there is no more night.

8. *An exemplification of the requirements of the moral law in respect to our neighbour.* Love to man, verified in continual acts of varied benevolence, the characteristic of Job's life. Such love the requirement of the second part of the Decalogue. Job's life and character no more than is required by the law of God from each individual according to his means and opportunities. Every shortcoming of it, sin. Hence the universal character of men as transgressors of the Divine law (Rom. iii. 23). Job himself, with all his integrity and benevolence, still a sinner as coming short of that law. Every mouth stopped, and the whole world guilty before God (Rom. iii. 19). An example of perfect obedience to the law of love found only in one of Adam's children.

9. *Job exhibited in this chapter as a type of Jesus Christ the Righteous.* The picture Job draws of himself only fully and perfectly realized in him who "did no sin," and who "went about, doing good" (Is. xi. 1—5; lxi. 1—3). Christ, the second Adam, the only perfect man. His life, even more than Job's, an exhibition of the beauty and excellence of the moral law, as well as a fulfilment of it. Christ fitted, therefore, to be our representative and head in a new covenant (Rom. v. 12—19). His perfect fulfilment of the law, for our sakes—(1) As a pattern for our imitation. (2) As a proof that He was what He professed to be—the Son of God and Saviour of men. (3) To give value to His death as a sacrifice and satisfaction for sin, Himself being without spot, and a sweet savour to God. (4) As a substitution for the perfect obedience required of each individual. (5) As the image and character to be reproduced in all who are united to Him by faith, as the members of that family of which He is the head and representative.

CHAPTER XXX.

THE CONTRAST.—JOB'S SOLILOQUY, CONTINUED.

With his former state of happiness and honour Job now contrasts his present misery and degradation. His object as well to show the grounds he has for complaint as to ease his burdened spirit. Probably now sitting in the open air, near his own residence, outside the city. Still among the ashes, and covered from head to foot with the worst form of leprosy. Abandoned by his wife and domestics, and viewed by his pious visitors as suffering the penalty of past transgressions perhaps secretly committed, he is at the same time frequently surrounded by a rude rabble, especially of younger persons, who now, like the young men who mocked Elisha, deride him for his former piety and present affliction; perhaps taking a spiteful revenge for his former reproofs. These persons, whose character and condition, as well as that of their fathers, Job describes, probably the remains of the Horites who had been conquered and dispossessed by the Idumœans, to whom Job's ancestors belonged, and who had now for some time been in possession of the country (Gen. xiv. 6; xxxvi. 20, 21; Deut. ii. 12, 22). Some of those Horites had probably been enslaved by their conquerors, while others, to preserve their liberty, had fled into the desert and taken refuge among the mountains.

I. **Job describes the class of persons by whom he was now treated with scorn and insult** (verses 1—8). These were—

1. *Younger than himself.* Verse 1.— "But now they that are younger than I have me in derision." Derision a bitter aggravation of affliction. Christ's experience (Matt. xxvii. 27—31; Luke xxiii. 34—37). Such treatment from juniors an aggravation of the trial. Seniors habitually treated with respect, and veneration paid to age among the orientals, especially in Arabia. Another aggravation in Job's case that he had formerly been treated with deference, not only by the youth but even by aged men, himself being still comparatively young (chap. xxix. 8). A sign of great corruption in morals when seniors are treated with disrespect, still more with derision—especially when these are in affliction and distress. Sad state of society when the youth are rude and insolent, and particularly towards those who suffer, whether from age, poverty, or affliction. David's prayer (Ps. cxliv. 11, 12).

2. *Base-born.* "Whose fathers I would have disdained to set with (in the same employment; or 'to set over,' as keepers; or 'to rank in equality with') the dogs of my flock." A large number of dogs required for Job's seven thousand sheep. Dogs anciently employed, as now, both for watching flocks and dwellings (Is. lvi. 10). Job's language in reference to these men probably from their character and conduct rather than their condition. Observe—(1) Sad when men, made in the image of God and capable of engaging along with angels in the highest and most honourable services, are inferior in usefulness and condition to the dogs that guard a flock of sheep, and from want of principle unfit to be entrusted even with such an employment. Dogs in the east esteemed unclean and treated with little consideration (Ps. lix. 14, 15). (2) *The character of sin to degrade men beneath the brutes.* Verse 8.—"They were the children of fools (or 'worthless, wicked men' —both by birth and imitation); yea, children of base men" (*Heb.*, "of men without a name"—with no reputation except a bad

one—men of low birth and still lower character). Parentage of great account in the east. Felt to be a disgrace, as well as a loss, to be born of base and wicked parents. Children unable to help their birth; yet often "like father like child." Persons supposed to bear the character as well as the features of their parents. The education and moral training of the children of bad or base men usually neglected. Such children grow up in a morally poisonous atmosphere. The taint of the parent usually attaches more or less to the children. A man's parentage and education often indicated by his character and conduct. Children often inherit both the parents' vices and their consequences. To exult over the wretched sufficient evidence of a base extraction. An aggravation of Job's trial and degradation, to be "held in derision" by youths of such low and base parentage. The contempt of the vile a bitter trial to an ingenuous spirit. David's experience (Ps. xxxv. 15). Verified in that of Christ (Matt. xxvii. 27—31). The class of persons here described such as, from their character, were unable to obtain any respectable —however humble — employment. Job's example in regard to them to be imitated. Important for masters and heads of families to look well to the character of those whom they employ, even in the humblest situations. David's resolution (Ps. ci. 6, 7).

3. *Feeble and useless.* Verse 2.—"Yea whereto might the strength of their hands profit me, in whom old age was perished?" (or, "in whom the vigour of manhood was lost;" or, "in whom there was no expectation of their ever reaching old age," whether from their vices or their mode of life,— neither having strength to work themselves nor wisdom to direct others). Job's reason for treating them as he did;—in this case the clause applied rather to the fathers than to the sons. Observe—(1) No uncommon thing for vices, as well as inadequate means of life, to enfeeble the frame and induce premature old age and death. Races by such means often stunted in stature as well as enfeebled in mind, and often die out. Often the case with the aborigines of lands taken into possession by a foreign race. Well if the vices, as in the case of the North American Indians and others, have not been imported by the foreigners themselves. (2) True religion favourable to physical as well as spiritual growth and development. Muscularity the natural outcome of a healthy Christianity. God's truth and service beneficial to man in all his aspects. (3) Godliness no less profitable to races than to individuals. Humanity itself either deteriorated by vices and their consequences, or

elevated by religion and morality. (4) Physical vigour and longevity among the features of the millennial period and the reign of righteousness upon earth. "The child shall die an hundred years old, and the sinner, being an hundred years old, shall be accursed. As the days of a tree shall be the days of my people, and mine elect shall long enjoy the work of their hands" (Isa. lxv. 20—22).

4. *Wretched and famished.* Verse 3.— "For want and famine they were solitary (or, 'afflicted,'—'desolate,' as in Isa. xlix. 21; or, in 'extreme want and hunger'); fleeing into the wilderness (as unfit for civilized life, or as loving the solitude and independence of the desert, or finally from a sense of guilt and shame as evil-doers; or, 'gnawing' and feeding on the wilderness), in former time desolate and waste (or, 'the night or darkness of the solitary waste'); who cut up mallows (or purslain, a species of halimus; a saltish plant growing in deserts, beside hedges, and by the sea-shore, and used as food by the poor) by the bushes, and juniper roots (or, 'roots of the broom,' a plant abundant in the sandy plains of Arabia) for their food " (or ' to warm themselves,'—the stems of the juniper or broom being used for fuel, as the berries and roots were for food). These men probably worse off for food than were David's dogs. No fault however of Job's. Some prefer the most wretched fare to following an honest calling. One of the effects of sin, *somewhere*, that men are in any degree destitute of the proper means of life. Abundant provision originally made by the Creator for man's comfortable subsistence (Gen. i. 29). Man, continuing in obedience, would have eaten of the good, not only of Paradise, but of every land. The finest of the wheat and honey out of the rock the promised portion of obedient Israel (Ps. lxxxi. 16). The earth in consequence of man's sin, made to yield him thorns and thistles (Gen. v. 18). Vice and indolence in some, with tyranny and oppression in others, still continue want and misery in the world. Among the blessings of the better time coming under the Prince of Peace, is, that "the earth shall yield her increase," and men "shall eat and be satisfied" (Ps. lxvii. 6, 22, 26; Isa. lxv. 21, 22).

5. *Excluded from civilized society.* Verse 5. —"They were driven from among men,—to dwell in the cliffs (or 'clefts,'—perhaps rather 'the horrid gloom') of the valleys (ravines or torrent-beds), in caves of the earth and in the rocks. Among the bushes they brayed (like wild asses, for thirst or hunger; or 'groaned' from want and misery): under the nettles (or brambles) they were gathered together" (they huddled together; or "stretched themselves," as all

the resting-place they had). To dwell in valleys in the East a mark of vileness. The rocks of stony Arabia abundant in caves. The text descriptive both of the country and the manners of the inhabitants. A people in that region anciently known as Troglodytes, or dwellers in caves. Such places the usual resort of some at least of the inhabitants of a subjugated mountainous country, as well as of the lowest and most lawless among the people. The fastnesses of the mountains in Wales the last resource of the ancient Britons. Dens and caves the refuge of the persecuted worshippers of Jehovah in the days of Ahab and at other times (1 Kings xvii. 4; Heb. xi. 38). The retreat of the Christians of Madagascar. The parties mentioned in the text expelled from the cities and inhabited parts of the country on account of their vicious conduct and disreputable character. Evil-doers in a state to be improved or expelled. The diseased limb, however, only to be cut off when all means of cure have failed. Time not to be lost in purging either Church or State of corrupt and incorrigible members. "One sinner destroyed much good." "Evil communications," &c. David's resolution as king of Israel and type of Messiah: "I will early cut off all evil-doers from the city of the Lord " (Psa. ci. 8).

6. *Depraved in character and conduct.* Verse 5.—"They cried after them as after a thief " (in the way of threatening, or in order to their apprehension, or to warn others of their character). Verse 8.—"They were viler than the earth " (or, "they were whipped out of the land," viz., for their evil deeds) perhaps one of the results of Job's careful administration of justice, for which the wretched vagabonds, or their sons, now make retaliation on the humbled magistrate (Prov. xx. 8, 26).

The section brings us face to face with a portion of the lowest stratum of humanity and the dregs of society. Such found in most countries, Britain not excepted. The result not merely of vice and indolence in themselves and their fathers, perhaps for generations, but also probably of oppression and neglect on the part of their superiors. Their existence in a country often, under Divine Providence, a retribution. Probably due to Christianity that the description in the text was not verified in the British refugees among the mountains of Wales, and even in the Saxons after the Norman possession. The waifs and roughs, thieves and city Arabs, in the slums of London, perhaps as much the result of harsh treatment and neglect as of personal depravity. Church and State in general only now beginning to wake up to a sense of duty in regard to this class of society, when the case has become next to unmanageable. The great problem of the present day—What is to be done for the reclamation and elevation of the sunken masses? Much capable of being done both by Church and State, under the impulse of loving hearts and the direction of enlightened heads. The Gospel of the grace of God, suitably presented and lovingly applied, the Divinely-appointed, and therefore the most efficient, means of restoring fallen humanity. Embraces in the contemplated objects of its operation the lowest grades of society in every land. The commission of its Divine Author: "Go ye into all the world, and preach the Gospel to every creature." Possesses in itself, and along with its faithful ministration, a power sufficient to elevate the lowest and reclaim the most utterly lost of the human family. "The power of God unto salvation to every one that believeth." "Mighty through God to the pulling down of the strongholds" of ignorance and vice. Has already proved itself adequate to this end. Has achieved its triumphs both among the profligates of Corinth, and the Bechuanas of Caffraria. The glory of Christianity, that its greatest, and perhaps most numerous, trophies have been from among the lowest classes of society. "Not many wise men after the flesh, not many mighty, not many noble are called; but God hath chosen the foolish things of the world to confound the wise; and God hath chosen the weak things of the world to confound the things which are mighty: and base things of the world, and things which are despised hath God chosen, yea and things which are not, to bring to nought things which are" (1 Cor. i. 26—28).

Christianity suited to all classes and conditions of men. Views all men as brethren. Teaches the unity of the race. "God hath made of one blood all nations of men" (Acts xvii. 26). The Gospel an enemy to caste of every description. All nations and all classes represented by it as equally the purchase of the same precious blood of the Son of God (1 Tim. ii. 6). The countless multitude of the redeemed before the throne gathered out of every nation, and kindred, and people, and tongue (Rev. vii. 9). One of the precepts of Christianity, "Honour all men" (1 Pet. ii. 17. "Fraternity," and "equality," as well as "liberty," emblazoned on the Gospel banner. Corresponding responsibility involved in regard to its possessors. Only a Cain asks: "Am I my brother's keeper."

Solemn inquiry for every possessor and professor of the Gospel: Am I faithfully attempting to perform my part, however humble, in raising up the sunken masses of

my brethren at home and abroad, by communicating to them that Gospel which has already done so much for many and for me? Am I, like the Master I profess to follow, while contemplating, whether with the eye of the body or of the mind, the multitudes that are as sheep without a shepherd, "moved with compassion towards them," and *so* moved as, like Him also, to reach forth a helping hand? or, Am I still verily guilty concerning my brother?

II. The treatment received from these persons (verses 9—14). Enlarged on by Job, as indicating how deeply he felt it. Particulars specified.

1. *His sufferings and afflictions made the subject of their coarse jests and ribald mirth.* Verse 9.—"And now I am their song (accompanied with a musical instrument); yea, I am their byword" (or jest, probably both from his former piety and present sufferings; perhaps, also, as the rich man brought low, the proud Emir humbled, and the secret oppressor punished). Similar treatment experienced by David, and by David's Lord and antitype (Psa. xxxv. 15; lxix 12). Christ, in His deepest affliction, taunted with His former trust in God and charity to men, while now neither delivered by God nor able to deliver Himself (Matt. xxvii. 43; Luke xxiii. 35). The prophet Jeremiah in his humiliation also the song of his ungodly countrymen (Lam. iii. 14, 63). In Job's case this treatment from the rabble less to be wondered at after the conduct of his pious friends. Note—The lower classes of the Arabs addicted to scurrility and abuse. Indulge freely in the streets and bazaars in satirical and abusive songs upon their rulers and superiors. Clever in extemporising verses, which they usually accompany with the music of a drum, tambourine, or lute.

2. *Shunned with abhorrence.* Verse 10—"They abhor me; they flee far from me." Their abhorrence of him from—(1) His loathsome disease. (2) His lying apparently under the Divine malediction. (3) His supposed wickedness and oppression as the cause of it. His miserable disease, instead of evoking sympathy, caused him only to be avoided as a pestilence or a sight too loathsome and shocking to be looked upon.

3. *Treated with insult and contempt.* "They spare not (either as doing it abundantly and repeatedly, or as casting off all restraint) to spit in my face" (or, in my presence). Note: Orientals seldom spit but for the purpose of insult, and much more frequently spit on the ground before the party they wish to insult than on his face or person, though both are done. To spit out before another an expression of the greatest contempt (Deut. xxv. 9).

Frequently done by Mohammedans in respect to Christians, whom they regard as infidels and dogs. So great the affront in the East, that when done even by a father in regard to his daughter, the shame of the thing required her to shut herself up in her tent or apartment for a whole week (Num. xii. 14). Sad contrast in Job's case with his former honour (chap. xxix. 8—11). This deep insult put more than once upon the Son of God while standing as our substitute. Predicted (Isa. l. 6). Realized (Matt. xxvi. 67 ; xxvii. 30).

4. *All restraint in regard to him cast off by the rabble around him, in consequence of his affliction.* Verse 11.—"Because he (the Almighty) hath loosed my cord (dissolved my strength and authority; or, according to another reading, 'his cord,'—giving loose reins to his anger), and afflicted (or humbled) me, they have also let loose the bridle before me" (have cast off all restraint in my presence, and treat me with unbridled insolence). All Job's afflictions ascribed by him to God as their first Author. His cord now loosed by Him, a sad contrast to his fond anticipation (chap. xxxix. 8—11). Observe—*The wicked sometimes allowed to say and do whatever their pleasure may suggest or their malice invent.* This now done by Job's enemies—(1) As if it were a merit to treat with insult one who appeared the object of Divine execration. (2) From the absence either of power in himself or inclination in others to restrain them. The same experienced by the Saviour from the soldiers, servants, and others, when in the hands of his enemies (Mark xiv. 65; xv. 16—20).

5. *Violently pushed by rude youths, who employed every method to annoy and distress him.* Verse 12.—"Upon my right hand (—the place of accusers; also where he should otherwise have been most able to defend himself,—thus chosen for greater insult and contempt) rise the youth (*Hebrew*, 'brood,' —so called in disdain); they push away my feet (probably stretched out as he sat or lay among the ashes), and raise up against me the ways of their destruction" (or, "their destructive ways,"—the ways by which they may attack and destroy me, like the raised ways or banks of a besieging army, 2 Kings xix. 32). A wicked and mischievous band of city youths, like those who mocked Elisha at Jericho, now surround and assault him on set purpose to annoy and do him injury, as an army employing every means they can contrive to overthrow the beleaguered fortress. A picture of deeper degradation and misery hardly conceivable; all the darker from the contrast afforded by the previous chapter. Yet, even this only a shadow of

the outrages endured by the King of kings when "made a curse for us" (Matt. xxv. 3, 4, to the end of that and the following chapter).

6. *His sufferings increased by the rabble, who seemed to take pleasure in adding to his affliction, and completing his overthrow.* Verse 13.—"They mar (cut up) my path (annoying me whenever I attempt to walk, and preventing all escape or access to me from without), they set forward my calamity [as if it afforded them profit as well as pleasure], they have no helper" (persons of the lowest and most worthless character). So Christ in His last sufferings reviled by the thieves that were crucified with Him (Matt. xxvii. 44). Observe—A mark of deepest depravity to take pleasure in another's calamity, and to add affliction to those already afflicted. Edom and other nations severely threatened for similar conduct in regard to humbled Israel (Ob. x. 15; Zech. i. 15). The experience also of David and David's son (Ps. lxix. 26).

7. *His utter ruin eagerly sought by the rabble multitude about him.* Verse 14.—"They came (or come) upon me as a wide breaking-in of waters (or, 'as by a wide breach'—the figure of a siege still continued); in the (or, like a) desolation (or, 'under the crash or ruin,' as of the falling walls and buildings of the breached fortress; or, 'with a tumult,' or 'shout' of triumph) they rolled (or roll) themselves upon me" (as a storming party entering the breach). Implies—(1) The number of those seeking to distress and overthrow him. (2) Their eagerness in their wickedness. (3) Their actual mischief.

The section affords an affecting view of the depths of Job's aggravated and accumulated sufferings. As if the sudden and peculiarly melancholy death of his whole ten children; the loss of his entire property; his personal suffering from a most loathsome and distressing disease; his being made the object of aversion by his wife and domestics, and of suspicion and reproach by his friends —as if all this had not been enough, he is subjected to the coarsest treatment and most unfeeling mockery from a low rabble, who take a fiendish pleasure in insulting him and adding to his affliction. Observe—

1. *Impossible to say to what suffering a child of God may be subjected in this world.* Sometimes all the powers of wickedness in earth and hell apparently let loose against him, while at the same time suffering under distressing dispensations of Divine Providence. No trial so sharp but a godly man may meet with it. If Satan has one dart in his quiver more fiery than another, he may shoot it at him. In respect to outward

181

trials and sufferings, but for the inward comfort and future hope afforded them, believers, sometimes, of all men the most miserable (1 Cor. xv. 19). Tribulation and persecution promised by the Master. This, at times, abundantly and amazingly realized. Witness the sufferings of the martyrs of Lyons, Smyrna, and elsewhere, in the second century. "Tortures by racks, by pincers, by faggots, by the tossings of wild beasts, by being seated in burning [iron] chairs, that the fumes of their roasting flesh might come up about them, amid scoffs and jeers from the rabble, when a word of retraction would have saved them." See *Dickinson's Theological Quarterly*, July, 1875, p. 389.

2. *Nothing strange for a child of God to fall from esteem into contempt and disgrace* (Matt. v. 11). Hatred and reproach their promised fare. Mockery not the least painful and effective species of persecution (Heb. x. 32, 33; Gen. xxi. 9 compared with Gal. iv. 29).

3. *The depravity of the human heart, which is capable of conduct such as is ascribed to Job's rabble persecutors.* "Murder," in its worst form, proceeding out of it (Matt. xv. 19). Capable of inflicting deliberate injury on those already deeply afflicted and suffering, from the mere gratification of a fiendish pleasure in witnessing it, or from a diabolical hatred of moral excellence in the sufferer.

4. *The intense malevolence and cruelty of Satan, the author of these aggravated sufferings on the part of Job, and the instigator of those wretched creatures whom he found or made his ready tools, in rendering his suffering as bitter as it could possibly be.* Nothing wanting on Satan's part if men are not as wretched and miserable as himself.

5. *The mutability of outward happiness and popular favour.* None ever enjoyed both in a higher degree than Job, and none ever, for a time, so entirely stripped of them. The fickleness of "fortune" and popular applause proverbial. The "Hosanna" of to-day the "crucify Him" of to-morrow. To-day a silken couch—to-morrow a scaffold. To-day Paul is ready to be worshipped as a divinity; to-morrow he is dragged out of the city and all but stoned to death. The believer's comfort.—(1) That all these vicissitudes are under his Heavenly Father's appointment. (2) That his real happiness is elsewhere and far above the reach of change.

6. *The love of Christ in submitting, for our sake, to sufferings and indignities which are only foreshadowed in those of the Patriarch.* In the last eighteen hours of His life on earth all the bitter ingredients indicated in this chapter were infused into the cup of suffering appointed for Him as our substitute

182

to drink. "He was made a curse for us," and therefore abandoned to every species of human endurance. The Gospel narrative presents us with a scene of suffering which only finds anything approaching a parallel to it in the case of the Patriarch, as exhibited in this and preceding chapters.

III. Reverts to his personal affliction, more especially as from the hand of God (verses 15—18). Laments.—

1. *The sad reverse in his condition.* Verse 15.— "Terrors are turned upon me (or, 'things are changed'—tables are turned with me; or, 'I am overthrown,' like a stormed fortress; or, 'trouble,'—carrying consternation with it, like the terror in a city taken by storm,—'pursues me') ; they (the terrors or calamities) pursue (like the besiegers when entering the breach they have made in the walls; or, 'thou pursust') my soul (*Heb.*, 'my nobility' or princely state —perhaps a term for the soul from its nobler nature) as the wind [pursues and drives along the chaff—*i. e.* vehemently and irresistibly]; my welfare (all the happiness and comfort of my life) passeth away as a cloud " [which leaves no trace of its former presence and can no more be recalled]. Observe :—(1). *Sad reverses from a happy and prosperous condition among the most painful of human trials.* (2) *Soul terrors the greatest troubles.* These not unknown to a child of God (Ps. lxxxviii. 15, 16). Amazement and consternation among the ingredients of Christ's cup (Mark xiv. 33, 34).

2. *His inward grief, expressing itself in continual groans and lamentations.* Verse 16.—"And now my soul is poured out upon me (or, 'within me,' as if dissolved in grief; *Heb.*, 'pours itself out,' *i.e.*, in tears and groans) ; the days of affliction have taken hold (or fast hold) of me" (like armed men entering a besieged city—denoting the violence of his troubles ; "days of affliction," as indicating its continuance and the sad contrast with his former happy experience). Observe—*Days of affliction, sooner or later, and of longer or shorter continuance, to take hold of each* (Eccles xi. 8). Happy then to have one with us who "in all our afflictions is afflicted " (Is. lxiii. 9). His promise (Is. xliii. 2). Christ's presence with us in the furnace quenches the violence of the fire (Dan. iii. 25 ; Heb. xi. 34).

3. *His bodily sufferings.* Verse 17.—"My bones are pierced in me (*Heb.*, 'from off me ') in the night season (or, 'night pierceth my bones from off me,'—*i.e.* with acute pains, usually most severe in the night) ; and my sinews (or 'my gnawing pains ') take (or find) no rest." Acute and gnawing pains added to all Job's other afflictions. Satan accom-

plishes his wish and goes the full length of his permission,—"Touch his flesh and his *bones*." The bones sensible of the most acute and severe pain. The affliction carried into his very bones. Severe suffering usually expressed by reference to the bones (Ps. li. 8; Is. xxxviii. 13). An aggravation of pain and suffering when endured in the night while others enjoy rest, and when one's own exhausted nature requires repose. Night also the season in which sorrow sinks deepest.

4. *The pollution of his garments and the changed appearance of his skin in consequence of his disease.* Verse 18.—"By the great force of my disease is my garment (either *literally*, in consequence of the purulent discharge from his sores; or *figuratively*, his *skin* so changed in its appearance that he could scarcely be recognized): it bindeth me as the collar of my coat" (vest, tunic, or inner garment—his loose outer garment being now so stiff with gore and matter as to sit as close to his person as his tunic; or, 'it—the disease—bindeth me about like my vest;' sitting as closely, constantly, and completely upon me as my tunic). A sore aggravation of disease—(1) When it pollutes our garments and disfigures our persons—(2) When it appears likely to yield neither to time nor treatment.

5. *Degradation coupled with extreme debility.* Verse 19.—"He (God, or, 'it,' the disease) hath cast me into the mire (as a wrestler seizing his antagonist by the throat and throwing him to the ground; or, hath rendered me filthy and abominable as one cast into the mire), and I am become like dust and ashes" (as low and mean, as weak and powerless, as the ashes on which I sit; or, I am reduced to dust and ashes, deprived of vital energy, and more like a corpse than a living man; his disease such as to give his body the appearance of clods and ashes, from its dried scabs and filthy ulcers). Observe—Piety enables us to keep an eye upon God as the supreme and sovereign Author of all our troubles. In one sense our troubles as truly from God, as in another from Satan, the world, or ourselves. God the ultimate Author, whoever or whatever may be the immediate instrument or occasion. No trouble but by His purpose and permission. Satan and the world only God's hand in afflicting and chastening His children. Satan's demand in regard to Job: "Put forth thy hand upon him;" God's answer, "He is in thine hand." Paul's thorn in the flesh from Satan, yet given by God (2 Cor. xii. 7). Better to think of God the *first* cause in our trouble, than of man or any other second cause. "I was dumb, I opened not my mouth; because Thou didst it" (Ps. xxxix. 9).

IV. Directs his complaint against God Himself (verses 20—22).

1. *As disregarding his prayer in his affliction.* Verse 20.—"I cry unto thee, and thou dost not hear (or hearken, so as to help and deliver) me; I stand up (in frequent and earnest supplication; or, I stand, continue waiting and expecting an answer), and thou regardest me not" (or "thou considerest me" [and my case], but dost not answer or afford relief). Observe—(1) Crying to God a familiar exercise with Job. Good for us to have the path to the mercy-seat a well-trodden one. (2) Job not only *prayed* in his affliction, but *continued* to do so. Unlike the hypocrite (chap. xxvii. 10). (3) Standing a usual and Scriptural posture in prayer (Gen. xviii. 22; Jer. xv. 1; Matt. vi. 5; Luke xviii. 11—13). The early Christians usually *knelt* in prayer on every day of the week, except *the Lord's-day*, when they *stood*, as a posture more befitting a day of joy and triumph. (4) Sometimes one of the most painful trials to an afflicted child of God, to pray, and *continue* praying, without any apparent attention to his prayer on the part of God. The trial of David and of David's Lord in his deepest affliction (Psa. xxii. 1, 2; Matt. xxvii. 46). (5) God's regard to our prayer not to be judged by immediate appearances.

Answers to Prayer.

Believing prayer heard, though followed by no immediate or direct answer. Prayer offered through the Holy Spirit's assistance never unheard or unanswered. Answers to prayer not restricted to time or form. Sometimes, the thing itself not granted, but something better in its stead. So with Paul (2 Cor. xii. 8, 9). With Christ (Luke xxii. 42, 43). Sometimes petitions for temporal benefits not granted, that those for spiritual and better ones may be so. The withholding an answer sometimes a greater blessing than the answer itself. God not a mere force, but an intelligence acting according to infinite wisdom and judgment in the bestowment of His mercies. "The absurdity of Tyndall's famous 'prayer-test' was, that it regarded God as simply a force in nature, and proposed to experiment with it to see just what it would do. . . . . The impossibility of knowing the motives which actuate God must for ever render the expectation of receiving an invariable answer to any prayer absurd in the extreme. The very fact that our prayers are sometimes answered and sometimes denied, and that the answers when granted are sometimes modified and often delayed, is itself proof that we are dealing with a great intelligence, whose acts are governed only by his own will and purposes."—*Rev. Jacob Todd, M.A., in Dickinson's Theological Quarterly,* July, 1875, p. 369. True and acceptable prayer carries in it submission to the Divine will. A part of every such prayer, understood if not expressed,—Not my will, but thine be done. Christ our exemplar in prayer (Luke xxii. 24). Himself the example of His own teaching (Matt. vi. 10). Believing prayer like seed, whose temporary disappearance in the earth is necessary to its production of fruit. All the tears of God's people put into His bottle, and all their prayers recorded in His book (Ps. lvi. 8). All Job's prayers at length abundantly answered, even in this life. Perhaps the most of believers' prayers only to be answered after they have ceased both to pray and live. Better, in trouble, to pray for patience to endure it, and grace to improve it, than for deliverance out of it.

2. *As acting towards him with apparent cruelty and hostility.* Verse 21.—"Thou art become cruel to me (*Hebrew*, 'Art turned into a cruel one unto me') ; with thy strong hand thou opposest thyself against me," (or, 'carriest on a bitter hostility against me ;' or 'liest in wait for me'). One of the severest things Job ever uttered in regard to God, indicating the bitterness of his grief at being thus treated by Him as an enemy. Observe— (1) *The flesh has never, any more than Satan, anything good to say of God.* (2) *The flesh makes the most grievous mistakes in its judgments of God and of Divine things.* Says of God what is exactly true of the devil, and the very opposite of what is true of God. God is love, and Satan the impersonation of cruelty. His name *Satan* denotes "an adcersary," and is closely allied to the word Job employs in speaking of God. Satan the opposer of every man's happiness, and especially the adversary of believers (1 Peter v.8). (3) God may, for wise purposes, in a little wrath hide his face from his children "for a moment," and in apparent wrath may "smite them," though really in love (Isa. liv. 8; lvii. 17; Rev. iii. 19). Even this not the case at present in regard to Job. While Satan was bruising, God was praising him. (4) Job's experience in the text, without the sin, realized by his great Antitype when uttering the cry, My God, my God, why hast thou forsaken me (Matt. xxvii. 46). For our sakes, that satisfaction might be made for man's sins, God obliged to assume the aspect of "a cruel one" to His own beloved Son. The bitterest element of the cup given him, as our surety, to drink.

3. *As sporting with his sufferings, and giving him up to destruction.* Verse 22.— "Thou liftest me up to the wind (like the grain thrown up from the threshing-floor by the

winnowing shovel against the wind) thou causest me to ride (tossest me up and down, or carriest me away) upon it" (as the chaff of the threshing-floor when separated from the wheat, or as, any light substance made the sport of the wind and carried away by it). Observe—(1) Job, under the misleading suggestions of the flesh, views God as sporting with his sufferings, while, in reality, glorying in him before principalities and powers as his faithful servant, who had not his like upon earth. (2) What Job here ignorantly and unbelievingly ascribes to God, very like what Satan desired to do with the disciples of Jesus in the night of their Master's betrayal (Luke xxii. 31, 32). The thing Satan was actually doing now with Job.

4. *As filling him with terror and making an utter end of him.* "Thou dissolvest my substance" (or, my health and soundness, as well from terror as disease; or "Thou dissolvest me, Thou terrifest me;" or, according to another reading, "Thou dissolvest me in the tempest's crash"). A tragic picture of inward as well as outward distress. Vague terror and deep depression of spirits among the effects of Job's peculiar disease. Trouble of soul the soul of all trouble. Terrible experience, when in affliction and trouble God is viewed as dealing with us in anger. Sometimes the temporary experience of a believer. Sure to be the unending experience of every impenitent unbeliever. God's terrors able to dissolve the firmest substance, and to terrify the stoutest heart. "A fearful thing to fall into the hands of the living God."

V. Reflects upon the future (verses 23, 24).

1. *Anticipates death as the result of his present sufferings.* Verse 23.—"For I know that thou wilt bring me to death, and to the house appointed for all living" (the grave, or the earth, according to Gen. iii. 19; the book of Genesis, in some form or other, most probably in Job's hands). Job's language that of dejection and despondency, not without an alloy of petulance. Faith again at the ebb. Despondency one of the effects of his disease. Sense and sight said : " He will slay me—this disease must be fatal ; " only faith could say : " I shall not die but live." Observe—(1) The flesh ever apt to draw hasty and wrong conclusions from God's dealings in Providence. (2) God acknowledged by Job as the dispenser of all His afflictions, and as the disposer of all events. None go down to the grave till God brings them there, though some are brought before their time. The keys of death and the eternal world in Christ's hands.

The grave the house appointed for all living.

Declares the general law relating to humanity. Only two known exceptions. More to be made at the Lord's second advent. Believers then changed without tasting of death (1 Cor. xv. 51, 52; 1 Thess. iv. 15—17). Till Christ shall come, the grave the appointed receptacle for humanity. Job mistaken as to the time and occasion of his death; no mistake as to the fact of it. Every disease, if not strictly "unto death," yet brings us nearer to it. In regard to the issue of our trouble, God often better than our fears. Paul's case (2 Cor. i. 8—10). God as able to bring up from the grave as to bring down to it. The times of each in His hand. Useful in affliction to remember our mortality, and to regard death as the possible, if not the certain, result of it. From the universality of the grave as "the house appointed for all living," we learn—(1) *A lesson of humility.* Pride ill becoming in any creature,—preposterous in those who in a few years at most will have only a dark chamber in the earth of a few cubic feet for their dwelling, with the worms as their nearest companions, and actually making a banquet of their flesh. Such a dwelling awaiting the prince equally with the peasant. (2) *Earnestness in attending to present and important duty, more especially in seeking the eternal welfare of ourselves and others connected with us.* Opportunity for attending to the concerns of eternity confined to this life. The exhortation of Divine wisdom—"Whatsoever thy hand findeth to do, do it with thy might; for there is no work, &c., in the grave, whither thou goest" (Eccles. ix. 10). "The night cometh when no man can work." (3) *The evil of sin.* The grave not originally "the house appointed for all living." Death to mankind the result of transgression. "In the day that thou eatest thereof thou shalt surely die." "By one man sin entered the world, and death by sin." "The wages of sin is death." No grave but sin has dug it. Terrible evil which has filled the world with sepulchres and dead men's bones. Sad to be in love with that which has proved the murderer of the race. So great an evil must require a corresponding means for its expiation and removal. (4) *The inflexible character of the Divine law.* The sentence against transgressors of that law fulfilled, though a whole race must be reduced to death. Adequate satisfaction to be made to it before the grave can close its mouth or yield up its dead to an eternal life. That satisfaction, through Divine compassion, already made. "By man came death;

by man came also the resurrection from the dead." "The wages of sin is death; but the gift of God is eternal life, through Jesus Christ our Lord." "I am the resurrection and the life; he that believeth in me, though he were dead, yet shall he live; and whosoever liveth and believeth in me shall never die." "He suffered for our sins, the just One in the room of the unjust." "All we like sheep have gone astray; and the Lord hath laid upon him the iniquity of us all. He was wounded for our transgressions. By His stripes we are healed. For the transgression of My people was he stricken. He hath made his soul an offering for sin. He bare the sin of many" (1 Cor. xv. 21; Rom. vi. 23; John xi. 25; Is. liii. 5—12). (5) *True wisdom to seek a better than an earthly portion.* The 'house appointed for all living' the end of all mere earthly enjoyments and possessions. Sad to spend our time only in the pursuit of such, and to be found at last with nothing we can carry with us beyond it. (6) *The grave the vestibule to two other houses, both eternal in their duration, but immensely different in their character.* The one of these a home of light and beauty, peace and purity, life and health, joy and song, where death is unknown and no tear is shed. The other one of darkness and despair,—'weeping, wailing, and gnashing of teeth.' Solemn and important question for each—which of these shall be my home? "Except a man be born again, he cannot see the kingdom of God." "Without holiness no man shall see the Lord."

2. *Despairs of help being afforded in answer to his prayers, and looks only for relief in the grave.* Verse 24.—"Howbeit (or surely) he will not stretch out his hand (in the way of help and deliverance) to the grave (now when I am already on the verge of it; or, 'surely prayer avails nothing when he stretches forth his hand,' viz., to smite or to slay); though they (or men) cry in his destruction" (the destruction sent by him—while he is visiting with destruction). The verse, however, may also be read as expressing the assurance of rest in the grave: "Howbeit he will not stretch out his [afflicting] hand to the grave (so as to afflict in or beyond it); in the destruction He sends there is deliverance." Or even as justifying prayer in such circumstances as this: "Howbeit, do not men [still] stretch out the hand [imploring help] in ruin, and utter a cry on account of it in the destruction which is sent by Him?" Observe—(1) *The language of unbelief,—"There is no hope."* The flesh, even in a believer, ever ready in protracted trial and disappointed hope, to say, with Ahab: "Why should I wait any longer?" (2) *Faith in a believer has its*

ebbs and flows. Low water with Abraham's faith when he spoke to God of Eliezer of Damascus being his heir, and when he prayed that Ishmael might live before him,—as if he were to have no other son. Mounts and triumphs when he goes forth at God's command to offer up to God the heir of promise, believing that He was able even to raise him from the dead. Faith in its ebb with David when he said: "I shall one day fall by the hand of Saul." At its flow, when he wrote in the 118th Psalm: "I shall not die but live, and declare the works of the Lord." Faith high in Elijah when he sent for Ahab and told him to gather together all the prophets of Baal; low, when he fled from the face of Jezebel and sat down under the juniper tree, with the prayer "Take away my life, for I am no better than my fathers." Hard to believe when all appearances are, and continue to be, clean contrary to our prayers. The part of faith to hope against hope, having to do with a God to whom all things are possible, and who adopts as his title—"Thou that hearest prayer" (Ps. lxv. 2). (3) *Sweet consolation to a suffering child to know that he has at least rest and deliverance in the grave.* "Blessed are the dead that die in the Lord, for they do rest from their labours" (Rev. xiv. 13). Man cannot lay on his afflicting hand in the grave, and God will not. A believer's faith may not be able to see deliverance on this side of death, but clearly sees it on the other. (4) *A believer prays, although answers are withheld and there appears little prospect of any.* Prayer a necessity of his nature. A latent faith always in the renewed heart that God is gracious, and that He is the hearer and answerer of prayer.

VI. Expresses his disappointment and the grounds of it (verses 25, 26).

1. *The grounds of his disappointment.* Verse 25.—"Did not I weep for him that was in trouble? Was not my soul grieved for the poor?" His sympathy deep and real. Conscience bore its testimony to the sincerity of his charity. Could appeal to those around him for the general and genuine character of his compassion. The question affirmed by the admission of Eliphaz (chap. iii. 3, 4). Having shown sympathy and compassion to others when in trouble, he calculated on experiencing the same himself when in similar circumstances. The same thought expressed by the Psalmist, speaking as the type of Messiah (Ps. xxxv. 13, 14). A natural as well as Scriptural law—"With the same measure that ye mete withal, it shall be measured to you again (Luke vi. 38). True in respect to God, though sometimes for a time apparently otherwise. One of the laws of His kingdom,—"Blessed are the merciful, for they shall obtain mercy" (Matt. v. 7). Generally, though not always, true in relation to men. Job and Job's Antitype remarkable examples of the contrary. In Christ's case, unbounded compassion and tenderest sympathy repaid with cruelty and insult. An aggravation of trouble when sympathy and compassion are withheld where there is a just right to expect them. Mark of monstrous depravity when the sympathizing and compassionate are treated with unkindness and cruelty.

Job, according to the text, a beautiful example of Christian sympathy. The exemplification of the precept: "Weep with them that weep" (Rom. xii. 15). Remarkable manifestation of the grace of the Spirit in patriarchal times. May well put many living under the Christian dispensation to the blush. The great want in the Church of Christ, the Master's sympathy and compassion for the poor and afflicted. Yet the glory of Christianity and the evidence of its Divine character, that such a spirit has been so largely produced under it. Among its characteristic precepts are: "Be pitiful;" "Put on bowels of mercies" (1 Peter iii. 8; Col. iii. 12). Christ's compassionate spirit, in a greater or less degree, infused into all His members. The privilege as well as duty of believers, to be filled and pervaded with it (Eph. v. 18). Provision made for this in the present dispensation by the full bestowment of the Holy Spirit. Such sympathy and compassion the necessary qualification for Christian usefulness.

2. *The disappointment itself.* Verse 26.—"When I looked for good, then evil came unto me; and when I waited for (or expected) light (happiness and joy), there came darkness" (trouble and distress). Natural to expect happiness as the result of piety. Godliness has the "promise of the life that now is as well as of that which is to come" (1 Tim. iv. 8). Wisdom's ways pleasantness, and all her paths peace. Experienced as a matter of fact. The experience of Job himself previous to his calamities, and again after they were past. Promises of temporal happiness and comfort to be understood with an exception of needful trials. Fear of future trials not foreign to Job in the time of his prosperity (chap. iii. 25, 26; i. 5; ii. 10). Observe—(1) Trials as well as comforts necessary in a state of discipline. Darkness as well as light needful in the spiritual as in the natural world. (2) A believer's expectation, if good, always realized, though not always in this life or in the things of it. His trials and disappointments blessings as well as his comforts.

VII. Enlarges on his troubles (verses 27—31).

1. *Incessant inward as well as outward affliction.* Verse 27.—"My bowels boiled (with inward distress, as Lam. i. 20, or as the physical effect of his disease), and rested not (continued to do so without intermission, night and day); the days of affliction prevented me" (met me or came upon me suddenly and unexpectedly—an aggravation of the trouble).

2. *Continued grief.* Verse 28.—"I went (moved about) mourning (or black, in person or attire) without the sun." Not as the effect of exposure to the heat; or, in gloomy solitary places; or, in a state of dejection and sorrow. Reference perhaps to his experience previous to his disease, which probably kept him confined to his dwelling or the vicinity of it; enough in the loss of his ten children to occasion it.

3. *Public and unrestrained complaint.* Verse 28.—"I stood up [through deep earnestness and anguish], and I cried (as the expression of deep and uncontrollable grief, or as imploring relief and aid) in the congregation" (assembled for public business or Divine worship). Here also probable reference to the period in which he was still able to mingle with others and to appear in the public assemblies, and hence previous to his being smitten with his leprosy. Lepers excluded from society (Lev. v. 2, 3). Miriam, under the same disease, shut out from the camp seven days (Numb. xii. 15). King Azariah, when a leper, obliged to dwell in a "several," or separate house, and "cut off from the house of the Lord" (2 Chron xxvi. 20, 21). Usual for Orientals to give vent to their feelings in public.

4. *Solitary moaning.* Verse 29.—"I am a brother (by close resemblance) to dragons (or jackals, which roam in solitary places and utter doleful and hideous cries, especially in the night), and a companion to owls" (or ostriches, also remarkable for their loud nocturnal cries (Mic. i. 8).

5. *The disfigurement of his person, and internal physical suffering.* Verse 30.—"My skin is black upon me (or, becomes black [and falls] from off me, among the effects of his disease, hence called the black leprosy: the skin, however, also blackened by grief, Psa. cxix. 83; Jer. viii. 21; Lam. v. 16); and my bones are burned with heat" (as the result of internal inflammation, or expressive of inward distress, Psa. cii. 3).

6. *His whole experience one of sorrow and lamentation.* Verse 31.—"My harp also is turned to mourning, and my organ (or pipe) into the voice of them that weep" (as at funerals—the early practice of funeral

wailing still continued in the East). The harp, and organ or pipe, instruments of music earliest in use. Mentioned Gen. iv. 30. Indicative of the period in which the patriarch lived. Especially employed on joyful occasions. The language descriptive of a melancholy change from a joyous to a sorrowful experience. The sudden transition from previous joy an aggravation of present sorrow. Observe—(1) Job's previous life one rather of gaiety than gloom. True piety the sister of innocent pleasure. Wisdom's ways those of pleasantness. The voice of rejoicing and salvation heard in the tabernacles of the righteous. (2) The holiest heart and the happiest home liable to be overtaken by sudden and overwhelming sorrow. The major key often exchanged for the minor, and the song of gladness for the wail of grief. His Father's "house" the only place where the believer's sun never goes down, and his moon never withdraws itself. Heaven the only land where the harp and the organ are always in use, and the garments are always white.

Job held up in these tragic verses as an affecting picture of human distress. The inquiry suggested—why such grief and trouble under the administration of a benevolent Creator? Why its existence at all? Why in connection with comparative innocence? Why in the experience of a child of God? (1) The existence of suffering easily accounted for on the ground that sin is in the world. Sorrow and suffering the shadow cast by sin. Sin and suffering inseparably linked. Absence of sorrow impossible in a world of sin. Suffering to be viewed either—(i.) As the necessary and inevitable accompaniment of sin, as pain accompanies inflamation; or (ii.) as the infliction of a penalty, as punishment follows transgression in the state; or (iii.) as a kind and salutary discipline, like that employed by a father with his children. No absolutely innocent person in the world. The comparatively innocent necessarily suffer along with the guilty. Often suffer in consequence of the sin and suffering of others. (2) Suffering in a child of God part of the treatment necessary for his perfection and preparation for his eternal inheritance. A need-be for his heaviness through manifold temptations. Gold necessarily tried and purified in the fire. The believer's troubles necessary for the exercise and development of the graces of the Spirit. Made to conduce to the glory of God and the benefit of others. God sometimes glorified more in His patient than in His prosperous children. Suffering a theatre for the display both of the excellence and reality of true religion. Often the very result of the character and condition of a child of God. Such the special object of Satan's temptations and the world's persecution. By his renewed nature, made more sensible of the evil of sin within himself, and more deeply affected with the sufferings and sins of others. The glory and privilege of a child of God to be made a partaker of the afflictions of Christ, and for the same object (Col. i. 24). (3) Suffering and sorrow to be expected in the world as long as Satan is permitted to go up and down in it (chap. i. 7). This not always to be the case (Rev. xx. 1—3).

CHAPTER XXXI.

JOB'S SELF-VINDICATION.—HIS SOLILOQUY CONTINUED.

Concludes his speeches by a solemn, particular, and extended declaration of the purity and uprightness of his life. Especial reference to his *private*, as before to his *public*, conduct. Intended to silence his accusers and justify his complaints. Affords a picture of an outwardly and blameless character. A specimen, presented in beautiful language, of a pure morality accompanied with, and based upon, an ardent piety and genuine religion. Job asserts—

I. His chastity. Verse 1.—"I made a covenant with (or laid a solemn charge upon) mine eyes: why (or how) then should I look (or that I would not look) upon a maid" [to lust after her, as Matt. v. 28]. Speaks especially as a married man, and with reference to the sin of adultery. Already beginning to prevail in that early period, particularly with the rich and powerful. Hence Abraham's apprehension and temptation (Gen. xii. 11—15); and Isaac's, (Gen. xxvi. 7—10). Observe—

1. The text the language of *holy resolution.* The soul to act as lord of the body. The body with its members, organs, and senses, to be kept in subjection (1 Cor. ix. 27). The avenues to temptation to be guarded. The eye the inlet of lust. *Occasions and temptations to sin to be guarded against as well as sin itself.* The neglect of Job's resolution the occasion of David's fall and broken bones (2 Sam. xi. 2—4; Ps. li. 8). The Saviour's rule—"If thine eye offend thee"—prove a constant or frequent occasion of sin by awaking lust—"pluck it out"—remove the occasion of sin at whatever cost (Matt. v. 28). Eve's looking on the forbidden fruit the occasion of her own fall and the ruin of millions of her offspring. Lot's wife looking back on Sodom the cause of her petrifaction into a pillar of salt. Dinah's idle curiosity in visiting a heathen city to see its women, the loss of her own chastity. Achan's looking on the golden wedge and Babylonish garments the loss of his life (Josh. vii. 21). Samson's sleep on Delilah's lap the loss of his locks (Judges xvi. 19). "Look not on the wine when it is red" (Prov. xxiii. 31). David's (or Daniel's ?) prayer: "Turn away mine eyes from beholding vanity" (Ps. cxix. 37). Christian and Faithful in Vanity Fair refused even to look upon its wares. The contrast of the text in 2 Peter ii. 14, "Having eyes full of adultery."

2. Job's *reasons* for his resolution. (1) *His preference for a better portion.* Verse 2. —"For what portion of God is there [in such a case] from above? and what inheritance from the Almighty on high ?." Job taught to distinguish between present pleasure and future bliss, and between the mere gratification of lust and the enjoyment of true happiness. No gratification of the senses to be compared to the enjoyment of God's favour. A man must either forego the pleasures of sin or the joys of heaven. Nothing unclean admitted within the New Jerusalem. The gratification of sinful passion incompatible with the enjoyment of God's presence. Observe—(i.) *In order to the resisting of temptation and avoiding of sin, important to "have respect to the recompense of reward"* (Heb. xi. 26). Thus Moses chose rather to suffer affliction with the people of God, than to enjoy the pleasures of sin, which are but for a season (Heb. xi. 25). Having this respect, Mary chose the good part, and turned her back on the world ; *not* having it, the rich young man chose the world, and turned his back upon Christ. (ii.) *Necessary to choose between the enjoyment of sin and the enjoyment of God, and between a portion in this world and one in the next.* The whole tenour of a man's life here, and the whole eternity of his experience hereafter, determined by the choice he makes between the two. (iii.) God not only the Bestower of a believer's portion, but the portion itself (Ps. xvi. 5). Such portion to be desired in preference to all earthly and sensuous enjoyment, as—*First:* More excellent in itself, and more becoming man's better nature as a moral and intellectual being. *Second:* More satisfying to such a being, and to one made capable, as man is, of enjoying his Maker's friendship. *Third:*

More enduring, the one terminating at the farthest with death, the other extending throughout eternity. *Fourth:* Attended with no remorse. *Fifth:* Followed by no penalty. (2) *His dread of the consequences of sin.* Verse 3—"Is not destruction to the wicked? and a strange punishment (a terrible calamity or 'alienation'— viz., from God and all good) to the workers of iniquity?" Reference to the "terrors of the Lord" important in persuading ourselves, as well as others, to the avoidance of sin (2 Cor. v. 11). Christ's argument, "What shall a man be profited, if he should gain the whole world and lose his own soul?" Better to enter into life with one eye or one foot, than having two eyes or two feet to be cast into hell. Better lose everything than lose heaven. Every loss light compared with the loss of the soul. Observe—(i.) *Destruction certain to the wicked and impenitent.* The wicked turned into hell, and all the nations that forget God (Psa. ix. 17). (ii) *No earthly calamity equal to that which must one day overtake the ungodly.* The destruction of the Old World by water, and that of Sodom and Gomorrha by fire, only a foreshadowing of the destruction of the impenitent at the final judgment. Inconceivable terrors involved in the sentence: "Depart from me, ye cursed, into everlasting fire, prepared for the devil and his angels." (Matt. xxv. 41). "Everlasting destruction from the presence of the Lord, and from the glory of his power (2 Thess. i. 9). Such destruction the righteous penalty of wilful transgression of the Divine law, rebellion against the Divine government, and refusal of the Divine mercy. Natural that whatsoever a man soweth that he should also reap. Destruction and misery the flower and fruit of sin. Sin is misery in the seed; misery is only sin in the bloom. (3) *The recollections of God's constant inspection.* (Verse 4.)—"Doth not he see my ways, and count all my steps?" (or actions,—every separate act or passage in my course on earth) Omniscience a necessary attribute of godhead. An open eye the Egyptian hieroglyphic for deity. "Thou God seest me," the guardian of Job's life. Not easy to sin under the gaze of the broad eye of the Almighty. Few so hardy as to break the Queen's commands with the Queen herself looking on. The practice of sin the result of forgetfulness of God. The language of the heart if not of the lips of the ungodly,—No eye shall see me (ch. xxiv. 15). To walk before God the easy and natural way to be perfect and upright (Gen. xvii. 1).

II. **His honesty, uprightness, and freedom from covetousness (verses 5—8).**

"If I have walked with vanity (lived in the practice of falsehood and hypocrisy), or if my food hath hasted to deceit (to the commission of a fraud); let me be weighed (*Heb.*, 'let him—or any one—weigh me') in an even balance (*Heb.* 'in the balances of righteousness,') that God may know my integrity (should there be any doubt in the matter, which however is impossible). If my step hath turned out of the way (the straight way, or way of truth and uprightness, the only way that men should walk in), and mine heart walked after mine eyes— (gone out in covetous desire after the possession of what I have seen, as Ahab's heart went after Naboth's vineyard, — the eye being the inlet of covetousness as well as of lust), and if any blot (or stain of wrongdoing, unjust gain, or bribe for the perversion of justice) hath cleaved to my hands (in the transaction of any business with my fellow-men, or in the discharge of my duty as a magistrate and a judge); then let me sow, and let another eat; yea, let my offspring (or my produce) be rooted out." The language—

1. *Of conscious innocence and integrity.* Job able unhesitatingly to appeal to his neighbours and to God Himself in the declaration of his honesty and uprightness both in private and public life. So Samuel at Gilgal (1 Samuel xii. 3; and Paul at Miletus (Acts. xx. 18—20, 33 — 35). Job's character as here given by himself only that already given by God.

2. *Of, in some degree at least, self-ignorance and pride.* Job apparently still too confident in his own righteousness. Though upright in his external dealings, and blameless in the eyes of men, yet, weighed "in the balances of righteousness," even Job found wanting (Rom. iii. 9, 10, 19, 23). Much self-knowledge yet to be gained by him. Job yet to take the place of the publican—"God be merciful to me a sinner" (chap. xl. 4; xlii. 5, 6).

3. *Of sincerity.* A mark of uprightness, when we are not only willing but wishful, if we have done wrong, to suffer for it. David's case (Ps. vii. 3—5. Paul's Acts xxv. 11).

Job's imprecation suggests that, in the providence of God, *punishment in this world is often according to the nature of the sin.* Cruelty and wrong done to others often punished by the same being experienced by ourselves. Injustice in our gains punished by a blight on our substance. Same principle acknowledged in the next sin specified.

III. **His freedom from adulterous desires and practices.** Verses 9—12.— "If mine heart hath been deceived by (or enticed towards) a woman (especially one married—temptation from a maid spoken of already, verse 1); or if I have laid wait at my neighbour's door (watching the opportunity of his absence); then let my wife (my *own* wife) grind (become an abject slave; Exod. xi. 5; Is. xlvii. 2; and concubine) to another, and let others bow down upon her."

Adultery apparently prevalent in the time of Job and the writer of the book (chap. xxiv. 15). Job declares his freedom from the sin as an exceptional thing among the great men of his time and country. A sin to which his riches and power afforded, as in David's case, a strong temptation. Not uncommon in patriarchal times for the great to take another man's wife, though at the expense of her husband's life. Hence Abraham's and Isaac's fear for their wives' chastity and their own lives—the one in Egypt, and both in Gerar (Gen. xii. 12; xx. 2; xxvi. 7). One of the ten commandments in the Decalogue expressly directed against this sin. Its commission punished with death (Lev. xx. 10; Deut. xxii. 22). The sin apparently prevalent in the time of David and Solomon (Ps. l. 18; Prov. vi. 24—29; vii. 5—9; and of the later prophets, Jer. v. 8; ix. 2; Ezek. xviii. 6). Common among the Jews in the time of the Saviour (John viii. 3—9). The Pharisees and Rabbis themselves said to have been notoriously guilty of it (Rom. ii. 22). The destruction of Jerusalem and the Great Captivity under the Romans ascribed by the Talmud to its prevalence for forty years previous to that event.

Job's *reasons for abstaining from this sin.* Verse 11.—

1. The *heinousness of the crime itself:* "For this is an heinous crime." Sin to be avoided on account of its heinousness and malignity, apart from its consequences (Jer. xliv. 4). Adultery the most heinous form of covetousness and theft. The most aggravated wrong that can be done to another. Inflicts the deepest wound and in the tenderest part. Robs him of honour and home. Covers his family with shame. Defilement of a man's wife worse to endure than her death. Adultery a species of murder. The ruin of the injured man's peace, and often leading to bloodshed and death.

2. *Its consequences.* These were—(1) *Civil and judicial.* "It is an iniquity to be punished by the judges"—probably authoritative umpires or arbitrators in the case of any serious charge between man and man, with power to inflict appropriate penalty—usually the elders of the people (Deut. xxi. 2; Josh. xx. 4). Adultery a capital crime,

190

not only among the Jews but other nations of antiquity. The magistrate appointed by God to be a terror to evil doers (Rom. xiii. 1—4). Some sins only cognizable by God; others punishable by man. A special heinousness in a crime punishable by the civil magistrate. (2) *Natural and providential.* "For it is a fire that consumeth unto destruction, and would root out all mine increase." Sin in general, and sins like adultery in particular, a "fire taken into the bosom" (Prov. vi. 27). Its tendency to destroy comfort, health, reputation, family, estate; and ultimately the soul itself in endless perdition. One single act brought constant trouble into David's house and lasting sorrow into his heart. Sin destructive in its own nature; and some sins naturally more destructive than others. Many, if not all, sins carry with them their own punishment.

The imprecation in the text strongly declarative of Job's innocence. The evil imprecated, the very last a man would wish to himself. The penalty invoked in accordance with the nature of the offence. "By what a man sins by that is he punished." —*Jewish Proverb.* David's adultery with Bathsheba is punished with incest between his son and daughter, and the defilement of his concubines by his own son. His murder of Uriah is punished by the murder of his incestuous son by the hand of his own brother (2 Sam. xiii. 16).

IV. His justice and humanity to his servants or slaves. Verse 13.—"If I did despise the cause (or rights) of my manservant, or of my maidservant (my bondman or my bondwoman, my male or female slave), when they contended (had any controversy) with me." In the East, masters viewed as having absolute right over their servants or slaves. These considered a portion of the master's property. Were not permitted to appear in a court of justice against him. Might therefore be the object of any oppression without human redress. Job's conduct towards his slaves the opposite of that of an oppressor. Probably exceptional, and just such as became a professed servant of the true God. His slaves treated by him, in the case of any complaint, as having rights equal with his own.

The *grounds* of this treatment of his slaves or servants:—

1. *The consideration that for his conduct towards them he was amenable to God.* Verse 14.—"What then should I do when God riseth up? (to examine into my conduct, or to execute judgment on me as a transgressor, or finally, to plead the cause of the oppressed slave), and when he visiteth (for

the examination of conduct or the punishment of offences) what should I answer him" (for such conduct, so as to escape His anger)? Observe—(1) *The fear of God an effectual restraint on Job and all good men.* Joseph's case: "How shall I do this great wickedness, and sin against God?" The principle of Nehemiah's upright and disinterested conduct (Neh. v. 15). (2) *A day coming in which God makes inquisition into the conduct both of masters and servants, rulers and ruled.* The highest as well as the lowest amenable to His tribunal. (3) *God viewed by the natural conscience as a righteous and impartial judge.* (4) *Justice even in respect to the most outcast, a duty written on the conscience of mankind.* (5) *Men helpless against God's determination to punish the transgressor.* The most powerful tyrant feebler than the puniest insect before Him.

2. *As having the same Creator, and mode of creation.* Verse 15.—"Did not he that made me in the womb make him?" Master and servant the similar work of the same Creator, and therefore both equally valued and cared for by Him, and to be treated on equal terms by each other.

3. *As having the same nature.* "Did not one fashion us in the womb" (or, "did not He fashion us in one and the same womb—one by similarity, not numerically). Both formed in the same manner and possessed of the same human nature. A woman's womb the origin of both (Mal. ii. 10). The fundamental equality of mankind thus strongly asserted. The sentiment confirmed by the Apostle—"God hath made of one blood all nations of men," &c. (Acts xvii. 26). The Negro and the Papuan with the same essential features of humanity as the European. The slave possessed of the same faculties and powers, both moral and intellectual, as his master. The points in which men naturally differ from each other small and few compared with those in which all are alike. Men in a proper sense brethren, of whatever nation or class in society. The language of Job strikes at the root of slavery as justified by inferiority of race. Equality between master and servant, in the eyes of God, the teaching of the New Testament. Slavery not expressly forbidden, but principles inculcated which necessarily lead to its overthrow as Christianity advances. The views expressed by Job, in respect to man, of an advanced character for that period of the world. Only even now becoming universally acknowledged and acted upon by the Christian Church. Sentiments and practice of an opposite kind till very lately prevalent in a large portion of the Christian world. Even Christians justified the poet's satire—

" Man finds his fellow guilty of a skin
  Not coloured like his own ; and having power
To enforce the wrong, for such a worthy cause
  Dooms and devotes him as his lawful prey."

V. His benevolence and kindness to the poor. Verses 16, 17.—"If I have withheld the poor from their desire (their due wages, or rather the perquisites for which they looked as something belonging to them), or have caused the eyes of the widow to fail [by long withholding from her the expected help or redress]; or have eaten my morsel (or bread) alone, and the fatherless have not eaten thereof." Claims of the *poor* constantly recognized in the law of Moses. Perquisites appointed for them in the harvest and in the vintage (Lev. xix. 9; xxiii. 22) ; in every seventh year (Exod. xxiii. 11) ; and in every third year's tithes (Deut. xiv. 28, 29). Kindness and readiness to help the poor strictly enjoined (Deut. xv. 7—11). Their wages to be promptly paid them (Lev. xix. 13). Observe—Help as well as justice to the poor to be not only rendered, but rendered *promptly.* He gives twice who gives at once.—*Latin Proverb.* Job's conduct the opposite of that of the unjust judge in the parable (Luke xviii. 2, &c.).—Provision made by the Mosaic law for the *widow* in common with the poor in general. Their perquisites the same (Deut. xix. 21). Her raiment not to be taken to pledge (Deut. xxiv. 17). Herself not to be harrassed or afflicted (Exod. xxii. 22). A curse pronounced on those who should wrong her or "pervert her judgment" (Deut. xxvii. 19). Job, probably long before the law was given, careful to afford the poor and the widow their just rights, and to fulfil their reasonable expectations. The law from Sinai a Divine sanction to duties already performed by many without it, through the law written on the conscience, and the principle of grace infused by the Holy Spirit.—Kindness to and care of the *fatherless* also strictly enjoined by the Divine law. These objects of sympathy and compassion usually joined with the poor and the widow. Job's table open to the poor and needy. Common in the East to admit poor persons and strangers to their table or to send them portions from it. Hospitality a cardinal virtue among the Arabs. To be cultivated as a Christian grace (Rom. xii. 13; Heb. xiii. 2). Enjoined as a Christian duty (Luke xiv. 13). "Ready to distribute," a New Testament precept (1 Tim. vi. 18). The section suggestive of the duty of

Kindness to the poor.

Reasons and motives for its exercise—

1. The desire to relieve suffering and extend happiness.

2. The claim the poor have upon us as fellow-creatures and partakers of our common humanity. A Divine principle that where there is lack on the part of any member of the great family, it should be supplied out of the abundance of others (2 Cor. viii. 13—15). All living creatures, according to their nature, claim our help in suffering circumstances. Still more those of our own flesh. Kindness and benevolence to the poor and destitute allied to justice. Love a debt we owe to all our brethren. Kindness to the poor only one form of that love (Rom. xiii. 8—10).

3. The principle that we should do to others as we would that they should do to us in similar circumstances (Luke vi. 31).

4. The will and authority of our common Maker and Parent.

5. The example of the heavenly Father (Luke vi. 35, 36).

6. The special example of Christ, who "for our sakes became poor that we through his poverty might become rich" (2 Cor. viii. 9). His life a going about doing good.

7. The manner in which God has identified the cause of the poor with His own, and in which Christ has done that of His disciples (Prov. xix. 17; Matt. xxv. 40, 45).

8. Active kindness to the poor a fruit of the Spirit, and an instinct of the new nature created in a believer after the image of God, (Gal. v. 22; Col. iii. 10—12).

Lower and less worthy considerations—

1. The pleasure in the exercise of the benevolent affections, in relieving the sufferings and contributing to the happiness of others. The luxury of doing good.

2. The remembrance of our own liability to poverty and suffering, and our possible need of the help and sympathy of others.

3. The reward in an approving conscience and the "blessing of those who were ready to perish" (chap. xxix. 13.)

The exercise of kindness and benevolence marred by the introduction of selfish elements.

Kindness to the poor and needy to be—

1. Free and spontaneous.

2. Disinterested and pure from selfish motives.

3. Sincere and undissembled.

4. Prompt and seasonable.

5. Unwearied and persevering.

6. Self-denying as far as is necessary.

7. Impartial and general.

8. Up to our ability and opportunity.

9. Judicious and discriminating. Help given to the poor, without judgment and discretion, may be more injurious than beneficial. Our charity, like God's, to be directed by "wisdom and prudence" (Eph. i. 8). Relief not only to be given, but given to the proper *objects* and in the proper *form*.

10. Hearty and cheerful. Kind deeds to be accompanied with kind words and kind looks (Rom. xii. 8). The *manner* of the deed often as important as the deed itself.

Job's *reason* for his assertion, with stronger affirmation of it. Verse 18.—"For from my youth, he (the fatherless) was brought up with me as with a father, and I have guided (helped or comforted) her (the widow) from my mother's womb" (a strong hyperbole, meaning, "from my earliest years"). To assert more strongly his benevolence, he assigns a reason for it, and adds something in regard to its exercise. With him the practice was nothing new. Benevolence was his natural disposition. Speaks of it as something born with him. Kindness to the widow and fatherless had been practised by him from his earliest years. Had grown with him into a habit or second nature. Much of this habit probably due to the character, and care of his parents. Neither the name of his father nor mother mentioned; but their eulogy unintentionally written in these words. His home a pious one, and his up-bringing according to godliness. Care early bestowed by his parents on his moral training. Observe, in respect to—

Early moral training—

1. *Some born with dispositions naturally more benevolent than others.* Such a disposition a favour from the Author of our being. Responsibility connected with its cultivation and exercise. Natural disposition to benevolence not necessarily followed by the wise, persevering, and self-denying practice of it. In Job's case, the disposition fostered by his parents, and improved by himself through the constant exercise of kindness to the poor and needy. All probably born with more or less of such a disposition to begin with. A fragment of the Divine image imparted in creation. The least of it capable of increase through cultivation and practice. Its introduction in early life possible, and to be expected under the Christian economy and the dispensation of the Spirit. The natural disposition of children often an inheritance from their parents.

2. *Children capable of being trained to the exercise of the benevolent affections.* To be

trained to "minister" and to show kindness to the poor and suffering, one of the most important parts of a child's education. Such education more especially devolving upon the parents, and particularly the mother. Under the parents' careful and constant attention, habits of good-doing capable of being formed in early life.

3. *Early habits of benevolence, among the principal means of forming the character in after years.* A child trained to such habits may become, in a greater or less degree, a Howard or an Elizabeth Fry. A Nero only the development of a child allowed to take pleasure in torturing a bird, or sticking a pin through a fly. The child the father to the man. Job resumes the declaration of his humanity and benevolence, and asserts it in respect to *clothing* as well as feeding the poor. Verses 19, 20.—"If I have seen any perish for want of clothing, or any poor without covering (by night or by day); if his loins have not blessed me (in gratitude for my clothing them), and if he were not warmed with the fleece of my sheep" (or lambs, woven into cloth to serve him for a garment by day and a coverlet by night). Clothing the poor a needful form of benevolence in Arabia as well as in Britain. The cold of winter at times severe, all the more sensible after the extreme heat of summer. The nights often as cold as the days are hot. Clothing especially manufactured from the wool of sheep; a coarser kind from the hair of the camels. The earliest kind of clothing the skins of animals (Gen. iii. 21). The next step a garment made of the wool woven into cloth. Sheep chiefly valuable in the East on this account. The wool not only a beneficent provision for the animal itself, but for man who was to be its keeper. One of the sons of Adam, and the first martyr, a keeper of sheep (Gen. iv. 2).

Clothing the poor repeatedly mentioned in Scripture as one of the duties of charity. One of the forms of loving service rehearsed by Christ from the judgment-seat, as having been performed by the righteous on Himself in the person of His followers. (Matt. xxv. 36). The duty enjoined by the Baptist as a proof of true repentance—"He that hath two coats let him give to him that hath none." The name of Dorcas now a household word, from her kindness in clothing the poor. Perhaps as many perish for want of clothing as for want of bread. To be feared that garments lie in the chest, or hang in the wardrobe, which ought to clothe the "loins" of the poor. "The boards of my floor can well want carpets while so many of the poor around me want clothes to their backs" (*Fenelon*).

13

Declares, further, his humanity *negatively.* Had never used intimidation or violence in regard to the fatherless, nor used his influence in court to their disadvantage. Verse 21.—"If I have lifted up my hand against the fatherless (either to threaten or oppress him,—to 'smite with the fist of wickedness,' Is. lviii. 4), when I saw my help (or advantage, or those who were ready to support me) in the gate" (or court of justice, where a controversy was pending between us). Observe:—

1. Humanity exercised as well in what we refrain from doing as in what we do.

2. A strong temptation to the rich and powerful to take advantage of their position in a dispute with the poor. Cases of complaint against injury usually decided in the east by the opinion of the judge or Kadi, or by the voice of the majority of elders. A man of power and influence easily able to carry a case in his favour against the weak and defenceless. Such cases of complaint probably not infrequent where one man possessed such numerous flocks and herds, and carried on so extensive a husbandry. The greatest man in the land of Uz might easily have used his power and influence in such a case, but had ever refrained from doing so.

3. As much principle often required to abstain from taking advantage of our position and influence in a dispute with others, as to bestow a positive benefit. Jezebel's wickedness displayed in her counting upon her power with the elders and nobles in the court to obtain the vineyard of Naboth (1 Kings xxi. 7—13).

Closes the declaration of his humanity to the poor with an *imprecation* in case of guilt. Verse 22.—"Then let mine arm (the upper arm, from the elbow upwards) fall from the shoulder blade, and mine arm (the fore-arm, between the wrist and the elbow) be broken from the bone" (or upper arm to which it is attached). Reference to the whole of the preceding declaration in regard to his humanity to the poor, but more especially to the last-mentioned particular—"If I have lifted," &c. The punishment imprecated always corresponding with the offence supposed to have been committed. On the same principle, Cranmer held his right hand over the burning pile to be first consumed, as the member which had signed the recantation made against his conscience and against the truth. The penalty conceived justly to fall especially on the member or organ which was more especially concerned in the offence. Men convicted of theft among the Copts not unfrequently found with their hands cut off.

Adds a *reason* for his declared conduct.

193

Verse 23.—"For destruction from God was a terror unto me, and by reason of his highness, I could not endure" (either to commit the sin or meet His wrath). Similar sentiment expressed in verses 3 and 14. The reason given with reference to all the particulars of his conduct just mentioned, but more especially to the last. Observe—

The fear of God a good man's preservative against sin. Seen in the case of Joseph and Nehemiah as well as of Job. The consideration of God's displeasure against the sinner and the punishment threatened against the sin, *one* motive for resisting temptation and practising good, though not the highest. Rather the last source of defence against temptation when others fail. Better to abstain from sin and practice good, from hatred to sin itself and from love to God and good-doing, than from fear of His wrath. In Gospel exhortations to resist temptation and to do good, appeals rather made to the believer's gratitude for mercies received, to his position and privileges in Christ, and to the example of his Divine Master and Father, than to his fears of punishment and the Divine anger. Fear a right and important motive, but rather for the servant than the child. "Ye have not received the spirit of bondage again to fear, but ye have received the spirit of adoption, whereby we cry: Abba, Father" (Rom. viii. 15). Yet a loving and right-minded child will fear to offend a father, even more than a servant fears to offend a master. Love a more powerful principle than fear; yet fear may be called in to help when love is not sufficiently strong in itself.

V. Declares his freedom from idolatry both in its spiritual and external form, both secret and open, in heart and in life (verses 24—28). Specifies the two leading forms of idolatry—Mammonism and Sabæism—the trust in and love of *riches*, and the worship of idols in the ordinary sense of the word; here that of the *sun and moon*. The one the idolatry of the *heart*, the other that of the *outward act*. Job clears himself from both.

1. From *Mammonism*, or the trust in and love of riches. Verses 24, 25.—"If I have made gold my hope, or have said to the fine gold, thou art my confidence; if I rejoiced because my wealth was great, and because mine hand had gotten much." (Note—the language of idolatry,—"Mine hand had gotten," instead of—"the Lord had given"—the language of a servant of God). Job abjures as forms of

Heart-idolatry,

1. *Trust in riches.* Riches naturally and

194

easily trusted in by an unrenewed heart. Money a defence (Eccles. vii. 12). Answereth all things (Eccles. x. 19). Trust apt to be placed in riches for happiness in general. More particularly—(1) For acquisition of the means of life and sources of enjoyment. (2) For defence against suffering and the assaults of others. (3) For power and position in the world. *Trust in money a common form of idolatry.* "Soul, thou hast much goods laid up for many years; take thine ease," &c. Trust in Himself required by God from His intelligent creatures. That trust transferred to any other person or thing, in God's sight idolatry. Trust in riches contrasted in the Scriptures with trust in God (Ps. lii. 7; 1 Tim. vi. 17). The former characteristic of the ungodly; the latter, of the righteous. Believers cautioned not to trust in uncertain riches, but in the living God (1 Tim. vi. 17). Trust in riches incompatible with entrance into the kingdom of God (Mark x. 24). The rich man not to glory in his riches, but in the Lord (Jer. ix. 23, 24; 1 Cor i. 31). God and not riches to be trusted in for our daily bread. Hence the petition: "Give us this day," &c. Man's life not in the abundance of the things he possesses. Liveth not by bread alone, but by every word of God (Matt. iv. 4). Riches not given to be trusted in, but to be employed by us as stewards, in the service of the Master and for the benefit of others as well as ourselves, in obedience to His will and in dependence on His blessing.

To trust in riches instead of God not only wicked but *foolish*, as—(1) Riches are uncertain, and may soon and suddenly cease to be ours. (2) They are unable to render us either safe or happy even while we possess them. (3) They fail to meet the most important exigences of our nature as moral and responsible creatures. (4) They are unable to accompany us into another world.

The *possession* of riches to be distinguished from *trust* in them. Money well employed, a *blessing*; when allowed to usurp the place of God as our trust and confidence, a *curse*. The young man in the Gospel an example of trust in riches, notwithstanding a great appearance of piety and morality. Unable to give them up to follow Christ, because looking to *them* to make him happy rather than to God. A test as to whether we are trusting in riches—Am I ready cheerfully to give them up at God's will and for God's service? And, What proportion of my substance do I give for the extension of His kingdom, and the promotion of His cause in the world?

2. *Love of riches.* Job neither *trusted* in his wealth nor *rejoiced* in it. Riches a good,

but not the chief good. If riches increase, the heart not therefore to be set upon them (Ps. lxii. 10). Observe—(1) *Not money, but the love of it, the root of all evil* (1 Tim. vi. 10). A lawful, as well as an unlawful, rejoicing in our possessions (Deut. xii. 7; Eccles. ii. 7; iv. 26). Lawfully rejoiced in, when viewed not as what our own hand has gotten, but as what God has given; and not as given for our own exclusive enjoyment, but also for the benefit of others and the Master's service. Riches loved and idolized— (i.) When their acquisition and enjoyment afford us more pleasure and delight than the possession and enjoyment of God. (ii.) When we are more concerned about the acquisition and increase of them than about the enjoyment of God's favour and the advancement of His cause. (iii.) When we find it difficult to give up any considerable portion of them at God's will and for the promotion of His glory in the world. (2) *The love of money incompatible with the love of God* (Matt. vi. 24; 1 John ii. 15). Hence covetousness, or the love of riches, idolatry (Col. iii. 5; Eph. v. 5). Supreme love to God as the All-good, required of His intelligent creatures, as truly as as undivided trust in Him as the Almighty. (3) *Love of riches distinct from a proper appreciation of them.* Riches as merely possessed by us, a *blessing;* a *curse,* when they possess *us.* As a mere possession, they are worthless; as a means of doing good and glorifying God, invaluable. Job's wealth not taken from him either for his *trust in* it or his *fondness of* it, any more than for his unlawful acquisition of it, or any evil use which he made of it.

Job taught by the Holy Spirit as well as by the light of nature, to view heart-idolatry, or the worship of riches, as heinous in God's sight as outward idolatry, or the worship of sun and moon. The view confirmed in the New Testament (Eph. v. 5).

2. Job equally abjures the *second* form of idolatry, the worship of fictitious divinities, or of idols in the ordinary sense of the word, —here, that of the heavenly bodies, especially the *sun and moon.* Verses 26, 27.—"If I beheld the sun (*Heb.* 'light,'—a poetic name for the sun, which from its luminous atmosphere has been constituted a fountain of light to the earth and other planets), when it shined [in its glorious effulgence], or the moon walking in brightness (advancing like an orb of burnished silver in her course through the heavens); and my heart (the seat of the affections, and required in worship) hath been secretly [while I have outwardly been a worshipper of the only true God, and because afraid of the consequences of open idolatry,] enticed [by their appearance of majesty, glory, and beauty, and by the false views already beginning to be entertained regarding their divinity], or my mouth hath kissed my hand" [in token of my adoration of these luminaries (1 Kings xix. 5; Hos. xiii. 2)]; (*Heb.,* "My hand hath kissed my mouth"—the *heart* leading in the sin, and the *hand* following; inward affections being manifested by outward actions). The idolatry here indicated known as *Sabæism,* from the Hebrew word *Saba,* "a host," denoting the worship of the "host of heaven," or the heavenly bodies (Deut. xvii. 3; 2 Chron. xxxiii. 3). Originally the worship of "light" or fire, and afterwards connected with that of the sun, moon, and stars, as its great reservoirs and sources as well as symbols. The heavenly bodies, especially the sun and moon, among the earliest objects of idolatrous worship. This form of idolatry especially prevalent in Chaldæa, where probably it had its origin. Babylon called the mother of harlots. The worship of the sun and moon an early form of Arabian idolatry. The moon the great divinity of the ancient Arabians. Still an object of great veneration with Mahommedans. Hence the symbol of the Crescent. The Caaba at Mecca originally a temple dedicated to the moon. Abraham's relatives and neighbours in Chaldæa addicted to this form of idolatry. His place of residence—"Ur of the Chaldees," probably so called from *Ur,* "fire;" or from *Or,* "light." At Mugheir, believed by some to be its modern representative, the ruins have been discovered of a temple dedicated to the moon, and resembling that of the sun at Babylon.

These luminaries worshipped originally as representatives of deity, then as deities themselves. Viewed as the great prolific powers in the universe, and the bestowers of all earthly blessings.

The worship of the sun and moon ultimately that of almost the whole known world. Prevalent among our own ancestors. The names of the first and second days of the week, monuments of its existence among the Anglo-Saxons. Temples of Apollo or the sun, and of Diana or the moon, formerly stood in London, the one on the site of Westminster Abbey, the other on that of St. Paul's Cathedral.

The object of Jehovah in making Israel his elect nation to preserve them from the practice of this idolatry, and thus to have witnesses for Himself and His truth in the world (Deut. iv. 19). The practice of it in Israel's degeneracy the cause of their captivity in Babylon (Ezek. viii. 16; 2 Kings xxiii. 5, 11). Observe—(1) *Fallen humanity prone to put the creature in the place of the*

13—2

Creator. Early lost the true idea and knowledge of God through departure from and alienation to Him. "Did not like to retain God in their knowledge" (Rom. i. 28). Hence objects remarkable either for majesty, beauty or utility, worshipped in His stead. The source and essence of idolatry (Rom. i. 25). (2) *Difficult for fallen human nature to use the creature without abusing it.* Objects of nature to be viewed, not with idolatrous fondness or admiration of the creature, but with admiration, love, and praise to the Creator. Nature to lead up to nature's God, not away from Him. Indication of idolatry in man, when

> "The landscape has his praise, but not its Author."

(3) A mark of advanced enlightenment, that Job mentions with the same breath, trust in and love of riches, with the worship of the heavenly bodies, as equally idolatrous and offensive in the sight of God. (4) In Job's time the knowledge and worship of the true God greatly on the decrease; yet His faithful worshippers still to be found. "Left not himself without witness" (Acts xiv. 17).

Job's *reason* for abstaining from idolatry either in its spiritual or external forms. Verse 28.—"This also were an iniquity to be punished by the judge (or, 'a judicial iniquity;' idolatry still in Job's days considered a punishable crime; afterwards, by the law of Moses, to be punished with death, Deut. xvii. 2—7); for I should have denied ('lied to' or against) the God that is above" (in place, power, dignity, and excellence). Observe—

1. *The heinousness of a sin to be a principal reason for its avoidance.*

2. *That heinousness to be especially seen in its relation to God.*

3. *Trust in and love of riches, as well as the external worship of a created object or image, a denial of the true God.* All idolatry a denial of God. (1) In the boundless excellence of His being. (2) In the spirituality of His nature. (3) In His infinity and omnipresence. (4) In His moral as well as natural perfections. (5) In His sufficiency for our happiness and safety. (6) In His sole right to the trust, love, and worship of His intelligent creatures.

4. *God not only denied by our words, but by our works.*

5. *All trust in and worship of the creature, a lie against God.* A lie in the right hand of every idol-worshipper, whether of man, money, or of the sun and moon (Is. xliv. 20).

VI. Denies all vindictiveness in reference to enemies. Verses 29, 30.—"If I rejoiced at the destruction of him that hated
196

me, or lifted up myself (in exultation or insult) when evil found him; neither have I suffered my mouth to sin by wishing a curse to his soul" (or, by asking for his life, *i.e.*, the removal of it in an imprecation). Observe—

1. *Even a good man not without enemies.* Hatred from the world promised by Christ to His disciples (Matt. x. 22). A blessing pronounced on those who, for His sake, experience it (Luke vi. 22). A woe on those of whom all men speak well (Luke vi. 26). Hatred from the world a consequence of not being of it (John xv. 19). Christ Himself the great object of the world's hatred (John xv. 18). The ground of that hatred his testimony against its works (John vii. 7). Those spared the world's hatred who partake of its character (John vii. 7). "They that forsake the law, praise the wicked; but such as keep the law, contend with him" (Prov. xxviii. 4). Hence the enmity of the wicked against the good. This enmity experienced by Job.

2. *A good man known by his conduct towards his enemies.* The mark of an unregenerate heart to cherish ill-will against an enemy or to take pleasure in his misfortune. Hatred of a foe the prompting of fallen nature and the spirit of heathenism. "Revenge is sweet,"—the language of the Great Murderer. To rejoice in the fall of an enemy, the sin of the Edomites in relation to Israel and the cause of their punishment (Obadiah 12, 13). The sin forbidden in Prov. xxiv. 17. The contrary disposition enjoined both in the Old and New Testaments (Prov. xxv. 21; Rom. xii. 20). Christ's command to his followers, not only not to rejoice in the evil that overtakes an enemy, but to pray for and promote his welfare (Matt. iv. 44). *Noble minds rejoice in the opportunity of befriending a foe.* Instances recorded even of the heathen returning kindness for insult. Pericles having been followed to his door by one who had been railing against him, offered him his servant to light him home. Augustus invited to supper the poet Catullus after he had been railing against him. Nothing more common among men than vindictiveness, and nothing more contemptible. *Our best revenge on an enemy is to forgive him and treat him kindly.* To wish evil to him who hates us makes us as bad, or worse, than himself. The New Testament rule in such cases.— "Overcome evil with good" (Rom. xii. 21). In accordance with His own precept, Christ prayed for his murderers (Luke xxiii. 34). Commissioned His heralds of mercy to begin with those who had clamoured for His blood (Luke xxiv. 47). His spirit and conduct imitated by His followers. The first Christian

martyr died with a prayer on his lips for those who were stoning him to death (Acts vii. 60). Job's religion afterwards embodied in the Gospel. Though living in the patriarchal age, Job exemplified the spirit of Christianity. The new commandment only a new edition of the old. An advance however in the moral teaching of the New Testament as compared with that of the Old. Job instructed not to hate an enemy; the Christian taught to love him. Christianity teaches not only not to wish a curse to an enemy, but to pray for a blessing to him.

3. *The teaching of God's Spirit and the character of God's children always essentially the same.* That teaching and character a transcript of His own nature. God's example that of forgiveness and kindness to enemies. The carnal mind enmity to God. Mankind enemies to God in their mind by wicked works (Rom. viii. 7; Col. i. 21).

4. *Special guard to be placed upon the mouth.* A sinful thought or feeling not to be allowed utterance. To be *suppressed* instead of being *expressed.* An aggravation of sin in the heart to give it expression with the lips. Bodily organs not to be employed as the instruments of sin.

VII. Job declares his humanity as a householder (verses 31, 32).

1. In his kindness to his *domestics and inmates.* Verse 31—" If the men of my tabernacle (those residing under his roof, whether as domestics, retainers, or other inmates,) said not, Oh, that we had of his flesh! we cannot be satisfied " (or, " Who is there that was was not satisfied with his flesh ?"—*i.e.*, with his hospitality, 1 Sam. xxv. 11; or, according to some ancient versions, " If they said, Who will give us of his flesh, that we may be satisfied," as complaining of not having sufficient food, or longing for the better supplies on his own table). Job able to appeal to his own domestics and the inmates of his dwelling for evidence of his humanity, more especially of his bounty to them and his liberality to others. No niggard in his own house. Treated his servants not only with justice, but kindness. Gave them not only food, but of the best kind, and plenty of it. Made them sharers of the best that was on his own table. Had no feast but they partook of it. Observe—(1) *A good man will be kind and liberal to his domestics* (Col. iv.1). (2) *Well when, as masters, we can appeal to our servants for our character, and when they can bear an honest testimony in our favour.* Servants and inmates of our house, likely to be the best judges of our character and conduct. (3) *Good to make our house a*

home *for others as well as ourselves.* A Christian duty to "bring the poor that are cast out to our house " (Isa. lviii. 7). " I was a stranger and ye took me in" (Matt. xxv. 35). Job's house never without the objects of his charity. The widow and the fatherless, the stranger and the destitute, frequent guests at his table. Note—Customary for wealthy Arabs to slaughter sheep or camels for the supply of their household. "Broad dishes" the glory of an Arab chief, as necessary for the entertainment of his guests.

2. In his hospitality to *travellers.* Verse 32 —" The stranger did not lodge in the street (for want of a house to receive him, it being difficult to obtain accommodation in Oriental towns and villages *then,* as it is still, except with the sheikh or a Christian); but I opened my doors to the traveller" (or, as *margin,* "to the way," as if to invite and welcome the traveller passing by). Pleasing picture of Oriental manners, corresponding with those of patriarchal times (Gen. xviii. 1—4; xix. 1, &c.). Job an example of the New Testament precept— " Use hospitality *without grudging* " (1 Peter iv. 9). " Given to hospitality," more than merely " showing " it (Rom. xii. 13). " Be not forgetful to entertain strangers,"—not merely your relatives or acquaintances (Heb. xiii. 2).

VIII. Clears himself from secret and concealed transgressions. Verses 33, 34. —" If I covered my transgressions as Adam (in allusion to Gen. iii. 8; or, 'like men,' as Hos. vi. 7—as men are wont to do after the example of their first father), by hiding mine iniquity in my bosom (from impenitence or hypocrisy, or both): Did I fear a great multitude (or, 'because I feared,' &c.; or as an imprecation—'Then let me fear,' &c.), or did the contempt of families (or tribes) terrify me (so as to conceal my sin or neglect my duty to the stranger; or, 'because the contempt, &c., terrified me;' or, 'let the contempt, &c., terrify or crush me '), that I kept silence [instead of acknowledging my transgression, or opening my mouth in behalf of the oppressed stranger,— like Lot, Gen. xix. 6—8, or the old man of Gibeah, Judges xix. 22—24], and went not out of the door ?" (for fear of detection, or to avoid the danger and self-denial connected with my duty to the stranger; or, as continuing the imprecation, "let me be silent," &c.). Observe—

1. The best not free from transgressions, both against God and men. Job a perfect man, yet acknowledges transgressions. "Not a just man on earth that doeth good and sinneth not " (Eccles. vii. 20).

2. Natural to men to conceal their transgressions. Adam's conduct imitated by all his children (Gen. iii. 8). ·

3. Men with much outward morality and religion may still be guilty of secret sins. The case with the Scribes and Pharisees in the days of the Saviour. Job more than suspected of it by his friends. Hence his concern now to clear himself of such hypocrisy.

4. The fear of man often more powerful in leading men to conceal their guilt, than the fear of God in leading them to confess it. The ungodly more afraid of man's shame than of God's wrath.

5. Just that secret crimes should be followed by popular contempt and ignominy as their penalty. A day coming when secret transgressors, who have successfully covered their crimes in this life, will awake to "shame and everlasting contempt" in the next (Daniel xii. 3).

6. A good man has no need either to fear the populace or shun the public eye. A good conscience a man's best armour. "Be just and fear not."

7. A good man more afraid of God's displeasure than of man's contempt. The sin of men, that they are more afraid of man and the "multitude" than of their Maker. "Who art thou, that thou shouldst be afraid of a man that shall die, and of the Son of man that shall be made as grass, and forgettest the Lord thy Maker?" (Is. li. 12, 13). "Fear not them which kill the body, but are not able to kill the soul" (Matt. x. 23).

8. The part of an honest and sincere heart, to confess transgressions both before God, and, when necessary, before man. A Christian's first duty, to confess his transgressions to God; his next, to confess them to man if he has injured or offended him. "Confess your faults one to another," a New Testament precept (James v. 16). Confession *to* God necessary to forgiveness *from* God (Prov. xxviii. 13; 1 John i. 8, 9; Ps. xxxii. 3–5). Frank confession a mark of true repentance. Examples: Zaccheus (Luke xix. 8); the penitent thief (Luke xxiii. 41); the converts of Ephesus (Acts xix. 18, 19).

9. A good man not deterred from duty, either by the fear of numbers or the contempt of neighbours. Example: Lot in Sodom (Gen. xix). Milton's famous picture of the Seraph Abdiel—

"Faithful found
Among the faithless, faithful only he;
Among innumerable false, unmov'd,
Unshaken, unseduced, unterrified.

198

His loyalty he kept, his love, his zeal;
Nor number, nor example, with him wrought
To swerve from truth, or change his constant mind,
Though single."

VIII. Job's final desire and challenge. Verses 35—37.—"O that one would hear me! (or 'O that I had one to hear me!'—an impartial judge or umpire in the controversy between the Almighty and himself, so that his case might be fairly tried and decided upon). Behold, my desire is that the Almighty would answer me (or, 'here is my mark' or signature, i.e., to the declaration he made of his innocence— 'let the Almighty answer me,' and prove me guilty if He can); and that my adversary had written a book (or, 'and let mine adversary write a book' or bill of indictment against me, as in courts of law; or, 'and [O that I had] the book [or indictment which] mine adversary has written against me!') Surely I would take it upon my shoulder (as a thing of which I was not ashamed, but which I was willing that every one should see and know), and bind it as a crown to me (as a thing in which I rather gloried as my honour and ornament, being persuaded that all the charges contained in it would be found to be groundless). I would declare unto him (viz., the umpire or judge) the number of my steps (all the various passages of my life); as a prince— (with the boldness and confidence of an innocent man assured of coming off victorious, instead of the faltering step and downcast look of a culprit) would I go near unto him" (instead of avoiding him like Adam in the garden, as conscious of guilt).

This lofty passage is, perhaps, the strongest declaration of his innocence that Job had yet made, probably intended as the *finale* of his pleadings, and the climax of his protestations. The three following verses, with the exception of the last clause, probably standing originally somewhere before the present passage; or, what is less likely, as a still farther vindication of his character.

The passage stands as a proof of his conscious integrity. Expresses his continued desire to have a fair and impartial hearing of his case, with the conviction that he would be declared free from the sins which were either openly or by implication charged upon him, and from any such transgressions as to merit his present sufferings. The adversary with whom he wishes to contest the matter, mainly God himself who seemed to treat him as a guilty person. His three friends also his adversaries, but only as taking up the view of his character which God himself seemed to take from the way in which He was now dealing with him. God seemed to have charges against him of which he was entirely unconscious. His friends declared that such charges must exist. Job denied there there was any ground for them. Hence his great desire that the matter may be fairly examined into and decided.

This desire of Job, now soon about to be granted, and that in his favour. Not however to be done till he has been taught some necessary and important lessons. Though having the truth on his side in the controversy, his spirit and language not always what they ought to have been. His error in declaring his innocence in too decided a manner, and in carrying his declaration almost, if not altogether, to the point of self-confident glorying and self-righteous pride. At times not only bitter in his spirit and language towards his three friends, but petulant and irreverent towards God. The present winding up of his speeches sounded like a declaration that *he* was righteous, whatever God might be in the matter; in other words, that he was more righteous than God. Too much overlooked the fact—(1) That he, in common with all mankind, was guilty before God, and had given sufficient occasion to be visited with stripes even more severe than those from which he was now suffering; (2) That God is infinitely holy, just, and good, and would do nothing with any of His creatures but what was perfectly right; (3) That God might have wise objects in view in dealing with him as He did, which, though now hidden from him, He in His own time would show—as, for example, his own purification, God employing his sufferings as the goldsmith does the furnace for purifying the gold; (4) That God, as Creator, has the right to do with His creatures as He pleases without doing anything either unjust or unkind, and that it is the creature's part to be passive and submissive in His hand— Job's actual conduct at the beginning of his trials.

The steps between this last speech of Job's and the declaration of his integrity on the part of the Almighty, occupied in correcting these errors, and in bringing him to a juster view of himself, and to a better state of mind in regard to God. Observe :—

1. *No flesh allowed to glory in God's presence*—(1 Cor. i., 29). One of the great objects of the Bible to teach men this truth. The proper place for fallen man before God, even at his best, is the dust. Tendency to pride in the best. Imperfection stamped

on all human excellence. Like Moses, Job speaks unadvisedly with his lips. Utters what is rash before God, which he afterwards repents in dust and ashes. Not yet the perfect man who "offendeth not in word" (James iii. 2).

2. *Only one way of going near to God as our judge with boldness and confidence.* Not that of Job, as in ourselves righteous and innocent; but as sinners, accepting of and trusting in the blood and righteousness of Jesus Christ as the only ground of our acceptance before God (Heb. x. 22.) "Surely shall one say, in the Lord have I righteousness. In him shall all the seed of Israel be justified and shall glory" (Is. xlv. 24, 25).

IX. **Job finally clears himself of injustice in his business transactions with his fellow-men.** (Verses 38—40).— "If my land (probably the land which, like Isaac, he rented and cultivated for his own use) cry against me (as dishonestly acquired or oppressively cultivated,—like Abel's innocent blood shed by his brother's hand (Gen. iv. 10), or that the furrows likewise thereof complain (*Hebrew,* 'weep together,' as in sympathy with one another, and with the owners whom I have wronged by occupying their land without paying duly for its use, or with the labourers whom I have oppressed by employing them without a fair remuneration for their work;—a beautiful and bold personification to increase the effect) : if 1 have eaten the fruits thereof without money (in payment either to the proprietor for the occupancy of his land, or to the labourer for his work in cultivating it), or have caused the owners thereof to lose their lives (either directly by violent means in order to obtain their property, or indirectly by withholding the just payment for its occupancy) : let thistles (or thorns) grow instead of wheat, and cockle (or noxious weeds) instead of barley." Observe—

1. *One of the most testing points in reference to a man's character, how he carries on his business and conducts his transactions with his fellow-men.* Constant temptation to over-reach and take advantage. Tendency in fallen human nature both to withhold from others their just due, and to exact more than our own. The business principles of the world often the reverse of those of the Bible. That of "Buy cheap and sell dear," liable to be carried out to the extent of fraud and extortion. Christianity and sound morality teach us to give every man a fair price for his labour or his goods, and to ask no more than a fair price for our own. The maxim, "Business is business," sinful if understood as meaning that business is

exempted from the same rules of morality as are applied to other branches of conduct. *Defectiveness in commercial morality one of the sins of the day* In the race for riches, men tempted, even in a Christian land, to commit the sins which Job here solemnly abjures—receiving labour, goods, or money, without giving a just equivalent. The temptation not always resisted to sell articles that are something different from what they are represented to be. The severe reproof of the Almighty, directed in the Bible against those who oppress the hireling of their wages (Mal. iii. 5; James v. 4). A woe pronounced on him "who buildeth his house by unrighteousness and his chambers by wrong; that useth his neighbour's service without wages, and giveth him not for his work," (Jer. xxii. 13).

2. *Even professedly religious men tempted to follow the world in untruthful and unfair modes of conducting business.* The practice of over-reaching and extortion apparently prevalent in Job's time and country. Extortion on the part of rulers, proprietors, and dealers in the East, notorious. The practice of a Turk or Arab in demanding an exorbitant price for his goods, as common as that of the governor or employer in giving the merest pittance for the labourer's work. Extortion and excess among the prevailing sins of the Pharisees in the days of the Saviour (Matt. xxiii. 25). Job careful to resist the temptation to a common sin. Renounced filthy gain. No canker in his gold and silver. No rust on his money to witness against him either here or hereafter, and to eat his flesh as it were fire (James v. 3). Had neither sought to buy cheaper nor sell dearer than justice and humanity demanded.

3. *Dishonesty found on the side of buyers as well as of sellers.* (1). In not paying duly for goods delivered; (2). In depreciating and cheapening down an article, in order to get a bargain, or to obtain it at a price below its value. "It is naught, it is naught, saith the buyer; but when he is gone his way, then he boasteth" (Prov. xx, 14).

4. *The mark of a true servant of God, to be "faithful in that which is least."*

5. *The part of a follower of Christ, to commend his Master's religion by exhibiting a sterling morality in his daily life.* "Whatsoever things are true, honest, just, lovely, and of good report," &c. (Phil iv. 8).

6. *Murder committed in more ways than one.* Indirect as well as direct murder. The life-blood of the poor may be drained by oppressive work and inadequate remuneration. Hearts broken by fraud and oppression in *civil,* as well as by inhumanity and cruelty in *domestic* life.

7. *Wrong done to another often recompensed by loss incurred by ourselves.* A curse imprecated by Job on his land as the righteous penalty of wrong, if done by him either in acquiring or cultivating it. Another example of the maxim: As the sin, so the punishment. Job probably reminded of the curse pronounced on the ground, first for Adam's sin and then for Cain's (Gen. iii. 17, 18; iv, 11, 12). Suggests another evidence that Job was well acquainted with Genesis.

"The words of Job are ended." Probably followed the final protestation of his innocence in verse 37. Job's "words" spoken partly by the flesh and partly by the spirit. Were partly those of an enlightened and sanctified believer, and partly those of a yet unhumbled sinner. Were at last partly commended and partly reproved by the Almighty. Have been recorded for our instruction and comfort, but not all of them for our imitation. Began with justifying and speaking well of God; ended by speaking well of himself. Contain some of the most elevated sentiments and glorious truths ever conceived by human mind or uttered by human lips. Viewed in connection with his extraordinary sufferings, and the circumstances in which they were uttered, they exhibit a marvel of Divine grace, in enabling the sufferer to possess his soul in patience, and "to glorify God in the fires." Afford the picture of a man as perfect as fallen nature admitted of in the ages previous to the advent of Christ and the dispensation of the Spirit. Observe— *Words ended in their utterance not ended in their effect.* By these words of Job, he "being dead yet speaketh." The effect of words, for good or evil, often experienced for generations and centuries after they have been spoken or written.

"Nothing is lost: the drop of dew,
    That trembles on the leaf or flower,
Is but exhaled to fall anew,
    In summer's thunder shower;
Perchance to shine within the bow,
    That fronts the sun at fall of day;
Perchance to sparkle in the flow
    Of fountains far away.
So with our words; or harsh or kind,
    Utter'd, they are not all forgot;
But leave some trace upon the mind,
    Pass on, yet perish not."

J. *Critchley Prince.*

CHAPTER XXXII.

INTRODUCTION AND SPEECH OF ELIHU.

The place of Elihu, introduced in this chapter, that of an umpire stepping forward of his own accord, under the promptings of zeal and conscious knowledge, to decide the controversy between Job and his three friends on the one hand, and between Job and the Almighty on the other. His speeches contribute to the solution, as showing reasons why Job might be afflicted as he was, without being what his friends suspected him to be—a secretly bad man, and also as pointing out wherein he erred—namely, in his too strongly justifying himself, and almost censuring the Almighty. His speeches preparatory to the appearance and address of Jehovah, who follows up what Elihu had begun. Elihu in relation to the Almighty, like John the Baptist in relation to Christ. Observe—(1) An honour to be, like Elihu, a *peacemaker*, in seeking to compose disputes between brethren, and to remove a believer's controversy with God. (2) A high privilege to be, like Elihu also, a *forerunner* in preparing the way for God himself. Precious to be sent, like the seventy disciples, to preach in places where Christ himself is to come (Luke x. 1).

I. The occasion of Elihu's introduction.

Verse 1.—" So these three men ceased to answer Job, because he was righteous in his own eyes."

The great object of these friends, to make Job out to be a secret transgressor, and so deserving the sufferings inflicted on him. This view of his case required by their false theology in respect to the Divine government—God viewed by them as necessarily punishing sin and rewarding virtue in this life. Failing to convince Job that he was a bad man, and guilty of such sins as had justly drawn upon him God's severe judgments, they " ceased to answer Job." Their arguments only in the direction of showing that bad men suffer in this life the consequences of their deeds, however secretly committed, and that good men are invariably prosperous and happy, even in this world. They had employed the last arrow in their quiver without making any impression, and now desist.

Their final charge against Job,—" He was righteous in his own eyes," partly false and partly true. False, as Job acknowledged himself a sinner (ch. vii, 20, 21; ix. 2, 3). True, but both in a right and wrong sense.

1. In a *right* sense. In the ordinary use of the term, Job a "righteous" man. This the Divine testimony given of him. The testimony also of his own conscience. His own heart " condemned him not." Conscious of having served God sincerely, earnestly, and perseveringly. Like Paul, could testify that he had " lived in all good conscience unto this day." Had exercised himself in having " a conscience void of offence both towards God and towards men." With this consciousness, Job necessarily and justly " righteous in his own eyes." Could not truthfully deny it, or honestly confess the contrary. So far Job simply believed and maintained he was righteous, because he *was* so. As a matter of fact, Job's sins *not* the cause of his sufferings (ch. ii. 3).

2. In a *wrong* sense. (1) As insisting too strongly on his own righteousness. (2) In ignoring or regarding too slightly the sins that actually adhered to him. (3) In being too prone to charge God with cruelty and injustice in dealing with him as He did. (4) In being much more careful to justify himself than his Maker. His eye so entirely on his own integrity and uprightness as to overlook and forget his short-comings and offences against the Divine law. Righteous before men, he failed to see and acknowledge himself, as he ought, guilty before God. Job still very much in the condition of Paul before his journey to Damascus—"alive without the law" (Rom. vii. 9). The commandment was yet to " come," in order to his dying in his own eyes as a sinner, and having his mouth stopped as guilty before God (Rom iii. 19). Job yet to learn and realize more deeply than he had yet done, that in God's sight no man living can be justified (Ps. cxliii. 2). This change in his views and experience soon about to take place. What the three friends failed in doing, God Himself was about to accomplish, first and in part through the instrumentality of Elihu ; afterwards and more especially, by the manifestation of Himself (ch. xlii. 5, 6). Observe—(1) *Possible to have a conscience void of offence towards God and men, and yet to require to be humbled as a sinner before God.* (2) *One of the objects of the law of God, to strip men of self-righteousness.* (3) *The great aim is the knowledge of sin* (Rom. iii., 20; vii. 7). (3) *The great aim in the Holy Spirit's mission into the world, to convince men of sin and of a better righteousness than their own, in order to their accep-*

tance with God (John xvi. 7, 10). What was to be done in Job's case by the appearance of God Himself and the ministry of Elihu, now done by the inward operation of the Holy Ghost and the ministry of the word. (4). *Self-righteousness the great enemy to our peace, as well as to our acceptance before God through the righteousness wrought out for us by the Son of God in our nature* (Rom. x., 34; Phil. iii., 4, 9).

II. **Elihu's Personality** (verse 26).
1. His NAME—"Elihu." Denotes—"my God is he,"or, "my God is Jehovah." Given at his birth, implies piety on the part of his parents. His name a profession of the faith of his parents, and probably intended to be that of his own. Elihu constantly reminded of the true God by his very name. Probably given him to serve as a guard against advancing idolatry. That object gained. Much in a name. More meaning in names given to individuals, and more importance attached to them, in early times and in the East, than now and with ourselves. Scripture names generally significant. Observe—(1) Wise in parents to impress Divine truth by every suitable means on the minds of their children from their earliest days, and to keep God before them as they grow up. (2) Not enough to know that Jehovah is the true God, but that He is *our* God. God is to be appropriated as our own God in Christ. "My God," the language of faith and love,—"O God thou art my God" (Ps. lxiii. 1). The first confession of Christ after his resurrection: "My Lord and my God" (John xx. 28). Such appropriation of God and self-consecration to Him, the will of God concerning us (Jer. iii. 4, 19, 22). In the covenant of grace, of God gives Himself over to the believing sinner as his God in Christ (Jer. xxxi., 33; Heb. viii. 10).
2. His PARENTAGE. "Son of Barachel." Elihu the only individual in the poem whose parentage is recorded. Possibly in order to distinguish him from others of the same name, or because his father was a well-known and distinguished man in the country. Possibly because Elihu was yet a young man, and required thus to be distinguished. The addition of the father's name the ordinary way of naming men in the East, except when the party was advanced in years, or a person of great distinction. The name of Elihu's father significant as well as his own. Denotes—"the blessing of God," or "God hath blessed." God's goodness and blessing probably recognized by his parents in the gift of a son. Well to mark God's hand in in our ordinary mercies. Piety not only in Elihu's parents but his grand-parents. A precious blessing to have a pious ancestry.

202

—*The privilege of all in Christ to be a "Barachel."* God "hath blessed us with all spiritual blessings in Christ Jesus" (Eph. i. 3). Barachel, having realized the blessing expressed in his name, the more anxious that his son should do the same, and should be able to say: "The Lord is my God." Hence called him Elihu. Parents enjoying the blessing of a covenant-God themselves, likely to be made a blessing to their children. Elihu the worthy son of a worthy father. "Grace does not run in the blood, but often runs in the line."—*P. Henry.* Elihu distinguished for his piety and wisdom even while a young man. Reflected honour on the father whose name was connected with his own. Only truly pious children a real credit and honour to their parents. "My son, if thy heart be wise, my heart shall rejoice, even mine" (Prov. xxiii. 15).
3. His COUNTRY. "The Buzite." Buz the second son of Nahor, Abraham's brother (Gen. xxii. 21). A city of this name in Arabia Deserta, mentioned in connection with Dedan in Idumæa (Jer. xxv. 13). The name of the city and the country around probably derived from Buz, Nahor's son. Buz himself a Syrian. Probably some of his descendants emigrated south-westwards into Idumæa or Arabia. Buz a brother of Uz, from whom the country of Job probably took its name. Job and Elihu thus perhaps not very distantly connected. The Syrians in general already tinged more or less with idolatry. Hence the command to Abraham to leave his country and his kindred. Idols or images, probably kept as household gods, found in the family of Laban, Nahor's grandson (Gen. xxxi. 19). Strange gods worshipped by Terah the father of Abraham and Nahor (Josh. xxiv. 2, 15). Barachel probably an exception. Hence the piety and wisdom of his son. Due to sovereign grace, that generally some are "among the faithless, faithful found." Saints in Nero's household.
4, His KINDRED. "Of the kindred (or clan) of Ram." Ram probably the same as Aram (1 Chron. xxix. 10, with Matt. i. 3, 4). Ram or Aram a son of Shem, and the father or brother of Uz (Gen. x. 23; 1 Chron. i. 17). Another, the son of Kemuel the son of Nahor, and the brother of Buz and Uz (Gen. xxii. 21). A third and later Ram or Aram, the father of Amminadab and grandfather of Nahshon, the prince of the children of Judah at the time of the Exodus (1 Chron. ii. 9—10; Num. i. 7, 2, 3). From Ram or Aram, Syria had its name, Mesopotamia, the country between the rivers—namely, the Tigris and the Euphrates, also hence called Padan-Aram, or the Plain of Aram. Hence the Syriac and Chaldaic

language called the Aramaic, traces of which appear in the Book of Job, but more especially in the speeches of Elihu.—This particularity in the description of Elihu significant, as—(1) An evidence of the historic truth of the poem; (2) Indicative of the important place he occupies in the controversy, and the part he contributed to its solution ; (3) Expressive of the honour put upon Elihu himself as the most enlightened of the speakers. "Them that honour me I will honour."

5. His AGE. "Young." Probably even younger than Job. A remarkable peculiarity in his case. The other speakers elderly, and even aged men (verse 6). Unusual in Arabia and the East for young men to take part in a religious controversy. Observe — *Grace and wisdom not confined to age.* John the most beloved and devoted of the Apostles, believed to have been the youngest, Paul, when chosen to be the Apostle of the Gentiles, a young man. Timothy, his friend and deputy while but a youth. Jesus among the doctors in the temple at the age of twelve. Daniel, Shadrach, Meshach and Abednego, distinguished for piety and wisdom at an early age.

III. Elihu's Character. To be gathered from the history and from his own speeches.

1. *Ardent and zealous.* Hence his anger both against Job and his three friends (verse 2), and his eager endeavour to correct their mistakes. Full of matter, and eager to deliver himself of it (verses 18, 19).

2. *Modest.* Conscious of his youth, he waits till all the other speakers had nothing more to say (verses 4, 11). Hesitating and afraid to deliver his opinion (verse 6). Spoke at length, only because inwardly constrained to do so, and conscious of having something to say on the subject (verse 18). Ascribes what knowledge and understanding he had to the Spirit of God (verse 8). The appearance of inflation in his language probably due to Oriental poetry, and to the apologetic style which he assumes in introducing himself.

3. *Enlightened.* Indicated in his speeches. Answered neither by Job nor his friends. The only speaker not censured by the Almighty. Jehovah's address to Job a continuation of his own.

4. *Candid and impartial.* Neither justifies Job, though desirous of doing so; nor yet, like the three friends, suspects and condemns him as necessarily a wicked man. Speaks his mind, without either fear or favour, as amenable to his Maker (verses 21, 22). Reproves Job, without, like the others, losing his temper.

Elihu may be viewed—(1) As, in character, name, and the attitude he assumes in the controversy, a type of Christ in relation to the Pharisees and doctors of the law, as well as in his office of mediator and revealer of the Father; (2) As, in his character and speeches, an example to pastors and preachers of the Gospel.

IV. His motives and reasons for entering into the controversy.

1. *His displeasure with Job and his three friends.* Verses 2, 3.—"Then was kindled the wrath of Elihu (Oriental expression for strong disapprobation and displeasure); against Job was his wrath kindled, because he justified himself rather than God (or, "made himself more righteous than God). Also against his three friends was his wrath kindled, because they had no answer [to Job which was solid and satisfactory], and yet had condemned Job" (as a hypocrite and secret transgressor). Elihu, angry with Job for his offence against God ; with his friends for their offence against Job.

Observe—*anger, not always sinful.* "Be ye angry, and sin not" (Eph. iv. 26.) Anger may be either holy or unholy. Shewn by God Himself. God "angry with the wicked every day." Felt and exhibited by Christ. "Looked round about" upon his Pharisaic adversaries and opposers "with anger" (Mark iii. 5). Anger a principle or passion implanted in our nature for wise and holy objects. Only right when—(1) *Directed against a proper object.* This not always the case with creature anger. (2) *Excited by a just or sufficient cause.* Human anger often excited by a *bad* cause, still more frequently by an *insufficient* one. Jonah first angry at Nineveh's repentance, and then at the loss of his gourd. (3) *Held under due control.* Uncontrolled anger a sinful passion—a sin itself, and leading to many others. (4) *Accompanied with love.* Jesus wept over the objects of His anger (Luke xix. 41). 5. *Not long continued.* "Let not the sun go down upon your wrath" (Eph. iv. 26). Anger may *enter* the breast of a wise man, but *rests* only in the bosom of fools (Eccles vii. 9). Anger in fallen creatures apt to be sinful. Hence spoken of as a work of the flesh (Gal. v. 25). Believers exhorted to put it away (Eph. iv. 31). Anger in fallen men like gunpowder in the hands of children—useful but dangerous Often sinful even in good men. Excluded Moses, though the meekest man on earth, from the promised land (Num. xx. 10, 12). Anger safest where directed against the sin rather than the sinner. Causeless anger murder in the heart, and often leading to murder in the act. Excessive anger a species

203

of madness. The New Testament rule— "Slow to speak, slow to wrath." "Not soon angry," a precept necessary both for ministers and people. One feature of charity or love that it is "not easily provoked (1 Cor. xiii. 5).

2. *The inability of the three friends to answer Job.* Verse 3—"They had found no answer." Verse 10—Therefore I said, hearken unto me; I also will shew mine opinion. Behold, I waited for your words; I gave ear to your reasons (your arguments, or your views ; *Margin,* ' your understandings '), whilst (or till) ye searched out what to say. Yea, I attended unto you (or 'to your testimonies'), and behold, there was none of you that convinced Job (refuted or convicted him of error), or that answered his words" (solidly, suitably, and satisfactorily). Verse 15 —"They (*i.e.,* Job's friends,—the words addressed to Job, or to others present at the controversy as by-standers), were amazed (' struck down,' either by Job's arguments, his confidence in God, or his obstinacy in maintaining his innocence), they left off speaking. When I had waited (or simply, ' I waited '—spoken after an interval of silence, leaving room for remark), for (or but) they spake not, but stood still (persevered in their silence, or stood as dumb), and answered no more ; I said, I will also [though so much younger] answer my part (will contribute my part to the controversy); I also will show my opinion." Becoming in juniors to be silent in a discussion, till others, older and likely to be better informed on the subject, have said what they are able to say upon it. Modesty an ornament to all, but especially to youth. "Slow to speak," in most cases a safe rule. Jesus among the doctors, first *heard,* then asked questions, and then gave answers.

3. *The general bestowment of understanding by the Creator on mankind.* Verse 7.—" I said, days (men of advanced age) should speak, and the multitude of years should teach wisdom (understanding as to God's dealings and man's duty). But there is a spirit in man (mankind in general, without being confined to age), and the inspiration of the Almighty giveth them understanding. Great men (great either in age or position) are not always wise; neither do the aged (necessarily or exclusively) understand judgment (what is right either in doctrine or duty). Therefore I said, Hearken to me ; I also will shew mine opinion." Observe : (1) *To speak on great and important subjects connected with Divine truth, the especial right and duty of men of age and experience.* Growth in wisdom naturally expected to accompany growth in years. (2) *Wisdom not the monopoly of any age or class.* (3). *Intelligence the gift of God.* Christ the light that lighteth every man that cometh into the world (John i. 9). (4) *A preacher to speak in dependence on, and as the result of, Divine enlightenment.* "If any speak, let him speak as the oracles of God." The manifestation of the Spirit given to every [believing] man to profit [others] withal (1 Cor. xii., 7 ; 1 Pet. 4, 11. Three things necessary for every preacher of Divine truth—(1) A message given him by the Spirit. (2) The unction of the Spirit in delivering it. (3) The power of the Spirit to accompany it in the hearts of the hearers.

4. *His conviction, in opposition to the self-conceit of the three friends, that the subject under discussion was capable of receiving a more satisfactory treatment.* Verse 13—" Lest ye should say (or ' do not say'), We have found out wisdom ; God casteth him down, and not man" (his afflictions are to be viewed as coming in righteous judgment from the hand of God, and not from man ; or, "God must confute or overcome him and not man.") Either the language of the friends, as if they had said all that could be advanced on the subject, Job being now incorrigible to all but God himself; or the language of Elihu, as indicating that what he was about to advance was not the mere argument of man, but the teaching of God himself, by whose inspiration he was about to speak. "We have found out wisdom," generally the language of ignorance and pride, as if we ourselves had seen the whole truth in relation to a subject, and nothing more could be said about it. The language of many of the philosophers or wise men of antiquity. "Professing themselves to be wise." The name "philosopher," however, denoting a *lover of wisdom,* chosen in modesty by Pythagoras its inventor, to indicate, in opposition to many who called themselves "wise men,"that wisdom was not yet found out, and that all that men could pretend to, was to be lovers or seekers of it ; while both Socrates and Plato acknowledged the necessity of a Divine revelation, and anticipated the bestowment of it at some future period. "We have found out wisdom," still the language of a 'vain philosophy,' and of 'science falsely so called.' The boast of some modern as well as of ancient schools. Especially made at present in reference to the origin of man and of the universe. 'Natural Selection' to take the place of a personal and intelligent Creator. The Bible account of creation to be set aside, according to some, for the teachings or guessings of science, which yet is obliged to confess that it neither does nor can know anything certain on the subject. "I say," says one of those who think they have 'found out wisdom' on this subject, "that

natural knowledge, seeking to satisfy natural wants, has found the ideas which alone can satisfy spiritual cravings." On a subject, in regard to which science professes it has and can have no evidence and can give no certain account, on which its teachings are far from being in harmony with each other, and one connected with matters of infinite and eternal importance, — it would seem not a little wiser to accept the professed and sufficiently-accredited Divine testimony, however it is to be intrepreted, which has been preserved and handed down to us through nearly four thousand years; which has been received as such by Jesus Christ and His Apostles, and by the best men in every age, both before and since, who have had the opportunity of doing so; and is infinitely more calculated to meet the wants and circumstances of humanity, than the theory or guesses which some professors of science would give us in its stead.

5. *His having hitherto stood aloof from the controversy, and having arguments to produce which had not yet been advanced.* Verse 14. —" Now he (Job) hath not directed his words against me : neither will I answer him with your speeches " (either as to the matter or manner of them). Elihu proposes—(1) To bring new matter to bear on the subject under discussion, viz., God's providential dealings with men; (2) To speak in a calmer and more dispassionate tone than the three friends, as not having had anything irritating addressed to him by Job. The argument of the friends, that Job's sufferings proved him to be a transgressor. Elihu's object to show that afflictions and trials are often of a disciplinary character.—Necessary in a discussion—(1) To be able to say something new; (2) To keep one's temper.

6. *His deep interest in the subject, his consciousness of having much to say upon it, and his earnest desire to deliver it.* Verse 18.— "For I am full of matter : the spirit within me (Heb. 'of my belly' or heart) constraineth (or straiteneth) me. Behold, my belly (or heart, as John vii. 38) is as wine which hath no vent (or outlet for the escape of the gas generated in the course of fermentation); it is ready to burst like new bottles (or, like skin-bottles containing new wine undergoing fermentation; old skins being more liable to burst than new ones, Matt. ix. 17, 18). I will speak that I may be refreshed (relieved of the inward pressure to deliver what I have to say on the subject); I will open my lips and answer." In the East, a young man only justified in speaking in the presence of seniors, when he has much to say on the subject under discussion. Observe—The duty of Christians

in general, and of preachers in particular : (1) To be deeply interested in subjects pertaining to the Divine glory and the welfare of men. Well to be "zealously affected always in a good thing " (Gal. iv. 18). (2) To sympathize with the sufferings of a fellow-creature, and to seek in every way we can to alleviate them. (3) To obtain correct views as to the cause of afflictions, and the best way to improve them. (4) To communicate for the comfort and benefit of others what we ourselves have been taught in regard to Divine things. That preacher likely to profit who feels that he has something important to say, and is inwardly constrained to say it. Desirable for a preacher to have the prophet's experience,—God's Word as a burning fire shut up in his bones (Jer. xx. 9). " We cannot but speak the things which we have seen and heard" (Acts iv. 20). Paul pressed in the spirit at Corinth, and so testified to the Jews that Jesus was the Christ (Acts xviii. 5). Preachers needed who are ready to burst with the good news they have to communicate to their hearers concerning the great salvation of God. Such the preachers of the Gospel who at first turned the world up-side-down, and would do so again if found in any considerable number.

V. **Elihu's resolution to be plain and impartial in his discourse, and his reason for it.** Verses 21, 22.—" Let me not, I pray you, accept any man's person (shew partiality to any on the ground either of age or reputation), neither let me give flattering titles unto man (employing titles of honour and compliment, or speaking blandly and flatteringly, instead of plainly and honestly, and calling things by their right names). For I know not (am neither able nor willing) to give flattering titles; in so doing my Maker would soon take me away" (by some signal manifestation of His displeasure ; or simply, " my Maker will soon take me away," *i. e.,* by death : I shall soon appear in His presence and render an account of what and how I have spoken). The Orientals remarkable for their employment of flattering titles in addressing others. Observe—(1) *Plainness of speech in a preacher not incompatible with courtesy.* Paul an example of both. (2) *The preacher neither to be influenced by fear nor favour in delivering his message or performing his office.* His business not to please but persuade men, or to please only in so far as it may tend to their edification, and with that object (Rom. xv. 2 ; 1 Cor. x. 33, ix. 22). His duty to declare the whole counsel of God ; to speak necessary truth, however unpalatable ; to deliver his message faithfully, whether men will hear or whether they will forbear. (3) *Important recollection for a preacher*: "*My Maker will soon take me away.*" Good to speak "as a dying man to dying men." (4) *The remembrance of Christ's presence as a hearer the best safeguard to the faithfulness of the preacher, and the best means of deliverance from the fear of man.* Fear or flattery of man on the part of a preacher, an insult to his Master. Foolish as well as base to court the page's favour instead of the sovereign's. "That

man preaches before me as if he had the Almighty standing at his elbow"—*James the First, of one of his Court Preachers.* Latimer's introduction to his sermon before Henry the Eighth: "Remember, Hugh Latimer, that thou speakest before the king, and, therefore, take good heed to what thou sayest in presence of his majesty; but remember also, Hugh Latimer, that thou speakest before the King of Kings, whose servant thou art, and who shall one day call thee to account."

CHAPTER XXXIII.

ELIHU'S FIRST SPEECH.

Elihu addresses himself to Job on the subject of God's afflictive dispensations. Afflictions often disciplinary chastisements.

I. He bespeaks Job's careful attention to all that he has to advance.

Verse 1.—"Wherefore, Job, I pray thee, hear my speeches and hearken to all my words." Elihu speaks as one that had much to say. His speech, or perhaps rather *speeches*, much the longest of any in the controversy. Probably two speeches, separated by a pause or interval of silence (ch. xxxv. 1; xxxvi. 1). His statement—"I am full of matter," confirmed by the fact. His speeches, in this respect, perhaps in accordance with his age. Youthful speakers often wordy. The work of time and experience to learn to prune down our discourses and avoid multiplying words Elihu makes good his promise not to give flattering titles. Addresses Job by his plain name. A king of Spain complained that he lacked one who would speak plainly and faithfully to him without flattery and partiality. Elihu speaks with courtesy and respect as well as earnestness,—"I pray thee." "Be courteous," —a New Testament precept, to be especially remembered by all who endeavour to persuade others. Paul, an example of courtesy to his hearers. Often, like Elihu, employs the language of entreaty (Rom. xii. 1; Eph. iii. 4). A duty to give serious attention to *all* that an earnest and enlightened preacher has to say; still more that the inspired Word itself teaches (Deut. v. 27; Acts x. 35). Men not to listen to only as much as pleases them, or accords with their own views.

Elihu bespeaks attention on the ground—

1. *Of his own earnestness, and purpose to enter fully and intelligently into the subject.* Verse 2—"Behold, now I have opened my mouth; my tongue hath spoken (or speaketh) in my mouth," (*margin*, in or with "my palate;" the palate, or roof of the mouth,

used in articulate speech; perhaps referring to the distinctness with which it was his purpose to speak on the subject in hand). The expression: "I have opened my mouth," an Oriental one, indicating—(1) The setting of oneself to deliver a weighty and important discourse. Said of Jesus (Matt. v. 2). (2) Fulness of matter and readiness of utterance, as if the words were waiting for egress, and flowed forth spontaneously. Paul's request for the Church's prayers, that "utterance" (freeness of speech) might be given him, that he might "open his mouth boldly, as he ought to speak" (Eph. vi. 19; Col. iv. 3).

2. *Of his sincerity in what he says, as well as the clearness with which he will speak.* Verse 3.—"My words shall be of (or from) the uprightness (or sincerity) of my heart; and my lips shall utter knowledge clearly," (or "they," *i. e.*, his words, "shall utter the sentiments of my lips purely"—sincerely, clearly, and correctly). Elihu, anxious to appear to Job and the rest—(1) *As unprejudiced and sincere*—points in which the three friends had appeared to him to fail. Their views one-sided, and their minds prejudiced against Job on account of his extraordinary afflictions. Not always easy, though in the highest degree important, for a speaker to divest himself of prejudice, partiality and passion, and to be pure and sincere in his motives. Truth to be spoken without gall or guile. "Speaking the truth (literally, 'truthing it') in love." Truth often distorted through passion and prejudice. (2) *As expressing his views simply and distinctly.* Using plain language, and uttering exactly what he thinks, without fear or favour, mistiness or circumlocution. Plainness, simplicity and directness, important in every teacher of Divine truth. "All our learning necessary to make things plain."—*Archbishop Ussher.* Paul again an example to preachers,—"We use great plainness of speech" (2 Cor. iii. 12). The vision to be

made "plain, that he may run [at once for escape] that readeth it," (Hab. ii. 2). (3) *As uttering what is true and correct on the subject.* "Shall utter knowledge"—not fancies but facts, not mere opinions but truth. What Elihu promised he appears to have performed. No fault found at last by the Almighty with any of his utterances, as in the case of the three friends. A religious teacher to employ the greatest possible care, both by prayer and study, to have his discourses and instructions strictly in accordance with revealed truth and the circumstances of the case. "If any speak, let him speak as the oracles of God" (1 Peter, iv. 11). Care to be taken that the Word of God be not corrupted or adulterated (2 Cor. ii. 17). Preachers to utter not merely what they have heard or read, but what they "know" (John iii. 11; Acts iv. 20).

3. *Of his equality with Job as a creature of God.* Verses 4—7.—"The Spirit of God (either the Divine *power*, corresponding with 'breath' in the next clause; or, the Divine person so spoken of throughout the Scriptures) hath made me [in connection with thyself], and the breath of the Almighty hath given me life (as to Adam and all his children, Gen. ii. 7). If thou canst answer me, set thy words in order (produce and exhibit thy arguments) before me; stand up [as an opponent against what I have to say]. Behold, I am according to thy wish (or, 'mouth,'—referring to Job's words, chap. ix. 34, 35; xiii. 21, &c.; or simply, 'like thee') in God's stead (or, 'for God,' *i.e.*, to plead in his name; or, 'in relation to God,' *i.e.*, as his creature); I also am formed out of the clay. Behold, my terror (or overpowering majesty) shall not make thee afraid; neither shall my hand (or power as of a superior being) be heavy upon thee." Elihu, conscious of having no advantage over Job from his position, wishes him to listen at ease, and to answer with freedom. Those engaged in a discussion, to be able to speak on equal grounds and without fear from the authority and power of each other. "He must be confessed the better scholar who has thirty legions at his command,"—*Phavorinus* the philosopher, in reference to Adrian the Emperor. Observe:—(1) A sign of weakness in dealing with an opponent, to take undue advantage either of learning or position. (2) The wisdom and kindness of God, first in revealing Himself by one who became a partaker of our own nature, and then of employing not angels but men in the ministry of reconciliation. Elihu possibly designed by the Holy Ghost to be a representative and type both of Christ and His Apostles, as well as of all faithful preachers of the Gospel. (3) The record of man's

creation as found in the Bible, well known in the days of the writer of the Book. (4) The Holy Ghost probably known as a distinct person. Personality apparently here ascribed to Him. So in Gen. i. 2. Probably also in Gen. vi. 3. The breath or wind a Scriptural symbol of the Spirit, as proceeding from God, and mighty in His operation (Ez. xxxvii. 9—14; John iii. 8; Acts ii. 2—4). A plurity of persons recognized in the one Divine Creator (Gen. i. 26; so Job xxxv. 10—"my Maker," Hebrew, "my makers;" so Isaiah liv. 5). (5) The specialty in man's creation here referred to, such as to render him an intelligent being, capable of reasoning and uttering important truth.

II. States his complaint against Job (verses 8—11). His complaint not against Job's former life, but his present language. Verse 8.—" Surely thou hast spoken in mine hearing, and I have heard the voice of thy words." Elihu, till now, only an attentive listener. The best listener likely to be not the worst speaker. "Swift to hear, slow to speak." Reference made by Elihu to such passages as chap. ix. 17, 30; x. 7, &c. The grounds of his complaint in reference to Job's language—

1. *His maintaining his sinlessness.* Verse 9.—"Saying, surely I am clean, without transgression; I am innocent; neither is there iniquity in me." Given as the substance of Job's statements, rather than his exact language. Perhaps a mistaken or exaggerated representation of it. Yet according to the impression made by Job's speeches on the mind of a bystander. His expressions often rash, unguarded, and extreme. At times seemed to say all that is here imputed to him, although not intending it in the sense in which Elihu understood it. His intention probably only to maintain that he was not conscious of living in the known breach of any of God's laws, as he was suspected of doing, and that he was free from any such crime as to deserve, above others, the awful calamities with which he had been visited. Observe—(1) Easy, under strong feeling, to utter unguarded language, capable of being misunderstood. (2) Our duty to put the most charitable construction on the words of a good man, uttered at a time of suffering and excitement. (3) Job's error, that he maintained too vehemently his own innocence, and was more careful to vindicate himself than justify God. Personal depravity and imperfection the lesson he had yet to learn.

2. *His charging God.* Verses 10, 11. Job seemed to charge God—(1) With *fickleness and unkindness.* Verse 10.—"Behold, he findeth occasions (quarrels or

breaches of friendship, Num. xix. 34) against me; he counteth me for his enemy." Reference to Job's language in such places as chap. ix. 17; xiii. 24; xvi. 9; xix. 11; xxxi. 21. God's former friendship and regard viewed by Job as now changed without cause into enmity. A grievous mistake and reflection on the Divine character. God's love unchangeable (Jer. xiii. 3; John xiii. 1). His *face* may change, but not His *heart* (Is. liv. 7—10). God may *seem* to count a man His enemy, whom He *really* regards as His friend. Love and hatred on the part of God not to be always gathered from His external dealings. Often the greatest love where there appears the greatest want of it. "You only have I known; therefore," &c. On the other hand, often the greatest anger where there appears none. Observe—The pride of the natural heart leading to vehement vindication of ourselves, may easily, in the darkness and confusion of our spirit under trouble, lead also to language reflecting on our Maker and His procedure. (2) With *treating Him unjustly as a criminal.* Verse 11.—"He putteth my feet in the stocks" (or clog,—either as a punishment or a means of preventing escape). Job's actual language (chap. xiii. 27). The child sometimes placed under temporary confinement while the servant or slave goes at large. (3) With *acting towards Him with undue severity and strictness.* Verse 11.—"He marketh all my paths" (as if watching for the least offence, in order to punish it). So Job seemed to say (chap. xiii. 17; xiv. 16; xxxi. 4). The flesh in a tried believer, constantly liable to mistakes in regard to God and His dealings. God, for Christ's sake, *forgets*, instead of *marking*, the offences of those who take hold of His covenant (Jer. xxxi. 34; Heb. viii. 12; x. 17). Casts them behind His back, and into the depths of the sea (Is. xxxviii. 17; Mic. vii. 19). Forgets the evil deeds of His faithful though imperfect servants, but remembers their good ones (Matt. xxv. 35—40; Heb. vi. 10). Treasures up their tears, but blots out their transgressions (Ps. lvi. 8; Is. 43 25).

III. **Condemns Job for such sentiments.** Verse 12.—"Behold, in this thou art not just." Job neither—(1) Correct in judging according to the facts of the case; nor (2) Just in his views regarding God. A man may be ordinarily just towards his fellowmen when he is very unjust towards God. Improper sentiments in regard to God and His dealings are injustice towards our Maker. This injustice charged upon Job rather than any iniquity in his past life.—Elihu gives his reasons for condemning Job for his language. "I will answer thee." Our speech to be with

208

grace, seasoned with salt [or wisdom], that we may know how we ought to answer every man (Col. iv. 6.) "Every one shall kiss *his* lips who giveth a right answer." Elihu's main reasons for man's silent submission and acquiescence in all the Divine procedure—

1. *God's greatness in comparison with man.* Verse 12.—"God is greater than man." God greater than man in wisdom, power, and justice. Greater than man as his Maker, Ruler, and Judge. The natural inference from this—man, even the greatest and best, is not to strive with God. "Why dost thou strive against Him?"—quarrelling with and disputing against His procedure (Is. xlv. 9). God's greatness above man sufficient to exclude all murmurs and complaints, as—(1) *God is not to be required to give an account of his procedure to any of his creatures.* Verse 13.—"For (or because) he giveth not account of any of his matters" (or dealings). The reason why Job should have refrained from the sentiments he had uttered in regard to God, and why neither he nor any one ought to "strive against Him." God a sovereign who acts according to His own will, though never but in infinite wisdom, rectitude, and holiness. Monstrous presumption to think that the Creator is to be called to His creature's bar to answer for what He does (Ps. cxv. 3; Dan. iv. 35). God too great to stoop to defend His procedure against the cavils of rebellious worms. This the scope of Jehovah's own answer to Job afterwards. (2) *God is not to be comprehended by His short-sighted creatures.* Folly and presumption for man to think he is able to comprehend God's dealings, except as He is pleased to reveal and explain them. Hence the weakness and wickedness of censuring them.

> "As if upon a full-proportioned dome,
>   On swelling columns heaved, the pride of art!
> A critic fly, whose feeble ray scarce spreads
> An inch around, with blind presumption bold
> Should dare to tax the structure of the whole."

2. *God employs sufficient means for man's instruction, which are yet unheeded.* Verse 14.—"For God speaketh (in order to man's instruction and direction) once, yea, twice, yet man perceiveth (or regardeth) it not." Man does not perish from want of means on God's part for his preservation, but from inattention to them on his own. Not left without sufficient light for his guidance, were the light improved. God unwearied in His instructions to men. Means employed apart from a written revelation of His will. Some of these specified. Verse 15.—"In a dream (as in the earlier periods of the world), in a

vision of the night, when deep sleep falleth upon men, in slumberings upon the bed (a state between sleeping and waking); then He openeth the ears of men (communicates His will), and sealeth their instruction (impressing it upon their hearts as with a seal, or secretly conveying their instruction as in a sealed document), that he may withdraw man from his purpose (or intended work, as Abimelech, Gen. xx. 6; Laban, Gen. xxxi. 24; Balaam, Num. xxii. 12, 20, 31), and hide pride from man (by keeping him back from it)." "He [by these means when meekly and attentively received] keepeth back his soul from the pit (grave or corruption,—emblem of future punishment), and his life from perishing by the sword [of Divine judgment]." Thus God employs sufficient means of instruction to supply man's necessity though not to gratify his curiosity. Means still more abundantly employed in connection with inspired prophecy and a written revelation (Ps. cxlvii. 19, 20; Is. xxviii. 13; Heb. i. 1). These means often unheeded by man—(1) Through indifference and sloth; (2) Through worldliness and love of sin. A sufficient reason why Job and other sufferers should refrain from murmurs and complaints. Man is in a state of disobedience. God, in the exercise of mercy and compassion, employs means for his recovery, but often, through man's waywardness, without effect. No just cause for striving against Him. God only kind to man, till compelled to be severe. At first uses gentle means for his restoration. Only from necessity employs more painful ones, and still from kindness to man. Acts towards men not merely as a governor but as a father. His eye constantly upon them for their good. His object in his admonitions to men—

First : To " withdraw man from his purpose" or work. Sin properly man's work. " The thoughts of the imaginations of man's heart only evil from his youth " (Gen. vi. 5; viii. 21). God made man upright, but he hath sought out many inventions (Eccles. vii. 29.) Man's purposes and doings often such as if carried out would be ruinous both to themselves and others. Men kept back by God from many sins which they would otherwise commit.

Second : To " hide pride from man." Pride fallen man's besetting sin. Exemplified in the building of the Tower of Babel (Gen. xi. 4); in Pharaoh,—" Who is the Lord ?" &c.; in Sennacherib,—" By the strength of my hand I have done it " (Is. x. 13); in Nebuchadnezzar,—" Is not this great Babylon which I have built ? " in Herod, eaten up of worms, " because he gave not God the glory" (Acts xii. 23); even in good Hezekiah,—"his heart was lifted up " (2 Chr.

xxxii. 25). Pride at once the subtlest and most hateful of sins. Robs God of His glory and man of his peace. Founded on a lie, that we are something when we are nothing. Loathsome in a creature hitherto unfallen, monstrous in one already fallen. Insinuates itself into man's best actions and holiest feelings. Often the "fly in the pot of ointment." Can array itself in the garb of humility. " Lowliness " often made " young ambition's ladder." Possible to be proud of one's humility. Such a thing as spiritual pride. The sin of the Pharisee. The most loathsome of all the forms of pride. Doubtful if there can be such a thing as a " just pride." To be elated with pride the next step to falling into the " condemnation of the devil" (1 Tim. iii. 6). " Pride goeth before destruction, and a haughty spirit before a fall." God's aim to keep Israel back from pride (Deut. viii. 11—13). The sin that banished the angels from heaven and our parents from paradise.

" Cromwell, I charge thee, fling away ambition.
  By that sin fell the angels: how can man then,
  The image of his Maker, hope to win by it ?"

God hides pride from men—(1) By showing the hatefulness of it; (2) By discovering the consequences of it; (3) By removing the occasions of and temptations to it. Afflictions and trials often sent to keep men humble, and mercies withheld or removed which might prove the occasion of pride. True humility a fruit of the Spirit and a feature of the new man in Christ. To be learned at the feet of Jesus and in the shadow of His cross. Christ the only example of perfect humility (Matt. xi. 29; Phil. ii. 5—8.)

Third : To save men from the consequences of transgression,—to "keep back their soul from the pit." Sin's consequences, the pit of the grave, and that of which it is the emblem, the "bottomless pit"(Rev. ix.1). Death, in its full extent, the wages of sin (Rom. vi. 23; Gen. ii. 17; James i. 15). Some sins lead directly to temporal death; all sin to death eternal. Man composed of body and soul. The penalty of sin extends to both. The soul that sinneth it shall die. A first and second death (Rev. ii. 11). The former the shadow, the latter the substance. The first death, man's separation from the light of this world; the second, his separation for ever from the light and glory and blessedness of the next. The first to a believer in Christ, bereft of its sting and converted into a blessing; the second, only remediless unmitigated woe. The latter a necessity as well as righteous sentence. Sin its own misery and punishment. No peace possible to the wicked. Without holiness no man see the Lord. God's great object to save men from eternal death, and from sin which is its cause. Hence the giving up of His own Son as man's substitute. "Die man or justice must, unless," &c. Christ made "sin for us, that we might be made the righteousness of God in him." "By his knowledge shall my righteous servant justify many, for he shall bear their iniquities" (Is. liii. 11; 2 Cor. v. 21).

Perhaps another reason for man's acquiescence in God's procedure intimated in verse 14. "God speaketh (decreeth or purposeth) once, yea, twice, yet man perceiveth it not " (or, "but twice, or a second time, He—God Himself—does not consider it, so as to alter or improve it.) God's purposes founded on infinite wisdom and holiness, and therefore unchangeable.

IV. Passes to personal affliction as a means employed for man's benefit. Verse 19—22.—"He (man in general, or the man whose spiritual benefit God is aiming at) is chastened also with pain upon his bed, and the multitude of his bones with strong pain (or, 'and with incessant racking of his bones' Ps. xxxviii. 3; Is. xxxviii. 13); so that his life (or appetite) abhorreth bread, and his soul dainty meat (*Heb.*, 'meat of desire,' or meat otherwise desirable). His flesh is consumed (or pines) away, that it cannot be seen, and his bones that were not seen stick out (or, 'his bones are wasted away [so that] they are not seen"), yea, his soul draweth near to the grave, and his life to the destroyers " (the bands or pains of death as Acts ii. 24; "things causing death," as the *Latin Vulgate*; or simply, death itself, Hades or the invisible world, as the *Septuagint* or Greek version; or perhaps the angel of death—"him that hath the power of death" (Heb. ii. 14). Observe—

1. *Affliction the result of sin.* Affliction in general the consequence of the first transgression. Individual cases of affliction often the chastening for some particular offence. Thus the leprosy of Miriam, Gehazi, and King Azariah; the plague in Israel's camp in the Wilderness; the emerods of the Ashdodites; the disease of Herod. Diseases threatened to Israel as the consequence of disobedience (Lev. xxvi. 16; Deut. xxviii. 60) Sickness and disease also the disciplinary consequence of sin in the New Testament. Distinctly stated in 1 Cor. xi. 30; implied in James v. 15.

2. *Affliction of the body one of God's remedial measures for the welfare of the soul.* Diseases His servants. His to bring down to the grave. Diseases His rebuke for

iniquity. In His hand as the Creator and Ruler of the universe. Employed by Him as a father, under a dispensation of mercy, for the benefit of His children. A testimony that God is gracious and has purposes of mercy in reference to man. "Whom the Lord loveth he chasteneth, and scourgeth every son whom he receiveth." "He that spareth the rod hateth the child " (Prov. xiii. 24). Affliction no less employed by God as a fatherly chastisement because coming through secondary or natural causes. The causes themselves in His hand as well as the effects they are to produce. A part of His providential plan and government of the world He has made and cares for. His to bring the causes of disease to bear on the individual and in such a way as to produce the end. The Shunamite's child goes out to the reapers, and returns home with a sunstroke [and dies. Of God's ordering that the child was there, and that the sunstroke should happen and produce the effect which it did, while other children escaped. Diseases induced in a thousand ways, when apparently, but for the most trifling circumstance, they might have been avoided. The effect of a cause in producing disease dependent upon various circumstances, the same cause often operating differently in different cases. The circumstance determining the effect, in God's hands. This no reason why care is not to be exercised in order to avoid disease and prolong health in ourselves and others. Such care enjoined as a duty. "Do thyself no harm." "Thou shalt not kill."

3. *Afflictions thus often made blessings.* But for a dispensation of mercy through the provision of a Saviour, disease only a penalty and part of the curse entailed by transgression. "In the day thou eatest thereof thou shalt surely die." In the economy of grace, the very curse converted into a means of blessing. Blessing connected in the Bible with chastening (Ps. xciv. 10; Job v. 17). Corrections of instruction the way of life (Prov. vi. 23). Designed in mercy, not to ruin but to restore. "Mercy, when an affliction is a correction, not an execution.—*Brooks.* Affliction, as a correction, designed—(1) To *arrest the sinner in his sinful career;* (2) To *subdue pride;* (3) To *lead to thought;* The prodigal "came to himself," and said, &c.; (4) To *exhibit the emptiness and unsatisfying nature of a present world;* (5) To *bring to view death, judgment and eternity;* (6) To *bring sin to remembrance as the cause of suffering,*—"*Father, I have sinned,*" &c.; (7) To *give us to realize God as our Governor and Judge, on whom we are dependant and to whom we are amenable as His creatures;* (8) Thus to *bring to repentance.*

Chastening the theology of Christians,—

Luther. The workshop of the virtues.—*Ambrose.* The treasury of all blessings.—*Brentius.* King Alfred prayed that God would frequently send him sickness. Man often like the top that moves only when it is whipped.—*Brooks.* David's experience, that of most: "Before I was afflicted I went astray; but now I have learned to keep thy law." Affliction a bitter but salutary drug in the hands of a heavenly father. The digging about the tree to render it fruitful instead of cutting it down. Manasseh's iron chain better to him than his golden crown.

V. Describes the means and result of sanctified affliction. Verse 23—28.—"If there be a messenger with him (either divine, angelical, or human; here probably the last, as Haggai i. 13; Mal. ii. 7; Eccles. v. 6; Rev. i. 20; same word usually rendered angel, and applied both to Christ and His ministers; here, one sent or employed by God for the patient's spiritual benefit); an interpreter (one able to explain the meaning of the affliction and the way of improving it, probably a human spiritual teacher or enlightened friend, without excluding either the Great Teacher,—the Messenger of the covenant, who alone teaches to profit, or the Holy Spirit employed by Him and the Father, whose office it is to 'reprove [or convince] the world of sin, righteousness, and judgment'), one among a thousand (of rare intelligence, fidelity, and skill, Ecc. vii. 28); to shew unto man (here the afflicted person) his uprightness (either—(1) what he *should* have done, but which he has failed to do; or (2) his duty in his present circumstances; or rather (3) what may now restore him to a state of uprightness and acceptance with God, viz., repentance and faith in Him in whom, as our propitiation and substitute, we have righteousness and strength, Is. xlv. 24. Then (when these means have been employed and have operated successfully on the sick man's mind and heart in bringing him to humiliation, repentance, and faith) He is gracious (or favourable) unto him (has mercy upon him so as to pardon his sin and probably deliver him from his affliction, James v. 15, 16), and saith (decrees or commands—perhaps to an angel who may have the power given him to remove the disease, as John v. 4, or to Satan, who had the power of death committed to him, Heb. ii. 14): Deliver from going down to the pit (in the first instance, the *grave*, but probably including the idea of the bottomless pit (Rev. ix. 1), of which it was the symbol); I have found (provided or accepted) a ransom (what makes satisfaction for his sin, so that I can righteously forgive and restore him,—the great atonement, now laid hold of by the sick man

in repentance and faith). His flesh (as *one* of the results of his repentance and faith) shall be fresher, or more tender, than a child's (as in the case of Naaman when healed of his leprosy, 2 Kings v. 14). He shall return to the days of his youth (as Ps. ciii. 5). He shall (as a *second* result of his repentance and faith, and the fruit of his sanctified affliction) pray unto God, and He will be favourable unto him (—shall have both access to and acceptance with God); he shall see His face with joy (rejoice in the Divine favour and fellowship—a *third* and still more blessed result): for (in confirmation of these statements as to the results of sanctified affliction) He will render unto man His righteousness (will deal faithfully with him according to his conduct; in this case according to his repentance and faith; or, will restore to the sick man, on his repentance and faith, the righteousness which he lost by the Fall, but which is recovered in Jesus Christ the Second Adam, and given to the penitent believer). He looketh upon men (as the Omniscient Father and Ruler, as Ps. xiv. 2), and if any say (or as *margin*: "He [the sick man, as a *further* result and evidence of sanctified affliction] shall look upon men and say" [in confession and thanksgiving]; or, perhaps rather: "he shall sing [in praise of God, who has been so gracious to him] among or before men, and say ") : I have sinned and perverted that which was right (transgressed God's righteous laws), and it profited me not (or, 'and He has not requited me according to my deserts'); He will deliver his soul (or as *margin*, 'He hath delivered my soul ') from going into the pit, and his life (*margin*, 'my life') shall see the light" [both of this world and the next]. The passage indicates, in regard to

Sanctified Affliction,

First, the MEANS through which it is effected, viz.: *spiritual teaching*. Verse 23.— "If there be a messenger with him," &c. Spiritual teaching *always* necessary to the improvement of affliction. Ordinarily through a *human* teacher; always through a *Divine* one (Ps. xciv. 10). Something necessary to be *shown* to the patient. "To show unto man," &c. Observe—

1. *Affliction in itself not a blessing.* The blessing dependant on other things connected with it. Depends on the manner in which it works and in which the patient is inwardly exercised by it. "Worketh the peaceable fruits of righteousness in them that are *exercised* thereby" (Heb. xii. 11). Spiritual teaching necessary in order to this. "Blessed is the man whom Thou chastenest, O Lord; and *teachest* him out of Thy law" (Ps. xciv.

10). Affliction may either soften or harden; as fire softens wax and hardens clay.

2. The *exhibition of Divine truth to the patient necessary to the improvement of his affliction.* Not only *prayer* to be made *for* him and *with* him, but suitable *truth* to be presented *to* him. Implied in the term "interpreter." His office to "*show*" to the sick man. The spiritual teacher *at least* as necessary to the patient as the physician. *Truth* to be *exhibited* for his *mind*, as well as *medicine* for his *body*.

3. *The spiritual teaching usually through human instrumentality.* The *Divine* Teacher absolutely necessary; a human teacher usually the instrument. The New Testament rule (James v. 14). "Is any sick among you? Let him call for the elders of the Church," —who are required to be "apt to teach," and of whom at least *some* labour "in the word and doctrine" (1 Tim. iii. 2 ; v. 17). Therefore not only to *pray* with the sick man, but to *instruct* him.

4. *Great skill and fidelity required on the part of ministers and others in healing the sick.* "One among a thousand." Easier to preach to a thousand hearers than to minister wisely and faithfully to one sick-bed. Study and prayer necessary for the bed-room as well as the pulpit.

5. *The part of the visitor of the sick to "show" to the patient " his uprightness"*—the *personal righteousness* in which he has failed, the *imputed righteousness* which he may yet obtain, and which he is now to seek, receive, and rejoice in, and the *present duty* required of him, viz., humiliation, repentance, and faith in the provided sacrifice. Hence the visitor's need of knowledge both of the law and of the Gospel; of sin and the way of salvation from it. By the law is the knowledge of sin; by the Gospel the knowledge of salvation. The visitor to be able to point the patient to the Saviour as God's way of righteousness for the sinner—"the end of the law for righteousness to every one that believeth" (Rom. x. 4), "and made righteousness to all who are in him " (1 Cor. i. 30).

Second, the RESULTS of sanctified affliction, or of repentance and faith on the part of the patient. Verse 24.—"Then," &c. The results varied and precious. Chiefly spiritual, in the patient's mind and *soul ;* partly and frequently also in his *body.*

1. *Experience of the Divine mercy and forgiveness.*—" Then he is gracious unto him." God, as a righteous and holy God, able only to exercise forgiving grace and mercy in certain circumstances and. on certain conditions. " *Then* He is gracious to him,"— when these things have taken place. The gracious inclination and purpose already there; the outlet or manifestation of it pre-

212

vented till the patient's repentance and faith. Mercy provides the means for its own outflow to sinners. Repentance and faith necessary to the experience of pardoning mercy ; but even these of mercy's own providing (Acts iii. 19 ; v. 31).

2. *Deliverance.*—" Deliver from going down to the pit." This deliverance probably twofold—the one a picture of the other. (1) Deliverance from *temporal* or *physical death*, which seemed impending. (2) More especially, deliverance from eternal death,— the object of the chastening. The death, which is the consequence and wages of sin, now averted in the patient's repentance and faith. Hence the *ground* of this deliverance —" I have found a ransom." In regard to the

Ransom.

Observe—

1. *The meaning and application of the term.* In Hebrew, literally a *covering.* Hence something to cover transgression ; a ground of pardon (Ps. xxxii. 1). An atonement, or what satisfies justice, and makes it righteous to forgive transgressors. The name given to the mercy-seat or lid of the ark in the Holy of Holies; called also in the New Testament the Propitiation, from the atonement made on it by the sprinkled blood of the sacrifices (Lev. xvi. 14). Hence also, anything done, suffered, or paid as an atonement or ground of deliverance. Thus the intercession of Moses for Israel (Exod. xxxii. 20); and the censer taken into the camp by the zeal of Phinehas (Numb. xxv. 13). The price paid for the redemption of a captive. Egypt given for Israel's ransom (Isa. xliii. 3). The ransom, in reference to men, whatever God may please in His wisdom and goodness to appoint. Appointed according to the nature of the case and the deliverance afforded. Repentance and amendment on the part of a nation, made a ground of forgiveness and deliverance from threatened punishment. Thus Nineveh saved from predicted destruction. The existence of one truly righteous man in Jerusalem, in the days of Jeremiah, a ground of forgiveness to the whole city (Jer. v. 1). So the existence of ten righteous men in Sodom. Ahab's humiliation the ground of the deliverance of himself and the kingdom from threatened punishment during his own life-time (1 Kings xxi. 29). Confession of sin, with the prayer of faith on the part of the sick, made in the New Testament the more immediate ground of forgiveness, and consequent restoration to health (James v. 15, 16). Christ's death the only ransom-price of a sinner's deliverance from eternal death (Matt. xx. 28).

2. The *actual ransom in the text.* As the ground of the sick man's deliverance from eternal death, the ransom that provided by God Himself for the purpose—the *death of His own Son as a substitute for sinners*—to be exhibited in our time (1 Tim. ii. 6). That death typified and held forth as the ransom for sinners and the ground of their forgiveness and deliverance from death eternal, in the sacrifices slain and offered up in the patriarchal and Levitical age (Lev. xvii. 11). That death a full satisfaction to Divine justice for the sins of the world (1 John ii. 2). Through it, God able to be just while justifying the ungodly who believe in it (Rom. iii. 25, 26). Without shedding of blood no remission (Heb. ix. 22). The significance of sacrifices as typifying this ground of forgiveness understood by Job (chap. i. 5 ; xlii. 8).

3. *This ransom "found" or provided by God Himself.* "God so loved the world that He gave his only-begotten Son" (John iii. 16; Rom. viii. 32). The ransom found in His own bosom (John i. 18). The deliverance of the sick man the result of this ransom appropriated by and applied to him on his repentance and faith. That repentance and faith the ground or occasion of his deliverance from *temporal* death; the Lamb "slain from the foundation of the world," the ground of his deliverance from death eternal (1 Peter i. 20). Impossible for any but God to provide such a ransom. Man unable to provide a ransom for his brother even from death temporal (Ps. xlix. 7—9). Christ slain as the Ransom, the power and the wisdom of God (1 Cor. i. 23, 24). The words in the text the language of *joy,*— "I have found," &c. God "delighteth in mercy." Hence rejoices in finding a righteous way for its exercise. The father rejoices over the return of his prodigal or long-lost child, and the means of securing it. Similar language employed in reference to David as the type of Messiah (Ps. lxxxix. 19, 20).

3. *Restoration to health,* among the results of sanctified affliction. Verse 25.— "His flesh shall be fresher," &c. This probably included in the command: "Deliver from going down to the pit." The power to deliver from temporal death and to restore from the brink of the grave, in the hand of the Almighty. The command needs only to be given or power put forth. The Divine command as effectual in restoring to life and health as at the creation in producing light : "Let there be light, and there was light." The centurion's faith in regard to Jesus the Son of God : "Speak the word only and my servant shall be healed." *Diseases God's servants, to come and go at His bidding.* The leper's faith : "Lord, if thou *wilt,* thou *canst*

make me clean." All nature, visible and invisible, under the Divine control. The command or will of Jehovah obeyed through all the material universe. "He spake and it was done." *Recovery from sickness dependant not on the skill of the physician, but on the will of the Almighty.* Till God says : "Deliver from going down," &c., all remedies fruitless. When He speaks the word, the simplest becomes effectual. A plaster of figs laid on Hezekiah's boil at the prophet's prescription, the means, at God's will, of saving the king's life (Is. xxxviii. 21). The power of

Healing the Sick,

claimed by God in regard to *Israel* (Exod. xv. 26; xxiii. 25; Deut. vii. 15). Ascribed to Him in regard to men in general (Ps. ciii. 3 ; cvii. 20). Exercised by Christ as a proof of His Divinity and Divine mission as the Messiah (Luke vii. 20—22). The same power communicated by Him to the Apostles as credentials of their Divine commission and of the truth of their doctrine (Mark iii. 15). The power communicated also to the seventy (Luke x. 9); and promised to believers in general (Mark xvi. 18). Continued in the New Testament Church as one of the "spiritual gifts" (1 Cor. xii. 9, 28). Exercised through the elders of the Church in connection with the prayer of faith and anointing with oil (James v. 14—16). Healing still imparted in the Church in answer to believing prayer. The institution at Mannedorf, in Switzerland, an evidence. The healing in the text in connection with repentance and the forgiveness of sins. The affliction sent on account of sin and with a view to the individual's repentance and salvation, most likely to be removed when, and only when, the end has been secured. Repentance and faith, followed by forgiveness and peace with God, even on *natural* grounds among the most likely means of restoration to health. Sin being the cause of sickness, natural that the removal of the cause should be followed by the removal of the effect. Thus forgiveness of sin followed by restoration to health (James v., 15, 16; Matt. ix., 2—6 ; Ps. ciii., 3). Hezekiah restored to health when God cast all his sins behind his back (Is. xxviii., 17).

4. *Access to God and acceptance with Him in prayer, a* FOURTH result of sanctified affliction. Verse 26.—"He shall pray unto God, and he will be favourable unto him."

Prayer

the natural and necessary consequence of a graciously awakened conscience, of submission to God, of repentance, and of faith in the Divine mercy. The testimony concerning penitent Saul in Damascus: "Behold he prayeth." The prayer of the awakened and penitent sick man at least as much for forgiveness of sin as for restoration to health. With sanctified affliction, prayer becomes his "vital breath." The penitent and believing unable to live without prayer. Prayer the happy privilege of the child of God. A precious mercy in itself, as well as the means of obtaining more. Accepted prayer the result of the Spirit of adoption, crying "Abba Father," and of the Spirit of grace and supplication making intercession within us (Rom. viii. 15, 26; Zech. xii. 10). A heart to pray not always present with the need of prayer. Prayer, though made, not always accepted (Prov. i. 28; Is. i. 15). In sanctified affliction, prayer not only made but accepted: "He will be favourable unto him." Prayer only accepted when offered in penitence and faith. Believing prayer the channel for the best of all favours. The key that opens the cabinet of God and unlocks the treasures of heaven. God's favour, the fountain of all blessing, experienced through believing prayer. The Divine invitation: Seek ye my face. His face, or favour, not sought in vain (Ps. xxviii. 8; xxiv. 6; Is. xlv. 19). A mercy to be able to pray; a still greater one to have our prayer answered. A praying heart both preceded and followed by Divine mercy.

5. *Reconciliation with and joy in God.* "He shall see his face with joy." So the penitent prodigal in respect to his father (Luke xiv. 22—24). Reconciliation with God the sinner's greatest blessing. The object aimed at by God in the gift and sacrifice of His Son (2 Cor. v. 18, 19; Acts x. 36; Eph. ii. 16; Col. i. 20—22). Aimed at in his chastenings (Hos. ii. 6, 7, 11—20). Reconciliation with and joy in God the fruit of faith in Jesus Christ (Rom. v. 1, 11). The spiritual healing of the penitent patient (Matt. v. 8). A foretaste of heaven thus enjoyed as the result of sanctified affliction (Rev. xxii., 4; Ps. xvii., 15). The sight of God's reconciled face here is heaven before coming to it—*Chrysostom.* No joy like that of seeing the reconciled face of God in Jesus Christ.

6. *Confession of sin, and praise to God for pardoning and restoring mercy,* a SIXTH result of sanctified affliction. Verse 27.—"He looketh upon men, and if any say, &c.; he will deliver his soul," &c. Probably better according to the *Margin*: "He (*i.e.*, the sick man now restored) shall look upon men and say, &c.; he (God) hath delivered my soul," &c. (1) *Confession of sin*: "I have sinned." A result and evidence of sanctified affliction. The language of the penitent prodigal (Luke

214

xv. 21). Confession of sin made in respect to (i.) Its iniquity and turpitude: "I have perverted that which was right." Observe —(*a*) God's will concerning us and his law given to us, only what is right. (*b*) *All sin a perverting of what is right.* Sin an opposition to God's holy will and righteous law. (ii.) Its hurtful consequences: "And it profited me not;" or, "he hath not rewarded me accordingly." No profit in sin. Its promises delusions. Its pleasures but for a season. No profit in gaining the world and losing the soul. Not only no profit in sin, but absolute loss. Its fruit shame, its end death (Rom. vi. 21). An ill exchange for the path of obedience (Hos. ii. 7). The righteous desert of sin eternal death (Rom. vi. 23). Sin an ill paymaster that sends all his servants away weeping. —*Trapp.* Observe—(i.) *Confession of sin an evidence of genuine repentance.* Such confession made not feignedly, as by Saul (1 Sam. xv. 24); nor forcedly, as by Pharaoh (Exod. x. 16), and by Achan (Josh. vii. 20); nor despairingly, as by Judas Iscariot (Matt. xxvii. 4); but sincerely, freely, and hopefully, as by David (Ps. li. 3, 4, 12—14. (ii.) *Confession of sin an accompaniment of pardoning mercy.* Preceding it (Ps. xxxii. 5; 1 John i. 9; Prov. xxviii. 13). Following it (Ezek. xvi. 63).—(2) *Praise for pardoning and restoring mercy.* *Margin:* "He shall look on men and say," &c., or, "He shall sing among men," &c. Examples: Hezekiah (Is. xxxviii. 19, 20); David (Ps. xxx. 1— 12). Praise, God's due for mercies received (Ps. l. 23; cxvi. 12, 13). Mercies doubly sweet when accompanied with a grateful heart and thanksgiving to their gracious Author.

VI. **Re-asserts these gracious dealings of Divine Providence.** Verses 29, 30.—" Lo (the fact worthy of careful notice, both from its truth and preciousness), all these things worketh God oftentimes with man, to bring back his soul from the pit (the grave, and that state in eternity of which it is the symbol), to be enlightened with the light of the living" (made glad with the joy of those who are truly and spiritually alive). The "things" referred to, God's chastening men for sin by bringing them to the verge of the grave, and then restoring and blessing them upon repentance. Observe—

1. The *frequency* of such dispensations,— "Oftentimes." Not *always*. All not visited alike with chastening and affliction. God sovereign in his dealings. But *often*. Multitudes thus graciously visited. God merciful and gracious. Intent on man's welfare. Chastenings a greater proof of his love than the want of them (Rev. iii. 19). An ill sign

for a man when God will not spend a rod upon him.—*Brooks.*

2. The *object* of them,—"To bring back his soul," &c. God's object in chastening men, their present and eternal welfare. "He [chastens] for our profit, that we may be partakers of his holiness" (Heb. xii. 6, 11). This is all the fruit to take away his sin (Is. xxvii. 9). Man by nature in a state of darkness and of death. God's object in affliction to deliver him out of it. Brings his body to the verge of the grave to save his soul from going to a deeper pit. Danger of temporal death made a means of deliverance from death spiritual and eternal. The true penitent, one who was dead, but is alive again (Luke xv. 32). Life only in the favour and image of God. Heaven rather than earth the place of the living (Matt. xx. 32).

VII. Invites Job to reply, and urges attention to his further remarks.

Verses 31—33.—"Mark well, O Job; hearken unto me: hold thy peace and I will speak. If thou hast anything to say, answer me: speak, for I desire to justify thee (or 'thy justification' or 'righteousness'). If not, hearken unto me: hold thy peace, and I shall teach thee wisdom." Observe—

1. *Opportunity to be given to reply or object to our statements.* The benefit of inquiry or after-meetings in connection with special or missionary services.

2. In the absence of objection or reply, respectful attention the more to be expected.

3. Hearers to be convinced that we speak from a simple desire for their own benefit. The desire of the preacher of the Gospel, the justification of the hearers through their acceptance of Jesus as the Lord their Righteousness (Jer. xxiii. 6). Christ the way of a sinner's justification. The way provided by God, and the *only* way. "The end of the law for righteousness to every one that believeth" (Rom. x. 4).

4. The hearer's character and case to be viewed in the most favourable light that truth admits of. The contrary the case with Job's three friends. Hence Job's irritation rather than conviction. Elihu takes up a contrary position, and Job is silent.

5. *True "wisdom," to understand the character and dealings of God, and to act in humble submission to Him under those dealings.* This wisdom taught by Elihu, and ultimately learned by the patriarch.

CHAPTER XXXIV.

ELIHU'S SECOND SPEECH.

Probably after waiting for a reply from Job, and none being forthcoming, Elihu resumes. Verse 1.—"Furthermore Elihu answered (took up speech), and said." Job's silence probably indicative of the effect produced by Elihu's first speech. Elihu now addresses himself partly to the three friends and others present, and partly to Job himself. The first part of his speech addressed to the former. In the preceding chapter, Elihu vindicates God's goodness; in this, His justice.

1. His introduction. Verse 2—4.

1. *Bespeaks their careful attention, and appeals to their sound judgment.* Verse 2.—"Hear my words, O ye wise men (the three friends, and perhaps others), and give ear unto me, ye that have knowledge." Observe—(1) Wisdom and knowledge required to judge correctly of statements made respecting things pertaining to God and His moral government. (2) The part of a wise man to give earnest attention to what is advanced on such subjects. (3) A wise speaker willing

to be corrected by men of judgment and understanding.

2. *Invites an impartial examination of his statements.* Verse 3.—"For the ear trieth words, as the mouth tasteth meat." Observe—(1) *Man is furnished by his Creator with means for testing statements on moral and religious truth, as well for trying the food which he is to eat.* (2) *Private judgment in reference to such subjects man's duty as well as his right.* His duty carefully and impartially to examine, and so either to adopt or reject. The Bereans commended, because they not only "received the word with all readiness of mind," but "searched the Scriptures daily whether these things were so" (Acts xvii. 11). The New Testament rule—"Prove all things; hold fast that which is good." "Believe not every spirit; but try the spirits whether they be of God." "Why even of yourselves judge ye not what is right?" "Judge ye what I say." (1 Thess. v. 21; 1 John iv. 1; Luke xii. 57; 1 Cor. x. 15). The Old Testament rule: "Cease, my son, to hear the instruction that causeth to err from the words of knowledge:" "To the

law and to the testimony; if they speak not according to this word, it is because there is no light in them" (Prov. xix. 27; Isaiah viii. 20).

3. *Exhorts to a faithful treatment of the subject in hand.* Verse 4.—"Let us choose to us judgment (let us examine among ourselves, and choose as our conclusion what is the right view of the case): let us know among ourselves (learn, and so acknowledge and adopt) what is good" (right and true on the subject in hand). Like that of the Saviour: "Judge not according to appearance, but judge righteous judgment" (John vii. 24). And that of the Apostle: "Be transformed by the renewing of your mind, that ye may prove what is the good and acceptable and perfect, even the will of God" (Rom. xii. 2). Observe—(1) The part of a wise man to contend, not for victory, but for truth; (2) What is right and true alone is good. A false view and a wrong course never, in the end, a profitable one.

II. **Elihu's charge against Job.** Verses 5–9.—" For Job hath said," &c. Job's language, rather than his life, the subject of Elihu's censure. The friends had, by inference, condemned Job's life *previous* to his affliction; Elihu condemns, as a matter of fact, his language *under* it. His general charge against Job, that he seemed to *accuse God of acting unjustly towards him.* More especially—

1. That he *justified himself as righteous.* Verse 5.—" For Job hath said: ' I am righteous,'—'without transgression,'" *i.e.,* such as to merit such treatment. Reference to such parts of Job's speeches as chap. ix. 17; xiii. 18; xvi. 17. Job maintained his innocence in opposition to what his friends suspected and believed, and to what his present calamities seemed to indicate. This, even in Elihu's judgment, improperly maintained by Job, as reflecting on his Maker's character and government. Job's language, though relatively true, yet too strong and unqualified, and apparently uttered in a self-righteous spirit. Declarations of personal righteousness like those of Job, unbecoming in a sinner. Lawful for a man boldly to declare his righteousness only as he is righteous in Christ. "Surely shall one say: In the Lord have I righteousness: in Him shall all the seed of Israel be justified, and shall glory" (Is. xlv. 25).

2. That he *charged God with injustice and wrong in the way He treated him.* (Verse 6) —"God hath taken away my judgment (deprived me of my righteousness in treating me as a guilty person; or, has put aside my righteous cause); my wound is incurable

(or grievous) without transgression" [on my part to deserve it]. Job's actual language (ch. xxvii. 2). Observe—(1) *Complaint against God's dealings an implied challenge of His justice.* (2) *God's righteousness to be acknowledged in all the circumstances of our lot.* The proper language of a sufferer: "The Lord is righteous:" "He hath not dealt with us after our sins (2 Chron. xii. 6; Jer. xii. 1; Ps. ciii. 10).

3. That he *had used contemptuous language in regard to God.* Verse 7.—" What man is like Job (or, 'what man is there like Job,' —a man having so high a character for piety), who drinketh up scorning like water?" Reference to Job's daring and irreverent language, in which he challenged God to a controversy on his case, and appeared to make his own righteousness less questionable than God's in the matter. Such language used by Job *frequently,* and with apparent *eagerness* and *pleasure,* like a thirsty animal taking a large draught of water. Same metaphor employed by Eliphaz in reference to mankind, and with respect to sin in general (ch. xv. 16). Job's language unusual in *any,* but especially in a person of his character. Observe—(1) *Perseverance and pleasure in doing or saying what is wrong a serious aggravation of the sin;* (2) *A grief and offence to the godly when a pious man is found speaking or acting in a way unlike himself.* Thus Abraham in Egypt; David in the matter of Uriah; Peter in the high priest's palace. David's prayer always necessary: "Keep back thy servant," &c.; "Set a watch before my mouth," &c. (Ps. xix. 12—14; cxli. 3).

4. That he *appeared to adopt the language and sentiments of the ungodly.* Verse 8.— " Which goeth in company with the workers of iniquity, and walketh with wicked men," —namely, in using such language and adopting such sentiments. Observe—(1) *The part of the ungodly to entertain unjust thoughts of God, and to speak irreverently in regard both to Himself and His dealings.* (2) *A godly man to be careful not to countenance the ungodly in their views and language, either by what he says or does.* (3) *The views and language of the ungodly in reference to God and His dealings to be carefully avoided, as well as their company.* (4) *A man appears to be the companion of those whose language, views, and practices he adopts.* The proper language of a godly man: "I am a companion of all them that fear thee" (Ps. cxix. 63). His prayer: "Gather not my soul with sinners" (Ps. xxvi. 9).

5. That he seemed *to deny that there was any benefit in true religion* (ver. 9). "For he hath said, It profiteth a man nothing that he should delight himself in

God." True piety also characterised, though by a different Hebrew word, in ch. xxvii. 10, as a *delighting in God*. The expression in the text indicates—(1) To have friendly and familiar intercourse with God; (2) To have pleasure in such intercourse; (3) To make it one's care to please God; (4) To be satisfied with Him as one's portion. The character of the godly to walk with God, and have delight in such walk (Gen. v. 22—24). Observe—*True religion a delighting oneself in God* (ch. xxvii. 10).

Delight in God

Is—(1) Characteristic of the godly, and that which distinguishes them from the world. (2) Enjoined as a duty (Ps. xxxvii. 5; Phil. iii. 1; iv. 4). Gladness required in serving him (Deut. xii. 12, 18; xxviii. 47; Ps. c. 2; Is. lxiv. 5). (3) Promised as a reward of piety, especially in regard to the Sabbath (Job xxii. 26; Is. lviii. 14). Implies—
1. The *excellence and loveliness in God*. God worthy to be delighted in—(1) In Himself and His perfections; (2) In what He has become to us in and through Jesus Christ.
2. The *inwardness and spirituality of true religion*. True religion a thing of the *heart*; the seat of delight. Not a thing of *form or ceremony*; or of *bodily service*; or of *mere morality* or *outward obedience*. A thing of delight, because a thing of *love*.
3. The *happiness and pleasantness of true piety*. Not only *causes delight*, but *is itself* a *delighting*. Wisdom's ways pleasantness and peace. Delight and pleasure a necessary accompaniment of true religion. God the object of true religion, not as a Being merely to be feared or served, but *delighted in*. God sufficient in Himself to fill every intelligent creature with joy. His favour *life*; His loving kindness better than life. Believers though not *seeing* Christ, yet *believing* and so *loving* Him, rejoice in Him with joy unspeakable and full of glory (1 Peter i. 8).
Delight in God shewn—
1. By *holding fellowship with Him*. We cultivate the society of those we delight in. Hence true religion a "walking with God," (Micah vi. 8; Gen. v. 22; vi. 9).
2. By *obeying His will and seeking to please Him*. Impossible willingly to disobey or grieve the person we delight in. To "walk with God," and to "please God," spoken of in Scripture as one and the same thing (Gen. v. 22, 54, compared with Heb. xi. 5).
3. By *ceasing to love and delight in the world*. Impossible to love and please two masters of opposite characters. The love of the world incompatible with the love of God (Matt. vi. 24; 1 John ii. 14, 15). The

world a crucified thing where Christ is delighted in (Gal. vi. 14).
4. By *attending upon His ordinances*. His ordinances the means of fellowship with God, and helps to the enjoyment of Him. His banqueting house, where His banner over us is love (Cant. ii. 4). The sanctuary and the Sabbath a delight when God Himself is so (Ps. xxvi. 8; lxiii. 1, 2; lxxx. 1, 10; Is. lviii. 13).
5. By *cheerfully acquiescing in His appointments*. Delight in a person leads to delight, and at least to a cheerful acquiescence, in what he says and does. Strictly true in regard to God, all whose sayings and doings are known and believed to be right.
The profitableness of true religion, or "delighting oneself with God," apparently denied in some of Job's expressions, as ch. ix. 22, 23; xxi. 7—15. The reference, however, only to this life and the outward dispensations of Divine Providence. The language ascribed by Elihu to Job never really used by him. His employment of it Satan's great object. At times strongly tempted to it. Suggested by his wife. Asaph tempted in like circumstances to employ it (Ps. lxxiii. 12—14). The language of unbelief (Mal. iii. 14). Godliness profitable to all things. Has the promise of both worlds (1 Tim. ii. 8; vi. 6).

III. **Elihu's defence of God against Job's cavils and complaints.**—(Verses 10—30). First addresses himself to the three friends and those present at the debate. Verse 10.—"Therefore hearken unto me, ye men of understanding." Afterwards addresses his discourse to Job himself. Verse 16.—"If now thou hast understanding, hear this; hearken to the voice of my words." Elihu's self-imposed task, "to justify the ways of God to man." Intelligence in the hearers required to judge of statements made on such a subject. Elihu's arguments are—
1. *Iniquity and injustice incompatible with the Divine nature.* Verses 10—12. —"Far be it from God (as a thing profane to think of) that He should do wickedness, and from the Almighty that He should commit iniquity. For, the work of a man (or the *reward* of his work) shall He render unto him, and cause every one to find according to his ways. Yea, surely God will not do wickedly, neither will the Almighty prevent judgment" ("act unrighteously," or "pass an unrighteous sentence"). Injustice not merely denied of God, but denied as a thing not for a moment to be thought—as a thing utterly incongruous with His nature as God, and not possible to be found in Him. The idea of iniquity

incompatible with the idea of God. God's ways to be believed to be just and right, simply because they are His, and because they cannot be otherwise. The thought of injustice and wrong in God to be repelled with loathing and execration, as profane and abominable. Observe—(1) Some things to be not simply denied, but execrated; as injustice in God. Others to be not so much argued, as simply but strongly asserted; as that God is just (Rom. iii. 4, 5). (2) A man finds according to his ways either in this life or the next. Every work brought into judgment (Ecc. xi. 9; xii. 14; 2 Cor. v. 10; Rev. xx. 12). Sentence against an evil work only not speedily executed (Ecc. viii. 11). Sin sometimes punished in this life in the natural course of things which God has established. Sometimes punished by special and unexpected acts of His Providence, as in the case of Herod (Acts xii. 23). The impenitent sinner escaping punishment all through life is overtaken at last, and finds "according to his ways." The rich man dies and is buried, prosperous and luxurious to the last: but "in hell he lifted up his eyes, being in torments" (Luke xvi. 23).

2. *Injustice incompatible with God's absolute supremacy and independence as the Creator and Governor of the Universe.* Verse 13.—"Who hath given him a charge over the earth (or, committed the earth to his charge, as a superior commits a charge to a subordinate)? or who hath disposed the whole world?" (—placed the universe in the state in which we find it). Observe—(1) As Creator, Proprietor, and Supreme Ruler of the Universe, God can be under no temptation to injustice. To be unjust would be to wrong Himself. (2) God accountable to no superior. That the world exists at all, and is ruled by Him, is not from necessity imposed upon him, but from the benevolence of His own nature. God therefore to be called to account for his doings by none of His creatures.

3. *Man dependent on God's mere goodness for life and all he enjoys.* Verses 14, 15—"If He set His heart upon man (or, 'against man,' to deal strictly with him according to his deserts; or, 'if He directed His attention only to Himself'); if He gather (or 'He would gather') unto Himself [as its author, (Ecc. xii. 7)] his spirit and his breath [which He first breathed into man's nostrils to make him a living soul, Gen. ii. 7]; all flesh shall (or should) perish together (as at the general deluge, Gen. vi. 3, 17), and man shall (or should) turn again unto dust" [according to the original sentence pronounced on man after the Fall, Gen. iii. 19]. Observe —(1) *Man's life and breath entirely in the*

hands *of God.* Given by God at first, and only continued at His pleasure. In Him we live, and move, and have our being (Acts xvii. 28). (2) A *sinner's continuance in life the fruit and evidence of Divine goodness.* His life forfeited to justice as a transgressor of the Divine law (Gen. ii. 17; Rom. vi. 23). (3) Injustice or wrong, therefore, on the part of God to His creatures, entirely out of the question. Hence (4) murmuring and complaining against God to be for ever silenced: "Wherefore doth a living man complain" (Lam. iii. 39).

4. *Injustice on the part of God incompatible with His being the Ruler of the Universe.* Verses 17, 19—"Shall even he that hateth right govern? (*Heb.*, 'bind,' as with authority and law; or 'bind up,' as a wound or fracture, a ruler being properly a 'healer,' Is. iii. 7). And wilt thou condemn him that is most just (or, 'him that is at once just and mighty?') Is it fit to say to a king (even an earthly sovereign), thou art wicked (*Heb.* 'Belial,' wickedness), and to princes, ye are ungodly? How much less to Him that accepteth not the persons of princes, nor regardeth the rich more than the poor? for they all are the work of His hands." Observe—(1) The *mere fact of God being the Supreme Ruler of the Universe a sufficient proof of His justice.* Justice implied in the rule even of an earthly sovereign. An unjust ruler to be regarded as a monster—an exception to the ordinary course of things, and soon therefore coming to an end. The exercise of justice necessary to, and therefore supposed in, the continuance of government. "He that ruleth over men must be just" (2 Sam. xxiii. 3). Abraham's plea: "Shall not the Judge of all the earth do right?" (Gen. xvii. 25). God just, because mighty. (2) *Rulers under the most solemn obligation to be just.* If the charge of iniquity is not to be made by the subject, it is not to be incurred by the sovereign. (3) *Rulers to be not only just, but beneficent.* A ruler to be a healer. The State more or less sick and wounded by sin and its consequences (Is. i. 5, 6; Jer. viii. 22). The part of a ruler to heal and bind it up—by just laws, wholesome authority, wise institutions, and godly example. The ruler a healer only as he rules "in the fear of God" (2 Sam. xxiii. 3). Examples: Hezekiah; Josiah; Alfred. (4) *Reverence due to rulers and those in authority.* Rulers not to be reviled by their subjects (Exod. xxii. 28). God's vicegerents and representatives, and therefore called by his name (Ex. xxii. 2; Ps. lxxxii. 1, 6). (5) *God impartial in His government.* As His creatures, all on an equal footing in His sight. Differences among men disregarded by God. No difference of treatment either

from fear or favour. Hence (i.) warning to the sick; (ii.) comfort to the poor; (iii.) example to rulers and magistrates.

5. *Judgments inflicted on sinners, especially on powerful oppressors.* Verses 20—28. "In a moment (suddenly and speedily) shall they die (or, 'they—*i.e.*, the ungodly—especially the rich and powerful—die,' viz., under the infliction of Divine judgments), and the people (as distinguished from the princes) shall be troubled (or 'are troubled,' viz., by the judgments inflicted) at midnight (unexpectedly and in a time of quiet and security, as 1 Thess. v. 2), and pass away (as at the Deluge, and the destruction of the Cities of the Plain, or as by earthquakes, &c.): and the mighty shall be (or are) taken away without hand [of man, or any human agency or violence]. For His eyes are upon the ways of man (both rulers and ruled), and He seeth all his doings. There is no darkness nor shadow of death where the workers of iniquity may hide themselves [from His eye, or elude His vengeance]. For He will not lay upon man more than is right, that he should enter into judgment with God (giving him occasion to complain of being punished beyond his deserts; or, ' He does not direct His attention long to a man for him to go to God in judgment,' as if needing long investigation into his case in dealing judicially with him). He shall break (or he breaks) in pieces (by His judgments) mighty men without number (or without enquiry), and set others in their stead (putting down one and setting up another, as Ps. lxxv. 7). Therefore (or, for) he knoweth their works, and he overturneth them in the night (or 'in a night;' or 'he turneth night upon them,' *i.e.* the night of calamity and death, as in the case of Belshazzar, Dan. v. 30; and of Herod, Acts. xii 23; so that they are destroyed. He striketh them (by His judgments) as wicked men (—as other wicked men; or, 'because they are wicked men') in the open sight of others. Because they turned back from Him (or, from following after Him, viz., by adhering to His service and obeying His commands), and would not consider [seriously and attentively] any of His ways [whether in Providence or precept, so as to 'stand in awe and sin not']: so that they cause [by their oppression] the cry of the poor to come unto Him, and (or, so that) He heareth the cry of the afflicted." Observe—(1) *Judgments manifestly inflicted on tyrants and oppressors, a proof of the justice of the Divine government.* "The Lord is known by the judgment which He executeth" (Ps. ix. 16). History full of such judgments. (2) *The ungodly often overtaken and cut off by Divine judgments unexpectedly.* This still to be the case (1 Thess. v. 3). (3) *Impos-*

sible for the wicked, either by power or prudence, to escape God's righteous judgments. God omniscient as well as omnipotent. His eye as penetrating as His arm is powerful. (4) *Ungodly men and oppressors often visited with signal and manifest judgments, as a warning to others and a testimony to the justice of the Divine government.* "So that a man shall say: Verily there is a reward to the righteous; verily there is a God that judgeth in the earth" (Ps. lviii. 11). Open sinners often made open sufferers. (5) *Perseverance in His service, and consideration of His word and works, required by God of His intelligent creatures, whether rulers or ruled.* The want of it regarded by Him as a grievous sin. (6) *Disobedience and neglect in regard to God, as well as oppression and cruelty in regard to man, the frequent ground of suffering in this life, and, if unrepented of, the certain cause of misery in the next.*

6. *The dependence of all upon God for quietness and comfort.* Verse 29.—" When He giveth quietness (or forgives), who then can make trouble (or condemn)? and when He hideth His face (as in displeasure, or as withdrawing His help and favour; or ' When He hideth the face,' *i.e.*, condemns, or treats as a condemned criminal), who then can behold Him (enjoy His favour, or reverse the sentence of death)? Whether it be done against (or towards) a nation, or against a man only?" Observe—(1) *God the Sovereign Dispenser of quiet and comfort to individuals.* His to forgive or to condemn. His sentence irreversible. Hence the prophet's challenge in the person of the Messiah (Ps. l. 7—9), and the apostle's triumph in the name of believers (Rom. viii. 31—34). The part of God to give peace (Ps. lxxxv. 8; Is. xlv. 7; lvii. 19). Able to make even a man's enemies to be at peace with him (Prov. xvi. 7). Speaks peace and gives rest to an awakened sinner's conscience. To do this, the object of—(i.) The atoning death of Jesus. (ii.) His resurrection, as declarative of the Divine acceptance and efficacy of His death. (iii.) His ascension into heaven and session at God's right hand as the Advocate of believing sinners. (iv.) The mission of the Holy Ghost as the Comforter and Witness-bearer of the Saviour's work (Rom. viii. 34; xv. 16). Quiet and rest to the troubled conscience the object of the Saviour's mission (Is. lxi. 1—3 ; Luke ii. 10). His invitation and promise (Matt. xi. 28). Peace and rest the fruit of faith in Him (Is. xxvi. 3; Rom. v. 1; xv. 13; Heb. iv. 3). (2) *God the Dispenser of rest and quietness to nations and Churches.* To nations (1 Chron. xxii. 9, 18). To Churches (Acts ix. 31). Nations and men equally in God's power (Is. xl. 15—17). His to make wars to cease to the ends of the earth (Ps. xlvi.

9); to make peace in our borders (Ps. cxlvii. 14); or in righteous judgment, to stir up one nation against another (Is. xiii. 17). (3) None able to frustate God's work and purpose, whether of mercy or of judgment (Is. xxvii. 3, 4; xliii. 14).

7. *The Divine benevolence in the judgments inflicted on oppressors.* Verse 30.—"That the hypocrite (or profligate) reign not, lest the people be ensnared" (or, "That there be no ensnarings or offences to the people"). Observe—(1) *Kings and rulers subject to God's ordination* (Rom. xiii. 1). His to say who shall and who shall not reign. His prerogative to put down one and set up another (Ps. lxxv. 6, 7). Examples: David set up instead of Saul (2 Sam. vi. 21); Jeroboam as ruler of the ten tribes instead of Rehoboam (2 Chron. xi. 4). (2) *A grievous evil to a people when a "profligate, wicked prince" rules over them* (Ps. xii. 8). (3) *God's benevolence seen in His cutting short the reign of profane rulers* (Ez. xxi. 25). Men usually not suffered long to continue in the power which they abuse. The reason,—God is careful of the welfare of mankind. (4) *A people apt to imitate the example of their rulers.* An ungodly king a snare to his subjects. A dissolute prince makes a dissolute people. Example: The reign of the second Charles. (5) *God's benevolence, as seen in the judgments He inflicts on tyrants and oppressors, an evidence of the justice of His government.* A benevolent Being cannot be unjust.

IV. Man's duty under the Divine chastisements. Verses 31, 32.—"Surely it is meet to be said unto God, I have borne chastisement, I will not offend any more: that which I see not, teach thou me: if I have done iniquity, I will do no more." Elihu performs to Job the part of the messenger and interpreter he himself describes (chap. xxxiii. 23). Teaches what is man's

Duty under Chastisement.

1. To *turn to God.* Verse 31.—"It is meet to be said unto God." The afflicted to direct himself to God, who is dealing with him, and against whom he has sinned. God's object in chastisement to bring the individual to Himself. Thus the prodigal, in his distress, returned to his *father.* God's call under chastisement: "Return unto the Lord thy God" (Hos. xiv. 1). His complaint against Israel, that they returned, but not to *Him* (Hos. vii. 16, 10). God both speaks to us in chastening, and wishes to be *spoken to :* "It is meet to be *said* unto God:" "Take with you *words*, and turn to the Lord" (Hos. xiv. 2). No benefit from affliction till we speak to *God* in it.
220

2. To *acknowledge and accept the chastisement*: "I have borne chastisement." God's will that His chastening should be accepted and acknowledged. The condition on which He promised returning mercy to Israel (Lev. xxvi. 41, 42). The language of penitent Israel: "Thou hast chastised me, and I was chastised" (Jer. xxxi. 18). The mark of a humbled heart, to accept or submit to chastisement (Lev. xxvi. 41). Divine chastening neither to be despised nor despaired under (Heb. xii. 5). The prophet our example under chastisement—"I will bear the indignation of the Lord, because I have sinned against Him" (Mic. vii. 9). Divine chastisement to be borne—(1) submissively; (2) Patiently; (3) Humbly; (4) Lovingly; (5) Thankfully. The chastisement of a believer not that by a master, but by a father. To be borne not as a slave, but as a child. The lesson Job now needed especially to be taught.

3. To *confess our sin.* "I have done iniquity." God's aim in chastisement to bring us to confession of sin. "Only acknowledge thine iniquity" (Jer. iii. 13). Forgiveness and mercy promised only upon confession (1 John i. 9 ; Prov. xxviii. 13).

4. To *resolve upon amendment.* "I will not offend any more. If I have done iniquity, I will do no more." The language put into the mouth of penitent Israel: "What have I to do any more with idols? Neither will we say any more to the work of our hands: Ye are our gods" (Hos. xiv. 8, 3). Mercy promised to those who confess and *forsake* their sins (Prov. xxviii. 13). To abandon what we confess, the only proof of sincerity. The offence to be avoided may be either one of omission or of commission; may be either in spirit or demeanour, in heart or in life. God jealous over His people's inward affection as well as their outward conduct : "I have somewhat against thee, because thou hast left thy *first love.* Remember, therefore, from whence thou art *fallen,* and *repent,* and do the *first works ;* or else," &c. (Rev. ii. 4, 5).

5. To *pray for Divine teaching.* Verse 32.—"What I see not, teach thou me." A mark of humility and sanctified affliction when we seek and ask for Divine teaching. That teaching needed and desired—(1) In regard to *sin.* Sin the cause of suffering, and occasion for chastisement. To be seen and known in order to be confessed, forsaken, and forgiven. To be shown both as to its nature and its prevalence in ourselves. But little of sin seen by us in comparison with the sad reality. Much both of the malignity and demerit of sin at first unknown to us. Much sin unseen by us as existing in ourselves, both in heart and

in life. "Who can understand his errors?" "Cleanse thou me from secret faults" (Ps. xix. 12). David's prayer (Ps. cxxxix. 23, 24). The mark of sincerity to desire to *know* our sin, instead of cloaking or palliating it. (2) In regard to *duty*. The penitent onlypartially acquainted with his duty. His desire to know the Lord's will in order to do it (Ps. lxxxvi. 11). The penitent's inquiry that of Saul on the way to Damascus, "Lord what wilt thou have me do?" (Acts x. 6).

V. Elihu's reproof of Job (verses 33, 35). —The reproof directed—

1. Against *his murmuring and discontent.* Verse 33.—" Should it be according to thy mind? he will recompense it, whether thou refuse or whether thou choose, and not I? (or, 'According to *thy* mind, shall he recompense it, *i.e.*, thy conduct,—because *thou* refusest and *thou* choosest, and not I?'—the words supposed to be uttered by God himself): therefore speak what thou knowest" (*i.e.*, as to how God shall treat thee—spoken in irony). In Elihu's judgment Job's spirit and language under his afflictions open to severe censure—(1) On account of its *rebelliousness.* As if not God but Job himself were to rule in the matter of his treatment and appointment of his lot. The part of rebellion to wish to take the mode and measure of our chastisement out of God's hand into our own. This rebellion implied in all murmuring and discontent under trials. The language of piety and duty : " Not *my* will, but thine, be done :" "The cup that my Father hath given me, shall I not drink it?" (Luke xxii. 42; John xviii.) (2) On account of its *pride.* The highest pride to think to arrogate to ourselves the distribution of rewards and punishments, or to prescribe how God shall deal with us. Murmuring and discontent imply the supposed possession of a wisdom superior to our Maker's.

2. Against his *ignorance.* Verses 34, 35. —" Let men of understanding tell me, and let a wise man hearken unto me (implying that Job had not spoken as such). Job hath spoken without knowledge, and his words were without wisdom." Observe— (1) To cavil with our Maker's treatment of us, indicative of ignorance both in regard to God and ourselves. Job's want of knowledge and wisdom indicated in—(i.) Erroneously judging of God's dealings with him; (ii.) Sitting in judgment on those dealings at all; (iii.) Wishing to enter into controversy with God on the justice of them; (iv.) Charging God with undue severity in them. Thereproof given by Elihu seconded afterwards by the Almighty himself. Job's

ignorance and want of understanding in what he had spoken afterwards acknowledged and repented of. (2) Humbling to subject ourselves to the reproof which we have administered to others. Job now reproved for what he had at first reproved his wife. (3) God's dealings with us not according to our ignorance, but His wisdom. (4) The disposal of our lot best left in God's own hands.

VI. Elihu's desire in regard to Job. Verses 36, 37.—"My desire is," &c

1. *The desire itself.* Verse 36.—" That Job may be tried unto the end" (fully, or more literally, "unto victory,"—until the end has been served in Job's humiliation and confession; the wish granted (ch. xli. 4, 5; xlii. 2—6.) Observe—(1) *Elihu's earnestness and zeal indicated in the wish with which he concludes his final speech.* A speaker should exhibit *warmth* as well as *wisdom.* People more likely to be persuaded when logic is accompanied with *feeling.* A preacher's light rather to resemble that of the sun than the moon. (2.) *Elihu's wish apparently exhibits more zeal for the truth than sympathy with the tried.* Wishes Job's trial still further to be continued. Apparently inconsistent with his former profession. The wish, however, both wise and benevolent, though apparently harsh. The best wish for the afflicted is that the affliction may produce the effects intended by it,—the spiritual benefit of the sufferer. Better the continuance of a trial than its premature removal. To have affliction removed before the heart is humbled, a curse rather than a blessing.

2. *The ground of the desire.* Verses 36, 37. —These are—(1) His apparently *ungodly sentiments.* "Because of his answers for (among, with, or like) wicked men." Some of Job's utterances apparently in favour of ungodliness, and only found in the lips of ungodly men. Sad when a godly man appears, even for a short time, to pass over to the side of the wicked, either in the sentiments he utters or the conduct he exhibits. An aggravation in the open sin of the godly that it associates them for the time with the workers of iniquity (Ps. cxli. 4). Care needed under temptation, lest we utter what may appear to favour ungodliness, and afford an excuse to the ungodly. Job's "answers" afterwards recalled and deeply repented of. (2) His *obstinacy and rebellion.* "He addeth (or will add) rebellion to his sin." A distinction between sin and rebellion. So between the sin of ignorance and the presumptuous sin. The latter much more heinous. "Sin" committed through the

infirmity of our nature; "rebellion," through the perversity of our choice. Believers sin; unbelievers add rebellion to their sin. Noah and Abraham, David and Peter, *sinned;* Pharaoh and Saul, Judas and Herod, *rebelled* in their sin. Sin greatly aggravated by rebellion and stubbornness in it. In Job's case, rebellion only at times approached. Was Satan's desire, and would probably have been his victory. Elihu's wish to prevent this result. Rebellion far from Job's heart and intention. The lips may sometimes utter what the heart abhors. (3) His *pride and contempt.* "He clappeth (or will clap) his hands among us." The token of triumph and contempt. Job victorious in the contest, but, in Elihu's judgment, had carried himself unbecomingly in his victory. Though victorious in the argument, not yet humbled in his spirit. Had not yet recanted his bold and irreverent language, and seemed still to glory in his innocence. Carried himself as victor not only over men, but God himself. Elihu's desire to correct this unseemly spirit. (4)

The *impiety of his language.* "He multiplieth (or will multiply) his words against God." Job's language had at times appeared to assume this character. Irreverent and rebellious language a heinous sin. God's complaint against Israel in the days of Malachi: "Your words have been stout against me" (Mal. iii. 13). Words ordinarily the index of the heart (Matt. xii. 34). The characteristic of the ungodly to speak against God. The sin as early as the days of Enoch, before the flood (Jude 14). That for which Christ will execute judgment on the wicked at His second appearing (Jude 15). For every *idle* word that men speak they shall give account at the day of judgment; still more for every rebellious one (Matt. xii. 37). The confession of Isaiah that of every child of God (Is. vi. 5). The character of men universally. The believer's lips touched with the live coal from off the altar, and their iniquity taken away (Is. vi. 7). A "pure language" (or lip) one of the gifts of grace (Zeph. iii. 9).

CHAPTER XXXV.

ELIHU'S THIRD SPEECH.

After a second pause, and no reply, Elihu again resumes. Renews his reproof of Job, and attempts to answer some of his cavils. Verse 1.—"Elihu spake moreover," &c.

I. **Reproves Job for his improper language.** Verses 2, 3.—"Thinkest thou this to be right (or, 'Dost thou reckon this for judgment') that thou saidst," &c. Probably a sarcastic allusion to Job's vehement complaints about the want of "judgment." *Care necessary that we do not ourselves offend in that for which we are forward to blame others.* "Judge not that ye be not judged." Job's *language* rather than his life still the subject of Elihu's reproof." Job reproved—

1. *For maintaining his righteousness to be greater than God's.* Verse 2.—"My righteousness is more than God's,"—allusion to such passages as ch. ix. 30—35; x. 15. The supposed meaning rather than the exact words of Job's speeches. Job had maintained that his life had been pure and righteous, and that he was, notwithstanding, treated by the Almighty as wicked. The natural inference from the complaint—Job thinks himself more righteous than God. Job, judging from present appearances, often tempted to believe this. The same conclusion only avoided by the three friends by

their falsely maintaining that Job must be a hypocrite and bad man. The error of both parties, that of judging of God's justice from His *present* dealings. Neither of them fully aware that God, for special reasons, may allow a godly man to be very severely tried. Their error that of the period in which they lived. A future judgment not yet fully revealed. The pious inclined to expect rewards and punishments in the present life. The peculiarity of Abraham's faith that he acted as one "that looked for a better country, that is, an heavenly;" content meanwhile to live as "a stranger and pilgrim on the earth" (Heb. xi. 13—16). Hence Abraham, not Job, the "father of the faithful." The nature of faith to give substance and reality to things hoped for, and the certainty of conviction as regards things not seen (Heb. xi. 1). Observe—(1) *In judging in regard to God and His dealings, apart from faith, men certain to fall into error.* Job's error and consequent irreverent language, the result of defective faith. (2) *Inferences from our language often such as we ourselves should be shocked at.* Probably Job himself would have recoiled from the language here ascribed to him. (3) *A good man responsible not only for his words, but from the inference that may justly be drawn from them.*

2. For *appearing to maintain that piety was*

profitless to its possessor. Verse 3.—"For thou saidst, what advantage will it be unto thee (viz., that thy life has been righteous and pure)? and what profit shall I have if I be cleansed from my sin (or as *margin—* 'more than by my sin')?" Another inference from Job's actual language, closely connected with the former one. Job maintained that his life had been pure, and that, notwithstanding, he was a most grievous sufferer. Inference: Job maintains that piety brings no profit. True, if such sufferings continued through life, and there were no hereafter. Job's real assertion, however, that in the *present* life, piety did no save its possessor from suffering. "If the scourge stay suddenly, He mocketh at the trial of the innocent" (ch. ix. 23). Satan's challenge that Job only served God for present advantage, and that when this was withdrawn, he would cast off his religion. His great object to accomplish this. The temptation from Job's wife. Against this, Job maintained that he was a righteous man, although he suffered so unusually, and that he would hold fast his religious character and conduct at all hazards (ch. xiii. 15). Observe—The sentiments ascribed to Job, the language of *unbelief.* Entertained by the unbelieving Jews in the days of Malachi (Mal. iii. 14). Even the godly tempted at times to employ such language (Ps. lxxiii. 13). *The opposite of the truth.* Godliness *profitable unto all things* (1 Tim. iv. 8). Yet the godly often called to suffer severely in the present life. "Through much tribulation we must enter the kingdom" (Acts xiv. 22; Rev. vii. 14; 2 Tim. iii. 11—12).

II. **Elihu answers Job's cavils.** Verse 4, &c.—" I will answer thee and thy companions with thee,"—either the three friends and others present, some of whom perhaps appeared inclined to coincide with Job; or more generally, all those who entertained sentiments similar to those he had expressed —like ch. xxxiv. 8. Observe—(1) *The duty of the godly to be ready to answer for God and to correct the errors of brethren.* "Every one shall kiss his lips that giveth a right answer" (Prov. xxiv. 26). Believers to know how they "ought to answer every man" (Col. iv. 6). (2) *Believers* to be careful with whom they associate, and whose sentiments they espouse.—Two considerations employed by Elihu to silence Job's cavils:—
I. God's infinite superiority to, and absolute independence of, His creatures. Verses 5 —8. "Look unto the heavens and see; and behold the clouds which are higher than thou (hence, God who dwells above them not only incomprehensible to His creatures, **but** independent of and unaffected by them).

If thou sinnest, what doest thou against him? if thy transgressions be multiplied, what doest thou unto him? Thy wickedness may hurt (or affect) a man as thou art; and thy righteousness may profit (or affect) the son of man" (mankind, thyself or others like thee, but not God). Observe—(1) Men apt to think they lay God under an obligation by their piety or morality. God's happiness not capable of being increased or diminished by His creatures doings (Ps. xvi. 2; Jer. vii. 19). His creatures unable to give Him what is not already His own (1 Chron. xxiii. 14; Rom. ii. 35, 36). No good either possessed or practised by man but is received from God Himself. (2.) Man apt to forget the distance between the creature and the Creator. Infinite condescension on the part of God to regard man as He does. David's language that of wisdom and piety: "Lord, what is man that thou art mindful of him?" (Ps. xviii. 4; cxliv. 3.) Self-humiliation in God to behold the things that are in heaven and on the earth (Ps. cxiii. 6). Condescension and love on His part, that He receives glory from, and has pleasure in, those that fear and love, serve and trust in Him (Ps. l. 25; cxlvii. 11). (3.) Man himself affected for weal or woe by his own conduct (Is. iii. 9, 11; Prov. viii. 36; ix. 12). Reaps what he sows now, either here or hereafter (Gal. vi. 7—9.) Life and death, happiness and misery, the respective fruits of righteousness and sin (Prov. ii. 19) (4.) *A man's conduct not only productive of weal and woe to himself but also to those around him.* In the constitution of the world, one creature made to depend upon, and be affected for good or evil by, another. Each made either a blessing or a curse to his neighbour. One man's sin likely to be another's misery as well as his own. The piety of one the profit of another as well as of himself. A godly man a blessing to the neighbourhood; an ungodly one its bane. Both a conscious and an unconscious influence exercised by each on those around him, either for good or evil. *Unconscious* often more effective than *conscious* influence. Each responsible to God for both. A man with a loving and Christlike spirit a perpetual benefaction. Such a spirit perceived in society as the perfume carried about on one's person. All men like boys writing with invisible ink. An impression left upon thousands by our spirit, words, and conduct, to be only known and seen hereafter.—*H. W. Beecher.* (5.) The sky over our head fitted to correct man's low and erroneous conceptions of the Divine Being. Profitable to "look unto the heavens," and to study the lessons taught by the starry firmament. The nocturnal sky "Nature's system of Divinity." God's ever open Bible

"His universal temple, hung
With lustres, with innumerable lights,
That shed religion on the soul, at once
The temple and the preacher.—
His love lets down these silver chains of light
To draw up men's ambition to Himself,
And bind his chaste affections to His throne.—
One sun by day, by night ten thousand shine,
And light us deep into the Deity."

2. The cause of men's continued misery and God's apparent disregard, to be found not in God but in themselves. Verses 8, 13.— "By reason of the multitude of oppression, they make the oppressed to cry (or simply, 'men cry'); they cry out by reason of the arm of the mighty (the violence of tyrants and the ungodly rich). But none saith (under his trouble, in a grateful remembrance of past mercies and prayerful dependence for present aid), where is God my Maker (*Heb.,* 'my makers,' as Is. liv. 5; Ecc. xii. 1; probably with allusion to Gen. i. 26—indicating the plurality of Divine persons and the fulness of Divine perfections in the one God), who giveth songs in the night? who teacheth us more than (or 'above') the beasts of the earth, and maketh us wiser than the fowls of heaven. There (in their afflicted and oppressed condition) they cry, but none giveth answer, because of the pride of evil men (who cause them by their cruelty and violence to cry out under their affliction). Surely God will not hear vanity (vain prayers that are destitute of faith or piety, and only extorted by suffering); neither will the Almighty regard it" (viz., so long as they remain impenitent). From the whole passage, Observe—(1) *Men often made to suffer grievously from the oppression and tyranny of others.* Witness the Israelites in Egypt (Ex. i. 2). Possible allusion made by Elihu to the case of Job himself. (2) *Men's cries under oppression and trouble not always followed with Divine deliverance.* "They cry, but none giveth answer." (3) *The reason of such unanswered cries not in God, but in the sufferers themselves.* Elihu indicates some

Reasons for continued suffering.

1. *Men do not pray to God in their affliction.* They "cry" and "cry out," but do not pray. Men's cries in trouble often not *to* God but *against* Him. Sufferers often cry to men, and cry out *of* men, without praying to God. All cries not prayer. Cries in suffering only heard and answered when they are *cries to God.*

2. *Prayer made in trouble not answered, because not right prayers.* "God will not hear vanity." God hears only the prayer of piety or of penitence—the prayer of His servants or of those who desire to become such. No promise to impenitent prayers.

"God heareth not sinners," continuing such (John ix. 31). "If I regard iniquity in my heart, the Lord will not hear me" (Ps. lxvi. 18). "When ye make many prayers, I will not hear; your hands are full of blood" (Is. i. 15). "He that turneth away his ear from hearing the law, even his prayer shall be abomination" (Prov. xxviii. 9; i. 28—30). "Ye ask and receive not, because ye ask amiss, that ye may consume it upon your lusts" (James iv. 3). Penitence and purity necessary to prevailing prayer. "I will that men pray everywhere, lifting up holy hands without wrath and doubting" (1 Tim. ii. 8). The prayer of the upright is God's delight (Prov. xv. 8). The sacrifices of God are a broken spirit (Ps. li. 17). Men may kneel upon their beds without being humbled in their hearts (Hos. vii. 14). Prayer is vanity when—(1) Without sincerity; (2) Without repentance; (3) Without faith. Prayer without faith is like faith without works,— dead, being alone (James ii. 17). Earnest and believing prayer either receives the thing asked or something better.

3. Deliverance not experienced, *on account of forgetfulness of God.* Verse 10.—"None saith, where is God my Maker?" Men suffering at the hand of others apt to think more of the creature than the Creator (Is. li. 12, 13). God not acknowledged by the unregenerate either in their mercies or their afflictions. God's object in afflicting men, to bring them to Himself. The prayer of the sufferer unanswered till the object is secured, or answered in wrath (Ps. civ. 15). Affliction blessed when men turn to God and inquire after Him. Men, since the fall, naturally forgetful of God. Forgetfulness of God the sin that fills hell with inhabitants (Ps. ix. 17). Men under suffering apt to inquire after men's help rather than God's. Asa, in his affliction, sought not unto the Lord, but unto physicians (2 Chron. xvi. 12). Righteous that God should disregard men who willingly forget Him. Seriously to inquire after God the first step in true repentance. Observe—God to be remembered in affliction as our "Maker." Our Maker, who is also our Redeemer, has the best right to our remembrance. To turn to Him who made us, our first duty in affliction. He who made us cannot but be able to help and deliver us. Our wisdom, when suffering at the hands of men, to turn from the creature to the Creator. Sin to be acknowledged in not having served and followed our Maker. In consequence of the Fall, God to be inquired and sought after as one who is lost. Affliction naturally finds men "without God in the world" (Eph. ii. 12). God however to be found. Not far from every one of us. Savingly found in Christ (John xiv. 6; 2 Cor. v. 17).

4. *Deliverance not vouchsafed on account of ingratitude for past mercies.* "Who giveth songs in the night." Past songs not to be forgotten in present sufferings. A thankful remembrance of past mercies the best way to obtain present deliverances. Remembrance of past triumphs a precious help under present troubles. "Because Thou hast been my help," &c. (Ps. lxiii. 7). The recollection of God's past kindness David's sweetest comfort in his most crushing trial (Ps. xlii. 6). Forgetfulness of Divine mercies one of our greatest sins (Is. i. 2, 3). The natural heart forgetful of God's benefits as well as His being. The part of grace to resist this tendency (Ps. ciii. 2).

Two reasons on the part of God why He should be remembered and sought to under affliction and suffering:—

First reason: He gives

Songs in the Night.

Observe—

1. *What He gives.* "Songs." God the giver of songs. Songs the expression—(1) Of *joy and gladness*; (2) Of *praise and thanksgiving.* God happy Himself, and delights in making His creatures happy. According to His nature to give songs rather than sorrows. To give joy, His delight; to cause sorrow, His strange act. God is love; and the nature of love to give songs. The songs that God gives are—(1) The *sweetest*; (2) The *holiest*; (3) The *most lasting.* Satan also gives songs,—short songs the prelude to lasting sorrows. The world gives songs—songs often sung to a heavy heart. All songs but those that God gives to be one day turned into howlings (Amos viii. 3). The instrument gives forth its sweetest music under the hands of Him that made it.

2. *When He gives songs.* "In the night." *First:* In the *natural night* (Ps. viii. 8). Night the time of reflection and meditation. Satan makes men *howl* upon their beds; God makes them *sing* upon them (Hos. vii. 14; Ps. cxlix. 5). God gives songs when there is nothing else to give them—in the night. Paul and Silas sang praises at midnight (Acts xvi. 25). Musing on our bed the fire burns, and we rise at midnight to give thanks (Ps. xxxix. 3; cxix. 62). *Second:* In the *night of trouble* (chap. xxxvi. 20). God gives songs in the night—(1) Of personal affliction; (2) Of temporal adversity; (3) Of painful bereavement; (4) Of persecution from the world; (5) Of spiritual darkness and desertion; (6) Of death and its solemn approaches (Hab. iii. 17, 18; Acts xvi. 25; Hos. ii. 14, 15; Ps. xxiii. 4). No night of trouble too dark for God to give songs in it. Jesus sung a hymn with His

disciples in the darkest night of His earthly life. John sung songs of joy and praise as an exile in Patmos, and Paul and Silas as prisoners in Philippi. God gives songs to His people when it is night to others as well as themselves. Israel had light in their dwellings when all Egypt was covered with darkness.

3. *How God gives songs in the night.*—(1) By *bringing into trouble*; (2) By *comforting under it*; (3) By *delivering out of it* (Hos. ii. 14; Ps. xxiii. 4). The songs God gives, generally "songs of deliverance" (Ps. xxxii. 7). God puts songs into the mouth by putting gladness into the heart (Ps. iv. 7). Puts a new song into our mouth by setting our feet upon a rock (Ps. xl. 2, 3). God gives songs in the night by sending and showing us a Saviour (Luke ii. 8). The office of Jesus to give "the oil of joy for mourning, and the garment of praise for the spirit of heaviness" (Is. lxi. 3).

Second reason: He "teacheth us more than the beasts," &c.—(1) His *special regard* to His intelligent creatures, a reason for their seeking to Him in time of trouble. God cares for the lower animals, how much more for man? Man made rational and intelligent after his Maker's likeness. (2) The *faculties* with which God has endowed man, a reason why he should seek Him in trouble. Reason given to enable us to know God, and to understand that He is the helper and deliverer of all who truly seek Him. To be in trouble without inquiring after God, more the part of a *beast* than a man. Beasts cry in their sufferings, but unable to think of God in them. Sin degrades men below the brute creation. Beasts howl but cannot pray: men can pray but do not. Faculties given to *beasts* to apprehend the creature: to *man* to apprehend the *Creator.* A beast able to know the will of his master; a man to know the will of his God. Understanding given to the beasts to enable them to attend to their *bodily* wants and those of their offspring; a higher understanding given to man to enable him to attend also to his *spiritual* wants and those of others. Beasts endowed with sufficient intelligence for the preservation of themselves and others in their *present life*; man endowed with an intelligence to enable him to secure happiness for himself and others in the *life to come.* The understanding or instinct of the lower animals ever the same; the understanding of man capable of continual increase.

III. Elihu exhorts Job to patience and hope. Verse 14.—"Although (or 'even when') thou sayest thou shalt not see Him (enjoy His returning favour; or, 'thou dost not see Him,' *i.e.*, understand His procedure), yet judgment is before Him (He ever acts according to judgment; or, 'the case is before Him'—under His consideration); therefore trust thou in Him."

Notice—

1. A *temptation* or *complaint supposed.*—(1) *A temptation to despondency.* "Thou sayst thou shalt not see him." Job at times hard pressed with it (chap. xvii. 15). Yet enabled to overcome it (chap. xix. 26, 27). The part of believers to resist temptation (Ps. xlii. 5—11). To a believer the sun is only hidden by a cloud, not set. The hiding of God's face no proof that He neglects our cause. Is glorified when He is trusted in the dark (Heb. iii. 17, 18). Or—(2) *A complaint of darkness.* "Thou sayest thou dost not see him." Job's trial that he was unable to comprehend God's dealings (chap. ix. 11). God's dealings with His people often dark, mysterious, and incomprehensible. Christ's words to Peter spoken for the consolation of tried believers through all time,—"What I do, thou knowest not *now;* but thou shalt know hereafter" (John xiii. 7).

2. *A truth stated.* "Judgment is before him." God's dealings may be dark, but are never doubtful. While clouds of darkness are round about Him, justice and judgment are the basis of His throne (Ps. xcvii. 2; lxxxix. 14). Purposes of wisdom and goodness in every event, though unknown to us. A God of truth and without iniquity. The cause of the poor and afflicted believer never really, though sometimes apparently, overlooked. "I have seen, I have seen, the affliction of my people in Egypt, and I am come down to deliver them." Joseph's case in the pit and then in the prison. Jacob's in Canaan: "All these things are against me." Job's case at present. Believers made to pass through fire and water, but are brought out into a wealthy place (Ps. lxvi. 12).

3. *An exhortation addressed.* "Trust thou in him."

Trust in God.

The believer's grand recipe in darkness and trouble. Implies—(1) Faith; (2) Hope; (3) Patience. Faith in God's promise and perfections; hope of His deliverance; patience to wait His time for it. God delivers His people, but in His own time and way. Tarry thou the Lord's leisure. The vision is for an appointed time; though it tarry, wait for it (Ps. xxxvii. 7—34; Hab. ii. 3) Sinners not immediately punished, nor saints immediately delivered. Trust in God founded in the knowledge of Him. They that know Thy name will put their trust in Thee (Ps. ix. 10). God to be trusted in, not an idol

bearing His name; God as revealed in His Word, not as formed by our own imagination. To be trusted in as a God of justice as well as mercy. True trust in God founded on the atonement of His Son. God in Christ the revealed object of a sinner's trust. Christ the only way to the Father. Trust in God implies trust in—(1) His goodness; (2) His wisdom; (3) His faithfulness; (4) His justice; (5) His power. God in Christ to be trusted in by the sinner for pardon; by the saint for purity. To be trusted in by believers —(1) In deepest darkness; (2) Under greatest discouragements; (3) In danger and difficulty; (4) In the absence of all help from ourselves and others; (5) In the face of all appearances. Trust, the grace that brings the greatest glory to God and the greatest comfort to ourselves (Isa. xii. 2; Rom. iv. 20).

IV. Elihu reproves Job's obstinacy.

Verses 15, 16.—"But now because it is not so, he hath visited in his anger (or, 'because it is not so [that] his anger has visited,' viz., Job, for his irreverent and unbecoming speeches), yet he knoweth it not in great extremity (or, 'and He [viz., God] hath not taken severe cognizance of his transgression'); therefore doth Job open his mouth in vain (in vain and foolish complaints against God, without either reason or success); he multiplieth words without knowledge" [either of God or himself]. One of the most obscure passages in the book. Elihu's object to reprove Job either—(1) Because, while God was chastising, Job was still sinning by his rebellious murmurs; or (2) Because while God was forbearing to punish Job's irreverent speeches, Job still continued to indulge in them. Observe—(1) An evil case—(i.) when God chastises, and we are either blind to the chastening or harden ourselves under it; (ii.) when God's forbearance is abused to a continuance in sin. (2) A child of God not always like himself in temptation and trial. Asaph's confession: "So foolish was I, and ignorant; I was as a beast before thee" (Ps. lxxiii. 22). A believer never entirely free from his old carnal nature in this life. Innate corruption liable at times to break out with great violence. God's forbearance required as well in the case of a saint as of a sinner. David's prayer needful for every child of God: "Keep back Thy servant from presumptuous sins" (Ps. xix. 13). A strict watch required to be kept over heart and lips in time of temptation and trouble. A tendency in the best to impatience under intense and protracted suffering. New Testament grace required in order to fulfil the New Testament precept: "Rejoice evermore; in everything give thanks" (1 Thess. v. 16, 17). The beiever's privilege as well as duty to "glory in tribulation" (Rom. v. 3). Not too much, under the New Testament supplies of the Spirit, to be "strengthened with all might,

according to His glorious power, unto all patience and long suffering with joyfulness" (Col. i. 11).

CHAPTER XXXVI.

ELIHU'S FOURTH SPEECH

No reply being made to Elihu's preceding address, he resumes. Verse 1.—"Elihu also proceded and said." His object to bring Job to a more becoming state of mind in reference to God's dealings with him. Aims, like Job's three friends, at showing that God is not to be charged with injustice by any of his creatures.

I. His Introduction (verses 2—4).

1. *Bespeaks Job's farther patience and attention.* Verse 2.—"Suffer (wait for, or bear with) me a little, and I will show thee that I have yet to speak in God's behalf" (or, "that there are yet arguments for God"). Elihu makes good his own statement: "I am full of matter." "The words of a man's mouth are as deep waters; and the wellspring of wisdom as a flowing brook." "Counsel in the heart of man is like deep water, but a man of understanding will draw it out" (Prov. xviii. 4; xx. 5). The promise to believers in New Testament times: "Out of them shall flow rivers of living water" (John vii. 37). On the day of Pentecost, believers, filled with the Holy Ghost, spake with other tongues as the Spirit gave them utterance (Acts ii. 4). Observe—(1) Patient attention to spiritual teaching not always easy to the flesh. (2) Wise in a public teacher to draw as little as possible on the patience of his hearers. Brevity, as far as consistent with faithfulness to the truth and the hearer's interests, to be constantly aimed at. The matter spoken to be carefully arranged, and the words employed to be few and well chosen. Prolixity, digression, and repetition to be avoided. (3) Elihu's wisdom in making breaks in his discourse, and in pausing at times for a reply. His speeches four or five instead of one. (4) Well to be ready to speak for God, in the presence either of friends or foes. Elihu's task to speak as an advocate for God against Job, who had appeared to take the place of an accuser. The part of wisdom to know how to speak for God, and to give a suitable answer to men's cavils and complaints.

2. *Promises a thorough and satisfactory treatment of the subject in hand.* Verse 3.— "I will fetch my knowledge from afar" (from the widely-extended departments of God's

works; from principles long and everywhere acknowledged; from deep thought and mature consideration). Elihu's knowledge like Solomon's "deep waters." *Preachers to ponder and study well the subjects on which they are to speak.* Dr. Guthrie commenced his preparations for the Sabbath on the preceding Monday, and thus kept his discourses 'simmering' in his mind all the week. Sermons to carry evidence of close thought and thorough acquaintance with the subjects treated. To be confirmed by solid arguments and commended by apt illustrations.—The subject and aim of Elihu's discourse: "I will ascribe righteousness to my Maker." His subject—*the justice of God's dealings in Providence;* his aim—to *exhibit and defend that justice.* His arguments for God especially in relation to His righteousness as the Governor of the Universe. Job had apparently questioned that righteousness (ch. xxvii. 2; xxxiv. 5—12). Wise in preachers to have a *distinct subject* and a *clear aim* in their discourses.

3. *Assures Job of the sincerity as well as correctness of his sentiments.* Verse 4.—"For truly my words shall not be false (either *subjectively,* as spoken against my conscience to serve some by-end or selfish purpose—a sin of which Job had accused his three friends; nor *objectively,* as being untrue in themselves in relation to the subject treated, as if vindicating God's ways by unsound arguments). He that is perfect in knowledge (or, one sincere in his opinions and mature in his knowledge of the subject in hand—no novice or tyro, albeit young in years) is with thee." Observe—(1) *A religious teacher to be true both in himself and in his teaching.* Truth to be spoken, and to be spoken *as truth,* and not as *fiction.* The speaker to be true both in the manner and matter of his discourse. The truth to be spoken *in truthfulness.* What we speak to be *truth,* and to be believed and accepted by ourselves as such. "We speak," said the Model Teacher, "what we do know, and testify what we have seen." (2) *A preacher to be sound in his knowledge and in the use he makes of it.* Timothy exhorted to "study to show himself a workman that needeth not to be ashamed, rightly dividing the word of truth;" Titus, to use "sound speech that

cannot be condemned" (2 Tim. ii. 15; Tit. ii. 8). The means of attaining this: "Give attendance to reading; meditate upon these things; give thyself wholly to them; take heed unto thyself and unto the doctrine" (1 Tim. iv. 13, 15, 16). Teachers of others to be not babes but men of full age in understanding, whatever they may be in years (Heb. v. 12—14). The Scriptures given "that the man of God may be perfect, thoroughly furnished unto every good work" (2 Tim. iii. 17).

III. Elihu's defence of God (verses 5—15). "Behold," &c. What is about to be spoken is—(1) Worthy of all attention; (2) Patent to everyone, and not for a moment to be questioned. Elihu grounds his defence—

1. On God's *attributes.* Verse 5.—"God is mighty, and despiseth not any; he is mighty in strength and wisdom." Adduces—(1) His *power.* "God is mighty." Omnipotent and able to accomplish all His pleasure throughout the universe. Hence under no temptation to be unrighteous. Injustice allied to weakness. The mighty scorn to be unjust. (2) His *kindness.* "He despiseth not any." In opposition to Job's insinuation (chap. x. 3; xix. 7; xxiii. 13). Though mighty, He scorns not the meanest. Though high, He hath respect to the lowly. Slights no creature's cause or interests. The contrast of earth's mighty ones. No creature too minute or insignificant in God's eyes for His care and attention. A sparrow not forgotten before Him. His power no impediment to His providence. His greatness enables Him to pay attention to the tiniest insect as well as to the mightiest angel. To Omnipotence and Omniscience an atom an object of attention as well as a sun. God the universal Parent. All creatures, great and small, His own. All created by Him and for Him. All dependent on Him for life and all things. The universe a proof that He is mighty, yet "despiseth not any." The animalcule, invisible to the naked eye, a testimony to His condescension and care, as well as to His power and wisdom. The animating reflection of Mungo Park from the appearance of a small moss in the solitary African desert: "Can that Being, thought I, who planted, watered, and brought to perfection in this obscure part of the world, a thing which appears of so small importance, look with unconcern upon the situation and sufferings of creatures formed after His own image? Surely not." The attribute in the text appropriated by Jesus in reference to sinners applying to Him . for salvation. "Him that cometh unto me, I will in no wise cast out" (John vi. 37). His own incar-

228

nation and death on man's behalf the most illustrious confirmation of the text (Ps. viii. 4; Heb. ii. 6, &c.). (3) His *wisdom.* "He is mighty in strength and wisdom" (*Heb.,* "in strength of heart," perhaps including generosity and kindness, as parallel to the preceding clause). God's omniscience as real as His omnipotence. His wisdom equal to His power. In God infinite power directed by infinite wisdom and employed by infinite goodness. Scripture reveals God's *heart* as well as His *arm.* Hence God a Father and a Friend, instead of a tyrant and a terror to His creatures. The object of love and trust as well as of reverence and fear. The tiniest creature the monument of His skill. All nature a testimony to His heart as well as to His hand.

2. On God's *dealings in Providence* (verse 6). His dealings—(1) In respect to the ungodly. "He preserveth not the life of the wicked," *i.e.,* always. Suffers, or causes them, if continuing wicked, sooner or later, to perish. Usually, however, not till after long patience. Examples:—Pharaoh; Sodom and Gomorrha; the antediluvian world. The ungodly preserved for a time by God—(i.) For His own purposes (Rom. ix. 17); (ii). To afford space for repentance (Rom. ii. 4; 2 Pet. iii. 9—15). (2) In respect to the poor: "But giveth right to the poor,"—the oppressed and afflicted; not without respect to their *spirit* as well as their circumstances. Maintains their cause against oppressors, and sooner or later, in one way or other, delivers them. Example: Israelites in Egypt. Same truth in similar language (Ps. cxl. 12, and elsewhere in the Psalms). Applied by Jesus to His suffering Church (Luke xviii. 8). Maintained by Elihu against Job's complaints and frequent appearances. Might often suffered to take the place of right. Yet "there is a God that judgeth in the earth." The language of Elihu both a rebuke and an encouragement to Job. If poor, he should sooner or later have right given him, notwithstanding his complaint (chap. xxvii. 2). Observe—God's people "poor "in this world, both in respect to their spirit and their position. Their posture one of patience and hope. Their cause, however, maintained by God. "A righteous thing with God to recompense tribulation to them that trouble you, and to you who are troubled, rest with us, when the Lord Jesus shall be revealed from heaven" (2 Thes. i. 6, 7). *Then,* if not sooner, right given to the poor. (3) In respect to the righteous. First, in *exercising continual care over them.* Verse 7.—"He withdraweth not His eyes from the righteous," however they may seem at times to be overlooked and forsaken by Him. The case of

Noah already a well-known example. Joseph in Egypt an example of a later period. Righteous Abel died indeed by his brother's hand, but his blood not forgotten by Jehovah (Gen. iv. 10). The eyes of the Lord are upon the righteous (Ps. xxxiv. 15). The comfort of God's people in all circumstances. At times almost forgotten and questioned by the afflicted and tempted patriarch. "Thou God seest me," a well of refreshment for tried believers.—Second; in *exalting them.* "But with kings are they on the throne; yea, he doth establish them (or, "yea, kings on the throne, He doth even make them sit") for ever, and they are exalted." Even on earth the righteous often exalted, out of great affliction, to dignity and honour. Joseph and David examples. So far from neglecting the godly, God sooner or later exalts them,—sometimes to an earthly throne, always to a heavenly one (1 Sam. ii. 3; Ps. cxiii. 8). "Out of prison he cometh to reign" (Ecc. iv. 14). Every believer made a king as well as a priest (1 Pet. ii. 9; Rev. i. 6; v. 10). Their kingdom an everlasting one (Dan. vii. 18). *God's providence and care extended over godly rulers.* His eyes not withdrawn from kings on the throne. Earthly rulers from God Himself. "He putteth down one and setteth up another." "By Me kings reign" (Prov. viii. 15, 16; Rom. xiii. 1; Ps. lxxv. 7). Human rule an evidence and consequence of the Divine. Perhaps a direct allusion in the text to Job himself.—Third; In *correcting them.* Verses 8—12—"And if they be bound in fetters, and be holden in cords of affliction, then He sheweth them their work, and their transgressions that they have exceeded (or, 'wherein they have acted proudly'). He openeth also their ear to discipline (or, 'correction'—so as to hear the lesson which that discipline is intended to teach them), and commandeth that they return from iniquity. If they obey [the voice of the rod] and serve Him, they shall spend their days in prosperity and their years in pleasures (or 'delights'). But if they obey not, they shall perish by the sword [of Divine judgment]. They shall die without knowledge" (in their folly, or "before they are aware," *i.e.*, suddenly). Observe from the whole passage, in regard to

Divine Chastisements,

1. *Even the righteous may require correction.* True both in Old and New Testament times (1 Cor. xi. 30; Rev. iii. 19). In Elihu's judgment, Job's case at present. Though the godly may not live in sin, they may fall into it, and for a time continue in it. Examples: Noah; Abraham; David; Peter. Every sin has its root in a believer's heart.

"Foolishness bound up in the heart of a child, but the rod of correction driveth it out" (Prov. xxii. 15).

2. *The righteous not left to remain in their sin.* Correction employed to raise them out of it (Prov. xxii. 15). "As many as I love I rebuke and chasten; be zealous therefore and repent" (Rev. iii. 12). "For this cause (viz., sin in reference to the Lord's Supper) many are weak and sickly among you, and many sleep"—are dead (1 Cor. ii. 30). "When we are judged, we are chastened of the Lord, that we should not be condemned with the world" (verse 32). In Elihu's view, Job not proved to be a wicked man by his suffering, but a righteous one who has sinned, and whom God in His love is chastening.

3. *The object of chastisement to bring sin to our remembrance in order to repentance.* "He sheweth them their work and their transgressions." God's rod a speaking one (Mic. vi. 9). "Art thou come to call my sin to remembrance?"—the question of the widow of Zarephath to Elijah on the death of her son.

4. *Chastening, when improved, followed by a life of enjoyment.* God's rod, like Jonathan's, brings honey on the point of it. A rich blessing attendant on sanctified affliction (Ps. xciv. 10). Believers allured into the wilderness, that the Lord "may speak comfortably" to them (*Heb.*, "to their heart"). Their vineyards given them from thence, and the valley of Achor made a door of hope (Hos. ii. 14, 15).

5. *Chastisements, not improved, followed by still severer ones.* "If they obey not, they shall perish by the sword." Divine chastening neither to be despised nor fainted under (Heb. xii. 5).

III. Elihu administers reproof to Job (verses 13—17).

1. *By adducing the case of the ungodly.* Ver. 13.—"But the hypocrite (or ungodly) in heart (whatever they may appear in their outward life or in the eyes of their fellow-men,) heap up wrath (increasing the Divine displeasure against them by their continuance in sin, and their impenitent stubbornness under affliction—another solemn word for Job); they cry not (to God, as sinners for pardoning mercy) when He bindeth them (with the cords of affliction). They die in youth (that is, prematurely), and their life is (or 'becomes extinct') among the unclean" (*Margin*, "Sodomites,"—persons who by prostituting their bodies abridge their lives; with possible allusion to the men of Sodom, or more likely, to those who prostituted themselves in heathen temples in the service of their abominable

deities). Observe—(1) *A fearful case when
a man is "a hypocrite in heart."* Christ's
most solemn woes pronounced on hypocrites.
Sad to be an open sinner; still more to be
a secret one. Necessary to look to our outward life; still more to look to our heart
(Ps. cxxxix. 23, 24). (2) *The wrath of God
the reward of sin, whether open or secret.*
God angry with the wicked every day (Ps.
vii. 11). The wrath of God revealed from
heaven against all ungodliness and unrighteousness of men (Rom. i. 18). (3) *That wrath
capable of being removed by repentance and
faith, or increased by impenitence and unbelief.* "He that believeth in the Son hath
everlasting life; and he that believeth not
the Son shall not see life, but the wrath of
God abideth on him" (John iii. 36). Wrath
treasured up to themselves by the impenitent
against the day of wrath (Rom. ii. 5). (4)
*The mark of a hard and impenitent heart
when prayer is not made to God in affliction.*
(5) *Sin the cause of an unhappy life, and
often of a premature death* (Ps. lv. 23; 1
Cor. xi. 30). (6) *Awful to live among sinners; still more awful to die among them.*

2. *By showing God's conduct towards the
humble and afflicted.* Verse 15.—"He de-
livereth the poor in His affliction, and openeth
their ears in oppression," to receive instruction. A reminder to Job of what had been
his duty and what might have been his experience. Observe—(1) *Affliction of various
kinds, whether from men or otherwise, allowed
by God for wise purposes.* (2) *One of these
purposes is to receive instruction.* Divine
chastening connected with Divine teaching
(Ps. xciv. 10). "Hear ye the rod" (Micah
vi. 2). (3) *Accepted chastisement usually
followed by imparted deliverance* (Lev. xxvi.
41, 42). Deliverance may be either—(i.)
By removing the affliction; (ii.) By removing the afflicted to a better world; or
(iii.) By filling his soul with comfort and
raising him above his affliction.

3. *By applying the whole to Job's own
case.* Verses 16, 17.—"Even so would He
have removed thee out of the strait into a
broad place where there is no straitness (or,
'out of the wide mouth of distress which
has no bottom'); and that which should be
set on thy table should be full of fatness.
But thou hast fulfilled the judgment of the
wicked (approving their way, imitating their
example, and incurring their punishment):
judgment and justice take hold on thee" (or,
"will hold their place,"—causing thee still
to suffer in consequence of thy rebellious
speeches, instead of being delivered, as thou
wouldst have been, hadst thou meekly submitted to the Divine chastening and justified
God in thy affliction.) Job's sin, in Elihu's
judgment, that like Israel, instead of meekly

accepting the Divine chastisement, he chafed
and kicked against it "like a bullock un-
accustomed to the yoke" (Jer. xxxi. 18).
Observe—(1) *The way to have chastisement
removed is meekly and patiently to submit to
it, and to seek its improvement* (Lam. iii. 25—
32, 39—41; Mic. vii. 9). (2) *An easy thing
with God to remove us out of the deepest distress and to bring us into enlargement and
comfort.* The experience of the Israelites a
common one with God's children (Ps. lxvi.
10—12). (3) *A well-supplied table a gift
of God's providence to His obedient children.*
God able to give richly all things to enjoy.
Promises that our bread shall be given
us, and our water shall be sure. Teaches
his children both how to abound and
how to suffer need. Prepares a table
for them in the presence of their enemies,
and makes their cup to run over (Ps.
xxiii. 5). (4) *If God's people sin with
the ungodly, they must expect to suffer with
them.* God's dealings characterized by "judgment and justice," as well with saints as
with sinners. Sin shown to be abominable
and malignant wherever it is found. Sons
not exempt from stripes (Ps. lxxxix. 32).

IV. Elihu's warning. Verses 18—21.
—"Because (or since) there is wrath [on
the part of God], beware lest He take thee
away with His stroke (or chastisement): then
a great ransom cannot deliver thee. Will
He esteem thy riches? No, not gold, nor all
the forces (or exertions) of strength." Observe—(1) *Appearance of wrath on the part
of God not necessarily wrath.* Job's afflic-
tious not the effect of wrath. Elihu, in this
respect, almost as much in the dark as Job's
three friends. Love and hatred on the part
of God not known by present treatment
(Eccles. ix. 1). Yet (2) *Suffering often an
indication of displeasure.* "For the iniquity
of his covetousness was I wroth, and
smote him." "In a little wrath I hid
my face from thee for a moment" (Is.
liv. 8; lvii. 17) (3) *Believers and others,
under chastening, to beware of further
provoking God's displeasure by obstinacy and
rebellion.* (4) *Chastisement, not improved,
may end in death* (1 Cor. ii. 30). (5) *No
human power or worldly riches able to divert
the Divine displeasure.* All Herod's wealth
unable to save him from the worms that ate
him up (Acts xii. 23). (6) The language of
Elihu to be taken as in general a

Warning to Sinners.

1. *Their* DANGER. "There is wrath." God
angry with the wicked every day. The
wrath of God revealed from heaven against
all sin. Must exist till sin is atoned for, re-

pented of, and forgiven. Sin draws to itself the lightning of Divine wrath. That wrath displayed in the expulsion of the angels from heaven, of man from paradise, and of the Jews from their own land. Exhibited in the destruction of the Old World by water, and of the Cities of the Plain by fire. Most of all seen in the suffering and death of the Son of God standing as the sinner's Surety. God's wrath must consume either the sinner himself or his substitute. The meaning of sacrifices. Christ the thunder-rod that drew down that wrath on Himself in order to draw it off from man. God's wrath is—(1) *Righteous*—the just reward of sin; (2) *Holy* —infinitely removed from sinful passion; (3) *Intolerable*—as the wrath of man's Creator and Judge; (4) *Unabatable and unremovable* by creature power. That wrath all the more dreadful to the impenitent and unbelieving as the "Wrath of the Lamb" (Rev. vi. 16).

2. *Their* DUTY. "Beware, lest He take thee away with His stroke." Implies—(1) *An awaking to consciousness and consideration of one's peril.* "Stop, poor sinner, stop and think!" (2) *A halting in one's present course.* Illustrations: The prodigal at the swine-trough; the penitent thief. (3) *Earnest inquiry as to the way of deliverance.* Illustrations: The converted murderers of Jesus on the day of Pentecost—Men and brethren, what must we do? Saul of Tarsus —Lord, what wilt thou have me to do? The Philippian jailer—Sirs, what must I do to be saved? No safety but in the Lord's own way. Any other ends only in death. (4) *Immediate obedience to Divine direction.* That direction—Believe on the Lord Jesus Christ. Behold the Lamb of God. Come unto Me and I will give you rest. No safety for a sinner but at the cross where the wrath alighted and was extinguished. Dangerous to delay in obeying the direction. Let not to tarry in all the plain. No safety till inside of Zoar. An hour after God shut Noah and his family in the ark, too late for refuge. A step outside the City of Refuge, and the manslayer might perish. The three thousand at Pentecost gladly received the Word and were baptized. The jailer believed and was saved before daybreak. "Behold, now is the accepted time; behold, now is the day of salvation!" "To-day, if ye will hear His voice, harden not your heart."

3. *Their* DOOM, *if neglecting it*: "Then a great ransom cannot deliver thee." No chance of deliverance after death to the unsaved sinner. A "great ransom" already provided. Nothing less than the blood of God's own Son made flesh. Able to satisfy Divine justice for the sins of a world. Delivers every sinner who trusts in it. De-

livered the thief upon the cross, Saul the persecutor, and Christ's own murderers. A cloud of witnesses, both in heaven and on earth, to the value of the ransom. Available, however, only on this side of death. After death the judgment. An impassable gulf fixed between heaven and hell. Purgatory a priestly fiction. Rejectors of Christ's proffer here, punished with everlasting destruction from His presence hereafter. The hand that shut Noah in the ark shut all the world out. The blood of Jesus pleads for pardon to all who trust in it,—punishment on all who trample on it (Heb. ix. 13, 14; x. 26—29). A day when even the blood of God's Son cannot save a soul. Much less anything else. How shall we escape if we neglect so great salvation?

V. Elihu's admonition. Verses 20, 21. —"Desire not the night (of death,—probable allusion to Job's wish, chap. vii. 15), when people are cut off in their place (or, go up [as chaff in a whirlwind] 'to their place'). Take heed, regard not iniquity; for this hast thou chosen rather than affliction" (or, "meek submission;" or, "in consequence of affliction"). Job's temptation twofold: (1) To desire death rather than continuance in his present affliction; (2) To sin or cast off religion in consequence of it. The latter especially Satan's aim. Observe—

1. *No sin to which a believer may not be tempted.* "Scarcely a temptation except that of covetousness, which Luther did not experience."—*Spurgeon.* The Head tempted to the grossest of all sins,—the worship of the devil for worldly gain and worldly glory; no marvel if the members should be so too. No attainment in grace sufficient to exempt a believer from temptation. Christ taken to the *Holy City* to be tempted, and there placed on *a pinnacle of the temple.* Temple-pinnacles, places for the most terrible temptations. The measure of grace shown not in being free from temptations, but in overcoming them. Gold, not pinchbeck, submitted to the crucible.

2. *Temptations only sinful when succumbed to.* Job sorely tempted to curse God, yet only blessed Him. Tempted to renounce religion, yet only clung to it the closer. Not temptation, but sinning in it, hurts the soul.

3. *Common to be tempted to sin in order to escape suffering.* Christ tempted to distrust God and work a miracle, to escape the pangs of hunger. Daniel tempted to abstain from prayer, to escape the lion's den. The three captive youths tempted to worship the golden image, to escape the fiery furnace. Peter tempted to deny his Master, to escape his fate. Cranmer tempted to recant, to escape

231

the fires of martyrdom. Believers tempted to choose sin rather than suffering, yet, through grace, prefer suffering to sinning. Peter repented of his sin, and met a martyr's death. Cranmer recanted his recantation, and embraced the flames.

VI. Elihu directs attention to the Divine perfections (verses 22, 23). "Behold," &c. With a view to bring Job to submission, he exhibits—

1. *The power of God.* Verse 22.—"God exalteth (*i.e.*, men; or simply, 'is exalted') by His power." God exalted in Himself, and exalts the lowly. None so reduced but Divine power can restore him. Exalted Joseph from a dungeon to the throne of Egypt. God's power employed as well in exalting the humble as in abasing the proud.

2. *His condescension.* "Who teacheth like Him?" (or, who is like Him as a teacher, ruler, or master?) God's power makes Him a ruler; His condescension, a teacher of His creatures (Ps. xciv. 10). Observe in reference to—

Divine Teaching:

1. *Its excellence.* As a Teacher, God is—(1) Perfectly acquainted with the *subjects which He teaches*, and which we require to be taught. (2) Understands the *capacity and capabilities of the taught.* (3) Knows the *best and most effectual way of teaching them.* (4) Able by His power to *give effect to His instructions.* Instructs with a strong hand (Is. viii. 11). (5) *Has patience* with the dulness of His scholars. (6) *Carries them to the highest degree of knowledge.* Makes them ultimately to know even as they are known (1 Cor. xiii. 12). (7) *Exalts them* by His teaching to *His own moral excellence.* Conformity to His own image the end of His teaching. The effect of human teaching often to make men proud. Knowledge puffeth up. God's teaching *humbles* while it exalts. Human teaching often leaves men depraved and immoral. Attainments in knowledge not always attainments in virtue. Divine teaching purifies the *heart*, while it enlightens the *mind*. God teaches men in order to save them.—2. The *necessity* of Divine teaching. As fallen men, need Divine teaching to restore them. "Alienated from the life of God through the ignorance that is in them" (Eph. iv. 18). Men need teaching that gives *life* as well as *light*. One of Christ's offices as Redeemer, that of Prophet or Teacher. Is made "wisdom" to us as well as "righteousness," &c.—3. The *means* of Divine teaching: God teaches (1) By His *Word*; (2) By His *works*; (3) By His Providential dealings; (4) By His Spirit. His teaching connected with His chastening

(Ps. xciv. 10).—4. The *subjects* of Divine teaching God teaches us to know—(1) *Ourselves*, both as creatures and as sinners. The celebrated maxim: "Know thyself," only truly learned under Divine teaching. (2) Our *duty*, both to God, our neighbour, and ourselves. (3) Our *happiness*—wherein it consists, and how it is secured. (4) *Virtue* or holiness—its nature, excellence, and means of attainment. (5) *Sin*—its nature, malignity, and consequences. (6) *Salvation*, or the way of deliverance from sin and its effects. (7) *God Himself*, in His being, His perfections, and the relations He sustains to mankind. (8) *Jesus Christ*, in His person, His offices, and His work as our Redeemer (John xvii. 2, 3).

3. *His supremacy and independence.* Verse 23.—"Who hath enjoined Him His way?" (has charged Him how He is to act, and may call Him to account for His conduct). Deity admits of no superior or director. From the Creator's tribunal no appeal to a higher court.

4. His *justice and holiness.* "Who can (will or dare to) say to him, Thou hast wrought iniquity?" Connected with preceding clause. (1) There is none to charge God with a dereliction of duty. (2) There can be no ground for such a charge. Iniquity possibly found in human rulers; none in the Supreme. The creature's interests safe in the hands of the Creator. Iniquity in God the ruin of the universe. The blasphemous presumption supposed in the text, implied in all quarrelling with God's providence. The sin to which Job had been chiefly tempted. The temptation to which men under severe trials are especially exposed.

VII. Job's duty in reference to the Creator and His works. Verse 24.—"Remember that thou magnify his work (both his actual working and the products of it), which men behold (or 'praise'). Every man may see it; men may behold it afar off" (so glorious and conspicuous is it). Observe—(1) *Trouble apt to shut out God and His work from our thoughts.* The tendency of suffering and trial to draw our attention more to ourselves than our Maker. In dwelling on our own griefs, we are apt to forget His glory. (2) *Our duty, as intelligent creatures, to observe and magnify God's work.* God's works made to be remembered (Ps. cxi. 4). (3) *Man's distinction, as a creature, that he is capable of admiring and praising God's work.* Other creatures only capable of rendering unconscious praise. The lower animals made to rejoice in the *effects* of God's work; man to praise and magnify the work itself. Man alone of terrestrial creatures capable of perceiving the wisdom, power, and goodness in the Creator's work. Hence (i) his greater capacity for happiness; (ii) his responsibility. (4) *God's work such as to demand the praise and admiration of intelligent creatures.* His work honourable and glorious (Ps. cxi. 3). His works the reflection of Himself and the exponents of His perfections. The heavens declare His glory. All His works praise Him. Infinite wisdom, power, and goodness impressed on the work of His hands. His attributes displayed as well in His work of Providence as of creation. (5) *God's work admired and praised by men, especially the good, in all ages.* "The works of the Lord are great, sought out of all them that have pleasure therein" (Ps. cxi. 2). Some of the earliest poetry hymns in praise of God's work. (6) *God's work everywhere visible and conspicuous.* "Every man may see it; man may behold it afar off." God never without a witness to Himself from His works, giving rain from heaven and fruitful seasons (Acts xiv. 17). His work threefold—

1. *Creation.* In creation, God calls into existence and gives shape and character to what thus exists. Creation itself a fact of reason and revelation. Everything must have a cause, and marks of design prove a designer. The *process* of creation briefly indicated in the beginning of the Book of Genesis. The Scriptures "by far the most ancient and the only thoroughly trustworthy record" of the work of creation. Other accounts preserved in various heathen countries, doubtless, in their origin related to the Hebrew one. Nearly all commence, like that of Genesis, with a primitive chaos of matter, empty and dark, on which the Creator acted. Science able to say nothing as to the one first cause. Its instruments inadequate to discern the spiritual cause, asserted by the Bible to be behind all natural phenomena. Knows, and can know of itself, nothing of the origin of the world, either in regard to the matter composing it or the forces operating in it. The language in Genesis that of accommodation. Every creation-act accomplished by a *word of command*, as the fullest representation of the kind of power exerted. The work, both as to matter and form, simply a *will* on the part of the Creator. Materials for later stages in creation ready at hand in the results of the earlier. At each stage a special *fiat*, consistent with a gradual development, and new Divine impulse. A perfect universe not created at once, but slowly built up step by step.—*Warrington's Week of Creation.* What appears at first as the results of one period of creation actually that of many. The rocks

disclose a series of creations previous to that of man, separated from each other by thousands of years. The rocks themselves, to a large extent, the result of those previous creations. Limestone rocks almost entirely composed of the remains of shell fish. The *products* and proof of God's creation-work everywhere before us. Embrace both the visible and the invisible, the material and the spiritual. Man both spiritual and material—a microcosm or universe in himself. God's works of creation claim our admiration both for their magnitude and minuteness; their multiplicity and variety; their perfection and beauty; their complexity and order; their extent and mutual adaptation.

2. *Providence.* Consists in the preserving and governing the creatures made, and conducting them to the end for which they were created. The creatures dependent on God for their preservation as well as their creation. In Him we live and move, as well as have our being. The end of creation the Creator's own glory. His work of Providence the steps by which that end is secured. Its operation discovered in what at first sight appears to have been the work of creation. The creatures whose remains lie imbedded in the rocks, and to a considerable extent compose them, the ancient objects of God's providence. The formation of the rocks themselves due to the same providence, acting for millions of years previous to man's appearance on the earth. Provision made by God's providence, in those distant ages, for man's future residence and comfort, as well in the coal-beds prepared for his fuel by the growth of primeval forests, as in the rocks which should furnish the soil he was to cultivate, and the material with which he was to build his dwelling. God's work of providence extends to the lowest as well as the highest of His creatures. The fall of a sparrow under His direction as well as the revolution of a world. The animalcule, invisible to the naked eye, cared for by it as well as the sun with its diameter of a million miles. That work embraces the rise and fall of empires, the progress and decay of states, and the affairs of the humblest individuals that compose them. All history but the exponent of Divine providence. Its operations continually before our eyes, and often such as to arrest the attention even of the thoughtless. Visible in the miseries and calamities, as well as in the blessings and deliverances experienced among men. Under Divine providence, virtue in general, and in the end, rewarded, though frequently permitted, for a time, to be tried and purified by suffering —the case exhibited in this book. Vice in general, and in the end, punished, though often allowed, for a time, to prosper and

triumph. Many things in God's work of providence, as in that of creation, mysterious to us in our present imperfect condition. Among these the permission of evil. His providence seen, not only in permitting it, but in overruling it for His own glory—"from seeming evil still educing good."

3. *Redemption.*—Properly a special part of God's work of providence. Its most glorious part, and that to which both creation and providence are subservient. Redemption the deliverance and restoration of fallen men by the incarnation and life, the suffering and death, the resurrection and ascension of the Son of God, as well as by the mission and operation of the Holy Ghost. The work in which God has chosen, most of all, to exhibit His perfections. "To the intent that now unto the principalities and powers in heavenly places, might be made known by the Church, the manifold wisdom of God" (Eph. iii. 10, 11). God's work of Redemption established upon man's fall, which it includes as its foundation. Embraces the call of Abraham, and the selection of a part of his posterity to be, for a time, the special field of its development, preparatory to the extension of its blessings to all the nations of the earth. Included, as a farther preparation, the union of the nations in successive universal empires, culminating in the Roman, in which the work was to receive its principal development. Embraced the mission of the Apostles for the proclamation of the Redemption among all nations, and the establishment of the New Testament for its experience and further exhibition. Included the destruction of Jerusalem and the dispersion of the Jews, thus terminating a religion of symbols after it had served its purpose, and affording a standing evidence to the truth of the Scriptures which announce and unfold the Redemption. Comprehends the spread of the Gospel and the conversion of the nations to Christianity, with all the events, movements, and arrangements of Divine providence conducing to it; as—the general diffusion of the Greek language as the channel for the early promulgation of the Gospel; the free communication among the nations, through the extension of the Roman empire and its universal net-work of roads; the breaking up of the Roman Empire, and the settlement of the Northern nations in the provinces of Southern Europe; the persecutions of the Church, and the dispersion of its members and teachers; the preservation of a faithful remnant in the midst of corruption and apostasy in the Church itself; the Reformation, and the various steps conducting to it, as the revival of learning, the invention of printing, and the general aspiration after liberty; the discovery

of America, and the planting, in its northern portion, of a nation of Protestants who should occupy it with the Gospel, and disseminate it in its purity and power in other lands; the increasing power and influence of Protestant nations, as England and Prussia, and the decay of Popish ones, as Spain and Portugal; the discovery of the maritime passage to India, and the subsequent transfer of its numerous millions from the sway of a Popish to that of a Protestant nation; the defeated attempts of Mahommedanism to overspread Europe, and of Popery to crush Protestantism in England and the Netherlands; the French Revolution, which aroused both the Church and the world, preparing the one to communicate and the other to receive the Gospel; the almost simultaneous formation of societies for the spread of the Gospel in foreign lands, as the Bible, Tract, and Missionary Societies of Great Britain; the overthrow of the Pope's temporal sway by the Italian people, and the crippling of the power of France which had been its chief support. The work of redemption the sum of all God's dealings in providence. All past history but the unravelling of God's eternal plan concerning our race, and the working out of that redemption provided for it. Redemption both the key and the keystone of history. Runs through its entire course, like the scarlet cord said to run through all the cables of the Royal Navy. Finds its realization in the conversion of every believer's soul.

VIII. Returns to the perfections of God as exhibited in the operations of nature, especially in the production of rain and the phenomena of a thunderstorm. Verses 26—33.—"Behold, God is great, and we know Him not (or, 'and we know not'—how great He is), neither can the number of His years be searched out (is from everlasting, and therefore incomprehensible to us). For he maketh small the drops of rain (or, 'draweth up [by evaporation] the watery particles' from land and sea to be formed into rain): they pour down rain according to the vapour thereof (or, 'according to His vapour'—the quantity of vapour thus collected by Him; or, 'they fine [or filter] the rain from His vapour; or, 'instead of His mist,' alluding to Gen. ii. 5, 6), which the clouds do drop and distil (instead of pouring them down in destructive and overwhelming floods) upon man abundantly. Also, can any understand (or, does any consider) the spreadings of the clouds (either as to mode or measure), or the noise of His tabernacle (the thunder-crash that proceeds from the clouds, which form His pavilion, Ps. xviii. 11)? Behold, He spreadeth His light (or lightning) upon it (or, 'over Himself,' Ps. civ. 2), and covereth the bottom (*Marg.*, 'the roots') of the sea (namely, with the light or lightning which penetrates the ocean's depths, or with the dense cloud spread over its surface; or, 'he covereth Himself with the bottom of the sea, *i.e.*, with the waters exhaled from it, and formed into clouds). For by them (the clouds, or these operations in the atmosphere) judgeth He the people (either in the bestowment of benefits or the infliction of chastisement); He giveth meat in abundance (by imparting fertility to the earth). With clouds He covereth the light (or the sun, the great reservoir and source of light to the earth, its opaque body being surrounded with a luminous atmosphere; or, 'He covereth both His hands with lightning'); and commandeth it not to shine by the cloud that cometh betwixt (or, 'commandeth concerning it—the lightning—in its striking,' or as to where it shall strike). The noise thereof sheweth concerning it (or, 'His thunder declares concerning Him,—His presence, power, and majesty), the cattle also concerning the vapour" (or concerning Him as He ascends [in the storm]; or, "a magazine of wrath against iniquity").

The whole paragraph sublime, but, on that account, obscure and difficult.—Contains a highly poetical description of a gathering thunder-storm, probably the storm-cloud out of which the Almighty was about to speak, and which was already making its appearance and giving forth its pealing thunder. From the whole, observe—

1. God in Himself infinitely above our comprehension, but discernable in His works of creation and providence.

2. Elihu's first illustration of God's power and wisdom drawn from meteorology. God seen in objects and operations the most minute as well as the most majestic. The phenomenon of rain one of the most interesting evidences of His being and perfections. The atmosphere the Divine laboratory for the irrigation and fructifying of the earth. To fill the cloudy reservoirs with water exhaled from the land and sea, and then to form the contents into rain, and send it down in refreshing and fertilizing showers,—a process as interesting and wonderful as it is beneficial

and little regarded. The whole operation carried on by the Divine Ruler according to laws of His own establishment. The process no less His own, and no less requiring His hand and direction, that it is carried on according to established laws.

3. The formation and descent of rain generally understood by the scientific, though much of the process still remains a mystery. "Can any understand [fully] the spreadings of the clouds?" The operation intended, like all other works of God in nature, to engage the attention and employ the study of His intelligent creatures. Engaged the thoughts of devout men in Job's day, when natural processes were much less understood than at present. Not considered, because so common. "Doth any consider the spreadings of the clouds?"

4. All nature a magazine of means prepared by the Almighty, to be employed by Him, either in judgment or in mercy. His goodness exhibited in the copious or softly falling shower; his terrible majesty and awful displeasure against sin, in the forked lightning and crashing thunder. Even the irrational creatures gladdened by the one, but alarmed and terrified by the other. All the elements of nature under the Almighty's control. The lightning-flash or thunderbolt has its commission from the Creator. "He commandeth concerning it where it shall strike." Alexis, the friend of Luther, is struck dead by a flash of lightning, while Luther himself, close by his side, remains unhurt.

5. The voice of Nature as well as of Revelation, that the Almighty is present in the thunder-storm. "The noise thereof showeth concerning him." God no less in the thunder because its reverberation is according to natural and tolerably understood laws. The report of a musket no less dependent on the hand that draws the trigger, that it is produced by the same laws. Every reason why the thunder-cloud should be designed and employed by its Divine Author, among other purposes, as his celestial artillery against His impenitent and rebellious adversaries (ch. xxviii. 22, 23).

6. Unspeakably blessed to have the Almighty for our Father and friend; terrible beyond conception, to have Him for our foe.

CHAPTER XXXVII.

ELIHU'S FOURTH SPEECH CONTINUED.

now heard) my heart trembleth (beats with awe) and is moved (or leaps) out of his place." Awe, a natural effect of loud reverberating thunder, even when its cause is better understood than it was in the days of Elihu. Pealing thunder intended as a display of God's solemn majesty as Ruler and Judge of mankind. Hence, accompanied the giving of the law on Mount Sinai (Exod. xix. 19). Only a consciousness of having the Almighty for our Father and friend through Jesus Christ, can or ought to give assurance and composure amid the cracking thunder and flashing of the storm.

I. Elihu calls Job's attention to the thunder-storm. Verses 2—5.

—"Hear attentively the noise of His voice (in the thunder), and the sound that goeth out of His mouth. He directeth it (the thunder, or the flash that precedes it) under the whole heaven (or, ' under the whole heaven is its darting), and His lightning unto the ends of the earth. After it (*i.e.*, the flash) a voice goeth; He thundereth with the voice of His excellency, and He will not stay (or delay) them (the lightning, or other accompaniments of the thunder) when his voice is heard (or, "one cannot track them, though His voice hath been heard"). God thundereth marvellously with his voice; great things doeth He which we cannot comprehend." The magnificence and terror of a thunder-storm similarly described by the Psalmist: "The voice of the Lord is upon the waters," &c. (Ps. xxix. 3, 10). Also, but with less sublimity, by the Poet of the Seasons:—

"'Tis listening fear, and dumb amazement all,
When to the startled eye, the sudden flame
Appears far South, eruptive through the cloud;
And following slower, in explosion vast,
The thunder raises his tremendous voice.
At first heard solemn, o'er the verge of Heaven,
The tempest growls; but as it nearer comes,
And rolls its awful burden on the world,
The lightnings flash a larger curve, and more
The noise astounds: till overhead a sheet
Of lurid flame discloses wide; then shuts
And opens wider; shuts, and opens still
Expansive, wrapping ether in a blaze.
Follows the loosened aggravated roar,
Enlarging, deepening, mingling; peal on peal
Crush'd horrible, convulsing heaven and earth."

Observe—

1. *The terrors of a thunder-storm to be viewed as manifestations of the Almighty.* The thunder, however caused, truth and piety regard as "the noise of His voice." "God thundereth marvellously." The teaching of universal consciousness as well as of the

236

Bible. No reason why the Almighty should not have witnesses, in His own universe, to His terribleness as well as to His tenderness. God no less in the thunder-storm, because we are allowed to understand a little of the way in which, and the laws by which, He is pleased, ordinarily, to produce it.

2. *Those sublimities in nature to be attentively regarded by us.* "Hear attentively the noise of His voice." The thunder-peal to be listened to as proclaiming—(1) The presence of God in the Universe; (2) His power and majesty; (3) The terribleness of His displeasure; (4) The vengeance awaiting the impenitent. Fitted and intended, among other things, to arouse the sinner to a sense of his guilt and danger. God's voice calling him to secure, in time, a place of refuge for his soul in Christ—"the covert from the tempest" (Is. xxxii. 2). "This voice came for *your* sakes" (John xii. 30).

3. *The elements of nature all under God's control.* "He directeth it under the whole heaven."

4. *The omnipresence of God suggested by the velocity and reach of the lightning-flash.* "His lightning [is] to the ends of the earth." The passage of the electric fluid over thousands of miles instantaneous. Hence its wonderful and now extensive employment in telegraphy.

5. *God's operations in the atmosphere, as elsewhere, marvellous, and even still full of mystery.* "God thundereth marvellously: great things doeth He which we cannot comprehend." The thunder marvellous—(1) In its production; (2) In its terribleness; (3) In its effects. The nature of that which produces the thunder, and to which we give the name "electricity," still a mystery. Philosophers uncertain as to whether it is a fluid or a force, matter or a mere affection in matter. The latter now regarded as the more probable opinion, though for convenience, electricity is still spoken of as a fluid. Like heat, it appears to pervade all material substances, existing in each in a certain ordinary proportion, then imperceptible to the senses. Bodies capable of being overcharged with it, or made to have more than their ordinary proportion, and then of discharging the excess into some neighbouring body, so as thus to regain their usual condition. Its discharge or passage from one body to another, accompanied with a shock and a spark, or flash of light. The shock produced by electricity, artificially collected, able to throw down the strongest ox; and the heat produced by the spark or flash, able to melt the hardest metals. Lightning, the flash accompanying the passage of the fluid from a surcharged cloud either to another cloud or to the ground, its

general reservoir. The excess of electricity collected in a cloud during the heat of Summer, sometimes immense. Hence the terrible effects often attending its discharge. Thunder the sound produced by the explosion. Such explosions ordinarily made to serve a beneficent purpose, by restoring the air to a healthy condition. Capable, however, under the Divine direction, of serving other ends. All nature but the Almighty's instrument—

"A capacious reservoir of means,
Framed for His use and ready at His will."

Man acquainted, in some measure, with what are the forces operating in natural phenomenon, and what are the effects they produce; but the nature of the forces themselves a mystery. How they come to exist, and how they act and produce their effects, a greater mystery still.

II. Describes other Divine operations in nature. Verses 6—13.—"For He saith to the snow, be (or fall) thou on the earth; likewise to the small rain, and to the great rain of His strength (*Marg.*, 'and to the shower of rain, and to the showers of rain of His strength;' or, 'to the heavy shower of rain, and to the heavy shower of His violent rains'). He sealeth up (by these vehement rains or by the cold of winter about to be described) the hand of every man (stopping his labour in the field (Ps. xx. 4); or 'He putteth His seal on the hand of every man,' as a door or bag is sealed so as not to be opened but by the authority of Him who sealed it); that all men may know His work (or agency; or, 'that all men whom He hath made may know'—that is, the effect of His power as operating in nature, and their dependence upon Him). Then (at the time of these rains and cold of winter) the beasts go into dens and remain in their places. Out of the South cometh the whirlwind (from the sandy desert of Arabia, such as overthrew the house of Job's eldest son, ch. i. 19; Zech. ix. 14; Is. xxi. 1); and cold out of the north (or "from the scatterers;' *Marg.*, 'the scattering wind,' the north wind, which disperses the clouds and driveth away rain, Prov. xxv. 23). By the breath of God is frost given (or, 'ice congealeth'), and the breadth of the waters is straitened (or, 'the expanded waters are made solid,' namely, by being congealed). Also by watering (or 'in irrigating,' *i.e.*, the earth), He wearieth the thick cloud (by causing it to move from place to place; or 'He burdeneth' it, *i.e.*, with moisture; or, 'He presseth it,' in order to yield its contents, like a water-skin, which is pressed in order to empty it; otherwise, 'the brightness dispelleth the thick cloud'):

He scattereth His bright cloud (*Marg.* "the cloud of His light," the cloud on which He causes the light of His sun to shine; or, 'His light [or sun] scattereth the cloud'—cumulous or *stack* clouds being usually dispersed at noon; otherwise, 'the cloud of His lightning'—that from which the lightning issues). And it is turned round about by His counsel (or, 'it moves round in circuits by His guidance'—literally, 'by His steerings'): that they may do whatsoever He commandeth them upon the face of the world in the earth (over the whole habitable globe). He causeth it (*i.e.*, the cloud with its watery contents) to come (*Heb.*, 'to find,' *i.e.*, its place or object), whether for correction, or for His land, or for mercy" (or, "whether it be for a rod or tribe, or for His land or earth, viz., to fructify it,—verily [it is] for mercy;" or, "whether for correction to His land, or for mercy"). The last verse, as the text stands at present, obscure in the connection of its different clauses, while the general sense is sufficiently obvious. On the whole section, observe—

1. *All nature, with its various operations and phenomena, under God's direction and subject to His will.* (1) *Snow.* "He saith to the snow, be thou, and snow and vapour as well as stormy wind fulfil His word (Ps. cxlviii. 1). "He giveth snow like wool" (Ps. cxlvii. 16). Snow and hail reserved by Him against the time of trouble (ch. xxviii. 22, 23). The snow no less the Almighty's servant, because we happen to know that when the condensed moisture in the atmosphere is congealed by the temperature being reduced below the freezing point, its particles descend in the form of snow. Serves a beneficial purpose in regard to the earth, in contributing to its irrigation, and especially in keeping it at a moderate degree of cold, and so protecting the germs of vegetation from the effects of frost. Made to serve other purposes of a providential, and sometimes of a judicial nature. Snow remarkable for the beautiful and variously-shaped crystals of which it is composed. (2) *Rain*—"Likewise to the small rain," &c. The rain-cloud parts with its contents only when God commands it, and *as* He commands, whether in the soft gentle shower or in the drenching down-pour that floods the fields and obstructs the labours of the husbandman. Every cloud does not necessarily descend in rain. If the cloud happens to be made warmer, either by the sun or by a current of dry warm air mixing with it, the watery particles are again dissolved into invisible vapour. Although we can explain the circumstances under which clouds are formed, 'there is a difficulty in understanding how the minute particles of water, of which they

are composed, are upheld so long in the air as we often see them, without any tendency, apparently, to descend. It is only, as would appear, when some unknown cause brings several of the particles together, so as to form drops of some size, that they begin to fall; and then, in their descent, they meet more and more particles, and thus become larger as they approach the ground.—*Chambers' Introduction to the Sciences.* (3) *Heat* and *Cold.* "Out of the south cometh the whirlwind, and cold out of the North." The waters poetically said to be congealed by the breath of His mouth. Heat and cold continued to the earth according to His promise made after the flood. Their degree in any particular part of the earth's surface dependent on the situation of that part in relation to the sun, so as to receive its rays more or less directly or obliquely. The cold most intense and continued at the poles, as from the obliquity of the earth's axis they receive so little of the solar rays. The heat greatest about the equator, for the opposite reason. The air there, becoming rarefied by the heat, ascends, from its greater lightness, to occupy higher regions, while the cold air from about the poles rushes in to fill its place. Intermediate places rendered colder by the cold air thus passing over them. Frost and ice no less from God, that we know that when the heat of the atmospheric air falls below a certain point, hence called the *freezing point,* water begins to freeze and is changed into ice. (4) *Clouds.*—Here said to be "turned round, or in circuits, by His counsels," or literally, His steerings.' God the almighty and omniscient pilot of the universe, whose hand is ever on the helm, and who steers those mighty vessels with their watery contents, according to His will. Every motion of the clouds directed by Him and made to serve the purpose which He designs. Each little speck of light fleecy cloud, as well as the huge heavy-laden *stack,* observed by His omniscient eye, and guided by His almighty hand. The clouds among the most important ministers of Divine providence in nature. No less so because we know that they are formed by a portion of air, saturated with vapour, having its temperature by any cause reduced, and so having its invisible changed into visible vapour.

2. *The purposes for which God employs the agencies of nature such as to serve His moral government of the world.* "Whether for correction," &c. These purposes always beneficent, or "for mercy," in the end, but sometimes in the way of correction, or a "rod." God's procedure towards mankind both judgment and mercy. Judgment His strange act; mercy His delight. "Mercy rejoiceth against judgment" (James ii. 13).
238

Yet judgment and correction necessary in a world of sin. The clouds ordinarily discharge their contents for the irrigation of the earth; but occasionally also for the destruction of person and property, man and beast. The ancient deluge, and inundations not unfrequent in our own time, examples of what ordinarily serves a beneficent purpose being employed also in a way entailing serious suffering and loss. Such corrections necessary and important—(1) As a testimony to Divine justice; (2) As proofs of the power of God to punish transgression; (3) As warnings against a course of sin. Punishment and its instruments no less necessary and proper in the Divine than in a human government. Yet, even in such cases, mercy remembered in wrath, and good to mankind educed. As in earthly governments, the inflicting of punishment one means of promoting the general good. Yet, in the Divine administration such corrections not always indicative of special demerit on the part of the sufferer. Sent for the trial and purification of the good, as well as for the chastisement and punishment of the bad.

III. Elihu calls Job's special attention to the works of God as seen in creation and providence. Verse 14.— "Hearken unto this, O Job; stand still and consider the wondrous works of God." The object of this summons, Job's humiliation and the silencing of his murmurs against God's procedure, from the consideration both of his ignorance and impotence. Verses 15—18. —"Dost thou know when God disposed them (or 'put His hand to them;' or, 'gave command concerning them,' in allusion to Gen. i. 3, &c.; or, 'imposed laws upon them,' in order to their preservation and the accomplishment of the end for which He created them), and caused the light of His cloud (the light that should illuminate His cloud, referring to the original command : 'Let there be light;' or, 'made the lightning of His cloud to shine,' as it was probably now flashing from the storm-cloud in their view). Dost thou know the balancings of the clouds (the manner in which they are poised and suspended in the air—probably another allusion to the creation, in reference to the waters above and below the firmament, Gen. i. 7), the wondrous works of Him Who is perfect in knowledge? How thy garments are warm (felt to be too warm by the greatly increased temperature of summer), when He quieteth the earth by the south wind (tranquillizing the atmosphere, and causing the piercing north winds to cease) ? Hast thou with Him (as His associate and companion in the work of creation—like the Divine Person designated Wisdom in Prov. viii.

22—31) spread out the sky (or firmament, Gen. i. 7) which is strong (as supporting in it the heavenly bodies) and as a molten looking-glass" (or mirror—those in the East being usually of polished metal, either brass or steel—the sky at different times resembling the one or the other, as the yellow or blue predominates). Observe—

1. *Serious attention to be given to the works of God around us.* "Hearken unto this, O Job," &c. Those works in themselves marvellous displays of power and wisdom. Every department of creation teems with evidences of Divine skill and Almighty power. The works of God in nature, both on the earth and above it, a study as interesting as it is profitable. Such study, according to opportunities afforded, a duty we owe to God as well as to ourselves.

2. *Much in the commonest phenomena of nature we are unable even still to understand.* Among these is *heat.* "Knowest thou how thy garments are warm when He quieteth the earth by the south wind?" Heat both a sensation and the cause producing it. As a cause of the sensation, its exact nature not known. Like electricity, pervades all the material world; but whether a thin and subtle fluid, or only a property or affection of matter—motion of some kind among the component atoms of bodies, philosophers not agreed, though now generally inclining to the latter opinion. Mystery still connected with its operation as well as its nature. Sometimes a great deal of it enters a body and disappears, or produces no apparent effect, the body feeling no hotter to the touch, nor shown to be any hotter by the thermometer. Thus a great deal of heat required to melt a piece of ice, yet the water from the ice feels as cold as the ice itself and affects the thermometer in the same way, the heat not having warmed the ice, but only changed it into a liquid state. The alternation of heat and cold, summer and winter, now known to be occasioned by a remarkable provision on the part of the Creator—the obliquity of the earth's axis in its revolution round the sun, that axis being twenty-three and a half degrees out of the perpendicular.

3. *Creation intended as a school for man's instruction.* "Stand still and consider the wondrous works of God." Some of man's most useful lessons to be learned in the school of nature. These lessons both in reference to God and ourselves. God's greatness and our own littleness never more realized than in the intelligent contemplation of the arrangements in nature in relation to the earth, and of the mechanism of the heavens, of which the earth forms a part. Of God's work in creation we understand but little: still less of His secret purposes and provi-

dential procedure; least of all, of Himself. The origin of the universe, except as God reveals it, entirely hidden from our knowledge. Science, of itself, able to teach nothing as to the fact of creation, or of the first great cause, except that there is one—an intelligence infinite in power and wisdom. The distance of the time when God first "disposed," or put His Almighty hand to the work, far beyond man's conception, millions of years being revealed in the earth's strata as antecedent to man's existence.

IV. **Elihu ironically reproves Job's Presumption.** Verse 19.—"Teach us what we shall say unto Him (as you are so much wiser than we are, and are able to enter into controversy with the Almighty); for we [for our part] cannot order speech (so as to argue with Him) by reason of darkness (in ourselves generally, and in relation to God's purposes and procedure in particular). Shall it be told Him that I speak (—be declared as by a messenger sent to Him that I will speak and debate the matter with Him)? If a man speak (attempt so to debate with the Almighty), surely he shall be swallowed up (confounded and overwhelmed by the Divine Majesty). And now (at the very time Elihu was speaking—either the storm-cloud then hiding the sun from view, and obscuring the sky, or a rising wind having cleared away the clouds and revealed the sun in his effulgence; or speaking figuratively—now in this present life, or in this present time of trouble in which Job then was,) men see not the bright light (or the sun shining brightly) which is in the clouds (or, men cannot look upon the light, or the sun, as it shines brightly in the sky); but the wind passeth and cleanseth them" (*i.e.*, the clouds, thus revealing the sun which before had been hidden by them; or, "after the wind has passed and cleansed it," *i.e.*, the sky). Observe—

1. *Man's duty to cherish becoming views of his creature-unworthiness, and to cultivate reverence in speaking of and to the Almighty.* "Be not rash with thy mouth, and let not thine heart be hasty to utter anything before God; for God is in heaven, and thou upon earth; therefore let thy words be few" (Eccl. v. 4). The Lord's Prayer an example of the mode in which to address the Almighty. Teaches us to go to God as our Father, yet with deep reverence and humility. Contains only seven petitions, the three first having relation to God Himself, and each of them, with one exception, expressed in about half a dozen words. In the New Testament, God especially revealed as our Father through Christ; while through Him, as our Advocate with and our way to the Father, we enjoy the privilege of a free access to and filial fellow-

ship with God not generally known to the patriarchs and Old Testament saints (Eph. iii. 12; Heb. iv. 16; xi. 40).

2. *External nature to be viewed as a symbol of spiritual and Divine things.* (1) In reference to God *Himself.* The brightness of the unclouded sun apparently intended by Elihu to be viewed as a symbol of the majesty and glory of God. God's dwelling in that light which no man can approach to (1 Tim. vi. 16). If men are unable to contemplate the material sun without being blinded by its dazzling effulgence, how much less the glory of the Almighty Himself! Yet our happiness to see God—in a manner even here, and more fully hereafter. For this end God reveals Himself in Christ. The splendour of the Divine glory softened in the Son of God by the veil of humanity. Christ's name, "Emmanuel—God with us." In Christ, who is also our Brother, we see the Father (John xiv. 9). His glory beheld even here, as that of the only begotten of the Father (John i. 14). Purity of heart, given us in Christ, necessary in order to see God (Matt. v. 8; 1 Cor. i. 2). (2) In reference to *our own experience.* Elihu's language in verse 21 suggestive of the

Life of Faith.

1. *The believer's experience on earth often resembling a clouded sky.* "*Now* men see not the bright light." The face of the sun often hidden by a thick cloud. Times when even believers cannot see the light of God's countenance, and when His dealings with them are dark and mysterious. At best, while here, we know but in part, and see through a glass darkly. God's face often apparently hidden from believers in time of trouble. "In a little wrath I hid my face from thee for a moment" (Is. liv. 8). David's complaint: "Why hidest Thou Thyself in times of trouble" (Ps. x. 1). Job's case at present. A dark and cloudy day with Abraham on his way to Mount Moriah; with Jacob, on the apparent loss of his three sons; with Joseph in the prison; with Moses in Midian; with David at Ziklag; with Jeremiah in the dungeon; with Jesus on the cross. Believers, as well as men in general, find themselves while on earth hedged in by mystery on every side. Clouds and darkness contingent to us as creatures—still more as sinful ones. "What I do thou knowest not *now.*"

2. *To the believer there is bright light behind the clouds.* "Now men see not the bright light which is in the clouds." The bright light *there*, though men see it not. The sun still in the heavens, though a cloud

240

hide him from our view. Whatever clouds hide God from his sight or rest upon his path, a threefold light still shining to the believer. (1) God's unchanging *love* in Christ (Jer. xxxi. 3; John xiii. 1; Rom. viii. 38, 39); (2) God's everlasting *covenant* made with him in Christ, ordered in all things and sure (2 Sam. xxiii. 5; Is. liv. 10, lv. 3); (3) God's gracious *purpose* in Christ, to save him, and to make all things work together for his good (Rom. viii. 28—32; Eph. i. 3—14). The wheels of Divine Providence ever going straightforward to a believer's full salvation, however things may at times appear to himself. "Behind a frowning Providence He hides a smiling face,"—one of the truths intended to be taught by this very book.

3. *The time comes when the clouds are chased away.* "The wind passeth and cleanseth them." The light of God's countenance not always to be hidden to the believer. Cloud and mystery not always to rest upon his path. David's comfort in a time of darkness: "I shall yet praise Him for the help of His countenance;" "the Lord will command His loving-kindness in the daytime" (Ps. xlii. 5, 8). Micah's confidence: "When I fall, I shall arise; when I sit in darkness, the Lord shall be a light unto me" (Mic. vii. 8). He will not always chide. "For a small moment have I forsaken thee; but with great mercies will I gather thee" (Is. liv. 7). "I will see you again, and your heart shall rejoice." "What I do, thou knowest not now, but thou shalt know hereafter" (John xiii. 7; xvi. 22). The cloud passed away from Abraham on Mount Moriah, and he rejoiced in the renewed assurance of God's gracious purposes concerning his seed; from Joseph, and he saw himself next to Pharaoh on the throne of Egypt, preserving much people, and among them his own father and brothers, alive; from Moses, and he found himself at the head of all Israel, leading them out of Egypt, and worshipping with them at the mount where God had appeared to him; from David, and he saw himself occupying the throne of Saul and made a blessing to the people. So the cloud ultimately passed away from Job, and he saw himself richer than ever, not only in possessions, but in the affection of his friends and esteem of all his neighbours. A day coming which shall clear away all obscurity, and solve every enigma both in the Book of Revelation and Providence. Hence the lesson—(1) of *humility* and *modesty* in judging both of God's word and works; (2) of *patience* and *resignation* to the Divine will; (3) of *faith*, so as to walk in comfort and hope even in the darkest dispensations.

V. Winding up of Elihu's speech.
Verses 22—24.—" Fair weather (*Marg.*:
' gold ; ' *i.e.* golden splendour or effulgence
—a bright or golden sky) cometh out of the
north (or from the north wind which dis-
perses the clouds, Prov. xxv. 23) ; with God
is terrible majesty (of which that visible
splendour is but a shadow). Touching the
Almighty, we cannot find Him out (neither
in His being nor His prócedure) ; He is excellent in power and in judgment, and in
plenty of justice (whatever men may at any
time think of His dealings) : He will not afflict
(or ' oppress,' though Job was ready at times
to think so in reference to himself, or ' He
will not answer ' or ' give account ' of His
procedure to any of His creatures). Men
do therefore fear Him (or ' let men therefore
fear Him '—the conclusion of the whole
matter, Eccl. xii. 13) ; he respecteth (or
' feareth ') not any that are wise of heart " (as
Job thinks himself to be ; or "let each," or
"shall not each" of the wise-hearted fear
Him ; otherwise,—" none of the wise-hearted
seeth or comprehendeth Him "). Observe—
1. *The end of all true teaching, as of all
revelation, that men may fear God.* Elihu
concludes his speeches as the Royal Preacher
his discourses : " Let us hear the conclusion
of the whole matter,—Fear God and keep
His commandments, for this is the whole
duty of man " (Eccl. xii. 13). All consideration of God and His works, whether of
creation or Providence, to conduct to the
same conclusion. Everything in God and
His works fitted to lead men to fear Him.
That fear a holy reverence,—the fear of a
loving child in reference to a worthy father ;
not that of a trembling slave in reference to
a severe master. God's being and perfections,—His wisdom, power, holiness, justice,
goodness, and truth,—such as to render Him
the object at once of fear and love. A
loving fear required by God from His intelligent creatures. The rational creature's
whole duty summed up in such fear. Forgiving mercy intended to produce it (Ps.
cxxx. 4). Such fear not the growth of fallen
nature, but the production of Divine grace
(Jer. xxxii. 39, 40). The object of Christ's
redemption to deliver us from slavish fear
and implant the filial (Luke i. 74 ; Rom. viii.
15 ; 1 John iv. 18 ; 1 Peter i. 17—20).
2. *God too glorious to be contemplated by
fallen, and too great to be comprehended by
finite, man.* A terrible majesty with God,
only pictured by the dazzling brightness of
the unclouded sun. Seraphims veil their
faces with their wings as they stand before
Him. Fallen men conscious of being unable

to look on Him and live (Gen. xxxii. 30) ;
Judges xiii. 22). Declared by God Himself
(Ex. xxxiii. 20). Hence Peter's exclamation on beholding the traces of Christ's
divinity (Luke v. 8). In Christ, however,
God contemplated even by sinful men.
Heaven in beholding the glory of God.
Stephen's vision. Christ's prayer for His
people. The glorified see God's face (Rev.
xxii. 4). God not more to be *comprehended*
than *contemplated.* His thoughts a great
deep. Only the smallest portion of His
works at all understood by men. The
greatest among scientific men compared himself to a child gathering bubbles on the sea-
shore, while the ocean of knowledge lay
unexplored before him. The attempt to comprehend God compared by Augustine to that
of a child scooping a hole in the sand, and
attempting with its tiny shell to empty the
sea into it. God to be *apprehended* for our
own *comfort* and His glory by the humblest
peasant that sits at the feet of Jesus, who
reveals the Father ; not to be *comprehended*
by the highest seraph that folds his wings
before the throne. Heaven filled with adoring
wonder (Rev. xv. 3, 4).
3. *The interests of His creatures safe in the
hands of the Almighty.* " He is excellent in
power, and in judgment, and in plenty of
justice." In God is power to execute all
His will, and defend all who trust in Him ;
judgment and justice, to make only a right
use of that power. Justice His nature, and
judgment His administration. " He will not
afflict." In another sense He afflicts, but
even then not willingly (Lam. iii. 33). He
afflicts as a chastening ; does *not* afflict as an
oppression. " To crush under His feet all
the prisoners of the earth, the Lord ap-
proveth not " (Lam. iii. 34). God may
punish but not oppress. Has no pleasure in
the sinner's death. Judgment His strange
act, mercy His delight. Binds up the bruised
reed instead of breaking it (Is. xlii. 3).
4. *Comfort to Job and every tried believer
in Elihu's last words :* " He will not afflict,"
or oppress. How much less any of His own
children ! " Fair weather cometh out of the
north." The tempest may howl, and the
clouds lower, and the thunders roll ; but
after the storm comes a calm and serene
sky. The wind shall chase away the clouds
—albeit a north wind with its piercing cold.
Troubles are to a believer but a passing
storm. Weeping may endure for a night ;
joy cometh in the morning. We sow in
tears ; but in a little while we shall reap
with joy.

16

CHAPTER XXXVIII.

JEHOVAH'S ADDRESS TO JOB.

Elihu had now said all he intended. Possibly interrupted by the storm which had been gathering during his speech. Out of the storm-cloud, from which already issued thunders and lightnings, the Almighty was now to speak. The grandeur and sublimity of the scene not to be surpassed. Its only counterpart at the giving of the law on Mount Sinai (Exod. xix. 18).

I. The announcement of the Almighty's speech. Verse 1.—"Then the Lord answered Job out of the whirlwind" (or storm-cloud). Observe—
1. The *Speaker*. "The Lord"—Jehovah. A name (1) *Mysterious*; expressive of the mysterious attributes of Godhead—eternity, self-existence, unchangeableness, self-dependence—He Who was, is, and is to be. Equivalent to that given by God Himself at the burning bush: "I am," or "I am that I am." (2) *Gracious*; a covenant name. Assumed by God in relation to Israel as His chosen and covenant people—"Jehovah, the God of Israel." Indicates unchangeable faithfulness in the performance of His promises and covenant obligations. Especially revealed to Moses at the bush as expressive of the relationship to be established between God and Israel from that period. The pronunciation of the name lost to the Jews, together with their covenant relationship to the Almighty. Now known by them only as the name of four letters. "Adonai"— Lord or Master—substituted for it. The name as given in the text, probably indicative of the Israelitish authorship of the book, as well as in some degree of the period of its composition. The name applied in the Bible to three distinct persons in the Godhead— the Father, the Son, and the Holy Spirit. Here the Son intended as "The Word," or He by Whom the Godhead speaks and reveals Himself to man (John i. 1). Unspeakable condescension on the part of Jehovah to address Himself to fallen man in any other way than one of judgment.
2. The *speech*. "Answered." God's address to Job an "answer." Mercy implied in God's speaking to man at all. "God, who at sundry times and in divers manners spake in time past to the fathers," &c. (Heb. i. 1). Might have treated men as the fallen angels—with eternal silence. One of the greatest trials and griefs to the godly when God appears to be "silent to them"

(Ps. xxviii. 1). Saul's great misery that God answered him no more (1 Sam. xxviii. 15). Especial mercy when God *answers* men. Implies felt need and desire on man's part—sense of darkness, perplexity, want. God *still* answers men—by His written word, His Spirit, the lips of His servants, His providence. Especial mercy when *God* answers men. Job's three friends, and then Elihu, had answered Job, but without effect. The answer from God Himself needed. "None teacheth like Him." "I am the Lord that teacheth thee to profit." He speaks and instructs "with a strong hand" (Is. viii. 11). His word with power. The proper posture of men in relation to God that of Samuel: "Speak, Lord, for thy servant heareth;" or that of David: "I will hear what God the Lord will speak" (1 Sam. iii. 10; Ps. lxxxv. 8). God's answer to Job given according to his desire, yet not *such* as he expected. Intended not to vindicate Himself or His procedure, but to instruct and humble Job. Given to convince him of the sinfulness of his complaints and questionings, by showing him his own ignorance and littleness in contrast with Jehovah's omniscience and almightiness. Designed to show him his inability even to *judge* of His Maker's procedure, from his inability to explain the commonest operations in nature. The answer a prosecution of the argument of Elihu. Job apparently *silenced*, but not *convinced*, by Elihu's speeches. The address unequalled for majesty of sentiment and sublimity of language by any uninspired production either of ancient or modern times. The speech a daring flight for a poet, but sustained because *inspired*. The book of Job the sublimest poem in the world. "One of the grandest things ever written with pen—nothing written, I think, in the Bible or out of it, of equal literary merit."—*Carlyle*. This speech the sublimest part of the book.
3. The *party addressed*. "Job." Others present; possibly, however, without hearing, or at least understanding, what was spoken. Saul's companions on the way to Damascus saw the light, but "heard not the voice of Him that spake to him" (Acts xxii. 9). Yet, they "heard a voice, but saw no man" —hearing it without understanding its utterance (Acts ix. 7). A Divine voice, like thunder, spoke to Jesus in the presence of the people, understood by Him, but not by

them (John xii. 28, 29). Observe—(1) *Divine sovereignty.* The three friends in greater error than Job, yet Job only answered. Yet (2) sovereignty exercised in *justice and goodness.* Job alone desired an answer from God, and alone believed that such would be given. (3) *Divine mercy and kindness* in answering *Job.* His spirit at times all but, if not actually, rebellious, and his language petulant and irreverent—such as called for deep repentance. *God does not turn away from His sincere, though sinning, servants.* (4) *God's faithfulness to His people.* His answer a sharp *reproof* to Job. "As many as I love, I rebuke and chasten." *God loves His people too well to suffer sin upon them.* Saints often dealt with in an apparently rougher manner than even sinners. (5) The *particularity* of God's dealing with men. Job singled out in this address, as if the only person present. So always when God speaks effectually. "Thou art the man." "Zacchæus, make haste and come down." The Good Shepherd "calleth His own sheep by their name."

4. The *place.* "Out of the whirlwind." The tempest raised for this special purpose. Perhaps an ordinary storm-cloud now produced in the providence of God to be employed as His pavilion whence to issue this address. Natural for a storm to be chosen for such a purpose. Perhaps a similar storm employed in the giving of the law (Exod. xix 18). All nature under God's control, and ready at His call. The lightnings His servants, saying : Here we are (verse 35). A storm the symbol of judgment and the expression of power. The descent of the Spirit at Pentecost like the sound of "a rushing mighty wind" (Acts ii. 2). Divine interposition on behalf of David and David's Lord represented as connected with a storm of wind and hail, thundering and lightning (Ps. xviii. 9–14). Clouds, fire, and tempest accompany the Judge's descent at the last day (Ps. l. 3 ; Dan. vii. 10 ; 2 Thess. i. 8 ; Rev. i. 7). The whirlwind, or storm-cloud, now employed as expressive of—(1) The majesty of the Speaker ; (2) The weightiness of the matter ; (3) The power of the Almighty to accomplish His purposes, whether of mercy or judgment ; (4) The terribleness of His displeasure. Intended (1) To awaken more solemn attention ; (2) To convey a deeper impression of the power and majesty of God ; (3) To contribute to the object of the speech, Job's conviction and humiliation. Suitable as—(1) Accompanying a Divine reproof ; 2) On an occasion in which the power, justice, and providence of God had appeared to be called in question. The present case compared and contrasted with God's voice to Elijah in the wilderness

—a wind, earthquake, and fire, yet the Lord in none of them, but in "a still, small voice" which followed (1 Kings xix. 11, 12). Observe—(1) *All nature used as God's instruments.* The storm-cloud employed as His pavilion, and the whirlwind as His car (Ps. xviii. 10, 11). (2) *Terrible to have such a Being for our enemy ; blessed to have Him for our friend.* "A fearful thing to fall into the hands of the living God" (Heb. x. 31). (3) *God occasionally speaks to His people out of a storm.* Storms in the experience of believers ; but the Lord is in the storm, and speaks out of it. An ancient version of the text reads : "The Lord answered Job out of the whirlwind of grief." A Father's voice in every tempest of trouble that overtakes a believer. The voice, as in Job's case, may be one of *reproof,* but is, at the same time, one of *love.* "It is I ; be not afraid." "I will allure her into the wilderness, and I will speak comfortably unto her" (*Marg.* "to her heart"). What appears only to betoken wrath, and to threaten destruction, made to believers to be a channel of mercy. In Job's case the storm-cloud prepared the way for the sunshine that followed. Blessed for God to speak to us, though out of a whirlwind. A storm of any kind a blessing, if God speaks to us out of it. If God only speak to us, we may well leave the mode of His doing so to Himself. The same loving Father and faithful covenant-God, whether He speak in a whirlwind, an earthquake, a fire, or a " still, small voice."

II. The Reproof. Verse 2.—"Who is this that darkeneth counsel by words without knowledge ?" The question expressive of wonder and reprehension. "Who is this ?" Who so bold, foolish, and presumptuous ? The wisest and best incompetent to sit in judgment on the Divine procedure. The ground of God's reproof— "that darkens counsel by words without knowledge." Job not reproved for his previous life, but his present language. His language blamed not for its impiety, but its presumption and ignorance. Job "darkened counsel"—(1) By casting reflections on the Divine procedure, and so obscuring its brightness ; (2) Making that which is mysterious to us still darker by cavils and short-sighted reasonings. Great force in the expression. Man, by his carnal reasoning, and still more by his complaining, instead of clearing up what is dark in the Divine procedure, only makes it darker. Observe—

1. *All God's ways are " counsel."* "Counsel is mine and sound wisdom." Nothing in God's dealings but what is the result of an infinite wisdom and eternal

forethought. "Known unto God are all
His works from the beginning of the world."
Everything both actual and possible taken
into view by Him at one glance. His perfections enable Him not only to *know*, but to
choose and accomplish, what is best. Nothing unforeseen or unprovided for. A sparrow's fall not without God. His purposes
called His "counsel," because the result of
wisdom and forethought (Ps. xxxiii. 11;
Prov. xix. 21; Is. xxviii. 29; Acts ii. 23).
God's grace in Christ abundant towards us,
but "in all wisdom and prudence" (Eph. i.
8). Every event in Providence and every
trouble in a believer's experience, the filling
up of a wise and well-calculated plan, without any prejudice to man's freedom or lessen-
ing of his responsibility.

2. *Man, by reasoning about, and cavilling
against, God's dealings, only darkens the subject.*
Our duty in reference to God's procedure
not to reason and question, but to submit
and adore. The more that man, in his own
carnal wisdom, reasons about God and His
providence, the greater His perplexity and
confusion. To teach man's duty in reference
to the Divine procedure, the object of the
Almighty's present address. Its meaning,
"Be still, and know that I am God" (Ps.
lxvi. 10).

3. *Human reasonings in regard to God
and his dealings, apart from revelation, only
"words without knowledge."* Such reasonings
the mere thoughts and prattle of children
in regard to the administration of a kingdom.
God and His ways known only as He is pleased
to reveal them. "What I do, thou knowest
not now; but thou shalt know hereafter."
Our knowledge, while on earth, at best but
"in part"—fragmentary and piecemeal. God's
providential dealings seen hereafter as a
transparent sea of glass (Rev. xv. 2).

4. *All cavils and complaints against God's
dealings in providence only the result of
'ignorance*—"words without knowledge."

III. The Challenge. Verse 3.—"Gird
up now thy loins like a man (a valiant man,
ready to enter on a contest, as Job had wished
to do with the Almighty (ch. xiii. 22),—
spoken in irony and humbling reproof); for
I will demand of thee, and answer thou me."
Job's desire now granted, but not in the way
he expected. God "calls" (ch. xiii. 22), but
not to enter into a suit with Job in regard to
his past life. The questions put, not as to
what he has done, but what he knows and
is able to do. The object of them to shew
his folly and presumption in questioning his
Maker's dealings. His knowledge shown to
be ignorance, and his power perfect weakness. These contrasted with the wisdom
and power of God, as seen—(1) In His work
244

of creation; (2) In His work of providence.
A series of questions proposed which follow
each other like claps of thunder in the ear of
the silenced patriarch. The challenge intended to show Job his utter incapacity to
sit in judgment on God's procedure, and his
arrogance in arraigning it. Job reminded
by it that he is but of yesterday and knows
nothing, and that he is unable to put a
finger to the commonest processes of nature,
either in the inanimate or animate world;
while all has been seen, planned, and executed
ages before he was born, and is continually,
every moment, and in all places, executed still
by Him who is both Creator and Governor of
the universe. The questions such as to teach
us true Christian wisdom—*silence and submission in the presence of God's most mysterious and painful providences.* Observe—

1. *Man's proper character and behaviour in
relation to God's procedure, rather that of a
child than of a "man."* The things of God
hidden from the wise and prudent, but
"revealed unto babes." Our duty and interest in relation to God's dealings, to be-
have ourselves like "a weaned child" (Ps.
cxxxi. 2). "In malice be ye children, but
in understanding be ye men" (1 Cor. xiv.
20).

2. *In the presence of God, man's posture
to be rather that of a child than of a "man."*
In relation to our duty as Christians in the
world, we are to "quit ourselves like men
and be strong," but in the presence of God
to take the place of children. When
Jeremiah took the place of a child, God
made him "an iron pillar and a brazen wall
against the whole land" (Jer. i. 6, 18). The
"worm Jacob" taken by God and employed as
a "new sharp thrashing instrument having
teeth, to thrash the nations" (Is. xli. 15).

3. *Man's duty to "gird up his loins" in
order to work for God, not to debate with
Him.* The mightiest but a sorry match
for his Maker. "Let the potsherd strive with
the potsherds of the earth; but woe unto
him that striveth with his Maker" (Is. xlv.
9). "Who will set the thorns and briars
against me in battle." Man's glory and
honour, to contend *for* God; his disgrace
and ruin, to contend *with* Him.

IV. The Questioning. Verses 4—41).
—Embraces a wide field both in nature and
Providence. As suitable and appropriate to
humble man's pride in the present age of
advanced science, as in the days of the patriarch. The questions have relation to—

1. *Job's antiquity and God's creation of
the world.* Verses 3—7.—"Where wast
thou when I laid the foundations of the
earth? declare, if (or 'since'—ironically)
thou hast understanding. Who hath laid

the measures (assigned the dimensions and proportions) thereof, if (or since) thou knowest? or who hath stretched the line upon it (the measuring line, in order to regulate its form and dimensions for beauty and use)? Whereupon are the foundations thereof fastened ('its bases sunk')? or who laid the corner-stone thereof (rendering the fabric so firm as not to fall to pieces); When the morning stars (angels, figuratively so called from their splendour and early place in creation; or perhaps, literal stars, by personification) sang together (like the Priests and Levites at the foundation and finishing of the second Temple (Ezra iii. 10, 11; Zech. iv. 7), and all the sons of God (angels, so called from their Divine origin and resemblance) shouted for joy?" (participating with their Maker's joy in the perfection of the work and the prospects connected with it (Exod. xxxi. 17; Ps. civ. 31; Prov. viii. 31).

Observe—(1) *Man incapacitated from his very creaturehood, and especially his comparatively recent creation, for forming a judgment, apart from revelation, concerning God's purposes and procedure.* The plan of the world's government formed in connection with the creation of it. To form an unaided judgment of the former, man should have been present at the latter. (2) *Every thing connected with the*

Formation of the Earth,

indicative of infinite wisdom and power, but lying beyond man's present knowledge. Science confessedly ignorant of such a thing as creation, and of the origin of the universe. The rocks probably intended here as the "foundations" of the earth. These ascertained to descend several miles below the surface. The earth's crust known to the depth of eight or ten miles. Supposed, from calculation, to extend nearly twenty miles lower. The globe itself believed to have been at the beginning a mass of metal resembling quicksilver, and to have been launched into space in a state of extreme heat—being first, by a natural process, covered with rust and then with water. The first really solid ground believed to have been *granite*—a hard, fire-baked substance, prepared in the interior furnace of the globe for the pavement of the water-covered earth, and pressed, while in a soft state, by some enormous weight occasioned by the hot and burning metals that rested over it. Its hard stony masses afterwards, by some mighty agency, forced up to the surface; some portions being left under the waters, while others were driven up through them, and formed mountains and hills. The granite subsequently covered by various earths placed on it by the Creator, so as to

form the earth's crust. The granite itself formed out of *eight* of the sixty materials found in the crust of the globe, these forming three distinct bodies (quartz, mica, and feldspar), each so constituted as to answer the purposes for which it was required, viz. —to form by its union with the other substances a solid pavement, suitable to go round the globe. Streams of electricity supposed to have accompanied the mighty forces that lifted the granite, in mountain piles, up through the waters, causing it to crack and rend into four-sided blocks. The granite thus uplifted at various periods of the world's existence, and made the great storehouse whence mud, sand, and fragments have been supplied for the building up of the greater number of our rocks; its blocks grinding one against another, and its mountain surfaces being broken and crumbled into dust by the united action of frost, wind, and rain. The particles rolling down the rocky steeps, and falling into innumerable rills trickling down the mountain's side, believed to have been washed by them into the valleys below, to meet the river-floods; where they were ground and smoothed, through constant friction, into masses of sand, mud, and rubble, swept into the ocean, and driven still onwards by tides and currents, till they gradually sank down and formed flat beds or strata. Some of these strata thousands of feet in depth. Hardened into rock by the pressure of new beds over them, by the effects of heat, and by dissolved iron or lime percolating in water through the masses. Some of the loosened particles of granite falling into the surrounding waters, believed to have been spread in beds over the hot ocean floors, or piled up in hollow places between the sea-mountains; and having been there baked by the hot granite, to have formed what are called crystalline rocks of gneiss and mica slate, sometimes two miles in depth; while clay slate, several hundred feet in thickness, was further made from the same materials, and divided into its thin plates by the electric fluid having been sent through the mass of the slate mud. The earth thus said in Scripture to have been "founded upon the seas and established upon the floods" (Ps. xxiv. 2); an ocean of water having been the original covering of the globe, before the rocks were heaved up through its waters. In another sense, the earth without foundations, being hung "upon nothing" (ch. xxvi. 7), and kept in its place while moving round the sun, by the two opposite centripetal and centrifugal forces.

(3) *The formation of the earth and its preparation as a habitation for man, especially when viewed in connection with its future*

history, a work of such glory and excellence as to call forth the joyful songs of angelic spectators. The earth itself, before sin defaced it, and as it appeared on the day on which God rested from His work, a scene of matchless beauty. That must have been beautiful, and worthy of the songs of angels, which the Divine Creator himself pronounced "very good." From that earth, as probably in some degree made known at the time of its formation, angels themselves were to derive a large accession both to their knowledge and their joy (Eph. iii. 10; 1 Pet. i. 12; Luke ii. 10—14; Rev. v. 12). (4) *Angels of inconceivable antiquity.* Millions of ages since the foundations of the earth were laid in its granite rocks. Angels apparently spectators during the laying of those foundations as well as through the whole process of the earth's formation. Hence probably called "morning stars." God's elder children. Full of knowledge as the elder-born of creation. Happy they are who made to resemble them in character and to spend eternity in their society! (5) *That in God's works of creation on earth sufficient to occupy the songs of the highest created Intelligences.* How glorious then those works, and how worthy of our contemplation and praise! A lesson here intended for Job. The angels' joyful adoration exhibited for his and our imitation. God's works, whether of creation or providence, to be commended, not complained against nor cavilled at. A privilege to be the inhabitants of a world whose formation awakened the joyful songs of angels. If angels rejoiced and sung on account of its formation, how much more may we, if savingly interested in the redemption-work of Him by whom and for whom all things were made, and who, to save us, took our nature and became our elder Brother!

2. *The sea and its barriers of sand and rock.* Verse 8—11.—" Or who shut up the sea (probably the waters that covered the earth at the beginning of the Mosaic creation, Gen. i. 2) with doors, when it brake forth (perhaps from an underground abyss), as if it had issued out of the womb? When I made the cloud the garment thereof (perhaps the darkness or thick vapour that was 'upon the face of the deep,' Gen. i. 2), and thick darkness a swaddling band for it (the waters viewed as a new-born infant); and brake up for it my decreed place (or, 'appointed my decree over it '), and set bars and doors (in the sand and rocks, while preparing the sea and dry land, Gen. i. 9); and said : Hitherto shalt thou come, but no farther; and here shall thy proud waves be stayed."

The operations here referred to, in accordance with the account of the creation given in the book of Genesis. Darkness and dense vapour enveloping the globe and its watery

surface, the natural effect of the earth's internal heat acting upon the waters that covered it. According to geologists, the fiercest heat of the glowing globe probably checked from ascending into the air through the rusty covering spread over it; the change in temperature thus causing the steaming vapours in the atmosphere to fall down upon that covering in the shape of water, and so to surround the whole of the globe with one general primeval ocean. The "doors," or sandy and rocky barriers of the ocean afterwards formed, the result of upheavals and subsidencies at subsequent and different periods. The whole process the work of a wisdom and power surpassing our conception, and one far beyond the knowledge and comprehension of men. Observe—

The restraint imposed upon the rolling and dashing waves of ocean by a barrier of sand and rocks, the emblem of the restraint put upon the pride and rebellion of intelligent creatures. Fallen *angels* restrained within the bounds assigned them by the Almighty. ' Reserved in everlasting chains under darkness unto the judgment of the great day (Jude 8). Their liberty to tempt and do mischief only such as He is pleased to allow. Such restraining power frequently exhibited by the Saviour when on earth. In their endeavours to crush the Church, allowed to proceed so far and no farther. So with wicked *men* and the Church's human adversaries. Herod "stretched forth his hand to vex certain of the Church." Had already slain one apostle and was intent on the murder of another, when he is smitten by an invisible hand and miserably dies (Acts xii. 1, &c.). The reformation under Luther took place immediately after the Pope and his adherents, at the Lateran Council in 1514, rejoiced that not a single voice was raised against his authority throughout the whole world. The power of the Moslems arrested at Tours by Charles Martel in 1492, when it threatened to subdue the whole of Europe, as it had already done a large portion of it. The Invincible Armada, by which Philip II. of Spain expected to crush the Reformation in England, with its troops drawn from all quarters, after three years of preparation, carrying, as it did, the instruments of torture by which the heretics of England were to pay the price of their desertion from Rome, was destroyed almost without hand when on the very eve of accomplishing its purpose. *Deus flavit, et dissipantur.* "God blew and they are scattered." "Hitherto shalt thou come, but no farther, and here shall thy proud waves be stayed." The "gates of hell" may send forth its raging legions against the Church of Christ, but "shall not prevail against it." The interests of the Church as a whole, and of every believer composing it, safe in the hands of such a God and Saviour.

3. *The vicissitude of day and night.* Verses 12 —15.—"Hast thou commanded the morning (to succeed the night) since thy days (since thou wast born, or, because thou hast seen many days); and caused the day-spring to know his place (the exact time throughout the year when it should arise); that it might take hold of the ends of the earth (spreading its light from one end of the earth to the other—from the eastern to the western horizon), that the wicked might be shaken out of it (as no longer able to pursue their deeds of darkness after the morning light has risen)? It (the earth) is turned as clay to the seal (*Heb.*, 'as clay of the seal,' as the clay under the impression of the seal, exhibiting forms and appearances which were not visible upon it before); and they (the objects on the earth's surface) stand [forth] as a garment (a beautiful, parti-coloured, and variously-figured robe clothing the earth, which during the night was entirely unseen). And from the wicked their light is withholden (these being, as the result of their evil deeds, deprived of the light either by imprisonment or death), and the high arm (their mighty power, or the arm uplifted for deeds of violence,) shall be (or is) broken " (in consequence of the light exposing their deeds and leading to their detection and punishment, and from courts of justice being in those countries usually held in the morning). Observe—(1) *One of the most striking examples of Divine wisdom, power, and goodness, afforded in the succession of day and night.* The result of the earth's daily rotation on its axis in its annual revolution round the sun, and the inclination of that axis from the perpendicular. The return of light every morning a mercy demanding devout thankfulness, and calling for adoring consideration of the Divine wisdom and goodness; all the more as this has been going on ever since the creation of the world. (2) *Man's feebleness exhibited in connection with the return of each morning's light.* Man unable to promote or hinder, hasten or retard, its return by a single moment. (3) Among other beneficial objects accomplished by the return of morning light, is its subserviency to God's moral government of the world, in checking the commission of evil deeds which can only be perpetrated under the cover of night, and in leading to their detection and punishment. (4) As every morning throughout the year exhibits afresh to man's view the earth arrayed in its beautiful garments, our duty is thankfully to recognize the goodness of God in an arrangement

which conduces so much to our comfort and enjoyment, as well as to our convenience.
4. *The depths of the* [ocean. Verse 16.— " Hast thou entered into the springs of the sea (the 'fountains of the great deep,' Gen. vii. 11; or 'the entangled thickets' or jungle in the ocean beds)? or hast thou walked (as on dry land) in the search of the depth ? " (penetrated and examined the depths of the ocean or its caverned recesses). Three facts connected with the ocean-depths exhibiting God's greatness and man's littleness. (1) *The unexplored vegetation found in the bottom of sea.* The bed of the ocean in many localities luxuriantly clothed with marine vegetation, to the extent of many hundred miles. These submarine forests and jungles thronged with living beings, while no eye of man rests on their hidden beauties. (2) *The great depth of water in some parts of the ocean.* Probable that, considering the greater extent of the ocean than of the land, the bed of the former descends to a depth considerably exceeding the highest mountains of the latter. In the North Atlantic, no bottom found in 1849 with a line of 34,200 feet, nearly equal to six and a half miles in length. In the South Atlantic, the depth reached, in 1853, of eight miles and three quarters. In these almost unfathomable depths, not a plant that vegetates; nor a creature that finds a home in those ocean-caves, but is open to God's omniscient eye, and is the object of his providential care. (3) *The existence of fountains in the bottom of the sea.* These fountains emit their streams of fresh water into the ocean from underground sources. In many places the water of the sea is fresher at great depths than at the surface, owing to the presence of such springs. A powerful jet of fresh water found in the Gulf of Spezzia, and others in the Persian Gulf and in the Bay of Xagua, south-east of Cuba.
5. *The earth's interior and the nether world of spirits.* Verse 17.—"Have the gates of death been opened unto thee? or hast thou seen the doors of the shadow of death ? " Two ideas suggested in these interrogatories. (1) *The earth's interior hidden and unknown to men.* The place of departed spirits often represented as in the interior of the earth, probably from the body being buried beneath its surface (1 Sam. xxviii. 8—15). The earth's interior entirely unknown to man. Rocks of various kinds known to constitute its crust to the depth of eight or ten miles. This crust supposed to extend perhaps fifteen miles further—an extent, however, of which nothing is known. The space beyond, probably an immense cavern of subterranean fire, heating the lower parts of the crust, and occasioning hot springs and volcanoes, which

from time to time force up flames, lava, and red-hot mud. (2) *The world of spirits unknown and unpenetrated by men while in the body.* Of that world nothing is certainly known except as revealed in the Word of God. Man unable to penetrate its hidden regions except by bursting the bars of his corporeal enclosure. Views of the abode of *happy* spirits sometimes vouchsafed to favoured men on earth, probably while in an ecstatic state (2 Cor. xii. 2—4; Rev. iv. 1—11; vii. 9—17). Persons miraculously restored to life unable to report their observation and experience in the spirit-world. Glimpses of heaven occasionally afforded to believers, especially when already arrived at its confines. Human power or science unable to draw aside the veil that conceals the world of spirits from our view. Mysteries connected with the state of the dead not revealed. One thing certain;—a heaven of joy or a hell of woe awaits men after death, according as their character prepares them for one or the other. Fallen angels "reserved in chains under darkness to the judgment of the great day," with temporary liberty allowed, in the mean time to perhaps a part (Jude 6; Luke viii. 18—31).

6. *The earth's extent.* Verse 18.—"Hast thou perceived (as in one glance) the breadth of the earth? declare if (or since) thou knowest it all." The language adapted to the ideas then prevalent in regard to the earth. Its form and extent equally unknown in the days of the patriarch. The earth then thought to be a vast plain with inequalities on its surface, stretching to an unknown extent, and bounded on all sides by the ocean. More recent observation and study have ascertained, with sufficient accuracy, both the figure and the dimensions of the earth. In consequence however of its spherical figure, man's eye able to rest at any moment on but a small portion of its surface. The Eye of Omniscience every moment equally on every part of that surface, as well as on its secret depths.

7. *The origin and diffusion of light.* Verses 19—21, 24. "Where is the way [to] where [the] light dwelleth? and as for darkness (viewed as a substance, rather than as the absence of light), where is the place thereof (from whence it comes, or where it exactly begins)? that thou shouldst take it to (or 'seize it at') the bound thereof (where it begins and terminates), and that thou shouldst know the paths to the house thereof? Knowest thou (or 'thou knowest') it, because thou wast then born? or because the number of thy days is great? By what way is the light parted (diffusing itself over the earth every morning), which scattereth the east wind upon the earth?" (the solar

248

heat causing the air to ascend while colder air rushes in to fill its place, thus causing the wind, especially the trade winds, which blow for months from east to west; or, "which the east wind scatters upon the earth,"—the light rising in the east).

Light

naturally an object of special attention to early sages. Its emanation from the sun and other heavenly bodies obvious. The subject, however, still a mysterious one. According to Genesis, light created before either sun or moon. These bodies merely reservoirs or reflectors of light. The question still arose: What is light, and what is its origin? Philosophers still uncertain as to its nature. Doubtful whether an extremely thin and subtle fluid substance, or merely an agitation or undulation of the ether, producing its effects in a similar way to that in which sound is produced; the undulations in the one case striking the *ear* and in the other the *eye*, and so producing the sensation of sound or light respectively. The former, till lately, generally believed; the latter now the prevailing theory. Light now viewed by men of science as *radiant force.* Uncertain whether, by the creation of light at the beginning, we are to understand the creation of the actual force itself, or that of the particular condition or medium of radiation, technically known as *ether*, supposed to permeate space and substance. The latter thought more probable. Of the source of light, the account in Genesis says nothing. Its existence or appearance followed the command : "Let there be light." That it came from an external source, previous to the sun's formation or appearance, seems evident from the alternation of light and darkness during the intervening days. Light ascertained, from the testimony of the rocks, to have operated on the earth ages before man's residence on it. The sun the centre of light, only as endued with a luminous atmosphere which envelopes its opaque body, but through which portions of that body are distinctly visible. The manner in which the light is "parted," or separated from its great solar centre, as much a mystery now as in the days of the patriarch. Known to occupy a certain time in reaching the earth. Its rate of travel ascertained to be about thirteen millions of miles in a minute, and the period required in reaching the earth, about eight minutes. Some of the laws according to which light operates, in recent times satisfactorily ascertained. Known to be composed of different coloured rays—red, yellow, and blue; their composition affording the white light, and their "parting" or separation, and partial blending, giving the various colours presented by different objects. Exhibited in their pure and blended form in the rainbow; the raindrops separating the rays and refracting them at different angles after the manner of a prism, and so producing the three primary and four secondary colours. The light emanating from the fixed stars generally like that of our own sun, but in some cases coloured; different stars appearing to be different colours. The question in regard to the *abode* of the light, perhaps referring rather to the sun itself, frequently called "the light," as being the centre and source of it to the earth. Represented as coming forth as a bridegroom "from his chamber" (Ps. xix. 4). The question : Where is that chamber? The earth's annual revolution round the sun and daily rotation on its own axis, not then known. The sun supposed to move from east to west, as it *appears* to do. But whence he rose, and where he remained after setting, a mystery. The Ptolemaic theory of the earth being the centre of the system, and the sun, &c., moving round it, finally succeeded by the Copernican or Newtonian, which places the sun in the centre, at the distance of ninety-five millions of miles from the earth. The sun *appears* to rise in the east and move towards the west, from the earth moving on its axis from west to east. The opposite hemispheres of the globe naturally illuminated and in darkness alternately once in twenty-four hours, the period of one rotation on its axis.

8. *The snow and hail.* Verses 22, 23. "Hast thou entered into the treasures of the snow? or hast thou seen the treasures of the hail, which I have reserved against the time of trouble, against the day of battle and of war?" Snow and hail known to be the effects of cold in the higher regions of the atmosphere; the former being condensed vapour congealed before it is formed into drops, and the latter the drops themselves congealed in their descent to the earth. Usually brought by cold winds from the north; their treasures therefore, to those living north of the equator, apparently in the northern regions. These regions probably unknown in the days of Job. The treasures of the snow and hail, however, rather in the higher parts of the atmosphere, where man has not been able to penetrate. Spoken of as "treasures" from their vast abundance, and as being apparently stored up in the clouds. Snow and hail among the Creator's instruments in His government of the world, employed often in a way of judgment. Hail especially an instrument of destruction to the crops of the field. Employed as one of the plagues on Egypt

(Exod. ix, 14); and as the means of discomfiting the combined forces of the Canaanites (Josh. x. 11). To be, perhaps, still more grievously employed among the judgments to be inflicted on the kingdom of Antichrist, forming part of the seventh and last vial (Rev. xvi. 21). The sufferings and destruction of Napoleon's Grand Army, in 1812, mainly due to the snow and cold of a Russian winter. Snow and hail among the Almighty's reserved treasures for the discomfiture of His and His Churches' adversaries, to be probably employed in the "battle of that great day of God Almighty,—in the place called in the Hebrew tongue Armageddon" (Rev. xvi. 14 —16).

9. *Rain.* Verse 25—28, 34, 37, 38.— "Who hath divided a water-course (conduit or channel) for the overflowing (inundation or pouring forth) of waters [in the form of rain], or a way for the lightning (or flash) of thunder (the usual precursor of rain in the east, ch. 28, 26 ; Zech. x. 1); to cause it to rain on the earth where no man is [to care either for the ground or the beasts that live upon it]; on the wilderness, where there is no man [but only the inferior animals to be provided for]; to satisfy the desolate and waste ground; and to cause the bud of the tender herb to spring? Hath the rain a father? Canst thou lift up thy voice to the clouds, [commanding] that abundance of waters may cover thee? Who can number the clouds in wisdom (or 'muster' them as an army for the purpose for which he requires them (2 Kings xxv. 29)? Who can stay (or 'lay,' so as to empty) the bottles of heaven (the clouds, resembling in their form and use the dark-coloured water-skins employed in the East), when the dust groweth into hardness (is fused into a solid mass), and the clouds cleave fast together (thus forming soil for cultivation, instead of mere dust,—the effect of continued drought)?" Still points to the mysteries of meteorology, even yet but imperfectly understood, but evincing a wisdom and a power altogether Divine.

Four circumstances connected with rain here alluded to as exhibiting God's greatness and man's littleness. (1.) *That the rain does not descend in one mass of water from the clouds, but in innumerable channels or tiny rills.* Who makes these channels? what has man to do with the forming of them? Man, as in Egypt, makes channels for conveying the water from the well to irrigate his garden or his field; but who makes those channels that convey the water down from the clouds? (2) *The mysterious production of the rain, by the conversion of invisible into visible vapour, and its condensation into drops, which increase in size as they fall to the ground.* This atmospheric process unknown in the days of Job, and still a mystery of Divine power and wisdom. "Hath the rain a father?" (3) *The preparation for the rain by the lightning or electric flash, dissolving the rain-cloud by reducing its temperature, or otherwise.* Drops of water known to result from the combination of the two gases of which water is composed, through the introduction of an electric spark. But what power is it which so manages that mysterious element or force called *electricity*, as to produce the copious and fertilizing showers? "Who hath made a way for the lightning?" (4) *That the wilderness receives a supply of rain as well as inhabited places.* Proof of its abundance and the riches of Divine goodness. No stinting with God, neither from want of ability nor willingness to bestow. Enough and to spare with Him. Even the beasts in the solitary waste provided for. His also to make even the solitary place to be glad for His people, and to cause the desert to rejoice and blossom as the rose (Is. xxxv. 1). Divine power and goodness able to turn the wilderness into a fruitful field as seen in the oases in African deserts (Is. xxxii. 15). (5) *That the clouds are so managed as to be made the means, by their filling and emptying, like so many huge water-skins, of irrigating the earth and ministering to man's necessities.* Who so musters those clouds, like a general his forces, taking account of their number, size, &c., as to have them ready for his service, and to bring them together whenever he pleases to employ them? Who disposes and empties those bottles of heaven? 10. *The dew.* Verse 18.—"Who hath begotten the drops of dew?" Another of the mysteries of nature. Dew long supposed to *fall* on the ground during the night. But whence its fall? There is no cloud. No one ever saw it fall. The process better understood in modern times. The dew rather a formation or deposit than a descent. The moisture in the saturated air, in consequence of the greatly reduced temperature during the night and its contact with the cooler ground, condenses on certain substances and forms drops, like those which stand on the wall of a room, when the air, which has been saturated with moisture, is suddenly cooled by the reduction of the temperature. Usually falls, or is deposited, in clear cold nights after a warm day. Hence found with us especially in autumn. Most copious in warm climates, where the days are hot and the nights often cold. In eastern countries, as in Judæa, the want of rain often compensated by the abundant dew, in cooling and moistening the ground, and in refreshing and promoting

vegetation. Hence the frequent allusion to it and to its beneficial effects found in the Scriptures (Gen. xxvii. 28; Deut. xxxiii. 13, 38; Ps. cxxxii. 3; Prov. xix. 12; Is. xviii. 4). Frequently employed for comparison and metaphor. The Word of God compared to it from its influence on the soul (Deut. xxxii. 2). The people of God compared to it from their influence on the world (Mic. v. 7). God Himself compared to it in relation to his people (Hos. xiv. 5). The converts of Christ compared to it both from their number and beauty, especially as seen in the morning of the resurrection after the night of the tomb (Ps. cx. 3).

11. *The ice and hoar-frost.* Verses 29, 30.—"Out of whose womb came the ice? and the hoary frost of heaven, who hath engendered it? The waters (in consequence of the cold) are hid as with a stone (or, 'being made as a stone'), and the face of the deep (any collection of water) is frozen" ('held bound' or 'holds itself together,' *i. e.* is congealed). Ice known to be water rendered solid by the loss of its natural heat, which keeps its particles separate and so preserves it in a liquid state, but which the water gives out to the atmosphere in contact with it in consequence of the great reduction of its temperature. Hoar-frost simply the dew frozen before it has been formed into drops. The temperature of the atmosphere that to which these and almost all the phenomena of meteorology are due. This again due to the radiant force, or light, as including heat, imparted by the sun to the earth, and then again dispersed into space. Heat an element or force pervading all bodies, and keeping their particles at a certain degree of expansion. Suddenly withdrawn from nature, the globe would shrink into a much smaller compass; what is now in a gaseous state would become liquid; the liquid would become solid; and all vegetable and animal life on the earth's surface would instantly perish. On the other hand, an opposite result would ensue from a much increased degree of heat. Solids would become liquid or be consumed, while liquids would be converted into vapour. The wisdom, power, and goodness of God seen in so tempering the heat given forth from the sun, that both the atmosphere and the earth are in their present ordinary condition. Times indicated by the rocks when a different state of things existed. A time indicated in the Scriptures of truth, when it will be otherwise again (2 Pet. iii. 10, 12).

12. *The heavenly bodies.* Verse 31—33.— "Canst thou bind (restrain, or perhaps unite) the sweet influences (or delights, or according to another reading, 'bonds') of Pleiades (*Marg.,* 'Chimah, or the Seven

Stars'), or loose the bands of Orion? (*Marg.*, 'Chesil,' or the Fool or, Impious one; a magnificent constellation appearing in winter, and therefore connected with stormy weather, hence probably the Hebrew name. Orion a warrior in Greek mythology; the name given from the supposed resemblance of the constellation to a giant or hero; the 'bands' of Orion either the rigours of winter, which bind up vegetation, or the invisible tie which connects the numerous stars that compose it, the telescope revealing myriads more than are visible to the naked eye, particularly in the nebula seen in the belt of the figure). Canst thou bring forth Mazzaroth (*Marg.*, 'the [twelve] signs of the Zodiac,' appearing successively through the twelve months of the year), in his season? or, canst thou guide Arcturus with his sons? (probably the constellation known as the Great Bear, or the Plough; the Hebrew and Arabic name *Aish* denoting the Bier, the four stars in the body of the Bear forming the Bier itself, and the three in the tail, its 'sons' or attendant mourners: the constellation appropriately said to be 'guided,' not brought forth, —being visible all through the year, and appearing continually to move round the centre which we call the North Pole). Knowest thou the ordinances of heaven (or laws of the heavens)? Canst thou set the dominion (or influence) thereof in the earth?"

The attention of eastern sages directed at an early period to the stars, their time of appearing, and their supposed influence on the earth. Their successive appearance indicative of the seasons of the year and the time suitable for agricultural and other pursuits. Stars early grouped into figures or constellations, to which names were given from their supposed resemblance to terrestrial objects. Twelve of these appeared to rise or come into view successively in the course of the year, thus marking the twelve months. Their names, the Ram, the Bull, &c. These twelve groups or constellations, called the twelve signs of the Zodiac, probably what is here meant by Mazzaroth. The name perhaps identical with one denoting "abodes," as indicating the different stages of the sun in his apparent annual course. Said to be "brought forth," because apparently so; their appearance being probably due to the earth's progress round the sun. Natural things spoken of in the Bible rather as they *appear* to be, than as they are in reality.

The Pleiades or Seven Stars, a group or cluster of stars in the constellation or Sign of the Bull. Their Hebrew name *Chimah*, denoting a heap or cluster, probably given from their appearance. Appears about the middle of April. Hence associated with the

season of spring, whence its Latin name— Vergiliæ. The name in the text its Greek one, from a word denoting to "sail"; as indicating the time when navigation might be safely commenced. The "sweet influences," or delights, ascribed, according to the present text, to the Pleiades, as marking the arrival of Spring. The genial change in the weather accompanying the appearance of this constellation, hailed as not merely necessary to vegetation and the sustenance of man and beast, but as also contributing in a high degree to man's comfort and enjoyment. The season of

Spring

loved and celebrated in all ages, as the season—(1) Of returning *brightness and sunshine*, after the clouds and gloom of winter. (2) Of *warmth and comfort*, after the cold and tempests of preceding months. (3) Of *revived life*, both in the vegetable and animal creation—the natural world appearing to burst forth as from a state of death. (4) Of *freshness and beauty*, as seen everywhere in the verdure of the fields, the foliage of the woods, and the flowers of the garden and the meadow. (5) Of *joyousness and gaiety*, exhibited in the melody of birds and hum of insects that fills the air, the flitting butterfly and the sportive fish. (6) Of *love*, as seen especially in the birds that now pair and build their nests, and warble their affection to one another. All nature appears to rejoice and put on festal attire, and man participates largely in the "sweet influences" of Spring.

> " Now that the winter's gone, the earth hath lost
> Her snow-white robes; and now no more the frost
> Candies the grass, or casts an icy cream
> Upon the silver lake or crystal stream;
> But the warm air thaws the benumbèd earth,
> And makes it tender; gives a second birth
> To the dead swallow; wakes in hollow tree
> The drowsy cuckoo and the humble bee.
> Now do a choir of chirping minstrels bring
> In triumph to the world the youthful spring
> The valleys, hills, and woods in rich array
> Welcome the coming of the long'd-for May.
> Now all things smile."

Spring fitted and intended—(1) To *awaken gratitude* to its Divine and bountiful Author, who gives us again to rejoice in "the sweet influences of the Pleiades." Then, if ever, is to be said: "All thy works shall praise Thee, O Lord; and thy saints shall bless Thee" (Ps. cxlv. 10). (2) To serve as an *emblem of the spiritual spring*—(i.) *When the soul is renewed and quickened to spiritual life* by the Holy Ghost, and Jesus arises on it as "the Sun of righteousness with healing in His wings." Man's natural state, in consequence of the Fall, one of winter and spiritual death. Christ came into the world and comes into the soul as the reviving Sun, to impart life, and fruitfulness, and joy. The Spirit, the Lord and Giver of life, employed by Him to breathe upon the soul and renew its life. (ii.) *When the believer,* under the same Divine influence, is *restored to liveliness and comfort,* and to the "joys of God's salvation," after a season of darkness, deadness, and tempest. (iii.) When both the *Church and the earth* itself shall be *renewed in life and beauty* at the Lord's advent and the resurrection of the just. A new life then imparted to the believer's body after the winter of the tomb, and a new earth created out of the ashes of the present one, wherein shall dwell righteousness (2 Pet. iii. 12, 13 ; Rom. viii. 21—23). The Bridegroom's call to the Church then fully realized : "Lo, the winter is past ; the rain is over and gone ; the flowers appear on the earth ; and the time of singing is come, and the voice of the turtle is heard in our land : Arise, my love, my fair one, and come away" (Cant. ii. 11—13).

The Pleiades, especially the brightest star in the cluster, called Alcyone, recently ascertained to be the centre or axle round which the Solar System revolves, the sun carrying with it the earth and other planets with their satellites, and moving in the direction of the constellation Hercules. The number of stars seen in the cluster, with the aid of a good telescope, nine or ten times as many as those visible to the naked eye. The distance of the group from the sun, thirty-four millions of times greater than that of the sun from the earth. The "influences" of the Pleiades upon the earth, in so attracting it with the whole Solar System as to carry it round it at the rate, it is supposed, of four hundred and twenty-two thousand miles a day, in an orbit which it will require many thousands of years to accomplish, probably unspeakably greater than was dreamt of in the days of Job. Yet perfectly known to Him who asked the question : Canst thou bind the sweet influences of the Pleiades ? and who Himself communicated to the group its mighty power of attraction. The Hebrew name, interpreted by some as denoting a pivot or hinge, in striking accordance with this recent discovery of science."—*See an article on the subject from Dr. McMillan in Dickinson's Theological Quarterly for April,* 1875.

The "ordinances of heaven," or laws governing the motions and influences of the heavenly bodies, much better understood now than in the time of the patriarch. The

discovery of these laws one of the greatest achievements of modern science, associated with the names of Newton, Kepler, and Laplace. The laws themselves of a different nature from that contemplated by early sages. The law of *gravitation,*—by which bodies and the particles which compose them act upon each other according to their bulk, with an attracting force which increases as the squares of their distance from each other decrease,—found so far as observation has been able to penetrate, to operate through all space. This law, in connection with another,—that of the *vis inertiæ* of bodies operating as a *centrifugal force,* or the tendency of a body to move on in a straight line when once put in motion—that by which the earth and other planets, with their attendant moons, are preserved in their orbits and carried round the sun. The same law in operation among the fixed stars, some of which are observed to revolve round each other. Each star thus preserved in its own place in the heavens. The same law that which carries our solar system round its centre in the Pleiades, and which probably carries the Pleiades themselves round some other centre hid far away in the unexplored depths of our galaxy ; and, possibly, the galaxy itself, with its countless millions of worlds, round some other centre,—perhaps the glorious throne of their Almighty Creator.

The *conservation of force*—or the fact that none of the natural forces—heat, light, electricity, mechanical motion, magnetism, and chemism,—is either created or annihilated in any of the material processes of the universe, but is only *transformed*—either taking the place of or giving place to an equivalent amount of some other force—pronounced by the late Professor Faraday to be "the highest law in physical science which our faculties permit us to perceive." Yet, how little it is that we know of the "ordinances of heaven," or laws of the material universe, we are reminded by the well-known language of one of the greatest discoverers of those laws. According to the authority just quoted, the idea of gravity as varying inversely as the square of the distance, apparently in direct opposition to the principle of the conservation of force ; involving, as it appears to do, the creation and annihilation of power to an enormous extent, simply by the change of distance,—a result equal to the "highest acts our minds can appreciate of infinite power upon matter." Here science, notwithstanding her amazing progress in unfolding the mysteries of the universe, is at a stand. Besides her ignorance of the nature of the forces which she has succeeded in discovering, she is unable to explain the apparent opposition between the two highest physical laws with which she is acquainted. These "ordinances of heaven," as not only "known" but established by the Almighty, singularly expressive of the infinite power and glorious majesty of "Him, with whom we have to do."

The "dominion" or influence of the heavenly bodies upon the earth, also a subject transcending man's present knowledge. The influence of the sun alone upon the earth still full of mystery. Science teaches us that on the light or radiant force (including heat) imparted by the sun, depend well nigh the whole of the phenomena of meteorology; being the cause not only of the temperature of the earth, but of the moistness of the atmosphere, of winds, of clouds, of dew, of rain, of ocean-currents, and of "every one of the elements which, variously combined and conditioned by the earth's external features, go to make up climate."— *Warrington's Week of Creation.* Changes in the condition of our own atmosphere, and so of the weather, believed to be connected with changes in the atmosphere of the sun. The influence of the moon upon the earth, especially upon its waters, well known. A portion of heat discovered to reach us even from the fixed stars. The chemical influence of the solar rays on bodies exposed to the light also well known. The very existence of vegetation dependent on that element or force in those rays called actinism or chemism. Even metals and rocks unable to be exposed to its influence without undergoing a change in consequence of it. The "dominion" or influence of the heavenly bodies, especially of the sun, doubtless intimately connected with the physical forces now known to man, and found to be so correlated as to be capable of producing and being resolved or transformed into each other. Man so far from "setting" that "dominion" in the earth, that he even yet very imperfectly understands it.

13. *Lightning and meteors.* Verses 35, 36.—"Canst thou send lightnings that they may go and say unto thee : Here we are? Who hath put wisdom in the inward parts (perhaps 'into the dark masses' of cloud or 'into the airy dartings')? or, who hath given understanding to the heart (not here the word always translated 'heart,' but one elsewhere denoting a picture, image, or imagination, as in Is. ii. 16 ; Lev. xxvi. 1 ; Ps. lxxiii. 7,—perhaps the forms of the clouds, or the shooting meteors)? " Human powerlessness seen in relation to the lightning. Man able to draw down electricity from the thunder-cloud, and by a suitable apparatus to obtain vivid electric sparks and flashes from the atmosphere. But his feebleness in the presence of this mysterious agent shown in the

fact that such attempts have been known to be followed by instant death. Although uncontrollable by man, the lightning yet obedient to the command of its Maker. Its origin in the electricity of which the earth is the reservoir. The earth thus shown to contain within it the elements of its own destruction, which only await the bidding of their Creator to do their work.

The allusions in the 36th verse uncertain. The reference to celestial phenomena favoured, if not rendered certain, by the context. Clouds or meteors probably in view, as objects far beyond man's control, but serving the wise purposes of their Creator as if themselves endowed with intelligence. The first clause possibly a reference to the Aurora Borealis, the well-known lights arising from electricity, and seen sometimes at night shooting up in streams from the northern part of the sky; their motions, especially as seen in more northern latitudes, sometimes amazingly quick and their forms rapidly changing. The second clause of the verse may be an allusion to the phenomenon known as Meteoric Showers or Falling Stars. These meteors usually visible in clear weather about the middle of November. Myriads of small stars appear to shoot out in all directions with the rapidity of lightning, and then suddenly disappear. The nature and origin of the phenomenon still undetermined. To man the motions of these meteors appear in the highest degree arbitrary. But even these, like the lightning-flash, are under the direction of infinite wisdom and in accordance with the will of their Creator. "Not an object in nature left to the reckless sway of chance. All things adjusted with unerring wisdom, managed by infinite power, and overruled for good with paternal care."— *Duncan's Philosophy of the Seasons.*

According to the English version, the questioning in the 36th verse will relate to—

14. *Human reason and intelligence.* "Who hath put wisdom in the inward parts," &c. "Wisdom" and "understanding" used to denote reason and intelligence, or the first of the three great classes of mental faculties —the intellect, the emotions, and the will; the intellect including both the *cognitive* or *knowing,* and the *reflective* or *reasoning* faculties. The "inward parts" and the "heart" spoken of as the seat of these faculties. The *brain* now more correctly regarded as the seat and organ of the mind. Three things suggested by the questions in reference to the

Human Intellect.

(1) *Reason and intelligence proper to man.* "Wisdom" found in man's "inward parts,"

and "understanding" in his "heart." Man distinguished from the brute creation by the possession of these faculties of the intellect. Thus qualified to know, love, and intelligently to serve his Creator, to contemplate the works of God around him, to reason on subjects of the most varied and highest import, and to prepare for another and a better life. Only so much "understanding" possessed by the lower animals as to qualify them for the preservation and enjoyment of the present life, and for the propagation and preservation of offspring, as well as to render them, in various respects, serviceable to man. Reason and intelligence in man not something merely differing in degree from the instinct of other animals, but differing from it in kind. Intellect that which allies him both to angels and to God Himself. Constitutes a large portion of the image of his Creator in which he was created. Existed in a much higher degree before sin disordered and depraved his nature. Men now "alienated from the life of God through the ignorance that is in them, because of the blindness of their heart" (Eph. iv. 18). The faculties themselves, however, still in existence as man enters the world. Their development the work of time. That development affected by circumstances, and the means employed for it. Education the great means of developing the mental faculties. The intellect of races and families progressive or retrograde according to such development. The degree of intellect different in different individuals, constitutionally and from birth. This difference, doubtless, in some cases the result of circumstances, but more generally from the good pleasure of the Creator, who even in this respect "divideth to every man severally as He will" (1 Cor. xii. 11). The degree as well as the development of intellect connected with the condition, size, and configuration of the brain, which forms its seat, and is the organ through which it acts. (2) *Reason and intelligence imparted to man by the Creator.* Wisdom "*put*" into the inward parts; "*given*" to the heart. The mind or intellect entirely different and distinct from the material organ through which it acts and manifests itself. Reason and thought not a mere force existing in and belonging to the brain as a material substance. The brain the *seat* and *organ* of thought, not its *cause.* Mind not the production of other physical forces, as heat is transformed into electricity; but something *superadded* to the material organization. Man's physical frame formed out of the dust of the ground, after which God "breathed into his nostrils the breath of life, and man became a living soul" (Gen. ii. 7). Man thus made to partake of an intellectual as well as an immortal nature,

which rendered him what his Maker designed him to be—a reflection of His own image (Gen. i. 26). The art, science, and skill of man mediately or immediately the gifts of God. The language of the prophet applicable not merely to agriculture, but to all the arts and manufactures, and to all the sciences which elevate the human mind and distinguish the most enlightened of the human species: "This also cometh from the Lord of Hosts, who is wonderful in counsel and excellent in working" (Isa. xxviii. 29). The language of the Almighty concerning Bezaleel, the son of Uri, true of any other similarly eminent in any of the arts of civilized life: "I have filled him with the Spirit of God in wisdom, and in understanding, and in knowledge, and in all manner of workmanship, to devise cunning works," &c. (Exod. xxxi. 3). "In the hearts of all the wise-hearted I have put wisdom" (verse 6). (3) *The impartation of reason and intelligence to man a special exhibition of Divine power and wisdom.* "*Who* put wisdom in the inward parts?" Thought and reason the highest manifestation of power in a creature. Man thus placed far above other creatures greatly his superior in size and physical strength. Able thus to fulfil his Maker's purpose concerning him and the commission given him, to "subdue" the earth and "have dominion" over all other living creatures (Gen. i. 28). Made by the possession of his mental faculties a fellow-worker with God. Enabled, by working upon the materials placed at his hand, to produce other works of power, both of a material and an intellectual nature. Qualified to invent and construct works which are themselves the admiration of others and the multiplication of power. A Watt and an Arkwright enabled to produce machines by which, with a little water and fuel, one man is able to do the work of twenty or a hundred, and the strength of draught-horses can be entirely dispensed with. By a simple apparatus, provided through the human intellect, man is enabled to employ the lightning to convey his messages, and to hold almost immediate fellowship with distant countries and continents. As a co-worker with his Maker, he is enabled, by the faculties which God has given him, to convert the wilderness into a fruitful field, and to cause the desert to "rejoice and blossom as the rose." If God thus puts wisdom and understanding into man, and endows him with so much power, how great the wisdom and power of the Creator Himself!

15. *Beasts and birds of prey.* Verses 39—41—"Wilt thou hunt the prey for the lion (or lioness), or fill the appetite of the young lions, when they couch in their dens and

abide in the covert to lie in wait? Who provideth for the raven his food? when his young ones cry unto God, they wander (or, 'and wander,' or 'are famished') for lack of meat." Passes from inanimate to animated nature. The present section properly belonging to the next chapter. Begins with beasts of prey. Their food provided for them by the Creator Himself, by bringing other animals, which they are enabled to overcome and feed upon, within their reach. Some animals formed, by their physical structure, to live upon others. Their character as carnivorous given them by God, who provides for them the sustenance for which their bodily organization is adapted. Even the fierce lioness provided with her food by God. Beasts of prey, with all their ferocity, only a portion of the great family for which the Creator daily provides. But how powerless is man in their presence! How unable to provide for them! Man, since the entrance of sin into the world, obliged to employ his intellect in destroying, instead of supporting, such animals.

The "raven" probably mentioned in contrast with the lion. The largest of the sparrow-order of birds. Feeds on carrion as well as fruit and small animals, and is known even to carry off poultry. An unclean bird, and of little apparent significance; yet the raven cared for by the Creator equally with the noble and majestic lord of the forest. His Divine providence, directed even to the young of the raven, when forsaken by the parent bird, or early expelled by it from the nest. Not a cry of these young ravens but enters into the ears of the great and gracious Creator (Ps. cxlvii. 9). Their cry viewed as directed to Himself as their parent and provider. God cares and provides for the meanest as well as the mightiest of His creatures. A twofold lesson for man. (1) To be *kind to animals*, and, when not injurious or destructive, *attentive to their wants*. (2) To *trust in God* while doing His will. The lesson taught by Jesus to his disciples : "Consider the ravens; for they neither sow nor reap; which neither have store-house nor barn : and God feedeth them : how much are ye better than the fowls?" (Luke xii. 24). "The young lions do lack and suffer hunger; but they that seek the Lord shall not want any good thing" (Ps. xxxiv. 10).

CHAPTER XXXIX.

JEHOVAH'S ADDRESS CONTINUED.

Continuation of the questioning. Job now pointed to the animal creation; the passage from inanimate to animated nature having been made at the 30th verse of the previous chapter, instead of the beginning of this. Specimens or representatives of the various great classes of animals adduced—first beasts, then birds, then the inhabitants of the water, or of both land and water. The animals referred to mostly those of the wild class, or in a wild state, rather than domestic or domesticated ones. Exhibited for the most part in their native character as coming from the hand of their Creator. The animals selected distinguished for some special property, habit, or instinct, as indicative of the Creator's power in making, and His Providence in caring for them. The object of the references to reprove and humble Job, by reminding him of the greatness, majesty, sovereignty, power, wisdom, and goodness of Him whose providential dealings he had been tempted to arraign. Many things in connection with the lower animals mysterious and incomprehensible to man; why not in connection with man himself? The manifestation of Divine power in the animal creation, as well as of Divine wisdom and goodness in providing for, sustaining, preserving, and governing the various tribes of living creatures, a sufficient argument to silence all objections and murmurs as to the justice of His providential dealings.

The appeal here made by Jehovah to animated nature an indication of man's duty, as far as he has opportunity, to observe and make himself acquainted with the structure and habits of the lower animals. The visible, and especially the animal creation, moreover, to be observed and studied *as works of God*, and as *expressive of His attributes and perfections, both as its Creator and Governor.* Man always and everywhere surrounded with memorials and lessons of God's character and providence. The works of nature, both animate and inanimate, intended by their Creator to be so observed and studied by men, that He may derive praise, and they both pleasure and profit. The language of an eminent philosopher (Sedgwick) as true of natural history as of the Newtonian philosophy : "A study affecting our moral powers and capabilities; teaches us to see the finger of God in all things, animate and inanimate, and gives us an exalted conception of His attributes, placing before us the clearest proofs of their reality; and so prepares, or ought to prepare, the mind for the reception of that higher illumination which brings the rebellious faculties into obedience to the Divine will." Constant reference in Scripture to the animal creation as illustrative of God's character and man's duty. Nature, or creation—God's own Book—ever open to our view. "Go to the ant, thou sluggard;" "Consider the ravens;" "Behold the lilies of the field,"—recorded specimens of Divine teaching.

The reference here made to the various animals, such as to indicate the pleasure and satisfaction with which the Almighty contemplates the visible works of His hand. In accordance with the Mosaic narrative, "God saw everything that He had made, and behold, it was very good" (Gen. i. 31). "The Lord shall rejoice in His works" (Ps. civ. 31). A sufficient reason why *man* should rejoice in them. The better a man is acquainted with God's works in general, and with the animal creation in particular, the greater the pleasure he will derive from them. After the lion and the raven, Job is pointed to—

1. *The Wild Goat or Ibex.* Verse 1.—"Knowest thou the time when the wild goats of the rock bring forth?" The wild goat, probably the animal known among naturalists as the Ibex—the Bedin of the Arabs—a bold and powerful animal, armed with two huge sweeping horns, curving over its back and often three feet long. Inhabits the most elevated summits of the highest mountain ranges in the whole eastern continent. Stands two feet six or eight inches in height, and is extremely active and vigorous. Vigilant and wary, it only descends during the night to pasture in the woods, repairing again at sunrise to the bleak mountain summits. "Its chase very arduous; the animal leading its pursuer, unless he can steal upon it unawares with his rifle, a dangerous track over steep and rugged mountain pinnacles, along the brink of precipices, and over fearful chasms; and when at last, hard pressed, often turning upon its foe with impetuous rapidity, and hurling him down the steep rocks." Its favourite haunts in Europe the Alps, the Apennines, the Pyrenees, and the Tyrolese mountains. Doubtful whether it or the *Paseng* of the Caucasus and of Persia (the *Capra Ægagra* of Cuvier), is the original stock of our domestic goat. The wild goat referred to as being so far beyond man's power to manage it, or even become familiarly acquainted with its habits. The "knowledge" intended probably not

simply that of mere acquaintance, but of care. "Knowest thou," &c., so as to attend to, watch over, &c. Certain animals so constituted that man may both become easily and thoroughly acquainted with them and their habits, and be able to attend to their wants and aid them in their emergencies. The case with others the reverse. The shepherd knows the time when his ewes are to lamb: but who knows "the time when the wild goats of the rock bring forth?" Hence, observe—(1) *A proof of the Creator's care over the animal creation.* With no human eye to observe the wild goats, and no shepherd's hand to aid them, God's eye marks and His hand helps them in their greatest difficulties. (2) *A lesson of humility and modesty.* Man ignorant of the time when the wild goats of the rock bring forth; how then shall he be able to fathom the designs and understand the reasons of God in His providential dealings? What presumption for a creature of so limited knowledge, even of the humbler works of God, to question the wisdom and justice of His moral government! (3.) *A comfort for God's tried people.* Even the wild goats of the rock have their time of parturition assigned them by their Creator. That time known, marked, and attended to by Him. How much more everything connected with His intelligent offspring, and most of all with those who love and fear Him! If God so watches over and cares for the wild goat, will He not much more watch over and care for *you?*

2. *The Hind, or Female Stag or Antelope.* Verses 1–4.—"Canst thou mark (or watch) when the hinds do calve? Canst thou number the months that they fulfil (knowing the period of their gestation, and waiting like the shepherd in regard to his ewes, till they bring forth their fawns)? or knowest thou the time when they bring forth? They bow themselves (or go down on their knees in their labour), they bring forth their young ones, they cast out their sorrows (put forth their young which occasion their pains). Their young ones are in good liking (sleek and in good condition); they grow up with corn (or, in the desert or open country); they go forth (to obtain food for themselves), and return not again unto them (viz., to the hinds, their mothers)." The animal more especially alluded to doubtless the gazelle, or Arabian antelope. Formerly numerous in Syria and Arabia. Seen in large herds, bounding over the plain with amazing fleetness. Resemble the stags in the lightness of their figure and the swiftness of their course. In Africa, the usual prey of the lion and the panther. Remarkable for their timidity, as well as for their elegance and beauty; especially for the

soft expression of their large, dark, lustrous eyes. The hind or female referred to is, like the ibex, an animal beyond human care and attention, but observed and provided for by its Creator. The providence of God noted in not only delivering the mother in her pangs, but in caring for her offspring. Without either man or mother to attend to its wants, the young fawn, under the care of its Creator, grows up sleek and well-conditioned. Observe—(1.) *The tenderness of the Creator's care.* Indicated by the special reference to the animal's labour—the time of its maternal "sorrows." Its labour said to be naturally with difficulty and pain. The animal, however, said to be taught by the instinct given to it, to employ an herb called *Siselis* in order to facilitate the birth. (2.) *Comfort to suffering believers.* The Creator not indifferent to the pangs of the hind. Will He be indifferent to the sorrows and pains of His intelligent creatures, made after His own image, and especially of His own redeemed and adopted children? If He attends to the labour of the irrational creatures, and marks the time when it takes place, is anything connected with His own children beyond his observation and regard? (3.) Humbling, that while the Creator makes the sufferings of such creatures the object of his care, man should occasion them in the prosecution of his sport. Touching picture, drawn by the greatest of uninspired poets, of a dying stag shot by the hunter:—

"The wretched animal heav'd forth such
  · groans
That their discharge did stretch his leathern
  coat
Almost to bursting; and the big round tears
Coursed one another down his innocent nose
In piteous chase."

3. *The Wild Ass.* Verses 5—8.—" Who hath sent out the wild ass free (unrestrained to roam at large)? or who hath loosed the bands of the wild ass (a different name in the original text from the former; *that* employed more in Palestine, *this* in Chaldea; both indicative of a rapid flight; the latter, perhaps, also of the animal's noise in braying)? Whose house I have made the wilderness, and the barren land (*Marg.*, 'salt places') his dwellings (or haunts). He scorneth the multitude (or din) of the city, neither regardeth he the crying of the driver (or officer compelling to public service —the animal enjoying his liberty in the desert, and defying all attempts to subdue and domesticate him). The range of the mountains is his pasture (or 'he searches or roams the mountains as his pasture'), and he searcheth out every green thing (as rare in the desert, his proper habitation)." The wild ass, an animal met with in great num-

bers in Arabia Petræa. According to the Arabs, perfectly untamable. In fleetness equal to the gazelle; to overtake it a feat which only one or two of the most celebrated mares have been known to accomplish. Its food the saltest plants of the desert. In the East, the symbol of uncontrolled freedom. Its name assumed by Persian kings. The wild independence of Ishmael and his descendants (the Bedouin Arabs) indicated by the same figure: "He will be a wild (*Heb.*, wild ass) man" (Gen. xvi. 12). A picture also of the wayward and self-willed (ch xi. 12; Jer. ii. 24; Hos. viii. 9). The wild ass here selected by the Almighty on account of its natural freedom from restraint and its wild enjoyment of its desert haunts. Referred to in order to show—(1) *The Creator's sovereignty,* in not only making some species of animals naturally wild and others tame, but making a similar difference in the same species. (2) *The Almighty's power over animated nature.* (3) *His universally extended providence.* The wild ass, though beyond man's power to overtake or capture, yet only one of the innumerable objects of Jehovah's care. Its freedom and wildness given by Him. Its abode in the wilderness appointed by Him. The salt plants of the desert given by Him for its support. Hence observe —(1) Man himself entirely in the Almighty's hands. (2) Jehovah's right to dispose of His creatures as He sees good. The potter has power over the clay to make out of the same mass vessels of various kinds and for various purposes (Jer. xviii. 6; Rom. ix. 21.) (3) Man, unable to give law to the wild ass, how much less to His Maker?—(*Henry*). (4) God, who has the wild ass entirely under His control, can easily subdue the wildest and most wayward human spirit. (5) Variety a characteristic in the Creator's works. Wildness and independence given by Him to the wild ass. The Almighty tied to no uniform type. (6) Man's true liberty, not that of the wild ass,—an unrestrained independence; but to be under willing, intelligent, and loving subjection to his Maker's laws. The liberty of a child of God not to be "without law to God, but under the law to Christ" (1 Cor. ix. 21). The true liberty that with which Christ makes his people free (Gal. v. 1). His yoke easy, and his burden light (Matt. xi. 30).

4. *The Unicorn.* Verses 9—12.—" Will the unicorn be willing to serve thee, or abide by thy crib (or, spend the night at thy stall, like an ox or other domestic animal)? Canst thou bind the unicorn with his band in the furrow (guide him with a rope or rein in ploughing thy field)? or will he harrow the valleys (or low grounds, especially suited for

tillage) after thee (after thy direction and following thy steps like the quiet ox,—the husbandman going before the harrow, though behind the plough)? Wilt thou trust him (have confidence in him as an animal helpful in the labour of the fields) because his strength is great? or wilt thou leave thy labour to him (thy grain, the fruit of thy labour,—to watch it by night while remaining on the threshing floor)? Wilt thou believe him that he will bring home thy seed (or grain, from the field after being reaped or threshed, like an ox yoked in the waggon), and gather it into thy barn (or granary)?" The animal here intended apparently one of the ox kind, probably the wild ox or oryx (*aurochs*),—the *urus* of the ancients, "generally but erroneously considered as the wild stock of our horned cattle." A savage animal that has now taken refuge in the great marshy forests of Lithunia, the Krapacs, and the Caucasus; but which formerly inhabited all the temperate parts of Europe. The largest quadruped proper to Europe — (*Cuvier*). The animal subdued with difficulty. Extremely powerful: hence the reference in the text. Probably the "strong bulls of Bashan" (Ps. xxii. 12). Once roamed freely in the forests of Palestine. Large herds of them still in the region beyond Jordan. Often mentioned by Arabian poets. Its two horns include a space of ten feet from tip to tip. The animal thought, however, by some to be a species of antelope with two horns, formerly abundant in Egypt and the south-west of Asia; described by Aristotle as one-horned, and appearing on the Egyptian monuments sometimes with one and sometimes with two horns. By others, the unicorn, or *reem*, thought to be the rhinocerus, one species of which—the rhinoceros of India—has only one horn. This well-known animal also one of enormous strength, being scarcely less in size than the elephant. That of India, sluggish in his movements, and wandering through his native plains with a heavy step. At certain times very dangerous, impetuously attacking every animal that attracts his notice. The African rhinoceros has a double horn, the principal one rising about nine or ten inches above the nose, and inclining backwards; the other immediately behind it, a short thick one. The Hebrew name (*reem*) generally translated in our English Bible the "unicorn," or one-horned. The animal, however, apparently spoken of as having two horns (Num. xxiii. 8; Deut. xxxiii. 17; Ps. xxii. 21.) Frequently mentioned in Scripture as distinguished for its strength. The *reem* of the Arabs an animal with two horns. The name apparently significant of its loftiness and power. The unicorn of heraldry long

258

thought a merely fabulous animal. Its existence, however, now contended for by some, who allege ancient and modern eye-witnesses of it. Its figure—a head like a horse, cloven feet, the tail of a boar, and one horn in the forehead. The representation of such an animal found among the ruins of Persepolis. The animal referred to in the text as one of huge strength, but beyond the power of man to render it serviceable to him in the works of the field. Fitted by its physical structure and great strength, to be employed like the ox or ass in agricultural pursuits; but, from its intractable condition, not to be subjugated by man for that purpose. The reference intended by the Almighty to remind Job of his own littleness and the power of his Creator. Observe— (1) *A lesson of humility and modesty for man.* If unable to bind and bring into his service an animal like the *reem*, how should he be able to contend with his Maker? If unable to rule a mere creature, how unfit to question the dealings of his Creator! (2) *The effect of sin.* The animals originally designed to serve man. Dominion over them given him by the Creator (Gen. i. 26, 28; Ps. viii. 6). That dominion forfeited by the Fall. (3) *The Divine sovereignty.* Some animals apparently such as by nature to be more useful and serviceable to man than others. God's reasons for endowing the animals with their various properties unknown to us. Mysteries in creation; no wonder if we find similar mysteries in providence.

5. *The Ostrich.* Verses 13—18.—"Gavest thou the goodly wings unto the peacocks? or wings and feathers unto the ostrich? (*Marg.*, 'the feathers of the stork and ostrich?' Or the whole verse may read thus: 'The wing of the ostriches moveth gaily: but is it the wing and feathers of the stork?"—a bird remarkable for maternal affection, of which the ostrich appears to be so deficient). Which (or because, since) she leaveth (or, deposits) her eggs in the ground, and forgetteth that the foot may crush them, or that the wild beast may break them (in the exposed place where she lays them). She is hardened (or acts hardly) against her young ones, as though they were not hers (or, 'for those which are not her own'): her labour (in preparing her nest, and sitting on her eggs) is in vain, without fear (she being without solicitude for the preservation of her young). Because God hath deprived her (or, 'made her forgetful') of wisdom (the prudence necessary for preserving her young), neither hath he imparted unto her understanding (such, or so much as he has implanted in the animals in general, usually called instinct). What time she lifteth up (or rouseth) herself on

high (erecting her head and body as well as her wings, the latter being used to aid her in *running* rather than flying), she scorneth the horse and his rider (when pursuing her in the chase)."

The ostrich referred to as an animal generally regarded as deficient in natural forethought, especially in reference to the preservation of her young (Lam. iv. 3), while endowed with extraordinary speed, so as to be able to secure her own safety by flight. One of the two known species (the *struthio camelus*) abounds in the sandy deserts of Arabia and Africa. This the ostrich mentioned here and elsewhere in the Bible. Attains the height of eight feet. So swift that no animal is able to overtake it. The wings white and black, not unlike those of the stork; furnished with the well-known loose and flexible, elegant and slender-stemmed feathers; and sufficiently long to increase the animal's speed in running, serving both for sail and oar. Being found in hot countries, the ostrich is content to lay its eggs, from thirty to fifty at a time, each weighing nearly three pounds, about a foot below the surface in the sand. Outside the tropics, however, she is said to brood over her eggs with great care, and courageously to defend her young. From the animal's known neglect of her young in Arabia, it is designated by the Arabs the "impious bird," as in contrast with the stork, which is called the "pious" one. Said to hatch her eggs only for a time, and to leave them frequently during the day at the least noise, going to a great distance and sometimes never returning to them. Plays and frisks about on all occasions, "moving her wings gaily," and would be always fanning and hiding herself with them. Her eggs left exposed to the view of the traveller and the foot of the wild beasts that frequent the desert. Often addled before she returns from her long absence in search for food. Sometimes, during her absence, found sitting on the eggs of another bird. Its sense of taste so obtuse that it swallows rags, leather, &c., and even pebbles and pieces of metal. The bird proverbially stupid. "More foolish than an ostrich," an Arab proverb. Its speed calculated by Dr. Livingstone to be about twenty-six miles an hour. The stride of one in the Sahara found to be from twenty-two to twenty-eight feet.

The "peacock" probably not intended in the verse. The word so rendered, quite different from that in 1 Kings x. 22. Literally, denotes "singing ones," and probably given to characterize the ostrich, distinguished for its cries. The peacock distinguished not so much for the beauty of its *wings* as of its

tail. Originally brought from India. First known in Palestine and Arabia in the time of Solomon, who imported it into his kingdom. Introduced into Europe by Alexander the Great. Its magnificent plumage, most splendid in a wild state, like the flowers of the field,—indicative of the Creator's pleasure in the beautiful, and of the beauty residing in Himself. In the peacock, the beauty apparently not accompanied with other excellencies.

From the whole section, observe—(1) *God's providential care of His creatures.* Provides for the young of the ostrich even when the care and affection of the parent fail. (2) *His sovereignty in the endowments of His creatures.* Instinctive care for the preservation of offspring strong in the animals in general; weak in the ostrich. "Wisdom and understanding"—whether in the lower form as in the brute creation, or in the higher, as in man—the gift of God. Its degrees in both cases according to His own pleasure. The ostrich endowed with remarkable speed, but with little sense. The stork, with much humbler plumage, yet gifted with much greater natural affection. An example related of two which had built their nest on the roof of a house in Delft, a town of Holland, and which, when the house was on fire, first endeavoured to carry off all their young, and when unable to do this, kept flapping their wings over them as if to cool the air; and at last, as the flames drew nearer, sat down over the nest to die with them. (3) *The various endowments of animals designed for man's instruction.* Intended to teach man both concerning God and himself. Some of those endowments designed for man's imitation; others the reverse. The stork an *example* to parents in regard to their children; the ostrich a *warning*. Indifference and neglect in regard to those committed to our care monstrous even in irrational creatures: much more so in *man*. Like the "labour" of the ostrich, that of parents and teachers often "in vain," from the want of "fear" and solicitude for the *preservation* of those for whom they have laboured. "*Those most likely to lose their labour who have least fear of losing it.*" While men sleep, the enemy sows his tares. Such solicitude especially needful in the case of children leaving the parental roof. Watchful care always necessary to guard the young against the influence of evil company, and the dangers incident from an ungodly world. Prayerful solicitude constantly required on behalf of those for whose spiritual benefit we have laboured, and in whom have appeared the beginnings of grace. Early grace watched over by God, but not therefore the less to be watched over by man.

6. *The Horse.* Verses 19—25.—"Hast thou given the horse strength (or courage, or rather both combined)? Hast thou clothed his neck with thunder (with the terror of his neighings; or, 'with lofty quivering mane'—the indistinctness of the figure heightening its sublimity)? Canst thou make him afraid as a grasshopper (or, 'bound like a locust')? The glory of his nostrils (or neighings) is terrible (or, 'a terror'—more especially to the Hebrews, little acquainted with war-horses, Jer. viii. 16). He paweth in the valley (or ' plain '—usually selected for the battle-field where cavalry were to be employed); and rejoiceth in his strength. He goeth on to meet the armed men (or, 'boldly he advanced against the weapons'). He mocketh at fear (what would cause fear in others), and is not affrighted (by all the terrors of the battle-field); neither turneth he back from the [face or presence of] of the sword. The quiver (or its contents, the arrows) rattleth against (or upon) him: the glittering spear and the shield (or, 'the flash of the spear and the lance'). He swalloweth the ground with fierceness and rage (in his impetuous eagerness for the fight): neither believeth he that it is the sound of the trumpet (or, 'standeth still when there is the sound of the trumpet'). He saith among (or at the blast of) the trumpets, Ha, ha: and he smelleth the battle afar off—the thunder of the captains (animating the hosts to the fight), and the shouting" (of the warriors).

The reference to the horse apparently suggested by the mention made at the close of the preceding paragraph, of "the horse and his rider." The war-horse here especially referred to. The description acknowledged to be unequalled anywhere for sublimity. Sufficient in itself to place the writer among the first of poets. The war-horse referred to as an example of courage and noble bearing. The reference intended to impress Job with the majesty of Him whose creature this noble and courageous animal is.

The horse exhibited in the text as the noblest specimen among inferior animals. Those of Arabia and Egypt especially famous. The horse believed to exist in Arabia, the home of the patriarch, in a finer condition than in any other country. Still the chief treasure of the Bedawin Arab. Formerly many of them in a wild state in the Arabian deserts: only caught in pits, and then subjugated through hunger and fatigue. Believed by the Arabs to be endowed with a nature superior to that of other animals, and to be next to man himself. At first employed by fallen man chiefly in war, yoked to a chariot in which the warrior stood. The earliest mention of them in connection with

the exodus of the Israelites from Egypt (Exod. xiv. 6—9). Probably employed in Egypt and elsewhere on state occasions (Gen. xli. 43). Used also early in the chase, apparently intended in verse 18. Among Egyptian monuments, only one of a horse and its rider, and that comparatively recent. Horses mentioned among the valuable possessions of Solomon brought up by him from Egypt. Among the ancient Assyrians used indiscriminately for war and hunting. Israel spoken of by Jehovah as His "goodly horse in the battle;" as endowed by Him with strength and courage, and employed for the conquest of heathen adversaries (Zech. x. 3). The horse, as distinguished for its beauty as well as its strength and courage, employed as a simile for the Church of Christ under the figure of a beautiful woman (Cant. i. 9). Elsewhere noticed in Scripture for his strength and eagerness for the battle (Ps. cxlvii. 10; Jer. viii. 6). Yet a vain thing for safety (Ps. xxxiii. 17).

From the description of the war-horse observe—(1) *The example of the Almighty in contemplating and admiring the works of His hand.* God represented as rejoicing in His works, whether the feathers of the ostrich or the spirit of the war-horse, the intelligence of a seraph or the piety of a man. A refined pleasure in contemplating and admiring the works of God; a *Divine* pleasure in contemplating them as such. God's example to be imitated by His intelligent children. (2) *An example exhibited in the war-horse, of courage and fearlessness in the discharge of duty and in the service of our Divine Master* (See again Zech. x. 3; Cant. i. 9). The courage and impetuosity of the war-horse too often imitated in a contrary direction (Jer. viii. 6). Man capable of being employed as Satan's war-horse as well as Jesus Christ's. The latter his glory and felicity; the former his disgrace and ruin. (3) *The war-horse, in some respects, a faint reflection of his Maker's excellence.* "Who would set the briars and thorns against Me in battle?" (Is. xxvii. 4). All creature excellence only a shadow of the infinite and uncreated excellence of the Creator. All endowments and excellencies found in the creature intended to lead the thoughts to the Creator as the source and sum of all excellence. (4) *Mystery connected with all God's works.* The horse, the noblest of God's irrational creatures, yet here admired by his Maker as displaying his excellence in what cannot but be regarded as, in many respects, Satan's work. The battle-field, usually the theatre of evil passions, and the delight of the enemy of God and man. Sin, the origin of all strife and warfare; yet war and battle not always sinful. Sometimes man's duty, and commanded by God. In some respects, the battle is the Lord's. The Lord of hosts mustereth the hosts for the battle. Nebuchadnezzar God's servant in his war against Tyre (Ezek. xxix. 17—20. War employed by God as His own terrible instrument in His government of the world. God's glory in overruling man's sin and Satan's malice to his own praise and the welfare of the universe. Napoleon and his battles, God's scourge for the benefit of Europe and the world. Yet on the field of Waterloo, "those terrible grey horses" a terror to him who had been the terror of the nations. "I have created the waster to destroy." A prospective use in many of God's creatures. The creature "made subject to vanity" through Adam's fall. The time to come when the creature, groaning and travailing in pain until now through man's sin, "shall be delivered from the bondage of corruption into the glorious liberty of the children of God" (Rom. viii. 20—22). The day hastening on, when the noble horse shall find other employment than rushing with its rider into the din of the battle, and careering among garments rolled in blood. The promise in connection with Christ's kingdom to be fulfilled: "They shall beat their swords into ploughshares, and their spears into pruning hooks; nation shall not lift up sword against nation, neither shall they learn war any more." "He maketh wars to cease unto the end of the earth; he breaketh the bow, and cutteth the spear in sunder; he burneth the chariot in the fire." (Is. ii. 4; Ps. xlvi. 9). The last inspired mention of the war-horse, and perhaps the last use of him as such, made in connection with "the battle of the great day of God Almighty," in the place "called in the Hebrew tongue Amageddon;" and with the symbolical appearance of the Faithful and True witness upon a white horse, clothed in a vesture dipped in blood, in righteousness judging and making war as King of Kings and Lord of Lords, and followed by the armies of heaven; these also "upon white horses, clothed in fine linen, white and clean" (Rev. xvi. 14—16: xix. 11—14, 18—21.

7. *The Hawk.* Verse 26.—"Doth the hawk fly by thy wisdom, and stretch her wings towards the south?" The reference to birds of prey and those feeding on carrion probably suggested by the battle-field mentioned in the previous section. The hawk, or falcon, selected as a specimen and representative of the feathered tribe, from the rapidity of its flight, and perhaps also from its being migratory in its habits. Birds of the hawk order (*accipitres*), placed by naturalists highest in the list, including not only hawks and falcons, but eagles and vultures. Are

among birds what the lion and other carnivorous animals are among quadrupeds. Known by their talons and hooked beaks, by which they seize and devour other birds and even the weaker quadrupeds and reptiles. Plumage dense and quills strong, giving them great power on the wing, and enabling them to pursue or pounce at once upon their prey. Perhaps the name in the text one of a generic kind, including all such birds of prey. Falcons, with naturalists, the second and by far the most numerous division of those predaceous birds that pursue their prey in the daytime. The greater number prey on living animals. The falcon proper, the most courageous bird in proportion to its size.—Two things in the text referred to as indicative of the wisdom of God in relation to the hawk:—

First: *Its Flight*—"Doth the hawk fly by thy wisdom?" The hawk mentioned by Homer as the swiftest of birds. The rapidity with which the hawk and many other birds occasionally fly, probably not less than at the rate of 150 miles an hour. A falcon escaping from Fontainbleau, in France, found to have reached Malta, 1350 miles distant, after twenty-four hours. The common falcon formerly employed in hunting, chiefly from its rapid flight. Builds her nest in the most elevated and inaccessible cliffs, whence she darts down with rapid wing upon her prey, descried at a distance. An inhabitant of northern latitudes, whence her flight towards the South. Second: *Its Migration.*—"Stretcheth her wings towards the south,"—as if for a warmer climate. Many animals, unfit to provide against the vicissitude of the seasons by varying the quantity or colour of their dress, enabled by the providence of God to protect themselves by shifting their quarters, so as to live throughout the whole year in a temperature suited to their constitution, and at the same time to obtain an abundant supply of food. The migration of birds an object of observation from an early period. "The stork in the heavens knoweth her appointed times; and the turtle, and the crane, and the swallow observe the time of their coming" (Jer. viii. 7). Birds of passage not confined to any particular order or tribe; nor distinguished by similarity in habits or kind of food. Some birds stationary in one district, migratory in another.

Observe—(1) *The wisdom of God in adapting birds for flight.* The general form of the body of birds, one best calculated for gliding with the least resistance through the air. Everything in its structure contrived to give it *lightness.* The horny materials of the feathers formed into hollow cylinders, exceedingly strong when compared with their weight. A similar shape given to the cylindrical bones, which are fashioned into tubes, with dense but thin sides; most of the other bones likewise made hollow, but containing only air. The neck exceedingly long and flexible, to enable the bird in flying exactly to balance itself, by bringing the centre of gravity precisely to the proper point. *The feathers of the bird a marvellous contrivance.* Made to consist of three parts—the quill, the shaft, and the vane. A mould made for every feather, "in what may be called a feather manufactory." This manufactory not merely in action once during the life of the bird, but at every time of moulting—generally once a year. The feather remarkable for its strength as well as its lightness. The vane of the feather so disposed that the impulse of the air occurs first where the feather does not yield. The wing adapted for flight by its striking the air below it with a certain force, and so causing a re-action of the air upwards exactly equal to it, the bird rising or sinking as the force of the stroke is greater or less than its weight. The wings also employed by the bird in steering its course, as the rower turns his boat by using only his right or left oar. The tail made to act as a supplementary organ for the same purpose. The tail, however—in addition to its serving as the rudder of a ship,—by expanding and offering a considerable surface to the air, fulfils some of the offices of a third wing, and serves also to poise the body of the bird. (2) *The wisdom and goodness of God in the migration of birds.* An admirable instance of the Creator's care, that birds are endowed with an instinct which enables them to know where and when to direct their flight, so as to find a more genial climate during the colder season in their native home. (3) *The hawk, as well as other migratory birds, an example to men in relation to God their Saviour.* "The stork, &c., know the time of their coming: but my people know not the judgment of the Lord" (Jer. viii. 7). Christ provided by the love of God, as the sinner's shelter from the certain storm of Divine wrath against sin. Men invited to dwell in Him as "in a peaceable habitation, and in sure dwellings, and in quiet resting-places; when it shall hail, coming down on the forest" (Isa. xxxii. 2, 18). The Saviour's complaint that sinners "know not the time of their merciful visitation." "O, Jerusalem! how often would I have gathered thy children together, as a hen gathereth her chickens under her wings, but ye would not" (Luke xix. 41—44; Matt. xxiii. 37).

S. *The Eagle.* Verses 27—30.—"Doth the eagle mount up at thy command, and make her nest on high. She dwelleth and abideth on the rock, upon the crag of the rock, and the strong place (or mountain-castle). From thence she seeketh her prey, and her eyes behold afar off. Her young ones suck up blood, and where the slain are, there is she." The eagle a species of the same order of birds as the hawk (*accipitres*), and belonging to the *falcon* genus. The largest of the genus, and the most powerful of all the birds of prey. Probably intended, however, to include *vultures* as well, especially the bearded or eagle-vulture (*Gypaetus*), which, rather than the eagle, feed on carrion. The bearded or eagle-vulture, though differing both in head and body from the eagle, yet resembling it in its robust form and general habits, except that it feeds on dead flesh, which the eagle rarely does. Equals, or exceeds, the largest eagle in size, and is found throughout the great mountain chains of the Old World. Apparently referred to in Mic. i. 16; as its head and neck are entirely destitute of feathers, which those of the proper eagle are not. The eagle referred to in the text on account of—(1) Its *lofty flight.* "Doth the eagle mount up," &c. Its great bodily power and ample wing fit the bird for a lofty and majestic flight. The eagle-vulture about four feet from the beak to the tip of the tail, and from nine to ten feet in the extent of its wings. The peculiarity of the eagle, to fly directly upward till out of sight. Its flight referred to by the prophet: "They shall mount up with wings as eagles" (Isa. xl. 31). Hence also said to have an eye fitted to gaze upon the sun. (2) Its *inaccessible abode.* "She maketh her nest on high," &c. The eagle, and the eagle-vulture, both select the most inaccessible pinnacles as the site of their eyrie. (3) Its *acute vision.* "Her eyes behold afar off." The sight of the eagle, as of birds of prey in general, remarkably acute. Such birds endowed with the power of pushing out and drawing in the lenses of the eye, as the object is more or less distant, so as to discern from its lofty abode the prey far beneath it, and to see it no less distinctly as it descends. (4) Their *appetite for flesh and blood.* "Her young ones also suck up blood," &c. The greater number of the *falcon* class of birds, to which the eagle belongs, feed on living prey, while the eagle-vulture, like birds of the *vulture* genus, also feeds on carrion. Hence the battle-field the great attraction for the latter. Eagles said only to drink blood. The young ones trained to this in the nest, to which the parent-bird brings the prey.

Observe from the section—(1) The *wisdom of the Creator* in respect to birds and beasts of prey. Exhibited—(i.) in providing that one class of animals prey upon another. According to the present constitution of nature, no other system could long exist except that which operated as a check on animal production, and preserved a balance of power between all creatures. (ii.) In providing by means of such animals' for the removal of dead bodies left on the surface of the earth. Vultures, and even eagles, among birds and wolves, jackals, and hyænas, among quadrupeds, employed by the Creator as the earth's scavengers—in removing its offal, and especially the carcases of animals, which would otherwise tend to corrupt the air with pestilential exhalations, and unfit parts of the earth for the abode of the living. (2) The *eagle viewed as an emblem.* May be regarded as an emblem— (i.) Of *God* Himself, in His tender care of and attention to the wants of His creatures. "Her young ones suck up blood." "As the eagle stirreth up her nest, fluttereth over her young, spreadeth abroad her wings, taketh them, beareth them in her wings; so the Lord alone did lead him' (Deut. xxxii. 11, 12). (ii.) Of *believers.* (*a*) In their *upward ascent.* "They shall mount up with wings as eagles." Believers' journey a heavenward one. Believers not to have their affection set on things on the earth, but to "seek those things that are above, where Christ sitteth" (Col. iii. 1, 2). The unregenerate burrow in the earth, as moles and worms; believers mount upwards, as with eagles' wings. The disposition to do so, from their new spiritual and Divine

nature; their ability, imparted by the Holy Spirit in connection with their waiting upon God (Isa. xl. 31). (*b*) In their *lofty and safe abode.* "They shall dwell on high; their place of defence is the munitions of rocks" (Isa. xxxiii. 16). Their dwelling in God Himself, the Rock of Ages. Their abode, the secret place of the Most High, under the shadow of the Almighty. Jehovah Himself their refuge and fortress. Their safe shelter, the Rock that is higher than they (Ps. xci. 1, 2,; lxi. 2, 3). (*c*) In their *spiritual vision.* Believers enabled to "see afar off" (2 Pet. i. 9). Once blind, but now see. Their eyes anointed with Christ's eye-salve (Rev. iii. 17). Believers behold, as in a glass, the glory of the Lord. Behold the glory of Jesus, as that of the Only Begotten of the Father (2 Cor. iii. 18; John i. 14). Endure, as seeing Him who is invisible. See promised glory afar off. Look at the things that are unseen and eternal (Heb. xi. 13, 27; 2 Cor. iv. 18). Behold, by the eye of faith, the King in His beauty, and the land that is very far off (Isa. xxxiii. 17). (*d*) In their *feeding, by faith, on the flesh and blood of the Lamb that was slain for them.* "Whoso eateth My flesh, and drinketh My blood, hath eternal life; he that eateth My flesh, and drinketh My blood, dwelleth in Me, and I in him. The bread that I will give is My flesh, which I will give for the life of the world" (John vi. 51, 54, 55).

CHAPTER XL.

JEHOVAH'S ADDRESS CONTINUED.

A pause in the Almighty's address apparently indicated in the commencement of the present chapter. The language in which it is resumed, together with the reply of Job immediately following, implies also a suspension of the argument, which seems only to be taken up at the fifteenth verse—when the Almighty spoke a second time out of the whirlwind. This is usually explained on the ground that Job's conviction and repentance, though expressed in verses 4 and 5 in reply to the Almighty's appeal in verse 2, were not yet sufficiently deep, and that the argument and means of correction are on that account resumed. It is conjectured, however, by some that an accidental dislocation of the parts has taken place, and that the first fourteen verses of the chapter originally followed the description of Leviathan and the first six verses of the succeeding chapter. In this way the narrative is believed better to correspond with the seventh verse of the forty-

second chapter, which seems to make the Almighty the last speaker; while the fourteenth verse of the present chapter forms a manifestly appropriate and impressive conclusion to the Divine address. Taking the narrative, however, as it stands in the text, we have—

I. **The application of the preceding address.** Verses 1, 2.—"Moreover the Lord answered Job and said: Shall he that contendeth with the Almighty instruct Him (or, 'will the corrector of the Almighty still contend with Him?' Or, 'is the disputer with the Almighty yet instructed')? He that reproveth God, let him answer it" (viz., the questions just proposed). Observe—

1. *A sin most offensive to God, to contend with Him by disputing the equity of His government and the reasonableness of His providential dispensations.* This Job's sin. The sin to which fallen human nature, even

263

in believers, is always liable. The sin into which Asaph felt himself falling (Ps. lxxiii. 2—15). Conspicuously the sin of Jonah.

2. *The contemplation of the greatness and sovereignty of God as Creator and Ruler of the universe, fitted to silence all questionings and complainings in regard to His providential procedure.* This the object of the Almighty's address, and of the reference made by Him to His power, wisdom, and goodness as seen in the creation, preservation, and government of the earth, with all the tribes of its inhabitants, as well as of the worlds above and around us, and of all the various forces and phenomena of nature. Such a Being can require no instruction from any of His creatures; and for even the highest of them to think to reprove Him for any of His doings can only be the summit of presumption and folly. All ground of complaining against God on the part of His creatures removed by His infinitely glorious perfections. Those perfections sufficient foundation for our most assured confidence in the Divine procedure. A Being possessed of such perfections able only to do what is wise, and just, and good. Enough to hear in the darkest dispensations: "Be still, and know that I am God" (Ps. xlvi. 10).

II. Job's Confession. Verses 3—5.— "Then Job answered the Lord and said: Behold, I am vile (mean and contemptible): what shall I answer Thee (either as to these questions or Thy conduct and procedure)? I will lay mine hand upon my mouth (in token of silence and conviction). Once have I spoken, but I will not answer: yea twice, but I will proceed no farther." In this confession observe—

1. *The discovery.* "I am vile." Abraham's acknowledgment—"Am but dust and ashes." All flesh grass. Man a worm. His days on earth as a shadow. But of yesterday, and knowing nothing. Even the nations less than nothing, and vanity. The question appropriate and becoming: "What is man that thou art mindful of him?" Vile in his origin, and creature-nature; much viler still in his character as a sinner. His proper place therefore in the dust, with his hand upon his mouth. Murmurings and complainings against God's procedure monstrous in any creature, but especially in one so vile as man. Note—(1) *God made man in his own image, but sin has made him vile.* The character of sin to debase; that of righteousness to exalt. Sin renders man rebellious against his Creator, injurious to his neighbour, brutish in himself. Sin, the abominable thing which God hates. (2) *Repentance changes men's views of themselves as well as of God.* Job's former language: "I am not

264

wicked." "I would go as a prince before God;" Now it is: "Behold, I am vile." The language of Saul, the Pharisee: "God, I thank thee that I am not as other men are;" that of Paul, the penitent: "I am the chief of sinners." (3) *Job's discovery a blessed one.* The result of Divine teaching and of God's revealing himself to the soul. Isaiah's acknowledgment when he beheld the glory of the Lord in the temple: "Woe is me! for I am undone, because I am a man of unclean lips." That of Peter on the discovery of Christ's divinity in the fishing boat: "Depart from me; for I am a sinful man, O Lord." This discovery the first step to Job's exaltation, and the exaltation of any sinner. "He giveth grace to the lowly." "He that humbleth himself shall be exalted." Pride and self-righteousness the greatest hindrances to a man's peace.

2. *Job's silence.* "What shall I answer thee? I will lay mine hand upon my mouth." No plea to offer (chap. xxi. 5; Jud. xviii. 19). A Divinely taught self-knowledge the effectual cure of a murmuring spirit. God's government of his creatures of such a character as to stop the mouth of every objector. A day at hand when every mouth will be shut, and all the world become guilty before God. The immediate result of the Spirit's work in conviction. Examples: The thief upon the Cross; Saul of Tarsus.

3. *His resolution.* "Once have I spoken, but I will not answer," &c. The proof of repentance to resolve not to repeat the offence. "If I have offended, I will not offend any more." "He that confesseth and *forsaketh* his sin shall obtain mercy." "Go and sin no more." Complete and unconditional surrender, the aim of the Holy Ghost in the sinner's conviction. Note—Job's sin that of his *lips*, and especially in relation to *God.* Sins of the lips to be repented of as well as sins of the life. Unbecoming thoughts and words in regard to God at least as punishable as injustice towards our neighbour. "Uprightings of judgment towards God as much a duty as uprightness of conduct towards man."—*Kitto.*

III. The Almighty's Challenge. Verses 6—14.—"Then answered the Lord unto Job out of the whirlwind, and said: Gird up thy loins now like a man (a hero or mighty man, as thou imaginest thyself to be—spoken in irony): I will demand of thee, and declare thou unto me. Wilt thou also disannul my judgment (judicial sentence, or justice in governing the world)? wilt thou condemn me, that thou mayst be righteous (in order to establish thy innocence—which Job appeared on the point of doing)? Hast thou an arm like God? or canst thou thunder with a voice like Him? Deck thyself now with majesty and excellency, and array thyself [like a God] with glory and beauty. Cast abroad (manifest on every side, or dart forth as lightnings) the rage (or overflowings) of of thy wrath [against the ungodly for their destruction]: and behold [with a withering glance] every one that is proud, and abase him. Look [with omniscient eye from the throne of the universe] on every one that is proud, and bring him low (by the infliction of condign punishment, and for the manifestation of thy power and justice); and tread down the wicked in their place (on the spot, however high in power and station). Hide them in the dust [of the grave], and bind their faces in secret (without public process, or in the darkness of a prison, like so many doomed malefactors—Est., vii. 8). Then will I also [as well as others] confess unto thee [with praise], that thine own right hand can save thee."

The Almighty's address from the storm-cloud renewed, not to explain and remove the mysteries in His providential dealings, for which there will be time enough hereafter, but still to further convince Job of his error in questioning the Divine justice, and more fully to humble him, by the exhibition of His own almightiness and man's littleness. From the challenge in the above section, observe—

1. The spirit and tendency of all murmurings against God's dealings with us is to "disannul" His decisions, and to maintain our own righteousnes as deserving better treatment.

2. Discontent and rebellion against the Divine procedure is virtually to "contend" with God, and enter the lists with the Almighty. "Let the potsherds strive with the potsherds of the earth; but woe unto the man that striveth with his Maker." A fearful thing to fall into the hands of the living God. "Who can abide when once he is angry." The wrath of a king like the roaring of a lion; what then the wrath of a God? The sinner must either submit by grace or be subdued by judgment. "Kiss the Son, lest he be angry, and ye perish from the way."

4. Pride the object of God's special displeasure. The sin of fallen angels.

5. Every sinner "beheld" by the omniscient eye of the Almighty. "No darkness or shadow of death where the workers of iniquity may hide themselves."

6. The proudest to be one day "brought low." Proud sinners humbled either in mercy or judgment. Those happy who willingly humble themselves before God, before they are *unwillingly* humbled *by* Him.

7. *Thorough humiliation and self-abasement*

required, in order to the reception of full salvation and spiritual comfort. Job for a time only partially humbled. The ploughshare of conviction to be driven deeper into his soul, before the seed of Divine consolation is cast into it. The knife to be still further applied, before the wound is finally bound up. God's kindness seen in thoroughly humbling the saint as well as the sinner. A crowning blessing, to be divested of the last remains of pride and self-righteousness. God empties in order to fill; humbles in order to exalt.

8. *The tendency of fallen humanity always to save itself.* The essence of all infidelity, Pharisaism, and self-righteousness. The spirit of Cain with his offering of first fruits, in contrast with that of Abel with his bleeding lamb. The Pharisee in the temple, with his—"God, I thank thee I am not as other men;" in contrast with the Publican and his —"God be merciful to me a sinner." Self-salvation the aim of most of the religion in the world, whether Pagan, Mahometan, Jewish, or Christian. Much of the religion of the cloister as well as of the synagogue. Penances, prayers, almsgivings, and so-called good works, often only so many different forms of self-salvation. Self-salvation usually the first attempt of an awakened sinner. Salvation by self the great impediment to salvation by Christ.

9. *Attempts to save ourselves only cured by the discovery of our own weakness.* To save ourselves implies a power nothing less than Divine. To be our own Saviour we must possess the attributes of Deity. The Saviour of humanity, when fallen, must be God as truly as the Creator of humanity itself. "God our Saviour"—two ideas necessarily connected. Salvation includes—(1) Satisfaction to Divine justice for sin; (2) Regeneration or the renewal of a sinful nature. Satisfaction for sin, which deserves endless death, only to be made by one possessing infinite dignity. Regeneration, or the creation of a new and holy nature in a fallen man, the work of a Divine power. The power required to save ourselves, that which can punish sin anywhere and banish it from the world. The sinner made to see his inability, in order to abandon his attempts at self-salvation, and to cast himself entirely on God the Saviour, the Lord Jesus Christ. The glory of the Gospel, that it reveals a Divine power put forth for man's salvation; and actually put forth in the case of all who believe it. Man's inability to save himself the ground of Christ's redemption. To exhibit that inability one of the objects of this book. "God, and not man, the sinner's Saviour—the substance of all revelation." —*Townsend.*

IV. **Description of Behemoth.** Verses

15—24.—"Behold now Behemoth, which I made with thee (or in thy neighbourhood); he eateth grass as an ox. Lo now, his strength is in his loins, and his force is in the navel (or muscles) of his belly. He moveth (*Marg.*, "setteth up") his tail like a cedar: the sinews of his stones (or thighs) are wrapped together (or interlaced). His bones are as strong pieces (or tubes) of brass (or copper); his bones (a different word from the preceding—probably a Syriac or Chaldaic one, and rather denoting the larger bones—his limbs) are like bars of iron. He is [in bulk and strength] the chief of the ways (or works) of God: he that made him can make his sword to approach him (or, 'hath given to him his sword'—the weapon —probably his hooked teeth or tusks, with which he might defend himself and attack others, but which he only uses in mowing down the grass for his food). Surely the mountains bring him forth food, where all the beasts of the field play (the animal harmless and herbivorous, notwithstanding his sword). He lieth under the shady trees (or lotuses), in the covert of the reed and fens (or marshes abounding on the banks of the Nile). The shady trees (or lotuses) cover him with their shadow; the willows of the brook compass him about. Behold, he drinketh up a river (or a 'river rages' or over-flows its banks), and [he] basteth not (to escape from fear of the consequences): he trusteth that he can draw up Jordan with his mouth. He taketh it with his eyes (or 'will any take him before his eyes?'—instead of using stratagem): his nose pierceth through snares" (or, "will any pierce his nose with hooks?"—as 2 Kings xix. 28; Ezekiel xxxviii. 4).

Uncertain what animal, if any one in particular, is intended by the description. The name "Behemoth," as a Hebrew word, simply denotes "beasts," or viewed as the plural of majesty, "the beast." So rendered in some of the ancient versions. The word, however, thought by some to be rather the Hebrew form of an Egyptian name for the animal, viz., *P-ehe-moth*, or the water-ox. The *elephant* generally understood by the older commentators to be the animal intended. Modern interpreters, however, decidedly in favour of the *hippopotamus*, or river-horse. The description believed to agree better with the latter; while the hippopotamus, being an inhabitant of the Nile and its banks, was much more likely to be familiarly known to the patriarch and the poet than the elephant.

Both the elephant and the hippopotamus belong to the class of animals termed by naturalists *Pachydermata*, or thick-skinned. The elephant comprehends the largest of the

living terrestrial animals that suckle their young. Its food is strictly vegetable. It is of a mild disposition, and lives in herds, which are conducted by old males. Those of the present day clothed with a rough skin, nearly destitute of hair. Are only found in the torrid zone of the eastern continents; the Indian elephant being found from the Indus to the Eastern Ocean, and in the large islands of the south of India; and the African one, from Senegal to the Cape of Good Hope. The African elephant not now tamed, although the Carthaginians appear to have employed it in the same way that the inhabitants of India do theirs. The hippopotamus has a very massive and naked body, with very short legs, so that the belly reaches to the ground, an enormous head, and a short tail. It lives in rivers and their neighbourhood, feeding on roots and other vegetable substances, and exhibits much ferocity and stupidity. Now confined to the rivers of the middle and south of Africa.—*Cuvier.*

The description apparently agreeing in every particular neither with the elephant nor the hippopotamus, the animal has been conjectured by some to be a now extinct genus; and by others to be rather a poetical personification of the great pachydermata— the idea of the hippopotamus being predominant. Extinct species of this class of animals found in a fossil condition. The great *mastodon* the type of the elephant, though of a different species—the principal distinction being in the shape and structure of the teeth; while the mastodon also possessed short tusks in its lower, in addition to those in its upper, jaw. This animal equalled the elephant in size, but with still heavier proportions. Its remains found in a wonderful state of preservation both in America and the Eastern Continent. The skeleton of one, almost entire, found in the valley of the Missouri, now to be seen in the British Museum. The animal supposed to have been more an aquatic, or swamp-hunting, quadruped than the elephant. A *mammoth*—a more recent animal of the same class—measuring from the fore-part of the skull to the end of the tail sixteen feet four inches, and twelve feet in height, discovered in Siberia in 1801, imbedded in ice, with its flesh, skin, and hair as perfect as if recently dead. The remains of another found, which is supposed to have been twenty-five feet high and sixty feet in length. Gigantic elephants, of nearly twice the bulk of the largest elephant of Africa or Ceylon, believed by Professor Owen, from the abundance of their remains, to have roamed in herds over the British Islands in the period immediately before the creation of man. The fossil remains of an animal discovered in the gypsum quarries of Paris and other parts of France, to which has been given the name *Palæotherium*, or the 'ancient beast,' and which seems to have combined the characters of the rhinoceros, the hippopotamus, the horse, the pig, and the camel; while its external appearance, as restored by Cuvier, approaches more nearly to that of the tapir. The animal supposed to have lived in marshy ground, and to have fed on the roots and stems of trees.

The Almighty's object in the description of Behemoth, to present to Job, in this gigantic and powerful animal, an evidence of His Divine power; and at the same time to teach him his own littleness, and the presumption of thinking to dispute with his Maker, or of questioning the justice of His procedure. The Creator, Preserver, and Governor of such creatures must be one who possesses sufficient power, wisdom, and rectitude to govern the world.

Observe—(1) Not merely do the heavens and the firmament over our head declare the glory of God, but every creature which His hands have made. The huge mammoth points to the irresistibleness of His power, while the almost invisible animalcule tells of the universality of His Providential care. (2) *The largest, as well as the least, of His creatures dependent on, and provided for by, the Creator.* "He giveth the beast his food." How much more will He care and provide for His own children made after His image! He Who constantly feeds the gigantic monsters of the land and sea can be at no loss to supply the wants of His trusting people. The happiness of believers that they are able to testify with David: "He hath made with me an everlasting covenant, ordered in all things and sure" (2 Sam. xxiii. 5).

CHAPTER XLI.

JEHOVAH'S SECOND ADDRESS CONTINUED.

Nearly the whole of the chapter occupied with the description of "Leviathan." The section remarkable for its grandeur and sublimity. The idea of terribleness and power conveyed in a variety of striking particulars. The image of a formidable monster vividly placed before our eyes. The details naturally often obscure. The most extended description in the Almighty's address and in the whole book. The object to exhibit the might and majesty of the Creator. "Such a power of description as to constitute in my mind an evidence of its inspiration."—*Dr. Chalmers.*

I. **The description itself.** May be divided under various heads.

1. The creature's *fierceness and indomitableness.* Verses 1—10.—"Canst thou draw out leviathan with an hook? or his tongue with a cord which thou lettest down (or, 'press down his tongue with a rein,' or perhaps 'a fishing-line')? Canst thou put an hook into his nose? or bore his jaw through with a thorn (*i.e.*, an iron hook resembling one—so as to lead him about as thou wilt, like other wild beasts, as Ezek. xxix 4; Is. xxxvii. 29). Will he make many supplications unto thee [to spare him]? Will he speak soft words [of persuasion] unto thee? Will he make a covenant with thee? Wilt thou take him for a servant for ever? Wilt thou play with him as with a bird? or wilt thou bind him for thy maidens (as a plaything for thy little girls)? Shall the com-

panions (the partners employed in taking him) make a banquet of (or on account of) him (after taking and killing him, or, will they 'make a bargain over him,' or 'dig pits for him, in order to take him)? Shall they part him among the merchants (to be sold like other animals)? Canst thou fill his skin with barbed irons? or his head with fish spears? Lay thine hand upon him; remember the battle [which thou hast rashly entered on], do no more (—do not, or thou wilt not, repeat it). Behold, the hope of him (of taking him, or overcoming him) is in vain (will be disappointed). Shall not one be cast down [with terror] even at the sight of him. None is so fierce that dare stir him up" (or awake him when sleeping).

2. *His powerful structure and terrible aspect.* Verses 12—24.—" I will not conceal his parts (or members), nor his power, nor his comely proportions (or, 'the grace of his array'). Who can discover the face of his garment (strip off his skin or the scales that cover it)? or who can come to him with his double bridle (or, 'enter into the doubling of his jaws,' or his double row of teeth)? Who can open the doors of his face? His teeth are terrible round about (or, 'the circuits of his teeth are a terror'). His scales (*Marg.*, 'the strong pieces of his shields,' *i.e.*, his strong shields or scales) are his pride, shut up together as with a close seal (or, 'as a close seal'—a seal sticking closely to the material on which it is im-

pressed). One is so near to another that no
air can come between them; they are joined
one to another; they stick together that
they cannot be sundered. By his neesings
a light doth shine, and his eyes are like the
eyelids of the morning (as he lifts his head
above the water.) Out of his mouth go
burning lamps, and sparks of fire leap out
(expressive of his hot fiery breath). Out of
his nostrils goeth smoke, as out of a seething pot or caldron. His breath kindleth
coals (live burning coals), and a flame goeth
out of his mouth. In his neck remaineth
(lodgeth) strength, and sorrow is turned
into joy before him (*Marg.*, 'rejoiceth;'
or 'terror danceth before him'—a bold
personification, indicating the terror and
dismay occasioned by his appearance). The
flakes (or pendulous parts) of his flesh are
joined together; they are firm in themselves;
they cannot be moved. His heart is as firm
as a stone; yea, as hard as a piece of the
nether millstone (or 'as the lower millstone')."

3. *His invincibleness and invulnerableness.*
Verses 25—29.—"When he raiseth up himself (out of the water) the mighty are afraid;
by reason of breakings (which he makes
while plunging in the water, or 'from the
destruction' which his appearance threatens,
or the 'terror' which it causes) they purify
themselves (or lose their recollection—are
bewildered). The sword of him that layeth
at him cannot hold (or stand) : the spear,
the dart, nor the habergeon (coat of mail, or
perhaps the javelin). He esteemeth iron as
straw, and brass (or the brazen weapon) as
rotten wood. The arrow cannot make him
flee; slingstones are turned with him into
stubble. Darts (or clubs) are counted as
stubble; he laugheth at the shaking of a
spear."

4. *His habits, motion, and supremacy
among beasts.* Verses 30—34.—"Sharp
stones are under him (or, 'his lower parts
are sharp potsherds'—the scales on his belly
resembling such); he spreadeth sharp pointed
things (or, 'a threshing cart,'—his sharp
spikes resembling the teeth of one) upon
the mire (*i.e.*, when he moves upon his belly,
whether on the soft shore or on the bed of
the river. He maketh the deep (the water
in which he mostly lives—whether sea, lake,
or river) to boil like a pot (from the agitation which he causes); he maketh the sea
(or river, to which the term is also applied)
like a pot of ointment (seething on the fire,
and emitting a smell which that of the
crocodile is said to resemble). He maketh
a path to shine after him (like the phos-
phorescent light sometimes produced by the
rapid motion of a ship); one would think
the deep to be hoary (from the white froth

and foam which the creature occasions by
his motions). Upon earth there is not his
like (or 'any dominion' to which he is
subject), who is made without fear [of any
assailant]. He beholdeth all high things
(looks down upon the loftiest creature with
disdain; or 'terrifies every boaster') ; he is
king (holds supremacy) over all the children
of pride" (or, 'ferocity'—all proud ferocious animals, such as the lion and other
beasts of prey).

II. The creature described. Opinions
various. According to the Greek translation used by the Apostles, a *dragon*. With
some a sea-monster. By almost all the old
commentators, understood to be the *whale*,
as in Ps. civ. 26. Now generally believed
to be the *crocodile*. The name apparently
denoting the *twisting* or *folding* one, and so
applicable either to a serpent or a crocodile.
The description more suitable to the crocodile
than any other known living animal. The
crocodile also, as an inhabitant of the Nile,
likely to be known both to Job and the
writer of the book. The more likely to be
the crocodile as connected with Behemoth ;
if that creature be supposed to be the hippopotamus, also a native of that river. A
familiarity with Egypt and its productions
on the part of the writer, apparently indicated by the poem.

The animal intended, however, conjectured
by some to be one of an extinct species of
the order of Saurians, the description corresponding in all particulars neither to the
whale nor the crocodile. By others, the
description thought to be rather, like that
of Behemoth, a poetical generalization; in
this case, for all monsters of the whale, serpent, or lizard tribes, the idea of the crocodile
being the predominant one.

The crocodile, an amphibious animal of
the order of Saurians, has a single range of
pointed teeth in each jaw. The tongue
fleshy, flat, and adhering close to the edges
of the jaws a circumstance which induced
the ancients to believe that the animal was
destitute of a tongue altogether. The back
and tail covered with very stout, large,
square scales or plates, so thick as easily to
repel a musket ball, those on the belly being
smooth and thin. The crocodile inhabits
rivers and lakes, and is extremely ferocious
and carnivorous. Found nearly twenty feet
long and five feet in circumference.

Another family of the same order is the
dragon (draco, *Linnæus*), supposed by some
to be the Leviathan, which is also mentioned
in Is. xxvii. as "the dragon that is in the sea."
The dragon of the naturalists distinguished
from all other animals of the order, by their
first six false ribs; which, extending outwards

in a straight line, and supporting a production of the skin, form a kind of wing, like that of a bat, but not connected with the four feet; and having sufficient power to enable them to leap from one branch to another, but not to rise, like a bird, into the air. They are completely covered with scales. The tongue fleshy and somewhat extensive; while a long pointed dewlap hangs under their throats. To this tribe of Saurians probably belongs the long-extinct reptile only found in a fossil state, and known by the name of *Pterodactylus.* This animal of a bygone world had a short tail, an extremely long neck, and a very large head. The jaws armed with equal and pointed teeth. The second toe of the fore foot so elongated as to make the foot double the length of the trunk, and probably serving to support some membrane which enabled the animal to fly. Enormous eyes enabled it to see in the dark twilight, while its jaws were furnished with sixty pointed teeth. Some specimens must have had a spread of wing exceeding sixteen feet. The Greek term *draco*, or dragon, generally used to designate a large serpent; while some ancient Greek writers speak of flying dragons. Some of them speak also of dragons with a crest or beard; which can only apply to the *Iguanas*, properly so called, and belonging to the same family as the dragons. In these the head is covered with plates, and the body and tail with scales; while along the entire length of the back is a range of spines, or rather recurved, compressed, and pointed scales; and under the throat is a pendant compressed dewlap, whose edge is supported by a cartilaginous process of the hyoid bone. Each jaw is surrounded with a row of teeth, while two small rows are on the posterior edge of the palate. An iguana, common in South America and the West Indies, measures about five feet in length. To the same family belongs the enormous fossil reptile known as the *Iguanodon*, a monstrous lizard, sixty or seventy feet long; its form resembling the iguana of the West Indies, with the addition of a horn, situated like that of the rhinoceros, and of about the same size. Other monstrous animals, living at the same period, and found as fossils, were equally or even more terrific in appearance. The *hylosaurus*, or forest-lizard, had a row of scaly fringes on its back seventeen inches long, which it had the power of erecting when advancing to attack its enemy or to seize its prey. The *megalosaurus* exhibited the structure of the crocodile and monitor, from forty to fifty feet in length. The *plesiosaurus* united to the head of the lizard, the teeth of the crocodile, a neck of enormous

length resembling the body of a serpent, with a body and tail of the proportions of an ordinary quadruped, and the paddles of a whale. The *ichthyosaurus*, or fish-lizard, was the ruling monster of the waters. In some of these the eye must have been twelve inches long and nine broad, protected by scales. The jaws, armed with one hundred and eighty conical teeth, were, in the larger species, six feet long, the whole length of the animal being thirty feet.

III. The Lessons from the Description.

1. *The resistless power and universal dominion of the Almighty.* This, the lesson mainly intended to be taught the patriarch himself. Indicated expressly by the Almighty in verses 10, 11: "None is so fierce that dare stir him up: who then is able to stand before me? Who hath prevented me (in rendering any service, so as to lay me under an obligation to him), that I should repay him? (words referred to by the Apostle in Rom. xi. 35). Whatsoever is under the whole heaven is mine." The inference obvious: If you are unable to stand before or resist any of these monsters of the land or sea, how can you stand before me, from whom they all live, and move, and have their being? How vain to think to lay Him under obligation to us, to whom all creatures, from the least to the greatest, belong as His own property, and on whom they depend every moment for existence! Hence—(1) *Humility and submission to God, with confidence in the justice of His government and the wisdom of His providential dealings, man's duty in all circumstances.* The Creator, Possessor, and Ruler of universal nature may well be believed to be infinite in His perfections, and trusted in as righteous, wise, and good in all His procedure. (2) *Terrible to have Him for a foe to whom the mightiest monsters of sea or land belong, as only an insignificant portion of His creatures.* "A fearful thing to fall into the hands of the living God." Unspeakably blessed to have Him for our friend. Our highest wisdom to secure, without delay, a personal interest in His favour and friendship, through the redemption and mediation of His Son Jesus Christ.

2. *The mysterious sovereignty of God in the formation of His creatures.* The same Divine hand the former of the harmless dove and the terrible dragon. The Creator of the lamb pleased also to produce the Leviathan. The useful ox and the destructive crocodile made to inhabit the same locality. Why God should have formed creatures of such terrible aspect and ferocious dispositions,

clothed them with such impenetrable armour, and furnished them with such destructive weapons,—among the secrets of His Divine wisdom. All things made for Himself; even the wicked for the day of evil. For His pleasure all things are, and were created. No creature but made to show forth, in some way or other, the glory of His Divine perfections, and to secure some purpose or other in His all-comprehensive government. Variety everywhere displayed in the works of the Creator's hands. That variety directed by infinite wisdom, goodness, and justice.

3. *God's works of creation worthy of all admiration.* His works such as to bear to be taken to pieces and viewed in detail. The better known, the more admired. Exhibited by God himself for our admiration. " I will not conceal his parts." The crocodile, or the dragon, as truly worthy of admiration as the noble war-horse. Job pointed to the Leviathan as an object of beauty and gracefulness as well strength and power. If God sees beauty in the crocodile, what beauty then in many of His other works! Objects in creation doubtless viewed otherwise by God, angels, and unfallen men, than they are by creatures in a state of rebellion against their Creator, and, therefore, with their faculties impaired, and themselves at enmity with the rest of creation. Things viewed with terror by the consciously guilty and condemned, which might otherwise have only excited admiration. God's standard of beauty the true one. What God views with admiration and complacency certain to be viewed by His children with the same feelings, but for the effects of sin in their nature. Those effects entirely removed in a better state, when the universal song will be, " Great and marvellous are Thy works, Lord God Almighty ; just and true are all Thy ways, thou King of saints" (Rev. xv. 3). Interesting to mark in the above section the delighted contemplation by God on His own works. "Stamps a warrant of sacredness on our tasteful admiration of them."—*Dr. Chalmers.*

4. *The fact and effects of the fall seen in man's relation to the creatures.* Man originally made to have dominion over all the terrestrial works of the Creator's hands. Man fitted for such dominion, as created in his Maker's image. That dominion an obvious part of his natural right as a child of God. His intellectual nature, placing him so immensely above the brute creation, such as to warrant the expectation of it. That dominion enjoyed by Adam in a state of innocence, when he gave names to all the creatures. Naturally and justly forfeited, however, and lost by man's rebellion against his Creator. Rebellion justly followed by

attainder. Rights naturally forfeited by rebellion against an earthly sovereign. Hence, but for sin, the crocodile and the tiger as harmless to man, and as much under his subjection, as the cow or the dog. The dominion forfeited by the first Adam, regained and restored by the second. Christ, the Second Man, without sin, made Ruler over all the creatures as man's representative. Was in the wilderness forty days with the wild beasts, as Adam was with them in Paradise (Mark i. 13). The lions at the feet of Daniel in the den, a specimen of what may be "in the regeneration." All things reconciled in Christ. The members made partakers with the Head in the restored rule of creation. In the kingdom of Messiah, a state of things indicated which will probably have its external and physical, as well as its internal and spiritual, aspect : "The wolf also shall dwell with the lamb, and the leopard shall lie down with the kid, and the calf, and the young lion, and the fatling together, and a little child shall lead them ; and the sucking child shall play on the hole of the asp," &c. (Isa. xi. 6—9).

5. *An emblem afforded of the great adversary of man.* That adversary named in Scripture, "the Dragon, that Old Serpent, which is the Devil and Satan" (Rev. xx. 2). Under the figure of Leviathan, "the dragon that is in the sea," mention made by the prophet (Isaiah xxvii. 1) of some powerful adversary and oppressor of the Church and people of God; whom the Lord, when he comes "out of his place to punish the inhabitants of the world for their iniquity," will punish and slay "with his sore and great and strong sword." Perhaps some human oppressor of the Church thus indicated, as Pharaoh, the great enemy of Israel, is spoken of under the same figure (Ps. lxxiv. 13, 14 ; Is. li. 9). The king of Egypt expressly called "the great dragon that lieth in the midst of his rivers" (Ezek. xxix. 3). These, however, exhibited as types of the great oppressor of man, called by Peter, "Your adversary, the devil, [that] goeth about like a roaring lion, seeking whom he may devour." The chosen form of that adversary, in his first and successful attempt upon the human race, that of a serpent. The Leviathan, as some kind of dragon, very generally understood by early Christian writers as allegorically representing the dragon and old serpent of the Revelation. Parts of the description impressively applicable to our great adversary, and very frequently employed by evangelical writers and preachers as illustrative of his character. Leviathan may be viewed as an emblem of Satan in respect to—(1) *His loftiness and dignity as a creature.* Satan a

fallen angel; probably one of the highest, if not the very highest of the heavenly hierarchy. (2) *His fierceness and cruelty.* Satan a murderer from the beginning, sparing neither age, sex, nor condition. (3) *His power of inflicting mischief and working destruction.* One of Satan's names Apollyon or Abaddon, viz., the Destroyer. (4) *The difficulty of overcoming him.* Satan not to be overcome by any mere human effort. The strong man armed who is only to be overcome by one stronger than he (Luke xi. 21). (5) *The universality of his sway.* Satan the god and prince of this world; the spirit that worketh in the children of disobedience; the ruler of the darkness of this world. Keeps his palace (our fallen race), and has his goods in peace until the stronger than he—the Lord Jesus Christ, the Mighty God, or God the Champion (Is. ix. 9)—comes upon him, overcomes him, and "divideth the spoils" (Luke xi. 21). "He is so strong that if all of us should combine against him, he would laugh at us, as Leviathan 'laugheth at the shaking of a spear.' . . . He is well armed at every point, and he knows how to arm his slave, the sinner, too; he will plate him from head to foot with mail, and put weapons into his hand against which the puny might of Gospel ministers and human

conscience can never prevail. Prejudice, ignorance, evil education—all these are the chain-armour with which Satan girds himself. A hard heart is the impenetrable breastplate which this evil spirit wears; a seared conscience becomes to him like greaves of brass; habitude in sin is a helmet of iron. The demon who possesses men is not to be wounded by our artillery."—*Metropolitan Pulpit,* Feb. 5, 1865. Bunyan's description of Apollyon, partly taken from that of Leviathan in the text. "Now the monster was hideous to behold: he was clothed with scales like a fish (and they are his pride); he had wings like a dragon, feet like a bear, and out of his belly came fire and smoke, and his mouth was as the mouth of a lion." But one conqueror of the great Leviathan—the Lord Jesus Christ; who took our nature, "that through death he might destroy him that had the power of death, that is, the devil; and deliver them who, through fear of death, were all their lifetime subject to bondage" (Heb. ii. 14, 15). But one weapon by which he can be wounded, "the sword of the Spirit, which is the Word of God" (Eph. vi. 17). "I have written unto young men, because ye are strong, and the Word of God abideth in you, and ye have overcome the wicked one" (1 John ii. 14).

CHAPTER XLII.

THIRD GREAT DIVISION OF THE POEM.—THE CONCLUSION.

The Almighty's address immediately followed by the catastrophe of the poem,—the repentance of Job, and the consequent change of his condition. What the three friends, and Elihu himself, had failed to do, Jehovah's voice at once accomplishes. "Where the word of a king is, there is power." No explanation given by the Almighty of the mystery of Job's sufferings, and those of other good men, or of the prosperity of the ungodly in this world. By the mere exhibition of the Divine perfections, objection is silenced and discontent removed; while the objector confesses his error, and deeply humbles himself on account of his presumption and folly.

From verse seven to the end, the narrative is given in prose, in the same style as the introduction in the first two chapters. The chapter stands connected with the preceding parts of the book, as the capital of the magnificent column of which the introduction is the base.

1. Job's Repentance.   Verses 1—6.—

"Then Job answered the Lord," &c. Repentance the happy fruit of sanctified affliction (Isa. xxvii. 9). Job's repentance expressed in few words. God requires not many words, but much faith. We have—

1. *A believing acknowledgment of God's omnipotence.* Verse 2.—"I know that Thou canst do everything, and that no thought can be withholden from Thee (*Marg.,* 'no thought of thine can be hindered'; or, 'no purpose is too high for Thee' [to accomplish]." One of Job's errors, apparently, that he had, in his heart at least, doubted God's omnipotence, as if He were unable either to punish the wicked as they deserved, or to deliver His servants out of trouble, or keep them from falling into it. Much of this secret infidelity lurking in the natural heart. Apparently easy and natural to believe that God is almighty and able to "do all things." Easy to profess it, but not so easy to act always upon the belief, and to have our heart and life powerfully influenced by it. The belief of God's almightiness at the bottom of all true religion. The faith that characterized

the worthies of the Old Testament (Heb. xi). Noah believed that God could destroy the world by a flood, and preserve himself and his family by the ark; Abraham, that He could give him a son when Sarah was past child-bearing, and that He could raise that son from the dead; Moses, that He could open a way for Israel through the Red Sea; Joshua, that He could cause the walls of Jericho to fall to the ground; Shadrach, Meshach, and Abednego, that He could deliver them from the fiery furnace; Mary, that, without her knowing a man, God could, according to His Word, make her the mother of the promised Saviour. This faith directed, in the New Testament, to Christ. "Lord, if Thou wilt, Thou canst make me clean." "Believe ye that I am able to do this?" "If Thou canst do anything, have compassion on us and help us. Jesus said unto him: If thou canst *believe;* all things are possible to him that believeth." The Roman centurion commended for believing that Jesus had but to speak the work, where He was, and his servant should be healed. When God speaks, faith—

> "Laughs at impossibilities,
> And cries, It shall be done:"

Mighty works wrought by means of faith in God's almightiness. The part of such faith to "remove mountains." "Nothing shall be impossible to you." The virtue of faith, that it arms itself "with that omnipotence it trusts." Faith honours God, and God honours it (Rom. iv. 20, 21). Hence, through faith, men "subdued kingdoms, wrought righteousness, obtained promises, stopped the mouths of lions, quenched the violence of fire, escaped the edge of the sword, out of weakness were made strong, waxed valiant in fight, turned to flight the armies of the aliens" (Heb. xi. 33, 34). Peace and restfulness of heart the fruit of such faith. "Thou wilt keep him in perfect peace whose mind is stayed on Thee, because he trusteth in Thee" (Isa. xxvi. 3). The character of unbelief and infidelity that it doubts God's omnipotence. "If the Lord should open windows in heaven might this thing be." "Why should it be thought an incredible thing, that God should raise the dead?"

God's "thoughts" only known to us as they are revealed by Him. When known, faith rests assured that they shall be accomplished; however unlikely and impossible they may appear to carnal reason. His "thoughts" or purposes respect—(1) Himself; (2) His Son, Jesus Christ; (3) His Church as a whole; (4) Each individual member of that Church; (5) The creation at large (Rom. viii. 21). His thoughts those of an infinite and eternal Being, who sees the end from the

beginning; of one perfect in knowledge, wisdom, justice, goodness, and truth. His thoughts the foundation of His procedure, and the plan according to which He acts in Providence.

The front of Job's offending in God's sight, and that of which he has now so deeply to repent,—his unworthy thoughts of God, and especially his unbelief in regard to God's almightiness. Observe—(1) *Grievous sin often in the heart in reference to God, when none may appear in the life in reference to men.* (2) *The cause of bitter repentance to a child of God, to find that he has sinned by indulging unworthy thoughts of his heavenly Father.* (3) *Much of God's Word and works intended to teach His children that He is able to do all things.*

God's *right* as well as *might* probably included in Job's acknowledgment. A maxim in law, that a man can only do what he has a right to do. God not only *can,* but justly *may,* do whatever He pleases. Has a sovereign right over all His creatures. May dispose of them and deal with them as He pleases. Job tempted at times to question this right, or, at least, to doubt whether it was righteously exercised. His language at the commencement of his trials not maintained to the close—"The Lord gave, and the Lord hath taken away; blessed be the name of the Lord." God's pleasure in regard to His creatures, *always* and *necessarily* only what is right.

2. *Humble acceptance of Divine reproof.* Verse 3.—"Who is he that hideth (or obscureth) counsel (or wisdom) without knowledge (or which is beyond his knowledge)?" Supply: Thou speakest justly; I am that foolish and presumptuous person. Reference to the Almighty's question in chap. xxxviii. 2. Observe—*A truly penitent heart humbly accepts of God's reproof.* An impenitent one rejects it and maintains its own innocence. Israel's sin greatly aggravated in God's sight by saying, when reproved by Him: "I am innocent" (Jer. ii. 35). The fifty-first Psalm David's penitent acceptance of the Divine reproof. Adam's impenitence seen in charging his sin upon Eve, and Eve's in charging hers upon the serpent. Saul, instead of accepting Samuel's reproof, laid his sin upon the people (1 Sam. xv. 1—26). To accept the punishment of our iniquity a proof of a humbled heart (Lev. xxvi. 41.)

3. *Penitent acknowledgment of ignorant and rash speaking.* Verse 3.—"Therefore (this being true of me, I acknowledge that) I uttered that I understood not; things too wonderful for me, which I knew not." Observe:—(1) *Much of our discontent and murmuring at God's procedure, the result of*

ignorance. Asaph's acknowledgment: "So foolish was I, and ignorant; I was as a beast before Thee" (Ps. lxxiii. 21). (2) *Most of what we say of God, except as guided by His Spirit, that which we do not understand.* Our words concerning God and His dealings in Providence mostly only the prattling of a child, without its innocence. (3) *God's purposes and ways in Providence, "too wonderful" for us, in our present state, to comprehend.* His thoughts "a great deep." For that deep, human reason unable to furnish a sounding-line. The part of piety and faith to trust God without seeking to trace Him; and to be assured that He does all things well, however much appearances may appear to speak to the contrary. Even God's dealings in reference to ourselves often "too wonderful" for us; much more those dealings in reference to the world at large. His operations in respect to outward and common things often such as we know not; much more those in respect to the renewing of our nature and the salvation of our soul. "As thou knowest not the way of the Spirit (or of the wind, John iii. 8), nor how the bones do grow in the womb of her that is with child; even so thou knowest not the work of God, who maketh all" (Eccles. xi. 5).

4. *His desire to take the place of a humble inquirer and learner.* Verse 4.—"Hear, I beseech Thee, and I will speak: I will demand (or ask) of Thee, and declare (or tell) Thou unto me" [things of which I am so ignorant]. Observe—(1) *The mark of true repentance to desire to know the Lord's will.* "Lord, what wilt Thou have me to do?" (2) *Man's proper place, in relation to God and His dealings, that of a learner and inquirer.* (3) *A humble, docile, and childlike spirit, man's true nobility.* The spirit and posture of a child, that of the great philosopher whose name has become inseparably connected with the achievements of modern science. (4). *Enough in God and His ways to give room for inquiry and learning throughout eternity.* Into the mystery of redemption with its glorious results, the angels represented as desiring studiously to look. (5) *Wise to take all our difficulties, whether in regard to Providence or grace, His work or His Word, to God Himself for their solution.* God His own interpreter. Those the most proficient in knowledge who go most to God and His Word for instruction. The disciples to be imitated who inquired in private the meaning of the Master's teaching in public. "What may this parable mean?" (6) *Necessary to be inquirers and learners ourselves in order to be teachers of others.* (7) *In Divine things especially, nothing rightly known except as we are taught*

it of God. Divine teaching the special bestowment on God's elect, and the first step in a man's salvation (John vi. 45). That teaching imparted to the humble (Matt. xi. 25; Isa. xxviii. 9; Ps. xxv. 9). The privilege of a child of God through life (Ps. xvi. 7; xxxii. 8).

5. *His confession to a different kind of knowledge of God from what he had before.* Verse 5.—"I have heard of thee (or 'heard thee') by the hearing of the ear; but now mine eye seeth thee." A perception of God's visible glory probably vouchsafed to Job, as to Isaiah in the temple with similar results (Is. vi. 1—5). An inward and spiritual apprehension of the Divine perfections doubtless mainly intended. This the object of the Almighty's address. Observe—(1) *Knowledge of God and His Son different in different persons, and in the same person at different periods.* That difference twofold: (i) In *degree.* Among believers, some are babes in knowledge, others full-grown men (Heb. v. 13, 14.) All our knowledge here comparatively that of a child (1 Cor. xiii. 9 —11. Knowledge obtained by "seeing," much more clear and satisfactory than that by "hearing." Same contrast in chap. xxix. 11; Ps. xlviii. 8. Much of our knowledge here obtained by hearing or report. Hence rather faith than knowledge. Knowledge hereafter rather from seeing than hearing. "They shall see God." "Now we see through a glass darkly, but then face to face." "We shall be like Him, for we shall see Him as He is." (ii.) In *kind.* This difference probably, as well as the former, indicated in the contrast. The difference between a believer's knowledge of God and that of an unbeliever, one of kind rather than of degree. The believer *sees* with the eye of faith what before he had only *heard* by report. Knowledge of Divine things by mere report rather that of a blind man in relation to colours. A knowledge of Christ after the flesh the utmost that a man in his unrenewed state can attain to. This superseded in a believer by a spiritual divinely given knowledge (2 Cor. v. 16; Gal. i. 15; Matt. xvi. 17). The testimony of the men of Sychar: "Now we believe, not because of thy saying; for we have heard Him ourselves, and *know* that this is indeed the Christ, the Saviour of the world." Mere traditional and educational knowledge of Divine things to be distinguished from that which is spiritual and saving. The defectiveness of the former as compared with the latter exhibited in Job's case. The invitation of the Gospel: "Come and see." "Taste and see that the Lord is good." The knowledge of the believer an experimental one,—not only a hearing, but a

tasting of the salvation of God. "If so be ye have tasted that the Lord is gracious" (1 Peter ii. 3). (2) *Much of God's dealing with believers and others, with a view to bring them to an experimental knowledge of Himself and His truth.* This the object of His dealings with Job. "*Now mine eye seeth thee.*" God often pleased to reveal Himself most in the rebukes of His providence. "I will allure her into the wilderness, and will speak comfortably to her" (*Marg.,* 'to her heart'—in an effectual way of instruction). Spiritual knowledge often one of the most blessed fruits of sanctified affliction. Often more knowledge of Divine things gained in one month or one week on a sick bed than in many years of previous experience. Such teaching one of the ends of affliction. "Blessed is the man whom thou choosest, O Lord, and teachest him out of thy law" (Ps. xciv, 10). (3) *A good man's knowledge of God and Divine things progressive.* The hearing of God to conduct to the seeing of Him. The path of the just like the shining light, shining more and more unto the perfect day. Knowledge under Divine teaching like the river in Ezekiel's vision—first up to the ankles, then the knees, then the loins, and at last a river to swim in. Saving knowledge like the restored sight of the blind man in the Gospel—first men seen as trees walking, then all things seen clearly. The greatest increase of knowledge awaiting the believer in another world. "Now I know in part (in fragments or piecemeal), but then shall I know even as also I am known" (Cor. xiii. 12). (4) *Danger of stopping short of a spiritual and experimental knowledge of God and Divine things.* Job's "*now*" to be desired, whatever it may cost us. Paul's resolution—"Henceforth know we no man after the flesh; yea, though we have known Christ after the flesh, yet henceforth know we him [so] no more" (2 Cor. v. 16). Professing Christians especially counselled by Christ to come to Him for the eye-salve of His Spirit, that they may anoint their eyes and see (Rev. iii. 7).

6. *His self-abhorrence, as the result of his perception of the Divine perfections.* Verse 6.—"Wherefore I abhor myself (or, 'I loath [my conduct and language]')." Observe— (1) The result of the Divine manifestation and address *immediate.* But little time required for the Spirit's teaching. Nothing unnatural in sudden conversion. Conviction and conversion the effect of the same teaching as in the case of Job. Other examples of the same suddenness: Isaiah in the temple; Zacchæus; the penitent thief; the three thousand on the day of Pentecost;

Saul on the way to Damascus; the Ethiopian eunuch; the jailor at Philippi, &c. (2) Job's language *the effect of the apprehension of the Divine character and perfections.* The natural effect of such apprehension is the perception of the enormity of all sin, and the discovery of our own depravity in particular — more especially of our sinful thoughts and words in respect to God and His dealings with us. Similar effect in the case of Isaiah in the temple: "Woe is me, for I am undone: because I am a man of unclean lips, and I dwell among a people of unclean lips: for mine eyes have seen the King, the Lord of Hosts" (Isa. vi. 5). Some effect on Peter at the miraculous draught of fishes: "Depart from me, for I am a sinful man, O Lord." That in ourselves and others which needs only to be rightly known to be abhorred.

"Vice is a monster of such hideous mien,
  That, to be hated, needs but to be seen."

That is, to be seen as Job saw it, in the light of God's character and perfections. All sin in itself filthy and abominable. Probably seen to be such even by the lost,—"an abhorring to all flesh." The right abhorrence of sin and of ourselves, that accompanied with true repentance. Judas abhorred himself, and committed suicide. (3) *Self-abhorrence a part of true repentance.* The pardoned and accepted penitent is ashamed and loathes himself for his sins (Ezek. xvi. 60—63; xxxvi. 25—32). Self-abhorrence a part of the believers sweetest experience, and will always accompany it. (4) *Sin infinitely loathsome to a holy God.* Sin seen by God exactly as it is. If loathsome to Job, still infected with it, how much more to his spotless Creator! Hence (i.) The long-suffering patience and forbearance of God, in bearing with a world of sinners. (ii.) The riches of His grace in providing for such loathsome creatures a Saviour and a substitute in the person of His own Son, and in taking them again for His own children. (iii.) The mightiness and preciousness of the Holy Spirit's operation, that renews and sanctifies the objects of the Divine abhorrence. (5) *Not the least favourable sign when we are most loathsome in our own eyes.* Cannot be worst with us when we see ourselves as God sees us. We are often worst when we think ourselves best. The Pharisee in the temple contrasted with the Publican. "God be merciful to me, a sinner," a better sign than —"God, I thank Thee that I am not as other men are." Job most commended by God when most loathed by himself. The believer most beautiful in God's eyes when blackest in his own (Cant. i. 5). (6) *Self-abhorrence a benefit to ourselves.* Has the tendency—(i.) To keep us from pride. (ii.) To render us forbearing and compassionate towards others. (iii.) To prepare us to act as intercessors on behalf of fellow-sinners. Job not directed to pray for his three friends till he was brought to abhor himself.

7. *His declaration of repentance and humiliation.* Verse 6.—"I repent in dust and ashes" —that is, sitting in them—a token of humiliation and repentance (Job. iii. 6 ; Luke x. 13). The catastrophe of the poem in these last words of Job. Probably one of the secret purposes of God in permitting the temptation and trials. Not intimated at the first ; but "known unto God are all his works from the beginning of the world." One of God's objects in all the temptations and sufferings of his children, their perfection. That perfection connected with their self-humiliation and repentance (Ezek. xvi. 61—63 ; xxxvi. 31). The aim of God in His dealings with His people, to humble them in order to their exaltation—to empty in order to fill them (Is. lvii. 15 ; lxvi. 2). Observe, in regard to

Repentance—

1. *The Nature of it.* A change of mind— of views, feelings, dispositions ; with a corresponding change of conduct. This change mainly in relation to God : hence, "repentance toward God." Job's repentance *inward*, but manifesting itself *outwardly*, both in his words and actions, negatively and positively. No more murmuring and discontent with his lot. No more unworthy thoughts of God. No more bitterness against his three friends. "Fruits meet for repentance."

2. *The Author of it.* God himself, through the agency of the Holy Ghost. Repentance directed *to* God is a repentance proceeding *from* God. The exercise of it our own ; the grace of it, God's. Every good and perfect gift, and true repentance among them, from the Father of lights. "Then hath God granted unto the Gentiles repentance unto life." "Peradventure God will give them repentance to the acknowledging of the truth." The Son of God the author of saving repentance equally with the Father. Christ "exalted by the Father's right hand to be a Prince and a Saviour, to give repentance unto Israel and the remission of their sins." The Holy Ghost sent both by the Father and the Son for this purpose. God himself the Author of Job's repentance, when the three friends and Elihu had laboured for it in vain.

3. *The Means of it.* The truth, as exhibited by the Holy Ghost. The exhibition of the truth regarding God and ourselves. The prodigal "came to himself"—had his eyes

opened to the truth as to his conduct and condition, as well as to the character of his father, and said : "I will arise and go to my father." Job's repentance after the Divine exhibition of the truth to him regarding God and his own sin. The aim of the Almighty in his prolonged address and the manifestation of Himself. "After that I was instructed, I smote upon my thigh" (Jer. xxxi. 19). Ministers and preachers directed "in meekness to instruct those that oppose themselves, peradventure God will give them repentance to the acknowledging of the truth." Repentance and remission of sins to be *preached in Christ's name.* The preaching of Christ as the Father's gift of love to sinners, and as the sinner's Substitute through whom we are invited back to God, one of the most effectual means of producing "repentance unto life."

4. *The Effects of it.* The reception of blessing. Job prepared by his repentance for the turning of his captivity, with all the blessings that followed it. "Repentance into life." Job further prepared for becoming *a blessing to others.* Only directed to intercede for his friends when he repented himself. Deep personal repentance necessary as a preparation for usefulness to others. Christ's most useful and honoured servants usually those who have been brought through the deepest exercises of self-humiliation and repentance ; witness Paul, Luther, John Bunyan. Isaiah's self-abasement and repentance in the temple preparatory to his answering : "Here am I ; send me." Peter's commission as a fisher of men preceded by his exclamation : "Depart from me ; for I am a sinful man, O Lord."

II. The Divine Verdict. Verse 7.—

"And it was so that after the Lord had spoken these words unto Job, the Lord said to Eliphaz, the Temanite, My wrath is kindled against thee and against thy two friends ; for ye have not spoken of me (*Hebrew*, 'to me ;' *Greek Version*, 'before me,'—the controversy viewed as carried on in the presence of the Almighty as umpire, as all controversies should) the thing that is right (solid or true), as my servant Job hath " (*Greek version*, 'against my servant Job '). Eliphaz particularly named in the verdict as having been the first and chief speaker, and probably the oldest and most distinguished of the three friends. Perhaps the others influenced by his sentiments and example. *Responsibility connected with age, position, and attainments,* Job spoken of by the Almighty as "my servant" in presence of the three friends, as before in the presence of Satan and the angels. Observe—(1) *God's judgment of his servants often very* different from that of men, and even of their fellow servants. (2) *God never ashamed to acknowledge his faithful servants.* One of the rewards of the faithful servant to be so acknowledged at the last day (Matt. xxv. 21; Rev. iii. 5). (3) *True godliness a thing that stands the fire.* Comes out as it went in, only purer. (4) *God often most pleased with us when we are least pleased with ourselves.* Job now loathing himself, and sitting in ashes. From the verdict itself observe—

1. *All disputes sooner or later settled by God Himself.* A reason for patience and forbearance, meekness and moderation in controversy. "Judge nothing before the time, until the Lord come, who both will bring to light the hidden things of darkness, and will make manifest the counsels of the heart" (1 Cor. iv. 5). One great lesson of the book to teach us to wait patiently for that day (James v. 7—11). The cause of God's servants sooner or later righted by God Himself. He who has a good and righteous cause may afford to wait.

2. *God's decision often very different from man's expectation.* The decision apparently expected by all but Job to be in favour of the three friends. God's judgment entirely the reverse. Job magnified and the friends mortified. "Man looketh on the outward appearance, but the Lord looketh on the heart." "Not he that commendeth himself is approved, but whom the Lord commendeth" (2 Cor. x. 18). Job's cause essentially good, though marred by many unbecoming utterances; the friends' cause essentially bad, though supported by many precious and excellent truths.

3. *God's views in regard to individuals and their conduct not to be readily gathered from appearances.* The three friends *seemed* to be enjoying God's favour, and only Job to be lying under His displeasure. Exactly the reverse of the reality. So with Jesus, and the priests and rulers who condemned him. "We esteemed him stricken, smitten of God, and afflicted" (Is. liii. 4). Men often stand differently in God's account from what they do in their own and that of their fellow men. "A light thing to be judged of you or of man's judgment" (1 Cor. iv. 4). God often most angry when there is least appearance of it. May be angry with men for what they are most proud of themselves.

4. *God sometimes displeased with otherwise good men, and those bearing a high character for piety and morality.* Such apparently the character of the three friends. What then the case of men living in constant and open rebellion against Him? "If the righteous scarcely be saved, where shall the ungodly and the sinner appear?" (1 Pet. iv. 18).

276

5. *God angry with men on account of things not rightly and truly spoken.* God's displeasure as truly against sinful words as sinful actions. "By thy words thou shalt be justified, and by thy words thou shalt be condemned" (Matt. xii. 37). The reason— "Out of the abundance of the heart the mouth speaketh." Generally, as a man's words are, so is he.

6. *God jealous of his own glory and the character of his servants.* The things not rightly and truly spoken by the three friends were—(1) *In regard to God Himself.* So English version. (2) *In regard to His servant Job.* So Greek version. Their sin in regard to Himself, that they gave an unjust view of God as always visiting the ungodly in this life with tokens of his displeasure, and that the righteous are uniformly free from outward strokes. Their sin against Job the consequence of this—in making Job out to be a great, though perhaps secret, transgressor. The character of God's servants as dear to Him as His own. "He that toucheth you, toucheth the apple of His eye" (Zech. ii. 8). God requires that we not only speak zealously *for* Him, but truthfully *of* Him.

7. *God's anger against sins of omission as well as sins of commission.* "Ye have not spoken," &c. Not enough that we do not speak stoutly and blasphemously *against* Him. Do we speak truly and faithfully *of* him?

III. The Direction. Verses 8, 9.—

"Therefore take unto you seven bullocks and seven rams, and go to my servant Job, and offer up for yourselves a burnt offering; and my servant Job shall pray for you: for him will I accept; lest I deal with you after your folly (or 'impute folly to you, so as to punish it), in that ye have not spoken of me the thing which is right, like my servant Job. So Eliphaz the Temanite, and Bildad the Shuhite, and Zophar the Naamathite, went and did according as the Lord commanded them: the Lord also accepted Job" [in his intercession for his friends, according to verse 8]. The direction twofold, having reference to both parties in the controversy; involving humiliation to the one, and giving honour to the other.

1. In reference to the *three friends.* These directed as penitents to seek pardon and reconciliation with God through Job's mediation. Observe—(1) *God reproves only in order to reconciliation.* (2) *Pardon and reconciliation with God possible under a dispensation of mercy.* Our happiness that God's anger against us for sin may be turned away. Unspeakably awful were that anger to be everlasting. Yet this the case

of all who continue impenitent, and who reject the Saviour that God has provided (John iii. 36). (3) *God takes the first step in the matter of a sinner's reconciliation with Him.* Gives direction to Eliphaz about the means of securing it. Our quarrels with God begin on *our* part; reconciliation on *His.* "God was in Christ reconciling the world unto himself. Now then we are ambassadors of Christ as though God did beseech you by us" (2 Cor. v. 21). (4) *With God alone, not only to say whether there should be reconciliation with Him on the part of sinners, but how the reconciliation was to be effected.* "In vain they do worship me, teaching for doctrines the commandments of men" (Matt. xv. 9). To be reconciled with God we must comply with God's prescription.

The friends directed to *offer sacrifice.* Repentance implied; yet the direction not to *repent* as Job had done, but to *take a burnt-offering.* No reconciliation between God and man without sacrifice. No reconciliation without forgiveness of sin, and no forgiveness without satisfaction to justice, and no satisfaction without sacrifice. Hence all covenants made by God with men accompanied with sacrifices. Animal sacrifices appointed before and under the Law of Moses as the means of reconciliation with God. These only types or figures, for the time, of the true sacrifice, the woman's Seed; the bruising of whose heel by the Serpent in his suffering and death was to take away sin (Gen. iii. 15). Impossible that the blood of bulls and goats should make satisfaction for human transgression. Its object impressively to teach that without shedding of blood and the substitution of life for life, there is no remission (Heb. ix. 18—23). The promise of a Divine-human Saviour and Substitute never to be lost sight of. Every slaughtered victim but pointed to that Substitute.—*Seven* bullocks and *seven* rams here prescribed; to indicate (1) *The heinousness of sin* which is to be atoned for; (2) *The sufficiency of the great Sacrifice* provided to take it away; (3) *The insufficiency of every other.* The same number frequently offered under the law (Lev. xxiii. 18). Observe—*All sin to be at once confessed and taken to the blood of Christ for its forgiveness.* "If we confess our sin," &c. (1 John i. 7, 9). The conscience kept clean and peace maintained by constant confession to God (not to a priest), and faith in the sacrifice offered on Calvary.—The friends to *go to Job with their offering.* Thus expressing both their penitence and their faith. The act humbling to themselves, but honouring to Job. The first last, and the last first. Job had humbled himself before God; they

must humble themselves before him. Having joined in accusing him, they must join in seeking his mediation. Job *alone* to be regarded in the matter of acceptance; yet the friends to "go" to him. So Christ alone regarded as the ground of a sinner's acceptance with God, yet sinners to go to Him in penitence and faith. "To him shall men come; in the Lord shall all the seed of Israel be justified, and shall glory" (Is. xlv. 24, 25). Job apparently to officiate as priest in presenting the friends' sacrifices to God. This usually done, *before* the law, by the head of the family or the eldest son; under the law, by Aaron and his sons after him, as types for the time being of the great Priest—one not after the order of Aaron, but of Melchizedec, who was at once both priest and king; and made a priest immediately by God himself, without either predecessor or successor in the office. Job here exhibited as another type of the great High Priest, through whom we draw nigh to God.

2. In reference to *Job.* Job directed to "pray" for the friends, and to mediate with God on their behalf, with a view to their pardon and acceptance. In a sinner's reconciliation with God, sacrifice not to be without prayers. As a priest, Job must pray as well as offer the sacrifice for the friends. So Christ, the true Priest of our profession, offered in the midst of this sacrifice on the cross, the prayer: "Father forgive them;" and on the night immediately preceding it, the prayer in the Upper Room—a specimen of the intercession which He is ever making for His people within the veil. In the prayer as well as in the sacrifice offered up by Job, the friends doubtless united. So we are exhorted, "having such an High priest who is passed into the heavens," to "come boldly to the throne of grace, that we may obtain mercy, and find grace to help us in every time of need" (Heb. iv. 18). God's promise in regard to Job—"Him will I accept." *Him,* not you. Him, and you in him, for his sake. So men accepted with God not in themselves or on their own account, but in Christ and on Christ's account. Believers made "accepted in the Beloved." "The Lord is well pleased for His righteousness sake." (Eph. i. 6; Is. xlii. 21). Observe—(1). *Believers, being accepted in Christ, not only find acceptance for themselves in their prayers, but for others also.* The honour put upon Job, that put upon all Christ's members, who in Him are made "kings and priests unto God." (2) *Acceptance with God the thing to be aimed at in all our prayers and services.* Duties not only to be discharged and prayers offered, but their acceptance to be sought and looked for.

(3) *Acceptance certain, where there is obedience to God's commands and faith in His Son.* "Him will I accept." Acceptance itself certain—the time and manner of its manifestation with God Himself. Part of the Spirit's work to testify it. Also made known by its effects, and indicated in Providence. God's promise sufficient. (4) *The person to be first accepted, then the prayer or service.* "Him," his *person*, "will I accept." (5) *God's method to accept and bless one man for the sake of another.* So in temporal matters—God blessed Laban for Jacob's sake, and Potiphar for Joseph's sake (Gen. xxx. 27; xxxix. 5). This principle at the foundation of the Gospel and the scheme of redemption. Sinners pardoned, accepted, and blessed on Christ's account,—the whole plan of salvation. The Gospel thus found in Job as elsewhere in the Old Testament. The Scriptures testify of Christ.

Job honoured by being made a priest in behoof of his friends, *after his deep humiliation, his severe suffering, and their proud contemptuous treatment of him.* So with Christ — sufferings first, then "the glory which should follow." So with Christ's members—"If we suffer with Him, we shall also be glorified together." Job *prepared*, by his previous suffering and humiliation, for the honour now put upon him. Much of the painful discipline of God's children doubtless intended to qualify them for the exercise of their priestly office. Believers thus much more able to sympathize with others. "A deep distress hath humanized my soul."—*Wordsworth.* So Christ Himself suffered, that He might be a merciful High Priest. Prosperity, honour, and extensive usefulness, only safe when preceded by humiliation. Christ's most honoured servants usually those who have been most humbled under the mighty hand of God. "Before honour cometh humility." Job thus honoured after his rejection by his friends, a type of Christ exalted at God's right hand, as "a Priest upon His throne," after His rejection by the priests and rulers. "The stone which the builders rejected is become the head of the corner."

The honour put upon Job *God's highest testimony in favour of His servant.* The Divine testimony—(1) To his *faith* ; (2) To the sincerity of his *repentance* ; (3) To the uprightness and excellence of his *general character.* To be a priest and an intercessor for others, implies—(1) Deep consciousness of the evil and demerit of sin which necessitates such an arrangement; (2) High regard for the honour and interests of God, and the claims of His justice and government; (3) Tender compassion and love towards those for whom the duty is exer-

278

cised; (4) A forgiving spirit towards those who are enemies to ourselves. Believers most Christlike when interceding for others. To pray for ourselves is human ; to pray for others Divine. Job's general character and power as a man of prayer and intercession for others, indicated in the only other passage in the Old Testament where his name occurs. Mentioned as such in connection with Noah and Daniel, in Ezekiel xiv. 14. The privilege and duty of believers in the New Testament to pray for others, and to mediate their reconciliation with God by publishing Christ and persuading men to be reconciled to God through Him (2 Cor. v. 19—21). Only known in eternity how great the blessing derived by the world and individual men from the intercession of faithful and loving believers. In answer to their prayers, sickness removed and life spared ; prison doors opened ; nations preserved in tranquillity ; preachers of the Gospel aided and blessed in their work ; sinners awakened and souls saved (Gen. xx. 7, 17; James v. 14—16; Acts xii. 4—7; 1 Tim. ii. 1, 2; Col. iv. 3, 4; 1 John v. 14—16; James v. 16—20).

Job's praying for his friends an evidence—(1) Of the heartiness of his forgiveness of them; (2) Of the sincerity of his repentance. His prayer the most effectual means of opening their eyes and softening their heart. Ministers often more useful by their prayers than by their preaching, Saul probably impressed more by Stephen's praying than by his disputing.

IV. Job's Deliverance. Verse 10.— "And the Lord turned the captivity of Job, when (or while) he prayed for his friends." Observe—

1. *The Author of the deliverance.* "The Lord turned," &c. Job's trouble began from Satan's malice ; his deliverance, from God's mercy. No mischief done by the serpent, but can be undone by the woman's Seed. God able to deliver from Satan's malice, but Satan not able to hinder God's mercy. God Himself the deliverer both of His Church collectively and of His people individually. "When the Lord turned again the captivity of Zion," &c. (Ps. cxxvi. 1). "I was delivered out of the mouth of the lion : and the Lord shall deliver me from every evil work" (2 Tim. iv. 17, 18). See also 2 Cor. i. 10.

2. *The Deliverance itself.* "Turned the captivity of Job." His trouble a captivity. His *outward* condition resembling such. Stripped of all his property; separated from his friends; sitting on an ash-heap, as in the mire of a dungeon; his body covered with sores and filth. Strictly a captivity, as being for the time delivered into Satan's

hands, who treated him with all the rigour he was capable. Bodily affliction and outward trouble perhaps more frequently from Satan than we are aware. "Ought not this woman whom Satan hath bound, lo, these eighteen years," &c. (Luke xiii. 16). Job's captivity an *inward*, as well as an outward one. Job, in his affliction, held bound by his own spirit, as well as the spirit of evil. To a child of God, the most real and painful captivity to be shut out from God's sensible favour and fellowship, and to be shut up in spiritual darkness and desertion. Job's captivity turned, as being now released both from Satan's hand and his multiplied sufferings, whether external or internal. His disease removed, according to Elihu's teaching (ch. xxxiii. 24, 25). What His servants say in words, God Himself confirms by deeds. His disease probably removed as quickly as it had been inflicted. Diseases often instantaneously removed by the finger of God. Examples : The leprosy of Miriam, Gehazi, and the lepers in the Gospel. God's plaister as broad as Satan's sore. Job now also restored to the light of God's countenance and the sensible enjoyment of His favour and friendship. Also according to Elihu's doctrine (ch. xxxiii. 26). These deliverances and blessings followed by others afterwards narrated : plenty instead of poverty ; the affection of friends instead of their alienation ; a numerous and happy family instead of a desolate household.

The deliverance of Job a type—(1) Of the deliverance wrought by the Father for Christ, in terminating His sufferings, raising Him from the dead, and exalting Him to His own right hand in glory. (2) Of the deliverance of believers at death. Their departure a release ; a harvest of joy after a seed-time of tears ; a morning of gladness after a night of weeping. (3) Of the deliverance to be wrought for the Church and for creation at large at the resurrection of the just,—the binding of Satan, the emancipation of the creature from the bondage of corruption, and the creation of the new heavens and the new earth " wherein dwelleth righteousness."

3. *The Time of the deliverance.* "When he prayed for his friends." Observe—(1) *We are often best promoting our own welfare when praying for that of others.* According to the principles of the Divine government, that we should be most blessed ourselves when most solicitous about the happiness of our fellow-men. "The liberal soul shall be made fat." "He that watereth others shall be watered himself." "There is that scattereth and yet increaseth ; and there is that withholdeth more than is meet, and it tendeth to poverty." Selfishness the greatest

hindrance to our happiness. The ocean receives the influx of rivers as it exhales its waters into the air. The earth receives rain as it gives its moisture to the plants that grow on it. The clouds are replenished as they distil their treasures on the earth. To seek mercy and deliverance for others often the shortest way of obtaining it ourselves. (2) Job, in experiencing deliverance when praying for his so-called friends (often to him real enemies), typical of the Lord Jesus Christ. His deliverance and exaltation immediately subsequent to His prayer, "Father forgive them, for they know not what they do."

V. **Job's increased possessions.** Verses 10, 12.—"Also the Lord gave Job twice as much as he had before. So the Lord blessed the latter end of Job more than his beginning : for he had fourteen thousand sheep, and six thousand camels, and a thousand yoke of oxen, and a thousand she-asses." The "end of the Lord" now seen, "that the Lord is very pitiful" (James v. 11). God's thoughts towards his suffering people, "thoughts of peace and not of evil, to give them an expected end" (Jer. xxix. 11). Job seen to be right in blessing God both while giving and taking away. God takes away from His own only in order to give more. Every apparent loss to a believer a real gain. As easy with God to give riches as to take them away. His to give power to get wealth, by blessing honest endeavours: Made Jacob rich in spite of all Laban's endeavours to prevent it. Easy with God to restore what either Satan or man may take from us. Observe—(1) *God takes care that none loses by serving Him.* What is lost in God's service is made up with more than compound interest (Matt. xix. 29). God a liberal rewarder. Gave Job not only as much as he had lost, but its double. Raised faithful Joseph from a dungeon to a palace ; and, from a slave, made him prime-minister of Egypt. Valentinian lost his tribuneship for Christ, and was ultimately made Emperor. (2) *The faithful believer's latter end always better than his beginning.* Bildad's words true of every believer (chap. viii. 7). A good man's last days and last comforts generally his best. At eventide light. The best wine reserved by God for his obedient children to the last. As yet unknown what He has prepared hereafter for them that love Him (1 Cor. ii. 9). (3) *God able to do more than we either ask or think.* Job only asked to be shown why he was so severely afflicted and wherein he had sinned. God removes the affliction itself, and makes him twice as rich as he was before. Job only thought to remain practising repentance in dust and ashes. God not only withdrew him from his ash-heap, but restored him to more than his former dignity and prosperity. (4) *Believers often prepared for greater blessing by previous suffering and humiliation.* Prosperity more difficult to bear than adversity, and requires preparation for it. Job prepared for his great increase of wealth by his previous troubles, and the self-abasement which preceded it. Believers prepared for being glorified with Christ by being made first to suffer with Him. Comfort in the thought that present troubles may be only the preparation for future triumphs. (5) *The history of the Church and the world, as well as of individual believers, foreshadowed in the experience of Job.* The sufferings of the Church and of believers in this present time "not worthy to be compared with the glory that shall be revealed." The creation itself to be "delivered from the bondage of corruption into the glorious liberty of the children of God." The new earth "wherein dwelleth righteousness," to experience a blessing, and yield an abundance unknown since the entrance of sin (Rom. viii. 18—22; 2 Pet. iii. 13; Ps. lxvii. 4—7).

VI. The changed conduct of friends.

Verse 11.—"Then came unto him all his brethren, and all his sisters, and all they that had been of his acquaintance before, and did eat bread with him in his house: and they bemoaned him, and comforted him over all the evil that the Lord had brought upon him; every man also gave him a piece of money (*Greek* version, 'an ewe-lamb;' *Latin* version, 'à sheep;' same word used only in Gen. xxxiii. 19, and Josh. xxiv. 32), and every one an ear-ring of gold." This friendly conduct due to the favour of God. Included in the turning of Job's captivity. "When a man's ways please the Lord, he maketh even his enemies to be at peace with him,"—much more his friends. Job's relations and acquaintances probably now more influenced by God's hand on *them*, than by the removal of His hand from *him*. God's favour shown to Jacob in turning Esau's heart towards him, and causing Jacob to "see His face as the face of an angel." God's hand formerly recognized by Job in the alienation of some of his friends; now doubtless acknowledged by him in the affection of others. The hearts of men, whether friends or enemies, "in the hand of the Lord, who turneth them whithersoever He will." The former alienation of friends no small ingredient in Job's cup of sorrow. Their present affection no trifling element in his restored happiness. Friendship the wine of life. "Poor is the friendless master of a

world." Heaven itself sweetened by the presence of loving friends.

They "did eat bread in his house." No small joy to Job after his long isolation, that, his leprosy being now removed, he could have his friends partaking of a meal with him in his own house. Type of Jesus with His friends around Him at the marriage-supper of the Lamb. So also, after His resurrection, the scattered disciples gathered again to Him, and "ate and drank with Him" during the forty days of His sojourn with them (Acts. x. 41).

The visit one of congratulation as well as condolence. "They bemoaned him and comforted him," &c. Talk of past griefs an enhancement of present joy. Observe— (1) *God gives not only compensation but consolation to His suffering children.* "As one whom his mother comforteth, so will I comfort you" (Isa. lxvi. 13). God at no more loss for instruments to comfort His children than to correct them. (2) *Consolations come best in God's time.* Satan's malice in keeping back these friends before, now over-ruled for the enhancement of Job's restored happiness. (3) *Patience to have her perfect work.* "The Lord, after ye have suffered awhile, make you perfect, strengthen, stablish, settle you." The consolation of these friends all the sweeter, now that Job, after the dark night is over, can rejoice in the sunshine of God's favour. Yet Job still a mourner and needing consolation. His hearth still desolate, with neither son nor daughter at his board. No absolute freedom from trouble till we reach the land where the inhabitants shall no more say, I am sick; and where all tears are wiped away.

They comforted him "over all the Lord had done unto him." God's hand in Job's troubles acknowledged by the friends as well as himself. Observe—(1) God the Author and Dispenser of our trials, whatever the instruments. Safest and best in our trouble to regard the *first* cause, rather than secondary and subordinate ones. God to be acknowledged in all events as ordering all things by his His Providence, even to the fall of a sparrow. Evil, as well as good, from the Lord, however He may please to send it. Acknowledged even by Satan— "Put forth *thine hand* now," &c. (2) *Praise due to God for His grace in sustaining under past troubles, and His mercy in delivering out of them.* These, as well as sending the troubles, among the things which the Lord had done to Job. Such praise to mingle with our consolations. So Jethro, after coming out to meet Moses, praised God on hearing of "all that the Lord had done unto Pharaoh and to the Egyptians for Israel's sake, and all the travail that had come upon them by the way, and how the Lord delivered them " (Exod. xviii. 8—11). A picture of heaven and the enhancement of its joy.

The friends *brought presents to Job*, according to the custom of the country. These probably intended—(1) To testify their affection and esteem; (2) To contribute to the restoration of his estate. The sincerity of our friendship and affection evinced by what it costs us. The extent of our sympathy with the suffering measured by what, according to our ability, we contribute to their relief.

VII. Job's Second Family. Verses 13—15.

" He had also seven sons and three daughters. And he called the name of the first, Jemima; and the name of the second, Kezia; and the name of the third, Keren-happuch. And in all the land were no women found so fair as the daughters of Job : and their father gave them inheritance among their brethren." Children given to Job to take the place of the former one, and to sooth the sorrow for their removal. Given in the same number and proportion of sex. As easy with God to give children as riches. Observe—(1) *God's compassion and liberality towards His children.* Job to have every loss made up to him, even to his deceased children. God keeps account of His servants' losses, in order to make them up, either here or hereafter. (2) *Pious children not lost but gone before.* The reason why Job's cattle are doubled, but not his children. The former strictly lost, but not the latter. Those dying in the Lord not lost, but hidden from our view. Job's godly children, buried under the ruins of their dwelling, now only waiting to welcome him to the Father's house. All to be received again in body and spirit at the resurrection of the just. His children, therefore, really doubled, as well as his riches—ten with himself on earth, and ten with God in the better country. Precious comfort to pious parents in the death of their infant or believing children. These only separated from them for a time by a thin veil. The star goes out of sight with us only to shine in another hemisphere. Those not lost who are sleeping in Abraham's bosom. Those not to be considered as lost to us who are found to Christ. Those hardly absent who are in their Father's house. Such removals sanctified to believing parents. Children and friends departing in the Lord, only a part of the "plenishing" of our future home, making heaven more home-like. Help to make up the "sublime attractions of the grave." A purifying and elevating influence in the thought, that while a part of us is on earth, another part is glorified in heaven.

The fact fitted to turn our natural sorrow into a sacred joy.

" Who could sink and settle to that point
Of selfishness—so senseless who could be,
As long and perseveringly to mourn
For any object of his love, removed
From this unstable wild, if he could fix
A satisfying view upon that state
Of pure, imperishable blessedness
Which reason promises, and Holy Writ
Ensures to all believers ? "— *Wordsworth.*

Job, as made the father of a new family after his restoration, a type of Christ after His resurrection and ascension—receiving, as the eternal Father, or Father of eternity, the Gentiles as His children in the place of the Jews, who had previously constituted the covenant family, but who through unbelief were now for a time cut off. " Behold, I was left alone ; these, where had they been " (Isa. xlix. 20—23). " Instead of the fathers shall be the children."

Job's second daughters distinguished for the beauty of their persons. God not only gave children, but well-favoured ones. An enhancement of the gift. God's gifts to his tried people often come with a special mark of their origin upon them. A beautiful countenance pleasant to look upon. A reflection of the beauty which is in Him who is the sum and source of all beauty. Beauty vain as compared with grace, but in itself no mean gift and a fit accompaniment to a gracious spirit. A shadow or image of the beauty of holiness. The sweetest countenance, that which is lighted up by the inward grace of the Spirit. The beauty of the outward man made prominent in the Old Testament; that of the inward man in the New. New Testament females not praised for their beauty, but for their love and good works (Rom. xvi). Christ's second, or Gentile family, given Him after his ascension, distinguished for their spiritual beauty. The Holy Spirit only then given in his fulness. The promise then fulfilled: " Thy people shall be willing (liberal, princely, or free-will offerings) in the day of thy power, in the beauties of holiness " (Ps. cx. 3).

The names of Job's second daughters recorded. A mark of honour. The names of many of Christ's daughters recorded in the New Testament; those of all of them in the Book of Life (Rom. xvi. 1—15; Phil. iv. 3). The names of Job's daughters significant, and probably given to indicate at once the beauty of their person, and the sweetness of their disposition; as well as to commemorate the mercy of God in his own deliverance. " Jemima " denotes "a dove," or dovelike; but may include in it the idea of "day." " Kezia " is the Cassia, a fragrant spice. " Keren-happuch " is either " the

Horn of Paint," or "the Inverted Horn;" according to the Greek version, the Horn of Plenty. Thus perhaps Job praised the God of his life for changing his night into day, giving him the oil of joy for mourning, and turning again his captivity as the streams in the south. True piety will not forget God's benefits.

Job's estate divided among his daughters as well as his sons. Indicative—(1) Of his riches; (2) Of the excellent character of his daughters; (3) Of the harmony and love existing in his family. Job's second, no less than his first children, distinguished for their unity and mutual affection. Children a blessing when love unites them to one another, and to God as their common Father. Believing women, as well as men, made heirs of God and joint-heirs with Christ the Elder Brother. In Christ, neither male nor female, bond nor free (Gal. iii. 28; Col. iii. 11).

Job's Age and Death. Verses 16, 17.— "After this lived Job an hundred and forty years, and saw his sons and his son's sons, even four generations. So Job died, being old and full of days." Observe—

1. *His Age.* His years thought to have been doubled as well as his estate. In this case, seventy years old at the time of his trouble, and two hundred and ten at the time of his death. Thus attained a greater age than either Abraham or Isaac. Hence earlier than either of them, though probably during part of his life contemporary with one, if not both. Corresponds with the internal evidence of the book. To be remembered in reading his speeches. His troubles all the more keenly felt as occurring before he had reached, for that period of the world, the meridian of life. His death not until he had reached, even for that period, a good old age. Length of days a part of wisdom's wages (Prov. iii. 16). Job's short season of trouble and adversity succeeded by a long life of comfort and prosperity. *God a rich rewarder of his faithful servants.* Joseph thirteen years a slave; eighty a prime-minister. Our light affliction, which is but for a moment, worketh for us a far more exceeding, even an eternal weight of glory. Weeping endureth for a night, joy cometh in the morning of a nightless day. Short toil, long repose; short conflict, endless triumph. A temporary cross, an eternal crown. Every tear of God's faithful servants a seed which shall one day produce a rich harvest of ceaseless joy.

2. *His Experience.* Spared to see not only his children, but his children's children, "even to the fourth generation." The promise of the Old Testament (Ps. cxxviii. 6; Prov. xvii. 6). Mentioned as the happiness of Joseph in Egypt (Gen. l. 23). Job still more abundantly compensated for the loss of his former family. The words of Eliphaz made good in his experience (chap. v. 25). Died, not only old, but "full of days." Satisfied with the days given him, both as to their number and character. Now as willing to die as ever he had been wishful to live. Ready now, like Simeon, to depart in peace, his eyes having seen God's salvation. Had experienced the goodness of the Lord in the goodness of the living; and now, like Jacob, waited for his salvation in a better world. Had, like David, "served his generation by the will of God;" and now ready, like a tired and happy child, to fall asleep. Comes to his grave, as Eliphaz had said, "like a shock of corn, fully ripe." The evening of his days a tranquil sun-down. At eventide light. Typical of millennial blessedness in the evening of the world. A numerous family of the "Everlasting Father," like the drops of dew from the womb of the morning. His children all in holy and happy fellowship. No more falling out of the brethren by the way. No adversary nor evil occurrent. No Canaanite in the house of the Lord. Satan bound, and no more allowed either to deceive the nations or molest the Church.

3. *His Death.* "So Job died." Piety no exemption from death. Till Christ Himself comes, the grave receives the members as well as the Head. Death to Job no king of terrors. The messenger from his Father's house with a—"Well done, good and faithful servant; enter into the joy of thy Lord." The good fight fought, the weary warrior only called off from the field. Had already experienced great deliverances, but was now to experience the greatest of all. A king and a priest on earth, Job died, like all believers, to exercise his royal and priestly office in a land never stained with tears, and in a temple never defiled with sin.

FINIS.

Notes.

CHAPTER I.

VERSE 5 : " *Have sinned and cursed God in their hearts.*" Various opinions as to the meaning, in this passage, of the Hebrew word here rendered " cursed." בֵּרְכוּ (or *bērechoo*) the *Piel* (transitive or intensive) form of the verb בָּרַךְ (*bārach*) to kneel, generally meaning to "bless ;" *i.e.*, to cause to kneel, such being the usual attitude in receiving a blessing. The word, however, is generally believed to have also the opposite meaning of "cursing." So GESENIUS, who compares it with the Arabic اِبْتَرَكَ (*ibtaraka*), and the Ethiopic, *bāraka*, both having the opposite meanings of blessing and cursing. 1 Kings xxi. 10, where the same form of the verb occurs, is referred to as a clear case in which it is used with the meaning of *cursing*. The same word which is twice employed by Satan (chap. i. 11; and ii. 5), and once by Job's wife (chap. ii. 9); where it is no doubt used in the same sense as in the verse before us. This use of the word in two opposite senses variously accounted for. LEIGH, in his "Critica Sacra," connects these opposite meanings on the ground that the word expresses what a man ardently wishes or calls for, whether it may be good or evil, salvation or perdition. CAREY, in his "Notes on Job," connects them by observing that both blessing and cursing are acts of religious worship represented by " kneeling," the relation between them being like that of *precor* and *imprecor* in Latin. Others account for this use of the word on the principle of *Euphemism* ; blasphemy having been so abhorred by the ancients that they avoided the very term, as the Latins used *sacrum* for *execrandum*. So VATABLUS, DRUSIUS, and COCCEIUS. Perhaps a better way of accounting for these opposite meanings of the word, is that adopted by CODURCUS, who classes it with those verbs in which the *Piel* form gives a *privative* meaning, and so makes it convey an idea the opposite of that originally implied in it. Thus חָטָא (*khata*) to " sin " has its *Piel* form, חִטֵּא (*khitte*), to " put away sin," to expiate it or free

from it; עֶצֶם (*'etsem*), a "bone," gives a verb in the piel form עִצֵּם (*'itsem*) to " break the bones." WEMYSS explains this double and opposite meaning on the ground of irony or antiphrasis ; "they may have blessed God," *i.e.*, "may have offended Him "(!) The most satisfactory way for the word being used in this sinister sense, and one very generally adopted by modern interpreters, is that of giving it the meaning of " bidding farewell to," and so of " renouncing ;" it being customary on parting with a friend, to wish him farewell. So *valere* in Latin and χαίρειν in Greek are known to be used (TERENCE, *Andria* iv. 14; EURIPIDES, *Medea*, 1044. This view of " renouncing " is adopted by SCHULTENS, J. H. MICHAELIS, LOWTH, DE WETTE, &c. HUFNAGEL renders the word "forgotten." EWALD and HIRZEL: "forsaken." ZÖCKLER, in LANGE's Bible-work, observes that it indicates a hostile farewell.

Many, however, prefer to retain the original meaning of blessing, but under various aspects. AMBROSE, JEROME, AQUINAS, MAYER : Have sinned, and blessed God for their good cheer. COCCEIUS : Have sinned, and blessed God for their success. SANCTIUS : Have sinned in the way they blessed God ; viz., being puffed up by their riches and prosperity. BROUGHTON, CARYL, and POOLE : Have blessed God too little, or have lightly regarded Him ; thus approaching to the sense of cursing. Some supply a negative particle, or give a negative meaning to the copula (*cato*), as in Ps. ix. 18; Prov. xvii. 26; "have sinned and not blessed God." So CALVIN, GOOD, and SANCTIUS. BOOTHROYD and YOUNG retain the idea of blessing by giving the copula the sense of "though ;" "have sinned though they blessed God." Others do the same by rendering אֱלֹהִים (*elohim*) not " God," but " the gods; "—meaning the idols of the heathens or angelic beings; " have sinned and blessed the elohim or gods." So ADAM CLARKE, PARKHURST, and Dr. LEE, who explains by : " Have inclined to idolatrous practices," and refers to Isa. lxvi. 3, as giving the same expression. The word, however, being without the article, would seem to require to be rendered either "God" or simply "god;" and, as SCOTT the translator of Job has observed, no mention is made in the book of any other god or gods than the true one.

The ancient and later versions vary in their way of rendering the word. The SEPTUAGINT, according to the ordinary edition, has: "Have thought evil against God," in which it has been followed by the COPTIC; while the COMPLUTENSION has: "Have blessed God." In the ITALA, or older Latin version, it is: "Have cursed the Lord;" while the VULGATE has: "Have blessed God." The SYRIAC has: "Have mocked." The ARABIC: "Reproached." The CHALDAIC: "Provoked to anger." COVERDALE: "Have been unthankful to God." LUTHER, like the Vulgate: "Have blessed God." MARTIN's French version: "Have blasphemed God." DIODATI's Italian: "Have spoken evil of God."

Verse 11. "*And he will curse thee to thy face.*" (*Margin:* "If he curse thee not.") The clause susceptible of a variety of interpretations. The two particles at the commencement אִם לֹא (*im lo*) "if not," variously rendered and understood. By most they are regarded as expressive of an oath; with the rest of the form of imprecation understood; as, "may I perish," or such like; *i.e.*, "if he will not curse thee," &c. So VATABLUS, PISCATOR, HUFNAGEL, and ZOCKLER, who makes the expression equivalent to "verily." DATHE supplies, "Let me be accounted a liar," *i.e.*, "if he do not curse thee," &c. SCHULTENS thus views

the words as expressive of Satan's impudence and contumacy. Others supply "see;" *i.e.*, "if he will not," &c. So CAREY. Some who retain the sense of "blessing" in the verb, render the particles, "if not;" *i.e.*, "if thou do not smite him, then, no doubt, he will bless thee to thy face, or in thy presence." So Dr. LEE, COLEMAN, YOUNG, &c. SANCTIUS, following the Vulgate, renders the verb in the past tense, as expressive of *habit,*—"[See] if he hath not [merely] blessed thee to thy face." *i.e.*, hypocritically. ADAM CLARKE: "He will bless thee (or be pious) according to thy appearances for him." GOOD and BOOTHROYD interrogatively: "Will he still bless thee?" TOWNSEND: "Then he will bless thee in thy presence," as he has hitherto done. Job thus to be proved a mercenary worshipper according to either sense of the verb: If thou smite him he will curse thee to thy face; if not, he will still bless thee, but only to thy face. The same meaning of "renouncing," however, probably attached to בֵּרֵךְ (*bĕrēch*) here as in ver. 5; only, as has been remarked by NOYES and others, the phrase is stronger here, as importing an utter and public renunciation of religion as a vain thing. So SCHULTENS, DATHE, UMBREIT, ROSENMÜLLER, STICKEL, &c. BARTH, in his "Bible Manual," has: "He will renounce or even blaspheme thee to thy face." MERCER: "He will curse thee," *i.e.*, deny thy providence, and say it is vain to serve thee. Similarly POOLE: "He will reproach thy providence." It is well known that the heathen frequently reproach their gods in misfortune:" *Deos atque astra crudelia vocat.*"

CHAPTER II.

VERSE 4. "*Skin for skin; yea, all that a man hath will he give for his life.*" The expression "skin for skin" acknowledged to be a proverbial one. Its precise meaning not so obvious, though its general drift, as used by the Evil One, is sufficiently apparent. The Septuagint and Vulgate translate as we do; the one rendering the preposition by ὑπερ, and the other by *pro.* The Chaldaic has: "Member for member." So BERNARD, who renders the words: "Limb for limb." Martin's French Version has: "Every one will give skin for skin." Some, as PARKHURST and WEMYSS, render the phrase: "Skin after skin." Others, as PINEDA and TIRINUS: "Skin upon skin," *i.e.*, all skins; or, according to POOLE, all outward things. YOUNG

translates: "A skin for a skin." The meanings thus reducible to four:—

1. *The skin of another for one's own skin.* So VATABLUS, TIRINUS, SEB. SCHMIDT, MAIER. "Skin," in this view, is regarded by some as equivalent to "body," as in chap. xvi. 15; xviii. 13; xix. 26; like Horace's "*Pelliculam curare jubet.*" So ROSENMÜLLER and HUFNAGEL. By others it is viewed as equivalent to "life:" what a man holds as dear to him as his skin, *i.e.*, his life, he will give to save his life. So GESENIUS and HUPFELDT, after ORIGEN who says: "A man will give a skin, which is sold for money, to save his own skin, *i.e.*, his life." Others: Job will give the skin of his cattle, even that of his children, to

save his own. So GREGORY, EPHREM SYRUS,
MERCER, PISCATOR, DRUSIUS, NOYES, &c.
Like that of Terence: "*Proximus sum
egomet mihi.*" In this view, the proverb is
explained by what follows.

2. *Like for like*; *i.e.*, any one gives
that; men part with anything for a full
equivalent. So CODURCUS, HIRZEL, CONANT:
Equivalent for equivalent. MAURER: Job
may well give up the rest to keep his life.
FAUSSET: One thing for another. EWALD:
All is subject to barter. UMBREIT: One
article is given for another; but life is
dearest to all: Job is satisfied so long as he
is not obliged to give up *that*. CODURCUS:
The origin of the proverb in the general
practice of barter, or in the use of animals
instead of men in sacrifice. POOLE: Skins
or spoils of beasts in early ages the most
valuable property men could acquire; hence
became the chief representative of property.
GOOD and BOOTHROYD: "Skin "an equivalent
for riches, furniture, &c. PINEDA and SCHUL-
TENS: In the expression "skin for skin,"
GOOD thinks the word issued in two different
senses,—property is given for life. COBBIN
remarks that probably ransoms used also
to be paid in skins. CAREY sees in the
proverb a sort of *reductio ad absurdum:* a
man will not part with his skin unless you
supply him with another; on no terms will
he part with his life: hence Job, to save his
life, will part with his religion.

3. *Limb for limb*; or, one thing parted
with to save the rest: a less noble member
will be given up for a nobler one, as an arm
for a head. So MENOCHIUS, MUNSTER,
A. CLARKE, &c. The view of some of the
fathers: a man will put up his hand to ward
off a blow from his eye. So GREGORY, OLYM-
PIODORUS. Dr. LEE: Men willingly give
up a worse thing for a better: hence, much
more will a man give up all he has for his life.
COCCEIUS: Job can easily afford to part
with all while he keeps his life,—his possessions being as it were a skin or covering to
his person to protect and warm him: the one
of them—the less valuable—he easily lets
go to keep the other. So SCHLOTTMANN,
DELITZSCH, and ZÖCKLER in Lange, who
regards the life to be preserved as not so
much the animal or life-function, as the soul
which causes and conditions it.

4. *Skin upon skin*. So Dr. THOMASS, in
The Homilist: " like—sovereign after sovereign; all the sovereigns a man has," &c.;
"skin," equivalent to property; life dearer
than all. Job willing to have skin upon skin
taken from him to save his life. SCHULTENS
remarks that the Arabs call possessions
the outer skin—friends and relations the
inner one. According to OLSHAUSEN, the
meaning is: So long as thou dost not touch

his person, he will not attack thee. COLE-
MAN thinks an allusion is made to the
terrific skin-disease with which Satan purposed to afflict Job. CONANT regards the
rendering of the copula *caw* before "all"
by "yea," as embarrassing the sense, by
anticipating the reader's judgment of the
relation of the two clauses, and proposes to
read it as usual: "*And* all that a man hath,"
&c. UMBREIT, and after him FAUSSET,
would put "skin" and "life" in the two
clauses in antithesis to each other, and render
the copula "but." So DE WETTE: People
give up other things; but they take care of
their life—the highest value put upon *that*.
According to BARNES, the idea is: If Job
was so afflicted as to have his life endangered,
he would give up his religion to save it.

VERSE 7. "*Smote Job with sore boils.*"
The Septuagint and Vulgate, followed by
MARTIN and DIODATI in their French and
Italian versions, render the words which
describe Job's disease, "a bad or malignant
ulcer." The word שְׁחִין (*shekheen*) which we
render "boils," derived from a root not used
in Hebrew, but appearing in the Arabic سخن
(*sakhana*) to be hot, inflamed, fevered. Job's
disease, according to GESENIUS, NOYES, and
others, a kind of black leprosy, formerly prevailing in Egypt (Deut. xxviii. 27); called
Elephantiasis, from the skin being covered
with black scales, and from the mouth, feet,
and legs swelling enormously, while the body
becomes emaciated. The disease not attended
with great pain, but with much debility of
the system, uneasiness, and mental depression. Both Pliny and Lucretius speak of
it as a disease peculiar to Egypt; the former
calling it, "*Ægypti peculiare malum.*"
PISCATOR and CASTALIO render the singular
noun collectively "ulcers;" as our English
version, "boils." MORUS renders it: An
inflammation. VATABLUS: Pustules,—boils
from heat, such as were inflicted on Egypt
(Exodus ix. 10), and threatened to Israel
(Deut. xxviii. 27). GRYNÆUS, after SCHUL-
CENS: An inflammation, of which the ulcers
were the effect. ADAM CLARKE queries
whether it was not the small-pox. GOOD
makes it: Burning ulcerations,—the *baras*
of the Arabs. WEMYSS: Foul ulcers. LEE:
A burning disease. FRY: A sore ulcer.
CAREY: A malignant ulceration,—the disease nearly proving fatal in the case of
Hezekiah (Isaiah xxxviii. 1—21); in Job's
case, of a very virulent form. The
Homilist: One universal inflammation.
FAUSSET: A burning sore. CONANT, after
EWALD, observes that the singular here has
the effect of a collective. So HEILIGSTEDT:
Malignant ulcers. ZÖCKLER, in Lange,
regarding it as the *Elephantiasis*, speaks of it

285

as the Arabian, or worst kind of leprosy; called also *lepra nodosa*, or *tuberculosa*, from the greatly swollen lumps, or boils, which give to the extremities the appearance of an elephant's legs, whence its name. BARNES, after GOOD, calls it a universal ulcer, attended with violent pain and constant restlessness; named by the Arabs, *gudham*, and said to produce a grim, distorted, lion-like set of features, hence called *Leontiasis*. CHRYSOSTOM observes that it made Job like Lazarus, but in a far worse condition. The Jewish doctors say that the disease, in Job's case, lasted a whole year; while SUIDAS—we know not on what grounds—makes it to have continued seven.

CHAPTER III.

VERSE 5. "*Let the blackness of the day terrify it.*" Margin, "*Let them terrify it as those who have a bitter day.*" The expression בְּכִמְרִירֵי-יוֹם (*chimrire-yom*) gives rise to two classes of interpretations, according as the initial letter is regarded as a part of the noun, or as a particle. In the former case, it is best rendered "obscurations, or darkenings of the day:" from כָּמַר (*chamar*), an unused root, signifying "to be dark, or blackened, as with heat." So GESENIUS, who thinks the reference is to eclipses, always regarded by the ancients as portending calamities. The view also of BOCHART, NOTES, FAUSSET, ZÖCKLER, in "Lange," &c. The first of the two nouns is thus regarded as an augmentative; the simple form כְּמִירָא (*chemira*, from כְּמַר *chemar*, "to be dark, or sad"), being applied in Syriac (Matt. xvi. 3) to a dark and lowering sky. So SCOTT, who translates it "greatest sorrows," and in his metrical version: "Boding signs from all the quartered sphere." LEE classes it with a sort of superlative in Arabic words signifying colours, &c., formed by reduplicating the last radical letter, and occasionally introducing a long vowel; and so renders the expression "blackest things of the day"—blackest terrors. Of the earlier interpreters, JUNIUS and TREMELLIUS render the words: "Darkness of the day." COCCEIUS: "Blacknesses of the day,"—dark, hot, pestilential vapours. PAGNINUS, VATABLUS, and PISCATOR: "Heats, or vapours, of the day." The Tigurine translators: "Most burning heats of the dog-days." Bishop HALL: "A continued darkness." Among later expositors, GOOD has: "Blasts of noontide"—the *simoom*, or hot wind of the desert. FRY: "Black blasts of the day." BOOTHROYD: "Thunder-clouds, blackening the day." JENOUR: "Black darkness by day." CAREY and CONANT, after GESENIUS: "Darkenings of the day." BERNARD: "Black vapours." OLSHAUSEN, DILLMANN, and DELITZSCH: "Darknesses of the sun," as from clouds.

HERDER, viewing the expression figuratively: "Blackness of misfortune." UMBREIT understands by it: "Magical incantations which darken the day." GROTIUS and CONURCUS regard the first noun as used for כְּמִיר (*chimre*) or chemarims, a name given in the Old Testament to certain idolatrous priests (Zeph. i. 4; Hos. x. 5; 2 Kings xxiii. 5), and thus denoting "priests of the day,"—astrologers, who distinguish the character of days as lucky and unlucky, like the Roman "*prefecti fastorum.*"

If the initial letter כ, however, be viewed not as a part of the noun, but as a particle, it may be regarded either as one of comparison, or of emphasis. In this case, the noun מְרִירֵי (*merire*) will be viewed as derived from מָרַר (*marar*) "to be bitter," as in Deut. xxxii. 24. So the translators of the ancient versions appear to have understood the expression. The Septuagint has: "Let the day be cursed;" or, according to GRABE's emendation: "Let the day be troubled." The VULGATE: "Let the day be involved in bitterness." The TARGUM, SYRIAC, and AQUILA: "As bitternesses of the day." So MARTIN's French: "As the day of those to whom life is bitter." DIODATI's Italian: "The bitterest days." MERCER and MORUS, like our marginal reading: "As those bitter in days." MUNSTER, after the Syriac: "The bitternesses of the day." SEB. SCHMIDT: "As bitternesses of day,"—rather to be so called than day itself. SCHULTENS: "As it were, the bitter things of the day," —viz., misfortunes. ROSENMÜLLER: "According to the bitternesses of the day"— calamities which render a day black and ill-omened, as Amos viii. 10. ADAM CLARKE: "The bitterness of a day." YOUNG: "As the most bitter of days." LE CLERC derives the word, as the Septuagint appears to have done, from אָרַר (*arar*) "to curse:" "as those who curse the day."

VERSE 8. "*Who are ready to raise up their mourning;*" Margin: "*A leviathan.*" A

286

clause which has also two classes of interpretations, according as the noun לִוְיָתָן (*liyathan*) is regarded as derived from לָוָה (*larah*) "to twist into folds," and so meaning a serpent, or sea-monster, as in all the ancient versions; or from לָיַךְ (*layak*) "to mourn," and so denoting lamentation, as in our authorised version. Of the other two words in the clause, הָעֲתִידִים (*ha-'athidhim*, from עָתַד ('*athadh*), unused in Hebrew but found in Chaldaic; in the *Pael* form, עַתֵּד (*attedh*) "to appoint or prepare," like the Arabic عَتَد (*attedu*, Vth. conjugation, to be skilled in an art), rather denotes, "those who are skilled, or expert." So Schultens, Gesenius, Noyes, and Zöckler. The Septuagint has : "He who is to rouse up," &c. The Vulgate : "Those who are prepared," &c. So the Targum, Aquila, and Symmachus, as well as Luther, Martin, and Diodati. עוֹרֵר (*'orer*), properly "to raise up from sleep," as Ps. xliv. 23. So De Wette : "To wake up." Scott, observing that the sign of the infinitive is omitted, views the expression as a periphrasis for the future tense of the indicative, according to the Syriac idiom. The same appears to have been done by the translator of the Septuagint.

Of those who regard the noun as derived from לָוָה (*lueah* = لَوَى) "to twist," with the final syllable תָן (*tan*) as the terminative form of the noun, are Bochart, Schultens, Dathe, and Gesenius, who understands by the word a serpent of the larger kind, especially, as in chap. xli. 1, a crocodile. The Septuagint, followed by the Coptic and the Itala, renders it, "the great whale." The Vulgate leaves the word untranslated, "Leviathan." According to Noyes, the word is a common name to denote monstrous animals of different kinds, here perhaps a monstrous serpent. Barnes : Used here to to represent the most fierce and powerful of animals. Zöckler : The great dragon—the enemy of the sun and moon—which, according to an ancient superstition, seeks to cause darkness by swallowing them up. According to Grotius, Codurcus, and Seb. Schmidt, the persons in the text are represented as skilled in stirring up monsters by magic incantations. Döderlein and Umbreit understand, "charming of serpents." According to Osiander, Noyes, Barnes, and others, the reference is to sorcerers, or persons supposed to possess the power of

making any day fortunate or unfortunate, or even to call forth terrific monsters from the forest or the deep, in order to gratify their own malice, or that of others, of whom Balaam is viewed as an example. Wemyss has : "Skilled in conjuring up Leviathan." Dr. Chalmers understands : "Magicians or conjurers who raise, or pretend to raise up, infernal spirits by their spells. Hitzel, Hahn, and Schlottmann : the Constellation called the Dragon, between the Great and the Little Bear, or some other of the same name. So Maurer, who refers to the words of Horace as a parallel : "*Quæ sidera excantata voce Thessala lunamque cælo deripit.*" Lee, understanding the whale, or some other monster, translates : "Who are ready to stir up a leviathan,"—which, he adds, none but the most desperate would do. Bernard : "Ready to arouse the crocodile." Conant : Skilled to rouse the Leviathan." Hufnagel observes that the expression is probably employed to denote the undertaking of a most perilous task. Jenour renders it, "Prepared to stir up the Leviathan to battle;" *i.e.*, persons who have life, and are prepared to expose themselves to certain death. So Boothroyd, who observes that in chap. xli. 8—10, to arouse Leviathan is represented as inevitable destruction. Various other allusions are conjectured to be made in the expression. Reference is supposed by some to be made to the invocation of Typhon, the author of destruction, whose symbol was the crocodile, such as is found on a papyrus roll from Thebes. So Carey, who also thinks an allusion may be made to an ancient custom of the Egyptians in hunting the crocodile on a particular day, and then, after killing it, throwing its dead body before the temple of their god. Faucett thinks a reference is made to those who claimed the power of controlling or rousing up wild beasts at their will. Calmet sees an allusion to the Atlantes, a people of Ethiopia, who were ready to kill and eat the crocodile. Sir G. Wilkinson, quoted by Carey, refers to the Tintyrites, who were expert in catching and overcoming the crocodile in the water. Adam Clarke thinks that persons are meant who are desperate enough to provoke the crocodile to tear them in pieces. M. Henry thinks allusion is made to fishers who, being about to strike the whale or crocodile, curse it with the bitterest curses they can invent, in order to weaken its strength (!) Some of the older interpreters, as Cocceius, Tirinus, and Cartwright, thought the allusion also to fishers, but as cursing under the vexations and disappointments of their calling. Hutchinson, of Edinburgh, regarded the allusion as made to mariners, who, in a storm, curse the day they went to sea, and are ready by their wishes to evoke the sea-monsters to swallow them up. CHAPPELOW, followed by COBBIN, thinks those persons meant whose business it was to curse the days esteemed ominous and inauspicious. SANCTIUS accounted for the expression on the ground that in execrations men commonly introduce things that are most horrible, as the leviathan. SCOTT, in his metrical translation, has: "Rouse fierce Leviathan from his oozy bed ;" and adds, that probably the crocodile is meant, and that as it is natural to lament those who so miserably perished with bitter imprecations on the disastrous day, Job calls for the assistance of such language. Another construction of the words has been proposed, and has been adopted by SCHULTENS, and ROSENMÜLLER: "Let those who are skilled in that art, curse or brand it (his birthday) as the day that rouses up Leviathan" —as the dire mother of direst evils. Similarly COLEMAN: "as men promptly curse the day that evokes the crocodile from the deep." Leviathan was regarded by AMBROSE, and the fathers in general, as another name for Satan, whom Christ was to encounter and overcome. GREGORY thought the persons in the text to be those who fell by the devil's deceit. GUALTHER supposes them to be those who evoke Satan by incantations and witchcrafts. OSIANDER regards the word as equivalent to רְפָאִים (rephraim) the "spirits of the dead" mentioned in chap. xxvi. 5. (in the E.V. "dead things"); and considers it here as denoting the Evil One, and spectres in general. By most of the earlier interpreters, who regarded the word as denoting some monster, the *whale* was the creature understood. So COCCEIUS, SCULTETUS, JUNIUS and TREMELLIUS, &c.

The sense of "lamentation," as in our authorised version, from לָיָה (layah)= אָלָה (alah) "to mourn," was generally preferred by the earlier translators, as PISCATOR, MERCER, PAGNINUS, MORUS, MONTANUS, and VATABLUS. MARTIN, in his French version, has: "Who are ready to renew their mourning." DIODATI, in his Italian: "Always ready to make new lamentations." FRY renders the passage: "who are ready at raising their lamentations;" but supposes that the word is derived from לַ (loo), "O that ;— this syllable perhaps being the commencement of the solemn dirges or ululations of hired mourners, still common in the East; like the ἐλελελελεῦ of Io in Prometheus Vinctus, the *ulula* of the Irish, and the וְלוּלוּ (ululu) of the Arabians. According to TOWNSEND, the ideas of mourning and Leviathan are combined,—the mourning and that which was the cause of it; the

allusion being to the idolatrous persecuting power that afflicted the Church of God between the commencement of the empire of the first Ninus, or Nimrod, and the calling of Abraham ; and to the too late repentance of those who cursed the day when they gave their assistance to the founding and consolidating of that empire.

VERSE 14. "Which built desolate places for themselves." הַבֹּנִים (habbonim), "who built up," not "who built again." So ZÖCKLER, as against CASTALIO, GOOD, and others. CAREY: "Who were building," i.e., when overtaken by death. חֳרָבוֹת (kharābhoth), plural of חָרְבָּה (hhorbah) dryness, desolation, from חָרֵב (kharebh), to be dried up, devastated; waste places, ruins: "who built ruins for themselves," i.e. splendid edifices, as palaces or tombs, soon to become ruins or great stone heaps. So GESENIUS, UMBREIT, WINER, NOYES, CONANT, ZÖCKLER, and most moderns. VULGATE: "Who build solitudes for themselves." The SEPTUAGINT appears strangely to have read the word as the plural of חֶרֶב (kherebh), a sword. The TARGUM, SYRIAC, and ARABIC, like the Vulgate, have: "Solitudes," or "desert places." So MARTIN and DIODATI. LUTHER: "The wilderness." PAGNINUS: "Solitary places." DRUSIUS: "Destroyed places." CASTALIO: "Ruins," fallen palaces or towers. MERCER and VATABLUS, like the Vulgate: "Solitudes." JUNIUS: "Splendid buildings in desolate places, where no one would have expected such." JENOUR: "Waste places." BOOTHROYD: "Ruins of former cities." GOOD: "Ruined wastes." YOUNG: "Wastes." LEE: "Places now desolate." PINEDA, followed by SCHULTENS, DÖDERLEIN, CAREY, and others, think the reference is to sepulchral monuments, as the pyramids. PARKHURST: "Dreary sepulchral mansions, where the body is *wasted*, or consumed." SCOTT, the translator, thinks that sepulchral grottoes are meant, such as those at Thebes, or the pyramids : "Whose burial mansions load the desert plains." MICHAELIS regards the words as equivalent to חֲרָמוֹת (kharāmoth), and translates it, "temples, shrines, mausoleums." ZÖCKLER observes that, though πι-χραμ (pi-chram, "the temple"), is the name given to the pyramids, it is, perhaps, not the same with חָרְבִּית ; and that if mausoleums are intended, they are not necessarily those of Egypt. HIRZEL, with EWALD, DELITZSCH, STICKEL, &c., thinks mausoleums or pyramids are to be understood, and points to the ruins of Petra. BARNES observes that some of the most wonderful sepulchral monuments are found in the land of Edom to this day. TOWNSEND thinks the reference may be to the building of the Tower of Babel. The expression לָמוֹ (lamo), "for themselves," is understood by some as meaning: "To make their name immortal." So MERCER, VATABLUS, DRUSIUS, ADAM CLARKE. CODURCUS: "In order to display their wealth and power, enjoy retirement, or form new colonies." GRYNŒUS: "To resist all-destroying death." CAREY: "For their own tombs." COLEMAN: "As habitations for themselves, either while living or dead." NOYES thinks that the expression is so nearly pleonastic that it may be omitted. BARNES, on the other hand, thinks it full of emphasis; the ruinous structure being made for themselves alone. UMBREIT sees in it Job's irony breaking out from the black clouds of melancholy.

CHAPTER XIX.

VERSE 23. "O that my words were now written!" The "words" understood as either—(1) Those now to be uttered. So JEROME, PISCATOR, CARYL, HENRY, &c. As an everlasting monument of his faith in the resurrection.—MAYER. Such as would come within the inscription on a rock; therefore, those contained in verses 25—27.—SCOTT. Or (2) Those which he had already uttered in defence of his innocence. So MERCER, NOYES, &c. All the declarations he had already made of his integrity, together with his solemn appeals to God.—WEMYSS. BARTH, in his "Bible Manual," combines both: "The words of his lamentation and sorrow misunderstood by his friends, as well as those of his hope, which he was now about to utter." GREGORY understood not so much his "words," as his sufferings. "Words" put for the things themselves.—POLYCHROMIUS. Instead of "written," WEMYSS and KITTO would read "recorded." CAREY: "Engraven." SCOTT says: "Written, perhaps, on linen: painting on linen very ancient among the Egyptians; the use of papyrus a later invention."

"O that they were printed in a book!" בַּסֵּפֶר (bassēpher) "in the, or a, book;" סֵפֶר (sēpher) from סָפַר (sāphar) to shave, engrave, write. וְיֻחָקוּ (veyukhākoo) "and were printed, or engraved;" Hophal form of חָקַק (khākak) to cut, make an incision, engrave. So GESENIUS. PISCATOR, however, thinks that the verb חקק does not mean to "engrave," but to "delineate" or "paint," and refers to Isaiah xxx. 8; xlix. 16; Ezek iv. 1. MERCER observes that the order of the words is inverted, and translates: "That they might be engraven in a book." JUNIUS and TREMELLIUS: "Carved out." PAGNINUS: "Written out." SCULTETUS thinks that the first clause indicates simple writing; the second, writing in an entire book, or among histories or public records. So SCHULTENS understands בַּסֵּפֶר: "in a public record, in which more remarkable events were registered." J. H. MICHAELIS translates: "Who will put them into the book, that they may be engraven?" GRYNŒUS: "Engraven for eternal remembrance in all time to come." ADAM CLARKE: "Fairly traced out in a book, formed either of the leaves of the papyrus or on a sort of linen cloth." KITTO: "Engraven on a tablet of wood, earthenware, or bone." SCOTT observes that letters were supposed by Sir Isaac Newton to have been invented by the Edomites, from whom Moses learned them when he fled into Midian. NOYES renders the words: "O that they were marked down in a scroll!" CONANT: "In the book, where all might read them," as indicated by the presence of the article. CAREY thinks some particular book intended, perhaps that part of the Bible then extant, containing the records of the Creation and the history of the Antediluvian World. ZÖCKLER, however, thinks this unnecessary, and translates: "In a book,"—any book, or skin prepared for writing.

"That they were graven with an iron pen and lead in the rock for ever!" יֵחָצְבוּן (yekhatsebhoon), Niphal, or passive form of חָצַב (khatsable), to cut, or cut out; "were cut." So GESENIUS and J. H. MICHAELIS. KITTO: "Graven." WEMYSS: "Sculptured." BOOTHROYD: "Cut deep." לָעַד (la-adh) from עָדָה ('adhah, to pass); עַד (adh), primarily, a passage or progress; then perpetuity. GROTIUS conjectures the reading to have been לְעֵד (le'-edh) "for a testimony," which agrees with the version of the

Septuagint. בָּעֵט (be-et), "with a pen;" עֵט (ēt) being, according to Gesenius, a pen for writing on stone or metal. "And with lead," *i.e.*, poured into the letters carved with the iron pen for greater distinctness. So JARCHI, PISCATOR, BOCHART, JUNIUS, SCHULTENS, UMBREIT, and most of the moderns. The TIGURINE version, however : "In lead." So the VULGATE : "With a plate of lead." LUTHER : "Upon lead." A. CLARKE : "On leaden tablets." WEMYSS, BOOTHROYD, and KITTO : "On rolls of lead." TOWNSEND quotes PAUSANIAS, who says that near Helicon he was shown some leaden tablets, on which were engraven the works of HESIOD. TIRINUS observes that writing tablets among the ancients were made not only with wax, but *lead*, as is seen in the ancient tombs of Fabricius and Valesius, near Naples. It is known that with the Romans public acts were inscribed on leaden plates, as well as brazen ones. PLINY ("Nat. Hist., xiii. 11) says: "Formerly people wrote on the leaves of the palm and the inner bark of certain trees: afterwards, public monuments were written on rolls of lead ; and soon after, private ones on linen and wax." SCULTETUS observes that for security against fire, Job wishes the inscription to be also in a rock. So MERCER, PISCATOR, JUNIUS, and TREMELLIUS. PAGNINUS and MONTANUS, however, translate: "In stone." PINEDA: "On a pillar of stone." CODURCUS and SCHULTENS think the allusion is to sepulchral pillars, with epitaphs inscribed on them. SEB. SCHMIDT translates: "On tables of stone." POCOCKE remarks that hieroglyphical characters are cut in the rock in the tombs of the kings at Thebes. SCOTT observes, from GREAVES, that an inscription of one line in the same characters is found in the second pyramid. LEE, after SCHULTENS and HALES, notices that it was customary with the ancient Arabs of Yemen to inscribe their precepts of wisdom on the rocks, in order to preserve them. HUFNAGEL observes that Orientals appear to have been accustomed to make inscriptions on the rocks. NIEBUHR saw such in his travels. Those high up on the rocks, at the Nahr el Kelb, near Beyroot, now pretty well known. A. CLARKE remarks that all the modes of writing then in use are apparently alluded to in this passage.

VERSE 25. "*For I know,*" &c. Various opinions as to the nature and object of Job's present declaration. It has been viewed (1) as *a confession of his faith*, in opposition to the calumnies of his friends. So DRUSIUS, &c. More especially of his faith in the promised Redeemer. So SCHULTENS,

MICHAELIS, ROSENMÜLLER, HALES, GOOD, PYE SMITH, &c. Of his faith in a future judgment for the vindication of his character. So SCOTT. Of his faith and hope in reference to the resurrection of the body. So CAREY, &c. Of his faith in the Redeemer, and an assured expectation of a happy resurrection.—CARYL. M. HENRY calls it "Job's creed or confession of his faith," declaring that he sought a better country (Heb. xi. 14), and appealing to the coming of the Redeemer. A. CLARKE says: "Job speaks prophetically ; pointing out the future redemption of mankind by Jesus Christ, and the general resurrection of the human race." Dr. CHALMERS observes that—"To the consolations of a good conscience, Job adds those of a far-seeing faith." Others view it as (2) the declaration of *an expectation which the close of the book shows to have been fulfilled*. So KITTO. An expression of the conviction that he should himself see the restoration of his honour and health ; and that, although reduced to a perfect skeleton, he should be gladdened by an appearance of God on his behalf, and not on that of the others. So CHRYSOSTOM, JOHN of Damascus, and some of the early Greek Fathers; also some of the Reformed, as MERCER, GROTIUS, LE CLERC ; those on the Continent with rationalistic tendencies, as JUSTI, KNOBEL, HIRZEL, STICKEL; supernaturalists, as DATHE, DÖDERLEIN, BAUMGARTEN-CRUSIUS, KNAPP, AUGUSTI, UMBREIT ; even some of the directly orthodox, as v. HOFFMANN and HAHN ; and in our own country WEMYSS, STUART, BARNES. Some regard it as (3) the expression of his *hope of seeing God in a spiritually glorified condition beyond the grave*. So EWALD, SCHLOTTMANN, DELITZSCH, DILLMANN, ZÖCKLER, DAVIDSON in his Introduction ; and of Jewish interpreters, ARNHEIM and LOWENTHAL.

The force of the Copula at the beginning of the sentence has been variously understood. "For :" as in our English version. So the VULGATE, DUTCH, GENEVA, COVERDALE, and SCHULTENS. "Since," or "because :"—the older Hebrew interpreters. "Indeed :" so the SYRIAC, ARABIC, CASTALIO, PISCATOR, COCCEIUS, JUNIUS, and TREMELLIUS. "But :" LUTHER, DE WETTE, EWALD, LEE, CONANT, &c. DIODATI has : "Now." MERCER and PAGNINUS : "Also." MONTANUS : "And truly." SCULTETUS : "Yet"—notwithstanding my complaints. MENOCHIUS and DRUSIUS : "Yet,"—whatever you object to me, and although you continue wicked. DELITZSCH : "But yet." COLEMAN : "Verily." PYE SMITH : "Surely." FRY : "That." ZÖCKLER : "And." PINEDA observes: "The expression יָדַעְתִּי (yadhá'ti) 'I know,' excludes all doubt, as in Gen. xlviii. 19." SCULTETUS: "Implies the faith which is both knowledge and trust." GRYNŒUS and HIRZEL: "The conviction that will not be shaken by opponents." The "I," emphatic—"I know, if you do not," So FAUSSET, HIRZEL: "I, for my part," in opposition to those who deny him. GRYNŒUS: "I, in whom the arrows of God and man are now sticking, as in a wicked person."

"*My Redeemer liveth.*" גֹּאֲלִי (*goali*) from

גָּאַל (*gaal*) to redeem, deliver; my Redeemer. So GESENIUS. COCCEIUS: From

גָּאַל (*gaal*) to claim as one's own, as Ps. cxix. 154; Isa. xliii. 1; Ruth iv. 6; Ps. lxxiv. 2; Isa. xlviii. 20; used also of things sold and consecrated: hence to redeem:

גֹּאֵל (*goel*), a relative who can claim or vindicate the honour, life, goods, &c., of another as his own (Lev. xxv. 25; Ruth iii. 13). SCULTETUS: Properly, a blood relation, who claims or recovers the alienated goods of a near relative, or himself from slavery, or demands his blood, if slain at the hands of the slayer (Num. xxxv. 12). GROTIUS: A deliverer, in a general sense. SCHULTENS and ROSENMÜLLER: An avenger. GRYNŒUS and PYE SMITH: A deliverer or avenger; here pointing to the Messiah. UMBREIT: A blood-avenger—meaning God who should appear as his avenger before his death. LEE and HALES: An avenging Redeemer; viz. God, who should clear him of all charges. TOWNSEND: His Redeemer, (1) As the restorer of his temporal prosperity; (2) The vindicator of his innocence; (3) The redeemer of his soul from sin and death: the several offices of the Goel united in the person of Jesus Christ, who took our nature and become our Kinsman. גֹּאֵל (*goel*) originally applied to a person whose duty it was to maintain the rights, interests, and reputation of a near relative, either by repurchasing his mortgaged inheritance, by marrying his widow and saving his family from extinction, by redeeming him from servitude, or by avenging his blood; applied elsewhere to God as a Deliverer from any kind of calamities. This believed, by some, to be the application here, without any reference to Christ. So MERCER, CALVIN, GROTIUS, LE CLERC, PATRICK, WARBURTON, HEATH, KENNICOTT, DATHE, DODERLEIN, Dr. WETTE, BARNES, &c. GESENIUS:

גֹּאֲלִי חָי (*goali khai*), "my Redeemer liveth,"—God Himself will deliver me from these calamities. STICKEL observes: גָּאַל

(*goel*) here used without הַדָּם (*haddam*), "of blood;" hence employed in the more general sense of a judicially valid intercessor and deliverer of life and property. So OLSHAUSEN and CONANT. Here a deliverer, not an avenger of blood. On the other hand, FAUSSET observes: Job uniformly despairs of restoration and vindication in this life (chap. xvii. 15, 16); therefore the allusion here to a vindication in a future life. According to MERCER, the Redeemer here is God the Father. So called as delivering the godly from their troubles. GROTIUS: The view of the Jews and Socinians; but the office only appropriately ascribed to God the Son, man's Kinsman; and so always understood elsewhere. Redemption peculiarly ascribed to Christ. Job's Redeemer the God-man, the "living one," yet standing on the earth. SPEIFFER: The Incarnate Word. PINEDA, TIRINUS, SCULTETUS, &c.: The opinion of the fathers as well as of the earlier and modern evangelical interpreters in general. EPHREM SYRUS: A prediction of the incarnate Emmanuel. MUNSTER: "Of the Messiah, as the first-fruits of them that slept." COCCEIUS: Christ is Redeemer, as (1) Near of kin, (2) Redeeming by that right; (3) Taking the prey from the unrighteous possessor, and that without paying him any price; (4) Paying a price to the true proprietor. All redemptions and deliverances of the Church and people of God ascribed to Christ, as Zech. ix. 11; Isa. lxiii. 9; Gen. xlviii. 16. TOWNSEND observes: Job, in the age of error, may be considered as the faithful witness in his day to the hope of the Messiah. BARTLE, in his "Bible Manual," remarks: Though having no well-defined conception of the Messiah as his Redeemer, Job yet expresses his expectation that God would prove a Redeemer to him, and the Vindicator of his innocence. PINEDA: In the expression "My Redeemer," Job declares his singular love to Christ, as in the expression "My brother" (1 Kings xxx. 32). CARTWRIGHT: Job appropriates Christ to himself, and calls Him his own.

חָי (*khai*) "liveth" or "living;" always lives, is immortal and eternal. So DRUSIUS and MENOCHINS. CARTWRIGHT: "Liveth," without distinction of time as past or future; God the Eternal I am: Christ, as God, lives *from* eternity, while, as man, believes *to* eternity: "Liveth,"—hath life in Himself as the Prince of life; also denotes His strength and power, as Ps. xxxviii. 19. COCCEIUS: "Job opposes the Redeemer's life to his own death: perhaps, also, alludes to the death of the Redeemer Himself" (Rev. i. 18). SCULTETUS: Although he shall die

291

for me, yet is He the true and living God; the faith of the Old Testament saint is a true and saving faith in Christ (Gen. xlviii. 16; Acts iv. 12; xv. 11). JUNIUS: "My Redeemer liveth;" therefore, though men may bury my cause in oblivion, it remains safe with God. Others read: My Redeemer is the Living One. So SCOTT, PYE SMITH, Dr. HENDERSON. HALES translates: My Redeemer is living. Dr. THOMAS, in the "Homilist": My living Redeemer; like אֵל חַי the living God,—having life in Himself.

"*And that he shall stand at the latter day upon the earth.*" A clause very variously interpreted and understood. אַחֲרוֹן (*akharon*) from אָחַר (*akhar*, to remain, tarry, or be behind; here rendered "at the latter day;" properly "the last," but may be used adverbially, with בְּ or לְ understood, as in Isa. viii. 23; xxx. 8, &c.; and then meaning "at last." "At length he shall stand (or appear) on the dust," *i.e.*, on the earth. So GESENIUS, HEILIGSTEDT, MAURER, NOYES. Or "Over the tomb," as EWALD, ZÖCKLER, and others. To witness for him: DELITZSCH. To protect him: FAUSSET. To deliver him: ZÖCKLER. Ancient translators seem to have read the verb variously; as אָקוּם "I shall rise." So the VULGATE: "At the last day I shall rise from the earth." יָקִים "He shall raise up." So the SEPTUAGINT: "He shall raise up my skin on the earth." יָקוּם "He shall stand up or appear." So the SYRIAC and ARABIC: "In the end he shall appear on the earth." The TARGUM: "And afterwards his redemption shall rise upon the earth." In this way THEODORET read the word: "The last one shall rise upon the dust, or the tomb." So most of the translators at and since the Reformation. LUTHER, however, following the Septuagint, has: "He shall hereafter awaken me out of the earth." But the Dutch and French (MARTIN's) versions: "He shall remain the last on the earth." DIODATI's Italian: "At the last day he shall stand over the dust." VATABLUS: "He shall stand over the earth," *i.e.*, in heaven. GROTIUS, CASTALIO, LE CLERC: "At the last he shall stand over the dust," or earth. MERCER, COCCEIUS, SCULTETUS: "The latter or last One, he shall stand over the dust," *i.e.*, on the earth, as being to remain for ever. The TIGURINE: "In the last time he shall stand over the dust," applying his power over it. BROUGHTON: "He shall rise upon the

dust," *i.e.*, from death. JUNIUS "The latter one or last man," &c.,—living again in the resurrection and at the coming of Christ, compared with the former or first man, as in 1 Cor. xv. 42; perhaps Christ understood. MONTANUS: "The last one shall rise again from the dead," alluding to Christ, the first-fruits of them that slept; or, "He shall stand over the dust," *i.e.*, those lying in the dust. COCCEIUS: "The last," as never leaving us, or as remaining after all enemies are destroyed; or, last in life, alone immortal, ruling over death and the dust; or, as my deliverer, demanding me from the dust, having abolished the claim of death. SCULTETUS and GROTIUS: "Shall stand over the dust," as conqueror, raising it to life. CODURCUS: "The last shall stand over the dust," at the last judgment—the Son of God and the *goel* of our race. DRUSIUS and CARYL: "The last one," viz., the Redeemer. So SCHULTENS: "The last man"—an epithet of Christ—"He shall stand over dust,"—the dust of the grave, to claim this flesh from the spoiled prison of death; shall come as the avenger of a good cause and of oppressed innocence, and will put the crown of righteousness upon my head. GRYNÆUS: "The last," for, "At the last day." So WEMYSS, GOOD, DATHE, DÖDERLEIN: "At last he shall appear on the earth." HALES: "At the last day he shall stand over the dust," *i.e.*, over mankind—shall rise in judgment. FRY: "At the end he shall stand upon the earth." LEE: "In the last age or hereafter" (the "last days" of the prophets and apostles). CONANT: In after time. So NOYES, BARNES, HENDERSON. KITTO: "Hereafter or at last." Many of the moderns, however, prefer the other rendering of אַחֲרוֹן, viz., "the last one." So both the MICHAELISES, STICKEL, MAURER, HEILIGSTEDT, DE WETTE, DELITZSCH, SCOTT, PYE SMITH, Dr. ALEXANDER, FAUSSET. ZÖCKLER says: "As the last one," surviving all, with special reference to Job himself. ROSENMÜLLER: "He shall stand to assist or avenge the dust, *i.e.*, the dead." HUFNAGEL, viewing עָפָר (*aphar*) as from عدو "an enemy," has: "He shall stand over or overcome my enemies." A. CLARKE: He shall be manifest in the flesh, and shall stand over them who sleep in the dust, or who have been reduced to dust. CONANT: "He shall stand up," &c., as a judge, and will decide the case in my favour, as Ps. xii. 5; xliv. 26; or, "On the dust," *i.e.*, on the earth, including the sense of *vileness*. NOYES: "Dust," probably emphatic, as contrasted with heaven, the residence of the Creator. DÖDERLEIN understands by "dust" the patriarch himself reduced to dust and ashes. So Zöckler: "The dust of my decayed body or of my grave." Kennicott: "Over this dust." Dr. Alexander: "By my dust."

The drift of this sublime declaration thus variously understood. By most the sentence is viewed as declarative of Job's assurance regarding the promised Redeemer and future resurrection of the body. Castalio: The reference is to the resurrection of Christ, to be followed by that of all men. The arguments in favour of this view, as given by Cocceius, Schultens, and others: (1) The sublime preface; (2) A final judgment threatened by Job to his friends (verse 26); (3) His thoughts obviously lifted above this world, and the tone of his discourse now and henceforth more hopeful than before; (4) All hope in this life already given up (xvii. 5); (5) The opinion of the fathers, as Jerome, Augustine, Cyprian, Gregory, &c.; (6) The interpretation of the Targum and the Septuagint; (7) The wish that this testimony should be read after his death, perhaps on a sepulchral pillar; (8) The certainty expressed by him as resting on the immovable foundation of faith, that his Redeemer would come; (9) The simplicity of this interpretation; (10) Its agreement with the argument and scope; (11) The truth of the thing itself; (12) The majesty of the words; (13) The joyful hope exhibited by the patriarch; (14) The oneness of the Spirit in patriarchs, apostles, and all the faithful. Townsend observes: These words have always been interpreted by the Church as expressive of the patriarch's faith and hope in a spiritual Redeemer, who should restore him after the death of his body; hence embodied by the Churches of Rome and England in their offices for the dead. Lee speaks of the passage as "a recognition of the first promise made to Eve, and therefore a prediction of the Messiah." Jerome, in his Epistle to Pammachus, says: "None speaks so plainly of the resurrection after Christ, as Job does before Him." The passage was also applied by some of the Rabbis to the Messiah. Thus R. Hakkodesh: "God shall be seen in our flesh; as Job testifies. Out of my flesh I shall see God." The reference to an existence beyond the grave, apart from the resurrection of the body, understood by some modern interpreters, as Schlottmann, Zöckler, Conant, &c.

According to an opposite view, the reference is to a *figurative* resurrection of Job, and his restoration to a better condition in this life. So Grotius, Mercer, Calvin, (who yet fluctuates between the two opinions,) Chrysostom, Ambrose, Theophylact, &c.

The argument in favour of this view, as given by Mercer, Rosenmüller, Barnes, and others: (1) Its agreement with the history; (2) Its harmony with other passages of Scripture where a resurrection is spoken of, as Ezekiel xxxvii.; (3) The views of the Hebrew writers, who, in searching for proofs of the resurrection, never mention this passage; (4) The doctrine of the resurrection not likely to be found in this place of the Old Testament alone, nor in the Old Testament at all; (5) Job's restoration to prosperity and happiness solves the difficulty of suffering innocence; (6) The expectation of restored health naturally kept by the poet before Job's mind; (7) The assurance of restoration natural to one conscious of suffering innocently; (8) The language fairly interpreted, not necessarily implying a reference to a future and literal resurrection; (9) Such a view inconsistent with the argument, and with many other places in the book; (10) The resurrection never referred to as a topic of consolation either by Job or his friends; (11) Such a view wholly in advance of his age; (12) All that the words fairly convey met by the supposition that they refer to the events at the end. Stickel observes, that the decision of the mystery is given in the Epilogue without the immortality of the spirit being in the remotest manner touched; and adds, that Job's vindication required to be on the earth, and before those who were acquainted with the matter, or the inscription would be meaningless. Noyes: The idea of the resurrection inconsistent with the general design, the course of the argument, the connection of the discourse, and several express declarations, as vii. 7, 8; x. 20—22; xiv., *passim*. Ewald however, on the contrary, asserts: That through the certainty of that truth alone could the contest be victoriously carried on; while the more respectable of the reformed Biblical interpreters essentially agreed with the Vulgate in understanding the passage of a literal resurrection. So many Orientalists and Hebraists, as Schultens, both the Michaelises, Welthausen, Rosenmüller, Good, &c. Conant observes, that the views of early Christian fathers, who differed in their interpretation of the passage, are of little account on either side, having been based on the defective translations of the Septuagint, the Itala, and the Vulgate.

"*And though after my skin worms destroy this body*" (וְאַחַר עֹורִי נִקְּפוּ זֹאת ve-akhar 'ori nikkephoo zoth.) These words variously rendered and understood. נִקְּפוּ (nikkephoo, from נָקַף "to strike, or cut;" Piel from, to destroy; or, according to some, from

293

קַף=נָקַף "to surround." GESENIUS, in 1829, rendered the passage: "After they have destroyed my skin (equivalent to, 'After my skin has been destroyed'), this shall be," viz., that God shall appear. In 1840, he preferred to render it: "After my skin, which they shall have destroyed, this shall be." The SEPTUAGINT has: "he shall raise up my skin on the earth, which has endured such things." The VULGATE, followed by COVERDALE and LUTHER: "Again I shall be surrounded with my skin." TARGUM: "After my skin shall have been taken away, or burnt up, this shall be," viz., that my Redeemer shall remain the last. SYRIAC: "After this has spread all over and around my body." DIODATI: "However, after my skin, this body be corroded." MARTIN: "When, after my skin, this shall have been devoured." DUTCH: "After my skin has been eaten." TIGURINE: "After they (the Trinity) have surrounded this with my skin." CASTALIO: "After this (my body) shall be surrounded with my skin." MONTANUS and PAGNINUS: "After they have bruised this my skin." MUNSTER: "After [worms] shall have gnawed this body." JUNIUS: "After [worms] shall have pierced this, when I wake up,"—reading עוֹרִי ('oori) instead of עוֹרִי (ŏri). PISCATOR: "Although after my skin they (worms) pierce this,"—supplying כִּי (chi), or אִם (im). MERCER: "After my skin (corroded and consumed with my whole body), they (the worms in my ulcers, or my extreme pains) have shaken this (viz., his body,—not named, as so deformed, but pointed to)." COCCEIUS: "After they have stripped this that remains of my skin, or this my skin,—the whole of it, even to this particle; or, after my skin has burst, there shall be this,—pointing to his body." VATABLUS: "After my skin (has been perforated,) pains have broken this [mass of bones]." GROTIUS: "Although not only my skin, but also this (the fat that is under it), disease has consumed." DE DIEU: "After my skin has been consumed, they (my redeemer) shall make this to follow," viz., that I shall see God. SEB. SCHMIDT: "After my skin has ceased to be," viz., after my death. CALOVIUS, and GERHARD: "After my being raised up, this (all I see with my bodily eyes) shall be destroyed." J. H. MICHAELIS: "When, therefore, after my skin, worms shall have despatched this." LE CLERC: "If after my skin they have crushed this to pieces." HALES: "After my skin has been mangled thus." SCHULTENS: "After they (my pains and ulcers) have bruised my skin in this manner." STOCK:

"After they shall have swathed my skin, even this." KENNICOTT: "After they (my adversaries) have mangled me thus." J. D. MICHAELIS, and SCOTT the translator: "My skin, which is thus torn, shall become another," *i. e.*, shall be renewed. DÖDERLEIN: "I shall cast away my skin," understanding אחר for אָאחר. WEMYSS: "Though this skin of mine is thus corroded." GOOD: "After the disease has destroyed my skin." PYE SMITH: "Has cut down my skin." ADAM CLARKE: "After my skin they (diseases and afflictions) destroy this [wretched composition of misery and corruption]." ROSENMÜLLER: "When after my skin this [body] has been broken into fragments." BOOTHROYD: "If after my skin this [body] be destroyed." DE WETTE: "After my skin, which has been mangled, even this here." So EWALD, HIRZEL, and ZÖCKLER. NOYES: "Though with my skin this body be wasted away." DELITZSCH: "After my skin, which is thus mangled." CONANT, SCHLOTSMANN, and CAREY: "After this my skin shall be destroyed." BARNES: "Though after my skin the flesh be destroyed;" or, "after my skin has been pierced through thus." FAUCETT: "Though after my skin (is no more), this [body] is destroyed,"—the body not deserving to be named. FRY: "After I awake shall this be brought to pass,"—reading, like Junius and Calovius, עוֹרִי instead of עוֹרִי.

מִבְּשָׂרִי "Yet in my flesh shall I see God." (mibbesari),—literally, "from my flesh,"—variously translated and understood. The VULGATE has: "in my flesh." The TARGUM: "Out of my body." MARTIN (French): "From my flesh." DIODATI (Italian): "With my flesh." PAGNINUS, MONTANUS, MERCER, PISCATOR, JUNIUS and TREMELLIUS: "Out of my flesh." CASTALIO: "From my body." VATABLUS: "After my flesh has been wasted," or, "After the affliction endured in my flesh." So R. NACHMANN. MERCER: "Out of so great affliction of my flesh." COCCEIUS: "Out of my flesh," not put off, but received. CALVIN: "In my flesh,"—after I have been restored to a new state,—uncertain what. So GRYNŒUS: "Out of my revivified flesh." BROUGHTON: "From my flesh,—I being raised and clothed with flesh." GUSSET: "Out of my flesh, as my abode." J.H. MICHAELIS: "From out of my flesh." KENNICOTT: "Even in my flesh." ADAM CLARKE: Either, "See Him in my renewed body," or, "See Him as my kinsman in my flesh and blood." FRY: "Of my flesh," *i. e.*, of my nature and kindred, as Gen. ii., 23. LEE: "From or out of my flesh," *i. e.*, while still in it. KITTO: "In his flesh before he died, or in his flesh restored to soundness." BARTH (Bible Manual): "When the flesh is raised up"—in the re-animated glorified body. FAUSSET and ROSENMULLER (Second Edition): "From my renewed body," as the starting point of vision, as Cant. ii. 9,—the next clause proving bodily vision to be meant. STICKEL: "Without my flesh,"—as a mere skeleton; Job now comes to the point in which God, according to Satan's desire, "touched his bone and his flesh;" with only his life spared. MAUREN: "After my flesh has been all wasted away, yet still in the body." So CHRYSOSTOM, UMBREIT, HIRZEL, HEILIGSTEDT, HAHN, NOYES. BARNES: "Yet even without my flesh," COLEMAN: "Apart from my flesh." EWALD: "Without my flesh," *i.e.*, as a glorified spirit. So VAIHINGER, SCHLOTTMANN, DILLMANN, DELITZSCH, ZOCKLER.

"*I shall see God.*" According to PISCATOR, CONURCUS, and others, Job foretells the incarnation of the Divine Word. MERCER: "I shall contemplate him,"—discern His power, providence, and goodness in preserving me." GROTIUS: "Shall experience him propitious to me." So HUFNAGEL and ROSENMULLER. COCCEIUS: "Shall behold him in beatific vision," as Ps. xvi. 11; xvii. 15; Matt. v. 8; 1 John iii. 2. MENOCHIUS: Shall see Christ with bodily eyes, but his Divine Essence with the eyes of the mind. SCHULTENS: Shall then see God face to face, since access to him is denied me in this life; shall see God in glory,—not the God-man who is the *Goel.* SEB. SCHMIDT: Shall see God incarnate as the Messiah. DODERLEIN: From my condition, I shall understand that God wishes well to me and approves my life. LE CLERC: The expectation fulfilled when God spoke to him out of the whirlwind. STICKEL: Expresses the expectation of a vindication of his innocence before his death, though it should be only in the last moments of his life. So HOFMANN. NOYES: Shall see God interposing in my favour. DELITZSCH: Shall see God spiritually after death; Job's hope, not that of a resurrection, but of a life beyond the grave, and so a breaking through the idea of Hades. EWALD: Refers to the immortality of the soul in the spirit-world. Dr. THOMAS, in the Homilist: Refers to bodily, not mental, vision; the resurrection of the dead found taught here as resulting upon the advent of the Messiah. So AUGUSTINE: Job prophesies of the resurrection; "I shall be in my flesh when I see God." So CLEMENS ROMANUS, ORIGEN, CYRILL of JERUSALEM, EPHREM SYRUS, AMBROSE, EPIPHANIUS, JEROME, LUTHER, &c.

Verse 27. "*Whom I shall see for myself.*"

"See," repeated for emphasis: LEE. לִ (*li*), literally "for me or myself," variously understood. The SEPTUAGINT renders the passage: "Which things I know in myself." VULGATE: "Whom I myself shall see." MERCER: "Whom I shall discern to be for me, by His kindness in preserving me." SCULTETUS, "For me," *i.e.*, for my good. So MONTANUS, PISCATOR, PAGNINUS, and COCCEIUS. JUNIUS and TREMELLIUS: "The same that I shall see for me." CASTALIO: "Whom I indeed myself shall see." VATABLUS: "I shall enjoy the sight of Him to my salvation." COCCEIUS: "Whom I shall see, not angry but abounding in love, to my life and joy, or as mine." MUNSTER: "On my side." So KENNICOTT, HALES, SCOTT, WEMYSS, BOOTHROYD, CODURCUS: "Whom I even contemplate as standing by me." GROTIUS: "I, I say, with these eyes shall see him,"—לִ being emphatic. GRYNŒUS: "Whom I shall see as favourable to me, or as eternally mine." J. D. MICHAELIS: "For myself." So GOOD, BARNES, Dr. ALEXANDER. Dr. CHALMERS: "For myself and my own comfort." Dr. THOMAS: "In my proper personality." COLEMAN: "As my own." NOYES: "As my friend." KITTO: "Interposing on my behalf." FAUSSET: "For my advantage." So HEILIGSTEDT, MAURER, PYE SMITH. ZOCKLER: "For my salvation." DELITZSCH: "Whom I shall see, I, for my salvation." DE WETTE: "Yea, I shall see Him myself." CONANT: "Whom I, for myself, shall see." So SCHLOTTMANN. SCOTT: "Expresses more explicitly and emphatically his faith that in a disembodied state he should see God." CAREY: "Whom that I may see as my own," the object of the desire in the last clause. BARTH: "Anticipates partly his justification, and partly compensation for his sufferings." ADAM CLARKE: "Speaks as having a personal interest in the resurrection as in the Redeemer."

"*And my eyes shall behold.*" The Septuagint translates רָאוּ (*raoo*) as past: "Which things mine eye hath seen." So MONTANUS, CODURCUS and COCCEIUS: "My eyes have seen." The latter explains by saying: "The eyes of my mind have seen and tasted beforehand in my heart the vision of God by the illumination of the Holy Spirit." CODURCUS translates: "I myself have seen with these eyes; " and adds, "applying to himself the resurrection common to all the saints." MERCER renders the verb as present: "Whom my eyes see —not corporeally but spiritually: I contemplate His power with the eyes of my mind." Junius, followed by Caryl, has: "Whom I myself shall see with these eyes, being restored, though now I be entirely dissolved." Munster has: "Inasmuch as I myself shall behold him." Schultens views the words as equivalent to—"I believe the resurrection especially of myself." Rosenmuller: "I shall see with the eyes of my renewed body." Hufnagel: "I shall yet experience that God makes me happy." Dr. Thomas, in the Homilist, observes that רָאָה (*raah*) implies bodily vision.

"*And not another.*" זָר (*zar*) from זוּר (*zoor*) to "turn aside;" a stranger. The word differently understood. Gesenius renders it here "an adversary." "So Pineda, Bolduc, Stickel, Carey. Mercer, Montanus, and Pagninus: "A stranger." So De Wette and Michaelis. Conant observes that זָר denotes only a national enemy, and translates: "Another." So Schlottmann. Vatablus has: "Another," with "for me" understood. So Drusius, Cocceius, Grotius, Mercer: "I who know my pain and grief and not a stranger." Osiander: "Not a hypocrite," a stranger in faith and hope. Scultetus and Codurcus: "In this body and not another," as Isa. xxvi. 19. Henry: "He and not another for him shall be seen;" or, "I and not another for me." Caryl: "I myself, the very man who now speaks, and not changed into another;" intimating a personal resurrection. So Gregory and Beza. Mayer: "To show that as Christ lives again after death, so shall all the faithful, and that in the same bodies in which they lived before." Grynæus: "Not only *your* eyes, who in this might think you had a precedency over me." Hales: "Not estranged from me." So Kennicott, Dathe, Umbreit, Wemyss, Scott, Pye Smith. A. Clarke: "Not a stranger, who has no relation to human nature." Boothroyd: "Not another's [eyes]." Delitzsch: "I and not another person."

"*Though my reins be consumed within me,*" כָּלוּ כִלְיֹתַי בְּחֵקִי (*caloo chilyothai bekheki*) literally: "My reins are consumed in my bosom." So Gesenius and others; understanding: "From desire and longing for this consummation." The Septuagint has: "All things have been fulfilled to me in my bosom." Vulgate: "This my hope has been laid up in my bosom." Targum: "My reins are consumed in my bosom." Syriac: "My reins are consumed on account of my cause." Coverdale: "My reins are consumed within me, when ye say," &c. Geneva version: "My strength has been consumed

and destroyed." Vatablus: "My bowels have failed from affliction." Scultetus: "From sorrow and pain." Le Clerc: "From indignation." Mercer: "My reins have been consumed in my bosom"—בְּחֻקִּי (in my bosom) expressing the greater violence of his pain. Piscator and others supply, as in our authorized version: "Although." Codurcus has: "My desires have been fulfilled in my bosom." The Tigurine translators view the expression as equivalent to: "Which alone is my desire." Similarly, Caryl and Henry: "I have nothing more to desire." De Dieu: "My reins are consumed with desire in my bosom," as Ps. lxxxiv. 3. So Scultetus: "I also faint with desire of seeing him." Cocceius and Schultens: "With desire of seeing him clearly and openly." Dutch annotators: "With desire of obtaining so great a blessing." Seb. Schmidt connects with what follows: "Because ye say," &c. Schultens regards the words as part of the desired inscription. J. H. Michaelis: "From desire of him, or of it, my reins are consumed in my bosom." So Gregory: "I burn with desire of enjoying that wished-for time." To the same effect, J. D. Michaelis, Dathe, Rosenmuller, De Wette, Patrick, Wemyss, Scott, and Zockler. A. Clarke: "My reins, *i.e.,* my desires are spent;" equivalent to: "Though now apparently at the point of death." Kennicott: "All this have I made up in my own bosom." Pye Smith: "The thoughts of my bosom are accomplished." Boothroyd: "Accomplished shall be the desires of my breast." Lee: "When my reins," &c.; connecting with the preceding. Homilist: "Should my reins have been consumed," &c.

Verse 18. "*Seeing the root of the matter is found in me.*" For בִּי (*bi*) "in me," upwards of a hundred of MSS. have בּוֹ (*bo*) "in him." The expression שֹׁרֶשׁ דָּבָר (*shoresh dabhar*), literally, "the root of a word or matter," very variously understood. The interpretations reducible to four:—(1) A ground of accusation; (2) A ground of dispute; (3) The true faith; (4) A holy life. The first and second are the most probable, and now generally adopted: "[How] shall we find the root of the dispute or ground of accusation in him?" So Gesenius, Delitzsch, Noyes, Carey, Zockler, and others, reading נִמְצָא (*nimtsa*) as first person plural in Kal. The Septuagint has: "And find the root of the word in him." Vulgate and Targum: "And let us find the root of a word against them." Luther: "And find a matter against him." Coverdale: "We have found an occasion against him." MARTIN (French): "Since the foundation of my words is found in me." DIODATI (Italian): "Since the root of the word is found in me.' So MONTANUS, MERCER, VATABLUS, PAGNINUS, PISCATOR, JUNIUS, and TREMELLIUS. COCCEIUS: "And the root of the matter has been found in me," or is in me; change of person for "in him." Mercer understands the expression as implying Job's innocence. CODURCUS: "And that the cause of the quarrel is in me." So DE DIEU, POOLE, and SCHULTENS. GRYNÆUS: "The cause," &c. viz., that I'am a wicked man, and so deserving the calamities. HUFNAGEL: "Why sought we the cause of his misfortune in himself." AQUINAS, JEROME, BEDE, SANCTIUS, understand by "The root," &c., the words which Job had spoken, or some other charge which the friends brought against him. According to TIRINUS: "An occasion of calumniating him." OSIANDER: "Of chiding him." The Dutch annotators regard it as the affliction he endured, or the confession he had just made. COCCEIUS: "The ground of speaking boldly." VATABLUS: "Truth and innocence." PISCATOR: "Solid arguments." GROTIUS: "A good foundation." CODURCUS translates: "The root of the question;" and understands it of the faith and hope of the resurrection. According to the Assembly's Annotations: "The root of the Divine Word, or promise of a Redeemer." J. H. MICHAELIS and SED. SCHMIDT understand the expression as: "The foundation of his faith." KENNICOTT and SCOTT have: "The truth of the matter." HALES, with the Dutch annotators: "The strength of the argument." The TIGURINE: "The foundation of the matter of salvation." CARTWRIGHT: "Integrity of heart; the grace of God; true faith." So MAYER, SIMON, J. D. MICHAELIS, BARNES, and FAUSSET. LE CLERC: "The Word of God." BARTH: "The assurance he has just expressed." GOOD translates: "When the root of the matter is disclosed in me." WEMYSS: "Since there is no ground of accusation in me." FRY: "A ground of accusation is invented against me."

CHAPTER XXXII.

VERSE 2. *"Elihu"* אֱלִיהוּא "my God is He;" or, according to some: "My God is Jehovah." Various opinions concerning him, both as to his personality, speeches, and character. He has been considered by some as Balaam, the son of Beor. So JEROME, BEDE, LYRA, and some Rabbins. BEDE saw in him a type of the enemies of the church. Bishop WARBURTON thinks him to have been Ezra, the scribe. Some, as COLEMAN, have supposed him to be the Son of God—a manifestation of the Second Person of the Trinity in the form of a man; a prelibation of His incarnation; what Melchizedech was to Abraham. HODGE regards him as a representative character of the Messiah. KITTO makes him a comparatively obscure and unknown person. According to KIEL and others he was a fourth friend of Job. ZOCKLER understands him to have been a near kinsman of the Patriarch, and not belonging to the party of friends. According to GREGORY: A mere braggadocio; full of pride and vainglory; had the knowledge of God, and boasted of it not a little: from his pride and self-conceit, a type of those who, being left to themselves, become proud of their knowledge. So CODURCUS and MICHAELIS regard him as "highly conceited." STRIGELIUS sees in him an example of an ambitious orator, full of ostentation and audacity. So HERDER, UMBREIT, HAHN, DILLMANN. Professor TURNER speaks of him as manifesting a degree of veneration for Job and his friends, but speaking as an inflated youth, wishing to conceal his self-sufficiency under an appearance of modesty. According to VAIHINGER and others, he attempts to give a solution of the problem, but cannot. An entirely opposite view, however, is taken of him by AUGUSTIN, CHRYSOSTOM, AQUINAS, BRENTIUS, CALVIN, SCHULTENS, SCHLOTTMANN, ZOCKLER, and most of the defenders of the authenticity of the speeches ascribed to him. According to COCCEIUS and others, he "excelled in modesty, as in wisdom." CARPZOV: "Younger, but not inferior to the others in piety." SCULTETUS: "Rightly, but too severely blames Job's speeches." SCOTT, the translator, observes that the sacred writer bears witness to his modesty, and that Job's attention evidences the pertinence of his speeches; while his plan for humbling Job was pursued and completed by the Almighty Himself. According to HUFNAGEL, he defines the state of the question; hits the true point of view in relation to Job's conduct more than his predecessors, neither suspecting his piety, nor charging him with vice, but objecting to his impatience, and a finding fault with Divine Providence: with much power of comprehension and real goodness of heart, he has, however, too little experience. KEIL, who defends him, observes that it was not necessary to mention him in the preface; as parties were only introduced when they were to act or speak. According to ZOCKLER, he is only introduced to point out the sinfulness and perversity of Job's speeches, and to humble his pride; his part

in the poem no breach of the connection between Job's speeches and God's, and not superfluous, though leaving the mystery unsolved. Elihu the only one of the speakers whose genealogy is given: hence, thought by LIGHTFOOT and ROSENMULLER to have been the author of the book.

CHAPTER XXXIX.

VERSE 13. "*Gavest thou the goodly wings unto the peacock, or wings and feathers unto the ostrich?*" (MARGIN: "The feathers of the stork and ostrich.") The whole verse very variously rendered. In the first member, instead of "the peacock," the term רְנָנִים (*renanim*) is more correctly translated "ostriches," being derived from רָנַן (*ranan*) to "sing, or utter a shrill sound," and applied to the ostrich from its shrill nocturnal cry. So BOCHART, SCHULTENS, GESENIUS, and others. Other reasons given for this translation: (1) The authority of Jerome; (2) The resemblance in the meaning of רְנָנִים and יְעֵנִים (*ya'anim*),—the latter being the ordinary name of the ostrich; (3) The alacrity of the ostrich depending all on its wings; (4) The ostrich otherwise not named. The ostrich is literally the "crying bird;" the Arabs being accustomed to name things rather from their character. So REISKE and FAUSSET. The word in the text first rendered "peacock," by POMARIUS, and then hesitatingly adopted by PAGNINUS, MONTANUS, VATABLUS, MERCER, &c., and all modern versions: BOOTHROYD. נֶעֱלָסָה (*ne'elasah*) here rendered "goodly," is rather the Niphal of the verb עָלַס ('*alas*) to "rejoice, exult," as in chap xx. 18; or, according to others, to make a vibrating noise. GESENIUS renders the word: "Moveth joyfully." SCHULTENS: "Is full of exultation; is always moving." According to MERCER, the word is rarely found in Scripture, but is cognate with עָלַץ ('*alatz*) or עָלַז ('*aluz*) to "exult, or triumph." DRUSIUS, COCCEIUS, and SCULTETUS render the clause: "The wing of the peacocks is joyful, or moves joyfully. VATABLUS: "Is full of joy and pleasure." MERCER: "Does the wing of the peacock exult joyfully from thee?" PAGNINUS: "The peacock exults in its wings." GROTIUS: "Canst thou give the exulting wings of the peacocks?" MUNSTER:

298

"A wing to exult, or to be exulted in." MONTANUS: "The wing of the exulting ones is joyful." DODERLEIN: "She is one that exults with sounding wing"—supply, "does she fly by thy wisdom?" STICKEL: "The ostrich rejoices with fluttering wings." HUFNAGEL: "Joyfully move the sounding feathers and wing." MICHAELIS: "To the morning dawn the ostrich lifts its wings." UMBREIT: "The wing of the ostrich [which] lifts itself joyfully." HERDER: "A wing with joyous cry is uplifted yonder." SCOTT and BOOTHROYD: "The wing of the ostrich is triumphantly expanded." STOCK: "Is set to flutter." GOOD and WEMYSS: "The wing of the ostrich tribe is for flapping." PARKHURST: "Quivers, or flutters up and down." ROSENMULLER: "Exults." COLEMAN: "Flaps exultingly." NOYES and FAUSSET: "Moveth joyfully." LEE: "In the exulting wing of the ostrich [wilt thou put thy trust?]" BARNES: "The wing of the exulting fowls moves joyfully;" not their beauty, but their exulting, joyful, triumphant appearance being the object of attraction. FRY: "Is the flapped wing of the ostrich from thee." CAREY: "The wing of the ostrich thrilleth joyously." CONANT: "Waves exulting." DE WETTE: "Swings joyfully." ZOCKLER: "Flaps joyfully." Of the ancient and earlier versions, the SEPTUAGINT has: "The wing of the rejoicing ones;" leaving נֶעֱלָסָה untranslated. The VULGATE: "The wing of the ostrich is extolled." SYRIAC: "The wing of those that praise is lifted up." ARABIC: "The wing of praise." TARGUM: "The wing of the wild cock, which sings and exults." SYMMACHUS: "The wing of exultation grows around." AQUILA: "The wing of the praising ones folds up." COVERDALE: "The ostrich, whose feathers are fairer," &c. LUTHER: "The feathers of the peacock are finer," &c. MARTIN (French): "Has thou given to the peacock that plumage which is so brilliant." DIODATI (Italian): "The wings of the peacock, are they beautiful by thy doing?"

The rendering of the second member of

the verse (אִם־אֶבְרָה הֲסִידָה וְנֹצָה) (im ebhrah hasidhah ce-notsah) equally various. According to GESENIUS, אֶבְרָה (ebhrah) from the unused Root אָבַר (abhar), probably "to be strong, able to mount aloft;" a pinion or strong feather: distinguished from כָּנָף (canaph) a wing, and נֹצָה (natsah) a common feather. PISCATOR, and some earlier interpreters, make the word, which is elsewhere a "feather," to be here an "ostrich." The SEPTUAGINT leaves the words נֹצָה and הֲסִידָה untranslated. The VULGATE has: "[the wing of the ostrich is extolled] like the wing of the heron and the hawk;" reading נֹצָה as if יָץ or נָצָה. SYRIAC and ARABIC: "It flies, and comes, and builds its nest." COPTIC: "If the stork and ostrich could comprehend it;" which seems to be as destitute of meaning as the Septuagint itself. COVERDALE: "[Fairer] than the wings of the sparrow-hawk." LUTHER: "Than the wings and feathers of the stork." MARTIN (French): "Or to the ostrich [gavest thou] the wings and the feathers?" DIODATI (Italian): "Has the ostrich its feathers and plumage from thee?" MERCER, VATABLUS, and PAGNINUS: "Is the wing of the stork and its feathers so?" i.e., is it joyful or a cause of pleasure? or, has the stork such a wing and plumage? or, is it from thee? MUNSTER: "Or hast thou given wings and plumage to the stork?" SCULTETUS: "Or the wing of the stork and ostrich?" GROTIUS, PISCATOR, JUNIUS, and TREMELLIUS: "Or feathers to the stork and ostrich?" COCCEIUS: "Or if you wish a larger wing, that of the stork and ostrich." CASTALIO, including the preceding member: "Which are more noble, the wing of the ostrich, or the feathers and plumage of the stork?" So OSIANDER: "Are the wings of the ostrich more elegant than the wing and feather of the stork?" TIGURINE version: "The wing of the ostrich bears the palm, if you compare with it the wing or feather of the stork." BOCHART: "[The wing of the

ostrich exults]; verily the wing of the stork and the feathers;" i.e., which are verily a wing and plumage as is in the stork; or, the wings, I say, of the stork? כ being understood as in Genesis xix. 9; the ostrich being not so much a bird as a beast; whence the Arab proverb: "The ostrich is neither bird nor camel;" and its name among the Persians, the camel-bird, as resembling a camel in its neck, height, and walk, and a bird in its bill and feathers. SIMON: "Does it resemble the tail and feathers of the stork?" SCHULTENS: "Is its wing and plumage an affectionate one?" with allusion to the stork. HUFNAGEL and MICHAELIS: "The ostrich flies like the stork and the hawk." DODERLEIN: "With the feathers of the stork and the hawk." STOCK: "Hath her affection taken wings and flown away?" PARKHURST: "But is it the wing of the stork and it: plumage?" STICKEL: "Is it the stork-like, affectionate, pinions and feathers?" EWALD: "Is it a pious pinion and plumage?" אִם being interrogative. DE WETTE: "Is his wing also affectionate, and his plumage?" SCOTT: "Is it the pinion and feathers of the stork?"—not like the stork, providing for the security of its young. UMBREIT: "Is it not like the quill and feathers of the pious bird the stork?"—is it like the pious bird? surely not. NOYES: "But is it with loving pinion and feathers?" CAREY: "Is the feather and plumage that of the stork?" BARNES: "Has it the wing and plumage of the stork?"—flying without being endowed with the wings of the stork, and contrasted in its habits with those of that bird. BOOTHROYD: "Her pinions and feathers as those of the stork." COLEMAN: "Truly they have goodly pinions and plumage." FRY: "Or is the swollen pinion and plumage from thee?" LEE: "Or are her choice feathers and head-plumage from thee?" GOOD and WEMYSS: "But the wings of the stork and the falcon are for flight." ROSENMULLER: "Truly its wing and plumage is like that of the stork." ZOCKLER: "Though, is it a pious pinion and plumage?"

CHAPTER XL.

VERSE 15. "Behold now behemoth." Various opinions as to what is meant by the term "behemoth." According to GESENIUS, בְּהֵמוֹת (behemoth) is the plural of בְּהֵמָה (behemah, from the unused Root בָּהַם baham in the Xth conjugation, "to be dumb"),

a quadruped of the larger sort, living on the land; here the plural of majesty, denoting a large quadruped: the hippopotamus. So BOCHART: the river-horse or hippopotamus; like the Leviathan, an inhabitant of the Nile: the termination וֹת (oth) however, being, according to Bochart, not the sign of the piural, but of Egyptian singular, the animal being Egyptian. The SEPTUAGINT has: "Beasts." TARGUM: "The animal." The VULGATE, SYRIAC, and ARABIC, like the English Version, leave the word untranslated. MERCER, CASTALIO, and COCCEIUS, like Gesenius, consider the plural to be used on account of the great size of the animal. GROTIUS thinks it equivalent to "the animal of animals;" *i.e.*, the most excellent animal. According to MAIMONIDES, the term includes all land animals of monstrous size. So apparently the Septuagint. DR. LEE, in like manner, renders it "the beasts." The term, however, generally regarded as denoting a distinct species of animal, as—(1) distinct species are described in the former chapter; (2) It is here compared with other species; (3) The description is not suitable to all beasts of the field. The animal intended formerly regarded very generally as the *elephant.* So most of the earlier interpreters, both Catholic and Reformed, and all the Hebrew expositors. So the Geneva and Dutch versions, and the Italian of Diodati. According to MERCER: "Some animal larger and more monstrous than the elephant. Modern interpreters generally consider the *hippopotamus*, or river-horse, as especially intended. Bishop PATRICK says: "Not the elephant, which never lies among the reeds, but an animal of that region—the hippopotamus. CONANT: "The river-ox, the appro-priate name of the animal commonly known as the hippopotamus, or river-horse, the word being probably its Egyptian name. ROBINSON and CALMET derive the name from the Egyptian "*pe*" (the definite article "the"), "*ehe*," an ox, and "*mouth*," water: the water or river-ox, the name being modified like other foreign words. According to KITTO, the word is the plural of excellence; denoting the chief and most powerful of herbivorous animals known to Job, and living in his neighbourhood. GOOD thinks neither the elephant nor the hippopotamus exactly intended, but an animal now extinct. So A. CLARKE. FAUSSET thinks the description agrees partly with the elephant and partly with the hippopotamus, but exactly in all the details with neither; and that it is rather intended as a practical personification of the great Pachydermata or Herbivora, the idea of the hippopotamus being predominant. According to REISKE and BYTNER, the word indicates "beasts" in general; the peculiar name not being here given, as unnecessary, from the description. COCCEIUS, FRY and others, view the animal, called "the beast" by way of eminence, as one and the same with Leviathan. SAMUEL WESLEY queries whether it is not the animal alluded to by the Psalmist (Psalm lxviii. 30): "Rebuke the company of the spearman;" *Margin*: "The beasts of the reeds;" BOOTHROYD: "The wild beasts of the reeds."

CHAPTER XLI.

VERSE 1. "*Canst thou draw out Leviathan with a hook.*" The term "Leviathan" (לִוְיָתָן) rendered here by the SEPTUAGINT, SYRIAC, and ARABIC, "the dragon." The VULGATE and TARGUM leave it untranslated. Almost all the earlier interpreters understood the *Whale* to be the animal intended. BEZA and DIODATUS among the first to incline for the *Crocodile.* GROTIUS remarks: "From terrestrial he passes to marine animals." SANCTIUS is uncertain which animal of the whale kind is meant; and observes that the *Balæna* would not be unknown to Job, as being found, according to Pliny, in the Arabian Gulf. CODURCUS remarks that the whale is found in the Mediterranean Sea. According to DRUSIUS, some large unknown fish akin to the dragon is meant. SCHULTENS, with the Hebrew interpreters, thinks the animal to be a terrestrial dragon. LEE: "A sea monster in general; though the description rather suits the *whale*, and more particularly one of the Dolphin tribe, the *Delphinus Orcus Communis*, or common Grampus." KITTO: "A sea monster: here the crocodile. FAUSSET: "Literally, the twisted animal, gathering itself into folds: a poetic generalization for all cetacea, serpentine, and saurian monsters, especially the crocodile; described after the river horse, both being found in the Nile. Bishop PATRICK observes that the whale is not armed with scales, nor impenetrable, nor creeping on the earth; and that therefore the *crocodile* is the animal intended. S. WESLEY remarks that the crocodile was probably once in Palestine; a town named Crocodilopolis, or the city of the Crócodile, having stood in the neighbourhood of Mount Carmel. A. CLARKE thinks some extinct animal of the waters is probably intended. DODERLEIN thinks the word a general name of a very large and cruel beast, the real name being gathered from its attributes.

CHAPTER LXII.

VERSE 11. *"A piece of money."* According to Gesenius and others, קְשִׂיטָה (*kesitah*), from the unused root קָשַׂט = قَسَطَ (*kasata*) to "be just or true;" whence قِسْطُون (*Kistoon*) "balances;" a certain weight of money, equal to about four shekels (Gen. xlii. 35, xxxiii. 19, compared with xxiii. 16). According to SCHULTENS, a stater, or lump of gold exactly weighed. SEPTUAGINT: "A lamb." So ABULWALID and ABEN EZRA. VULGATE: "A sheep." So SYRIAC, ARABIC, and COVERDALE. LUTHER; "A fine groschen." MARTIN and DIODATI: "A piece of money." So the early translators and expositors in general. GROTIUS and MERCER, after the Rabbins: "A coin with the figure of a sheep struck upon it." SCOTT: "Some species of current coin," from Gen. xxxiii. 19, compared with Acts vii. 16. HUFNAGEL: "Apparently a piece of silver, not a coin. NOYES: "Pro-bably a lump of silver of a certain weight. UMBREIT: "The metal weighed out, not coined. MICHAELIS: "A weight which cannot be defined." LEE: "Not a stamped coin but a certain weight. CAREY: "A weight in the form of a lamb, used for weighing money;" as seen on Egyptian monuments, one being weighed against three rings. TOWNSEND: "Something weighed; each piece weighing four shekels." KITTO: "Probably a present of silver, the value of a lamb." BARTH: "A piece of money; a weight of gold or silver: a coin probably with the figure of an animal upon it." FAUSSET: "The term used instead of a shekel: a mark of antiquity. MAGEE and HORN: "Good reason to understand it as signifying a lamb." WEMYSS: "A girdle." BOOTHROYD: "Term derived from a Hebrew word denoting 'to be pure,' hence 'pure metal,' proved money." GRYNÆUS: "Symbol of Job's tried fidelity."

General Index.

www.ingramcontent.com/pod-product-compliance
Lightning Source LLC
Chambersburg PA
CBHW031339070726
47496CB00017B/1304